Microsoft® Access®
Small Business Solutions

Microsoft® Access®
Small Business Solutions

State-of-the-Art Database Models for Sales, Marketing, Customer Management, and More Key Business Activities

Teresa Hennig, Truitt Bradly,
Larry Linson, Leigh Purvis,
Brent Spaulding

WILEY
Wiley Publishing, Inc.

Microsoft® Access® Small Business Solutions: State-of-the-Art Database Models for Sales, Marketing, Customer Management, and More Key Business Activities

Published by
Wiley Publishing, Inc.
10475 Crosspoint Boulevard
Indianapolis, IN 46256
www.wiley.com

Copyright © 2010 by Wiley Publishing, Inc., Indianapolis, Indiana

Published simultaneously in Canada

ISBN: 978-0-470-52574-6

Manufactured in the United States of America

10 9 8 7 6 5 4 3 2 1

Library of Congress Control Number: 2009939784

To my parents ... whose lives have inspired me to enjoy and make the most of life's challenges and opportunities, and to find joy in sharing with others. Momma's radiant smile will light up a room, and her friendly, positive attitude brings happiness to everyone around her. Papa exemplifies the principles to live by: to be good to your neighbors and to have respect for yourself and others. He is "the salt of the earth," weathered yet softened by love and devotion. And Dad, the best friend and mentor anyone could have. May we all attain his ability to relish the unique gifts that life has to offer. They have taught me to learn from experiences and to appreciate the good in others. I am truly blessed to have three wonderful parents.
May we all enjoy the precious moments that we have to share with those who are most important to us.

—Teresa

To my mother and father, my daughter, and my son for inspiring me; to my high school bookkeeping teacher, Betty Oglesby, for igniting the slow burning fuse that eventually lead to my degree in accounting; and to my English 102 instructor at West Texas A&M, Dr. Jerri L. Williams, who encouraged me to explore and expand my technical writing skills.

—Truitt

For my children, Larry, Alan, and Lee-Ann, and grandchildren, Asa, Mandie, Melanie, and Ben—their unconditional love and continuing support and encouragement makes it all worthwhile. And to my friend and colleague, Kathy Lee Brown, whose devotion to saying it right and her way with words has made my contribution much more readable.

—Larry

To Hannah and C for being my reason to keep going and also the reason to stop and enjoy life. To my Mam and brother Gavin for the never ending support; I wouldn't be where I am without you. And to my Dad whose voice still carries on and drives me to be the best I can be.

—Leigh

To my wife and our eight children who have loved me, encouraged me, and prayed with me throughout the entirety of this adventure!

—Brent

About the Authors

 Teresa Hennig loves challenges, solving problems, and making things happen. Her company, Data Dynamics NW, reflects her dynamic personality and her innate ability to quickly grasp a situation and formulate a solution. With a strong background in business management, Teresa provides cost-effective solutions tailored to meet her client's needs. Her projects span the gamut of industries from title search companies to telemarketing services, and from managing union contracts and negotiations to supporting health care services. Whether reviewing an existing program or deploying a comprehensive solution, her focus is on solving problems and empowering others. You can learn more about Teresa from her website, www.DataDynamicsNW.com.

In recognition of her expertise and dedication to the Access community, Teresa has been awarded Microsoft Access MVP (Most Valuable Professional) every year, since her first award in 2006. Like several of the authors, Teresa is one of the founding moderators on the new MSDN database design forum at http://social.msdn.microsoft.com/Forums/en-US/category/sqlserver. Teresa continues to serve as president of both the Pacific Northwest Access Developer Groups (PNWADG) and of the Seattle Access Group (www.SeattleAccess.org) and publishes two monthly Access newsletters. Teresa is the lead author for *Access Programmer's Reference* (Wrox) and co-author of *RibbonX: Programming the Office 2007 Ribbon* (Wiley). The best part of being the lead author is being able to offer colleagues the opportunity to become published authors; for many it is truly "a dream come true."

Teresa's zeal for helping others has lead her to some amazing adventures—mostly to raise funds for various charities. On July 9, 2004, she triumphantly made it to the summit of Mt. Rainier. And nine days later, while on a pro-bono project to deliver an Access database to a teen clinic in Uganda, she was shooting Class 5 rapids on the Nile. Her next challenge event was in 2006, when she biked 220 miles in 2 days; raising money for Spinal Cord Society, in honor of her brother, Kirk. (And she *still* doesn't own or ride a bike!). At the encouragement of her Access group, Teresa's 2008 fundraiser was a sprint-triathlon. With a mere six hours of training, her attitude and dedication had her dancing across the finish line. Like so many things in life, this was yet another opportunity to be celebrated!

 Truitt Bradly was raised in West Texas and graduated from Hereford High School and West Texas A&M University. His first exposure to electronic databases was creating a membership database for a Masonic lodge as the lodge secretary in 1987. From that initial experience using PCFile II, a flat-file database, Truitt was hooked. He moved to Lotus Approach in the early 1990s and reluctantly switched to use Access 2 in 1996.

Truitt quickly realized that Access had extremely robust capabilities, especially when used with other Microsoft Office products, and was soon creating databases that automated existing manual procedures. He added VBA to his skill set beginning with Access 97.

In 2001, Truitt created his primary project using VB 6 to create an application based on an Access data file. The solution is still being used to calculate premium rates for group health insurance. The data portion of the application was migrated to a SQL Server and a web portal version was added using VB.net in 2003. Truitt continues to use and develop solutions in Access and looks forward to the release of Access 2010. Truitt received his first Microsoft Access MVP award in 2007, and he as earned the award each year since.

 Larry Linson, throughout his more than 50 years in the software development business, has been exposed to an extremely wide variety of business functions and has developed software applications to address them. Ever since relational databases emerged from a research project and an experimental database called *System R,* he has observed them, used them, taught others to use them, and consulted on applying them to address business issues. He has been a strong advocate of Access since it was first released and uses it daily for both business and personal needs. In his words, "Access is the best tool for creating user interfaces to relational databases that I have ever worked with, and I've worked with a lot of them."

Within a few months of Access' initial release, Larry founded, and still is one of the leaders of, an Access Special Interest Group (SIG) in the North Texas User Group (NTPCUG). As soon as it became practical for users who weren't primarily website developers to create websites, he built his first site for Access support. He currently maintains two such sites, one with Access samples and examples at `http://accdevel.tripod.com`, and another for SharePoint pages with Access information, references, and links for the NTPCUG Access SIG at `http://sp.ntpcug.org/accesssig/`. In 2003, Microsoft recognized Larry's contributions to the Access user community by naming him a Microsoft Access MVP and he has been awarded this distinction each year since.

Leigh Purvis is a consultant database developer from the north of England. He is the proprietor of Database Development and has been providing business solutions since 1998. Originally he worked primarily within the legal service sector, providing both proprietary and custom IT solutions which he continues to advance to this day. Over the years Leigh has also built successful databases for a wide variety of organizations including those involved in service, retail, wholesale, and manufacturing and production industries.

Leigh graduated with a Masters in Mathematics, but has since been captivated by databases, and in particular Access and SQL Server. He is a very active expert in various online forums and has written articles for *Access Advisor* (now known as *DataBased Advisor* and published online by Media Advisor) and as a result has been awarded a Microsoft Access MVP since 2007.

Leigh enjoys discovering ever more about Access development through reading, experimenting, answering questions, and providing solutions. He also likes TV, movies, real ale and, before databases consumed most of his time, recalls liking snooker and playing the guitar.

Brent Spaulding was formally educated as a mechanical engineer. His course of study focused on manufacturing systems. He has designed equipment and the programs used to control and monitor that equipment in a production environment. As his exposure to the manufacturing environment grew, his aptitude for integrating software to address the needs of the manufacturing environment grew. He has designed systems that have a wide range of focus; however, the majority of his applications were focused on needs born of his primary responsibilities as a manufacturing engineer—for example, product assembly analysis, equipment calibration logging, and manufacturing process management, which include product traceability, equipment condition monitoring, and process repeatability.

He has spent much of his professional career in the automotive industry designing equipment and supporting the production floor. In addition, he was responsible the integrating SCADA (Supervisory Control and Data Acquisition) systems, HMI (Human Machine Interface) systems, and CMMS (Computerized Maintenance Management System) applications into Manufacturing Process Management systems. Recently he has changed gears to join with a non-profit organization based out of Virginia as a software developer and database administrator. In July of 2007, he received the Microsoft Access MVP award which recognizes his talent and contributions to the Access community and has continued to be recognized as an MVP in each subsequent year. He spends much of his personal time learning and helping others on websites like Utter Access. His online alias is datAdrenaline. Brent currently lives in southern Indiana with his wife and children.

About the Contributing Authors and Technical Editors

 Jerry Dennison has over 17 years of professional experience designing and developing Microsoft Access database applications beginning with Access v1.0. He has been awarded the Microsoft Access MVP award for the past four years. He is an active contributor and administrator at Utter Access, the premier MS Access forum on the web. He is considered by many of his peers to be one of the foremost experts on the Forms of Data Normalization (a set of guidelines for relational databases developed by Dr. E.F. Codd). He has been selected as a co-author for the upcoming *Access 2010 Programmer's Reference* (Wrox).

Jerry currently lives in Easley, SC with his wife of 21 years and their two dogs; Duke and Duchess.

George Hepworth began his Access career by creating tools to track sales for the self-study materials he and his former colleagues created and sold, and to manage the results of continuing education exams administered to licensees. Realizing that Access databases were more interesting and rewarding than writing training materials, he moved to full-time Access development soon thereafter. Being self-taught, George believes any day on which he doesn't learn at least one new thing is a day wasted.

George is a Senior Development Advisor for Advisicon, a project management and development organization in Portland, OR, creating Access and Access/SQL Server solutions for clients primarily in the Portland area. Previously, George founded and operated Grover Park Consulting, (www.GPCData.com) specializing in resuscitating "owner-built" Access databases for small and medium sized organizations.

In his spare time, George is part of the administrator team, and a regular contributor, at Utter Access, the most popular Access support site on the Internet. In recognition of his expertise and community support, George has been recognized as a Microsoft Access MVP.

George holds a BS in English and an MA in TESL from Utah State University. And now, George's daughter and his money go to Washington State University.

 Doug Yudovich is the Director of Business Information for UW Physicians in Seattle. One of the BI department's primary responsibilities is developing database applications in support of various business needs for managing data. The applications vary in scope, from stopgap applications, to bolt-on tools, to mission critical-level applications that support up to 250 users. All of the applications use Access for the front end; with some using Jet as the database platform, and some use SQL Server.

Doug is also an administrator for the Utter Access forums. Joining UA in 2004, Doug progressed through the ranks (VIP, editor, administrator). UA is Doug's cyber home, where he shares his passion and knowledge in database design and information management with members who seek help, and with fellow developers discussing best practices. Doug is an active member of the Pacific Northwest Access Developer Group (PNWADG) and a presenter in the Seattle Access Group (SAG). Doug participated in two Developers' Kitchen events with the Microsoft Access product team to work on early development versions of Access 2010.

Due to his contributions to the Access developers' community in Utter Access, the user groups, and his work with the Access product team, Doug was awarded the Microsoft Access MVP award in April 2009.

Primary Technical Editors

 Arvin Meyer holds a degree in Business Administration, with a major in accounting, but instead of becoming an accountant he decided to go into the family cabinetmaking business. He got his first computer in 1981, and used computers extensively in bidding and construction takeoffs. In 1992, after discovering Windows 3.1, he began writing a computer column for a trade magazine. When Microsoft Access came on the scene in the fall of that year, he was hooked. He returned to college, studied programming and networking, and in 1994 wrote his first commercial database. In 1996, Arvin became a full-time database developer.

Today he is married and the father of twin sons. Arvin is active in the Microsoft newsgroups, and maintains the Access Web at www.mvps.org/access, an Access download site on his domain (www.datastrat.com), and several client websites. A Microsoft Certified Professional and Microsoft Access MVP, Arvin writes freelance technology articles, leads the Access Special Interest Group, is Vice-President of the Central Florida Computer Society, works as a consultant, and heads the development department of a software technology firm in Orlando, FL.

Armen Stein is the president of J Street Technology, a Microsoft Gold Certified Partner with a team of database application developers near Seattle, Washington. In addition to custom database development, J Street offers CartGenie, a complete e-commerce web storefront and shopping cart. Armen is a Microsoft Access MVP and MCP, and is President Emeritus of the Pacific Northwest Access Developers Group. He has taught college-level database classes, and has also developed and taught one-day training classes on Access and Access/SQL Server development. Armen has spoken at various user groups and conferences, including Microsoft TechEd in the US and Office DevCon in Australia, and he is co-author of *Access 2007 VBA Programmer's Reference* (Wrox). His other interests include activities with his family, travel, backgammon, Mariners baseball, and driving his 1969 Ford Bronco in the sun.

Credits

Executive Editor
Bob Elliott

Project Editor
Tom Dinse

Primary Technical Editors
Arvin Meyer
Armen Stein

**Technical Editors/
Contributing Authors**
Jerry Dennison
George Hepworth
Doug Yudovich

Production Editor
Daniel Scribner

Copy Editor
Expat Editing
Foxxe Editorial Services

Editorial Director
Robyn B. Siesky

Editorial Manager
Mary Beth Wakefield

Production Manager
Tim Tate

**Vice President and Executive
Group Publisher**
Richard Swadley

**Vice President and Executive
Publisher**
Barry Pruett

Associate Publisher
Jim Minatel

Project Coordinator, Cover
Lynsey Stanford

Proofreaders
Sheilah Ledwidge, Word One
Kyle Schlesinger, Word One
Maraya Cornell, Word One

Indexer
Robert Swanson

Cover Image
Comstock Images / Getty Images

Cover Designer
Ryan Sneed

Acknowledgments

From the group:

As a team, we can only express our respect and appreciation for all of the people who contributed to the content, editing and production of our book. We cannot say enough about Tom Dinse, our project editor, and his team. Suffice it to say that there is a lot more to writing a book than having the technical and subject matter expertise.

With a team of five Access MVPs, we anticipated a fun and easy project—after all, how hard could it be to put our thoughts into print? Several thousand hours later, we look at the thirty databases models and remember why we allocate 30% of the project time to gathering requirements and creating the tables. We couldn't have done it without the dedication of our technical editors, contributors, and colleagues. We started with Arvin Meyer and Armen Stein as our technical editors. Then we enlisted the help of Jerry Dennison, George Hepworth, and Doug Yudovich as tech editors and contributors. Our team of five soon doubled in size to ten Access MVPs. And we still had room for one more, so Jeff Boyce helped with some reviews.

On behalf of the entire team, I want to acknowledge and express appreciation for everyone else who contributed by sharing ideas, commenting on concepts, encouraging us, and most of all, understanding and making allowances for the time and energy that we all poured into this project.

We dedicated our energies to provide you with a resource that will pay for itself countless times on each and every project.

Teresa Hennig, lead author

From the authors:

Life is filled with opportunities . . . we should celebrate them all.

This project has presented opportunities for each of us to share our passion and expertise with Access, and to work with colleagues from across the country and ocean. I am honored to work with such an elite team of authors and tech editors; recognized as 10 of the best in the world. It is challenging to express how much your dedication, attitude, and support have meant to me. I can only say, "Thank you;" this has truly been a once-in-a-lifetime adventure. ;~)

Mere words cannot adequately express my gratitude for Tom's guidance and patience as he miraculously managed countless reviews of hundreds of files.

It is with heartfelt warmth that I express my appreciation for my family and friends. They are always there when I need them. They listen, encourage, and help in ways beyond measure. Family and friends are the priceless jewels in life that should never be taken for granted.

Teresa Hennig

I would like to thank the many members of UtterAccess.com for allowing me to expand my knowledge and skills by posting their questions about the many aspects of databases, and more especially the Utter Access Administrators, Moderators, and the VIPs for their unrelenting efforts to keep Utter Access the number one place to come for Access information in the world. Most of all, I would like to thank Teresa for keeping this train on the track.

Truitt Bradly

My thanks go to too many to list here. My late parents, Evelyn and L.Q. Linson instilled in me the desire to always do my best and the understanding that it takes an unrelenting dedication to the work ethic to accomplish that. Many helped me over the years and only asked in return that I help someone else when I could. Uncounted thousands posed questions about Access in person and on newsgroups—their real-world problems, along with my work, afforded exploration, discovery, and practice to make my Access work more successful. A few individuals stand out: the late Stan Ulam at Los Alamos, the late Burt Randolph at IBM, my friends Michael Kaplan and Arvin Meyer in the Access community, and Neel Cotten, Jim Wehe, Dan Ogden, Fred Williams, and the late Reagan and Connie Andrews in my user group. I offer special thanks to my friend and colleague Kathy Lee Brown—her knowledge of Access and business, keen editorial eye, and "sharp editorial pencil" made my parts of this book much more effective.

Larry Linson

I would like to thank Teresa, Larry, Truitt, and Brent for this amazing experience and sharing the wisdom they all have in such abundance. The editing team were also all fantastic, Armen, Arvin, Doug, and George. I must especially thank Jerry who worked valiantly on much of what I produced and Miriam for diving in and offering suggestions at a crucial time.

A very important thank you goes to both my colleagues and clients over the years, in particular to Archie, Carolyn, Mike and everyone who has worked for and with Courage & Co. and SDLT.co.uk over the last decade.

Long standing thanks go to friends: Paul, who truly introduced me to Access, Stuart, Lee, and Leah for listening to me go on over time. Most of all to my family: Hannah, Christopher, Mam, Gavin and everyone else for their support over the years. It means everything.

Leigh Purvis

With an undertaking like this book it goes without saying that it takes a lot of effort and cooperation, even when it feels like there is nothing left to give! I am humbled to have been asked to be a part of this extraordinary accomplishment. I am fortunate that the experiences I have gained through my education and professional career has sharpened the skills I have been blessed with to warrant the invitation. Despite any skill I may possess, it goes without saying that a feat like this book, let alone my portion of it, cannot be accomplished alone. With that, I would like to extend my gratitude to Glenn Lloyd and George Hepworth. The full list of people who have helped and encouraged me goes beyond the scope of this paragraph, but please know that my appreciation for the efforts, and counsel, of others I have benefitted from are greatly appreciated.

Brent Spaulding

Contents at a Glance

Contents

Foreword

There are many challenges to running a small- or medium-sized business. Whether it's dealing with your day-to-day internal demands, meeting the demands of customers, or competing against larger organizations with seemingly infinite resources, the key to survival is being more knowledgeable, nimble, and responsive.

Every business owner knows that technology is critical to managing operations, measuring performance, controlling costs, improving accuracy and compliance, and providing better services. But implementing the right technology and supporting it over time can often feel overwhelming and be very expensive.

You can purchase a commercial off-the-shelf (COTS) solution at a reasonable price, but it often requires modifying your processes to conform to the software. In some cases, that may be a good thing, but often, it's a partial solution that covers the basics without providing the ability to leverage the data and knowledge being collected.

Meanwhile, custom software solutions can be very expensive and require a professional software developer (or team) that is unlikely to know your business needs well. Designing and communicating your requirements, especially if you're not familiar with the whole software development process, can be a difficult experience for everyone. The results may be better than a COTS solution but can still be less than optimal, especially as your needs evolve.

The strength of Microsoft Access is that with the proper mastery of its features, you can create database applications that meet the needs of your organization quickly and cost effectively. Compared to more complex platforms, you actually have the ability to personally understand Microsoft Access and enhance its databases as your needs change.

The solutions provided in this book give you a head start to building your own systems and taking control of your destiny. By using these foundations, you can get up and running quickly, learn what these solutions can do for you, use them, then understand what else you need. You can either build those enhancements yourself or seek help from others to do so. Either way, you'll be much further along than if you started from scratch because you'll have tested solutions in your environment to extend and you'll understand them and their potential intimately.

Like your organization, well-designed software applications are like life forms. Healthy species grow and evolve over time in response to rapidly changing environments. Those that can't evolve go extinct. The world and your business aren't static. Having a strategy to rapidly create low-cost solutions to support your efforts is critical to success. Failure to do so is essentially giving business away to your competitors.

By responding faster and cheaper than your competitors, you can pursue more opportunities. While you can't expect a hit with every at bat, the more at bats you have, the more likely you'll score. And if you fail, you want to fail quickly and cheaply so you can move to the next great opportunity.

The software world is littered with failed projects. While new technology can make applications die a premature death, most applications become obsolete due to changes that have nothing to do with technology such as the economy, customers, regulations, competition, and so on.

Meanwhile, successful projects thrive and prosper in directions that were never envisioned originally. New customers, products, contracts, and laws can justify investments in features that weren't previously considered. Then there's the demand for new approaches once a solution gets used. I'm personally guilty of changing many software designs after deployment because I simply didn't know that what I originally requested wasn't what I really wanted. Unfortunately, it's nearly impossible to design what you want perfectly up front. That's why having a way to get up and running quickly and to respond to changing needs are so critical.

Leveraging your intimate knowledge of your organization's processes, requirements, and objectives, with the technology to address those needs, is extremely powerful. The examples in this book will get you up to speed quickly so you can go after opportunities, reduce costs, increase accuracy, and give your organization and yourself a significant competitive advantage.

Best of luck,
Luke Chung
President
FMS, Inc.

FMS, Inc. is the world's leading developer of Microsoft Access third party tools. Visit our website for extensive tips and resources for Microsoft Access development: http://www.fmsinc.com.

Introduction

Welcome to *Microsoft Access Small Business Solutions: State-of-the-Art Database Models for Sales, Marketing, Customer Management, and More Key Business Activities.*

Every small-business owner knows how important effective databases are to successful sales, marketing, and customer management strategies. Our goal is to provide you with both a structured learning process and functional database models so that you can create and modify solutions that will work best for your specific needs.

This book and companion CD provide and explain 31 database models that are ready to be incorporated into your solutions. They were created by an unparalleled team of 10 Access MVPs as the authors, contributors and technical editors with over 100 years of combined experience of working with Access. Their expertise, passion for Access, and dedication to the community have earned them recognition as being among the top Access experts in the world.

Access is increasingly used by small businesses to track vital information and more effectively and profitably manage those businesses, and this book is written to help with that effort. It will help employees and consultants who may lack expertise in relational database modeling, but who need to quickly develop a database solution.

One of the biggest challenges to any software solution is to identify and address the specific needs of the people and processes involved. That is where this book comes in. A properly designed database does more than record and store data, it can be an essential tool for managing operations, monitoring costs, improving performance and enhancing customer relations.

Who Should Read This Book

This book responds to the increased use of Access by small businesses and by departments within a business. Beneficiaries include small businesses, department heads, and anyone assigned to create a database solution, collect data, or to convert one or more spreadsheets into a functional database—from the novice to the seasoned database consultant.

It is an excellent resource for workers and consultants who may lack expertise in relational database modeling, but who need to quickly develop a database solution. Those who are new to database development will learn about the fundamental concepts for designing a database and progress into designing solutions that support real-world scenarios.

The explanations of the logic, interview material, and companion download files will also make this book an invaluable resource for experienced database developers and business consultants.

The book is also an excellent resource for colleges and business schools.

In addition to explaining how to design a relational database, this book delves into key business areas that are common to many database platforms. It not only shows how to design a database for a particular business center, but it goes through some of the interview processes that help tailor the database structure to a unique business scenario or to specific industry requirements. The examples are brought to life by the companion files that can quickly be modified to support a multitude of business models. The examples can also be combined to create comprehensive custom solutions.

Why choose Access? All levels of workers are becoming more tech savvy. Managers are used to having data literally at their fingertips. People are becoming more aware of the potential for instantly analyzing data and creating custom reports. This is driving the need for more people to use customizable databases. Our book will help people to quickly design a database so that they can capture, store, retrieve, manipulate, and report data. Since each situation is different, we placed a significant emphasis on explaining the interview process and determining what questions to ask. The explanations, sample interviews, and database models will help readers quickly become confident that they are creating a table structure that will serve their current and anticipated needs.

In addition to the traditional relational database models for transactional analysis, this book also discusses creating a hybrid database designed to support additional business analysis and historic comparisons.

How This Book Is Organized

The first chapter of our book serves as a roadmap to the rest of the book. It describes the contents of each chapter and talks about some of the highlights, techniques, and bonus materials that you will find. The next two chapters discuss the fundamentals of Access and of the relational data model.

It can be tempting to find the chapter that best matches your industry or needs and dive directly into creating and modifying one of the models that we provide. And, that might be the right approach if you've worked with Access and are already familiar with the terminology and concepts. But, if you are relatively new to database development, we encourage you to take the time to read Chapters 2 and 3 to get a solid foundation in the fundamentals. As you work through the examples later, you'll find that the time spent was well worth the investment.

The remaining chapters focus on business functions. We help you make correlations to your activities as we walk you through the process of identifying the business needs, critical information, and other requirements that help determine the data that needs to be recorded in your database. Most chapters provide a simple database design, and then incorporate numerous variations and options.

As we design the database models, we discuss applicable database concepts. This way, you not only build the database, but you also learn about methodology and techniques so that you can apply the principles to future projects. We also discuss alternative approaches and designs that can easily be adapted to support *real-world* scenarios.

The models provided in this book give you a head start to building your own systems and taking control of your destiny. By using these models as foundations for your solutions, you can get up and running quickly. As you learn what they can do, you will recognize what else you might need. You can either build those enhancements yourself or seek help from others. Either way, by starting with a proven foundation, you'll be much further along than if you started from scratch.

The models, examples, and interviews allow readers to quickly design solid solutions that will support current needs and facilitate future customizations. This book will more than pay for itself with the first application by reducing development time and by helping you to design a solid foundation that supports modifications and avoids needless challenges, delays, and rework. You may be amazed by how the right table structure can make it so much easier to create the forms and reports you desire. The returns will increase with each new project or modification—not only from the savings in development time, but also from more cost effective work-flow.

There are 10 appendixes that provide reference material and concepts that support and compliment the material in the chapters. In addition to the six in the book, there are four bonus appendixes on the CD.

We wanted the book to be as self-contained as possible so that it provides what you need, right at your fingertips. There was so much that we could not fit it between the covers of the book, but rather than forego valuable content, we have included one chapter and several appendixes on the CD. The bonus is that you can save the files to your computer, which allows quick searches, copy and paste, and click to open references. And, of course, you may want to print and store the hardcopy with the book.

What's on the CD-ROM

This CD includes 31 database files that correlate to the examples discussed in the book. The files are loaded with a wealth of details that compliment and expand on the discussions in their respective chapters. The files will help you understand the logic for the database models. By investigating them, you will learn more about the field properties and the relationships between the tables than could possible fit into one book.

By reviewing the companion files while going through a chapter, you can see first hand how a particular schema is being implemented. Not only that, but most of the groundwork has been done for you in the example database(s) for each chapter. This will save you lots of time when incorporating any of our models into solutions for your business.

As mentioned in the previous section, the CD also contains one bonus chapter and several appendixes. Appendix F, "What's On the CD-ROM," provides more information about the CD content and the system requirements. It also includes some useful troubleshooting tips that can help you avoid and quickly overcome a variety of challenges.

Introduction and Basic Concepts

In This Part

Overview and Road Map

You, like many others, either realize or are considering the probability that using a database will alleviate a lot of the challenges that you are struggling with to manage information. But you are not familiar with database technology, and you don't know the best place to start or what to expect. Maybe you've tried some templates, or looked at some packaged solutions, and determined that they were not the best fit for your needs. That's where this book comes in.

This is arguably the most comprehensive book about Access database designs that you will find. The companion CD provides 31 database models, guides, and bonus material–a total of 76 files! We have included numerous tips and techniques from database developers, based on real-life examples, and have provided ready-to-use models. As we went through the process of creating the tables, we provided practical advice, included alternatives, and incorporated some sidebars to help you deal with more complex scenarios. We've managed to consolidate this into a compact book that is easy to understand and implement—written without a lot of database jargon, and in a style that we hope is comfortable for you, the businessperson.

We wanted to cover the most common business scenarios and provide you with advice and guidance from business experts who are also recognized for their database expertise. We did that by forming a team of ten Access developers who have earned worldwide recognition as Microsoft Access Most Valuable Persons (MVPs). Moreover, to ensure that the material presented in any chapter isn't just based on one person's perspective or experiences, we assigned each chapter to a team of MVPs, based on their subject matter expertise. Then each chapter was reviewed by at least two other Access MVPs.

Each of us invested hundreds of hours to make this the single best resource available! Rather than wade through countless other books, with all the different concepts, terms, and opinions that entails, this book provides a resource that will help you design solid database solutions—solutions that will support your current needs and be flexible enough to expand and change in response to the dynamics of your business environment.

Collectively, the contributors to this book and databases have well over 100 years of combined experience with Microsoft Access! And we are especially proud to provide you with the Bonus Resource database in the files for Appendix E on the book's CD. It contains many of the tools, shortcuts, and resources that we use to create and maintain our own Access applications. The ADD_BonusResource.mdb can serve as the start of your personal database development toolkit.

One of the benefits of having such a large team was drawing on their diverse background and experiences so that we could expose you to a variety of styles and techniques. There are typically several ways to create a solution for most database needs, and by demonstrating different approaches to the design process we are giving you multiple ways to think about and solve your own business challenges. In going through the examples, you will find a style and model that works best for your particular scenario, which of course will vary according to what you are facing at any particular moment.

We based the models on our experiences and have incorporated aspects from numerous projects; and we encourage you to take a similar approach when building solutions for your projects. The naming conventions we used had to evolve as we progressed, so ensuring consistency in the final files required a considerable amount of effort and renaming. Consequently, you are likely to find some legacy terms, particularly in the descriptions of fields. Although this does not diminish the functionality in any way, we encourage you to update the field names and descriptions as you incorporate the tables and fields into your projects.

For each line of business, we provide you with a "base model" that demonstrates how we met a set of business needs or solved a common problem. Then we expand on that base model to give you the benefit of our experience and the different ways you may approach similar situations. That way, you can adapt our models to your own circumstances. By explaining some of the alternatives, including examples and consequences, we hope to impart a wide range of database knowledge, making it easier for you to apply the experience to other areas and to respond to unique situations.

We take advantage of this approach extensively in Chapters 6 through 10. If you look at Chapters 6, 7, and 10 together, you will not only learn about database models that support sales and marketing, you will also create some core modules that can be used in countless other areas. For example, you will learn how to design a database to support a questionnaire. Those models and techniques can be used for a multitude of purposes outside of marketing. We'll expand on that momentarily.

As you create the database models for a manufacturing and inventory process in Chapters 8 and 9, you will also gain a stronger understanding of what "normalization" really means with respect to database design. We have provided a structured approach for listing and analyzing each detail that is considered to be pertinent to your database.

As we do not expect you to be a database expert, we focus on demonstrating methods that are effective, yet easy to learn and relatively simple to implement. Even so, we've included some divergent approaches with arguably more advanced material because we think that it is important for you to try different techniques and to learn something new about database design in every chapter. The best approach, of course, is the one that works for you and has the best results.

Throughout the book we have been careful to emphasize four stages that are essential to good database development. You will investigate needs, evaluate the details, convert the details into tables and fields, and then review the relationships and model as a whole. The first two stages are critical to the planning process. During the third stage, you will experience several approaches to creating the tables and fields. The fourth stage ensures that the design is complete and meets your needs.

For many database projects, it is appropriate to allocate one-third of the entire time to planning. No, that is not a typo. The planning process can easily take one-third of the overall time involved from conceptualization to deployment. The time spent on investigation, interviews, development of the database requirements and specifications, and diagramming the data flow provides the foundation for the database project. With the solid foundation, you can proceed with confidence to create the tables, design the forms and reports, and finally, to test and deploy the solution.

While building dozens of carefully created database models, this book emphasizes sound database design in every chapter. We explain the concepts that you need to follow, and occasionally some pitfalls to avoid. As you will learn, many designs that initially seem well constructed cannot withstand the test of time. A poorly designed database can easily be locked into a format that limits modifications, leads to poor performance and frustrates both users and developers. By working through the examples in this book, you will learn how to create a solid database that will stand up to years of use, modifications, and expansion. You will understand the benefits of "normalization."

The first part of this book explains the underlying concepts of and fundamental principles for creating sustainable database designs. The subsequent parts discuss and demonstrate how to create database models for the main business functions. The chapter examples map well to the mission of a business or department. The end of the book includes 10 appendixes that provide a wealth of resources and reference material that complement and expand on the concepts discussed in the chapters. We wanted the book to be as self-contained as reasonably achievable, so that it literally provides everything you need, right at your fingertips.

Although each chapter is designed to stand alone, we recommend that you read through the entire book. Each chapter contains examples that reflect different concepts and features that can be incorporated into other scenarios. By working progressively through the examples, you will develop the experience and confidence to create and modify solid database solutions for a multitude of purposes.

The files are a great starting point for building your own solutions. You can use the files as they are, or select various tables and features from several files, to lay the groundwork for a new solution. This will save you a significant amount of time and provide a solid foundation for your applications.

Part I: Introduction and Fundamentals

The first three chapters provide some background information to help you understand the flow of the book, an explanation of the processes that we'll use, and the terminology and fundamental principles that form the cornerstone of relational database design.

Chapter 1: Overview and Road Map

This first chapter serves as a road map for the rest of the book. It describes the contents of each chapter, including highlights, techniques, and bonus materials that you will find. By reading Chapter 1, you will learn how the business functions and data management techniques from the various chapters relate to and complement each other.

Chapter 2: Elements of a Microsoft Access Database

After reading Chapter 2 you will be familiar with the different parts of a database, including the names and nomenclature you need to get started. The information you learn from this chapter, coupled with the information from Chapter 3, starts you off on a path to building efficient, reliable, and scalable databases to satisfy your business needs.

In Chapter 2, you will learn about the main database objects: the schema, tables, relationships, and queries. In a nutshell, the schema is the overall structure or plan of the database, normally expressed in a diagram; the tables hold the data; the relationships combine the tables; and queries are used to enter, view, or modify information from the tables. Each of these database elements is expanded upon with examples.

The database schema refers to the configurations, definitions, and rules that control how the data is entered, stored, and retrieved. There are additional controls built into the user interface, but our focus is on what you can do at the table level to define how your data will be stored and organized.

Each major subject is recorded in a separate table. The tables are comprised of fields and indexes. Each table contains any number of data records; and each record can contain numerous fields. The fields are used to store the individual details that make up a record. Indexes on the fields are used to organize the records within a table and help the database function more efficiently.

Relationships define the link that joins two tables together based on common key fields between them. You will learn each type of relationship that can be created: one-to-one, one-to-many, and many-to-many. You will also learn about referential integrity and how it can help you maintain clean data within your database.

Queries enable you to request data or perform an action on your data or table structure. They are predominately used to retrieve your data in a specific order based on values in the fields. We define different types of queries that you will use, and explain how to use joins to associate data from multiple tables.

With a basic understanding of how the tables and queries work with Access, you can then see how they are used to support a relational data model.

Chapter 3: Relational Data Model

The discussion of the relational data model (RDM) and normalization builds on the database fundamentals that were covered in Chapter 2. Together, these two chapters give you the terminology and the basics for understanding the RDM and how Access implements it. Although this chapter may seem somewhat academic, it provides an important foundation for understanding why and how you should organize data into appropriate tables and fields to support an efficient database.

This chapter covers some of the history of the RDM and its inventor. This is by far the most popular database model in use today. The same basic model used by Access is used in all other popular database programs, even the "heavy hitters" such as Oracle and Microsoft SQL Server. The model is based on mathematical set theory. What the inventor called a "relation" we now call a table. The purpose of the RDM is to store the data in a logical, consistent manner so you can later retrieve exactly the data you need to process and display it, or to create reports from it.

In addition to learning about the relational data model, you will learn a set of criteria known as the *normal forms*. The process of applying the normal forms, called *normalization*, helps build databases that follow the relational data model. While explaining the normal forms and normalization, we have tried to use terms that are as nontechnical as possible to reduce the possibility of confusion.

The discussions are accompanied by visual examples that demonstrate both what your data should look like when it complies with a normal form, and what the data might look like if it does not.

With a basic understanding of the fundamentals for database tables and designs, you are ready to start applying the concepts. You begin by creating a database for managing data about people, a subject that everyone is familiar with.

Part II: Dealing with Customers and Customer Data

People and organizations are topics you will find in many serious business database applications, regardless of the business function that the application addresses. The chapters in this section guide you through creating database models to manage information about people and organizations of all types.

In looking at customer relationship management, we will consider ways to leverage the data that you might have so that you can better serve your customers or clients, whether they are businesses, individuals, or any other entity.

The last two chapters in this part demonstrate how to create databases that support marketing processes and sales. When discussing marketing, we also provide some examples that demonstrate how to design questionnaires. You can easily apply the techniques to inspection reports, surveys, checklists, voting forms, and a multitude of other purposes.

Chapter 4: People, Organizations, Addresses

For those of you who cannot wait to dig into real-life examples, this chapter provides a wealth of them. People, organizations, and addresses are a good starting point because nearly everyone is familiar with, or needs to organize, data about people and organizations. We all deal with data about individuals, and most of us are members of some type of organization or association, whether business, noncommercial, or social. Many of you have likely used some form of computerized data, and you are probably quite familiar with the business functions described in the chapter. This type of data will be part of most of the business functions that you will be modeling in your new databases.

You'll take a look at two models for storing information about people and organizations: a simpler one that is appropriate for use with business functions that are not centered on people and organizations; and a more complex design suited for larger business functions that are more people- and organization-centric. The data you need in both is very similar, but they are modeled differently. In either case, it is quite likely that you'll want to modify them by adding fields for data that is specific to your database application. Adding fields is easy; structuring your table layout is not as easy.

In addition to explaining the models and how they correspond to various business functions, this chapter also includes some bonus tables, including some that are populated with reference data. This chapter provides several tables that are used in subsequent chapters.

Chapter 5: Customer Relationship Management

Feeling intimidated by the prices of market-leading customer relationship management (CRM) packages, or even by the lower-end packages and the costs of setting them up and running them? Here's something that will give you a lift: Enterprise organizations who buy those packages use them to manage aspects of their business that affect their relationships with their customers. You can do the same for your small to medium-size business with database applications that you create yourself, and for a fraction of the cost of the top-rated CRM packages. Moreover, because you develop them, you can easily tailor your applications to the exact way you do business. Even if you hire a database developer to help with the design and modifications, the overall costs can be significantly lower and the benefits markedly higher.

You will begin with a review of business functions, identifying particular activities in your organization that can affect customer relations, and considering the subjects and details that lead to the data you will need to gather, collect, and store. First, you consider people and organization information, a familiar subject if you just read the previous chapter. Then you proceed to business functions and communication with your customers; tracking your sales and service functions; marketing, advertising, and awareness campaigns; and sharing information within your organization. These are factors important to your relationship with your customers, and any improvements you can make in the way you handle them will help improve these relationships.

Note an additional ''bonus'' in creating your own applications—you can prioritize the business functions in whatever order you determine will be most beneficial to your organization. You can implement them one at a time on a schedule that fits your business workload and budget. This is a far better alternative to purchasing a package in which much of the expense is front-loaded and the generic functionality does not necessarily target the challenges you face or in the same order of priority.

Finally, if you want to examine some functions in more depth, you will see that later chapters use a different approach to address some of these same issues. You'll find separate chapters on marketing, sales, production, warehousing, inventory, and services. If you implement databases in those areas, you may be able to give yourself an added benefit. The files may provide a source for CRM data that you can use directly by linking to the tables, or you may be able to import selected data into your customer relationship management database.

Chapter 6: Marketing

Although no database can do the marketing for you, this chapter will show you how to create one that makes your marketing efforts more effective and efficient. It covers the important functionality that is included in almost every marketing solution, plus a few extra options. Of course, this chapter expands on what you have already learned about customers, addresses, and organizations. Among the highlights are three models for one of the most useful and diverse tools that you can design: the survey or questionnaire.

The first part of the chapter is focused on marketing campaigns. We start by addressing the data requirements, so you'll explore the needs, activities, and data associated with managing a marketing campaign. An important source of data for this is the existing customer base. Gathering and storing marketing information about your clients can easily be used to increase sales, improve product offerings, and realize many other similar opportunities. We'll explain how the tables support the collection and reporting of data as a marketing campaign progresses through the various stages, such as contacting prospective customers and following up on responses with targeted mailings. As we go through the process, we will create a database named c06Campaign.mdb.

The second section of the chapter explains how to create a model to support a questionnaire, which can be an effective tool for initiating contact, determining interest or satisfaction, and tailoring offerings to a customer's specific interests. We start by creating a basic survey-type questionnaire. This model is easy to create and maintain, and it should be sufficient for many of your needs. We'll also explain how to incorporate a few extra features while maintaining the basic design.

Then, you'll add to the file as we explain the concepts for a more complex design that allows a lot of flexibility for adding questions and functionality. We also demonstrate how to create an interactive questionnaire that uses the existing responses to determine subsequent questions—very much like the online surveys. The concepts used to support a questionnaire are applicable to a multitude of purposes, from marketing campaigns to inspection reports, and from satisfaction surveys to providing book reviews. We even included a bonus query, qryInterviews, that demonstrates how to bring the data together. You'll definitely want to add some more sample data and experiment with qryInterviews!

There are countless ways to leverage these techniques, enabling you to incorporate the tables and functionality into an unlimited number of projects.

This chapter expands on what you learned about organizations, people, and database tables, and provides a framework for creating a marketing database. Similar topics follow in subsequent chapters—for sales, services, and memberships.

Chapter 7: Sales

Sales is one of the most fundamental and comprehensive business areas to model; almost everyone is selling some sort of product. As with all of our examples, the first step is to gather information. You must understand the business rules concerning customers, orders, prices, taxes, quantities, deliveries, and so on. This leads to creating a list of business rules and database requirements. From this, you can determine the key subjects and details that need to be managed. The example we provide creates core tables for the subjects of customers, orders, products, and order details.

As we discuss the business scenarios and create the tables, we'll consider some alternative fields, along with their associated benefits and consequences. The first section of the chapter creates a basic model that will support a variety of sales operations. This is provided on the companion CD in the file c07Sales.mdb.

Next, the chapter covers a more complex model that includes additional requirements to support multiple price options and to identify the employees associated with the transactions. An additional table is added to support a new provision for notes, as shown in the file c07Sales_Complex.mdb.

The last segment of the chapter covers alternative design options and provides some powerful queries to demonstrate how to create customer invoices and calculate order totals. You will learn how to use a single table to store notes that relate to several subjects—somewhat analogous to using sticky notes. These features are provided in c07Sales_ComplexAlt.mdb.

After completing this chapter you should have a good idea of the design process and some alternative approaches. You will have several optional features that you can include in a variety of databases. With this, we are ready to transition our focus from people to processes. The next part of the book discusses areas related to process monitoring, including manufacturing, inventory management, and offering services. A central factor is that they associate a value with the time or process provided.

Chapter 8: Production and Manufacturing

If you are in a production and manufacturing environment, you know that a significant amount of information must be maintained. The database must be able to capture very detailed, process-specific information from the shop floor. It must also calculate and compile data to provide reports for all levels of staff and management. The example database in this chapter focuses on managing manufacturing processes. It will create alarms or notifications about processes that need attention, enable recording the deviations or changes that have been made to a process, and provide a common place to store and retrieve communications.

One special topic we will explore with you in this chapter is the self-referencing table, which is sometimes referred to as "bill of material processing," especially when it refers to the products being manufactured. This type of table is used to organize hierarchical manufacturing processes. You'll find this approach useful for many purposes, such as organizational charts, file structures, and menus.

As an added bonus, in the chapter file, c08ProductionAndManufacturing. mdb, we have included the forms and queries for displaying the data using a TreeView control. The TreeView control is a powerful tool for efficiently organizing and working with data. You often see them used for menus, file lists, process controls, and organization charts

We guide you through each of the steps needed to create a database model, from concept to implementation. Following a structured approach to normalization, we'll create a database that is compact, thorough, and scalable. In walking through these steps, you will learn how to make design decisions such as creating lookup tables (or domain tables), and when it is effective to create child tables. You will also look at one-to-many, one-to-one, and many-to-many relationships between tables.

Finally, you will take a guided walk-through of the database application's operation by following the standard workflow of a typical production work-day. From there, we move to the next chapter and create a database to manage inventory.

Chapter 9: Inventory Management

The goal of inventory management is to know what you have, how much of it is available, and where it is located. This chapter covers the four primary types of information needed to effectively monitor your inventory: products, vendors, storage locations, and inventory transactions—events that add or remove inventory. In addition to the necessary tables, the database for the chapter, c09InventoryManagement.mdb, also includes several queries that enable you to quickly retrieve data to support sound business decisions.

By recording transaction data, you can monitor for minimum stock conditions. Our sample database is developed in such a manner that by using the transactions table, you can calculate the quantity on hand of a product. You can also compare the in-stock levels with minimum stock conditions and determine how many replacement items to purchase to replenish your stock.

You will find that the Inventory Transaction table is a critical part of your database. It has a central role in the calculation of Quantity on Hand reports; for example, you will use Units Transacted to calculate Quantity on Hand. You also use this table to determine the rate at which products are used or sold. This will help you determine how much product you need to order and when to order it. As a bonus, we include a second database, c09PointOfSale.mdb, to emulate sales. It links to the inventory tables and automatically updates the quantity on hand.

Our database sample is designed to allow multiple vendors per product. Each vendor has its own price. In addition, pricing history is tracked, so you can see price trends by vendor and product. We also expand upon the vendors' contact information to provide the capability to store multiple addresses and contacts.

The locations in which you stock your products are managed through the use of a self-referencing table. As explained in Chapter 8, this is a special type of table structure that is highly effective for storing hierarchical information. The locations for storing products take on a hierarchical form that not only helps you group your data by varying levels of detail, but also enables you to easily manage your stock locations for each product.

Chapter 10: Services

A service can be thought of as payment for time, rather than a product. It is an agreement about the value of something performed in a period of time. As such, concepts for process management can be applied to tracking and recording services.

The cost of the service provided may be directly correlated with the time it takes, or it may depend upon how easily the provider can perform this task, especially if that provider can offer the service concurrently for many customers. In this chapter we will model the managing of appointments for a small service company, an events management example, and a process control example. We also create a process that will check for booking conflicts. The concepts can be applied to a multitude of scenarios where you need to check for or avoid overlapping tasks or subjects of any type. The pet grooming and boarding examples begin with the gathering of business rules. There are two different parts to one business: grooming and boarding, and appointments and events. Each has different requirements, so we will discuss them separately. The database for this example, c10Pets.mdb, includes the queries used to determine available openings. The chapter explains some important concepts and relatively advanced techniques related to managing schedules and booking appointments.

From appointments we move into planning complete events, and create a database to manage events, c10Events.mdb. The business scenario is for an events company that handles weddings and corporate events. The key subject areas include customers, events, venues, organizations, service types, and event details.

When you look at events from a process perspective, you can see that they can be broken down into a relatively pre-defined set of steps performed at various stages. For example, in a real estate title and sales business, the steps would likely include contact with clients, letters sent to inform parties of progress, completion and submission of documents, and inspections or searches performed on the property. We've included the file c10Events_Complex.mdb to provide some design alternatives that are not covered in the chapter, such as a centralized contact management layout that can be used to prevent duplication of phone numbers and addresses.

Having described the key business operations, the next part of the book shifts the focus to the administrative tasks related to financial data.

Part IV: Tracking and Analyzing Financial Data

In this part, we look at the financial side of a business. This follows a slightly different format; instead of each chapter being dedicated to a different business function, the tables are explained in Chapter 11, and the accounting functions are explained in Chapter 12.

The data stored in an accounting system can hold the key to a successful business, but only if it is used correctly. If the owners or management only use the data to meet the minimum required reports, important trends will be missed. Obviously, in order to take advantage of any strengths that an analysis may reveal, you must first perform the evaluation. Conversely, if you don't conduct the analysis, a weakness may be overlooked and earnings may suffer.

Chapter 11: Accounting Systems—Requirements and Design

An accounting database is not a solution that ensures a successful business, but rather an essential tool used to increase the chances of success. It is the business strategy systematically translated into financial numbers. The key to a successful accounting and budgeting system is the process used to prepare the projections. The data stored in an accounting system can hold the key to a successful business, but only if it is used correctly. In addition to supporting the reporting requirements, it is an invaluable tool for identifying trends and responding to novel activities.

This chapter covers the basic requirements and principles for an accounting system. We will discuss how to create and use a chart of accounts, the general ledger, subsidiary ledgers, and virtual subsidiary ledgers. You will learn how to create the necessary tables and how to establish the relationships between the tables.

In the discussion of subsidiary ledgers (subledgers), we demonstrate how to create a virtual subledger that uses the detail from the general ledger to create a view of the data, rather than use a separate table that is storing duplicate data. This technique ensures that the subledger always balances with the general ledger. Because the virtual subledger involves the use of queries, the chapter contains a detailed explanation of the queries, and we've included the actual queries in the chapter file, c11AccountingSystems.mdb.

The final section of the chapter describes the tables, queries, and steps used to support standard year-end accounting processes. After the accounting year has been closed, it is common to move data from active tables to *archive tables*. This also gives you the opportunity to create and use the queries needed to calculate and verify record counts and account balances.

After finishing the chapter, you should have all the necessary resources to create the basic model for an accounting system. The file that we create in this chapter is also used in Chapter 12.

Chapter 12: Accounting: Budgeting, Analysis, and Reporting

In this chapter, you will learn about recording financial transactions, working with budget data to perform analysis and create reports. Using the tables created in Chapter 11, the focus is now on understanding the accounting principles and creating the queries that support financial analysis and reporting. We'll illustrate the queries in Access design view as we explain the tables, fields, and criteria that you will need to use to retrieve data for your reports and analysis.

You will also learn how to create the managerial reports that are used to express formal financial goals and measure the financial results. And we will briefly discuss some of the basic concepts and explain the three major types of budgets: cash budgets, operating budgets, and capital budgets.

In addition to demonstrating how to create and use an operating budget, we discuss several helpful budgeting techniques. One example shows you how to allocate projections or expenses over a specified period of time. Because a lot of budget information and analysis is done in Excel, you will also look at different ways to import, export, and work with data in Excel.

After that, we demonstrate how to develop a base set of numbers that can be used to compare predicted and actual results. This enables you to identify any variances in budgeted vs. actual performance, and to perform ratio and financial analysis.

The final section explains how to use the data from the accounting system to create financial reports and analyze profitability. The two main reports are the balance sheet and the income statement, also known as the profit and loss statements. But before you can create the balance sheet, you need to have a trial balance, so we first explain how to create the queries that are used for the trial balance report. We'll then explain the process involved in mapping the data so that it will display on specified lines on the balance sheet and income statement reports. This is an impressive technique that you can apply to other areas outside of accounting.

Finally, we discuss several types of ratio analysis that are used to explain company performance. The main types of ratios are activity, profitability, and net operating. The query results are indicators that can help management make informed business decisions and take timely actions. Examining relationships between the statements and finding trends in those relationships is the definition of analyzing profitability.

That concludes the discussion of financial analysis. The next part of the book includes a chapter on intellectual property, followed by a chapter that covers a system for managing membership information.

Part V: Independent Areas

This part has three stand-alone chapters. Even if your projects don't fall directly into these areas, we recommend that you read the chapters. You will find many correlations to other business functions, so the concepts and techniques discussed in these chapters may benefit your other projects.

The chapters in this part are intended to help you combine concepts and models from multiple sources, and to work with data in other formats. One goal is to enable you to extend your solutions by leveraging available resources.

Chapter 13: Managing Memberships

Organizations with members abound in our society, and all but the very smallest of those will have to automate their activities in some way. This chapter covers several areas that are common to most membership organizations, whether they are formal or informal, profit or nonprofit, public or private. You'll learn how to manage several aspects of data about members, such as contact information, expiration dates, membership types and payment information, and the positions and officers.

Because organizations also hold events outside of the regular meetings and activities, we've included a section to incorporate event management. Rather than providing a full-fledged event-management solution, this material deals primarily with the planning, scheduling, and staffing of events; execution; and follow-up. Recruiting might be considered as a special activity, so we mention that here as well.

This database does not attempt to manage every aspect of a membership organization, but it does give you a good start by covering many common membership management needs. You could incorporate additional features based on functions covered in other chapters in this book or in existing programs that you or the organization might already use.

As you are preparing to create your membership database, you will also want to read the next chapter, "Implementing the Models." It describes a scenario for a not-for-profit organization and demonstrates how to incorporate the examples and data from several chapters and business functions into one database.

Chapter 14: Implementing the Models

This chapter demonstrates how to leverage the features that Access offers as a rapid database development tool. Instead of focusing on creating tables, we show you how to quickly create a solution for a not-for-profit organization by using tables from three other chapters and adding a few basic forms and reports. The application is designed to track membership information, billing and dues, donations, and sales.

The goal is not to create a slick-looking application, but rather to introduce you to several methods for creating forms, reports, and other user interface (UI) objects. We also demonstrate how to create several types of queries to combine data from multiple tables and to filter or limit the results to the specific records that you need. Our examples include parameter queries, select queries, and action queries. These become the record sources for the forms and reports that we create.

This leads directly to creating the forms and walking through the process of adding specific types of controls. We create 16 forms and subforms to provide a menu-driven system to manage member information, collect dues, identify products for sale, create invoices, and send e-mail. You will also learn how to create the reports to list products for sale, create an invoice, list invoices, and create a dues notification letter.

We want to show you how to use the features in Access to quickly create a solution. We have intentionally used several different types of forms, explaining how to create the record source, and even including a little bit of code to control how the forms work. We left the forms and reports in a relatively raw state to make it easy for you to follow the process and compare your work to our examples. Our emphasis is on retrieving and presenting the specific information that you want, rather than adding the format and style that you would display to users.

Once you have created the basic forms and reports, you can easily save them with new names, and then experiment with designs and styles to get just the look and layout that you'd like. We suggest that you create some standard sections that include your group logo and similar items. You can quickly copy these into other forms and reports as desired.

As you develop forms and reports, it is highly recommended that you make frequent backups of your work. Of course, it is easy to create a copy of the complete file, but returning to an early version does not always solve the problem if you are trying to recover from a corrupted object. Sometimes you will need to rebuild forms or reports, which can be quite tedious if they are complicated. It is much easier if you have saved your code to text. As a bonus, we've created a form that contains the instructions and code to save your forms and reports to text.

This is the last chapter that walks you through creating tables and databases. The final chapter in the book talks about working with data that is stored in formats other than Access.

Chapter 15: SQL Server and Other External Data Sources

The principles covered in this book are not only applicable to databases created for Microsoft Access; they are basically the same for Microsoft SQL Server, Oracle, and many other database platforms. The way we have gathered business rules, identified subjects and attributes and created tables, established table relationships, created queries, and created reports is the same for these enterprise relational data management systems as for Access. However, the software platform you choose can affect your design.

In this chapter, we discuss different data types used in SQL Server, and compare them to what is used in Access. Server functionality is covered in detail, so you will learn about the additional features of the client-server platform in the areas of programming, robustness, and the different software editions. We also briefly discuss why server designs often exhibit a preference for narrow and long tables, lookup tables, denormalizing, optimization, problem tables and conversions, and indexing.

There are brief discussions of using Access to work with data on a server with linked tables, pass-through queries and local table storage, as well as using Access Data Project (ADP) format. In additional to SQL Server, we mention some considerations for using SharePoint and provide a short section on working with CSV and XML formats.

The Appendixes

This book contains 10 appendixes that either provide additional reference materials or elaborate on concepts presented within the chapters, supporting and complementing the material presented there. By dividing the topics into printed and bonus items, we have provided extra examples and details to make this book as self-contained as possible.

Appendix A: Field Properties

In addition to specifying the data type for a field, you can also set several field properties to control what data can be accepted, how it will be displayed, and how it can be used. This appendix expands on some of the concepts you've learned in this book as you were creating the tables and fields. In several examples, we set specific field properties to control the type of data that a field can contain or to support relationships between the tables.

Rather than leave you to learn from experience, we are providing a functional database to explore field properties and to demonstrate how to leverage the properties to make it easier to efficiently manage your data. In addition to looking at the data types and field properties as they are used in the files provided, we look at some alternatives. We'll also discuss some helpful combinations for single and multiple field indexes. We end with a detailed explanation and demonstration of how to use Yes/No data types.

Appendix B: Relationships, Joins, and Nulls

The database models that we've created have relied on you to identify and define relationships between tables; when we created queries, we used joins between the tables. In this appendix, we take a closer look at the tools Access provides to manage those database components. We also demonstrate what effect the type of relationship or join has on the records that are returned by a query.

This appendix also includes a detailed discussion about nulls, which have an unknown value, and zero-length strings, which are known to have no value. The examples provided will not only help you understand how they occur, but also how to avoid or to leverage them in your projects. We end by exploring ways to create and use domain or lookup tables.

Appendix C: Resolving Relationship Triangles

In several chapters, we presented models for managing customer data that requires a customer to be categorized as either an individual or an organization, but not both. This type of either-or scenario is quite common, and is by no means limited to dealing with customers, or even people. As is often the case, implementing a table design to support this business rule leads to hard choices between options because there is more than one viable way to do it—and they all require controls in the user interface, or forms.

In this appendix, we take a quick look at two approaches and provide the minimal tables, forms, and queries to demonstrate how they are implemented. We start with a simplified interface that uses less normalized table design, and then we explain how to implement a similar effect with a more normalized table design. The extra benefit for you is having forms and queries that you can incorporate and modify to work for your own scenarios.

Appendix D: Measures—Financial and Performance

Measures are used to evaluate the performance of a business, or segments of a business. This appendix explains how to apply financial and nonfinancial data from both internal and external sources. Financial measures, like the financial ratios and ratio analysis discussed in Chapter 12, are specific to financial results. Performance measures can be, and often are, applied to data that is not strictly financial in nature, such as customer satisfaction. This appendix and the companion files provide instructions and examples that will help you to compile and analyze the data you need to make sound business decisions.

One benefit of using nonfinancial data is creating measures that are more easily compared to other companies. Comparing the dollar amounts of a small business to the dollar amounts of a large corporation would not provide you with a valid benchmark, but if a nonfinancial measure were introduced, such as units produced, a direct comparison of unit costs could be made.

Measures must fit the needs and goals of both management and the people doing and supervising the work. We explain how to create baseline data and benchmarks so that analysis can be done over a given period of time on both quantitative and qualitative measures. The appendix and companion database provide valuable examples of how to create queries to summarize the data.

Appendix E: References and Resources

When you first start searching for help online, the volume of results returned can be overwhelming. Not only do you need to find information that relates to your specific issue, you also need to know that you are getting good advice. This appendix shares some of the sites that we like to frequent and use when we are looking for inspiration and/or help. These include newsgroups, blogs, personal or group sites, and forums. Since most of the resources listed here are online, we have provided the information in electronic format as well as in the book.

The real jewel of this appendix is the database, ADD_BonusResource.mdb. While we were pulling together the sample databases for this book, we realized that we could provide an invaluable bonus just by compiling several of the database tools that we use into one convenient file. Therefore, in addition to providing the database models and explaining the rationale for their design, the Bonus Resource database includes some tools to help you analyze, work with, and create your own database solutions.

The database includes selected forms, tables, queries, and modules from the chapter files. We've also included several bonus modules from the authors that you will find to be helpful as you design and work with other database files. They will help you to efficiently create, manage, and analyze tables. We've also provided several pre-populated reference tables that you can copy into other applications.

Appendix F: What's on the CD-ROM

The material on the CD is arguably the most valuable part of the book. Of course, reading the chapters will help you understand the database models and the real-world scenarios that they are designed to support. By exploring and using the database models you will gain an in-depth knowledge of Access and save countless hours when creating your own solutions.

This appendix provides a brief summary of the directory *Access-DatabaseDesigns* that is provided on the CD. This contains 18 folders with 31 database files and several supporting documents. If you have any hesitation about purchasing this book, we encourage you to scan the list of database models. You'll immediately realize that we've provided an unprecedented compilation of models, guidance, and explanations.

You'll find a more complete list of files and benefits in the *Access-DatabaseDesignsCDGuide* and in the *File Guide* that is in each folder. These are Word documents, so you can easily print them.

With any project of this size and scope, there is always material that cannot fit between the covers of the book; but rather than forego valuable content, we have included one chapter and four appendixes on the CD. You can open the files from the Bonus Content button on the CD Content tab. By saving the files to your computer, you can quickly search, copy and paste, and click to open references—and, of course, you may want to print and store the hardcopy with the book.

Part VI: Bonus Content

Chapter B1 (on the CD): Knowledge: Intellectual Property, Structural Capital, and Intellectual Capital

"Knowledge is power" is an old axiom, but today a parallel statement could be that without knowledge, there can be no success. This chapter addresses three categories of knowledge that are important assets: intellectual property, structural capital, and intellectual capital.

Intellectual property is "knowledge that can be owned"—so you may need to protect it, and you may have to pay for the use of it. As we create a database, b1IPTracking.mdb, to track intellectual property owned by or used by your company, we'll discuss the issues involved with proving ownership, public domain and right to use, and with documenting associated costs and payments.

The second area, structural capital, refers to business assets that collect, store, and display information. This is the definition of your business processes, the procedures you follow, and the methods you employ to give your business an advantage. That advantage can quickly turn into a disadvantage if some of the information is lost. The model that we create, b1ProcessInfo.mdb, could be considered the modern replacement for the employee manual or handbook. It contains information about jobs (positions), business structure (departments), the work done in the departments, the business functions executed to perform that work, and any appropriate details.

The third area, intellectual capital, is knowledge about relationships with employees, suppliers, and customers. The discussion in this chapter focuses on creating database models to manage information relevant to relationships with employees and with suppliers. Customer relationship management is such a key area that we dedicated an entire chapter to it, Chapter 5.

The first model, b1EmployeeRel.mdb, manages information about employees. It provides tools to recognize their achievements and to record additional skills or expertise that they may have in areas not directly related to their job that might qualify them for a promotion or openings in different business areas. It can also be used as a job board, to post openings, and even to help evaluate applicants by comparing qualifications to requirements.

The second model, b1SupplierTrk.mdb, is for tracking your organization's dealings with suppliers. You can evaluate the timeliness and accuracy of orders and deliveries, the quality of material received, and amounts spent with given suppliers. Having this information will enable you to analyze which suppliers are the best choices for a continuing or expanded business relationship.

Appendix BA: Database and Business Terms

This appendix defines many of the database and business terms as they are used in this book. Our goal is to help you understand the terminology in the context that we used it—so the definitions will not necessarily mirror those found in other reference materials.

Appendix BB: Gathering Requirements

Often overlooked or short-circuited, the initial planning phase of database development should include a significant focus on clearly defining both the overall purpose of the database and the specific needs and requirements of the users. This information will become the blueprint for building a solid foundation for the final product: an efficiently working and useful database.

This appendix looks at the process of gathering and documenting the requirements that the database being developed must meet. The documentation helps to ensure that the user and the developer share the same expectations, and it provides a checklist to confirm that the necessary functionality and features are addressed. The emphasis is on asking questions, learning about existing processes, collecting examples of current and desired forms and reports, and learning what users expect and need from the program.

Appendix BC: Data Warehousing Concepts

The concept of a data warehouse is explained as an approach to tables that are specifically designed to make it easier to create reports. The table designs typically do not conform to the rules of normalization required in a relational database. Many of the tables will contain data that has been summarized, include calculated fields, contain repeating groups, and even have the same values stored in multiple tables.

Instead of the normalized designs that you've learned about for transactional tables, the data warehouse model uses fact tables and dimension tables. Fact tables include summarized data with pre-calculated values to make reporting easier and more efficient for the user. Dimension, or dim, tables are much like lookup tables in a relational database; they provide details that describe the data in the fact tables.

A warehouse can also be imitated using temporary tables, extracting data to create them on an ad hoc basis. The dim tables that describe the facts in the temporary fact tables can be added to the permanent set of tables as needed. You also use *temporary tables* or *work tables* to create a quasi-data warehouse in Access; but instead of emulating the fact and dim tables, you might combine these into larger *flat files* specifically designed and populated to support specific types of reports.

There are two key reasons to separate the data that you are analyzing from the live process data. One, it enables you to work with a snapshot of the data. Two, the data is in a flat file and no longer normalized. The snapshot allows you to run a variety of reports against the same set of data, which ensures consistency and avoids the risk of affecting the production data. Having all the data in one table makes it much easier and faster to perform calculations and comparisons. You may even add additional fields.

After creating some basic fact and dim tables, we explain how to create a query to filter and group the data for additional calculations. This demonstrates how using a simple data warehouse design or a temporary table not only makes it easier to create complicated reports, but also improves the performance of slow queries and reports.

Appendix BD: Database Platforms

In addition to understanding the principles of a good database design, you need to consider which platform is the most appropriate for your application and deployment scenario. A platform, in this instance, refers to the software (such as Access) or the combination of hardware and software (such as when using SQL Server) that enables your database application to run efficiently.

Several platforms support the relational database model. To help you determine the appropriate platform for a particular scenario, this appendix discusses some common platforms, along with their key limitations and benefits. The main aspects to evaluate include volume of data, number of concurrent users, data security, whether the data is accessed locally or over a network, and cost.

CHAPTER 2

Elements of a Microsoft Access Database

Regardless of the application you are designing, you need to be familiar with the terminology and the building blocks of database design. This chapter explains the terms and the elements of a database. While this book uses an Access database, the concepts are applicable to all databases. We are addressing the parts of the database providing the data storage of an application, rather than the user interface, typically viewed as the forms and reports.

The collection of data storage elements is referred to as the *schema*. In Microsoft Access the schema elements are known generically as *objects*, and include the following:

- **Tables:** are used to store data. Fields and indexes are essential parts of the table.

- **Relationships:** help to control the data by defining how tables are related.

- **Queries:** are generally used to request information from the tables, but can also be used to add or change information as well as to modify other schema objects.

The following sections expand on each of these schema objects, explaining what they are used for and how they are constructed. It is important that you have a basic understanding of these objects so that you can build a solid schema for your database.

Database Schema

When building or working with any type of project, whether it is a tree house or a database, it is important to have all the necessary parts, but that's not enough—you need a plan. If you're building a tree house, the plan will help you ensure a successful finished product. When you build a database, you also need the parts, or objects—tables, relationships, and queries—and you need a plan. The plan for your database is called the *schema*, which refers to how the objects interact. The schema comprises the configurations, definitions, and rules that control how the data is entered, stored, and retrieved.

NOTE There are additional controls built into the user interface, but this chapter focuses on what can be done at the table level.

In Access, as with almost any relational database management system (RDBMS, also sometimes referred to as RDM, or relational data model), the objects that make up the schema are hierarchically dependent upon each other. The core hierarchy of the schema used by the database engines used by Access (both ACE and Jet) is shown in Figure 2-1.

NOTE The term "database" is used very loosely in conversation. It is often used to describe the schema items that define the data. At other times, it is used to describe the application or user interface (UI) that is used when working with the data. In addition, "database" can be used to describe the entire system, including both the schema and the application. The term is also used to encompass a few other concepts as well. With such a variety of possible meanings, it's important to clarify how it is being used within a given conversation. In this chapter, and throughout the book, we use the term database primarily to describe the schema.

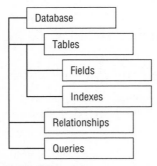

Figure 2-1: Access database schema hierarchy

Tables

A table is the primary object used within a database. The purpose of the table is to hold the data stored in the database. The number of tables in a database can range from one to hundreds. Each table should represent a collection of data about something that has a distinct existence as an individual unit. The collection, as well as the individual unit, is often called an *entity*. As you read through the chapters and work through the processes to build our model databases, you will also see us discuss things as the universe of *items* that are categorized or grouped into *subjects* and *details*. The subjects will typically become the tables and the details will become the fields. It is common for developers to also discuss tables as *entities* along with the *attributes* (fields or details) that are specific to the table.

Tables look like spreadsheets, but a table is *not* a spreadsheet. Within a spreadsheet, you can store, present, and perform calculations on data; but a table will only hold data. Databases use a table to store data, a query to perform calculations, and a report or form to present data. This separation of functionality provides the power and flexibility of a RDBMS such as Microsoft Access.

Since the table is the key object of our discussion, it is important that you become familiar with the components and terminology associated with tables. Table columns are called *fields*, and the rows are called *records*. While the number of records (rows) in a table can grow to a very large amount, with very few exceptions, when you are done with the design, your table will have a fixed number of fields (columns) and that number will not change unless there is a major redesign of the schema.

Each record represents the information for a distinct individual unit of the collection of data represented in the table. For example, if you have a table to store information about people, you will have one record for each person to be represented; so you may have dozens or thousands of records. Every record will have the same fields, whether they contain data or not.

Each field represents a specific piece of information—an *attribute*—that is used to describe the record. For example, when considering the attributes of a person, you may choose to create fields for first name, last name, and date of birth.

Figure 2-2 illustrates these concepts.

There are several different types of tables; and each type has a specific function and role that it is intended to serve. You should understand the purposes and benefits of each table type so that you can match the type of table to the role or process that you need it to perform. This will help you design a database schema that will efficiently store and retrieve your data. Table 2-1 describes several different types of database tables, provides examples for how they can be used, and lists ways they may be referred to.

Fields

The concept of the database field is relatively straightforward. A field stores a value that contributes to the full description of one record in the table.

In addition to the primary key, which we will define later, a record can be described with either a single field, as might be the case with some lookup tables, or it may require numerous fields. For example, a table with information about people may have dozens of fields. When you design the table and identify the required fields, you need to apply normalization rules. In essence, when you normalize a database, you are limiting each table to contain information about only one subject. This may sound like a simple thing to do, but you may be surprised at how the little things can trip you up. Normalization is discussed in depth in Chapter 3, ''Relational Database Model.''

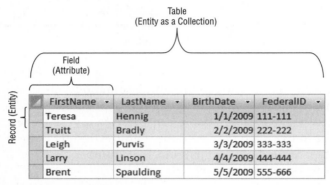

Figure 2-2: Table, record, and field

Table 2-1: Common Table Types Used in Applications

TABLE TYPE	COMMON TERMS	DESCRIPTION
Transactional	Normal Main Base Primary Operational	Transactional tables are used to store the core data of your application. They hold the business data that you capture and retrieve the most frequently. Depending on your application, the records can represent different activities, such as the following: Financial: Debits and credits Employment: Who works in what department and on what project Sales: Which client bought what product from each salesperson Transactional tables are the focus of data *normalization* efforts during the design phase of a database solution. You learn more about that in Chapter 3, ''Relational Database Model.''

TABLE TYPE	COMMON TERMS	DESCRIPTION
Functional	Lookup Junction (aka Intersection)	These types of tables provide a list of values to be used in specific fields in the transactional table (these values, called *foreign keys,* are covered in the next section). Examples might be a list of available classes for students, or a list of available products for purchase. The information contained in a look-up table may come from one table, or from several tables, as is the case with *many-to-many* relationships. Yet another term that will be explained shortly.
	Configuration	Sometimes you need to store values specific to the application's functionality so that the information can easily be retrieved as needed. Configuration tables are often used to store the location of the network drive that contains shared items, such as the company logo, or a list of objects that the application needs to cycle through when it is running.
	Temporary	You may use temporary tables to store data snapshots. Snapshots may be used to improve the speed of the reports, or to perform calculations that would otherwise require a complex series of queries. Temporary tables are also recommended as a staging area for importing data. They can be used to clean up or otherwise manipulate the data before adding to your transactional tables. Using a temporary table allows you to work with a copy of the data without locking or putting the "live" data at risk.
Archive	Archive Backup	Archive tables contain permanent data and often do not adhere to a normalized structure. In some cases they may be the primary data source for data warehousing solutions.

Every field in a table has properties, and the most important property is the Data Type property. The data type defines the kind of information you can store in that field. For example, if you set the field's data type to Date/Time, only dates and/or times can be stored in the field. The most forgiving data type is Text, because text will accept anything that is entered. That does not mean you should set all your fields to the text type, however. Using the right data type for the field ensures that you will capture good data, and helps you maintain the data integrity of your database.

NOTE The database engine that powers Microsoft Access is referred to by many synonymous terms: Access database engine, Access Connectivity Engine, ACE, the ACE database engine. All these terms refer to the same entity. ACE was introduced with Access 2007.

Earlier versions of Access, up through 2003, used the Joint Engine Technology database engine, also referred to as the JET database engine, the abbreviation JET, or the name Jet. Recent Microsoft documentation refers to "Jet," as a name, and not the acronym commonly used. Jet is the predecessor of ACE, thus the JET acronym or name is often present in ACE properties and documentation.

Table 2-2 lists the different data types available to you with the ACE database engine through the Access user interface, as well as their counterparts in the *SQL language* syntax used by ACE and Jet. To avoid confusion later, we want to clarify that that the lists of Data Types and Field Properties are based on what you will see in the table design view using Access 2007, so they are subject to change.

Table 2-2: Field Data Types Available in Jet/ACE

USER INTERFACE DATA TYPE	JET/ACE SQL DATA TYPE	DESCRIPTION
Text	TEXT	This can store text, numbers, and symbols. The field can contain up to 255 characters.
Memo	LONGTEXT	Memo represents an extended block of text. Memo fields can contain up to 65,535 characters if manipulated through a text box control in the user interface. If the field is manipulated through code, the field size is limited by the size of the database; so theoretically, it could approach 2 GB in one field alone.
Hyperlink	LONGTEXT	A memo field with an additional setting to indicate hyperlink data. Hyperlink fields can contain up to 2048 characters.
Number (Field Size = Byte)	BYTE	Unsigned integer; 1 byte. The values can range from 1 to 255.

USER INTERFACE DATA TYPE	JET/ACE SQL DATA TYPE	DESCRIPTION
Number (Field Size = Integer)	SHORT	Whole number; 2 bytes. The values can range from −32,768 to 32,767.
Number (Field Size = Long Integer)	LONG	Whole number; 4 bytes. The values can range from −2,147,483,648 to 2,147,483,647. This is the default field size for the Number data type, however the default setting can be manually changed in the Access options.
Number (Field Size = Single)	SINGLE	Single-precision, which means 7 significant digits with floating-point numeric values; 4 bytes. Negative values can range from −3.402823E38 to −1.401298E-45. Positive values can range from 1.401298E-45 to 3.402823E38.
Number (Field Size = Double)	DOUBLE	Double-precision, which means that the value has15 significant digits; 8 bytes. It uses floating-point numeric values. Negative values can range from −1.79769313486231E308 to −4.94065645841247E-324. Positive values can range from 4.94065645841247E-324 to 1.79769313486232E308.
Number (Field Size = Replication ID)	GUID	Global Unique Identifier (GUID); 16 bytes. The typical use for this data type is Replication. Replication ID is typically used as, but not limited to, a foreign key field to an AutoNumber. Although Replication itself is not supported in the Access 2007 or newer file formats, the Replication ID Field Size can be used in all versions of Access. Replication ID is a reference value which is unique in any context, so it has capabilities well beyond that of replication.
Number (Field Size = Decimal)	DECIMAL	A data type in which you can set the precision and scale of the numbers to be stored. The precision is the total number of digits allowed in the number. The scale is the number of digits to the right of the decimal place. For zero-scaled numbers, that is, numbers with no decimal places,

Continued

Table 2-2: (*continued*)

USER INTERFACE DATA TYPE	JET/ACE SQL DATA TYPE	DESCRIPTION
		the range is +/-79,228,162,514,264,337, 593,543,950,335. For numbers with 28 decimal places the range is +/-7.9228162514264337593543950335. The smallest non-zero number that can be represented as a Decimal is 0.0000000000000000000000000001. Please note that the Field Size of Decimal is not directly supported by VBA, but it can be used in VBA's Variant data type.
Currency	CURRENCY	Currency (scaled integer); 8 bytes. This will automatically display the dollar sign, or designated currency indicator, and show two decimal places. You can adjust the display through the field property settings. −922,337,203,685,477.5808 to 922,337,203,685,477.5807
AutoNumber (Field Size = Long Integer or Field Size = Replication ID)	AUTOINCREMENT	AutoNumber and its associated Field Size is a special data type the uses field size of Long Integer or Replication ID. Access will provide the values for fields with the AutoNumber Data Type. The value provided is either an increment of the previous value, or a randomly generated value. If the field size is set to Replication ID, the value is always random. To create a relationship with an AutoNumber field requires a field with a Number data type and field size of Long Interger or Replication ID, respectively. The Long Integer is the more common Field Size selected. Please see the respective data type and field size for more information.
Date/Time	DATETIME	Date/Time; 8 bytes. Dates are displayed in the short date format specified by your computer; times are displayed according to time format specified. You can change the display format by using the Format property of a control or field. Dates are stored in a numeric form equivalent to the data type of Number with a Field Size of Double. Values to the left of the decimal represent the date while values to the right of the decimal represent time.

USER INTERFACE DATA TYPE	JET/ACE SQL DATA TYPE	DESCRIPTION
		Midnight is 0 and midday is 0.5. Negative whole numbers represent dates before 30 December 1899, which has a numeric value of 0. The valid range is from January 1, 100 12:00 AM to December 31, 9999 11:59 PM.
Yes/No	BOOLEAN	A one-byte value that represents only two options: True or False; Yes or No; On or Off or -1 or 0. In ACE/Jet, the value returned by the keyword False is 0. The value returned by the keyword True is -1. Most database programs use 0 for False, but some use different values for True. SQL Server uses1 for True. One work-around is to use compare to not equal to 0 ($<>$ 0), by doing so, any value, other than zero, will produce a result of True for the comparison operation.
OLE Object	LONGBINARY	Binary data; 1GB. It is often used for images. The OLE Object cannot be indexed.
Lookup Wizard	Not Available	Launches a wizard that guides you through creating a field that will get its values from another table or from a list of values. The wizard will set the data type according to the selections you make in the wizard; it will typically be either Long Integer or Text.
Attachment	Not Available	Similar to attachments in e-mail. Images, spreadsheet files, documents, charts, and other types of supported files can be attached to the records in your database. Attachment fields utilize storage space more efficiently than OLE Object fields. This data type is available only in the Access 2007 format and higher.

You can find more information about the data types that are most often used in association with Microsoft Access at the following online location:

```
http://office.microsoft.com/client/helppreview.aspx?AssetID=
HV100480661033&QueryID=eyiFBPXGD&respos=1&rt=2&ns=MSACCESS.
DEV&lcid=1033&pid=CH101004451033
```

Alternatively, the same information is available in the Access help file under "Comparison of Data Types," or by looking up the help topic HV10048066.

NOTE Access 2007 introduced complex data types with two new fields: multi-valued and attachment. The attachment data type is described in Table 2-2. A multi-valued field has the unique capability to store more than one value associated with a single record. The data type of a multi-valued field can vary because the field itself is essentially an enhancement of an existing field, which already has a primary data type associated with it. These two data types, or fields, are only available in the ACCDB file format, and files containing those data types cannot be converted to MDB files.

Field Properties

Once you have selected the data type for a field, you will have the opportunity to use several related field properties. Field properties are specific to the data type, and they are used to help control and maintain the data.

By effectively using field properties, you can create a more friendly interface for users, improve the integrity of the data, and increase the performance of the database. Controlling what goes into a field can give you the ability to speed data entry, display your data in specific formats, and validate the data as it is entered.

Field properties are displayed when you open a table in design view. The properties are listed in a pane on the lower portion of the view using two tabs named General and Lookup. Table 2-3 lists the properties from the General tab. As we mentioned earlier, the list of available field properties is based on the data type of the field. Microsoft added a few new field types and field properties to Access 2007and the ACCDB file formats, so prior versions and the MDB file formats do not contain the entire list as presented in Tables 2-3 and 2-4.

Table 2-3: Field Properties (General Tab)

PROPERTY	DESCRIPTION
Field Size	This sets the maximum size of the data that you can store in the field. For text fields the value indicates the number of characters allowed. For numeric fields, you can chose from a list that defines the range of values the field can store. Table 2-2 explains each choice and the range the choice accepts.
Format	Used to set the format in which you wish to display your data. This setting will not affect the way the data is stored. This setting can be overridden at the form or report level by setting the format property of the control used to display the data. Format is often used in conjunction with currency and dates.
Decimal Places	Sets the number of decimal places you wish to make visible when displaying your numeric data. The database will still store all extra precision entered, so if you set 2 for number of decimal places and then a number such as 2.259854246 is entered, the complete value will be stored, but only 2.26 will be displayed.

PROPERTY	DESCRIPTION
Input Mask	Provides a pattern in which the data is entered into your field. Sometimes used for things like phone numbers or parts. Use with caution at the table level as this can also be done on the form used to collect the data.
Caption	The label given to your field when viewed on a form, report, or in datasheet view of a query or table. Using a caption can speed the process for creating forms and reports as the caption will become the default label for the field.
Default Value	The value given to a field automatically for new records. For a time stamp, this is often set as Now(). Be alert that Access puts a default value of 0 in number fields; but you can change that using the Field Properties.
Validation Rule	An expression that must evaluate to True in order to limit or constrain the data being entered into your table.
Validation Text	The text that your user will see if they enter data that does not meet the Validation rule criteria, i.e. returns False when evaluated by the Validation rule.
Required	Specifies whether you require data in the field. A record will not be saved until there is a value in every field that requires a value. This setting is particularly helpful for ensuring that all necessary data is obtained. You may need to provide an option for N/A to allow people to proceed with data entry and return later to provide the correct value.
Allow Zero Length	Specifies whether you will allow a zero-length string to be stored in text fields. A zero-length string is string without any characters, not even a space. Please note that a zero-length string is not the same as a special value known as a Null which is defined as: contains no valid data. You can learn more about these concepts in the help files for Access.
Index	Allows you to quickly define an index for the selected field.
Unicode Compression	Allows you to define how Access stores text. If set to yes, the text is stored with non-unicode characters. Unicode consumes two-bytes, where as non-unicode consumes one byte. Most applications do not require you to make changes to this property.
IME Mode	Input Mode Editor (IME) mode related to the language settings and the Kanji conversion mode. Options are presented to you with a combo box of choices. You can learn more about these concepts in the help files for Access.
IME Sentence Mode	Specify the sentence mode for the Japanese language and the IME. The options are presented to you with a combo box.

Continued

Table 2-3: (*continued*)

PROPERTY	DESCRIPTION
Smart Tags	Allows you to specify the smart tags for the field. Smart Tags allow you to quickly do common tasks with recognized patterns of information.
Text Format	Specifies the type of text, either Rich Text or Plain Text, of a field you have defined as a Memo field.
Text Align	Specifies the alignment of your field value within a control; this can also be modified on a case-by-case basis in forms and reports.
Show Date Picker	Tells Access to show a date picker control for your date/time data typed fields.
Append Only	Specifies whether or not a Memo typed field will allow edits of previously entered data. This property was added in 2007 and can be quite helpful for creating audit trails.

The list may seem extensive, so let us assure you that for the most part, you can create your tables and fields with minimum attention to the field properties. However, it is important for you to be aware of what they are and how to work with them, as well as of some of the more common uses.

The field properties on the Lookup tab are listed in Table 2-4. As with the properties on the General tab, the availability of these properties is based on the data type that you have selected for your field. For example the data types of Memo, Date/Time, OLE Object, Hyperlink, and Attachment do not have any available properties on the Lookup tab.

Table 2-4: Field Properties (Lookup Tab)

PROPERTY	DESCRIPTION
Display Control	The type of control that will be used when you view the field in datasheet mode of a table or query; or when you add the field to a form or report. The options are presented to you in a combo box and are dynamic with respect to the data type you have chosen for your field.
Row Source Type	The type of data that Access will use to create a list of items presented in a list box or combo box Display Control for your field.
Row Source	The source of the data for your combo or list box Display Control.
Bound Column	The column from the Row Source that will be saved in your table. The value selected can be from 1 to the number of columns, including hidden columns, that you have in your list.

PROPERTY	DESCRIPTION
Column Count	The number of columns you have in your Row Source.
Column Heads	Specifies whether or not to show column headings when displaying your list of items.
Column Widths	The widths of each column of your Row Source. Each column width is typically separated by a semi-colon (;). Please note that the semi-colon is the standard, however, the regional settings of your operating system can affect the separator used.
List Rows	The number of rows of data to display for a Display Control choice of combo box; if more rows of data exist than are set to display, a scroll bar is available to your users.
List Width	The total width of a list for a combo box list. If the width of the columns is greater than the width of your list, a horizontal scroll bar is made available to your users.
Limit To List	Limits the allowed values to the items in your list.
Allow Multiple Values	Allows you to accept more than one value from the Row Source to be stored in your field.
Allow Value List Edits	Specifies the ability to allow your users to edit the list of choices when you have selected a Row Source Type of *value list.*
Show Only Row Source Values	Specifies whether to display a stored value even if the value is no longer a choice in the list generated by your Row Source. This is useful if your Row Source is dynamic and you wish to see the data that is stored in your field, even if the value stored in your field is no longer a valid choice in the list of choices.

As you define your field properties, it is important to understand that many of the properties specified are *inherited* by the controls used to display your data on a form or report. That means that when you drag-and-drop fields onto a form or report, the controls used to display the data will inherit the table's field property settings. This essentially allows you to create default display settings at the table level.

When warranted, you can quickly modify the control properties on a particular form or report to adapt to a given situation. For example, in general you may want to set the Show Date Picker field property of a Date/Time typed field to *yes*. Setting the property at the field level of the table allows the controls you create with your field to inherit that property setting. However, on one form you may not want to show the Date Picker button, so setting the

Show Date Picker of your control to *no* tells Access to hide the date picker for that specific control.

> **WARNING** Defining your lookup fields at the table level can often lead to confusion of what is actually stored in your table. For example, setting the bound column to 1, then setting the column width to 0 for the first column, will cause Access to display the value of the second column of your combo or list box while viewing your table in datasheet view. However, the value stored in your table is from the hidden column of the list. The visual effect the datasheet view gives you is that the value from second column is stored in your table, which often will lead to confusion with searching and sorting.
>
> Lookup fields and combo box controls can be powerful and beneficial tools that you will find in almost every database. Along with the power comes some significant complexities and nuances. So we encourage you to study examples in the Access help files, books, and other online resources.

Indexes

After you have entered data into the database, you will want to be able to retrieve it. An *index* can be an effective tool to help the database retrieve data faster. If you are old enough to remember using a public library without a computer system, you will surely recall using the index cabinet. When you were looking for a specific book, you did not just roam the library hoping to find it — instead, you went to the index cabinet to find out where the book was stored. You could identify the right drawer based on either the name of the book or the author; and in that drawer, you would find the index card containing the information about the book and its location. A similar concept applies to the way indexes are used by the database engine.

Indexes are a valuable tool for the database engine, and the indexing itself is totally transparent to you as the database designer or user. When searching for values in a particular field, the database engine can optimize the search by using the key values associated with the index fields. In addition to ordering records and improving search performance, you can use indexes to prevent duplication of data in fields that are part of the key of a unique index. You will get a better picture of that in the upcoming example.

Indexes specify the order in which records are accessed, and therefore they enforce a rule or definition for your data. Indexes are built on existing fields in a table. Every table with a primary key will have at least one index: the field for the primary key. Access will automatically create an index on primary key fields and on fields that begin or end with the letters "id," "key," "code," or "num." You should not manually create an index on these fields as this will actually create two indexes on the field and cause undue work for the database engine. You can change the settings for the auto index fields in the Table Design Section of the Access Options.

As noted earlier, you can create an index on just about any field; and you can even include up to ten fields in one index. However, you can not create an index on a field with the data type of OLE Object. The field or combination of fields used for the index is known as a *key*. A key defined with two or more fields is known as a *compound key*. See Appendix B for a more detailed discussion of compound keys.

A *key value* is formed by concatenating the values from the fields specified for a key. For example, a key, or index, using LastName and FirstName from Figure 2-1 could be SpauldingBrent. If the index had a property that did not allow duplicates, you could not have another LastName-FirstName combination of SpauldingBrent; but you could have SpauldingTruitt. Indexes can be thought of as a single-column table containing the stored key values. Table 2-5 describes the different types of keys that are used to create indexes.

Table 2-5: Index Key Types

KEY TYPE	DESCRIPTION
Natural key	A field or combination of fields that has values which uniquely describe the entity being modeled by the table—for example, a serial number or VIN for a vehicle. A natural key means that there are no duplicates. Contrary to popular perception, a social security number is not a good choice for a natural key; not only is it not necessarily unique, but it is not an appropriate value to be stored in an Access database.
Surrogate key	An artificially created value, like an AutoNumber data type, that is created to uniquely identify a record in a table. The value of a surrogate key does nothing to describe the entity being represented by the record. The value for this key is generated by the system upon record generation. Usually, the surrogate key value is relevant only to the system that generated the key.
Candidate key	A field or combination of fields that meet the requirements for a *primary key*. That is, it cannot be blank and it uniquely identifies the record.
Search key	A field or combination of fields that are searched or ordered. The values of the keys do not need to be unique.
Relational key	A field or combination of fields that are used to relate tables, meaning that they create a relationship between two tables.

In addition to contributing to search optimization, you can use the `Index` property to ensure that there is no duplication of data in that field by setting the UniqueValues property to yes. The previous example with SpauldingBrent demonstrated how the unique value property for a multi-field key prevented two records from having the field name combination of SpauldingBrent.

With so many advantages, you must resist the temptation to create unnecessary indexes. Too many indexes can have a negative impact on database performance. Updates and additions to data often affect multiple tables, and tables with numerous index fields require the database engine to maintain and update the indexes associated with every table that is affected. In general, you should create an index for fields that are searched often, participate in a relationship, or are frequently sorted.

You can usually determine whether an index can function as the primary key for a table by asking the following question: Is the key value of the index unique? Although we strongly encourage you to use an AutoNumber field for the *primary key*, you can use a natural key. To be a candidate for a primary key, the index key must be unique, or be a natural key—although not every table might require a primary key. And, if you follow our example, all of your tables will use an AutoNumber for the primary key field.

There are often passionate discussions about which type of key you should use for the primary key index of a table: a *natural key* or a *surrogate key* (these terms are defined in Table 2-3). Although there is not a wrong answer, it is important for you to understand the ramifications of each option before deciding which approach you want to implement.

The two most important factors to consider when choosing between a natural or surrogate key are performance and maintainability. If you use compound keys to create relationships between tables, you will have to include each field in every related table. However, from an implementation and maintainability standpoint, that can quickly become tedious and time consuming. And, from a performance perspective, compound keys require the database engine to not only evaluate multiple fields for every record, but it has to evaluate every combination to ensure that the entire combination is unique. Even without doing the math, you can imagine how many potential combinations there are for 1,000 records with just two fields in a compound key.

In addition to the work that a database engine must do, you can also create some significant hurdles for yourself. If you use a natural key as the primary key or to build relationships, future changes to your business model that affect the natural key field will impact the database design. The natural key field will need to be changed and the values updated throughout the application —for every record in all of the related tables. This can be a complex and costly change to the system, not just monetarily, but also in terms of time and productivity. Using a surrogate key protects you from such an impact because changes to the business rules or processes will not change the value for any primary key.

We recommend a single-field primary key because of the clarity and simplification that it provides to the table and to the database as a whole. Adding a field to store a unique value that has no apparent relationship to the data in the record is known as using a surrogate key. In a Jet or ACE data file, you can use the AutoNumber data type to have Access create the unique values for a field. Regardless of the data type, the primary key field is often used for building relationships between tables and enforcing business rules.

TIP Using an AutoNumber data type for the primary key of every table can simplify database design and improve performance.

Our recommendation is to always assign a primary key for each table in the database. We also recommend that you use an AutoNumber data typed field as a single-field primary key. For additional candidate keys, you can create a unique index on any field that it is needed in order to maintain data integrity.

Relationships

Relationships are used to define the linked fields between the tables in the database. Similar to an index, a relationship defines a rule for your data and uses the types of keys just discussed. A relationship has a primary key and a foreign key.

The primary table in the relationship, referred to as the *parent table*, provides the primary key to the relationship. The secondary table in the relationship, known as the *child table*, provides the foreign key. The primary key and the foreign key must contain the same number of fields, and the related fields must have the same data type. For example, you could describe a relationship as follows: Table tblChildren using Field1 references Field1 from table tblParent.

WARNING Remember that both relationships and indexes use the term "primary key" but the meaning is different and does not necessarily refer to the same fields of the table.

Occasionally, developers will declare a compound key for the primary key index of a table, and add a single-field surrogate key for a unique index. Subsequently, when building relationships between tables, the single-field surrogate key is used as the primary key of the relationship instead of the compound key that is the primary key index. A surrogate key used in this fashion is called a *relational key*. This reinforces our earlier advice: We strongly recommend a single-field AutoNumber primary key for tables and relationships.

Relationships between two tables can be defined as either *one-to-many* or *one-to-one*. Although you will also hear about *many-to-many* relationships, in reality these are managed by using a junction table with two one-to-many relationships. You will see an example of these types of relationships in Figure 2-3. Before you get to the diagram, it will be helpful for you to understand a little more about table relationships. Review Table 2-6 to learn more about the three primary types of relationships that you may encounter and utilize in a database schema.

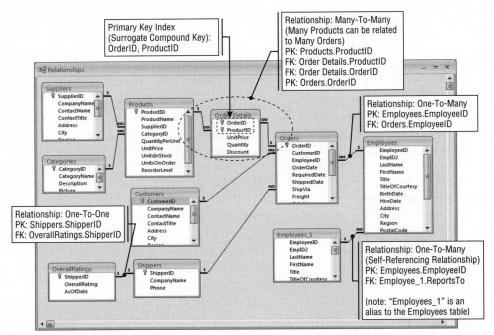

Figure 2-3: Table relationships

Table 2-6: Table Relationships

RELATIONSHIP	DESCRIPTION
One-to-one (1:1)	A single record in the primary table can be related to only a single record in the foreign table. For this type of relationship to exist, both the primary key and the foreign key must be unique.
One-to-many (1:M)	A single record in the primary table can have many related records in the foreign table. This is often described as a parent child relationship.
Many-to-many (M:M)	Multiple records in one table can have many related records in another table. To create this kind of relationship, you use a third table; a functional table, known as a *junction table*. The relationship is created by defining a one-to-many relationship between the junction table and each primary table. Every record in the junction table will store a unique value from each primary table, thereby making the junction table the foreign table in a one-to-many relationship with each primary table. For example, in a school, teachers will instruct many classes and each class can be taught by several different teachers. A many-to-many relationship is created to identify which classes a teacher will instruct, and this same relationship can report which teachers instruct each class.

With that background, you can now look at Figure 2-3, and understand how it provides a graphical representation of table relationships. To build on something that you may have used before, our figure uses the Northwind.mdb database for Access 2003 provided by Microsoft. The same features can be seen in the Microsoft-provided Northwind 2007.accdb database for Access 2007.

As we've explained, a relationship defines a rule for your data. However, your data will not magically follow that rule just because you've created a relationship between two tables. You can use a relationship attribute known as *referential integrity (RI)* to make the data comply by enforcing referential integrity. It is your choice whether the RI is enforced or not. As with other features, there are several options that allow you to control how relationships work. Table 2-7 describes how each option will affect your data.

TIP By now you understand how relationships relate one table to another table with a key value. However, that doesn't necessarily require two tables. An option that we often overlooked is the *self-referencing* table, this is created when both the foreign key and the primary key of the relationship come from the same table.

This type of table configuration can be very useful with a table that provides data for a TreeView control, (think of the folders and files displayed when you open the My Documents folder on your computer). You will also be quite familiar with another scenario for a self-referencing table: an Employees table that includes the roles and identifies the supervisor for each employee. The supervisor foreign key value uses the primary key of supervisor's record (from the same table).

Referring to Figure 2-3, the Employees table of the Northwind database shows a self-referencing relationship. In that case, the ReportsTo field is the foreign key of the relationship, and the EmployeeID field is the primary key of the relationship; and the relationship type is one-to-many. Notice that the same table (Employees) appears twice in the Relationships window.

Table 2-7: Referential Integrity Settings

OPTION	DESCRIPTION
Not Enforced	A relationship is defined, but there is not a requirement for your data to adhere to a rule. The foreign key value may hold any value; it is not limited to the values that exist in the parent table. This option increases the risk to the integrity of the data in the child table; and it can allow the child table to have records that do not relate to anything in the parent table, also known as an *orphaned record*.

Continued

Table 2-7: (*continued*)

OPTION	DESCRIPTION
Enforced	A relationship is defined, and your data must adhere to the rule. The foreign key value must exist in the set of primary key values; if this condition is not met, then a record change or modification will not be saved to the database. There is one exception: If a foreign key field returns Null, the foreign table records are not prevented from being stored. Null values can have specific effects when working with data. You will learn more about that in future chapters; and you can also find useful information in the help files for Microsoft Access.
Enforced-Cascade Delete	In addition to being enforced, this setting will also delete related records. If a record in the primary key table is deleted, then all the records with foreign key equivalents are deleted from other tables as well.
Enforced-Cascade Update	In addition to being enforced, this setting will also promulgate updates to related records. If the relationship's primary key is updated, then those updates are cascaded to the foreign key fields and values of related tables. This functionality is particularly useful with lookup tables. Keep in mind that AutoNumber fields cannot be updated in this manner, so if the relationship is built using an AutoNumber in the child table, it will not be updated using Cascade Update.
Enforced-Cascade Set Null	In addition to being enforced, this provides a way to maintain and control child records when the parent record is deleted. When a record in the primary key table is deleted, then all the foreign key equivalents in the child records are updated to Null. You can only set this feature through code, it is not an option listed in the relationship settings displayed by Microsoft Access.

Queries

Queries enable you to request data or perform an action on data. You can even do both with one query. Because there are several types of queries, you need to select the right query for the type of action that you want to perform. One of the great features in Access is that it provides several wizards that make it easy to create very complex queries. And, you can study these queries to learn how to create your own queries and query criteria.

A high-level overview of queries could be summed up by explaining the two basic types: *select queries* and *action queries*. Select queries are used to retrieve data from the database tables. Action queries are used to add, change, or delete data in the tables. You can use select queries to retrieve data from multiple tables or other data sources; and they can even perform calculations on the data.

Select queries offer a couple of hybrids including some that the Query Wizard will create, the Crosstab Query Wizard, the Find Duplicates Query Wizard, and Find Unmatched Query Wizard. You can also use a select query to collect and provide the data just about everywhere that a table can be used, including using a query within another query. When you use a query within a query, it is called a *subquery*.

Most select queries can be converted to an action query by changing the query type. The query names make them fairly self-explanatory. The action queries are: Make Table Query, Update Query, Delete Query, and Append Query. One of the unique benefits of the append query is that it provides a mechanism for manually inserting values into the AutoNumber fields. You can find good instructions and learn more using the Help files for Access.

When you use multiple tables in a query, you *join* them. A join is similar to a relationship, and in most cases the join will use the same fields that are used in the table relationship. However, unlike a relationship, a join is not a rule that governs the data as it is entered in your database. A join links tables together for the purpose of data retrieval. In other words, you use a relationship to govern data as it is being added to your database, and you use a join to shape data going out of your database.

When using the Query Designer in Access, you will notice that as you add tables to the query, the designer may automatically create a join between the tables. When this AutoJoin feature is enabled (the default setting), as you add tables that have a defined relationship, they will immediately be connected by a join that represents that relationship. If you add unrelated tables to the query, the Query Designer will try to identify fields with the same name and data type and then create a join on those fields; it will only create one AutoJoin per pair of tables.

As you work with queries, you will notice that the AutoJoin will not always be the join that you want to use in the query. You can modify or delete a join created by the AutoJoin feature and then create the join that is appropriate for your data needs. You can also keep the AutoJoin and add additional joins. This can be helpful to find records that match certain values in both tables or those that are missing a counterpart in the partner table.

NOTE You can disable the AutoJoin feature by going to the Object Designer's tab in Access Options. Under Query Design, you can uncheck the box for "Enable AutoJoin." You may find this to be overkill, as the AutoJoin can be helpful. But, it is very easy to manage the joins on a query-by-query basis. To remove a join in the Query Designer, select the join by clicking on the line, and press Delete on your keyboard. You can also right click the join line and select Delete from the popup menu. To add a join in the designer, click on the field you want to join in the first table, hold the mouse, and drag to the field in the second table you want to relate. The Query Designer will create the join for you. Right click on the join line and

select Join Properties to edit the join as needed. Please note that the location of Access Options may vary depending on the version of Access that you are using. The Access Help file is often a good resources for learning more.

Table 2-8 describes the different *join types*. These are basically categorized as an *outer join, inner join, cross join,* or *unequal join.* An outer join can take the form of a left join or a right join. Before you start spinning, we'll add some clarity by briefly explaining the concept of left and right joins. As you add tables to the Query Designer in Access, the tables are said to be added from left to right. Therefore, if two tables are added, the first is considered the left, and the second is considered the right. If a third were added, the second table would be considered the left when joined to the third, but the second table would still be the right when referencing the join to the first table. The bottom line is that in this context, right and left refer to the sequence of the tables.

Table 2-8: Join Types

JOIN	DESCRIPTION
Left (Outer)	Using the join field(s), the query will return all records from the left table and only the matching records from the right table.
Right (Outer)	Using the join field(s), the query will return all records from the right table and only the matching records from the left table.
Inner	Using the joined field(s), the query will return only the matching records from both tables. This is a default join, and it can lead to confusion as records that are not represented in both tables will not be included in the results.
Cross	Also known as a *Cartesian join*, the query will return each row from one table combined with each row from the other table. The results are called a *cross product* or a *Cartesian product*. To retrieve a cross product you do not explicitly join the tables in the query. Note that a cross join can return a large number of records. For example, if table1 has three records and table 2 has four records, a cross join of the two will yield 12 records (4 x 3).
Unequal	Unequal joins are based on the inequality of the joined field. This means that the join expression is based on the inequality of two values, rather than the equality. So, two record having the same value would be False and therefore not be returned by the query. However, two records with different values would be True and they would be returned—providing they meet all of the criteria. The inequality operator can be either greater than ($>$), less than ($<$), greater than or equal to ($>=$), less than or equal to ($<=$), or not equal to ($<>$). You can create unequal joins only when using the SQL view of a query.

JOIN	DESCRIPTION
Theta	Theta joins often use expressions to join the tables. For example, the join expression ([LeftTable].[Field1] * 20 = [RightTable].[Field1]) would join the records in the right table to the left table if the value of RightTable.Field1 is 20 times that of the LeftTable.Field1. Not all functions are supported in this join context.
	Theta joins are created in the WHERE clause of the query with cross-joined tables.
	Theta joins are not commonly used. And as you can see, they can be very complex and quite taxing on the database engine.

To illustrate a couple of the more common joins, we will again use tables from Microsoft's Northwind database. Figure 2-4 highlights how Microsoft Access 2007 represents a left and inner join in the Query Designer.

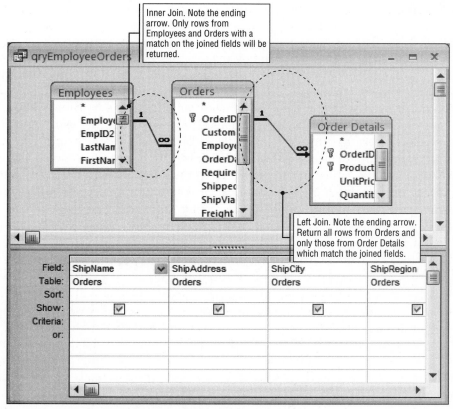

Figure 2-4: Join types in the Query Designer

Summary

From this chapter, you have learned about the database schema and its terminology. By now, you should be comfortable with using the term "schema" when referring to the three core objects—tables, relationships, and queries—along with the rules, definitions, and configurations that govern them. As you are designing your database projects, you will use the schema to help establish and enforce the rules for data entry, storage, and retrieval.

Within your tables, you store information in records that you define by creating fields. Using indexes, you can further define the tables by creating a known order for the database engine to sort and retrieve the data. You can also use indexes to constrain a field to a unique set of values. A key is defined as a field or set of fields that are concatenated to form a single value.

You create relationships between your tables by using a primary key and a foreign key. You can also define the type of relationship to help control the data by using one of three relationships. Although we often refer to three types of relationships: one-to-one, one-to-many, or many-to-many, the many-to-many relationship is resolved by using a junction table and creating two one-to-many relationships. The primary key uses values from the parent (primary) table of a relationship, and the foreign key uses values from the child (secondary) table. The fields that participate in the relationship must hold the same data type; and depending on how you set the referential integrity, the values in the foreign key may need to match the values available from the primary key.

And finally, you can use a query to add, retrieve, or modify data. You can use a select query to retrieve the data from one or many tables, and you can further refine the records that will be retrieved by changing the type of join used to relate the tables in the query. If you want to modify the data in the tables, or add or delete records, you can use an action query. As with select queries, you can join multiple tables to meet your needs. You can also use an action query to modify the schema itself, which is the obvious result of a make table query.

Now that you have a basic understanding of the elements of an Access database, including the effects of relationships and joins, it's time to learn about the relational database model. In Chapter 3, you will see how the concepts you learned from this chapter can be applied in various database management systems such as Access, SQL Server, Oracle, MySQL, and many others. You will learn the methodology for designing relational databases, and you will see how the proper design can create a remarkably powerful and effective solution for storing, managing, and reporting data about just about any subject or activity.

CHAPTER 3

Relational Data Model

In the database world, just like in the real world, people try to make sense of and organize information by breaking it down into manageable pieces. To help us in that process, we try to find a consistent approach. We organize papers and bills into folders, label them, and stuff them into a particular drawer of a particular filing cabinet. The reason we create consistent methods for storing things is simple: so we can find them again! Database systems try to do the same thing: provide a consistent method to create mechanisms for storing information. The *relational data model* (abbreviated RDM) provides a framework to break down information into logical chunks in order to promote a consistent and efficient means of storing information.

In 1969, the mathematician Edgar Codd proposed the concepts that underlie the relational model, which is arguably the most popular database model in use today. Although Codd is no longer with us, his legacy lives on in products provided by the leaders of the database world: Microsoft, Oracle, Informix, and many others.

Codd based his model on relational set theory. Online articles that explain relational theory are often written with a mathematical complexity that can be challenging. However, it is encouraging to know that you don't have to be a mathematician to understand the concepts of RDM, because the goal is similar to what we try to accomplish in our personal lives: a consistent, logical approach to storing information efficiently. Codd's application of set theory dramatically simplifies data storage concepts in a way that guarantees the integrity of the data as well as simplifies retrieval of that data.

In this chapter the relational data model is explained in understandable terms and language. As we progress through the chapter, we define a few key terms from the relational data model, and then transition to the terms used with database applications such as Microsoft Access.

After examining RDM, we explain the guidelines used by database developers in order to ensure that the relational data model is adhered to, specifically the guidelines known as the *normal forms*. The normal forms can be progressively applied throughout the development process in order to achieve a relational data model.

> **NOTE** You should not expect to gain a complete understanding of normalization and the relational data model just from reading the concepts and studying a few examples. However, after reading Chapter 2, "Elements of a Microsoft Access Database," and this chapter, and following the models in this book, you will have a strong foundation that can be built on as you create and work with databases.

The Basics

The primary factor of the relational model is the concept of *first-order predicate* logic. Clear as mud, right? Breaking it down, a *predicate* is a descriptive clause, detail, or statement about something. In other words, a predicate assigns a property to something. For example, in the simple sentence, *Access is cool!*, the phrase *is cool* forms a predicate, and *Access* is the object being described by the property. A first-order predicate, as well as the object being described by that predicate, can be given a type or name. In addition, a first-order predicate is one that directly relates to the object being described. Again, explaining with an example: *A person is named Brent, is male, and has a child that is male.* The object being described is a person. The first-order predicates for that person are: *is named Brent* and *is male*. The phrase *has a child that is male* is not a first-order predicate because another object, of the same type, is being described by the predicate.)

In Codd's relational model, a set of objects of the same type is known as a *relation*, but is most commonly referred to as a table; a first-order predicate is known as an *attribute* and typically referred to as a field; and each individual object in the relation is a *tuple* which is referred to as a record. In addition to those three terms, there is one more core term to toss into the mix: *derived relation*, which can be a query, as well as a view or stored procedure. A derived relation is simply a set of the tuples from a relation or a combination of relations. Those are the four primary terms that are used when fully describing what we know as the *relational data model* (abbreviated RDM).

Correlation to Microsoft Access

Not surprisingly, there are many other terms in the full description of the relational data model, but let's first translate the relational data model terms to the terms we use throughout this book (see also Chapter 2 for a discussion of these). Table 3-1 maps the relational data model terms to the more comfortable terms of Chapter 2.

Table 3-1: Codd's Terms, Their Access Equivalents, and Other Synonyms

RDM TERM	ACCESS EQUIVALENT	SYNONYM	DESCRIPTION
Database	Database	Data source	Collection of tables (relations)
Base Relation	Table	Base Table	Collection of records (tuples) that have the same fields (attributes), which describe an item of that collection. With rare exceptions, a table should have one, and only one, subject.
Derived Relation	Query	View, Stored Procedure	Collection of records, derived from one or more tables. Queries do not store data; they are used to retrieve and visualize or manipulate data.
Tuple	Record	Row	An individual item in a table, typically comprised of several fields
Attribute	Field	Column	A feature or descriptor of an item that the table represents (first-order predicates)

NOTE There are many other terms that are used in the relational data model. You will see them throughout the book and in other reference material. We will provide synonyms when we introduce a term, and you can refer to the Glossary at the end of this book to see our intended use.

To give you a better picture of how to use the terms from the relational data model, we have applied them to the image from Figure 2-2 in Chapter 2. The results are shown in Figure 3-1. As they say, a picture is worth a thousand words. So hopefully, we've saved at least a hundred.

As we discuss the relational data model, we will use a lot of terms that may be new or be used with a different meaning than you are accustomed to. It is more important for you to understand the concepts than to memorize the terminology. As you work through the remaining chapters of this book, you can always refer back to Chapters 2 and 3 for clarification or a refresher.

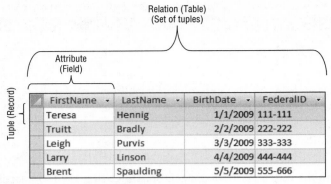

Figure 3-1: Relation, tuple, and attribute

A Little Deeper

The concept of first-order predicate logic supports the fundamental assumption of Codd's model which simply stated means that all data can be represented in one or more relations (tables) in Cartesian form. *Cartesian form* represents data in columns and rows. The approach defined by the relational data model allows the database designer to achieve the overall goal of providing a consistent method to create efficient mechanisms for storing information.

Relations, Relationships, and Keys

A relation is a set of objects that share the same type and can be described with the same set of first-order predicate identifiers. In other words, a relation is a set of tuples that have the same attributes. More simply put, a table (a relation) is a set of records that have the same fields. A table is the mechanism in the relational data model that stores values, or data, for each record.

The records of a relation have no set order, nor do the fields, thus making the data stored in the relation *commutative.* So, regardless of the order that the records or fields are presented, the set of data still means the same thing. (Think of simple arithmetic: no matter what order you list the numbers, they add up to the same total.) You will find that it can make your life easier to present the fields and data in a logical order, and it is great to know that you can change the order to fit your needs.

A field, or set of fields, used to sort or identify the rows of your table form what is called a key. In order for a key to identify a a single row, the key's value must be unique within the entire set of records within the table.

A relational database consists of several relations (tables) that store the data in a way that makes analysis possible. The tables of a relational database are categorized as either *transactional* or *functional.* For a full description of those two roles, please refer to Table 2-1 of Chapter 2.

Since the tables are based on first-order predicates (everything must directly relate to the stated subject), you might ask how *second-order predicates* are stored. To answer that question, we introduce the concept of a *relationship*, the bond that ties two tables together.

It can also be explained this way: in a relationship, a second-order predicate for one table is a first-order predicate for another table, and the link between them is a shared field value, or *key*. This shared value is often provided by placing a copy of the field or fields that uniquely identify the primary table in the second table.

NOTE With the terms *relation* and *relationship* being used to describe the *relational data model*, many assume that the *relational data model* got its name from the term *relationship*, but that is not the case. The term *relation*, with its original meaning of table is the root, in both semantics and concept, of the relational data model.

This concept may be best understood by considering Figure 3-2 using two relations from the Northwind database.

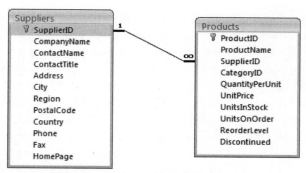

Figure 3-2: Relationship between two tables (relations)

On the left we have a relation implemented as a table named Suppliers, which has a series of first-order predicates, or attributes, implemented as fields that directly describe the subject of the table (CompanyName, ContactName, etc.). Suppose, as a database designer, that you also have a requirement to add the products each supplier makes. To help determine where the product data should go, you must first ask whether the data directly describes the supplier. If the answer is no, you need another table to store all the products a supplier provides. We know that a product is dependent upon a supplier, yet a product is a completely different object type than a supplier. Therefore the answer to the question of whether this data directly describes the supplier is "no" and you need to have a second table with its own set of attributes or fields to describe the products.

However, because a product cannot exist without a supplier, you need to have a way to associate the product with the correct supplier. You create that as a relationship between the two tables which is based on a common key, often called a *relational key*. All relationships involve two tables, a primary table and a referencing table.

> **NOTE** A referencing table is often called a *child table* or a *foreign table*, and a primary table is often called a *parent table*.

The relational key formed by one or more of the attributes (or fields) of the primary table of the relationship is called the *primary key*. The term *foreign key* is used to refer to the relational key created by one or more of the attributes, or fields, of the referencing table. When the referencing relation can have multiple records referencing the same primary record, the relationship is given the term *one-to-many*. If the referencing table's relational key is defined as unique for each record, then the relationship is given the term of *one-to-one*.

> **NOTE** The primary table is said to be on the "one" side of a relationship simply because only one record can be referenced by a record in the referencing table.

Another type of relationship is called *many-to-many*. A many-to-many relationship is actually a derived relationship that typically uses a third table, called a junction table, to create two one-to-many relationships. In most cases, the junction table will only have three fields: a primary key identifying the table and a foreign key from each of the two related tables. But, you can also add fields that have details unique to the newly created record, such as when you are recording the details of a sales order. That example is illustrated in Figure 3-3, where the table Order Details is the junction table of the many-to-many type of relationship. You can find more information regarding relational keys in Chapter 2, Table 2-4.

Derived Relations

A derived relation, implemented as a *query* in Access, is a computed set of records created from one or more tables. A query does not store any data. Queries gather data from one or more tables and perform *relational operations* on the data to create output, whether it is on screen, printed, or used for additional calculations. In general, relational operations take one or more sets of records and combine them into a single set of records. The common purpose served by a query is combining sets of records that are linked together with a relationship. The two tables, which are sets of records, are combined using what is known as a *join operation*. Conceptually, a join operation creates a result consisting of every combination of records from the two tables, but it filters out all records that do not match your join criteria. The join criteria are defined by the type of join and an expression that compares the keys from each table. For a list of join operations see Table 2-8 in Chapter 2.

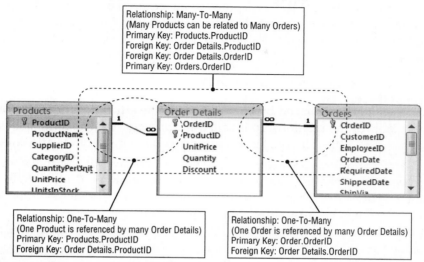

Figure 3-3: Many-to-many relationship

A join is similar in concept to a relationship. A join is defined between two sets of records (tables or queries) using keys that share the same value in each set of records. By that definition, joins and relationships sound virtually the same; however, a relationship governs the rules to which the data must adhere in order to be stored, whereas a join governs how you wish to combine the data you want to retrieve and report on from the tables.

Domains and Constraints

The complete set of valid values that populate a field (attribute) in a table creates the *domain* of that attribute. The domain of an attribute is often restricted to a fixed set of values allowed to be entered into that field. An example of this would be "only suppliers who are located in states west of the Mississippi." The restriction of values for a given attribute is known as a *constraint*.

A common way to create a domain constraint is to use a table to store acceptable values and then allow the user to make a selection. The tables that store the data are often called *domain relations* (domain tables—which are commonly known as lookup tables). Although the example given in the previous paragraph to describe the concept of a constraint was limited to one attribute, a constraint can also be placed upon an entire record or even the entire table.

Constraints that cover an entire relation or an individual record in a table are intended to enforce integrity of the data in that table. *Referential integrity* is achieved if the constraint defines a rule that links two relations together. Constraints can also define another form of integrity known as *entity integrity*. For example, an attribute that is deemed to be required over the entire domain is an entity integrity constraint. These are commonly referred to as required fields. The primary key for a table is the most common entity integrity constraint.

Normalization

The normalization process is a systematic approach to be employed when designing or repairing a relational database. After Codd introduced the relational data model, he presented *normalization*. Simply put, normalization is the process of applying a set of criteria that you evaluate during the development of your table structure to ensure that it adheres to the relational data model—and thereby providing data integrity and ease of use. In addition, if a person inherits an existing database, the normalization criteria can be used to evaluate any structural deficiencies to plan for restructuring, or to create an application that effectively handles the exceptions.

NOTE In this section, the terminology used shifts from the conceptual terms of the relational data model to terms that are used in a relational data model implementation, such as a Microsoft Access database. This has been done to make it easier to apply the concepts discussed by using the terms that appear in everyday applications you use to create database structures. The core terms are translated in Table 3-1 if you need to refer to them. In addition, you should note that the terms "column" and "field" are synonymous, as are the terms "row" and "record."

Objectives

The following sections describe the specific objectives that can be accomplished through proper normalization.

Objective 1: Prevent anomalies during data modification

Preventing anomalies during data modification is the primary focus of the normalization process. Data modification anomalies can be categorized into three types: update, insertion, and deletion. Simply stated, the anomaly is that after the change, the data did not end up being what you expected or intended.

You can see an example of a data modification anomaly in Figure 3-4, where LocationID 55 has two different values for LocationDescriptions. As a reminder, a *candidate key* is a field or set of fields that uniquely describe a record.

Normalization objects and concepts are largely based around candidate keys, which are defined in Chapter 2.

Candidate Key

tblEquipmentLocation			
EquipmentLocationID ▾	EquipmentID ▾	LocationID ▾	LocationDescription ▾
1	3	55	Column A, Aisle 4
2	5	55	Column A, Aisle 4
3	1	37	Mezzanine X
4	8	48	Metal Pit - South
5	10	22	Dock 4; Door 7

Figure 3-4: Data modification anomaly

The unwanted anomaly in Figure 3-4 is caused by the fact that the field LocationDescription has been modified in one record but those changes were not *cascaded* to any other records with the same LocationID. When you read the section "Normal Forms" later in this chapter, you'll see that the field LocationDescription should not even be present in this table.

Objective 2: Reduce the need for restructuring as new types of data are introduced, thus increasing the life span of application programs

Nearly all database applications experience growth with respect to data storage as well as capability. A fully normalized database allows the extension of a database structure while keeping most, if not all, of the pre-existing structures in place and unchanged. This inherent aspect of normalized databases enhances the longevity of applications that interact with the database.

Objective 3: Make the database more informative to the users

The relational data model implemented with normalization as the guiding design philosophy closely models how tangible items and concepts are related in the real world. The close correlation to real-world processes enable the database to be responsive and adaptable to a multitude of users and their dynamically changing needs.

Objective 4: Make the collections of relations, or tables, neutral to querying patterns

Querying normalized tables provides consistent results as the data and tables grow. As new pieces of data are added to normalized tables, queries are often unaffected. In addition, when you use normalized tables, your queries become more generalized, which enables them to be flexible as changes occur.

Objective 5: Reduce data entry steps

In a normalized database most data elements are stored once. The idea that data should only be entered one time and in one table, but used, or referred to, in several places is the premise behind related tables in a relational data model. This saves time with data entry and improves data integrity.

As an example, by entering a CustomerID into a CustomerOrder table, you are able to retrieve the information about the customer by looking up, or joining, to the Customer table based on the CustomerID that was input. So with a single input of data, you are able to retrieve an entire record of information.

Using the same example, data integrity increases by eliminating the opportunity to enter the same data in different ways. So if you correct a customer's name in one place, the Customer table, the update will appear everywhere the customer is referred to using the CustomerID.

Normal Forms

The process of normalization is used to ensure that the structure of an RDM database fulfills the five objectives we've just discussed, with the overriding purpose of preventing data anomalies. The degree to which a database design can avoid anomalies is measured by the level of normalization that can be attained by the database structure. These levels of normalization are defined by a set of progressive qualification groups called the *normal forms*. Each subsequent group of qualifications encompasses the prior group.

Codd's concept of normalization introduced what is known as the *first normal form*, or *minimal form*, expressed in shorthand as *1NF*. He soon followed this with the second and third normal forms. Over time, other people became involved in setting the normalization guidelines, which led to the six normal forms currently used in relational database design: first, second, third, Boyce-Codd, fourth, and fifth.

> **NOTE** In addition to the six normal forms used in relational database design, two more normal forms exist: domain/key and sixth. The domain/key normal form is often considered theoretical in nature. The sixth normal form deals with extending the relational data model into the time dimension. It is not appropriate to expand upon either in this book. If you would like to investigate the sixth normal form, we encourage you to check out *Temporal Data and the Relational Model: A Detailed Investigation into the Application of Interval and Relation Theory to the Problem of Temporal Database Management,* by Chris Date, Hugh Darwen, and Nikos A. Lorentoz (Morgan Kaufmann, 2002).

First Normal Form: Eliminate Repeating Groups

One criterion for the first formal form specifies that the table should faithfully represent the concept of a relation (table) in RDM. In addition, and arguably the most significant defining criterion for the first normal form, the table must be free of repeating groups.

In order to faithfully represent the concept of a relation, the table design must meet the following concepts of a relation in the relational data model:

- It describes one entity.

- The order of the rows and columns must be meaningless.

- No rows can be duplicated, thus requiring each table to have a primary key (contains a unique value).

- Every column value contains one value that is appropriate for the attribute being described—in other words, no blank fields.

The criterion stating that a table should not have any blank column values is disputed among many respected database designers and developers. This disagreement among the brightest minds of database development indicates that the requirement to attain the first normal form criteria is not etched in stone. This type of disagreement is generally the result of a difference of interpretation or a modification of a definition over time. For example, originally Dr. Codd defined a relation in such a way that blank values are not allowed for an attribute; however, as time progressed he accommodated the concept of a *null*, which simply means that a field (or attribute) value is unknown or undefined. Ergo the comment, "null is a value."

The most common way of stating the first normal form is that the table must be free of repeating groups. Repeating groups can occur across fields, within field values, and even between records. To explain further, let's look at a series of examples that attempt to handle the requirement to store multiple phone numbers for a person.

Repeating groups across columns is often easy to spot due to the naming of a table's fields, which are often enumerated or incremented in some way. Figure 3-5 shows columnar repeating groups.

tblPerson					
PersonID ▾	FirstName ▾	LastName ▾	Phone1 ▾	Phone2 ▾	Phone3 ▾
1	Brent	Spaulding	999-555-1213	999-555-1214	999-555-1212
2	Leigh	Purvis	999-555-1217	999-555-1216	999-555-1215
3	Truitt	Bradly	999-555-1214	999-555-1213	999-555-1215

Figure 3-5: Repeating group: across a column

Repeating groups within columns are also easy to identify. In this type of repeating group scenario, a field contains more than one value. Figure 3-6 shows repeating groups within a column.

| tblPerson | | | |
PersonID ▾	FirstName ▾	LastName ▾	Phone ▾
1	Brent	Spaulding	999-555-1213, 999-555-1214, 999-555-1214
2	Leigh	Purvis	999-555-1214, 999-555-1216, 999-555-1215
3	Truitt	Bradly	999-555-1214, 999-555-1213, 999-555-1215

Figure 3-6: Repeating group: within a column

NOTE Access 2007 introduced a field type extension called a *multi-valued field*. A multi-valued field visually appears like repeating groups within columns. Despite this visual appearance, the implementation of a multi-valued field is done in compliance with the normal forms. Although the table used in creating the normalized structure to hold the data for a multi-valued field is hidden from view, the data contained within it can be visualized, as well as edited, with a SELECT query containing an SQL statement similar to the following, which was created in the Northwind.accdb database supplied with Access 2007:

```
SELECT Products.ID AS ProductID
      , Products.[Supplier IDs].Value AS SupplierID
FROM Products;
```

Here, Products.[Supplier IDs] is a multi-valued field defined in the Products table. A word of caution when using this feature: Do not hide the bound column (a column width of 0 is hidden) of the row source for your multi-valued field in the table definition. By keeping that column visible, you will be able to see the raw data stored in the table, which is a significant benefit when you are troubleshooting problems.

Avoiding multi-valued fields will make your data structure easier to understand, and more portable to other database systems and older versions of Access.

Repeating groups within rows is often more difficult to spot when the entire schema is not known. But we've illustrated this in Figure 3-7, repeating the combined fields of FirstName and LastName in order to store multiple phone numbers for a person. Setting up a table in this manner increases the opportunity for future data modification errors. The key used is no longer a candidate key because it is no longer unique in the table.

WARNING The combination of first name and last name is not a good choice for a candidate key in an operational database. The combination is used here only as an example to explain a concept.

To create a design that complies with 1NF and also allows you to store multiple phone numbers for a person, the phone number field needs to be pulled out of the tblPerson table into a separate table, tblPersonPhone. Within the tblPersonPhone table, a foreign key column is created that references and links to a candidate key of the tblPerson table. A relationship can then be created between the tblPerson table and the tblPersonPhone table.

FirstName	LastName	Phone
Brent	Spaulding	999-555-1213
Brent	Spaulding	999-555-1214
Brent	Spaulding	999-555-1212
Leigh	Purvis	999-555-1217
Leigh	Purvis	999-555-1216
Leigh	Purvis	999-555-1215
Truitt	Bradly	999-555-1214
Truitt	Bradly	999-555-1213
Truitt	Bradly	999-555-1215

Figure 3-7: Repeating group: within a row

With that, you can easily create a query to join the tblPersonPhone table and the tblPerson table and present the telephone number data as shown in Figure 3-7. We have captured the entire process in Figure 3-8. It starts with the relationship between two tables, tblPerson and tblPersonPhone, and then displays data from each. You then see the SQL statement for the select query that combined the data from the two tables into the display of qryPersonPhones.

The 1NF-compliant design allows for consistent query results, proper key assignment, and avoids data modification anomalies. It also allows the data to grow as needs change for each person. For example, whether a person has one phone number or ten phone numbers, the 1NF design will accommodate the data.

Second Normal Form: Eliminate Redundant Data

The second normal form (2NF) includes the requirements set forth by the first normal form and adds a constraint dealing with columns that are not part of the candidate key. In less formal terms, the second normal form dictates that any column that is not part of a candidate key must be dependent upon the entire candidate key, and not just a portion of it. Figure 3-9, which is the same as Figure 3-4, displays redundant data in the form of the field LocationDescription simply because LocationDescription is solely dependent upon LocationID.

To adhere to 2NF, simply remove from the table shown in Figure 3-9 the field for the location description and rely on the LocationID field to create the link to the description stored in the location table (tblLocation). Figure 3-10 illustrates 2NF compliance, as well as a query definition that outputs the data with the same visual output as the table that violated 2NF. Note that in this figure, EquipmentID and LocationID are candidate keys in the table tblEquipmentLocation.

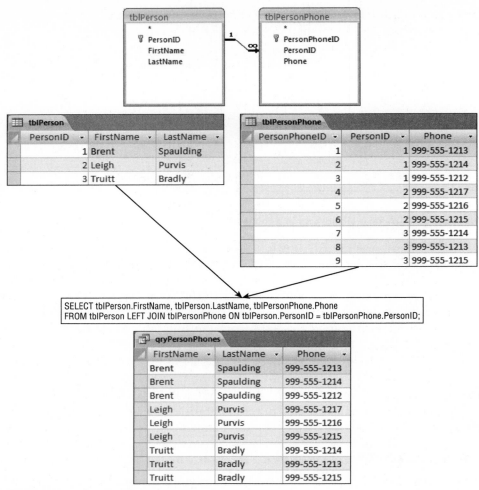

```
SELECT tblPerson.FirstName, tblPerson.LastName, tblPersonPhone.Phone
FROM tblPerson LEFT JOIN tblPersonPhone ON tblPerson.PersonID = tblPersonPhone.PersonID;
```

Figure 3-8: 1NF-compliant design

Figure 3-9: Second normal form violation

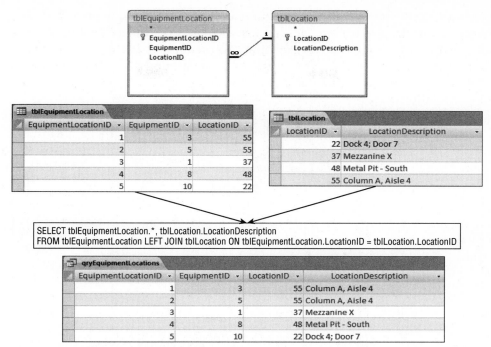

Figure 3-10: 2NF-compliant design

Third Normal Form: Eliminate Columns Not Dependent on a Candidate Key

The third normal form encompasses the criteria set forth by the second normal form, and adds a constraint dealing with columns that are not part of the candidate key, just like 2NF. To successfully adhere to the third normal form, a field that is not part of a candidate key must directly provide a fact about the key in its entirety. Making non-key fields provide information about the key as a whole is also a requirement of 2NF, but the subtlety in 3NF is that the non-key field must directly describe the entity represented by a candidate key. Figure 3-11 shows a violation of 3NF.

EquipmentID	EquipmentName	Department	Plant
1	Front End Loader	Assembly	1
2	Welding Robot	Body Weld	1A
3	Drop Lifter	Stamping	2
4	Rotator	Plastics	3

Figure 3-11: Third normal form violation

In Figure 3-11, EquipmentID is the primary key of the table. The fields EquipmentName and Department are non-candidate key fields that provide facts about the unique piece of equipment. The Plant field, however, describes a fact about the department, and thus is a violation of the third normal form. To correct this violation, a table relating equipment to department would have to be created. Figure 3-12 shows the table separation as well as the query definition needed to return records that visually represent what the previous 3NF violation displayed.

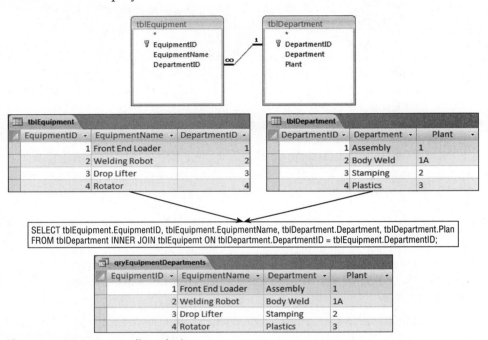

Figure 3-12: 3NF-compliant design

> **NOTE** Most developers would also separate out the Plant information into a lookup or domain table which is described briefly in the "Domains and Constraints" section earlier, and in more detail in Chapter 2. This could be done in such a way that a field named PlantID would be in tblDepartment as a foreign key to the primary key field of PlantID in a new table (named tblPlant).

Boyce-Codd Normal Form

The Boyce-Codd normal form (BCNF) is essentially a stricter version of 3NF. Typically, if a table meets 3NF, it will also meet BCNF; however, on some rare occasions BCNF will not be achieved. Because it is difficult to define the exact requirements for successfully attaining BCNF, we illustrate the form by explaining how tables that do meet 3NF might not meet BCNF requirements. To be in that situation, a table would have multiple compound candidate keys, with common fields between the keys. Figure 3-13 shows this violation of BCNF.

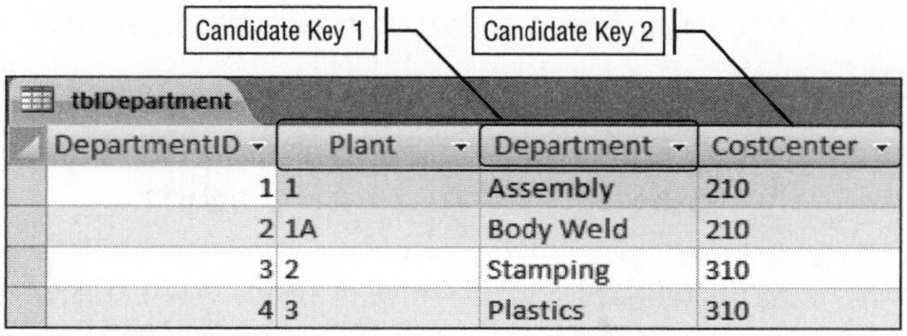

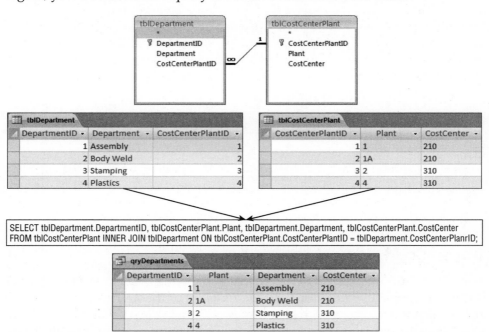

Figure 3-13: Boyce-Codd violation

In Figure 3-13 two candidate keys exist that both include the field Department, as illustrated by the overlapping ovals. In addition, suppose that you have a business rule that stipulates that only Plants 1 and 1A can use CostCenter 210; and that CostCenter 310 can be used by all plants except 1 and 1A.

At this point, we do not have a way of enforcing that requirement, because nothing prevents us from entering cost center 310 for plant 1.

To comply with the BCNF, you could move the fields for Plant and CostCenter to another table, create an index on those fields, and then relate that table back to tblDepartment. Figure 3-14 illustrates this solution by starting with the new table tblPlantCostCenter and creating a relationship to tblDepartment. Again, you would create a query to retrieve data from both tables.

Figure 3-14: BCNF compliance

TIP Most developers work with the intention of achieving a degree of 3NF with their database designs.

Fourth and Fifth Normal Forms: Isolate Multiple (Many-to-Many) Relationships

The fourth and fifth normal forms are very closely related because they both deal with isolating multiple relationships.

The forth normal form specifically indicates isolating independent multiple relationships. In other words, for a table that shares two or more many-to-many relationships, the fourth normal form specifies that each many-to-many relationship must be isolated. Figure 3-15 depicts a specification that warrants application of fourth normal form criteria. In this case, a product can be related to many suppliers and many customer orders. In addition, a supplier can be related to many products, and an order by a customer can be related to many products.

Figure 3-15: Specification requiring the fourth normal form

The fifth normal form specifically indicates isolating multiple relationships, just as 4NF does, but the twist is that the related tables of Supplier and Order from Figure 3-15 are also related to each other. Figure 3-16 depicts a specification that requires application of the fifth normal form. The specification is similar to the example in Figure 3-15, but an additional requirement specifies that a supplier can be related to many customer orders, and a customer order can be related to many suppliers.

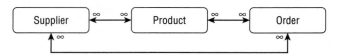

Figure 3-16: Specification requiring the fifth normal form

A common violation of the fourth and fifth normal forms is combining the relational keys into one connecting table in order to enforce the multiple many-to-many relationships. Please note, however, that in some situations having a single table holding relational keys enabling many-to-many relationships is completely valid and is not in violation of the fourth or fifth normal forms. The key to these normal forms is isolation of the tables used for the many-to-many relationships in such a way that these junction tables comply with the lower normal forms. Keep in mind that each level of form builds on and complies with the lower levels. Figure 3-17 illustrates a design that is suspect for violation of 4NF or 5NF.

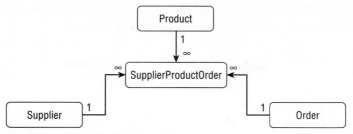

Figure 3-17: Suspect violation of 4NF or 5NF

Although violation of the fourth and fifth normal forms can look the same from a design perspective, the implementation of compliance to each form is somewhat different. Referring back to Figure 3-15, and knowing that each many-to-many relationship to the Product table is independent of one another, we need to create junction tables for each independent relationship. Figure 3-18 graphically shows this concept.

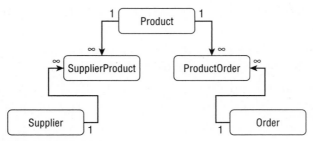

Figure 3-18: 4NF-compliant design

Figure 3-18 shows each many-to-many relationship that the table Product participates in. The compliant design for the fifth normal form involves adding another junction table to complete the many-to-many relationship specified between the Supplier table and the Customer Order table. Figure 3-19 illustrates the compliant design for the fifth normal form. And, as you can see, we no longer have a SupplierProductOrder.

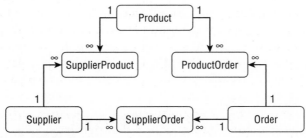

Figure 3-19: 5NF-compliant design

As you examine your tables for 4NF and 5NF compliance, keep in mind that a design as pictured in Figure 3-17 is not an automatic violation of either normal form. The violations occur when the junction table itself, SupplierProductOrder, does not comply with the other normal forms leading up to the 4th and 5th normal forms. This often becomes more of an issue as you add fields to junction tables.

When to Denormalize

As is true of many sets of guidelines or rules, sometimes it's necessary to break them. Typically, in a database adhering to relational data modeling and the normal forms, the decision to denormalize is done for performance reasons. The second most common reason designers denormalize is for sheer convenience.

Amazingly enough, even breaking the rules of normalization is regulated by guidelines (or perhaps it's more like a cautionary list):

- If the rules must be broken, then do so deliberately, with full knowledge of the impact.

- Document any decision to denormalize so that your successor understands both why the decision was made and the related ramifications.

- Ensure that any applications manipulating the data have been adjusted accordingly to accommodate the increased risk of data modification anomalies.

The ambiguity about when to denormalize often yields spirited discussion among database designers, so you can understand that the reasons and situations surrounding denormalization can be quite varied.

For example, some developers use TreeView controls as menus or navigation within their applications. When feeding data to the TreeView control, the TreeView control creates what is known as the FullPath. The FullPath is similar to the full path of a file in Windows Explorer. In one case, the data used to populate the TreeView control contained over 60,000 records. In order to improve the performance of loading the TreeView control data, VBA code was used to create a string that duplicated and saved the FullPath into an indexed field in a hierarchical table that subsequently provided the data for the control. Although this duplicated data, by using the stored, indexed data, the load time of the TreeView control was reduced by approximately 85%.

Note that not all denormalization scenarios pan out as well as this TreeView example. But if an application is suffering from performance issues, you should ensure that the structure is fully normalized before considering any steps to denormalized the structure. You may find that performance is quite adequate in a properly normalized structure.

Summary

This chapter discussed the relational data model (RDM) and normalization. The goal of the RDM is to store data in a logical manner so you can easily find it again!

You have learned that the core principle of RDM is to apply the concept of first-order predicate logic in creating a relation (table). A table is a collection, or set, of objects that are of the same type and that can be described with the same set of attributes or fields. The attribute values of an object contained in the table are the first-order predicate descriptors of that object. Each item, or object, in the set of objects contained in the relation is known as a tuple or record. RDM supports the concept of two types of relations: a base relation (table) and a derived relation (query). Each type visualizes a set of records, yet only the base relation stores the attribute values. The query simply visualizes or utilizes the data stored in one or more tables and/or queries.

A table is considered commutative, which simply means that the order of the records as well as the fields (attributes) does not affect the data. This nondependence on the order of items means that you can change the order in which records and fields are displayed without affecting the underlying data. We also explained why a base relation (table) cannot contain duplicate records. Each record must represent a unique entity within the table and be identified by a key. The key is comprised of one or more fields of the table.

You also learned that in order to store additional information that is not directly related to an item, you can use a second table and create a relationship through the relational keys. This is called second-order predicate information.

Relationships can be categorized as one-to-many or one-to-one. In addition, a many-to-many relationship can be formed using two one-to-many relationships related to a third table, called a junction table.

The relational data model is implemented with many different relational database management systems, including Microsoft Access or Microsoft SQL Server. Since we are providing Microsoft Access solutions, this chapter explained the correlating terms from RDM to MS Access. The four key terms are "relation" (known as a table), "derived relation" (commonly called a query), "attribute" (the fields that describe the subject of the table), and "tuple" (the records that make up the table).

The process of normalization was also covered. Normalization describes the criteria we use to guide the development of a relational data model in order to reduce the possibility of anomalies stemming from data modification. The progressive sets of criteria are as follows:

- First normal form: Eliminate repeating groups.
- Second normal form: Eliminate redundant data.

- Third normal form: Eliminate columns not dependent on a candidate key.

- Boyce-Codd normal form: Third normal form, but a little more strict.

- Fourth and fifth normal forms: Isolate multiple (many-to-many) relationships.

Along with all the information about how to ensure that a database avoids data modification anomalies with the normal forms, you also learned when it might be appropriate to denormalize your structure. Denormalization should only be done after considerable deliberation and with a clear understanding of the potential risks. Information about the database structure and denormalization will need to be considered by future developers and by anyone using the data, either directly or by creating an application to utilize the data.

Now that you have read Chapters 2 and 3, you should have a basic understanding about table design and relationships. We covered a lot of material here, with the expectation that you would refer back to these chapters as needed. This will help you work through the following chapters to help you build a database tailored to your needs.

Dealing with Customers and Customer Data

In This Part

People, Organizations, Addresses

What information do you need that spans all, or almost all, of the functions of your business or organization? Of course, that is information about people. Businesses and commercial organizations need to track, relate, and report information about employees, customers, suppliers, and vendors. Noncommercial organizations deal with information about members, sponsors, donors, and others.

So it is quite understandable that people and organizations are a key component of many database applications, regardless of the main business objectives. Managing the data can be quite challenging because the data often has multiple uses and can easily become fragmented or copied into multiple locations, and the more places that data is stored, the more difficult it is to update and ensure that it is consistent and accurate.

To complicate the matter even more, you will frequently discover additional kinds of data that you want to store. For example, in most business functions you don't need to know about the family of a person, but to enhance customer, employee, or member communications, that is useful information. You have several options for handling how you add this data to existing tables. An easy way to consistently use field properties is to copy an existing field—say, FavoriteColor—and rename it to SpouseName. Alternatively, add a new field named SpouseName, or you might add a separate FamilyMember table that includes spouses, children, significant others, and whatever other relations that you choose.

Consider the many places and tools you personally use to store information about people that you know. What would it take to have a central storage system that could manage all of the data relevant to each contact and to make it easy to look up the information by filtering on a characteristic or field? This simple exercise will help you visualize what might be involved when you set about designing a database for this purpose.

If you use an e-mail program, open it and look at the contact information. Although you will be looking at forms, not the underlying tables, you can deduce a great deal about the table design by considering the information and the ways that it can be entered and displayed. It will soon be obvious that most people have multiple accounts, and you may have part of their data stored on your computer, and other parts of their data online.

If you use more than one program for tracking personal information, you can see that they each store some of the same information, but that each program has some custom options. The list of similarities and differences is too extensive to cover here, but they indicate how important it is for you to consider not only what data you need to store, but also how it will be used.

You may be familiar with computer applications for personal information management (PIM) and for handling address book (AB) or contact information, so we use them as examples in this chapter. You will learn how to arrange the subjects into tables, and the details into fields that make up the records of those tables. We will show you how and when to create additional tables to incorporate related information. The tables are designed to store data that is common to a variety of organizational structures.

How This Chapter Is Organized

Two database structures are presented in this chapter. After looking at the questions to ask and the factors to consider, you can select the structure most appropriate for your needs, based on the characteristics of the real-world environment that you are modeling and how you need to use the data. Our focus in this chapter is to help you determine and create a solid foundation for storing, managing, and using data pertaining to people and organizations, but the examples we provide are not intended to represent the core of a full enterprise-level customer relationship management system. We definitely do not suggest that you use these sample tables to create your own PIM or address book database. As mentioned, there are many packages, both commercial and open source, for those purposes that cover all but the most unique or unusual needs.

Although the examples provided can be used as the foundation for a solution strictly focused on people and organizations, we assume that you will use these or similar tables in conjunction with other examples in the book. You might incorporate them as reusable parts of full business applications or you could share one set of people and organization information between your other business database applications. We hope you will find this chapter to be a useful tool for learning how to gather requirements for the data you include in your database applications, as well for designing those databases.

However, that is not to say that our examples would not support a more robust application. If you are seeking a contact management solution but are finding that the commercial packages do not fit your needs, then our examples will be of great benefit. By following the processes in this chapter, you will soon have the skills to customize these tables for use in conjunction with such an application, and we will cheer you on. In fact, even if you already have a PIM, AB, or contact management application, creating such an application might be a useful learning exercise before you leap directly into work on a database application for one of your vital business functions.

In this chapter, you learn how to store data specific to individual people or to particular organizations, along with other data associated with both people and organizations. You will review and consider options for using related tables to store information such as e-mail addresses and telephone numbers, and learn how to use a junction table to manage many-to-many relationships between the people and the organizations.

First you'll examine a simplified design for people and organization information that will work for many situations. Then you'll look at a slightly more complex design that provides additional flexibility. Of course, everything comes at a price, but don't be intimidated. In this case the price you pay will be the additional time and effort needed to both create the structure and then design the user interface, but you may be surprised to find that it is not burdensome.

In addition to explaining the models and how they correspond to various business functions, this chapter also includes some bonus tables. You will find a table for looking up the correct postal abbreviations for U.S. states, territories, and military "States" and Canadian provinces and territories. In the example database for this chapter on the CD that accompanies the book, this table is pre-populated with names and abbreviations. You may need to do nothing more than import it into your own application. It can be an invaluable tool for creating mailing and marketing solutions.

We've also provided a table for month, month abbreviation, and month number. Date manipulations are built into the VBA programming language used by Access, and into Access's expressions, but in many cases, especially when creating queries, you may find it simpler and easier to use this table instead of using date and time functions to perform calculations.

Now that you have a general idea of what you will be doing, we'll spend a little time reviewing some information about some of the fields.

Basic Field Information

To give you a start on creating the tables, we thought that you'd find it helpful to know a little about the fields that we use in nearly every table. So, we've compiled a series of notes that you can easily refer back to.

NOTE Item, subject, and detail are not, in general use, precise definitions. In this chapter, however, when we use the words without additional qualification they have the following meanings: *item* refers to a list of things to consider for inclusion in tables, *subject* refers to the topic of a table, and *detail* refers to something that will likely become a field in a table.

STANDARD FIELDS USED IN MOST TABLES

Primary and Natural Keys

Each table in this chapter, as with most tables in this book, uses an Access AutoNumber data type for the primary key. An AutoNumber field is a surrogate key, an arbitrarily defined value that will uniquely identify the record. As you'll recall from Chapters 2 and 3, using a single-field primary key makes it easier to create, understand and work with the relationships between tables and the joins used in queries.

Using an AutoNumber for the primary key does not preclude the table from having a different field (or combination of fields) that represents a natural key—real world data that uniquely identifies the record. Natural keys typically have the field properties of Required and Indexed with no duplicates allowed. This ensures that a value is stored in the field and that two or more records cannot have the same value.

Multi-Field and Unique Indexes

Indexes can include more than one field. You can use a multi-field index to ensure that any combination of field values does not occur more than one time by setting the index property to make it unique.

Junction tables often use a multi-field index on the two foreign keys. You can use the index property to ensure that the combination of these two fields will always be unique. In most cases, you also need to use the field property to make the field Required, so that each Record has to store a value.

In other cases, a single field (such as the main subject of the table) can be indexed with no duplicates allowed to insure that the content of the field is not duplicated. You will typically also make this a required field. Single field indexes can be created using either the field property or the index property.

Appendixes A and B provide an extensive discussion on field properties and relationships. A brief review of those two appendixes will give you a strong foundation for working on the examples throughout the book.

Audit Trail

Each data table may also contain fields that indicate who updated the record and when the record was updated. It may seem overkill to include this, but there may often be legal requirements or business rules that call for some form of audit trails. Before omitting these fields, you should make certain that your accountant and legal counsel concur.

In most Access database applications, you will have to use code or macros to collect audit trail data because the database engine does not provide this capability—at least not to the extent desired. However, many server databases, such as Microsoft SQL Server, provide support for logging all changes and thereby creating an audit trail.

Although these two fields do not provide a complete audit trail, they can identify when a record was created and if it is active. By setting the default value of the field to Now(), a Date/Time field can be used to automatically capture when a record was initially created.

You can also use a Yes/No field or a Date/Time field to indicate if a record is active or if it has been flagged as no longer used. Flagging a record is typically preferable to deleting the record, which may be illegal or cause data continuity problems.

Note Fields

Finally, transaction tables will typically have a "Note" field for optional comments about the record. Users may find it helpful to record a note if they're interrupted while entering data, and developers may use them when creating or testing the application. They can also store information that seems pertinent to the actual content of the record-something not specified in processing but perhaps useful to someone examining the record in detail.

No additional definition is required for these standard fields, so they will not be discussed each time they occur in the chapter.

MEMO FIELDS

You often hear advice against using Memo fields in transaction tables, primarily because the fields have been "subject to data corruption." If a table contains a Memo field that becomes corrupted, it is possible to lose all the data in that record, not just the data in the Memo field. Fortunately, the frequency of such corruptions has diminished significantly as network technology has matured and we are less likely to experience momentary outages and system interruptions that lead to data corruption.

Continued

> **MEMO FIELDS** *(continued)*
>
> An easy alternative is to move the Memo field to a related table, using either a one-to-one or many-to-one relationship. Chapter 7 provides a detailed discussion of how this can be implemented.

> **DATA RETENTION**
>
> You should exercise care and consult with your attorney on the nature of the information you keep on file. You are required to store certain information, but it is also prohibited by law and regulations to keep other information. Preserving information that is not required and that is not clearly useful to your business can, in fact, work to your disadvantage in future legal proceedings. Having too many records can also place an undue burden on systems and people trying to store and retrieve data.

Now that you know what we'll be covering and some of the basic structure that we'll be working with, it's time to get started with the project. The first step is to determine what data your database needs to store.

People and Organization Information Processing and Storage

Now we move on to dealing with the business functions and structuring the data to address them.

Personal Information Manager (PIM) or Address Book (AB) Basics

The basic functionality for a PIM or AB has the same or similar requirements as you'll find in other business functions that need to use people and organization data. Those requirements are as follows:

- You need to be able to view, add, change, and delete the information you decide you maintain about the people and organizations.

- You need to be able to view, add, change, and delete information that is related to the people and organizations but not stored with the people and organization data. Examples include telephone numbers, e-mail addresses, and in some cases postal address information.

- You need to be able to search by either person or organization to retrieve information to be displayed or printed as a report.

■ You want to be able to search or group by categories of person (minor, adult, customer, vendor, etc.) or type and category of organization when viewing or reporting information.

■ You want to be able to look up reference information used, such as the state and province postal abbreviations, categories for people, types of and categories for organizations, types of phone numbers, and types of e-mail accounts. Some of this reference information, such as state and province postal abbreviations, changes so infrequently that you won't want to expend a great deal of effort making it easy for the general user to view, add, change, and delete it. Other information, such as categories for people and organizations, should be made relatively simple for your application administrator to view, add, change, and delete. For example, with an age range category such as pre-school, children, teens, adult, and elderly, it might be desirable to change "elderly" to "senior."

■ You should consider whether there is any detail information that may change frequently and in a manner that would warrant a feature that allows users to perform a mass change. One example might be governmental categorizations, such as the type of business number and description used by the U.S. Census Bureau and Internal Revenue Service. This particular information isn't included in our examples, but it might be useful in your database(s) to support the business functions particular to your organization.

Questions to Ask

Collecting and storing information about people and organizations (and often the relationships between them) is a common need, but the amount of that information useful to a given business function varies. To determine how much and what type of information needs to be maintained, you need to ask key people associated with the business function (the sponsor or requester of the database application, knowledgeable users, and perhaps yourself) several leading questions such as:

■ *Do you need different information about people and organizations?* Is information about both people and organizations required, or only one or the other? If both, are both handled similarly, as in the case where either a person or an organization could be a customer? Or is information for the business function primarily about people? If so, is there a need to know which organizations a person is affiliated with? If the information you need is primarily about organizations, is contact information needed for people in various roles within the organization?

■ *How Will the Person Information Be Used?* How will the information about people be used for this business function? For example, if the business function simply requires contact information, you can choose items of information (called *fields* in an Access table) of a professional nature; but if the function has to do with maintaining a relationship with the person, you may choose more personal information about family, birthdays, or accomplishments. For more details about managing business relationships, see also Chapter 5, "Customer Relationship Management," and Chapter B1, "Knowledge: Intellectual Property, Structural Capital, and Intellectual Capital."

■ *How will organization information be used?* For this business function, how will the information about organizations be used? Different types of information may be needed for organizations that represent your vendors versus your customers, or you may want to keep certain information simply to be aware of the individual's association with an organization.

■ *Will people and organizations be treated the same?* Do you make the same types of contacts with people as you do with organizations? For example, are your customers only people, only organizations, or can they be both? Are people included only in their role within an organization, or does the business function primarily relate to people?

The answers to these questions will determine the structure of the tables that you need. If contact with an organization is to always be through the people who are affiliated with it, then most of the contact details will only be required to be associated with people. However, if you need to have complete sets of contact information for organizations as well as for people, then you will also need to establish direct links between the contact details and the organization.

■ *Are details of related tables frequently shared?* If multiple people, organizations, or a combination thereof might have the same telephone number, e-mail address, or physical address, then the contact details can be shared so that they only need to be maintained in one location. We explain how to do that by using a *many-to-many relationship* between the tables.

Items to Store

You should first consider the subjects that you want to store, retrieve, and manipulate information about—these subjects will serve as the basis for the tables you create for your database. For each subject, you will identify the details of interest. The details will become fields within the tables.

At this point, we can identify two key subjects: people and organizations. You may also think of related subjects, such as telephone numbers, e-mail addresses, delivery addresses, and other physical addresses. As you look into these, you'll likely think of using lists that provide state abbreviations, types of phone numbers, and even categories for contacts.

Once you have determined the key subjects, you need to identify all of the details that you want to record or track, commonly known as *requirements gathering*. This typically involves interviewing the key players and examining existing processes and reports. You can gain some valuable insight and tips from Appendix BB, "Gathering Requirements."

Looking at the universe of details that you need to manage leads to identifying the tables and how the information in each table will be integrated with other tables. In the following discussions, we italicize the items that we are considering as prospective tables or fields.

The Subject and Details of People

We'll start by identifying the details that you may need to record for people. In your business dealings with a person, one of the first requirements is for users to be able to identify the specific person—not just anyone named Larry. You may wish to consider including a person code if your organization assigns one—this might be an employee number or a customer number. You will probably find it useful to include a category such as friends, family, clients, and professional groups. Creating a category enables you to select and work with groups of people. For example, you might want to send holiday greetings to friends and family, or a newsletter to all of your clients.

You should also keep the person's name in whatever format is appropriate for your data. In English-speaking countries this would typically include separating the *first, middle, and last names* (even though some people have more than three). The separation is appropriate because in different scenarios, you may want to display or print the names individually or in a specific order, such as last name first. In most cases you will also want to keep address information, which is separated into the distinct parts we are familiar with—street, city, state, and country. Based on your scenario, you may also need to use other information, such as date of birth or date of first contact, last purchase date, client status, and even preferred method of contact.

The Subject and Details of Organizations

Just as with people, you must first be able to identify the organization. In your environment you might use an organization code—this could be a vendor number, a customer number, or another designation. You should also keep the organization's name, of course. You may also find it useful to include an organization type, as well as a category. This will enable you to split categories of organizations into subsets that share common characteristics.

Address information will again require several detail fields, and you will likely have several details based on your scenario, such as date of first contact with the organization. The list of details will grow as you review the activities involved to identify other information your business functions will require.

Other Subjects and Details

More often than not, your contact with either a person or an organization will be via e-mail or phone, rather than physical address. Therefore, these are good candidates for additional subjects, with the detail being a way to link the e-mail address or telephone number to a specific person or organization.

In addition to the actual data, another type of subject is the reference or lookup information. This type of information is provided in lists that can make it easier to enter, store, and retrieve data, and make data entry more efficient by limiting user options. We will store these lists in lookup tables.

In this example, we've already mentioned several items that can be useful as lookup tables, including a category of person and the type and category of organization. You may also want to use two other lookup tables, one for postal code abbreviations and one for country name.

Arranging the Data into Tables

In discussing the subjects, we've identified some key topics and how they relate to each other, as illustrated in Figure 4-1. The topics are the basis for creating the tables, and the discussion of details should help you decide which fields to include.

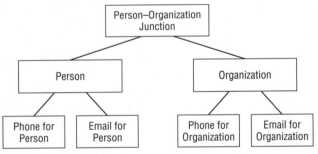

Figure 4-1: Overview of the Subjects

The subject of this database application is people and organizations, so it is logical for you to start by creating a table to contain information about people, which we'll name tblPerson, and another about organizations, named tblOrganization.

The Person Table

Information about the subject "people" can be collected in a table where each record represents a person and the information about that person. In our example, we name this tblPerson and translate the details of our earlier discussion into fields. The detail "person code" will become the field PersonCode. We will handle category by creating a field PersonCategoryID, which will contain the value of the primary key of the selected category from tblPersonCategory. (Primary keys are discussed in the "Standard Fields Used in Most Tables" sidebar earlier in this chapter.)

The details first name, middle name, and last name will translate directly to three separate fields for the name of the Person: NameLast, NameMiddle, and NameFirst. Each field may contain one or more words, as a first name can be Bobbie Jo, or Billy Bob. It may seem tempting, especially in a simple model, to combine the names and only store and use a full name. *Resist that temptation.* Sooner or later, you will need to sort the names by last name, or extract the first name for use in the salutation of an e-mail. The pain and difficulty involved in deconstructing a full name into its component parts outweighs any benefits you feel you will gain by having only one name field. Besides, you can easily combine, or concatenate, the name fields as needed. The Access expression to create a full name from the three components is simple (and can also be used in Access's VBA code programming language):

```
NameFull = [NameFirst] & (` ˝ + [NameMiddle]) & ` ˝ & [NameLast]
```

In the simple model for people and information (described later in this chapter), you will also store address information in several fields. We've described that in detail in the documentation for the tables in the example database. If you decide you need the details "date of birth" and "date of first contact," you might name them PersonBirthDate and PersonDateOfFirst-Contact. You will find detailed descriptions of the fields in the actual table documentation for our sample database, which follows in the sections headed "The Simple Model" and "The Complex Model," with descriptions of fields and screen captures of table design.

The Organization Table

Because you have separated people from organizations, you also need to create a table with records to represent each organization. An appropriate name for the table is tblOrganization. The detail "organization code" was intentionally omitted from our example, although we included a "person code." We did this to illustrate that an organization might use one but not the other. Should you need to include an identifier, an appropriate name for the field might be OrganizationCode. In the interest of readability and space, you could decide to abbreviate Organization as Org in all field names, but we'll use the complete word to provide continuity between the narrative and the sample file.

You can translate the detail "name" to a single field named Organization-Name. You can create a field OrganizationTypeID as a foreign key to the lookup table tblOrganizationType. In the example, the name of the category would also be selected from the tblOrganizationType, but since we are only providing one level of detail, we did not include a field for category. Having fields for both *types* and *categories,* where one is a subset of the other, would enable you to treat subsets of the organizations in your database in a hierarchy of groups with common characteristics.

Details about address information will be handled in fields in the same manner as we described for the People table. To include the detail "date of first contact," create a field named OrganizationDateOfFirstContact.

The Organization-Person Table

A person may be involved with multiple organizations, and an organization may be related to multiple people; this is a many-to-many relationship and requires a junction (or intersection) table to support it. Because this is "infrastructure," it was not discussed earlier as a subject or detail. The specific fields for this junction table will be explained when we start creating the tables. But as is common to all junction tables, it will contain a foreign key relating to a record in tblOrganization and a foreign key relating to a record in tblPerson.

The Phone and Email Tables

In the simple model of people and organizations, there is a Phone table for people, tblPhoneForPerson, and a Phone table for organizations, tblPhoneForOrg. Similarly, there are separate tables to store the e-mail addresses: tblEMailForPerson and tblEMailForOrg. This structure was chosen to simplify diagramming and to make it easier to understand the structure. In each of the Phone and Email tables of the simple model of person and organization data, there is a foreign key field that relates the record to the specific person in the Person table or the organization in the Organization table. In the complex model, Person and Organization are related to Phone and EMail using a junction table.

There are several viable options for managing contact information. To give you experience with other approaches, we will treat these tables differently in the complex model of people and organization information, which will be discussed later.

Reference or Lookup Tables

You can create a lookup table so that users can select data from a list of options. Lookup tables typically have one field that contains the unique record identifier for that table (the ID), and another field containing the information being looked up. For our example, you should create lookup tables for the category of person (tblCategoryOfPerson), and both the type and the category of organization (tblOrganizationType and tblOrganizationCategory). Other lookup information and tables which you might want to use are postal code abbreviation (tblStatesRef), and country name or abbreviation (tblCountryRef).

Determining the Level of Detail

To provide you with design options and learning opportunities, we consider two views or models based on the real world scenarios of people and organizations. The simple model serves well for many database applications, so that is our primary example. This model may be all that is needed for applications in which people and organizations are not the primary focus of the business function. It also serves well as a database to provide simple contact functions.

Later in this chapter we also discuss features useful where people and organizations are a primary focus of the business function. We explain and provide features to handle circumstances in which the additional complexity would be warranted.

The Simple Model

Addresses, in the simple model, are kept in the records for individual people and organizations. This works well when you only have one address per person or organization, which is a very common situation. Most people and organizations will have a telephone number or e-mail address, but they will frequently have multiple phone numbers or e-mail addresses, not just one. In the simple model, the phone number and e-mail address tables each have a *one-to-many* relationship with people and organizations.

In addition, although we are providing a simple model, we also include an example of a more complex relationship that is also quite common. Because one person can be associated with multiple organizations, and vice-versa, you need a way to represent this in your tables. This is known as a *many-to-many relationship*, which is resolved by creating a junction table.

The Person Table

The table tblPerson, shown in Figure 4-2, contains the standard fields, plus those listed below. Most fields are self-explanatory so there are minimal comments. For the purpose of clarity, we have included a table identifier in fields that may also appear in other tables. This is not a requirement but avoids confusion down the road.

PersonCode is a Text field containing the assigned code for this person (if used in your organization or useful in your database application). If this needs to be a unique value, you should set the field properties to have this field indexed and not allow duplicates.

PersonCategoryID is a Long Integer field that is used as a foreign key to tblPersonCategory. This is called a foreign key because it stores the value of the primary key of the selected record.

NOTE You will typically find it easy to recognize foreign keys, even if you are not familiar with the database or the person who designed it. In the majority of cases, the foreign key will have the same name as the primary key from the original table, so it is derived from the name of the table and has a suffix of ID. In addition, they will typically be a Long Integer data type. You can learn more about relationships and key values in Appendix B, "Relationships, Joins, and Nulls."

NameLast is a Text field containing the person's last name.

NameMiddle is a Text field containing the person's middle name.

NameFirst is a Text field containing the person's first name.

PersonAddress1 is a Text field that stores the first line of the person's address.

PersonAddress2 is a Text field that stores a possible second line of the person's address.

PersonCity is a Text field containing the name of the city of the person's address.

PersonState is a Text field containing the state, province, territory, and military "States" postal abbreviations for the U.S. and Canada of the person's address. Note that even if you are using a lookup table (also known as a reference or domain table) for state abbreviations, it makes perfect sense to store the abbreviation itself, rather than the value of the primary key. This logic applies to future instances of State—and other similar fields. You can find more information about lookup tables in Chapter 2, "Elements of a Microsoft Access Database," and in Appendix B, "Relationships, Joins, and Nulls."

If you choose to use the lookup table, and store just the abbreviation, you can still display the full name of the state when necessary by creating a join back to the table containing the state names and abbreviations. In that case, the abbreviations would need to be unique, and fortunately for us, they are.

PersonPostCode is a Text field storing the zip or postal code of the person's address.

CountryID is a Long Integer field that is used as a foreign key to the Country Reference table. In most cases, this is done equally well by storing the abbreviation for the country, as we did with state. This address structure is useful in the United States and a good many other countries, but not everywhere; if it is not suitable in your location, you may need to modify the fields defining an address.

PersonBirthDate is a Date/Time field that records the person's birth date, if known.

PersonDateOfFirstContact is a Date/Time field that records the date (and possibly time) of the first business or other contact, if known.

Next, we create the tables that are required to store multiple values related to the same record, such as e-mail addresses and phone numbers.

Field Name	Data Type	Description
PersonID	AutoNumber	Primary key, uniquely identifies this record
PersonCode	Text	Code as text (optional if useful in your application)
PersonCategoryID	Number	Foreign key to tblPersonCategories
NameLast	Text	Last Name
NameMiddle	Text	Middle Name
NameFirst	Text	First Name
PersonAddress1	Text	First Line of Address
PersonAddress2	Text	Second Line of Address
PersonCity	Text	City
PersonState	Text	State Abbreviation
PersonPostCode	Text	ZIP or Postal Code
CountryID	Number	Foreign key to tblCountryRef
PersonBirthDate	Date/Time	Birthdate, if known
PersonDateOfFirstContact	Date/Time	Date of First Business or Other Contact, if known
LastUpdatedBy	Text	User who last updated this Record
LastUpdatedDate	Date/Time	Date/time when this record was last updated
PersonNotes	Text	Optional, unstructured comments or notes about this record

Figure 4-2: The Person table

The Email For Person Table

The table tblEMailForPerson, shown in Figure 4-3, includes the following fields.

PersonID is a Long Integer field that is used to link to the person's record to which this e-mail is related, a foreign key to tblPerson.

EmailType is a Long Integer field that is used to indicate the type of e-mail address based on a selection from the lookup table, tblEmailType. This is called a foreign key because it stores the value of the primary key of the selected record.

Email is a Text field containing the person's e-mail address as text—for example, benbrown@acmewidgets.com.

Field Name	Data Type	Description
PersonEmailID	AutoNumber	Primary key, uniquely identifies this record
PersonID	Number	Foreign key to tblPerson
EmailTypeID	Number	Indicates type of e-mail address (foreign key to lookup table tblEmailTypes)
PersonEmail	Text	Email address
LastUpdatedBy	Text	User who last updated this Record
LastUpdatedDate	Date/Time	Date/time when this record was last updated
PersonEMailNotes	Text	Optional, unstructured comments or notes about this record

Figure 4-3: The Email For Person table

The Phone For Person Table

The table tblPhoneForPerson (shown in Figure 4-4) contains the fields required to store the phone numbers for individuals in tblPerson. In addition to the standard fields, you will need the fields described next.

PersonID is a Long Integer field that is used as a foreign key that identifies in tblPerson the record of the person who owns this phone number.

PersonPhoneType is a Text field that describes the type of phone: home, work, mobile, or pager. Alternatively, if you expect to be performing analysis using this field, and the consistency of the types would be beneficial, you can create a lookup table of types, and replace the Text field with a numeric foreign key to the lookup table.

PersonPhoneDisplayOrder is a Long Integer field that is used to specify the order in which to display the phone, if there are multiple phones for the related record.

PersonPhoneCountryCode is a Text field that contains the country code (all formats), a variable number of digits depending on the region. A value of 1 is the code for the U. S., Canada, and the Caribbean.

PersonPhoneAreaCode is a Text field that contains the three-digit area code (U.S./North American format only).

PersonPhonePrefix is a Text field that contains the three-digit prefix (U.S./North American format only).

PersonPhoneNumber is a Text field that contains the four-digit number (U.S./North American format only) or a variable-length number (other phone number formats).

The separate fields making up the phone number may be useful if you later use this information for detailed demographic analysis. For many applications, however, the area code, prefix, and phone number can be stored as one Text field instead of three. Whichever approach you choose, we recommend that you apply it consistently within an application.

PersonPhoneExtension is a Text field that contains the extension, if applicable.

Field Name	Data Type	Description
tblPhoneForPerson : Table		
PersonPhoneID	AutoNumber	Primary key, uniquely identifies this record
PersonID	Number	Foreign key to tblPerson
PersonPhoneType	Text	Type of phone: Home, Work, Cell, Pager
PersonPhoneDisplayOrder	Number	Order in which to display the phone, if multiple phones for related record
PersonPhoneCountryCode	Text	Country code (all formats) variable number of digits 1 = US, Canada, Caribbean
PersonPhoneAreaCode	Text	3-digit area code (US / North American Format Only)
PersonPhonePrefix	Text	3-digit prefix (US / North American Format Only)
PersonPhoneNumber	Text	4-digit number (US / North American Format); variable length number (Other)
PersonPhoneExtension	Text	Extension, if applicable
LastUpdatedBy	Text	User who last updated this Record
LastUpdatedDate	Date/Time	Date/time when this record was last updated
PersonPhoneNotes	Text	Optional, unstructured comments or notes about this record

Figure 4-4: The Phone for Person table

The Organization Table

Now that you have the table required to store information specific to people, we will create similar tables to store information about organizations.

Based on the scenario described earlier, we built tblOrganization, shown in Figure 4-5, to store the core information about the organization. Following the same process that you just completed, you can create the fields described next.

OrganizationName is a Text field that stores the name of this organization.

OrganizationAddress is a Text field that contains the first line of the organization's address.

OrganizationAddress2 is a Text field that contains a possible second line of the organization's address.

OrganizationCity is a Text field that contains the city.

OrganizationState is a Text field that records the state, province, or other political subdivision. Even if you are using a lookup table for state abbreviations, it makes perfect sense to store the abbreviation itself, rather than the value of the primary key.

OrganizationPostalCode is a Text field that holds the zip or postal code.

CountryID is a Long Integer field that is used as a lookup key to the Country Reference table. In most cases, this could be done equally well by storing the abbreviation for the country, as we did with states in the State Reference table.

OrganizationTypeID is a Long Integer field that is used as a lookup key to tblOrganizationType.

OrganizationDateOfFirstContact is a Date/Time field that records the date (and possibly time) of the first contact with this organization.

Once you have the central table to store the direct details about each organization, you can create the tables to store the information for fields that may have several values, such as email.

Field Name	Data Type	Description
OrganizationID	AutoNumber	Primary key, uniquely identifies this record
OrganizationName	Text	Name of this Organization
OrganizationAddress1	Text	First line of address
OrganizationAddress2	Text	Second line of address
OrganizationCity	Text	City
OrganizationState	Text	State, Province, or other Political Subdivision
OrganizationPostalCode	Text	ZIP or Postal Code
CountryID	Number	Foreign key to tblCountryRef
OrganizationTypeID	Number	Foreign Key to tblOrganizationType
OrganizationDateOfFirstContact	Date/Time	Date of first contact with this organization
LastUpdatedBy	Text	User who last updated this Record
LastUpdatedDate	Date/Time	Date/time when this record was last updated
OrganizationNotes	Text	Optional, unstructured comments or notes about this record

Figure 4-5: The Organization table

The Email for Organization Table

The table tblEMailForOrg (shown in Figure 4-6) is similar to the table for the e-mail addresses of individuals. You use the fields described next in this table.

OrganizationID is a Long Integer field that is used as a lookup field to store values from the table tblOrganization.

EmailType is a Long Integer field that indicates type of e-mail address. (This is a foreign key to lookup table tblEmailType.)

Email is a Text field that records an e-mail address.

Field Name	Data Type	Description
OrgEmailID	AutoNumber	Primary key, uniquely identifies this record
OrganizationID	Number	Foreign Key to tblOrganization
EmailTypeID	Number	Indicates type of e-mail address (foreign key to lookup table tblEmailType)
OrgEmail	Text	Email address
LastUpdatedBy	Text	User who last updated this Record
LastUpdatedDate	Date/Time	Date/time when this record was last updated
OrgEMaiNotes	Text	Optional, unstructured comments or notes about this record

Figure 4-6: The Email for Organization table

The Phone for Organization Table

Finally, you need a table to manage the numerous phone numbers that may be associated with a given organization.

The table tblPhoneForOrg contains the following fields, as shown in Figure 4-7.

OrganizationID is a Long Integer field that is used as the foreign key to a related record in tblOrganization.

OrgPhoneType is a Text field that describes the type of phone: home, work, mobile, or pager.

OrgPhoneDisplayOrder is a Long Integer field that is used to indicate the order in which to display the phone number, if multiple phone numbers exist for the related record.

OrgPhoneCountryCode is a Text field that contains a telephone's country code, which varies in number of digits in different regions.

OrgPhoneAreaCode is a Text field that contains a three-digit area code (U.S. /North American format only).

OrgPhonePrefix is a Text field that holds a three-digit prefix (U.S. /North American format only).

OrgPhoneTelephoneNumber is a Text field that stores a four-digit number (U.S. /North American format) or a variable-length number (other).

As noted earlier, in relation to the Phone for Person table, the area code, prefix, and phone number can be stored as "phone number" in a single Text field, unless you expect to later perform detailed demographic analysis.

OrgPhoneExtension is a Text field that records an extension, if applicable.

Field Name	Data Type	Description
⚷ OrgPhoneID	AutoNumber	Primary key, uniquely identifies this record
OrganizationID	Number	Foreign key to tblOrganization
OrgPhoneType	Text	Type of phone: Home, Work, Cell, Pager
OrgPhoneDisplayOrder	Number	Order in which to display the Phone, if multiple phones for related record
OrgPhoneCountryCode	Text	Country code, varying length depending on country/region
OrgPhoneAreaCode	Text	3-digit area code (US Format Only)
OrgPhonePrefix	Text	3-digit prefix (US Format Only)
OrgPhoneTelephoneNumber	Text	4-digit number (US Format); variable length number (Other)
OrgPhoneExtension	Text	Extension, if applicable
LastUpdatedBy	Text	User who last updated this Record
LastUpdatedDate	Date/Time	Date/time when this record was last updated
OrgPhoneNotes	Text	Optional, unstructured comments or notes about this record

Figure 4-7: The Phone for Organization table

NOTE In looking at the fields for tblPhoneForOrg, you will notice an anomaly in the name field for the primary key. When working with tables from other databases, you will often find that the table and field names do not exactly match the conventions that you have established for your own files. In some cases, it is easy to change, but in many cases, you will need to work with inherited names. In the table tblPhoneForOrg, the field PhoneID is an example of how you might retain the field name to facilitate exchanging data with the original source.

That completes the core tables that store the details specific to an individual or an organization. Next, we will create the lookup tables that store the lists of data from which users select, such as categories and states.

Lookup Tables

Lookup tables, as described earlier, provide an efficient way of obtaining faster and more accurate data entry, limiting the values in a field to a defined list, and increasing data integrity. We've used some in our sample database, and have also provided some reference tables that you can download as a bonus, so to speak. You might choose to use other lookup tables in your solutions.

Most lookup tables have a similar structure, so we only provide a brief explanation of each table. Following the guidelines for good relational database models, each of our lookup tables includes an AutoNumber primary key, whose name is derived from the table name with the suffix of ID.

NOTE The values are from a lookup table, and you can store either the primary key value or the text value. Deciding which value to store is typically based on how the data might change, how the data will be used, and the developer's personal preference. You can learn more about lookup tables in Chapter 3 and Appendix B.

The Person Category Table (a Lookup Table)

The list of categories in which you want to group people is included in tblPersonCategory. As shown in Figure 4-8, it has only one field that is unique.

PersonCategoryName is a Text field that contains the name of this category. Categories are whatever you find useful for your database application, e.g., member, vendor, or contractor.

Field Name	Data Type	Description
PersonCategoryID	AutoNumber	Primary key, uniquely identifies this record
PersonCategoryName	Text	Name of this Category
LastUpdatedBy	Text	User who last updated this Record
LastUpdatedDate	Date/Time	Date/time when this record was last updated
PersonCategoryNotes	Text	Optional, unstructured comments or notes about this record

tblPersonCategory : Table

Figure 4-8: The Person Category table

The Organization Category Table (a Lookup Table)

Next, we create a similar table for organizations. This table, named tblOrganizationCategory, is shown in Figure 4-9. It also has a single unique field.

OrganizationCategory is a Text field that specifies this organization's category. Examples of organization category could include commercial, non-profit, government, and religious.

Field Name	Data Type	Description
OrganizationCategoryID	AutoNumber	Primary key, uniquely identifies this record
OrganizationCategory	Text	Description of this category
LastUpdatedBy	Text	User who last updated this Record
LastUpdatedDate	Date/Time	Date/time when this record was last updated
OrganizationCategoryNotes	Text	Optional, unstructured comments or notes about this record

tblOrganizationCategory : Table

Figure 4-9: The Organization Category table

The Organization Type Table (a Lookup Table)

Within a category of organizations, such as services, you may have several types, such as office repair, printing, or delivery. We're using tblOrganizationType to store the list of specific types that are appropriate for our needs. Then, as shown in Figure 4-10, we can associate each type with a specific category by including the field from the category table. This table contains only two unique fields.

OrganizationCategoryID is a Long Integer field that is used as a lookup key to tblOrganizationCategory.

OrganizationType is a Text field that describes the organization type.

Field Name	Data Type	Description
OrganizationTypeID	AutoNumber	Primary key, uniquely identifies this record
OrganizationCategoryID	Number	Foreign key to tblOrganizationCategory
OrganizationType	Text	Type of organization
LastUpdatedBy	Text	User who last updated this Record
LastUpdatedDate	Date/Time	Date/time when this record was last updated
OrganizationTypeNotes	Text	Optional, unstructured comments or notes about this record

Figure 4-10: The Organization Type table

The State Reference Table (a Lookup Table)

Now we are ready to review some reference tables that can be helpful for managing contact information. We start with the table named tblStateRef. We have provided this in the example databases for this chapter on the CD that comes with this book. It is pre-populated with a list of U.S states, territory, and military postal locations, Canadian provinces and territories and their official abbreviations. The table, shown in Figure 4-11, has only two unique fields.

StateCode is a Text field that stores the postal code abbreviation for the state.

StateName is a Text field that contains the name of the state, province, or other locale for lookup.

Field Name	Data Type	Description
StateRefID	AutoNumber	Primary key, uniquely identifies this record
StateCode	Text	Postal code Abbreviation
StateName	Text	Name for lookup
LastUpdatedBy	Text	User who last updated this Record
LastUpdatedDate	Date/Time	Date/time when this record was last updated
StateRefNotes	Text	Optional, unstructured comments or notes about this record

Figure 4-11: The State Reference table

The Country Reference Table (a Lookup Table)

As we rely on the Internet and e-mail, it is becoming increasingly common to have contacts from around the world, so you may need to identify the country.

Having the official abbreviation for a country in a lookup table can help you quickly complete online forms, group contacts based on country, or even group countries into regions. We've provided a table, named tblCountryRef, complete with a few countries and their official abbreviations, as examples; the content is not intended to be nor represented as a complete list. If you make a lot of international calls, you may want to add a column for country or region code as used by the phone service. This table, shown in Figure 4-12, contains two unique fields.

CountryAbbreviation is a Text field that contains the abbreviation for the country's name.

CountryName is a Text field that contains the name of the country.

Field Name	Data Type	Description
CountryID	AutoNumber	Primary key, uniquely identifies this record
CountryAbbreviation	Text	Abbreviation for Country
CountryName	Text	Name of Country
LastUpdatedBy	Text	User who last updated this Record
LastUpdatedDate	Date/Time	Date/time when this record was last updated
CountryRefNotes	Text	Optional, unstructured comments or notes about this record

Figure 4-12: The Country Reference table

The EMail Type Table (a Lookup Table)

The table tblEMailType is shown in Figure 4-13. It contains the values used to classify e-mail by type, if you choose to do so in your database application. There is one field in addition to the standard fields.

EMailType is a Text field that describes the type of e-mail, which could include values such as work, personal, school, or mobile.

Field Name	Data Type	Description
EMailTypeID	AutoNumber	Primary key, uniquely identifies this record
EMailType	Text	Description of type of e-mail address, eg company, personal, mobile
LastUpdatedBy	Text	User who last updated this record
LastUpdatedDate	Date/Time	Date/time when this record was last updated
EMailTypeNotes	Text	Optional, unstructured comments or notes about this record

Figure 4-13: The Email Type table (a lookup table)

The Month Table (a Lookup Table)

As a matter of convenience, some developers like to use a table to store the various ways of displaying the month. We've provided tblMonth, which contains fields for the number, the full name, and the abbreviation, as shown in Figure 4-14.

MonthNumber is a Long Integer field that contains the number (1–12) of the month.

MonthName is a Text field that records the name of the month.

MonthAbbreviation is a Text field that stores the abbreviation for the month's name.

Field Name	Data Type	Description
⚿ MonthID	AutoNumber	Primary key, uniquely identifies this record
MonthNumber	Number	Number of the month
MonthName	Text	Name of the month
MonthAbbreviation	Text	Abbreviation of the month
LastUpdatedBy	Text	User who last updated this Record
LastUpdatedDate	Date/Time	Date/time when this record was last updated
MonthNotes	Text	Optional, unstructured comments or notes about this record

Figure 4-14: The Month table

That completes our list of lookup tables, but we have one more type of table to complete our example: a junction table.

Junction Tables

Simply described, a *junction table* is used to relate several items from one table with several items in another table. For example, consider classes and students. Each student attends several classes, and each class has multiple students. In Access, we resolve this by using a third table to store the foreign key to the related record. We also include a third field to store the primary key for the junction table itself.

You'll see how this works as you build the next table. One of the first things that you might notice is that when we refer to the junction table, we use a hyphen between the names of the two tables. This is a common way of indicating a junction table. Conversely, we do not use a hyphen referring to the tables in a one-to-many relationship. We've provided a detailed discussion in Appendix B, "Relationships, Joins, and Nulls."

The Organization-Person Table (a Junction Table)

Because each person can belong to several organizations and each organization is likely to be represented by several people, this creates a many-to-many relationship. We use a junction table to resolve this into two one-to-many relationships. Each person can have many records in the junction table, and each organization can have many records in the junction table; but each record from the junction table is associated with only one person and one organization.

For our database, we use tblOrganizationPerson. Each record in this table will contain the value that uniquely identifies a specific organization and a person, as shown in Figure 4-15. These will both be required fields.

OrganizationID is a Long Integer field that is used as a foreign key to the related organization's record in tblOrganization.

PersonID is a Long Integer field that is used as foreign key to the related person's record in tblPerson.

Field Name	Data Type	Description
OrganizationPersonID	AutoNumber	Primary key, uniquely identifies this record
OrganizationID	Number	Foreign key to tblOrganization
PersonID	Number	Foreign key to tblPerson
LastUpdatedBy	Text	User who last updated this Record
LastUpdatedDate	Date/Time	Date/time when this record was last updated
OrganizationPersonNotes	Text	Optional, unstructured comments or notes about this record

Figure 4-15: The Organization-Person table

Putting the Tables Together

Now that you have created all of the tables, you can see how they are related by looking at the relationship view, or schema. In database terminology, a schema is a diagram that shows how the tables are related. In the schema for the simple model, shown in Figure 4-16, you can see how relationships are formed by storing the primary key from one table in another table.

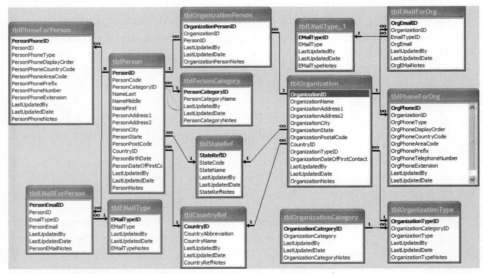

Figure 4-16: Relationship diagram of the simple model

Just to make it clear, the EMail For Person table and the EMail For Org table are both linked to the same EMail Type table, but two copies of the EMail Type table are shown (one with its name followed by "_1" because otherwise the relationship lines would be confusing).

Even a relatively simple database can start to look complicated as you add more tables, but understanding how the tables are related is fundamental to understanding how the data is managed in your application. Therefore, if you are faced with a complex situation, like our next example, you might find it helpful to break it into sections, and look at the tables and their relationships, one function at a time. If you'd like a refresher on creating and working with table relationships, we suggest that you review Chapter 3 and Appendix B.

Differences between the Simple and Complex Models

The primary difference between our simple example and the complex example is that some tables—the tables for people and the tables for organizations—have more information in common. Specifically, people and organizations may share email, phone, and address information. In the simple model that you just completed, we made the following assumptions:

- The person or organization using the database interacts with other individuals and small-to-modest-size organizations. For such an audience, it is reasonable to assume that a person or an organization has just a single address, and that address would not be shared with another person or organization. This enabled the simplicity of storing the address information directly in the tables for both the individual and the organization.

- Similarly, a person or an organization might have multiple e-mail addresses and multiple phone numbers and types, but for design purposes they do not share an e-mail address or a phone number with another person or organization. Please note that the design does not preclude more than one person using the same phone number or e-mail address. This results in a design for which e-mail addresses and phone numbers are kept in separate tables related one-to-many to the Person table and the Organization table.

> **NOTE** The most common way to implement a one-to-many relationship is by including a foreign key (a field that has a unique value) from the table on the "one" side of the relationship (often referred to as the *parent* table) in the table on the "many" side of the relationship (often referred to as the *child* table). This is typically accomplished by storing the value of the primary key from the parent record in the child record. This enables you to store the same parent value in multiple child records, while limiting each child record to having only one parent, ergo the term "one-to-many."

For a complex model, you will see how to manage data when the people and organizations have more data in common. For example, if several people are employed by the same organization, you can expect to have multiple people sharing the same postal addresses, e-mail addresses (such as an alias of `info@xyz`), or phone numbers. This creates the many-to-many relationship that you recently encountered. Even though the same data is involved, it requires a different table structure. To help you understand and apply this concept, we will explain it a little differently this time.

> **NOTE** You implement a many-to-many relationship in Access by creating a third table called a *junction table*. The junction table stores a foreign key from the two tables in the relationship. In addition, there are no differences between the "sides" of the relationship; the two tables are treated equally. For example, if you have tens or hundreds of people in your database related to one organization, each of those people may share one or more addresses. Furthermore, if the organization has subsidiaries in the same location, and each one is included in the Organization table, multiple organizations could easily share those same addresses. Each combination of address and organization or address and person will be represented by a record in a junction table.

In order to support the many-to-many relationships among e-mail, people, and organizations, and between phones, people, and organizations, you need to create several junction tables. Because the foreign keys will be stored in the junction table, you won't need a field to store a foreign key in the EMail or Phone tables, as you did when you created the one-to-many relationships in the simple model. Therefore, the tables for e-mail and phone numbers will be slightly different in this model.

Because address information is likely to be shared, you also need to create a separate table for addresses, and provide junction tables between the newly created Address table and the Person table, as well as between the Address table and the Organization table.

The Complex Model

Because the "business" data is similar, and only the structure of the tables is changed, we will look at an overview of the complex model. Using the basic structure of the simple model that you've just completed, we'll provide a full description of the tables that are different. However, for tables that are the same—such as all of the lookup tables in the simple model—you can find the full description in the previous example.

Figure 4-17 shows an overview of how data is related in the complex model. From this simple diagram, you can easily recognize the need for seven junction tables and three detail tables. The following sections explain the fields necessary for our two core tables—Person and Organization—and then explain the detail tables for address, e-mail, and phone. With those established, we can methodically create the junction tables.

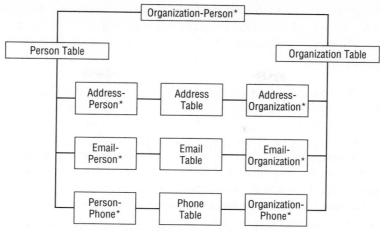

* Junction table supporting many-to-many relationship

Figure 4-17: Overview of subjects (complex model)

The Person Table

The table named tblPerson, as shown below in Figure 4-18, identifies the person, the person's contact information, and additional information about the person required to meet the business needs of the application. This might include details such as position or to whom the person reports. These items of information are stored in the following fields in the table:

■ **tblPerson : Table**

Field Name	Data Type	Description
PersonID	AutoNumber	Primary key, uniquely identifies this record
PersonCode	Text	Code as Text (optional if useful in your application)
PersonCategoryID	Number	Foreign key to tblPersonCategories
NameLast	Text	Last Name
NameMiddle	Text	Middle Name
NameFirst	Text	First Name
TitleID	Number	Foreign key to tblTitle
TitleSuffixID	Number	Foreign key to tblTitleSuffix
PersonBirthDate	Date/Time	Birthdate, if known
PersonDateOfFirstContact	Date/Time	Date of First Business or Other Contact, if known
LastUpdatedBy	Text	User who last updated this Record
LastUpdatedDate	Date/Time	Date/time when this record was last updated
PersonNotes	Text	Optional, unstructured comments or notes about this record

Figure 4-18: The Person table

PersonCode is an optional field used to store a code, typically as text, to identify the person. In order to uniquely identify the person, this needs to be a unique value. Because you want to avoid inadvertent duplication, you should set the field properties to have this field indexed and not allow duplicates.

PersonCategoryID is a Long Integer field that is used as a foreign key to the Person Category table. This might be the classification of worker, title, department or any other aspect that you need to record. You may require several similar fields.

NameLast is a Text field containing the person's last name.

NameMiddle is a Text field containing the person's middle name.

NameLast is a Text field containing the person's first name.

Resist the temptation to combine the name parts and only store and use a full name. As we explained when we were creating the Person table for the simple example, it is much better to have individual fields and then combine the data in any manner that you need.

PersonBirthDate is a Date/Time field that records the person's birth date, if known.

PersonDateOfFirstContact is a Date/Time field that records the date (and possibly time) of the first business or other contact, if known.

If you compare this to the simple model, you'll notice that all of the address fields have been removed, but you'll also see several fields that are the same in both the simple and complex versions of this table.

The Organization Table

Next, we created a similar table for organizations, tblOrganization, shown in Figure 4-19. Like the Person table, it no longer contains address information, as it did in the simple model. Because all of the contact information can be shared with persons and other organizations, this table does not contain any of the related foreign keys, so it only has three new fields.

OrganizationName is a Text field that contains the name of this organization.

NOTE Because you can anticipate several organizations having the same name, you cannot require this to be a unique value. Instead, you include features in the user interface, typically an Access Combo Box control, to display enough information to select the specific organization that you want. The Combo Box will likely become one of your favorite controls, when you begin designing and working with forms (which is a topic beyond the scope of this book).

OrganizationTypeID is a Long Integer field that is used as a foreign key to look up values in the Organization Type table.

OrganizationDateOfFirstContact is a Date/Time field that records the date (and possibly time) of the first contact with this organization.

Field Name	Data Type	Description
OrganizationID	AutoNumber	Primary key, uniquely identifies this record
OrganizationName	Text	Name of this Organization
OrganizationTypeID	Number	Foreign key to tblOrganizationType
OrganizationDateOfFirstContact	Date/Time	Date of first contact with this organization
LastUpdatedBy	Text	User who last updated this Record
LastUpdatedDate	Date/Time	Date/time when this record was last updated
OrganizationNotes	Text	Optional, unstructured comments or notes about this record

Figure 4-19: The Organization table

Now that you have the two core tables, you can create the tables for storing specific contact information that can be shared by people and organizations.

The EMail Table

tblEMail, as shown in Figure 4-20, contains the email addresses for people, organizations, or both.

EmailTypeID is a Long Integer field that is used to indicate the type of e-mail address (a foreign key to the lookup table tblEMailType). This could indicate whether the address is primary, home, work, and so on.

Email is a Text field that stores an e-mail address. There are options to store this as a hyperlink data type instead of text, but most programs will automatically convert a text version of an e-mail address to a hyperlink when you use the address.

Field Name	Data Type	Description
EmailID	AutoNumber	Primary key, uniquely identifies this record
EMailTypeID	Number	Foreign key to tblEmailTypes
Email	Text	E-mail address, sample: BenBrown@AcmeWidgets.com
LastUpdatedBy	Text	User who last updated this Record
LastUpdatedDate	Date/Time	Date/time when this record was last updated
EMailNotes	Text	Optional, unstructured comments or notes about this record

Figure 4-20: The EMail table

The Phone Table

The table tblPhone, shown in Figure 4-21, it differs from the Phone table in the simple model in that it doesn't contain a foreign key to either the Person table or the Organization table. Those relationships are accommodated by two junction tables, one between Organization and Phone and one between Person and Phone. We'll describe those shortly. For now, we'll create the fields for tblPhone.

PhoneType is a Text field that indicates the type of phone: home, work, mobile, or pager. The value is stored because the types of phones rarely change. If, in your environment, they do change more rapidly, replace this with a foreign key to a lookup table for phone types.

PhoneCountryCode is a Text field that records country code, a varying number of digits depending on region, for all formats. A value of 1 indicates U.S., Canada, and certain Caribbean countries.

PhoneAreaCode is a Text field that contains a three-digit area code (U.S./North American format only).

PhonePrefix is a Text field that holds a three-digit prefix (U.S./North American format only).

PhoneNumber is a Text field that stores a four-digit number (U.S./North American format) or a variable-length number (other formats).

As discussed when creating the tables for the simple model, the area code, prefix, and phone number can be stored in a single Text field, as "phone number." Having separate fields can be helpful if you need to perform detailed demographic analysis. Single fields may also be a benefit if you frequently receive large lists of contact data to clean and import into your system.

PhoneExtension is a Text field that contains an extension, if applicable.

As with the simple model, you could also include a field to set the display order.

Field Name	Data Type	Description
PhoneID	AutoNumber	Primary key, uniquely identifies this record
PhoneType	Text	Type of Phone: Home, Work, Cell, Pager
PhoneCountryCode	Text	Country code (all formats), variable length, value of 1 = US, Canada, Caribbean
PhoneAreaCode	Text	3-digit area code (US / North American Format Only)
PhonePrefix	Text	3-digit prefix (US / North American Format Only)
PhoneNumber	Text	4-digit number (US/ North American Format); variable length number (Other)
PhoneExtension	Text	Extension, if applicable
LastUpdatedBy	Text	User who last updated this Record
LastUpdatedDate	Date/Time	Date/time when this record was last updated
PhoneNotes	Text	Optional, unstructured comments or notes about this record

tblPhone : Table

Figure 4-21: The Phone table

The Address Table

The table, named tblAddress, has no counterpart table in the simple model because the address data was stored directly in the tables for Person and Organization.

You might start by creating the primary key and the field to identify the address type. Then, save some time by opening tblPerson in design view to copy and paste the address fields into the new table; then remove the prefix of people to end up with the field names shown in Figure 4-22.

AddressTypeID is a Long Integer field that is a foreign key to address type. Users will select from a list such as shipping, home, work, main, and so on.

Address1 is a Text field that contains first line of the address.

Address2 is a Text field that contains second line of the address.

City is a Text field that contains the city where the address is located.

State is a Text field that stores the state, province, or territory abbreviation. For validation that the abbreviation is typed correctly, this should be selected from a Combo Box in the user interface that has the State Ref table values as its Row Source.

PostCode is a Text field that holds the zip or postal code.

CountryID is a Long Integer field that is used as a foreign key to the Country Reference table.

Field Name	Data Type	Description
AddressID	AutoNumber	Primary key, uniquely identifies this record
AddressTypeID	Number	Foreign key to Address Type
Address1	Text	First Line of Address
Address2	Text	Second Line of Address
City	Text	City
State	Text	State, Province, Territory Abbreviation
PostCode	Text	ZIP or Postal Code
CountryID	Number	Foreign key to tblCountry Ref
LastUpdatedBy	Text	User who last updated this Record
LastUpdatedDate	Date/Time	Date/time when this record was last updated
AddressNotes	Text	Optional, unstructured comments or notes about this record

Figure 4-22: The Address table

Now that you have the tables for storing the information, you need to create the lookup tables that provide the lists for users to make selections.

Lookup Tables

There are four new lookup tables in the complex model that were not used in the simple model. The other lookup tables are identical to those in the simple model, so you use the tables that you've already created. Again, you can incorporate other lookup tables for example to obtain state abbreviations.

The Address Type Table (a Lookup Table)

This new lookup table is for listing the types of addresses. As shown in Figure 4-23, tblAddressType has only one unique field.

AddressType is a Text field that specifies the type of address. For a business, appropriate types might be billing or receiving (ship-to). For an individual, types might include office, home, shipping.

Field Name	Data Type	Description
☊ AddressTypeID	AutoNumber	Primary key, uniquely identifies this record
AddressType	Text	Type of Address
LastUpdatedBy	Text	User who last updated this Record
LastUpdatedDate	Date/Time	Date/time when this record was last updated
AddressTypeNotes	Text	Optional, unstructured comments or notes about this record

tblAddressType : Table

Figure 4-23: The Address Type table

The Role Table (a Lookup Table)

The table tblRole is shown in Figure 4-24 and allows lookup of the name of the role that a person has in an organization. It has three table-specific fields.

RoleName is a Text field that contains the short name for the role of an employee in your organization.

RoleDescription is a Text field that is optionally used for a longer description of the role.

RoleInactive is a Yes/No field in which Yes means the role is archived for historical purposes and no longer available to be assigned.

Field Name	Data Type	Description
☊ RoleID	AutoNumber	Primary key, uniquely identifies this record
RoleName	Text	Short name for the role of an employee in your organization
RoleDescription	Text	Longer description, if needed, of the role of the employe
RoleInactive	Yes/No	Yes - this is an archived role, no longer assigned to new records
LastUpdatedBy	Text	User who last updated this Record
LastUpdatedDate	Date/Time	Date/time when this record was last updated
RoleNotes	Text	Optional, unstructured comments or notes about this record

tblRole : Table

Figure 4-24: The Role table

The Title Table (a Lookup Table)

The table tblTitle, shown in Figure 4-25, contains the title by which the person is addressed in conversation, written communication, and postal address. It has two table unique fields.

TitleAbbreviation is a Text field containing the abbreviation of the title, such as Ms, Mr, Dr, or Rev.

TitleDescription is a Text field containing a longer description of the title, such as "Ms is for a woman (irrespective of marital status)" and "Doctor of Medicine."

Field Name	Data Type	Description
⚷ TitleID	AutoNumber	Primary key, uniquely identifies this record
TitleAbbreviation	Text	Title as used before name Ms, Mr, Dr, Rev
TitleDescription	Text	A fuller description of this title
LastUpdatedBy	Text	User who last updated this Record
LastUpdatedDate	Date/Time	Date/time when this record was last updated
TitleNotes	Text	Optional, unstructured comments or notes about this record

Figure 4-25: The Title table

The Title Suffix Table (a Lookup Table)

The table tblTitleSuffix, shown in Figure 4-26, contains the title suffix by which the person is addressed in conversation, written communication, and postal address. It has two fields in addition to the standard fields.

TitleSuffixAbbr is a Text field containing the abbreviation of the title, such as PhD, CEO, MA, or Col. USAF (Ret).

TitleDescription is a Text field containing a longer description of the title, such as "Doctor of Philosophy is the most advanced post-graduate degree in many fields of study," "Chief Executive Officer is the executive responsible for corporate policy," "Master of Arts is a post-graduate degree" and "Colonel, USAF (Retired) is a title for a retired United States Air Force officer."

Field Name	Data Type	Description
⚷ TitleSuffixID	AutoNumber	Primary key, uniquely identifies this record
TitleSuffixAbbr	Text	As used after name, e.g. on a postal address
TitleSuffixDesc	Text	A fuller description of this title
LastUpdatedBy	Text	User who last updated this Record
LastUpdatedDate	Date/Time	Date/time when this record was last updated
TitleSuffixNotes	Text	Optional, unstructured comments or notes about this record

Figure 4-26: The Title Suffix table

Junction Tables

As illustrated in the Figure 4-16 earlier in this chapter, the complex model relies on seven junction tables. You will use the junction table that we previously created to associate people with organizations, and create six new tables to support or resolve the other many-to-many relationships. They all have a similar structure, so you will quickly become familiar with creating and using them.

The EMail-Person Table (a Junction Table)

We'll start by creating a table named tblEMailPerson to associate people with e-mail addresses. As shown in Figure 4-27, there are really no "new" fields in this table. The first field is the AutoNumber primary key, and the table has three standard fields.

The remaining two fields are required to represent the many-to-many relationship between persons (tblPerson) and e-mail addresses (tblEmail). These two fields store the primary key for the selected record that represents a person and an e-mail address.

PersonID is a Long Integer field that stores the primary key from tblPerson as a foreign key.

EMailID is a Long Integer field that stores the primary key from tblEMail as a foreign key.

Field Name	Data Type	Description
EMailPersonID	AutoNumber	Primary key, uniquely identifies this record
PersonID	Number	Foreign key to tblPerson
EMailID	Number	Foreign key to tbEMail
LastUpdatedBy	Text	User who last updated this Record
LastUpdatedDate	Date/Time	Date/time when this record was last updated
EMailPersonNotes	Text	Optional, unstructured comments or notes about this record

Figure 4-27: The EMail-Person table

You can apply the same explanation about the fields to the rest of the junction tables, so we will just list the field names without the details.

The Person-Phone Table (a Junction Table)

Similar to e-mail addresses, each person may have several phone numbers and a phone number may be used by multiple persons. You use the junction table, tblPersonPhone, between tblPerson and tblPhone. We have included a field that can be used to determine the order in which numbers will appear, so this table has three unique fields, as shown in Figure 4-28.

PhoneID is a Long Integer field that stores the primary key from tblPhone as a foreign key.

PersonID is a Long Integer field that stores the primary key from tblPerson as a foreign key.

PersonPhoneDisplayOrder is a Long Integer field that determines the order in which this phone number will be displayed, if the person has more than one phone number. This allows each Person to set an individual display order, even if the phone is shared.

Field Name	Data Type	Description
🔑 PersonPhoneID	AutoNumber	Primary key, uniquely identifies this record
PhoneID	Number	Foreign key to tblPhone
PersonID	Number	Foreign key to tblPerson
PersonPhoneDisplayOrder	Number	Order in which to display phone number, if person has more than one
LastUpdatedBy	Text	User who last updated this Record
LastUpdatedDate	Date/Time	Date/time when this record was last updated
PersonPhoneNotes	Text	Optional, unstructured comments or notes about this record

Figure 4-28: The Person-Phone table

The Address-Person Table (a Junction Table)

Because we've already established that a person may have multiple addresses, such as a post office box and home address, and that several people can frequently have the same address, we again use a junction table to associate the two records. This table is named tblAddressPerson (see Figure 4-29). It contains the standard fields plus a field that uniquely identifies the person, and a field to uniquely identify the address. You might also include a field to store the display order if that will not be determined by the address type, which is stored in the Address table.

PersonID is a Long Integer field that stores the primary key from tblPerson as a foreign key.

AddressID is a Long Integer field that stores the primary key from tblAddress as a foreign key.

Field Name	Data Type	Description
🔑 AddressPersonID	AutoNumber	Primary key, uniquely identifies this record
PersonID	Number	Foreign Key to tblPerson
AddressID	Number	Foreign key to tblAddress
LastUpdatedBy	Text	User who last updated this Record
LastUpdatedDate	Date/Time	Date/time when this record was last updated
AddressPersonNotes	Text	Optional, unstructured comments or notes about this record

Figure 4-29: The Address-Person table

The EMail-Organization Table (a Junction Table)

At this point, you've created the junction tables required to manage the data for people. Your next step is to create similar tables for organizations. Like people, an organization may have several e-mail addresses. You might also find that one e-mail address can be associated with multiple records in your Organization table—for example, if a company has several subsidiaries co-located and using the same computer systems (sharing would be more common with physical addresses, but may occur with email addresses, too). To support this type of flexibility, we created a junction table named tblEMailOrganization, shown in Figure 4-30. Like the e-mail table for people, this table has only two unique fields.

EMailID is a Long Integer field that stores the primary key from tblEMail as a foreign key.

OrganizationID is a Long Integer field that stores the primary key from tblOrganization as a foreign key.

Field Name	Data Type	Description
EMailOrganizationID	AutoNumber	Primary key, uniquely identifies this record
EMailID	Number	Foreign key to tbEMail
OrganizationID	Number	Foreign key to tblOrganization
LastUpdatedBy	Text	User who last updated this Record
LastUpdatedDate	Date/Time	Date/time when this record was last updated
EMailOrganizationNotes	Text	Optional, unstructured comments or notes about this record

tblEMailOrganization : Table

Figure 4-30: The EMail-Organization table

The Organization-Phone Table (a Junction Table)

Again, in the same manner that you created the junction table for managing phone listings for people, you create tblOrganizationPhone to associate organizations with phone listings. As shown in Figure 4-31, we have included a field to stipulate the order in which numbers will appear, so there are three unique fields in this table.

PhoneID is a Long Integer field that stores the primary key from tblPhone as a foreign key.

OrganizationID is a Long Integer field that stores the primary key from tblOrganization as a foreign key.

OrganizationPhoneDisplayOrder is a Long Integer field that determines the order in which this phone number will be displayed if the organization has more than one phone number.

Field Name	Data Type	Description
OrganizationCategoryID	AutoNumber	Primary key, uniquely identifies this record
OrganizationCategory	Text	Description of this category
LastUpdatedBy	Text	User who last updated this Record
LastUpdatedDate	Date/Time	Date/time when this record was last updated
OrganizationCategoryNotes	Text	Optional, unstructured comments or notes about this record

tblOrganizationCategory : Table

Figure 4-31: The Organization-Phone table

The Address-Organization Table (a Junction Table)

The final junction table that you'll need for organization contact information is used to associate the addresses with each organization. Using the same approach as we did for people, create a table tblAddressOrganization, as shown in Figure 4-32. Because the address type is in the Address table, you do not need to include that here. However, similar to the management of phone numbers, you may want to include a field to specify the display or sort order. Our table includes two fields that are unique to this table.

OrganizationID is a Long Integer field that stores the primary key from tblOrganization as a foreign key.

AddressID is a Long Integer field that stores the primary key from tblAddress as a foreign key.

Field Name	Data Type	Description
AddressOrganizationID	AutoNumber	Primary key, uniquely identifies this record
OrganizationID	Number	Foreign key to tblOrganization
AddressID	Number	Foreign key to tblAddress
LastUpdatedBy	Text	User who last updated this Record
LastUpdatedDate	Date/Time	Date/time when this record was last updated
AddressOrganizationNotes	Text	Optional, unstructured comments or notes about this record

Figure 4-32: The Address-Organization table

NOTE When you are reviewing this table you will notice that the order of the subjects is reversed in the name of the primary key field. This illustrates some of the dilemma and challenges that you will encounter in many of your projects. It would seem logical to use organization as the prefix for the table and field names, but we also wanted to follow our convention of using alphabetical order for naming junction tables. As we were pulling all of the files together, we recognized the benefit of listing junction table names in alphabetical order to provide consistency as you copy tables from one database to another. In this case, the table name was revised but the name of the primary key was not. We encourage you to name the tables and fields to suit your needs, whether that is using abbreviations, reversing the names, or working with the files as-is.

The Organization-Person Table (a Junction Table)

Like the other junction tables, this one, named tblOrganizationPerson (shown in Figure 4-33), creates an association between two subjects, a person and an organization; but this table also provides additional information that is specific to that unique relationship. In our scenario, we are also identifying the title of a person and the role that he or she has within the selected organization.

NOTE The values are from a lookup table, and you can store either the primary key value or the text value. Deciding which value to store is typically based on how the data might change and the developer's personal preference. You can learn more about lookup tables in Chapter 3 and Appendix B.

For our example, tblOrganizationPerson requires the four fields described below in addition to the three standard fields.

OrganizationID is a Long Integer field that stores the primary key from tblOrganization as a foreign key.

PersonID is a Long Integer field that stores the primary key from tblPerson as a foreign key.

TitleSuffixID is a Long Integer field that is used as the foreign key to a lookup table (sometimes known as a "lookup key") called tblTitleSuffix, in reference to the person and organization. Some examples are CEO, CFO, Treas, and Secy.

RoleID is a Long Integer field that is used as a lookup key to tblRole, for the role of this person in this organization.

Field Name	Data Type	Description
OrganizationPersonID	AutoNumber	Primary key, uniquely identifies this record
OrganizationID	Number	in index with no duplicates, can be used as natural key
PersonID	Number	in index with no duplicates, can be used as natural key
TitleSuffixID	Number	use as lookup key to tblTitleSuffix, e.g., CEO, CFO, Treas.
RoleID	Number	use as lookup key to tblRole, role of person in organization
LastUpdatedBy	Text	User who last updated this Record
LastUpdatedDate	Date/Time	Date/time when this record was last updated
OrganizationPersonNotes	Text	Optional, unstructured comments or notes about this record

tblOrganizationPerson : Table

Figure 4-33: The Organization-Person table

Putting the Tables Together

Now that we've described all of the tables, we are ready to show you how they fit together. At this point, you've created several tables that each store pieces of information about a person or an organization, as well as junction tables required to connect the records. You've also created several lookup tables that make it easy for users to select values from lists of data; the lists can also be beneficial by limiting options to a predetermined set of values . All of those tables and relationships are illustrated in Figure 4-34.

If you follow the lines between the tables, you can see that the contact data is linked to each person and each organization. You can also see how tblOrganizationPeople links people with organizations.

You can use Access to draw a relationship diagram. Of course, you will have to choose the tables to be included and establish the relationships between them. The relationship diagram identifies and represents the relationships based on the field names and types. You can learn more about relationships in Chapter 3 and Appendix B.

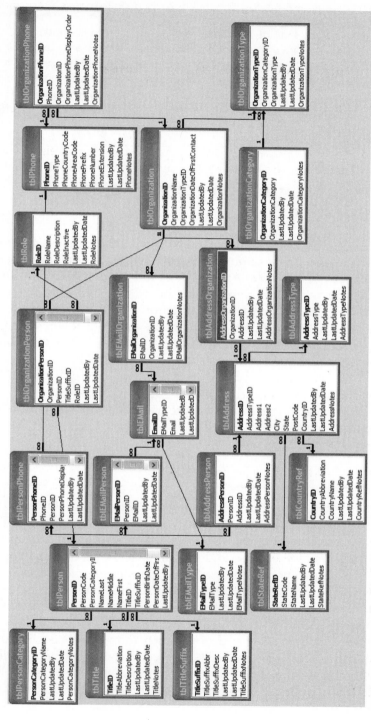

Figure 4-34: Relationship diagram of the Complex Model

Adding More Information about People and Organizations

If you need to record additional information about a person or organization, you can insert additional fields into the Person table or the Organization table. As an alternative, a separate table of business function–specific information can be created and related using a one-to-one relationship to the Person or Organization table. This type of table structure should only be used if the tables for Person and Organization are shared by multiple business functions and if, in your judgment, storing the data in a separate table will simplify managing and sharing it.

Information that can have several records associated with a person or an organization, such as appointments, events, or contact history, needs to be stored in separate tables. These would require additional junction tables similar to those used for contact information.

Summary

In this chapter, you learned how to create two databases to manage contact information for people and organizations. We started by discussing the purpose of the database and what we wanted to accomplish. We then considered sample questions that you can use to determine what level of detail you need to record. For example, you might include separate, unique pieces of data, such as a job title, or it may require allowing several similar items, such as having multiple phone numbers. In that case, you can also provide a way to specify the display order.

Based on the details needed and how much information is shared, you may be able to use a simple table structure, such as when there is limited data in common between people and organizations. Otherwise, if people and organizations might both use the same contact information, you can provide a more complex table structure.

Even in the simple model, you have the opportunity to create a many-to-many relationship to create the ties between records about a person and records about an organization. We explained how the data is related and managed using a junction table. This is a valuable model because you will frequently find scenarios that include this type of relationship.

You have examined tables describing people and organizations. In the simple model these tables include address information, but in the complex model people and organizations are each related many-to-many to a separate, shared Address table. You also examined a case for which there are separate Phone and E-Mail tables for people and for organizations (related one-to-many, in the simple model); and a case in which phone and e-mail information may be shared, and are therefore kept in separate tables related many-to-many to each of the People and Organization tables.

You have also seen that you can apply a category to people and to organizations, should you find that useful, as it enables you to group by category for searching or reporting in your database application.

As a bonus, we also discussed and provided some additional tables, not specifically and directly related to people and organizations. We've included tables with some official data that is commonly needed for addresses, such as the State Reference table, and another for referring to countries. We've also provided a table with month names, numbers, and abbreviations. The latter table can be used to eliminate some calculations with date-and-time functions that are built into Access's expression feature and its Visual Basic for Applications (VBA) language.

By working through the examples, you have not only created table structures that can serve as standalone solutions, you have had the opportunity to learn a lot about designing a database. As you read the other chapters, you can concentrate on the business functionality that they are describing and implementing; and as you complete other examples, you can incorporate the appropriate tables from this chapter to support your needs for contact information—a nontrivial aspect of many database solutions.

CHAPTER 5

Customer Relationship Management

What is the most important aspect of your business? Your relationship with your customers. Even dealings with your suppliers, your employees, and the lawn service are driven by the need to "do things right" so that your customers will be well-served and happy.

Customer relationship management (CRM) defines the methods businesses use to interact with their customers. The goal of CRM is to help you efficiently provide your customers with products and services, and give them prompt, courteous, and accurate responses to inquiries. CRM software focuses on enhancing your ability to save, retrieve, and use personal information crucial to the quality of your relationships with your customers.

While there are many CRM software packages available, the best-known of these are intended for large organizations, and are priced accordingly. They are designed to handle very large numbers—tens of thousands, hundreds of thousands, or millions—of customers. Packaged for enterprise-level organizations, they can cost hundreds of thousands of dollars to license, install, and set up, and additional tens of thousands each year to maintain and use. You might find a few other packages intended for mid- to large-sized companies with fewer customers, but they are still expensive and complex.

In this chapter, we offer you the alternative of creating a custom CRM database solution, one that is more appropriate for the size of your organization and tailored to serve your specific needs. We describe data that a small- to medium-sized organization can collect and look at how you can go about assembling that information. We also discuss how to set up the database tables where you will be storing it.

You will find that you can make immediate use of this data to improve communication with your customers. You can later analyze the information, either in a database application with custom programming, in a spreadsheet application (such as Microsoft Excel), or as you grow and move to a server back-end for data storage, you may use the analytical and reporting services of the server database. (Microsoft SQL Server, for example, incorporates exceptional tools for analyzing the data that it stores, and includes a highly-regarded Reporting Services component.) From your analysis, you can detect problems in your processes and make better decisions for the future. This may also lead you to incorporate modifications and enhancements to your database.

The information in this chapter can work well with that presented in the rest of this book. Because your customer's happiness is affected, directly or indirectly, by many areas of your organization, you might want to use those other topics as a guide to automating data handling in your organization. You can obtain and enter the data described in this chapter separately, or even better, as you create the database applications for those other functions, you can include the capability to capture and store the customer data that we describe in this chapter. If you opt for the latter approach, you'll not only reduce the time and effort required to put information into the database, but you'll reduce the opportunity for human error in transcribing the data.

In fact, you can capture most of the data needed for CRM from other business functions described in this book. You may not need all the fields from those functions, or you might need a few additional ones. But for simplicity of obtaining and using the data, it is likely to be effective to merely link to and use data that is already recorded in tables in the other business functions. You can leave extra fields intact and add the additional fields that are needed here. Keep in mind as you read this chapter that the tables shown here as separate tables may already exist elsewhere—so you may be able to link to or import data directly from the original tables.

Look also in other database applications, or other business functions in your database application if you are adding this to an existing database application. Look at what you can export from commercial, custom, or open-source software that you use in your business to see if you can make use of data that is already collected.

Several of the other chapters in this book explain how to create databases that can become data sources for a CRM solution. In particular, data from solutions built on the models for Chapters 7, "Sales," and Chapter 10, "Services," will be helpful; but solutions using the other models will typically provide valuable data about the people and organizations.

Six Core Topics of Customer Relationship Management

We describe six areas of business function that are of particular interest and importance for CRM. Each is included as a topic here, and all are included in the single example database for this chapter. The areas are:

- **People and organizations:** Collecting and maintaining information about your customers for communication and collecting additional information that you may later use in demographic analysis.

- **Customer information:** Using detailed information about your customers to improve and personalize your communication with them.

- **Sales:** Tracking the sales processes in your organization, generally and for specific customers, to identify areas where they can be improved.

- **Service:** Tracking service activities to identify areas of possible improvement, and also to spot problem trends in particular products or service offerings from your organization.

- **Campaigns:** Planning, executing, and tracking customer awareness campaigns. This function can also apply to special marketing efforts.

- **Internal Information Sharing:** Taking an active approach to ensure that anyone who may deal with customers is informed about appropriate items of information.

Now that we have identified the core topics, we will deal with each of them one at a time. Rather than just jump to identifying details and creating the tables, we'll take a moment to look at the approach we use.

Approach for Reviewing Core Topics

This section provides a brief review of the approach to help you understand the process that we are following. It can also serve as a guide for creating other databases for other purposes.

Basic Business Functions for the Topic

Within an organization, whether a for-profit business or a non-profit organization, you can identify topics, and within a topic, you identify business functions. The database design should support these business functions. Thus, the first step in our approach is to review and document the functions in your business that support the topics you identify. (The topics for CRM are listed in the "Six Core Topics of Customer Relationship Management" section earlier in this chapter.) You need to identify what is done, what information is needed, how to obtain the information, and how to record it.

With this, you will have identified the pertinent items to record in the database. Your next step will be to list, define, and group these items.

Items to Store

Some items will clearly be categories of information, which we call "subjects." Other items are clearly related information about the subject—we call those "details." Some will be less easy to identify as either subjects or details, but careful analysis and thought will allow you to identify them as one or the other.

The Subjects and Details of the Topic

You can start by outlining the subjects. Then you can determine which details directly describe each subject. You will typically need to make multiple passes through the data to ensure that you have all of the information that is required.

Some details can and should be broken down into component parts. For example, "name" is best stored as "first name," "middle name," and "last name." But things like "eye color" can't be further decomposed. Some items may be less easily broken out into details, but if you're persistent, you will be able to resolve most of those.

If you end up with a lot of unassigned details, it might be that most of them actually describe a subject that should be added to your list, rather than details describing another subject. If they are subjects, try to identify details that are associated with them and add those to your list. Otherwise, if they aren't subjects, you will need to determine what subject they describe.

Eventually, you will construct a list with subjects and related details. Don't despair if it doesn't always seem easy—it will become easier with practice.

Other Types of Subjects

Some subjects describe other subjects, and in many cases the relationship between subjects will be obvious. Sometimes these require special types of tables, such as a *junction table* used to resolve a many-to-many relationship. Occasionally the junction table will have additional details that describe the subject created by the junction. We explain how to create and use junction tables in the next section.

Another common type of table is the *lookup table*. We use lookup tables to provide selection lists. If you have a detail that identifies a characteristic of the subject, and the same values will be used over and over, that becomes a candidate for a lookup. An example of a candidate for a lookup might be "type of driver's license": motorcycle, private passenger vehicle, commercial (which may have categories based on weight or number of axles), private chauffeur, and public chauffeur.

Since the main field of most lookup tables provides selections lists for other tables, you should use field properties to make it a required field and set the Indexed property to Yes (No Duplicates).

Arranging the Data into Tables

To begin arranging subjects and details into tables and fields, it's convenient to draw or sketch an overview of subjects to determine their relationship, if any, to one another. You can do this by sketching a simple diagram. Don't get fancy, because your perception may change as you proceed, and it's nice to be able to erase and resketch parts of a diagram.

In some of the examples in this chapter, we include a diagram of subjects before discussing how to arrange the data into tables. This gives you a convenient overview of the main subjects for the business functions under consideration.

Then we review and consider whether, as is often the case, the identified subjects can directly be translated to tables, with the associated details becoming the fields. As we go through the process, we explain the concepts and best practices so that you will be able to use a similar approach on other projects.

We used a similar process to create the companion database for this chapter on the book's CD. We encourage you to review tables, fields, and relationships as we guide you through the steps to create them yourself. The file contains all of the tables that we use to support several business functions, and it incorporates tables from other chapters, too.

It is a matter of judgment whether the business functions can and should be combined into a single database, or whether separate database applications should be created for each. The decision is often based on the type and source of data involved, who will use it, and how it will be used. In this chapter, we combined the functions into one example database, but in Bonus Chapter B1 on the CD, "Knowledge: Intellectual Property, Structural Capital, and Intellectual Capital," we created separate databases for each example.

Now that we've explained the overall process that we use to create the tables, we will examine the tables themselves and explain the concepts and decisions that led to this design. We would like to remind you that the database in this chapter only illustrates the data model and has no user interface objects (forms or reports) or objects to support them (queries, macros, or modules). Those belong in a separate file that is known as the user interface, or UI. Designing the UI is beyond the scope of this book, but there are numerous resources to help you create a solution that is right for you. We've listed a few of our favorite resources in Appendix E, "References and Resources."

Tables in the Example Database for Each Topic

We will begin each topic by describing the table that seems most central to it, follow that with other, related data tables, and finish with junction and lookup tables.

The Table and Fields

For each table, we'll provide a brief description, followed by a short explanation of each field. We'll also explain various options, concepts, and techniques as they come up during the process. You will learn a lot by reviewing the figures in the chapter and the actual databases in the companion file for this chapter on the book's CD.

The following tables in this chapter, used in the example database, are identical to the same tables described in the complex data model in Chapter 4, "People, Organizations, Addresses": tblAddress, tblAddressPerson, tblAddressType, tblCountryRef, tblEMail, tblEMailPerson, tblEMailType, tblMonth, tblRole, tblStateRef, tblTitle, and tblTitleSuffix.

In some cases, either the table name or field names within the table were shortened for convenience or modified to adhere more closely to the naming conventions generally used in this book. The abbreviations or name changes should be obvious. Tables in this category are: tblAddressOrg (tblAddressOrganization), tblEMailOrg (tblEMailOrganization), tblOrg (tblOrganization), tblOrgCategory (tblOrganizationCategory), tblOrgPerson (tblOrganizationPerson), tblOrgPhone (tblOrganizationPhone), tblOrgType (tblOrganizationType), tblPersonCat (tblPersonCategory). The table names in parentheses are those of the original tables copied from the complex data model of Chapter 4.

MaritalStatusID, a foreign key to tblMaritalStatus, was added to tblPerson, to support anticipated processing, but all other fields are identical to tblPerson in the complex data model. And, PhoneTypeID, a foreign key to tblPhoneType, replaced the text field Phonetype in tblPhone, for flexibility, but all other fields are identical to tblPhone in the complex data model.

Review Chapter 4 for detailed descriptions and table design views of these tables.

Relationship Diagram Showing the Schema or Overview of the Topic

After we have discussed all of the tables that support a business function, we'll look at the relationship diagram to get an overview of the tables, fields, and relationships. This is often called a *schema* in database terminology.

DATA PRESERVATION

Don't delete information unless you must do so to preserve customer and individual privacy within the limits prescribed by law. The data may provide valuable insights into your customers' needs. Alternatively, if the data file becomes too large, you can archive some data or split the data file into multiple data files.

   You should preserve the data even if you are not currently using a CRM function. As you grow and automate more business functions, you may be able to use historic data to analyze your business and, perhaps, to implement a more robust analytical part of your CRM function, as discussed in this chapter. Information saved can be used again; information deleted often cannot be recreated.

STANDARD FIELDS USED IN MOST TABLES

This chapter uses the same standard fields described in Chapter 4. Refer to the "Standard Fields Used in Most Tables" sidebar at the beginning of that chapter for a discussion of primary keys, indexing, audit trail and notes. The subsequent sidebar in that chapter about memo fields applies here as well.

Customer Information

Whether you have software designated as a CRM application or not, think about what is at the heart of most of your business transactions. It would be an unusual business if your response to our opening question, "What is the most important aspect of your business?" was not, "People—my customers, my vendors, my members."

   If you are on good terms with the people with whom you do business, then it is very likely that you know some of the things that are important to them. Thus, the first topic we are going to address is information that you can use to improve your customers' view of you, and the second will be collecting information that you can use to analyze the demographics of your customers.

Improving Your Relationship with Your Customers

The goal of CRM is to improve the relationships you have with your customers. To do this, you rely on information that you can gather based on interactions with your customers. A key objective is to provide a means to ensure the quality and quantity of the information collected, and that it can be easily retrieved and used to demonstrate to your customers that you care and that you are personally interested in serving their needs.

If it seems somewhat cold to resort to a database to show your personal interest, remember that if your competitors seem to have better recall than you do, that is likely due to the software they use to keep track of a multitude of details about their customers. If your competitors are selling to, providing customer support for, or otherwise dealing with individuals who have big ticket orders, especially on high-end goods that are sold individually or in small lots, you can rest assured that the successful ones are using every technological advantage they have to improve their chances of success.

And, if you think about it, wouldn't you rather deal with a friend, someone who demonstrates an interest in you, than a stranger? So, a customer who considers you to be a friend, not just "someone trying to sell me something," will be more likely to purchase from you than from a competitor who hasn't established that friendly relationship. Perhaps equally important, is that when something goes wrong or just doesn't seem right in your transaction, they will tend to call you to work out the problem instead of just walking away and finding someone else to purchase from or deal with.

Gathering Data to Analyze in the Future

Collecting what may appear to be unrelated or irrelevant data might seem like overkill, but having this information can turn out to be a valuable business asset. Even if growth is not a primary goal for your company, you and your customers may benefit greatly from the edge that additional analysis might provide.

By recording the data now, you are ensuring that it will be available for detailed analysis in the future, so you need to be forward thinking, not just focused on today. The only downside is that you'll have a few more fields in some tables, and perhaps a few more tables; so you will spend a little more time on data entry. The upside far outweighs the extra effort, because in most cases once the chance to capture the data is gone, the data is likely gone for good.

As businesses grow, they use customer information grouped or sorted by city, state, zip code, area code, local telephone prefix, and personal characteristics (if they can determine those). This information can suggest where to open new locations for physical presence, the type of advertising to use, and who to target in advertising, awareness, and sales campaigns.

Basic Business Functions for People and Organizations

Since the business functions discussed in this chapter are centered on people and organizations, the business functions and the tables that we'll use are almost identical to the complex model described in Chapter 4. The detailed discussion of the people and organization information has not been duplicated here, so before you continue, you will find it beneficial to reacquaint yourself with Chapter 4's discussions on how to handle the data in the complex model. In the area that is directly taken from Chapter 4, we have only added one table to support our examples. We add the Customer table, named tblCustomer, to identify the customer.

Arranging the Data Into Tables

The core of our CRM system will be centralized on the customer, typically either a person or an organization. The primary difference between this solutions and the one described in Chapter 4 is that you will need to add a Customer table to identify the customer, as shown in Figure 5-1.

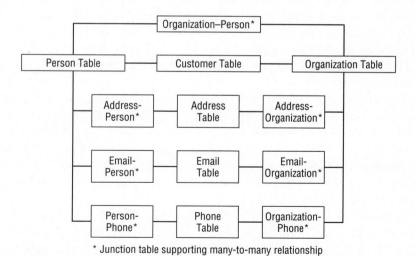

Figure 5-1: Diagram of subjects for CRM customers

As you can see from our diagram, this data model categorizes the customer as either a person or an organization. Although this approach introduces some complexity, it allows each group to have specific data requirements and provides maximum flexibility when adapting the model to your specific needs.

Before we jump into building the tables, you might want to review the discussion of standard fields in Chapter 4 to see if there are additional fields that are appropriate for your needs. Whatever list you choose can become the starting point for all of your tables. You can use a table template or start each table by copying the standard field into a table. You can then delete fields or add additional fields as appropriate.

Customer Table

The table called tblCustomer (shown in Figure 5-2), serves only to indentify customers, and to associate the customer data with the other data about the organization or individual. This is done by storing the value of the related PersonID or OrgID as a foreign key field in the customer record.

Data in this table will typically provide the starting point for finding a particular customer by joining this table in a query to tblOrg and tblPerson.

You will only need to add three fields in addition to the fields that are standard for each table (see the "Standard Fields Used in Most Tables" sidebar in Chapter 4).

CustomerName is a Text field that contains the customer's name. Providing the information is optional, but the field allows you to record a "commonly known as" name for your customer. If a specific name is not provided, you could use the person name or organization name that is associated with this customer record to identify or refer to this customer when you present the data on-screen or print it in a report. How you identify the customer, in detail, should be based on what will be useful and helpful in your business functions, rules, and practices.

PersonID is a Long Integer field used as a foreign key to the Person table to identify the person, if the customer is a person. This field is indexed, but with duplicates allowed, because one person may have multiple customer accounts.

OrgID is a Long Integer field used as a foreign key to the Organization table to identify the organization, if the customer is an organization. This field is indexed, but with duplicates allowed, because one organization may have multiple customer accounts.

It is important to note that a customer may be either a person or an organization but not both. As a result, you will find foreign keys to both tblPerson and tblOrg in tblCustomer, but only one of these foreign keys may contain a value at any given time. There are several ways of managing this at the time the data is entered. We've provided two approaches for implementing this type of model in Appendix C, "Resolving Relationship Triangles," together with the examples on the book's CD.

Field Name	Data Type	Description
CustomerID	AutoNumber	Primary key, uniquely identifies this record
CustomerName	Text	Optional -- if not supplied, choose and use the Person Name or Org Name
PersonID	Number	Foreign key to tblPerson
OrgID	Number	Foreign key to tblOrg
LastUpdatedBy	Text	User who last updated this Record
LastUpdatedDate	Date/Time	Date/time when this record was last updated
CustomerNotes	Text	Optional, unstructured comments or notes about this record

Figure 5-2: The Customer table

For details on how to create the other tables in this group, we again refer you to the discussion of the complex model in Chapter 4. We next work with the details associated with individuals.

The Person Table Grouping

It is often convenient to categorize the tables by the type of data they contain and how they are used, but in this business function, this is not easy. There are many details that can relate to several subjects. However, we can find a logical place to start based on our decision to identify a customer as either a person or an organization. Since we are all familiar with people, we'll start there. The tables which follow manage data about an individual person.

When considering people, you will want to think of areas and details that might help you both improve and expand your services. You may want to consider the possibility of cross-marketing or referring customers to other businesses, either now or in the future. With that in mind, you can see that the specific details that you capture in your database will vary depending on your business, your relationship with other businesses, and your plans for the future.

You will need to consider all of those factors when creating the tables related to the person—and to some extent to the organization. After you have a table to record information about a person (see Chapter 4), you should create a table to store information about their family.

The Family Member Table

We recommend a table to store information about family members, named tblFamilyMember (shown in Figure 5-3), to store information about family members of the individuals in the Person table. You might find this data to be invaluable for personalizing contacts with the person. Knowing about birthdays, anniversaries, and age (for example, at 16 kids can drive), can help you target marketing offers, acknowledge birthdays, and provide other personal touches. You will need to create the standard fields plus the following seven fields.

PersonID is a Long Integer field that is used as a foreign key. It identifies the person to whom this family member is related For performance, it is a good idea to index all foreign key fields. Because every family member should be associated with a customer record, we will make this a required field.

This brings up another issue. Although a family member can easily be related to several customers, the model that we are providing only accommodates a single connection. If your business requirements need to accommodate associating one family member with several people, then you can include another table, a junction table, to resolve the many-to-many relationship. You'll find several examples later in this chapter and throughout the book. For now, we'll proceed with the single relationship.

FamilyMemberNameFirst is a Text field that contains the first name of this family member.

FamilyMemberNameMiddle is a Text field that contains the middle name of this family member.

FamilyMemberNameLast is a Text field that contains the last name of this family member.

FamilyMemberNickname is a Text field that contains the nickname of this family member (e.g., Joseph might be "Joe," "Jody," "Hotshot," etc.).

TitleID is a Long Integer field that is used as a lookup, identifying the title to use.

FamilyMemberTypeID is a Long Integer field that is used as a foreign key to reference the type of family member.

We also need to create a table to record phone numbers (see Chapter 4).

Field Name	Data Type	Description
FamilyMemberID	AutoNumber	Primary key, uniquely identifies this record
PersonID	Number	Foreign key to tblPerson, identifies person to whom this family member is related
FamilyMemberNameFirst	Text	First name of this family member
FamilyMemberNameMiddle	Text	Middle name of this family member
FamilyMemberNameLast	Text	Last name of this family member
FamilyMemberNickname	Text	Nickname of this family member (e.g., Joseph might be "Joe", "Jody", "Hotshot", etc.)
TitleID	Number	Foreign key to tblTitle
FamilyMemberTypeID	Number	Foreign key to tblFamilyMemberType
LastUpdatedBy	Text	User who last updated this Record
LastUpdatedDate	Date/Time	Date/time when this record was last updated
FamilyMemberNotes	Text	Optional, unstructured comments or notes about this record

Figure 5-3: The Family Member table

That completes the tables required to capture the details related to people. Next, we will create the lookup tables needed to provide information for the lists that users will select from.

Lookup Tables

In this section we create all the lookup tables used within the "person" grouping. Several of these tables will also be used in the "organization" grouping. Lookup tables provide an excellent means to efficiently enter data. Selecting from a list is typically faster than typing in the information, and it avoids typos by limiting selection to the provided options. An added benefit is that having standardized entries makes it much easier to group and analyze data.

Lookup tables also provide the option of storing either the text value that the user sees, such as red, blue, or green, or a hidden value that you can specify, typically the primary key of the selected record. In our tables, the value of the primary key is stored as the foreign key in the main table.

A rule of thumb is that if you will rarely change the value displayed in the lookup, you can store the value; otherwise, it is typically best to store the foreign key. An example of a table where you have a reasonable expectation that the value will never change is the State Reference table. The values of the state abbreviations, values agreed by postal authorities in many countries, have never changed. New values that are added will not conflict with already-stored abbreviations.

The first lookup table that we create records marital status.

Marital Status Table (a Lookup Table)

This table, called tblMaritalStatus, is shown in Figure 5-4. It allows you to enforce consistency by listing the marital status terms you wish to use in your database application. You may wish to distinguish between single, divorced, widowed, and other options that may seem helpful to your marketing and customer relations. Keep in mind that you do not necessarily need to show the user all of the options. Just in case a status needed more explanation, we have identified two fields specific to this table.

MaritalStatus is a Text field that contains a brief description.

MaritalStatusExpanded is a Text field that contains an expanded description.

tblMaritalStatus : Table

	Field Name	Data Type	Description
🔑	MaritalStatusID	AutoNumber	Primary key, uniquely identifies this record
	MaritalStatus	Text	Brief description
	MaritalStatusExpanded	Text	Expanded description
	LastUpdatedBy	Text	User who last updated this Record
	LastUpdatedDate	Date/Time	Date/time when this record was last updated
	MaritalStatusNotes	Text	Optional, unstructured comments or notes about this record

Figure 5-4: The Marital Status table

The next table that we create lists types of family members.

The Family Member Type Table (a Lookup Table)

Named tblFamilyMemberType, this table provides the list of possible relationships that a family member can have with an individual. The key considerations for deciding what to include in your list are consistency and the level of detail appropriate for your database application. Again, we've added fields for both short identifier and a more detailed description, as shown in Figure 5-5.

FamilyMemberTypeDescription is a Text field that contains a short description of family member type. This field provides a selection list; we will use the field properties to make this a required field and set the Indexed property to Yes (No Duplicates).

FamiyMemberTypeExtendedDescription is a Text field that contains additional explanation of family member type.

	Field Name	Data Type	Description
	tblFamilyMemberType : Table		
🔑	FamilyMemberTypeID	AutoNumber	Primary key, uniquely identifies this record
	FamilyMemberTypeDesc	Text	Description of family member type
	FamiyMemberTypeExtDesc	Text	Additional explanation of family member type
	LastUpdatedBy	Text	User who last updated this Record
	LastUpdatedDate	Date/Time	Date/time when this record was last updated
	FamMemTypeNotes	Text	Optional, unstructured comments or notes about this record

Figure 5-5: The Family Member Type table

You also need the tables from Chapter 4 for title and suffix.

The Phone Type Table (a Lookup Table)

The table tblPhoneType, shown in Figure 5-6, contains a list of the phone number types used in your database application. It can be useful, when you are calling the individual, to know if you are calling a work phone (calls to a work phone are not often considered intrusive) or a home or mobile phone (which may cause the person to feel that you are encroaching upon their personal life). You may also need to know which, if any, of the numbers listed can receive a fax. You will only need to create one new field for this table.

PhoneTypeDescription is a Text field that contains the type of phone. Since this provides a lookup list, the field will typically have a field property of Required: Yes.

	Field Name	Data Type	Description
	tblPhoneType : Table		
🔑	PhoneTypeID	AutoNumber	Primary key, uniquely identifies this record
	PhoneTypeDescription	Text	Type of Phone
	LastUpdatedBy	Text	User who last updated this Record
	LastUpdatedDate	Date/Time	Date/time when this record was last updated
	PhoneTypeNotes	Text	Optional, unstructured comments or notes about this record

Figure 5-6: The Phone Type table

Other things that you may want to record in conjunction with a phone type or the phone number itself may include allowed or blocked times, customer preference, or do-not-call restrictions.

That completes the tables to hold the data for a person. We are now ready to create the tables for organizations.

The Organization Table Grouping

These tables are primarily concerned with data about the organizations you define as useful to your business database application. Only one table, tblOrg, differs from the organization tables described in the complex model in Chapter 4, and it differs only in the shortening of the table name.

Organization-Related Lookup Tables

The organization-related lookup tables for customer relationship management are identical to the tables of the same names in the complex model in Chapter 4, so it is not necessary to duplicate the table and field descriptions here.

Since we have confirmed that we have all of the tables required for the organization, we can now integrate them with the tables for person.

Overview of Person and Organization Information

A relationship diagram showing the tables that we have created for the people and organizations in the Customer Relationship Management database is shown in Figure 5-7.

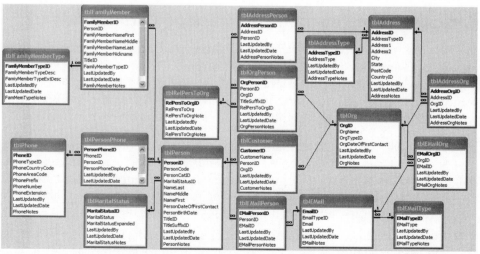

Figure 5-7: Relationship diagram showing the schema of person and organization information in CRM

These tables will become a central part of the process related to customer management. The next area that we'll design will allow you to track correspondence with customers.

Tracking Customer Correspondence

You can use the information that you've gathered about your customers and associated people and organizations as the basis for personalizing your correspondence by referencing specific individual details. Another facet of correspondence is tracking and linking it to a person, an organization, or a customer. All personalized correspondence will necessarily be to a person that is associated with a customer. The person may be the customer or may be associated with the customer through an organization. Therefore, it is necessary for you to have a way to search for the contact information in several ways.

We are about to create the tables required for recording the information for correspondence tracking. If you want to jump ahead, you can look at Figure 5-8, which provides a simplified drawing of the subjects involved. Once you've created the tables, you will see them in the relationship diagram in Figure 5-13, very much like the drawing in Figure 5-8. Because we've already explained some of the areas, we have omitted the details of the relationships of the person and organization tables and their associated lookup tables. You will find those details in the earlier part of this chapter as well as in the complex model in Chapter 4.

Basic Business Functions for Tracking Correspondence

In this discussion, *correspondence* refers to any form of communication between an employee of your organization and a customer. That could be a letter, an e-mail, a fax, a telephone call, a chat or IM session, or perhaps some other communication form not even available at the time this book was written. The following list describes business functions for correspondence:

- You must collect information for each tracked item of correspondence so that it can be represented as a single point of communication. To accomplish this, you will provide the users with appropriate data-entry and edit forms (also called *screens*) for recording information about the communication—either as it progresses or soon after.

- In case an error is encountered, you should provide a process that allows the user to change or delete all or part of the information. However, you will likely want to limit who has permission to edit the information, as you certainly don't want just any user to change predefined or mandated data.

- There should be sufficient identifying information about the correspondents and topics to allow searching through the data and to identify and select the specific communications for display or to print.

- You will need to group communications based on the same subject, and to be able to reconstruct the thread of correspondence about a subject.

- Additionally, you need the capability to maintain the lookup tables that provide selection lists.

As you can see, it is going to depend on the user to provide a lot of the information. There will be several controls and requirements needed. The focus here, though, is on creating the tables; designing the forms and other aspects of the user interface will come after you finish this book.

Items to Store

Similar to our other examples, the next focus is on indentifying all of the details that you need to record. This will take into consideration how you will use the tracked communications, as well as the limitations on some uses—both practical and imposed. For example, in many cases it is useful to be able to refer back to particular e-mail, letters, or phone calls and be able to precisely describe to the customer what was discussed. So you would want the details of the exchange, not just the date, subject, and parties involved.

WARNING You should exercise care and consult with your attorney on the nature of the information you keep on file. It is required that you store certain information, but it is also prohibited by law and regulations to keep other information. Preserving information that is not required and that is not clearly useful to your business can, in fact, work to your disadvantage in future legal proceedings. Having too many records can also place an undue burden on systems and people trying to store and retrieve data. The efficient storage and retrieval provided by a database can be of significant benefit when saving and working with data.

The Subject and Details of Customers, People, and Organizations

Since we have covered this area in great detail earlier and in other chapters, we will leverage the prior discussions rather than repeat the material. Instead we will refer you to the in the first section of this chapter as well as the detailed review in Chapter 4.

In the context of CRM, it may be useful to add a separate table of personal information about the employee and family or to add the additional fields to the information you keep about a person. You can use the table that you just created, the Family Member table, as your starting place.

The Subjects and Details of Correspondence

To record the information about your correspondence, you will need to address at least the following three key subjects:

- The identity of the correspondence, including:
  - the name or topic
  - the chronology (date and time)
  - the correspondents
- The business needs served by the correspondence, including:
  - the business reason
  - the goal of the communication
  - the outcome
- The content of the correspondence, including:
  - the summary and details
  - links to additional information, if applicable

These will become the basis for your core tables. As you review the data required, you will likely determine that you need additional details and tables.

Other Types of Subject

You should determine if there is a need or benefit to creating reference or lookup information. In this case, you have likely recognized that you would want to use lookup tables for the type of correspondence and for the role of an employee in your organization.

Arranging the Data Into Tables

Our discussion of subjects has provided you with guidelines for identifying the details and creating the tables that you will need to track correspondence. We've determined the need for correspondence, correspondence type, and correspondence detail. We've illustrated how they relate with the subjects of employees and customers in Figure 5-8. Since we have a business focus, we will limit our scope to correspondence at this level. If you choose to add correspondence for family members, you should first consider if benefits adequately offset the added complexity.

In addition to tables already discussed in the Chapter 4 and in the earlier part of this chapter, you will create some new tables. The discussion of the details from our list should help you to decide which fields to include. Of course, if you are creating a database tailored to your needs, your list may be somewhat different.

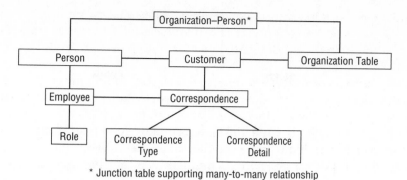

* Junction table supporting many-to-many relationship

Figure 5-8: Diagram of relationships for CRM correspondence

The Correspondence Table

You can collect the details about the subject correspondence into a single table; a good name would be tblCorrespondence. As we previously discussed the details, you should start with identifying information such as date and correspondence type. You would of course need to know the applicable details about the employee, customer, person, and organization. Information about those will be obtained from their respective tables by adding the primary key for the associated record as a foreign key.

There are several options for capturing the information about the content, such as a summary, a foreign key to detailed content information, and a hyperlink or Windows path and file pointer to electronically stored related documents. Finally, you may also want a method to record the business information like the reason for, goal of, and result of the correspondence.

That may seem like a lot of data for one table. But, as in the past, many items will not be stored directly in the table. And some of the details can be obtained from other tables.

Correspondence Detail

If you need to store long narratives, such as the body of a letter or details of a discussion, you will need to use a field with a capacity greater than the 255 character limit on a Text field. Access provides a memo field that allows you to store copious amounts of information, so that may seem like the logical choice for correspondence details. But memo fields have some drawbacks that are primarily associated with corruption.

As we noted in the "Memo Fields" sidebar in Chapter 4, improved technology has reduced the probability of corruption of a memo field. But the possibility is always there and the consequences can be devastating if you lose all the data in the same record, so you may want to be cautious and maintain the details of the correspondence in a memo field in a separate table. In the event that the memo field does become corrupted, this can limit the data loss to the memo field itself.

Our example includes several memo fields, so you will get to choose what will work best for you under different circumstances. Not all cases will necessarily warrant the same choice. For example, if you rarely expect to use the memo field, the associated risks are arguably lower, so it may be a safe bet to keep it in the main table for the sake of simplicity. However, if the memo field will grow or be changed frequently, it may be more susceptible to corruption.

DATA FILE MAINTENANCE AND BACKUP

The potential for corrupted data is just one of the reasons to establish routine procedures for file maintenance and backup. Two important tasks are to run the compact and repair process on the database and to make regular backups. The frequency for performing each depends on the size of the data file, the number of users, the types of processes, and the amount of data that might be lost. The process can be automated and scheduled to have minimal impact to the users.

The Employee Table

Additional information about the employee who is corresponding with customers can be useful. Although the desired details could be added to the Person table, we chose to create a new table for employee information that we want specifically for correspondence. The employee information you may decide to store includes the employee's role in your organization, and the dates that the employee began work for you, and the date the employee ceased to work for you; which will of course have some blank fields.

You may be wondering why we didn't include a field for the employee's name. Since we already have a table designed specifically for storing information about a person, we will leverage that here and use the approach of getting data from a separate table. So, you will need to store a foreign key to the Person table to retrieve the employee's name, e-mail, phone, and similar records.

You may also wonder why we might be duplicating information that is available elsewhere in an organization. That is a valid question and we have two primary reasons. One is to help you to design a standalone solution; the other is because some areas, such has personnel management, require confidential information and it is often better to not have direct links into their files.

Lookup Data

By using a reference or lookup table to provide lists of data, you can speed data entry while you are providing data integrity. In most cases, users are able to start typing an entry and it will auto-complete and move to the associated place in a list. The user can then select the correct item. This can minimize the opportunity for typos or having several versions of the same name.

USING LOOKUP TABLES INSTEAD OF VALUE LISTS

The data in an Access list box control or the drop-down list of an Access combo box control can come from a lookup table or a value list. We have chosen to use lookup tables for all of our lists as they make it easy use and provide several options to view and manage the data. By choosing the option to *limit-to-list* you can ensure that users can only choose one of your pre-defined values or names; they cannot enter other data or add items to the list. You will use a different process for adding values to the list.

Using a combo box gives you the opportunity to show related data in the dropdown list and to specify which detail is actually stored in the field of your table. Typically, you store the unique identifier for the lookup record in the data—a detail that the user does not even see. But you can also choose to store the value, such as the actual type of correspondence. In some scenarios, you may choose to store a different field that was included in the dropdown list.

Combo boxes and value lists are popular and powerful controls. You can learn a lot from the Access help files and from excellent examples online and in books that help you build the forms and reports of the user interface.

In our examples, we will store the primary key value from the lookup table as a foreign key in our main tables. To retrieve the data for display or printing you will need to join the lookup table with the data record. You will need to create two tables to serve as lookups for correspondence; they will have the lists for correspondence type and employee role.

LIMIT TO LIST

Why is it so important to limit the values used by employing lookup tables? That's a good question, and it has several answers. One of the benefits that you may not yet fully appreciate is data consistency.

If you or I are reading, and we see "mote" instead of "note," our brains translate for us, often without our realizing that we have just accommodated a misspelling. Computers, on the other hand, do not make that kind of adjustment. If you are searching for all correspondence of the type "note," the one

Continued

> ### LIMIT TO LIST *(continued)*
>
> with the "mote" misspelling will not be returned. It's often not feasible, and sometimes impossible, to add all the extra criteria to catch even common misspellings. Therefore, it is worthwhile to prevent typos and even valid variation, so that will not be an issue when your application goes operational.

Tables as Implemented in the Example Database

As described earlier, we did the analysis and created generic tables to serve the needs of several types of businesses. You may have modified your tables to provide optional or required features depending on your business needs.

We will continue with the tables from our example, which started with the people and organization model from Chapter 4. So, if you modified your tables, you will want to follow our process for incorporating the additional tables and fields that we are about to discuss. These are also provided in the sample database for this chapter.

The Correspondence Table

The core table for storing the correspondence details is called tblCorrespondence. It contains a summary of correspondence, identifies the correspondents, and has links to additional detail. As shown in Figure 5-9, you will need to add the following fields in addition to the standard fields.

Similar to the earlier discussion regarding customers being either an organization or a person, the correspondence can be associated with either an organization or a person, but not both. We again refer you to Appendix C to see some approaches for implementing this type of table relationship.

EmployeeID is a Long Integer field that is used as a foreign key to the Employee table to identify the sender.

CorresTypeId is a Long Integer field that is used as a lookup key to tbCorresType for obtaining the type of this correspondence.

PersonID is a Long Integer field that is used as a foreign key to the Person table to identify the addressee, if sent to a person.

OrgID is a Long Integer field that is used as a foreign key to the Organization table to identify the organization to which this correspondence applies, if appropriate.

CustomerID is a Long Integer field that is used as a foreign key to the Customer table to identify the customer to which this correspondence applies, if appropriate.

CorresDetailID is a Long Integer field that is used as a foreign key to the Correspondence Detail table, to a record containing detailed information about this correspondence.

CorresDate is a Date/Time field that records the date and time of this correspondence.

CorresSummary is a Text field that contains a summary of this correspondence. Keep in mind that as a text field, the summary will be limited to 255 characters. And, as a tip, you may need to change the field length, as the default field length for text fields is often 50 characters. To change field length, in table design view, click on the field, look at the area below the list of fields, and change the property Length. Please review Appendix A, "Field Properties," to learn more about the properties associated with each data type.

CorresReasonFor is a Text field that tells why this correspondence was initiated. You may want to limit this to a list, or to provide some suggestions for the user but also allow them to enter their own data.

CorresGoal is a Text field that states the goal of this correspondence.

CorresResult is a Text field containing an evaluation of the outcome of this correspondence. Again, this may be another area for using a list, which would facilitate analysis and tracking closure effectiveness.

CorresPathAndFile is a Text field that contains an Internet address or a fully-qualified Windows path and file name of an electronic document that is, or is related to, this correspondence.

tblCorrespondence : Table

Field Name	Data Type	Description
CorresID	AutoNumber	Primary key, uniquely identifies this record
EmployeeID	Number	Foreign key to tblEmployee (sender)
PersonID	Number	Foreign key to tblPerson (addressee)
CustomerID	Number	Foreign key to tblCustomer (addressee)
OrgID	Number	Foreign key to tblOrg (addressee)
CorresDetailID	Number	Foreign key to tblCorresDetail
CorresTypeId	Number	Foreign key to tbCorresType
CorresDate	Date/Time	Date and time of this correspondence
CorresSummary	Text	Summary of this correspondence
CorresReasonFor	Text	Why was correspondence initiated?
CorresGoal	Text	What was the goal of this correspondence?
CorresResult	Text	What was the outcome of this correspondence?
CorresPathAndFile	Text	Path and file name or hyperlink if document is stored electronically
LastUpdatedBy	Text	User who last updated this Record
LastUpdatedDate	Date/Time	Date/time when this record was last updated
CorresNotes	Text	Optional, unstructured comments or notes about this record

Figure 5-9: The Correspondence table

With the core table in place, we can create the additional tables that will store the related details.

The Correspondence Detail Table

The detailed record of the correspondence will be stored in the table named tblCorresDetail, shown in Figure 5-10. Since this is a memo field, we have chosen to put it in a table by itself. As we previously explained, it is not the high probability of corruption but rather the possibility and significant consequences of losing all the data in the same record that prompted us to use a separate table, just in case. Alternatively, if you wish to allow for multiple detail records instead of just one, you will need to include a foreign key to the Correspondence table in this record, instead of the foreign key to this table in the Correspondence record. However, since one record in the Correspondence table records only a single incident or instance of correspondence, rather than a chain or thread, one memo field will likely be sufficient. Because of this, there is only one table-specific field required.

CorresDetail is a Memo field that contains detailed information about this correspondence if the database is the principal or only source of detail. Since there is no purpose for the record if this field does not contain any data, the field properties will typically make it a required field.

Field Name	Data Type	Description
CorresDetailID	AutoNumber	Primary key, uniquely identifies this record
CorresDetail	Memo	Used if the database is the principal or only source of detail
LastUpdatedBy	Text	User who last updated this Record
LastUpdatedDate	Date/Time	Date/time when this record was last updated
CorresDetailNotes	Text	Optional, unstructured comments or notes about this record

Figure 5-10: The Correspondence Detail table

Next, we will create a table for the extra details that we think are important to know about the employees.

The Employee Table

To store the details about employees that we anticipate needing for correspondence, we will create the table called tblEmployee. As we touched on earlier, we are not attempting to link directly to systems that maintain official employee records. Instead, we will only be gathering and storing enough data to identify the sender of customer communications.

The Employee table has a one-to-one relationship with the Person table. In this case, every employee will be associated with a record in the Person table, but not every record in the Person table will have an employee record.

As shown in Figure 5-11, the table contains the standard fields plus four new fields.

PersonID is a Long Integer field that is used as a foreign key to the Person table, which for an employee contains the links to e-mail and phones, but not as much data as would be needed for a customer or customer organization's employee entry. To avoid duplicate employee records for the same person, this field will be indexed with no duplicates allowed. You will also use the field properties to make this a required field, as you do not want to have an employee record that is not associated with a specific record in the Person table.

RoleID is a Long Integer field that is used as a foreign key to the Role table.

EmployeeDateHired is a Date/Time field that records the date this employee was hired.

EmployeeDateLeft is a Date/Time field that records the date after which this employee is no longer an employee of your organization.

Field Name	Data Type	Description
EmployeeID	AutoNumber	Primary key, uniquely identifies this record
PersonID	Number	Foreign key to tblPerson
RoleID	Number	Foreign key to tblRole
EmployeeDateHired	Date/Time	Date this employee was hired
EmployeeDateLeft	Date/Time	Date this employee's employment ended
LastUpdatedBy	Text	User who last updated this Record
LastUpdatedDate	Date/Time	Date/time when this record was last updated
EmployeeNotes	Text	Optional, unstructured comments or notes about this record

Figure 5-11: The Employee table

The last two tables for this topic are lookup tables for correspondence type and employee role.

The Correspondence Type Table (A Lookup Table)

We will use a lookup table called tblCorresType, shown in Figure 5-12, to provide a list for choosing, or limiting, the types of correspondence identified as useful in your business application. In addition to the standard fields, you will only need to create one field.

CorresType is a Text field, containing the type assigned to this correspondence. To prevent duplicates, this should be indexed with no duplicates allowed. And of course, it should be required, so it is a natural key.

Field Name	Data Type	Description
CorresTypeID	AutoNumber	Primary key, uniquely identifies this record
CorresType	Text	Explanation of correspondence type
LastUpdatedBy	Text	User who last updated this Record
LastUpdatedDate	Date/Time	Date/time when this record was last updated
CorresTypeNotes	Text	Optional, unstructured comments or notes about this record

Figure 5-12: The Correspondence Type table

The final table in this module is for the employee role (see the Role table in Chapter 4).

Now that we've created all of the tables for correspondence, let's see how they fit with the tables we already have.

Tracking Correspondence Overview

To track the correspondence, you need to know the details about the item itself and the people involved. In our example, we are using one table to store the names of all of the people, whether they are a customer, a representative of an organization, or an employee. This table also provides the links to other information about the person. The table that stores the core information about correspondence is also supported by additional tables to store related details. The tables and their relations are illustrated in Figure 5-13.

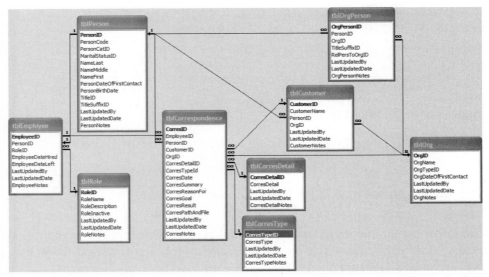

Figure 5-13: Relationship diagram showing the schema of correspondence items in CRM

This completes the discussion on correspondence. Next we explain how to track sales information.

Tracking Sales Information for CRM

Records of sales to customers apply not only to inventory and financial tracking, where they are helpful in resolving problems or issues that arise, but they are also vital to making informed decisions when you plan how to deal with the customers in the future.

It is likely that you already have the data that you need to make these types of business analyses. Using the information about delivered and paid orders, you can categorize customers by sales volume and other factors. Returns and post-shipment cancellations can also be significant in other analyses; and details about the products are useful input to yet more kinds of analysis. In each case, you will need to combine the specific details that are spread between sales records, order details, and invoice data into a single invoice table and also record the line items details for each invoice in a related table. Some information in this database application will summarize or simply be a copy of information stored elsewhere. And to preempt resistance to storing this type of data in your files, we will assure you that it is an accepted and often necessary practice. Even the priciest of CRM systems do not hold out the promise of "no duplicated data anywhere."

Items to Store

If you already have a system that adequately meets your needs for tracking sales you may only need to add a few fields or tables to capture some additional details that can be helpful to analysis and business decisions.

The area of sales, like correspondence, has plenty of pros and cons with regards to record retention. We said it before, but it is worth repeating; we advise that you exercise care and consult with your attorney about the nature of information you keep on file and how long you should retain it—certain information is required and other information is prohibited by law and regulations. Keeping information that is not required and is not clearly useful to your business can, in fact, work to your disadvantage in future legal proceedings.

With that said, let's move on with identifying the information that we want to track and store. We will be building on the tables and structure that we've created thus far in this chapter. So, if we've already created a table, we will merely explain how it will be used here and any additional fields that you will need to add.

The Subjects and Details of Sales

In order to analyze sales information, we'll need the information about invoices and their details.

An invoice can be described by breaking it down into four subjects with supporting details, which include:

- Identification of the invoice and sources, including:
  - the original invoice number
  - the original order number
- The individuals associated with the invoice, including:
  - the customer

- the customer's addresses for:
  - invoice
  - delivery
- the employee
- Associated dates, including:
  - the dates for the original order:
    - when it was placed
    - when it was expected to be delivered
    - when it was actually delivered
  - the dates when the invoice was:
    - sent to the customer
    - paid by the customer
- A financial summary, including:
  - the total amount (not necessarily a total of the detail lines)
  - the delivery charges
  - any other charges
  - the tax rate applicable at date of invoice

You need to address four details about the subject invoice detail (also known as an invoice line or line item detail).

- A reference to the (parent) invoice record
- A reference to the product type
- The quantity of product included in this invoice line
- The unit price as charged (as of—depending on your business rules—the date of order, date of invoice, or other)

You should consider the following details about the subject product:

- The product name
- The product identifying number or code, if any
- A product description and additional descriptive text
- An indication as to whether this product information has been archived for historical purposes or is still current or active
- A link to product category, if applicable

Other Types of Subjects

You should determine if there is a need for or benefit to creating reference or lookup information. In regard to invoices, you will likely benefit from a lookup table for the category of product. This can be useful in grouping and analyzing data.

Arranging the Data Into Tables

Our discussion of subjects has provided you with the basis for grouping the data and creating tables that you need to track and analyze sales data with respect to improving customer relations. In Figure 5-14, we have illustrated how the subjects and their resulting tables will be related to our existing tables for customers and employees.

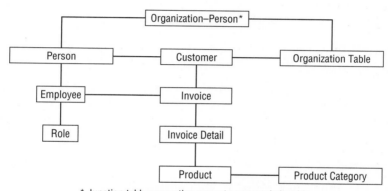

* Junction table supporting many-to-many relationship

Figure 5-14: Diagram of the subjects for CRM sales

We have already created the customer and employee tables, so we will only need to create a link to those in order to leverage the data in those tables and even the data in the tables that they relate to, such as the organization.

We will start with the core table for this area, the invoice table.

The Invoice Table

You can collect the details about the invoice into a single table. A good name for this would be tblInvoice. As discussed for the details, you should start by identifying the original invoice and the associated order. You can follow with information about individuals: a reference to the customer, the customer's address information, and a reference to the employee responsible for the sale or invoice.

The source of the historical invoice information will be from the invoices in the software used for your sales or services functions. You will often have links to other tables, but the sales information that is stored in the CRM database is consolidated and summarized for simplicity of subsequent analysis. The CRM module is not intended to handle sales or services.

The Invoice Detail Table

You can also collect the details about the subject "invoice detail" into a single table. A good name for this would be tblInvoiceDetail. Each record in this table represents a line item on the invoice, and so it will include a reference to record for the invoice in the Invoice table. Because there can be multiple invoice detail records for each invoice, there is a one-to-many relationship between an invoice and associated invoice details. You will also need a lookup reference to a product type, to record the actual product or item, the quantity, and unit price of the item sold.

The Product Table

To provide consistency, the details about the product can also all be held in a single table, which you may want to name tblProduct. The details that will become fields are product name, product number or code, product description, and the archived indicator.

The Product Category Table

Since this table will only be used to provide the list of categories to choose from, the only detail necessary in this table is the category name or description. You can add other information about the category that you believe would be helpful in your analysis of the data.

Tables as Implemented in the Example Database

As described earlier, we did the analysis and created generic tables to serve the needs of several types of businesses. You may have modified your tables to provide optional or required features depending on your business needs.

We will continue with the tables from our example, which started with the people and organization model from Chapter 4. So, if you modified your tables, you will want to follow our process for incorporating the additional tables and fields that we are about to discuss. The tables shown here are those in the example database that were added to collect and analyze customer data about Sales. These are also provided in the sample database for this chapter on the book's CD.

The Invoice Table

This table, called tblInvoice, contains information that can be collected from multiple tables that you'll find in the sample databases created in Chapter 7. As shown in Figure 5-15, you will need to add the following fields in addition to the standard fields.

CustomerID is a Long Integer field that is used as a foreign key to the Customer table.

PersonID is a Long Integer field that is used as a foreign key to the customer contact in the Person table.

DeliveryAddressID is a Long Integer field that is used as a foreign key to the Address table for the address to which the order was delivered.

InvoiceAddressID is a Long Integer field that is used as a foreign key to the Address table for the address to which the original invoice was sent.

InvoiceOrigNumber is a Text field that contains the original source invoice reference number.

InvoiceOrderNumber is a Text field that contains the original source order reference number.

EmployeeID is a Long Integer field that is used as a foreign key to the Employee table to identify the employee to contact about this invoice.

InvoiceOrderPlacedDate is a Date/Time field that records the date the order was placed.

InvoiceOrderDeliveryDateEstimate is a Date/Time field that records the date that the order was originally expected to be delivered to the customer.

InvoiceOrderDeliveredDate is a Date/Time field that records the date that the order was actually delivered to the customer.

InvoiceAmount is a Currency field that contains the total amount invoiced to the customer; this is not necessarily a sum of product prices as there can be various deductions and other charges. In many instances, you might expect this to be a calculated value, but in this case, it is simply information consolidated or summarized from an invoice.

InvoiceTaxRateApplicable is a double precision floating point number that contains the tax rate at the time of the order.

InvoiceDeliveryCharge is a Currency field that contains the amount of delivery charges as recorded at the time of the order or delivery, depending on your business practices.

InvoiceOtherCharges is a Currency field that contains other charges, e.g., special packing.

InvoiceSent is a Date/Time field that records the date and time that the invoice was originally sent to the customer.

InvoicePaid is a Date/Time field that records the date and time that the invoice was paid by the customer.

Field Name	Data Type	Description
InvoiceID	AutoNumber	Primary key, uniquely identifies this record
CustomerID	Number	Foreign key to tblCustomer
PersonID	Number	Foreign key to customer contact in tblPerson
DeliveryAddressID	Number	Foreign key to tblAddress
InvoiceAddressID	Number	Foreign key to Address table
InvoiceOrigNumber	Text	Original source invoice reference number
InvoiceOrderNumber	Text	Original source order reference number
EmployeeID	Number	Foreign key to tblEmployee identifies our employee to contact about this Invoice
InvoiceOrderPlacedDate	Date/Time	Date Order placed
InvoiceOrderDeliveryDateEst	Date/Time	Date order was originally expected to be delivered to customer
InvoiceOrderDeliveredDate	Date/Time	Date order was actually delivered to customer
InvoiceAmount	Currency	Total amount invoiced to the customer (not necessarily sum of product prices)
InvoiceTaxRateApplicable	Number	Tax rate at the time of the order
InvoiceDeliveryCharge	Currency	Amount of delivery charged at the time of the order
InvoiceOtherCharges	Currency	Other charges, e.g., special packing
InvoiceSent	Date/Time	Date invoice originally sent to customer
InvoicePaid	Date/Time	Date invoice paid by customer
LastUpdatedBy	Text	User who last updated this Record
LastUpdatedDate	Date/Time	Date/time when this record was last updated
InvoiceNotes	Text	Optional, unstructured comments or notes about this record

Figure 5-15: The Invoice table

Depending on your business model, you may also need to track things like late charges, subsequent price adjustments, and other incentives associated with a particular invoice.

Once you've created the table for the main invoice information, you are ready to create the table for the line item details.

The Invoice Detail Table

The table tblInvoiceDetail is used to capture the details about each line on the invoice that you may want for future analysis. In addition to the standard fields, it contains the following fields, as shown in Figure 5-16.

InvoiceID is a Long Integer field that is used as a foreign key to the parent record in the Invoice table. In the field property settings, this should be a required field.

ProductID is a Long Integer field that is used as a foreign key to the Product table for information about the product in this record.

Quantity is a Long Integer field that contains the number of products invoiced in this detail record or invoice line.

ItemPrice is a Currency field that contains the single-item price charged to the purchaser, at the date of order or delivery, depending on your business practice. This information is collected from the original invoice.

Field Name	Data Type	Description
InvoiceDetailID	AutoNumber	Primary key, uniquely identifies this record
InvoiceID	Number	Foreign key to Orders table
ProductID	Number	Foreign key to Product table
InvoiceDetailQuantity	Number	Number of this item type
InvoiceDetailItemPrice	Currency	The single item price (at time of order/delivery)
LastUpdatedBy	Text	User who last updated this Record
LastUpdatedDate	Date/Time	Date/ time when this record was last updated
InvoiceDetailNotes	Text	Optional, unstructured comments or notes about this record

Figure 5-16: The Invoice Detail table

The Product Table (a Lookup Table)

Next, you will need to create a table named tblProduct, that will provide the list of products that are, or were, available for sale. It describes the products in a record from the Invoice Detail table. In addition to the standard fields, it contains the following fields, as shown in Figure 5-17.

ProductCategoryID is a Long Integer field that is used as a foreign key to the Product Category table.

ProductName is a Text field that contains the name of this product.

ProductLineNo is a Text field that contains an identifying number or code, if there is one (optional).

ProductDescription is a Text field that contains a more extensive description of the product.

ProductInactive is a Yes/No (Boolean) field. Yes indicates that the product has been archived, so it is available for reference purposes only. This allows historic data to display properly. No indicates that the product is still actively sold. Again, you may want to set the default property of this field to No, so that when you add a new product type, it will initially be indicated as available for sale.

Field Name	Data Type	Description
ProductID	AutoNumber	Primary key, uniquely identifies this record
ProductCategoryID	Number	Foreign key to tblProductCategory
ProductName	Text	Name of this product
ProductLineNo	Text	Our identifying number(optional)
ProductDescription	Text	Descriptive text
ProductInactive	Yes/No	Yes = Archived for reference; No= this product is still actively sold
LastUpdatedBy	Text	User who last updated this Record
LastUpdatedDate	Date/Time	Date/time when this record was last updated
ProductNotes	Text	Optional, unstructured comments or notes about this record

Figure 5-17: The Product table

The Product Category Table (a Lookup Table)

The final lookup table is named tblProductCategory, which provide the list for selecting a category to be used with a product. In addition to the standard fields, it contains the following fields, as shown in Figure 5-18.

ProductCategory is a Text field that contains the name of the product category. In the field property settings, this should be a required field.

ProductCategoryDescription is a Text field that contains a fuller description of the category.

ProductCategoryInactive is a Yes/No (Boolean) field. Yes indicates that the category has been archived and is available for reference purposes. This allows historic data to be displayed properly. No indicates that the category has not been archived and that the category is active.

This is another instance in which you might want to set the default value for the field to No. As an alternative to a Yes/No field, you can create a date field to serve the dual purpose of indicating inactivity, and the historical record of when the category was inactivated.

Field Name	Data Type	Description
ProductCategoryID	AutoNumber	Primary key, uniquely identifies this record
ProductCategory	Text	Name of the category
ProductCategoryDescription	Text	Descriptive text about the category
ProductCategoryArchived	Yes/No	Yes = Archived for reference, but no longer assigned as a category
LastUpdatedBy	Text	User who last updated this Record
LastUpdatedDate	Date/Time	Date/time when this record was last updated
ProductCategoryNotes	Text	Optional, unstructured comments or notes about this record

Figure 5-18: The Product Category table

Now that you have created all of the tables, you are ready to see how they integrate with the existing tables for customers and employees.

Sales Information for CRM Overview

The schema for Sales CRM (shown in Figure 5-19), includes pertinent relationships to tables discussed in earlier sections of this chapter. To simplify the diagram, the secondary relationships to the earlier-defined tables are omitted. Because the requirements differ for use of information for tracking sales (as described in the Chapter 7), and for CRM (as described in this chapter), you will see that the tables are not identical.

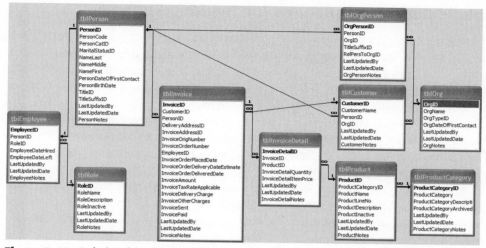

Figure 5-19: Relationship diagram showing the schema for sales information

It is important to remember that we are not creating a sales management solution. Our focus here is to provide a model for gathering and analyzing sales information in support of improving customer relationships. But, if the model we've provided meets your needs, by all means, use it as best you can. We also suggest that you review Chapters 7 and 10 for more detailed examples for the sales of products and services.

The next area that we'll discuss is related to providing service and support to your customers.

Tracking Service and Support Information

Many companies provide warranty support or service, offer free or for-a-fee technical support or service, user support or service, or offer add-on items or software for service and support. If your organization does any of these, you can identify and record the support, service, or products purchased or used by customers.

The product information will guide you in marketing support products. The information on support and service issues can also allow you to concentrate the support effort where it's needed to improve your service and support business processes. It will also help you identify areas of your own products that need to be improved.

Basic Business Functions for Tracking Support

Tracking service and support might seem to be collecting data for future analysis. But, in fact, your database application can be used to retrieve, sort, and report information that can be used immediately to manage operations, to ensure that appropriate follow-up contacts are made, and that the customer or client understands when the issue is closed.

First, you must define your business process. A convenient method often used is to have a customer contact on a service or support issue to "open an incident." An *incident* is defined simply as the chain of contact with a specific customer about a particular issue.

Then you must define what activities are performed in dealing with an incident. As always, planning ahead pays off. With a defined set of activities that allow flexibility to add additional activities as needed you can more easily train your service and support responders, and they will have the relevant information associated with an incident literally at their fingertips.

When a support or service incident is initiated, it should be immediately recorded in and retrievable from the database, even while the incident is still open. It also needs to accommodate the potential that a different support responder could respond to each call from the customer. We've all experienced this when we call tech support for help with a computer or cell phone.

You should also include the capability for the support responder (the employee who takes the call, or the employee to whom it is routed or escalated) to record the activity he or she performs, and to record information if the call is re-routed or escalated.

You must also define how to close the incident. Of course, you should include a way to display and report all of the open incidents to bring to the attention of your employees so that they can follow up. For analyzing performance in support and service, you should create reports that indicate particular areas requiring support, response times and results of support activities, and a way to categorize and rank the products requiring support.

Items to Store

Keeping in mind that our goal is to be able to analyze the effectiveness or impact that service and support have on customer relations, we need to capture information about incidents, products, and activities, and about the people involved. You may be able to pull much of this information from existing systems and records. And of course, you will continue to build on the framework that we've created so far.

The Subjects and Details of Tracking Support

To record the information about service and support, you will need to address the following three core areas: the incident, the response, and the associated documentation.

- Information you need to record and keep about an incident includes data that will:
  - identify the incident itself by:
    - briefly naming it
    - more extensively describing the incident
  - identify the people who initiated the incident, including:
    - the customer contact person
    - the employee with whom first contact is made
- Information you need to record about an activity performed in response to an incident includes data that will:
  - identify the activity, including:
    - the type of activity performed
    - a reference to the incident
    - a brief name for this activity
    - a longer description (also see incident document links, mentioned later in this list)
    - the date or date and time the activity occurred
  - provide a detailed status, including:
    - a reference to a predefined status, such as "customer contact," "responsibility reassigned," "progress," "completed"
    - the employee handling activity
    - the employee to whom the activity was reassigned, if applicable
- Information about (electronic) documents regarding the incident including:
  - the incident to which it applies
  - a description of document, brief and/or detailed
  - a link to the document, path, and file, or a hyperlink to the document

In creating this list, we also identified the need for one lookup table.

Other Types of Subject

To be able to group and report the effectiveness of different types of responses, you should consider a lookup table to list the type of activity that is provided in response to an incident.

Arranging the Data Into Tables

Our discussion of subjects has provided you with guidelines for identifying the details and creating the tables that you will need to track and analyze the effectiveness of responding to incidents. We've determined the need to collect details about incidents, the response activities, and the associated documentation. We've illustrated how they relate with the subjects of employees and customers in Figure 5-20.

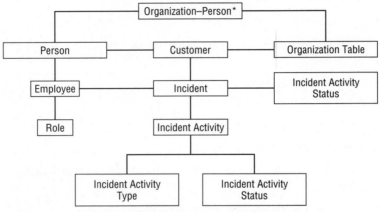

* Junction table supporting many-to-many relationship

Figure 5-20: Diagram of subjects for CRM tracking service and support

The following discussion of details should help you to decide which fields to include in your tables.

The Incident Table

You can create a table named tblIncident to collect the details directly related to the incident. This is the core table and will include the name and description of the incident, references to the customer contact person, and the employee with whom first contact is made.

Since our focus is on customer relations, we are only trying to capture sufficient details to measure and analyze how service and support are effecting customer relations. We are not including the details necessary for relating incidents to each other or to track an incident through multiple tiers of escalation.

The Incident Activity Table

Next, you need to create a table and name it tblIncidentActivity, to record the details about the response to the activity. The details include the type of activity performed, a reference to the incident, a brief name and a longer description for the response, and the date of the incident.

The table also uses three lookup fields to identify the status, the employee who took the in-call, and the employee to whom the activity was reassigned.

If you decide to allow multiple responses to an incident, then you may want to include additional fields. You will also consider what status you want to use to indicate that a response resulted in the need for a different response. This may require a new incident to be initiated.

The Incident Document Table

This table, called tblIncidentDocument, should include a reference to the incident table, descriptive text to describe the incident document, and a reference to the electronic document.

Depending on your business needs and your incident reporting system, you may need to get additional details from the incident report. Those would likely be added to the Incident Activity table.

The Incident Activity Type Table

By creating a table of this type, you will limit the opportunity for users to mistype or enter an activity that is not one that your organization uses. A good name would be tblIncidentActivityType. It should contain fields to provide both a short name for the type and a longer description for clarity.

The Incident Activity Status Table

For similar reasons, you should create a table called tblIncidentActivityStatus, which will include fields for the details related to the status of a given activity. This table will contain fields to provide both a brief name of the status and a longer description for clarity.

Tables as Implemented in the Example Database

Based on the description that we've provided about the business rules and needs, you can create the tables for tracking and analyzing responses to an incident. The details can be grouped into the following tables. These are also provided in the sample database for this chapter on the book's CD.

The Incident Table

This table, named tblIncident, shown in Figure 5-21, records and tracks support incidents. As the highest level view of support requirements it has standard fields and the following four fields.

IncidentName is a Text field that contains a short description of the support incident.

IncidentDescription is a Memo field that contains more detailed information about the support incident.

CustomerID is a Long Integer field that is used as a foreign key to the Customer table, identifying the customer receiving or requesting support.

EmployeeID is a Long Integer field that is used as a foreign key to the Employee table, identifying your organization's employee who was in initial contact with the customer—the employee who took the first call.

Field Name	Data Type	Description
IncidentID	AutoNumber	Primary key, uniquely identifies this record
IncidentName	Text	Short description of the Support Incident
IncidentDescription	Memo	Longer Description of the Support Incident
CustomerID	Number	Foreign key to tblCustomer, identifying customer receiving or requesting support
EmployeeID	Number	Foreign key to tblEmployee, identifying employee in initial contact with customer
LastUpdatedBy	Text	User who last updated this Record
LastUpdatedDate	Date/Time	Date/time when this record was last updated
IncidentNotes	Text	Optional, unstructured comments or notes about this record

Figure 5-21: The Incident table

The Incident Activity Table

This table, named tblIncidentActivity, shown in Figure 5-22, contains the record of the activities performed in response to a support incident. In addition to the standard fields, the table in our model includes the following fields.

IncidentActivityTypeID is a Long Integer field that is used as a lookup key to the Incident Activity Type table, indicating the type of this activity.

IncidentID is a Long Integer field that is used as a foreign key to the Incident table, to identify the support or service incident to which this activity applies. In the field property settings, this will typically be a required field.

IncidentActivityName is a Text field that contains a brief name for this activity.

IncidentActivityDescription is a Text field that contains a longer description. Entering a value in this field is optional. More information about the activity may also be available through the hyperlinks in the Incident Document table. If, in your database planning or in actual use, you see the need for more information than allowed by a Text field, change this to a Memo field type, or add a link to a table of Memos.

IncidentActivityDate is a Date/Time field that records the date this activity occurred.

IncidentActivityStatusID is a Long Integer field that is used as a lookup key to the Incident Activity Status table to indicate the status of this activity, e.g., "customer contact," "responsibility reassigned," "progress," "completed."

IncidentActivityEmployeeHandling is a Long Integer field that is used as a foreign key to the Employee table. The employee identified by this foreign key is the one handling the activity.

IncidentActivityEmployeeReassignedTo is a Long Integer field that is used as a foreign key to the Employee table if the activity is reassigned.

tblIncidentActivity : Table

Field Name	Data Type	Description
IncidentActivityID	AutoNumber	Primary key, uniquely identifies this record
IncidentActivityTypeID	Number	Foreign key to tblIncidentActivityType
IncidentID	Number	Foreign key to tblIncident
IncidentActivityName	Text	Brief name of this incident activity
IncidentActivityDescription	Text	Longer description (also see Incident Document Links)
IncidentActivityDate	Date/Time	Date this activity occurred
IncidentActivityStatusID	Number	Foreign key to tblIncidentActivityStatus
IncidentActivityEmployeeHandling	Number	Foreign key to tblEmployee
IncidentActivityEmployeeReassignedTo	Number	Foreign key to tblEmployee (if activity is reassigned)
LastUpdatedBy	Text	User who last updated this Record
LastUpdatedDate	Date/Time	Date/time when this record was last updated
IncidentActivityNotes	Text	Optional, unstructured comments or notes about this record

Figure 5-22: The Incident Activity table

You will notice that this table has two fields that each describe a relationship with the employee table. The fields IncidentActivityEmployeeHandling and IncidentActivityEmployeeReassignedTo are both foreign keys that store the values from the EmployeeID field in tblEmployee. Because a table cannot have two fields with the same name, we have given the foreign keys a descriptive name to indicate the purpose of the field. This is not uncommon, so you may run into similar scenarios in other projects.

The Incident Document Table

This table, named tblIncidentDocument, allows reference to supporting documents about a support incident, if applicable. Any document viewable on the network or by a hyperlink can be listed. If you use the hyperlink format or the complete network path the document will be accessed from the database using the "Application.Hyperlink" function of the Access Application Object. Since this table has a one-to-many relationship with the Incident table, you can record as many documents as needed about the same incident. In addition to the standard fields, you will need to create the following three fields as shown in Figure 5-23.

IncidentID is a Long Integer field that is used as a foreign key to the Incident table to identify the applicable incident. Since there is no reason to have a document about an incident if there is no incident, in the field property settings, this will typically be a required field.

IncidentDocumentDesc is a Text field that contains a short description of the document.

IncidentDocumentLink is a Text field that contains path and file or a hyperlink to the document. If your database is implemented with a Microsoft Access user interface, you can use this field with Access's Application.Hyperlink statement to hyperlink to (view and possibly modify) the document.

Field Name	Data Type	Description
IncidentDocumentID	AutoNumber	Primary key, uniquely identifies this record
IncidentID	Number	Foreign key to tblIncident
IncidentDocumentDesc	Text	Short description of document
IncidentDocumentLink	Text	Path and file or hyperlink to document
LastUpdatedBy	Text	User who last updated this Record
LastUpdatedDate	Date/Time	Date/time when this record was last updated
IncidentDocumentNotes	Text	Optional, unstructured comments or notes about this record

Figure 5-23: The Incident Document table

The final two tables for this module are lookup tables.

The Incident Activity Type Table (a Lookup Table)

This table, called tblIncidentActivityType, allows the assignment of specific "official" types to support activities. The user can either choose an incident activity type from a combo box or be limited to those defined by the application administrator. As shown in Figure 5-24, in addition to the standard fields, you need to create the following two fields.

IncidentActivityType is a Text field that contains a very brief description or name of the activity type. As the subject of the lookup list, this will be a required field and set the Indexed property to Yes (No Duplicates).

Field Name	Data Type	Description
IncidentActivityTypeID	AutoNumber	Primary key, uniquely identifies this record
IncidentActivityType	Text	Very brief description / name of activity type
IncidentActivityDescription	Text	Longer explanation of this activity type
LastUpdatedBy	Text	User who last updated this Record
LastUpdatedDate	Date/Time	Date/time when this record was last updated
IncidentActivityTypeNotes	Text	Optional, unstructured comments or notes about this record

Figure 5-24: The Incident Activity Type table

IncidentActivityDescription is a Text field that contains a longer explanation of this activity type.

The final table in this module provides a list for selecting the incident activity status.

The Incident Activity Status Table (a Lookup Table)

This table, called tblIncidentActivityStatus, shown in Figure 5-25, is a lookup table for the status of an activity. It can be used to limit the choices, as well as to ease use by providing the option for choosing items in a combo box or drop-down list. In addition to the standard fields, it includes the following two fields.

IncidentActivityStatus is a Text field that contains a brief description of status. In the field Properties, make this a required field and set the Indexed property to Yes (No Duplicates).

IncidentActivityStatusDescription is a Text field that contains a longer description of status.

Field Name	Data Type	Description
IncidentActivityStatusID	AutoNumber	Primary key, uniquely identifies this record
IncidentActivityStatus	Text	Brief description of status
IncidentActivityStatusDescription	Text	Longer description of status
LastUpdatedBy	Text	User who last updated this Record
LastUpdatedDate	Date/Time	Date/time when this record was last updated
IncidentActivityStatusNotes	Text	Optional, unstructured comments or notes about this record

Figure 5-25: The Incident Activity Status table

Now that we have created all of the tables for recording and analyzing service and support incidents, we can see how they fit with the existing tables for customers and employees.

Schema of Service and Support Tables

The relationship diagram in Figure 5-26 shows the schema or overview of the data tables and relationships for tracking service and support with the related tables for customers and employees.

We'll follow the same process with the next module, which relates to marketing and advertising.

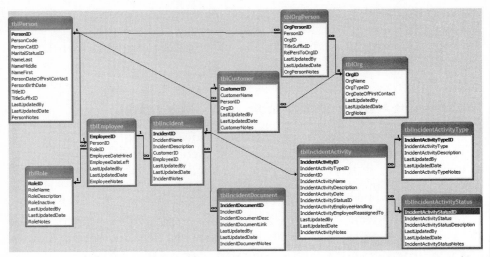

Figure 5-26: Relationship diagram showing the schema for Service and Support Tracking

Advertising and Marketing Campaigns, Targeted and General

Marketing campaigns can be general and directed at all of your customers, or they can be targeted to specific categories of customers. You may use information on the customers and previous business transactions to select the customers to whom you want to direct selected advertising and marketing. When setting up marketing campaigns, you may choose the customers most likely to be potential buyers based on their geographic location, the volume of purchases in past periods, the type of product or service they purchased, or a combination of these and other factors.

Additionally, tables for describing and tracking the activities and steps of marketing and advertising campaigns are shared between this topic and the following section.

Customer Awareness

It is useful to keep your customer's attention on your company, your products, and successful business transactions, whether or not you are trying to make an immediate sale or are exploring other immanent marketing opportunities. Planning and tracking campaigns to determine customer awareness falls into this area. The tables used for describing and tracking activities and the steps of customer awareness campaigns are shared with those in the preceding section. For tracking purposes, customer awareness campaigns are treated as just a type of advertising.

Basic Business Functions for Planning and Tracking Campaigns

Advertising and marketing campaigns are projects. An experienced and wise project manager once said, "There are only two times in the life of a project that you need to plan," and after a pause, he continued "early and often." To be successful, a campaign must be well-managed, and for it to be well-managed, the campaign manager or coordinator has to be able to record, view, adjust, and review information about the events and people associated with:

- What has to be done (we can call those activities)
- What has to happen to do those the things (call these tasks)
- Who has to do the things (people, either employees or contractors)
- When the tasks have to be done
- How the work is progressing

In order to capture and track the associated details, you'll need to provide for a way for the users and application administrator to:

- Define, set up, and maintain some standard values for document types
- Enter and maintain information about the campaign itself
- Enter and maintain information about the activities that comprise the campaign
- Enter and maintain information about the tasks that make up the activities.
- View, review, and act on the information using:
  - screens to display (forms)
  - reports to print

Items to Store

From the business functions and information requirements discussed, you can identify the main subjects and the details that need to be recorded about campaigns. It is from these subjects and details that you will begin to construct the database that will expedite planning and tracking the execution of your advertising and marketing campaigns.

The Subjects and Details of Planning and Tracking Campaigns

In this scenario, we address the following subjects and details related to campaigns. You may have other needs that should be included in your lists.

- Information you need to record and keep about campaigns, including:
  - identifying information: a name and description
  - references to people responsible for the planning
  - the employee in charge and/or an external or contract person
  - the tentative launch date
- Information about activities that make up a campaign, including:
  - identifying information, such as:
    - a reference to the campaign
    - a short name and a description
  - the people associated with the activity, an employee and/or an external or contract person
- Information about tasks that comprise an activity, including:
  - identifying information, such as:
    - reference to the campaign
    - a short name and a description
  - the people associated with an activity, an employee and/or an external or contract person
  - the planned start date and end date
- Information about campaign documents, including:
  - identifying information, such as:
    - reference to the campaign
    - a short name and a description
    - the date the document reference was added
  - the type of document
  - a link to the document

Other Types of Subject

You should consider the benefit of using a lookup table to provide a predefined list of document types.

Arranging the Data Into Tables

Based on the discussion about the details involved with marketing campaigns, we can group the data and create the tables. Figure 5-27 illustrates how the marketing information will be grouped and how it relates to our existing tables for employees and people.

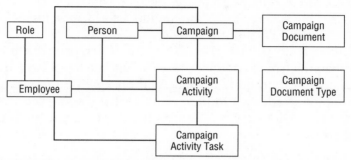

Figure 5-27: Diagram of subjects for CRM marketing campaigns

We will start with the table central to tracking the information about the marketing campaign.

The Campaign Table

To record the details about marketing and advertising campaigns you can create a table which we have named tblCampaign. This table stores the details directly related to each campaign. You need fields to identify information such as the name and description of the campaign, as well as references to the employee and/or external person or contractor associated with the campaign. You also should identify the date when preparation began, and the launch date.

You may also choose to include additional fields to indicate a status, the end date, and even a way to document a post campaign review.

The Campaign Activity Table

To record the various activities involved with the campaign, you can create another table, which we have named tblCampaignActivity. This table stores all the details directly relating to the campaign activity. It can have multiple records for a particular campaign, so it has a one-to-many relationship and is a child table to tblCampaign. It includes a reference to the campaign, name and description of the activity, and references to the employee and/or external person or contractor associated with the campaign activity.

The Campaign Task Table

Since each activity will likely have several tasks, you should create the table called tblCampaignTask. This will store all of the details directly relating to the campaign task. It can have many records relating to a given activity so it is a child table in a one-to-many relationship with the table tblCampaign. The fields will provide a reference to the campaign activity, name and description of the task, and references to the employee and/or external person or contractor associated with the specific task. You should also include fields for the start date and planned end date for the activity.

You may choose to use the planned end date for planning and charting progress. When the task is complete, you can update this with the actual end date. Alternatively, if progress tracking and on-time performance is critical, you may want to include an additional field so that you can preserve both the planned and actual end dates. You can apply the same principle to other dates in this module.

The Campaign Document Table

You can anticipate that a campaign will have numerous documents. So, you will need to create a table to record the details about each document. An appropriate name for this table is tblCampaignDocument. You will need fields to record the details directly relating to the document to identify the name, description, and date of the document, and a reference to the campaign to which it applies. If the document is electronically stored, you can also include a hyperlink to the file; if it is a physical document, you can describe the location where it will be found.

If you need to associate documents with specific activities or tasks within a campaign, then you could add a field in the activity or task table to reference the document itself.

The Campaign Document Type Table

This will be a reference or lookup table. By creating a lookup table, you will limit the opportunity for users to mistype or not remember the types of activity that your organization uses. We will name the table tblDocumentType, and it should contain a field that provides a short name for the type, e.g., "spreadsheet," "image," or "Word document."

Tables as Implemented in the Example Database

Based on the business processes that we've described, we can now create the tables to record the information about marketing campaigns for the purposes of analyzing their effect from a customer relations perspective.

We will continue using the tables from our example. So, if you modified your tables, you will want to follow our process for incorporating the additional tables and fields that we are about to discuss. These are also provided in the sample database for this chapter on the book's CD.

The Campaign Table

The table tblCampaign, shown in Figure 5-28, records the main details about the overall campaign, whether it is for customer awareness, advertising, or marketing. It uses the following fields to store the general information about the campaign.

CampaignName is a Text field that contains a short name for the campaign.

CampaignDescription is a Memo field that contains more extensive detailed information describing the campaign. You may determine that a text field is adequate for your purposes.

EmployeeID is a Long Integer field that is used as a foreign key to the Employee table to identify the employee in charge of the campaign.

PersonID is a Long Integer field that is used as a foreign key to the Person table to identify an external or contract person assisting management of the campaign.

CampaignPrepBeginDate is a Date/Time field that records the date preparation began or is planned to begin.

CampaignLaunchDate is a Date/Time field that records the date/time of the tentative launch date for this campaign.

Field Name	Data Type	Description
🔑 CampaignID	AutoNumber	Primary key, uniquely identifies this record
CampaignName	Text	Short name for campaign
CampaignDescription	Memo	Fuller description for campaign
EmployeeID	Number	Foreign key to tblEmployee
PersonID	Number	Foreign key to tblPerson
CampaignPrepBeginDate	Date/Time	Date preparation began or to begin
CampaignLaunchDate	Date/Time	Tentative launch date for this campaign
LastUpdatedBy	Text	User who last updated this Record
LastUpdatedDate	Date/Time	Date/time when this record was last updated
CampaignNotes	Text	Optional, unstructured comments or notes about this record

Figure 5-28: The Campaign table

After you create the Campaign table, you can create a table to record the associated activities.

The Campaign Activity Table

The table tblCampaignActivity stores the information about the activities in a campaign, the level between the campaign and the multitude of tasks required to accomplish it. This level or grouping might be assigned to a project leader or supervisor; in a simple campaign this might be the same person that performs the tasks. In addition to the standard fields, it includes the following fields, as shown in Figure 5-29.

CampaignID is a Long Integer field that is used as a foreign key to the parent record in the campaign table. In the field property settings, this should be a required field.

CampaignActivityName is a Text field that contains the short name for the activity.

CampaignActivityDescription is a Memo field, but a text field may be adequate for your needs. It contains a detailed description of the activity, and the content is optional but recommended.

EmployeeID is a Long Integer field that is used as a foreign key to the Employee table to identify the employee associated with this activity.

PersonID is a Long Integer field that is used as a foreign key to the Person table to identify a person external to your organization or a contract person associated with this activity.

Field Name	Data Type	Description
CampaignActivityID	AutoNumber	Primary key, uniquely identifies this record
CampaignID	Number	Foreign key to tblCampaign
CampaignActivityName	Text	Short name for Activity
CampaignActivityDescription	Memo	Description of Activity
EmployeeID	Number	Foreign key to tblEmployee - employee assoc with Activity
PersonID	Number	Foreign key to tblPerson - external or contract person assoc with Activity
LastUpdatedBy	Text	User who last updated this Record
LastUpdatedDate	Date/Time	Date/time when this record was last updated
CampaignActivityNotes	Text	Optional, unstructured comments or notes about this record

tblCampaignActivity : Table

Figure 5-29: The Campaign Activity table

The next table will provide the record of the final level of detail for the campaign.

The Campaign Task Table

This table, called tblCampaignTask, describes the lowest level of work that we are tracking on a campaign. Although a task is usually assigned to one or a limited number of individuals, we are only associating the task with the lead employee and/or a lead contact person. In addition to the standard fields, it contains the following fields as shown in Figure 5-30.

CampaignActivityID is a Long Integer field that is used as a foreign key to the Campaign Activity table to identify the activity this task is part of. Since the task should always relate to a campaign activity, in the field properties make this required.

CampaignTaskName is a Text field that contains the short name of this task. If your activities frequently repeat the same task, then it would be wise to replace this with a lookup key in this table to a lookup table of activity task names. You could, but would not have to, limit the users to choosing one of the predefined names, or allow the user to add a new task name if no appropriate name already exists.

CampaignTaskDescription is a Memo field, optional but recommended, that contains a fuller description of this task.

EmployeeID is a Long Integer field that is used as a foreign key to the Employee table to identify an employee associated with this task.

PersonID is a Long Integer field that is used as a foreign key to the Person table to identify a person external to our organization or a contract person associated with this task.

CampaignTaskStartDate is a Date/Time field that records the expected start date for the task.

CampaignTaskEndDate is a Date/Time field that records the planned completion date for the task.

tblCampaignTask : Table

Field Name	Data Type	Description
CampaignTaskID	AutoNumber	Primary key, uniquely identifies this record
CampaignActivityID	Number	Foreign key to tblCampaignActivity
CampaignTaskName	Text	Short name of Task
CampaignTaskDescription	Memo	Description of Task
EmployeeID	Number	Foreign key to tblEmployee - employee assoc w task
PersonID	Number	Foreign key to tblPerson - external or contract person
CampaignTaskStartDate	Date/Time	Expected start date for task
CampaignTaskEndDate	Date/Time	Planned completion date for task
LastUpdatedBy	Text	User who last updated this Record
LastUpdatedDate	Date/Time	Date/time when this record was last updated
CampaignTaskNotes	Text	Optional, unstructured comments or notes about this record

Figure 5-30: The Campaign Task table

Since a campaign can require numerous documents, you will need to record the relevant details about the documents.

The Campaign Document Table

This table, named tblCampaignDocument, records information about documents stored outside the database that are used in a campaign. If the document is accessible using a network connection, you can include a hyperlink to the file and be able to open the document from Access. In addition to the standard fields, you would need to create the following fields as shown in Figure 5-31.

CampaignDocumentTypeID is a Long Integer field that is used as a lookup key to the Document Type table to find the document type appropriate to this document.

CampaignID is a Long Integer field that is used as a foreign key to the Campaign table to identify the campaign this document is associated with. In the field properties, this is normally a required field.

CampaignDocumentName is a Text field that contains the short name of this document.

CampaignDocumentDescription is a Memo field, optional but recommended, that contains a fuller description of this document.

CampaignDocumentLink is a Text field that contains a path and file name or hyperlink to the electronically-stored document.

CampaignDocumentLocation is a Text field describing the location of the document if it is a physical document.

It is possible that both CampaignDocumentLink and CampaignDocument-Location could have values—an original physical document could have been scanned and stored electronically.

CampaignDocumentDate is a Date/Time field that records the date or date and time this document was added.

Field Name	Data Type	Description
CampaignDocumentID	AutoNumber	Primary key, uniquely identifies this record
DocumentTypeID	Number	Foreign key to tblDocumentType
CampaignID	Number	Foreign key to tblCampaign
CampaignDocumentName	Text	Short name of document
CampaignDocumentDescription	Memo	Description of document
CampaignDocumentLink	Text	Path and file name or hyperlink if document is stored electronically
CampaignDocumentLocation	Text	Location of the document if physical
CampaignDocumentDate	Date/Time	Date / time added
LastUpdatedBy	Text	User who last updated this Record
LastUpdatedDate	Date/Time	Date/time when this record was last updated
CampaignDocumentNotes	Text	Optional, unstructured comments or notes about this record

Figure 5-31: The Campaign Document table

The final table provides the list of document types.

The Campaign Document Type Table (a Lookup Table)

We use the Campaign Document Type table to limit documents to a list of predefined types that are used in your campaigns. This approach makes it easier for users to select a document type from a combo box or a drop-down list. This table has only one pertinent field, as shown in Figure 5-32.

DocumentType is a Text field that contains the type of the document, e. g., spreadsheet, Word, or image. In the field properties make this a required field and set the Indexed property to Yes (No Duplicates).

Field Name	Data Type	Description
⚷ DocumentTypeID	AutoNumber	Primary key, uniquely identifies this record
DocumentType	Text	Type of document (spreadsheet, word, image)
LastUpdatedBy	Text	User who last updated this Record
LastUpdatedDate	Date/Time	Date/time when this record was last updated
DocumentTypeNotes	Text	Optional, unstructured comments or notes about this record

tblCampaignDocumentType : Table

Figure 5-32: The Document Type table

Now that you've created all of the tables to record the key marketing details that are relevant to customer relations, you can see how the tables are related to our existing tables through the tables for employees and people.

Schema of Advertising and Marketing Campaigns

The overview or schema of tables and fields for advertising and marketing campaigns is shown in the relationship diagram in Figure 5-33.

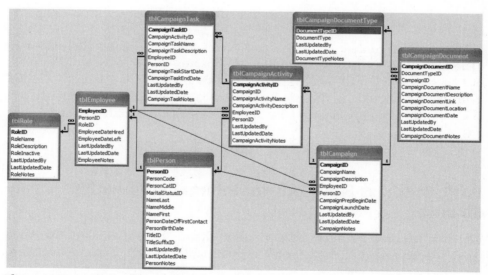

Figure 5-33: Relationship diagram showing the schema for an advertising and marketing campaign

Using the relationships established from the Campaign table to the Employee table and the Person table, you can leverage the data in all of the other tables that you've created.

Now that you've created several modules for collecting data about areas with great impact on customer relations, we will discuss some approaches to disseminating the data to the appropriate people.

Internal Information Sharing

The data described elsewhere in this chapter should be shared among internal functional groups within your organization. Sales of products are important to planning support needs and the burdens on both personnel and facilities. Service and support issues are important to the Sales department in addressing future sales and to the purchasing staff for the purpose of deciding on sources or negotiating with vendors for product changes and improvements.

At the most primitive level, sharing this information may be accomplished by permissions and authorization for personnel to access particular tables. But that approach relies on the employee to have or take the time, and to remember to check for updated information. A more effective approach is to define the types of information that various employees should be kept up-to-date on, and to then route e-mails, reports, and documents to the appropriate employees. They will still have to find or take the time to read and respond, but it's not easy to just "not remember" when the information shows up in your e-mail inbox, or arrives in your physical inbox with routing slip attached!

The specific content of additional tables relating people to data will depend on the needs of your individual business. CRM is one of the most business-specific areas that we cover in this book, so the tables included in this topic should be regarded as merely samples. You will almost certainly need to modify them to accommodate specific characteristics of your business.

Basic Business Functions for Internal Information Sharing

The data required for internal information sharing leverages tables that have been defined and discussed earlier in this chapter as well as some that were introduced in Chapter 4.

You will need to have information about people associated with your organization and document the information each person is authorized or directed to share. Depending on the business rules of your business, the people could be volunteers, employees, or contractors.

You will need to be able to categorize and mark information, and to automate information distribution in your organization.

You will be able to create multi-person distribution to share information, such as by e-mail, hard copy, or through shared access to a location. You can use queries to identify who should have access to or receive specific data.

Chapter 14, "Implementing the Models," provides an example of how to create personalized letters.

Items to Store

As stated earlier, information and information flow for this area differs so much from one business to another that you will need to learn some basic information about the subject and then personalize this model to reflect your individual business practices. In this section, we will discuss the items that you will save or store, and then group the details into the main subjects that they describe.

The Subjects and Details of Internal Information Sharing

The first subject and detail that you should consider is the type of infor-mation. This may appear to be nothing more than a lookup table, but classifying types of information is vital to efficiently sharing and using the information.

A second subject to consider is additional information about employees of your organization. This would include a link to information that you already have stored about the person, and the type or level of information they should share or have access to.

Contractors should typically be considered separate from employees. You need to determine what information to share with contractors, and whether the criteria are different than you use for employees. Keep in mind that contractors typically have not been subjected to the same kind of background checks, confidentiality requirements, or penalties for violations as your employees. Just as with employees, the information stored for this purpose is the type or level of information to be shared.

Arranging the Data Into Tables

We mentioned earlier in this discussion that the rules and needs associated with internal information sharing are often business-specific so the tables and fields will need to be tailored accordingly. In an information-intensive environment, a business that deals with sensitive and confidential data will require significantly more granularity in assigning data-sharing than in a warehouse or most manufacturing processes. In an environment which has strict privacy rules, you'll need to ensure that everyone who needs to know information has access to it, and that only those who have a need to know can view restricted information.

In its simplest form, information sharing can be implemented by adding a single field to the table where you maintain employee and contractor information, or it can be added to a related table that lists the types of information to be shared with this person.

For our example, we've chosen a solution that is a happy medium between complex and simplistic. The diagram of subjects, shown in Figure 5-34, shows how we will determine and control the information that a person can see based on the type of information.

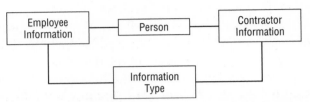

Figure 5-34: Diagram of the subjects for CRM internal information sharing

As indicated in the diagram, we will only need to create three tables to provide a system for identifying and limiting the data that a person can see, with consideration for whether they are an employee or a contractor.

The Person Table

The Person table, defined to maintain information on people, whether they are employees, contractors, or others, will not be repeated here. You should review earlier sections in this chapter and in Chapter 4.

The Employee Information Table

The Employee Information table serves as a junction table and contains a foreign key to the Employee table and another foreign key to the Information Type table. It resolves a many-to-many relationship between information types and the employees they should be routed to. You would use the field properties for both foreign keys to make them required fields and ensure that data is entered.

The Contractor Information Table

The Contractor Information table serves as a junction table to resolve a many-to-many relationship between a person in the Person table and the information types which should be routed to this contractor in the Information Type table. You would use the field properties for both foreign keys to make them required fields and ensure that data is entered.

The Information Type Table

The Information Type table serves as a lookup table. It contains the type of information by name, with an expanded description to assist in avoiding confusion.

Simplifying the Design

In many cases, you can just use employee or contractor status as one of a number of criteria, and combine the Employee Information table and the Contractor Information table into one Person Information table. This could simplify the design and implementation of the database.

The model that we're providing continues to use separate tables, as we have in our previous modules. We will continue working with the Person and the Contractor Information tables.

Tables as Implemented in the Example Database

The tables in the example database are described in the following discussion. But you should bear in mind that depending on the circumstances, environment, and practices in your own organization, you may have an even simpler design or a more complex one. The following tables are also provided in the sample database for this chapter on the book's CD.

The Information Type Table

This table, named tblInformationType, contains the information types that should be shared. There is one table specific field, as shown in Figure 5-35.

InformationType is a Text field that contains the name of this information type. Since this field provides the items for a selection list, in the field property settings, this will typically be a required field.

Field Name	Data Type	Description
InformationTypeID	AutoNumber	Unique key to this record
InformationType	Text	Name of this Information Type
LastUpdatedBy	Text	User who last updated this record
LastUpdatedDate	Date/Time	Date and time when this record was last updated
InformationTypeNotes	Text	Optional comment about this Information type

Figure 5-35: The Information Type table

The other two tables that you'll need are junction tables to manage the many-to-many relationships between employees and information and between contractors and information.

The Contractor-Information Table (a Junction Table)

This table, called tblContractorInformation, is a junction table to allow each contractor to have access to multiple types of documents and to allow each document type to be shared with multiple contractors. As shown in Figure 5-36, the table contains a link between the Information Type table and the Person table.

PersonID is a Long Integer field that is used as a foreign key to the Person table to identify the person (contractor). In the field property settings, this should be a required field.

InformationTypeID is a Long Integer field that is used as a foreign key to the Information Type table to identify the type of information to be shared with this contractor. In the field property settings, this should be a required field.

Create a multi-field index on the table including PersonID and InformationTypeID. In the index set the Unique property to Yes, to prevent recording the same relationship more than once.

Field Name	Data Type	Description
ContractorInformationID	AutoNumber	Primary key, uniquely identifies this record
PersonID	Number	Foreign key to tblPerson
InformationTypeID	Number	Foreign key to tblInformationType
LastUpdatedBy	Text	User who last updated this Record
LastUpdatedDate	Date/Time	Date/time when this record was last updated
ContractorInformationNotes	Text	Optional comment about this record

Figure 5-36: The Contractor-Information table

Finally, you need to create a similar table for employees.

The Employee-Information Table (a Junction Table)

This table, named tblEmployeeInformation, is a junction table that contains a link between the Information Type table and the Employee table. This allows each employee to have access to several types of documents and allows each type of document to be shared with several employees. You will need to create the following two fields, as shown in Figure 5-37.

EmployeeID is a Long Integer field that is used as a foreign key to the Employee table to identify the employee. In the field property settings, this should be a required field.

InformationTypeID is a Long Integer field that is used as a lookup key to the InformationType table. In the field property settings, this should be a required field.

Create a multi-field index on the table including EmployeeID and InformationTypeID; make it unique to prevent recording the same relationship more than once.

Field Name	Data Type	Description
EmployeeInformationID	AutoNumber	Unique key to this record
EmployeeID	Number	Foreign key to tblEmployee
InformationTypeID	Number	Foreign key to tblInformationType
LastUpdatedBy	Text	User who last updated this record
LastUpdatedDate	Date/Time	Date/time when this record was last updated
EmployeeInformationNotes	Text	Optional comment about this record

Figure 5-37: The Employee-Information table

As we mentioned, our approach only required three new tables. So now we are ready to see how they are related to our existing tables.

Schema Overview of Internal Information Sharing

The relationship diagram in Figure 5-38 shows the schema or overview of the three new tables used in our model for identifying and limiting the documents that a person can view. We've included the additional tables named tblPerson and tblEmployee so that you can easily see how the new business function can be incorporated into an existing database.

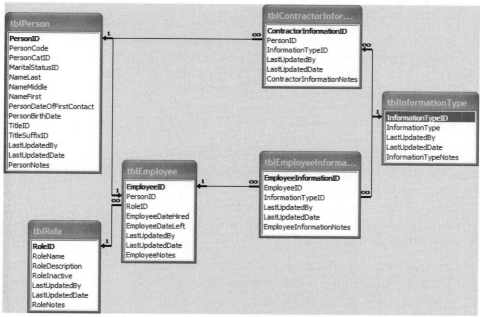

Figure 5-38: Relationship diagram showing the schema for internal information sharing

That completes the final example for this chapter. But you may also want to consider how your internal processes affect your customers and your relationship with them.

Improving Process Quality

Your records of activity about your internal processes can have a direct or indirect effect on your customers' experience with your organization. You should use information about your business processes as a part of the analysis you perform in support of your customer relationships. You can link, adapt from, or base the tables you use for this purpose on tables described in Bonus Chapter B1 on the book's CD.

Your own business or operation's specifics will determine what details of information you need to collect and the analysis you need to perform. Some might contend that this type of analysis, because of complexity and expense, is only feasible and valid for a larger company or "enterprise level" organization. Others would counter that, if you are not on top of your business processes and continually seeking means to improve them, you are doomed to failure. Only you can decide where your situation falls, whether at one extreme or the other or, more likely, somewhere between the two.

Summary

The best-known CRM software is intended for enterprise-level organizations, and it is priced accordingly. You may find that even less expensive packages still do not address the very small- to medium-sized business.

This chapter demonstrated that even simpler database software applications can improve the relationships that small businesses have with their customers. Since most of the data needed can typically be gathered in the normal course of running your business or organization, you may already have the details stored in various systems. By leveraging existing data, customer relationship improvements can provide a significant bonus for reusing business data and investing modestly to process it.

You have learned how you can apply database technology to manage factors you control that affect your customer relationships in several key areas including the following:

- **People and organizations:** You can collect and maintain information about customers for improving communication and to support demographic analysis.
- **Correspondence:** You can use detailed information about your customers to personalize your communication with them.
- **Sales:** You can track the sales processes in your organization to identify areas where your processes can be improved, both overall and with respect to specific customers or customer groups.

- **Support:** You can use information about support and service activities to identify areas for possible improvement within support and service generally as well as to spot problem trends in particular products or service offerings from your organization.

- **Campaigns:** You can plan, execute, and track advertising, marketing, and customer awareness campaigns.

- **Internal information sharing:** You can take an active approach to ensure that anyone who may deal with a customer is informed with the appropriate and relevant details.

By keeping customer relations in mind as you work through the other chapters in this book, you can ensure that you are capturing the data needed to analyze and improve customer relations. The perfect place to start is with marketing, the topic of the next chapter.

Marketing

Marketing is a complex subject—far too complex to cover completely in a single chapter. Often it contains large aspects of contact management—we dealt with that topic in earlier chapters, so you can use the information there to implement such requirements. For the purposes of this book, we have condensed coverage of marketing specific requirements into two sections: a generic marketing campaign database and a database to manage questions and responses for a questionnaire.

We start by creating a database for marketing with a design that is sufficiently generic to accommodate the marketing requirements of most organizations, rather than gear it toward a dedicated marketing company. To design the database, we consider what a marketing campaign consists of, the data that you need to use, and some concepts that will help reinforce what has been covered in other chapters.

Then we look at the questionnaire, a common tool that can be used to fulfill several roles in marketing database applications. For example, you can use a questionnaire to associate new and potential clients with their appropriate needs or to encourage horizontal sales to existing customers. This is done by determining if clients have other interests and needs that you could be fulfilling. The questionnaire is also a powerful tool for plain old market research.

Finally, in addition to supporting marketing campaigns, the questionnaire also functions as a standard resource that can be used in many applications outside of marketing. We explore that more when we get to the "Questionnaires" section.

The first step is to examine the data requirements and business needs; but before we get to that, we'll establish a basic foundation by reviewing some of the terminology that we will be using.

Database Terminology

In this chapter, as in other chapters, we'll progress by identifying the subjects, or entities, that make up the database. Each subject represents a real-world concept such as an order, customer, supplier, or invoice. The subjects typically become the tables in your database. Each subject will have various details that must be recorded, and these will become the fields of the tables.

The tables of the database all require a primary key to uniquely identify the records. These are AutoNumber fields which provide a sequential number value automatically. These primary key fields are named according to the table that contains them, with the "ID" suffix added. For example, a Customers table would be named "tblCustomer," and its primary key would be an AutoNumber named "CustomerID."

To work with the data, the tables must be joined together. The value of a primary key, which represents a record in the table, can be stored in a field in another table; that field is called a foreign key. For example, a table tblJob may have a foreign key CustomerID, which references the primary key from tblCustomers and indicates the customer to which that job record belongs. That design represents a *one-to-many relationship*—that is, the one customer record may appear in many jobs but a job belongs to a single customer.

A relationship can be created between two tables using the primary and foreign keys. This is a central concept for creating a relational database. The idea is that the fields in a table must all directly describe and relate to the subject of the table. Any fields that describe a different subject should be moved to a different table; that table can be related to others as appropriate. This is the essence of *normalization*, which is explained in detail in Chapter 3, "Relational Data Model."

A second type of relationship that you will often see between tables is called a *many-to-many relationship*. This requires a third table, referred to as a *junction table*, to serve as a link between the two main tables. The junction table is related to both original tables by storing a foreign key from each table. Occasionally this junction table will also contain additional data that is specifically and directly related to the link. You will often see that in sales, and we'll provide some examples in this chapter.

When you want to view the consolidated data in your application, you need to create a query that includes a *join* between the two tables and enables their data to be displayed as if it were in one table. In Access these queries are typically created graphically by using the query design view, but they can also be written directly using Structured Query Language (SQL).

Marketing Campaigns

A marketing campaign is a deliberate and multifaceted plan to generate a specific perception, typically about the desirability of a product. How this is to be achieved is carefully considered and implemented, as marketing campaigns can be very expensive affairs. Although many marketing firms or departments rely heavily on one particular methodology to create public awareness and perception of the product, a single marketing campaign often employs many strategies, progressing sequentially from one to another. This requires an application that can accommodate that progression.

The classic marketing example is advertising, whether it is in publications, online, on TV, or on the radio. Other common marketing activities include direct methods such as mass mailing and more targeted mail, telemarketing, cold visits, and sales appointments. Of course, there is also everybody's favorite, spam e-mail, which has even spread to SMS messages and other mobile technology. Some campaigns also employ more targeted e-mail based upon known contacts or information relating to interests or market sector.

These are only some of the contact methodologies available to marketers. And with new technologies and social activities constantly emerging, it is no longer possible to maintain a comprehensive list. Our model considers only a few, but this chapter also demonstrates how to use a generic version of that model. This will enable you to incorporate features that provide the versatility you need to accommodate new communication methods as you encounter them.

Other publicity options also exist, such as holding seminars or releasing articles, targeting either direct and open sales opportunities or under a guise such as education, with the product or service segued in.

A campaign could consist of one of these communication methodologies or it could employ several at different stages of the campaign—or simultaneously during the course of the campaign. It is quite common to run a campaign in stages, with initial broad public sweeps that become narrower and focus on more targeted, precision communications in later stages, with the end goal of legitimate sales leads.

NOTE You can often purchase targeted contact information from external sources. In this case, you are usually buying a database of companies and names. If this list of organizations and key contacts is something that you can acquire yourself, there's nothing preventing you from including that database as part of your marketing solution.

NOTE As mentioned earlier, each table should contain data about only one subject, but data from several tables can be pulled together to create the complete picture. We'll walk you through the process of identifying the necessary data, separating it into subjects, and then creating the tables and fields. As you are working through this chapter's example, we encourage you to refer to Chapters 2, "Elements of a Microsoft Access Database," and 3, "Relational Data Model," any time that you feel the need for a refresher.

Identifying Required Data Elements

With the vast number of options and differences in marketing campaigns, we are going to take a somewhat different approach to designing the database than you've seen in most other chapters. The final design will be comprised of several core areas that each have several tables. So rather than building the tables and fields one at a time, we will discuss all of the tables for a single core area at once. You might find it helpful to use this approach when designing a database for other business lines; this chapter will give you the opportunity to experience that process.

We'll start by identifying some of the general subjects, or data elements, that are the required parts of a marketing campaign. Those are the core subjects, as shown in Table 6-1. The initial list is deliberately broad, because we are keeping it generic to make it easier for you to tailor the process to a variety of scenarios.

Table 6-1: Core Subjects

SUBJECT	DESCRIPTION
Campaign	A description for reference
Marketed Product	The product (or service) marketed
Campaign Stage	The stage of the campaign
Communication	The method of contact to be used
Target Organization	The organization being contacted

At this point, the items listed are not necessarily destined to become either the subject of a table or a detail (field in the table) in your database. They represent the core areas that we can initially identify, but they need to be fleshed out. As you will see, each of the items may result in the creation of several tables and potentially dozens of fields. When you are working on other projects, you may also find that several of the initial items may become fields of one table.

Now we consider the items involved in conducting a campaign and communicating with target customers. You will often develop this sort of list by meeting with your colleagues, reviewing existing systems, interviewing a client, and using your own best judgment. The items initially identified will rarely form the complete list of data that will be stored in your database. Additional details will emerge as the design evolves. Table 6-2 describes the initial list of details that we will use for campaigns.

These represent the kind of details that need to be recorded about a marketing campaign. Some items in the list will represent more than one subject; others will be just one of several that relate to a single subject.

Table 6-2: Initial Marketing Campaign Details

DETAIL	DESCRIPTION
Campaign Name	Descriptive reference of the campaign
Campaign Product Name(s)	Name of product(s)/service(s) marketed
Campaign Product Description	Detail of the product
Campaign Stage Description	Stage in the campaign consisting of a particular type of communication
Campaign Reference Code	A code to help identify a successful stage
Communication Method	Phone/post address/e-mail
Communication Message	Content or purpose of the message
Communication Date	Date of communication
Target Organization	The organization being contacted
Organization Business Type	The type of organization contacted
Target Contact Name	The individual/role targeted if known
Organization Contact Details	E-mail/post address/phone number
Organization Contact Role	Position contact holds
Communication Result	The outcome. Ultimately a go/stop on further communication
Response	The actual spoken/written response, if any
Response Date	The date of response
Notes	Optional text information

To put these details into distinct tables, we need to consider each one individually to identify the unique subject(s) that it belongs to.

Assigning the Details to a Subject

Given the substantial list of details for a project, you'll need a system for assigning the details to the appropriate subject. This can be an iterative process; your initial grouping can be quite vague and will need to be refined as you progress.

Using our proposed list of subjects for our database from Table 6-1, we will attempt to assign each detail to one of the subjects. Table 6-3 shows this initial assignment.

Table 6-3: Assigning the Details to a Subject

DETAIL	IDENTIFIED SUBJECT
Campaign Name	Campaign
Campaign Product Name(s)	Marketed Product
Campaign Product Description	Marketed Product
Campaign Stage Description	Campaign Stage
Campaign Reference Code	Campaign Stage
Communication Method	Campaign Stage
Communication Message	Campaign Stage
Communication Date	Communication
Target Organization Name	Target Organization
Organization Business Category	Target Organization
Organization Contact Details	Target Organization
Target Contact Name	Target Organization
Organization Contact Role	Target Organization
Communication Result	Communication
Response	Communication
Response Date	Communication
Notes	Communication

If we hadn't already determined a core list of subjects for the project, they would come to light as we categorize the items listed. It doesn't really matter which way around you do it, however it is unlikely that you'll commence a new project without already having some idea of the major subject matters involved.

As you further isolate each subject, other relevant details about that subject will often become apparent. The content of your eventual tables will usually exceed the sum of your initial list of details.

Next we will discuss the core subjects in turn and explain our reasons for the assignments that we've made.

Campaign Stages and Communications

The distinction between a campaign and its stages was established at the beginning of this chapter. Each stage represents a unique phase in the campaign's progression; it is usually a concerted effort of communication to targeted organizations via a particular communication medium. For example, an initial mass e-mail stage followed up by letters or literature through the post and then another stage for telephone calls to follow-up with interested organizations.

In Table 6-3 we identified certain details that belong to the campaign stage, such as stage description and reference code. Although the communication method and the communication message may seem to describe an individual communication to an organization, they are actually related to a stage, i.e. all communications within a given stage will use the same method and convey the same message.

If these details became fields in the communication table, they would display a large number of repeating values as they would not vary across communications for each stage. This is a classic indication that they describe a different subject; in this case, that is the campaign stage.

If we consider all the campaign stages that could occur across all campaigns over time, then we can see that the communication method is going to repeat even as part of the campaign stage subject. For example, consider how many times you will see "e-mail" entered. This is a strong indicator that it would be beneficial to have a separate subject to represent the communication methods.

This brings us to the concept of the communications themselves. Communications always belong to a campaign stage and they also represent each single communication event or attempt made to reach an organization. Each e-mail or telephone call to an organization is a communication.

NOTE The requirement to record each physical communication could become a daunting task when it comes to mass mailings. It's possible that some form of automation of record generation may come into play. You may also use similar automation techniques for creating the e-mails or mailing labels.

Alternatively, you may choose to create sets of records by using a query. We'll explore how to create and use queries later in the chapter.

We have also determined that the details Communication Result, Response, and Response Date describe the subject Communication. These still relate directly to the communication made with the organization and therefore belong to the Communication subject. However, we will still examine their purpose a bit more closely.

The Communication Result, in particular, is an item of detail intended to express the outcome of the communication. It is a Text field that might store values such as "Not Interested," "No response," "Requested Further Information," or even the marketing ideal "Sales Meeting Arranged." However, it also must indicate whether an organization is open to receiving additional communication or if there are restrictions on the types of contact allowed. This could be enforced with another detail item such as "Continues," which uses a Yes/No data type to indicate whether there should be further communication.

With this review, we can identify the details related to communications as listed in Table 6-4.

Table 6-4: Expanded Communication Details

DETAIL	DESCRIPTION
Communication Date	Date of communication
Communication Result	Outcome description
Communication Continues	Outcome continue to contact
Response	The actual spoken/written response, if any
Response Date	The date of response
Notes	Optional text information

However, upon further review, we can also determine that the values of Communication Result and Communication Continues are related: whether or not communications continue depends upon the type of text entered. They consequently don't depend entirely on the communication and would exhibit repeating values; for example you'll see "Not Interested" entered many times with a corresponding "False" for Continues. This indicates that they describe a subject of their own. We'll call this new subject a communication result type.

Therefore, we will revise communication subject as in Table 6-5.

Table 6-5: Amended Communication Details

DETAIL	DESCRIPTION
Communication Date	Date of communication
Response	The actual spoken/written response, if any
Response Date	The date of response
Notes	Optional text information

This will be related to the new Communication Result Type subject shown in Table 6-6.

Table 6-6: Communication Result Type Details

DETAIL	DESCRIPTION
Communication Result	Outcome description
Communication Continues	Outcome continue to contact

As is so often the case, this new subject will eventually serve as a lookup table for convenient selection of values to describe the result of a communication.

NOTE Data such as the communication date and response date can be very useful when querying information. It's very simple to query the time between dates and to obtain averages and other aggregate details. This can guide future campaigns based on what was the most efficient means of communication for response speed.

Similarly, the entries from Result Type can be used to determine the proportion of communications that were met favorably as opposed to those which were terminated or ignored.

Descriptions of the Core Subjects

At this point, we have expanded our list of core subjects from four to seven. We can describe the core subjects as follows:

- **Campaign:** The primary subject representing the crux of any marketing effort.

- **Products:** The product (or potentially a service) that is being marketed by a given campaign.

- **Campaign Stages:** The anticipated phases that the campaign strategy is expected to involve. The stages may be adapted or increased/decreased as the campaign progresses, but together they describe the campaign process in full. Primarily, the stages will reflect communication efforts.

- **Campaign Communications:** The individual communications made to organizations, establishing contact or promoting the campaign product or service. Communications are related to the campaign stages that describes their effort and purpose.

- **Organizations:** The targets of the campaign communications and eventual sales opportunities. Each communication relates to an organization.

- **Communication Result Types:** The possible types of result of a communication. These both describes the result and indicate whether this communication should be the last to that organization.

■ **Communication Methods:** The list of possible communication methods that can be used in any marketing efforts. Apart from the direct communication methods this would include options such as publication advertizing.

Creating the Tables

In reviewing the campaign stages, communications, and contacts, we indentified several key subjects that will be represented by tables in our database. The next step is to create the tables. As explained earlier, we will build all of the tables related to a core area at one time. Much like a marketing campaign, we will break the process into several stages.

The first stage for creating the tables is to name the table and add the field for the primary key (PK), the fields that describe the subject, and the fields to represent related tables, the foreign keys (FKs). Like the primary key field name, the names for foreign key fields end with ID. Although the fields will store the primary key value of the selected record from a related table, users will see the data that it represents, such as the words E-mail or Mail.

Table 6-7 lists the initial fields for table tblCampaign, which represents the Campaign subject.

Table 6-7: tblCampaign

FIELD	DATA TYPE	DESCRIPTION
CampaignID	AutoNumber	Primary key
CampaignName	Text	A description for reference
ProductID	Long Integer	Foreign key to tblProduct

You'll notice that this table includes a foreign key to the Product table. The initial fields for tblProduct are listed in Table 6-8, and the fields for tblCampaignStage are listed in Table 6-9.

Table 6-8: tblProduct

FIELD	DATA TYPE	DESCRIPTION
ProductID	AutoNumber	Primary key
ProductName	Text	A description of the product

In tblCampaignStage, you see the foreign key related to tblCampaign. Similarly, the campaign stage itself will be referenced in the individual communication. The initial fields for tblCommunication are listed in Table 6-10.

Table 6-9: tblCampaignStage

FIELD	DATA TYPE	DESCRIPTION
CampaignStageID	AutoNumber	Primary key
CampaignID	Long Integer	Foreign key to tblCampaign
StageName	Text	A description for reference
CommunicationMethodID	Long Integer	Foreign key to tblCommunicationMethod
CommunicationText	Text	Message to be sent in marketing literature

Table 6-10: tblCommunication

FIELD	DATA TYPE	DESCRIPTION
CommunicationID	AutoNumber	Primary key
CampaignStageID	Long Integer	Foreign key to tblCampaignStage
OrganizationID	Long Integer	Foreign key to tblOrganization
CommunicationDate	Date/Time	Communication date
Communication ResultTypeID	Long Integer	Foreign key to tblCommunication ResultType
Response	Memo	The nature of the response
ResponseDate	Date/Time	The date of response
CommunicationNotes	Memo	Optional notes

This Communication table will reference other tables appropriate to the foreign keys it contains. In particular, the tblCommunicationResultType, which has the fields listed in Table 6-11.

Table 6-11: tblCommunicationResultType

FIELD	DATA TYPE	DESCRIPTION
CommunicationResultTypeID	AutoNumber	Primary key
ResultType	Text	Description of result type
Continues	Yes/No	Communication should continue

The communication is intrinsically related to the organization that is being contacted. The initial list of fields for tblOrganization are shown Table 6-12.

Table 6-12: tblOrganization

FIELD	DATA TYPE	DESCRIPTION
OrganizationID	AutoNumber	Primary key
OrganizationName	Text	Name of organization
OrganizationCategory	Text	Categorization of the organization
OrganizationAddress	Text	Postal address (multiple fields)
OrganizationEmail	Text	E-mail address
OrganizationPhone	Text	Telephone number
ContactName	Text	Name of contact
ContactRole	Text	Role of contact

Finally, Table 6-13 lists the fields for tblCommunicationMethod, which is a lookup table. This is used by tblCampaignStage to describe the method of communication.

Table 6-13: tblCommunicationMethod

FIELD	DATA TYPE	DESCRIPTION
CommunicationMethodID	AutoNumber	Primary key
CommunicationMethod	Text	Post/Email/Phone etc

As you develop the subjects for your database, you are focused on the marketing campaign. After the tables are designed, you want to review them to determine whether you have described each subject as completely as we might. As you are doing this, you will want to consider the business needs, table structure, user interface, and potential future needs. Initial requirement specifications are a vital source of your design, but the process needn't be static.

Creating Additional Fields

As mentioned previously, as you go through the campaign stages, your database design will often morph into new forms, suggesting extra fields. Changes are cheap at the beginning of the design process compared to later, so as you are designing the tables it is the perfect time to ask questions and ensure that you are considering the options that need to be addressed. In fact, it is a good practice to periodically challenge some of the premises for your design. For example, considering tblCampaign itself, a logical addition to its fields could be to include the start date of the campaign, as that could be before the first stage begins. Another option might be to allow recording of some financial information. Although such considerations could form a large part of the database itself, we will simply add a CampaignBudget Currency field.

Similarly, the tblCampaignStage will benefit from including a date field. Considering that campaigns may or may not run sequentially, including both StartDate and EndDate fields will enable various informative queries to be performed regarding the different phases of the campaign. We will also include a StageOrder field to give the stages a sequence of execution. It would be inappropriate to use an `AutoNumber` value for this purpose.

NOTE The intended order of the campaign stages may not exactly reflect the eventual entered dates. Although the StageOrder field indicates the sequence in which the stages are intended to occur, things do not always happen as intended. The actual dates will reflect the true sequence of events. Having both fields not only provides the information that you need, but also allows you to do various comparisons.

If we are to continue to develop our simplistic campaign budget checking, then each stage will need to record a budget. To that end, we will add the StageBudget field.

Inevitably, you will conceive of and incorporate more fields as appropriate to your own business requirements. This is just the beginning of that process, and we encourage you to make as many modifications as you need. Keep in mind that this database is intended to serve as a template for your own business's unique requirements.

Figure 6-1 shows the relationships between the core campaign tables, including the new lookup tables created for communication method and reply type.

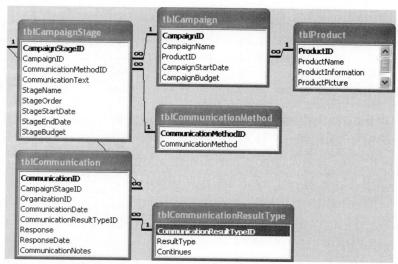

Figure 6-1: Relationships of the marketing campaign tables

Note the newly added fields, and in particular the budget fields from both tblCampaign and tblCampaignStage. By comparing these numbers, you can quickly determine whether the campaign is overspending. The following sidebar explains how to create the query to do just that.

CREATING A BUDGET ADHERENCE QUERY

To carry our example one step further, we will create a query to demonstrate how you can determine if your campaign budgets are being adhered to. We haven't included any detailed financial detail in this chapter's example, so this query will merely compare the campaign budget with the total of all stage budgets and respond with a simple Yes or No to indicate if they are at or over budget. This will tell you which campaigns are OK and which are over budget, but it is not intended to indicate the degree to which a campaign is either over budget or under budget. The following query design grid shows the query.

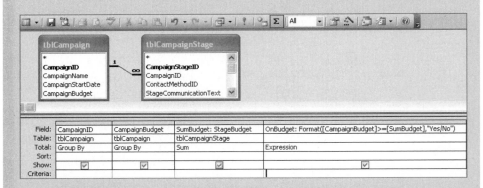

The query is an aggregate (totals) query, as indicated by the selected sigma ($\sum$) on the toolbar, which shows the Total row. A totals query enables you to summarize the rows—in this case, providing the sum of all stages grouped by each campaign. The calculated field OnBudget compares the original CampaignBudget field with our calculated SumBudget column, which adds together all the stages' budgets for that campaign.

The following code shows the query as it appears in SQL view. By studying the terms below and comparing them to the query grid, you can see what each part of the query does.

```
SELECT tblCampaign.CampaignID, tblCampaign.CampaignBudget,
    Sum(tblCampaignStage.StageBudget) AS SumBudget,
    Format([CampaignBudget]>=[SumBudget],"Yes/No") AS OnBudget
FROM tblCampaign INNER JOIN tblCampaignStage ON
    tblCampaign.CampaignID = tblCampaignStage.CampaignID
GROUP BY tblCampaign.CampaignID, tblCampaign.Budget
```

The results of this query will appear as shown below for the single campaign in the example file Campaign.mdb on the book's CD.

Reference Codes

Reference codes are a popular marketing technique for providing contacts with a reference number. This part of a promotion is used to encourage the contacted individual to act, and provides a means to identify the campaign stage. Reference codes are an excellent example of a subject-specific field.

The response fields in the communication table are important and well intended, but not every organization or individual targeted by marketing will respond or even be influenced immediately. In your own marketing endeavors, you have likely found that some recipients might not respond for weeks, months, or even years after the first contact; while others may respond in a manner that you hadn't anticipated. If contacts provide a reference number, however, you can still record their responses and use the reference number to identify which campaign stage or individual communication was successful. This provides another measure of the effectiveness of your strategy. Consequently, we will provide the option to specify a reference code at either the campaign stage or communication level by incorporating a ReferenceCode field into both tblCampaignStage and tblCommunication.

Therefore, the next step is for you to learn how to capture this data in a table. Although it's not required to capture this data in a table, a Campaign Reference Code parent table can be maintained to record the master list of all codes ever issued. By creating such a table, you can conveniently add any relevant data about the reference code, such as its purpose and the date that it was created. Including this type of information in the Campaign Stage or Communication tables would break the rule of limiting a table to details about only one subject.

Figure 6-2 shows the relationships of the Reference Code table.

Expanding Product Areas

As suggested earlier in the data analysis discussion, more than one product may be marketed for any campaign. It is equally possible that a product could feature in more than one campaign—for example, a product may be marketed yearly.

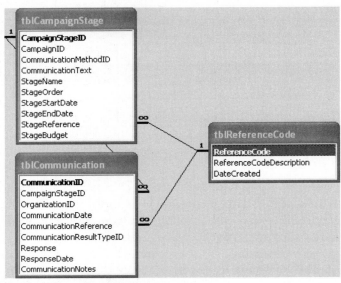

Figure 6-2: Relationships of the Reference Code table

Consequently, rather than relate the Product subject to the Campaign (refer to Figure 6-1), we require a many-to-many relationship. As shown in other chapters, this is resolved by using a link (or junction) table. In Figure 6-3, tblCampaignProduct performs that role, relating tblCampaign and tblProduct.

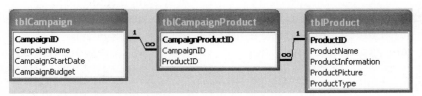

Figure 6-3: Relationships for the CampaignProduct table

Recall also that a campaign could revolve around an offered service, rather than a product. This wouldn't affect the rest of our design; although we have identified the subject as a product for the example, you could easily use it for service information as well. Indeed, we've added the ProductType field to tblProduct to store either "Product" or "Service" as a descriptive indication of this.

Creating the Tables Related to Organization

In this section we will identify and flesh out the tables that represent the subject of Organization. There are, in fact, several subjects that relate to an organization without being a direct part of it. If we consider tblOrganization as it was described in Table 6-12, then we can identify fields that require further expansion.

Organization Individuals

In Table 6-12, the fields ContactName and ContactRole describe the contact for the organization. These are deliberately brief descriptions and would likely involve several fields to describe the name alone. Fields should contain only one detail, so Title, Surname, and Forename need to be in separate fields. Similarly, because it is likely that more than one contact will exist for an organization, we need a separate contacts table that is related to tblOrganization. With that in mind, we can create tblOrganizationIndividual with the fields listed in Table 6-14.

Table 6-14: tblOrganizationIndividual

FIELD	DATA TYPE	DESCRIPTION
OrganizationIndividualID	AutoNumber	Primary key
OrganizationID	Long Integer	Foreign key to tblOrganization
Title	Text	Individual's title
LastName	Text	Surname
MiddleName	Text	Middle name or initials
FirstName	Text	First name
OrganizationRole	Text	Role of organization contact

We have kept the list brief, but you can make it as comprehensive as appropriate to contain the details you need to know about individuals. For example, in a marketing application geared towards organization contacts, you are unlikely to include details such as marital status or height, but you may have a reason to need them.

Of the fields in the table, OrganizationRole warrants discussion, as it both allows a free-form descriptive text and has the likelihood of repeated values being entered. For example, every organization will have a CEO, or a Manager, and so on; this is an indication that you may benefit from having a related table to describe the roles. We'll do that in tblRole, using the fields listed in Table 6-15.

Table 6-15: tblRole

FIELD	DATA TYPE	DESCRIPTION
RoleID	AutoNumber	Primary key field
RoleName	Text	Role text
RoleDescription	Text	Description of role's purpose
RoleInactive	Yes/No	Yes/No alternative to deleting

You will see the Inactive field option in several locations in this book. This field is used to indicate that the record is no longer current. By keeping the record, you can control whether it can be seen or used. This method is also used to conveniently limit lists that are displayed to users, while at the same time maintaining data consistency for current and historic values.

Figure 6-4 shows the tables which describe an organization's contacts.

Figure 6-4: Relationships of the OrganizationIndividual table

RELATIONSHIP TRIANGLES

Tables for organizations and people can represent a variety of subjects. They may be businesses, memberships, customers, employees, or individuals, among perhaps other designations. Regardless of the name used, the concepts for the table structure will remain the same. The primary differences in the tables will be determined by the type of information you use and whether the same type of information might apply to both an individual and an organization.

Managing the same type of data that might relate to two different tables to each other can result in complex table relationships. For example, both the organization and the individual will have phone listings, so all phone numbers could be stored in one Phone table. The challenge then becomes how to ensure that a specific phone record can be associated with only either an organization or an individual, but not both. You will likely encounter this type of scenario in several business functions.

There are countless ways for managing the relationships and the data; and they all involve both the table structure and controls in the user interface. An extensive discussion is outside the scope of this book, but the concepts are important, so we have provided a good introduction to the issue and some possible approaches to designing a solution in Appendix C, "Resolving Relationship Triangles."

Organization Communication Details

The contact information methods for organizations were listed in Table 6-12 as OrganizationAddress, OrganizationEmail, and OrganizationPhone. Again, one field apiece isn't enough to represent these items, particularly the address details. You can probably also see that more than one of these contact methods is likely to exist for each organization.

As before, we introduce new subjects as tables related to the parent Organization table. We will start by looking at the Address details, as listed in Table 6-16.

Table 6-16: tblOrganizationAddress

FIELD	DATA TYPE	DESCRIPTION
OrganizationAddressID	AutoNumber	Primary key
OrganizationID	Long Integer	Foreign key to tblOrganization
AddressType	Text	Purpose of address (e.g., delivery)
StreetAddress	Text	First line of address
StreetAddress2	Text	Second line of address, if it exists
AddressCity	Text	Town/city
AddressState	Text	State/region
AddressPostalCode	Text	Postal code

In a very similar vein, we can include tables to contain the e-mail and phone details. Each of these tables has a "type" field which describes the purpose of the record. Obviously there will be repeating values in the type field within each table and so a related "type" table is justified. Instead of maintaining three such "type" tables for each contact method, we can create an all-encompassing type description table which can be used to describe a type in tblOrganizationAddress, tblOrganizationEMail, or tblOrganizationPhone. This would have the fields listed in Table 6-17. Figure 6-5 shows some example data for such a ContactType table.

Table 6-17: tblContactType

FIELD	DATA TYPE	DESCRIPTION
ContactTypeID	AutoNumber	Primary key
ContactSubject	Text	Subject table it relates to
ContactType	Text	Type name
ContactTypeDescription	Text	Description of the type
ContactTypeInactive	Yes/No	Optional archive indicator

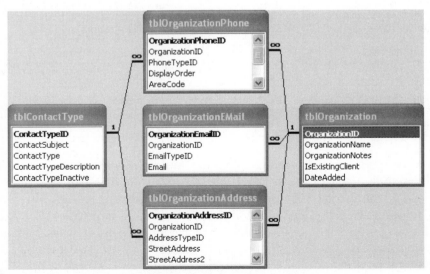

Figure 6-5: Sample data for ContactType table

These organization contact subjects are related as shown in Figure 6-6, which includes the Organization and the three contact detail tables.

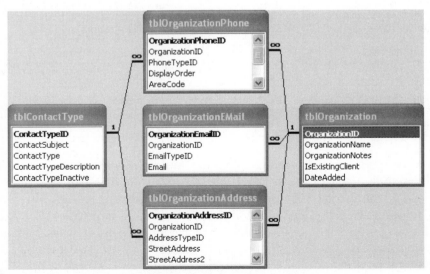

Figure 6-6: Relationships of the Organization Contact tables

Organization Types

For many reasons, it can be important to identify the type of an organization. Recall that tblOrganization contains a text field named OrganizationCategory that describes the type of organization—for example, "Legal Services." You can quickly discern that it will have repeating values, and therefore merits a related table. To help reinforce why this is a good idea, consider a user of the database who happens to enter the misspelled "Legl Service." Other users will be unlikely to find that record again from a search on that field. A lookup table that limits users to selecting values from a list will prevent such mishaps.

In this instance, we create tblOrganizationType with the fields listed in Table 6-18.

Table 6-18: tblOrganizationType

FIELD	DATA TYPE	DESCRIPTION
OrganizationTypeID	AutoNumber	Primary key
OrganizationType	Text	Type description

However, it is not always appropriate to limit an organization to only one type as a single organization may provide more than one service or have multiple interests. To indicate all of the types of services that an organization might provide, we need to use a table structure that can represent a many-to-many relationship. As before, we will use a junction table (link table) to create this relationship.

So, along with the Organization Type table, we also need a junction table to relate the organization with the organization type, as shown in Table 6-19.

Table 6-19: tblOrganizationTypeAssigned

FIELD	DATA TYPE	DESCRIPTION
OrganizationTypeAssignID	AutoNumber	Primary key
OrganizationID	Long Integer	Foreign key to parent organization record
OrganizationTypeID	Long Integer	Foreign key to tblOrganizationType
SelectedTypeOrder	Long Integer	Optional prioritizing field

Each record in the table tblOrganizationTypeAssigned relates to a selected organization with a selected organization type. We have also included the field, SelectedTypeOrder so that you can specify the display. For example, a value of 1 in that field could indicate this is the primary type of this organization, while there are other types selected with lower SelectedTypeOrder values.

For data consistency, it is a good idea to ensure that the same organization and type are only associated once. This is easily achieved by adding a unique index to the table across both the OrganizationID and the OrganizationTypeID fields, as is shown in Figure 6-7.

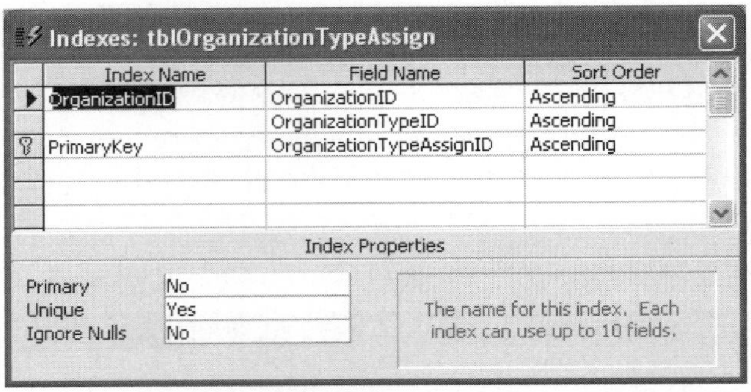

Figure 6-7: Multi-field unique index on tblOrganizationTypeAssigned

You can review and edit indexes for any table in the database. To open the Index window, open a table in design view and click the Index control on the Ribbon or toolbar. The Index control is the lightning bolt to the left of the table name, as shown in the upper-left corner of Figure 6-7.

At this point, you have completed the essential tables and fields for identifying the marketing campaign, its stages, communications, and the organizations to be contacted. Next we consider some additions to the design.

Further Campaign Subjects

As indicated earlier, your initial effort on paper will not always carry through to the final design. We've already expanded our example design just by fleshing out some details and features. In this section, you'll look at some extra considerations that could be added to enhance the database.

Targeted Organizations

Often a campaign is geared to target a specific set of organizations, rather than every one stored in your database. Although it is possible that you will choose to store only organizations that you wish to target, it is more likely that you will acquire a mass of records, only some of which you will want to include in a given campaign. For example, using the information stored in the Address tables, you could limit the selection to a specific region, perhaps by leveraging data in the postal code field or the phone area code field. With this in mind, the organization type is likely to be a vital statistic.

You would typically use a query to filter and selectively retrieve records based on certain criteria. For example, using the query designer in Access, you could create a query similar to the one shown in Figure 6-8 to retrieve the list of "Engineers" organization types with a phone prefix of "202."

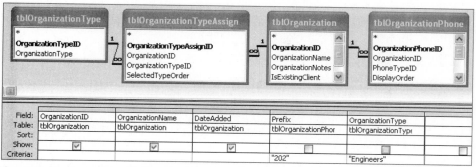

Figure 6-8: Query to retrieve specific types of organizations

The results could serve as your starting point to create the list of organizations for a specific marketing campaign. As you can see, it is relatively easy to create queries to obtain information from several tables.

> **TIP** Do not fear using multiple tables and joins in queries. While including a significantly large number of tables is not a good idea, a properly designed database should efficiently perform queries with the tables that are required. Using queries, you can pull together data from numerous tables and return only the information you require.

Such flexibility is the great thing about querying a database. You can change the query structure and criteria to suit your needs. You can also save and re-run a query, so that you can obtain the results when and as needed.

One downfall to managing a campaign based on the results of re-running a query is that the records in the tables may have changed in the interim. In other words, if new records (contacts) are added to the database after you have started a campaign, they could be included in the subsequent query executions. A campaign with multiple stages would then risk communicating with organizations that did not receive the earlier communications.

DATE ENTERED QUERY

One option to avoid such miscommunication is to include a field in tblOrganization to track the entry date of each record. Access's ACE engine doesn't provide this functionality natively but a default value property of `Date()` or

Continued

DATE ENTERED QUERY *(continued)*

`Now()` **for the DateAdded field would ensure it is always inserted. With that, you would limit the records to those that were added before your campaign began.**

This would require adding a field to your Organization table and including the appropriate criteria in your queries. This is illustrated in the query below.

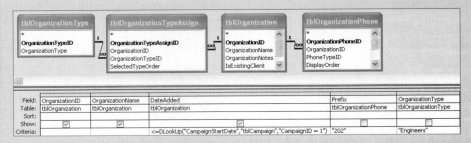

The criteria for the Prefix and OrganizationType are those shown in Figure 6-3. We also have criteria in the DateAdded field to compare against a looked up value of a specified campaign start date. We used the following criteria:

```
<=DLookUp("CampaignStartDate","tblCampaign","CampaignID=1")
```

This query can therefore be used as a source to ensure that only organizations that existed in your records before the campaign began will receive communications from that campaign.

One versatile option for identifying the organizations to be targeted by a campaign is to maintain a list of selected organizations. This is achieved with a link table between the campaign and organizations, such as table tblCampaignTarget with the fields as shown in Table 6-20.

Table 6-20: tblCampaignTarget

FIELD	DATA TYPE	DESCRIPTION
CampaignTargetID	AutoNumber	Primary key
CampaignID	Long Integer	Foreign key to parent campaign
OrganizationID	Long Integer	Foreign key to selected organization record

As in the tblOrganizationTypeAssign link table, the combination of CampaignID and OrganizationID is limited to a single entry by creating a unique index that includes both fields.

The entries in this table represent the organizations assigned to a given campaign. Its membership is predictable and fixed unless manually added to by the user. However, you may choose to establish the records by using an append query. You are then free to add and remove organizations from that list. We explain how to do this in the "Appending Records" sidebar.

APPENDING RECORDS

You can use an append query to insert a set of records into tblCampaign-Target. A query similar to that previously used to retrieve organizations that matched specified criteria can be made for this purpose. After creating the query, change the query type to an append query and enter the Append to table as tblCampaignTarget. The only field we need to insert into the target table is the OrganizationID.

An example of this query is shown below and can be seen as qryInsertToTarget in the Campaign.mdb file on the CD.

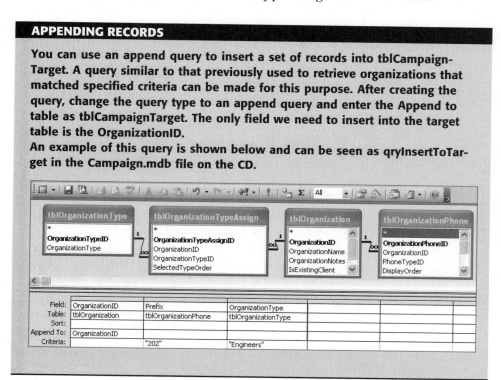

The initial communication of your campaign would be to the set of organizations stored in tblCampaignTarget. Each communication record would still store the OrganizationID that is being contacted. Subsequent communications may not be to all originally selected organizations, as some may be excluded from the process or targeted differently.

QUERYING FOR SPECIFIC LISTS

Querying for organizations that are still available from the original target list can be quite a complex procedure, but this example should be able to get the results you need. We start by considering what we want to select. We know we want the records from tblCampaignTarget, but we really only want those

Continued

QUERYING FOR SPECIFIC LISTS *(continued)*

that are not marked for no further communication in the current campaign. We achieve this by using two queries.

The first query, qryOrganizationUnavailable, shown below, selects all organizations that are excluded for selection using the Continues field as criteria.

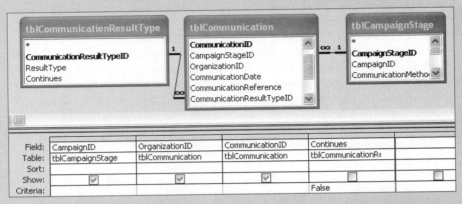

This returns a list of OrganizationIDs that should not be contacted. Next, we use this list as we select all organization records from tblCampaignTarget, but use a left outer join to ensure that we include only records which are not in qryOrganizationUnavailable based on the same OrganizationID and, vitally, the CampaignID (as we must not let other campaign results affect the one we're concerned with). This is accomplished using the query qryOrganizationAvailable, shown below.

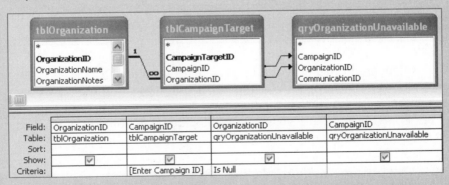

This query uses a parameter that enables us to enter a CampaignID indicating the campaign we're interested in. The "Is Null" criteria ensures that we exclude organizations that have records in qryOrganizationUnavailable. This query isn't a simple operation but it provides the results that we need. If nothing else, it's an excellent tool for learning about queries, subqueries, and joins.

Campaign Events

The campaign process and schedule described by the tblCampaignStage table is largely responsible for driving the sections of the campaign, particularly the communication initiatives. Although the table can be expanded to include other aspects of a marketing campaign, it shouldn't be cluttered with every noteworthy occurrence in the campaign. As a general rule, you should be able to define what will be stored in the campaign stages table before you even begin the marketing campaign.

To record unanticipated or exceptional processes, the model needs to include a means of separately recording them. Given that many such events can occur during the course of a campaign, we will use a related table and a one-to-many relationship to record the events. The question now is whether these events are related to a campaign or to a campaign stage? For more granular detail, we could consider that if they are related to a specific campaign stage then they are, indirectly, related to the campaign itself; but specifying at which stage an event occurred could provide a vital detail.

The details that we include to describe a campaign's events would be, at a minimum, a date, a name, and a description of the event. At this point, you could begin building the table, tblCampaignEvent, based on the fields listed in Table 6-21.

NOTE The EventDate field, as all Date/Time fields in ACE or Jet, can store both the date and time. While there are exceptions to almost every rule, you will rarely need to store a time value separately from a date value if they are both referring to the same point in time. Since the field holds both values they can be queried and displayed separately by repeating the field and changing the display format. The primary reason for storing the time component alone is for the convenience of users and those creating the forms and reports. This may become a benefit in an application that is heavily dependent on calculations and displays of time.

Table 6-21: tblCampaignEvent

FIELD	DATA TYPE	DESCRIPTION
CampaignEventID	AutoNumber	Primary key
CampaignStageID	Long Integer	Foreign key to parent campaign stage
EventDate	Date/Time	Date (and time) of event
EventDescription	Text	General description of the event
EventDetail	Memo	Memo field to allow greater detail

The fields listed in Table 6-21 will often provide all of the details needed to manage the critical information about an event. As you can see, the event is related to a specific campaign stage by storing the CampaignStageID in the events table. This allows you to have any number of events for a given campaign stage. And, since the campaign stage identifies the campaign, you do not need to store the CampaignID in this table.

You may choose to add other fields that you feel describe important information about the event. You may want an optional foreign key field to a list of your employees to describe who the event was most directly related to. Or you may want a field, such as the OLE Object data type, to be able to store almost anything you choose that is related to the event.

STORING ATTACHMENTS

As discussed in other chapters in this book, it's not a generally recommended practice to store binary objects such as large files in your database. It is much better to store a UNC (Unique Naming Convention) folder path to the file or just the filename itself if it is stored in a dedicated folder.

Since ACE was introduced in Access 2007, the Attachment data type has offered a more efficient means of storing files such as images in your databases. So, if you are using Access 2007 or newer with the ACCDB file format, you might enjoy the benefits of storing and previewing files within your database. However, Attachments are a uniquely Access concept that you won't find in other database platforms.

Figure 6-9 shows the tables in the relationship diagram.

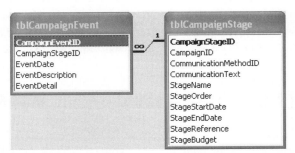

Figure 6-9: Relationship of the CampaignEvent and CampaignStage tables

As with the other tables, we have provided a relatively basic model and explained some of the aspects that you might consider when deciding how best to represent your activities. It is now your job to keep asking the questions so that you can tailor a schema to support your needs.

Keep in mind that these tables are the foundation for your application. It is much better (i.e., cheaper) to invest the time in planning the required schema than to suffer through using a poor design structure or redo dozens of forms and reports after the application has been deployed. Planning can easily take 30% of the time needed to create the entire database solution, including the forms and reports.

Summary of the Marketing Model

Now that we've worked through the process of analyzing the parts that make up a marketing campaign, it is time to see how they go together to represent the entire process. The completed database schema or relationship view, shown in Figure 6-10, provides a convenient way of seeing how all of the tables fit together.

We started with the core subjects of Campaign, Stages, Communications, and Organizations. These are now represented by groups of tables.

You can easily see how the peripheral items, such as the contacts, organizations, and addresses relate to and support the core subjects. And, based on the field names and the way the relationships are depicted, you can also decipher how the lookup tables can add efficiency and integrity.

You also saw how to create queries and use criteria to pull information from several tables while limiting the results to exactly what you want to use. These techniques can be expanded on and applied to create a variety of custom applications to manage your marketing campaigns. They are also valuable techniques to use in areas outside of the marketing arena.

We've covered a lot of material, but we have not yet considered one of the most common parts of a marketing campaign, something that often occurs before active marketing begins. It falls under the familiar term of "market research," but the database model of it is ultimately a variation on a concept that you can use time and again across a broad spectrum of applications. We are referring to the questionnaire.

Questionnaires

A fundamental part of successful marketing is to tailor the marketing campaign to the target audience. The questionnaire is one of the most common tools for learning about a prospective market.

Questionnaires come in all shapes and sizes. Some can be very complex while others are relatively simple. Examples of complex questionnaires include those with questions that branch off in different directions based on the answers given to previous questions. Simple questionnaires may involve only a few questions supporting only yes and no answers. We will look at a design that should work for most situations—one that is flexible and comprehensive enough to fill almost any questionnaire need.

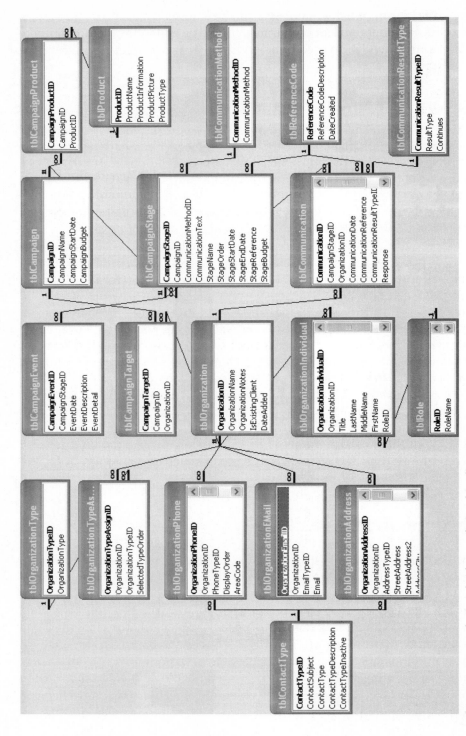

Figure 6-10: Marketing database relationship diagram

Just Questions and Answers

We begin by asking a question of our own. What does a questionnaire or survey need to model? That's simple: a list of questions and answers!

It sounds so simple—that is, until you start to consider all the different forms that questions and answers can take. For example, should you use leading, open-ended questions, fixed-response questions, or questions that allow multiple responses? Similarly, what is the best way to capture and use the responses you are seeking?

As we have done previously, we will begin with a relatively simple scenario so that you can learn the concepts involved. Then, we will expand the model to handle a more complicated scenario. First, though, we discuss a common but inappropriate design. This is not to confuse you, but rather to save you from needless mistakes and frustrations.

The Overly Simple Inappropriate Design

You may ask, just how simple is simple? Table 6-22 shows the answer: the questions form the individual fields.

You may be thinking that this looks like a great approach. It makes it easy to see the questions, and you could argue that each question is a detail that describes the questionnaire. So presumably you could argue that it supports the rules of good relational database design. The rebuttal is easy: each table could describe one and only one questionnaire. It would be a nightmare to manage a solution that required one table per questionnaire.

Table 6-22: Inappropriate Questionnaire Table

FIELD	DESCRIPTION
QuestionnaireID	Primary key field
Q1DoYouLiftObjects	1st question - Yes/No
Q2DoYouLiftEfficiently	2nd question - Yes/No
Q3DailyLiftingOccurrence	3rd question - Numeric
...	...

Each field is a single answer and data type for the question it asks. But what if you wanted to have a question that allows multiple options for the answer? Do you include a field for each potential option? In that case, a question with five options to choose from would require five fields with only one of them being used and the others left empty. And, what happens if you find out you needed a sixth option? You would have to revise the table, forms, queries, and reports. You can quickly realize that what might look like a convenient and simple design is really a subtle trap.

> **NOTE** Beginning with Access 2007 Microsoft has included the Multi-Value field data type. These complex field types do genuinely allow for storing multiple values within a single field; the relational structure is hidden from the developer and user. However, even this would only offer a partial solution as it allows multiple answers in a field but not multiple question options. And, since it isn't available in earlier versions of Access or in many other RDBMS platforms, we will not incorporate multi-value fields in our questionnaire.

The Simple Genuine Questionnaire

Now that you know what not to do, let's focus on how to create an appropriate design. Regardless of the complexity of the eventual design, you should always begin by considering the core subjects.

To design a questionnaire, you of course need to know the types of questions and the types of answers that will be allowed, and how the questionnaire will be conducted. For clarity, we stipulate for this example that each time a questionnaire is completed it will be called an *interview*. An interview represents an instance of completing a questionnaire, and includes both the question and the response.

And, since we are using the questionnaire in a marketing scenario, we will be interviewing organizations. Therefore, we wish to connect the organization to the answers they give during the interview process.

Identifying the Core Tables

With just a few quick questions, you have the basic information needed to create a simple database structure for conducting questionnaires. The core subjects can be identified as follows:

- **Questionnaire:** A template set of questions to be asked in an interview.
- **Questions:** The constituent questions which form the content of a questionnaire.
- **Interview:** The process of asking an organization those questions.
- **Organization:** The subject to which we ask the questions in an interview.
- **Answers:** The responses provided by the organization following the questions asked in the interview.

As in the marketing section, we will discuss the core tables all at one time, starting with the key fields. And, to model the basic process that we have just described, we will create the four tables as shown in Tables 6-23 to 6-26.

The fifth table, to provide the information about the organization, has been established previously; most recently in our marketing campaign model.

Table 6-23: Simple tblQuestionnaire

FIELD	DATA TYPE	DESCRIPTION
QuestionnaireID	AutoNumber	Primary key field
QuestionnaireName	Text	Name of this template (questionnaire)
QuestionnaireDate	Date/Time	Date (and time) of relevance
QuestionnaireDescription	Text	General expanded description

Because each question belongs to a particular questionnaire, the Questionnaire table is referenced from tblQuestion, which has the fields as listed in Table 6-24.

Table 6-24: Simple tblQuestion

FIELD	DATA TYPE	DESCRIPTION
QuestionID	AutoNumber	Primary key field
QuestionnaireID	Long Integer	Foreign key to tblQuestionnaire
QuestionText	Text	Descriptive text of the question
QuestionOrder	Long Integer	Order number of the questions
IncludeDetail	Yes/No	Include detail text with response

Together these two tables describe the information required to record a questionnaire, which is like a template set of questions to be asked. Each occurrence is an interview, which will be recorded in the fields listed for tblInterview as shown in Table 6-25.

Table 6-25: Simple tblInterview

FIELD	DATA TYPE	DESCRIPTION
InterviewID	AutoNumber	Primary key field
OrganizationID	Long Integer	Foreign key to tblOrganization
QuestionnaireID	Long Integer	Foreign key to tblQuestionnaire
InterviewDate	Date/Time	Date of interview occurrence
InterviewComments	Text	Optional relevant comments

Each interview has a set of answers. The answers are responses to specific combinations of the interview and the individual question which it is answering. The answers are recorded in tblAnswer, which contains the fields listed in Table 6-26.

Table 6-26: Simple tblAnswer

FIELD	DATA TYPE	DESCRIPTION
AnswerID	AutoNumber	Primary key field
InterviewID	Long Integer	Foreign key to tblInterview
QuestionID	Long Integer	Foreign key to tblQuestion
AnswerValue	Text	Actual answer given
AnswerComment	Text	Optional extra comment text

As you can see, tblAnswer is directly related to both tblInterview and tblQuestion. The Answer table stores the actual response to the question in a text field named AnswerValue. One benefit of the Text data type, is that it can store both text and numeric values.

The AnswerComment field is included as an optional field for additional information that is not accommodated in a different field. In the user interface, you can hide or display the field based on the question so that it only be visible for people to enter a response if the IncludeDetail field in tblQuestion is set to include details. Without this field, the answer is confined to the single value field AnswerValue.

This may work well for some questionnaire solutions. But as you select the data type, it's also worth considering how your database will be used in the workplace. If the response, like most other values, will likely need to be grouped, sorted, and searched, then you should anticipate exactly what users might be searching for—and how they will be searching.

For example, will users want to see all responses that contain numbers and have the responses grouped based on the number? If so, you need to factor in that text values will sort based on the position of the character, so numbers 1 through 11 will appear as 1, 10, 11, 2, 3, and so on. That isn't going to be the order that users expect. But, you are stuck with text or memo fields if you need to include narratives in the answers.

With all that in mind, you are ready to create the tables that were defined in previous Tables 6-23 to 6-26. These are included in the file Questionnaire_Simple.mdb on the book's CD. When you look at the tables in the relationship view, you should ensure that they have the relationships shown in Figure 6-11. If you are creating a new database, you will need to copy or import the tblOrganization from the marketing model.

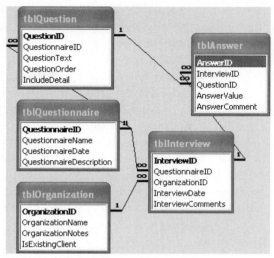

Figure 6-11: The simple questionnaire diagram

In looking at the relationship diagram, you can see that the interview is almost the central part of the design. It's at least as important as the questionnaire. This level of importance will remain true in the more complex models as well.

So, now that you've seen how to model a simple questionnaire, you are ready to add flexibility to accommodate additional common scenarios.

The Flexible Questionnaire

The first thing to consider is the types of situations you are likely to encounter that cannot be handled by the simple design. Two core issues immediately come to mind:

- Answers requiring a specific data type
- Questions that allow multiple answers

These introduce related and external issues to consider, such as identifying the data type expected from a question and storing multiple answers.

Specific Data Type Answers

Given that data types can be varied in a database, you have to choose what constitutes a reasonable set of options. In the simple model, all answer values were stored in a Text data type field regardless of what they actually stored: a yes/no, numeric, or text response. In this model, you want to use an appropriate data type field to store the answers.

Understanding the data types is necessary for determining a minimum set of data types that you might use. Boolean (Yes/No) values are stored as a required value of either 0 (False/No/Off) or -1 (True/Yes/On). Since these are numeric values, they can be stored in a numeric data type field. Even with a numeric data type in the table, you can still use the Yes/No type of responses on the form.

Another common field that you may need to consider is a date field. Dates are also stored as numeric values. Having analyzed the complete list of data types, we have determined that it is possible to use just two data types: Text and the numeric Double. With those two data types, we can simplify the table structure yet retain all of the benefits of the original data types, such as currency. We chose the Double because that allows a very wide range of numeric values to be entered and it can include decimal components.

The next task is to determine how to allow two different data types for a response. The previous schema used an Answer table with a single value field. So, one option might be to simply add one more field to provide the option for Text or Numeric value entries.

However, the inevitability that one of the fields will be empty usually points to a design flaw, which is typically fixed by introducing optional related tables. For our scenario, we've created a table for numeric responses and a table for text responses. That means you now require three tables to record the answer.

NOTE This situation is similar to the either-or structure that is illustrated in Appendix C. The two examples in that appendix are provided to demonstrate a couple of approaches for managing the data and relationships using the user interface.

The fields for the three tables are shown in Tables 6-27 through 6-29.

Table 6-27: Typed - tblAnswer

FIELD	DATA TYPE	DESCRIPTION
AnswerID	AutoNumber	Primary key field
InterviewID	Long Integer	Foreign key to tblInterview
QuestionID	Long Integer	Foreign key to tblQuestion
AnswerComment	Text	Optional extra comment text

This is the core table which represents the act of answering a question, however the actual answer itself is stored in a related table to allow for an appropriate data type to be used (either number or text). The numeric table is shown in Table 6-28, and the very similar text-based answer table is shown in Table 6-29.

Table 6-28: Typed - tblAnswerNumber

FIELD	DATA TYPE	DESCRIPTION
AnswerNumberID	AutoNumber	Primary key field
AnswerID	Long Integer	Foreign key to tblAnswer
AnswerNumber	Double	The typed Answer Value field

Table 6-29: Typed - tblAnswerText

FIELD	DATA TYPE	DESCRIPTION
AnswerTextID	AutoNumber	Primary key field
AnswerID	Long Integer	Foreign key to tblAnswer
AnswerText	Text	The typed Answer Value field

Together, these three tables will store the responses for all questions, as you can see from the relationship diagram shown in Figure 6-12.

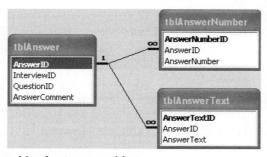

Figure 6-12: Relationships for Answer tables

The tables for text and numeric answers contain the actual responses, and tblAnswer relates the response back to the specific interview and question. This table also allows for including a comment about the answer.

Determining the Data Type for Questions

We have considered how to record answers of a specific type, but you also need to determine what you are asking and how you know what data type is appropriate for the specific question.

The solution is to include a field in the Question table that specifies the data type of the field that will store the answer. Based on our previous review of data types and responses we know that every response can be stored in a Text field or in a Number field with the field size of Double. However, the user interface needs to be able to have more control of the display for forms and reports—for example to display a number as currency. To accommodate this need, we will create a table to associate the data type of response expected with the necessary data type, either Text or Double, for storing the data. To provide an easy way for users to select the correct format, we'll use the lookup table called tblDataType, with the fields as listed in Table 6-30.

Table 6-30: tblDataType

FIELD	DATA TYPE	DESCRIPTION
DataTypeID	Long Integer	Primary key
DataTypeName	Text	Data type name
DataTypeUsedID	Long Integer	Foreign key to this table's DataTypeID

This table, which contains what is known as a *recursive join,* is commonly referred to as a *self-referencing table.* Recursive joins are foreign key links to their own table. In this instance, the DataTypeUsedID is a foreign key link to the DataTypeID field this table. This allows us to reassign the actual data type (for example, Currency) as either Text or Double as the response is recorded.

This table also demonstrates a rare exception for not using an AutoNumber as the primary key. We have specifically used a Long Integer for this DataTypeID so that we could use the values that are used by Access for the specific data type. For this technique to work as illustrated, you would need to use the same values, as shown in Table 6-31.

Table 6-31: tblDataType Example Values

DATATYPEID	DATATYPENAME	DATATYPEUSEDID
1	Boolean	7
4	Long Integer	7
5	Currency	7
7	Double	7
8	Date	7
10	Text	10
12	Memo	10

As we mentioned earlier, the Data Type table is a lookup table so that the person creating the survey can select the type of response expected to the question. This requires that the DataTypeId is listed as a foreign key in tblQuestion. You'll see that in Figure 6-13, after we discuss how to allow multiple-choice questions.

Multiple-Choice Questions

To provide answers to multiple-choice questions, the natural approach is to simply allow multiple answer records related to a given question. The previous example allows tblAnswer to contain a single answer that is related to the appropriate interview and question. We have just explained how to add the capability to allow an answer to have a response-specific data type. We will now show you how to leverage the ability to specify a data type as we incorporate yet another popular feature: the multiple-choice question.

The Question Options Table

We will start by considering how to include a question that will require or allow multiple options or responses. As in previous examples, to allow for multiple options, we will need another table. By creating a question option table related to the question table, we can now have one or more options for each question. Table 6-32 illustrates the fields we'll need to capture the options allowed for each question.

NOTE The sole purpose of this table is to provide specific allowable answers for any given question. This is particularly useful when you need to control the answer(s) given. If there are records in this table, then those values will be the only ones allowed as response(s) for the related question. Displaying and recording the responses will have to be controlled through the user interface. The typical approach is to transfer or append the response from the Question Option table to the Answer table. We will use the specified data type to determine the appropriate table for recording the response.

Table 6-32: tblQuestionOption

FIELD	DATA TYPE	DESCRIPTION
QuestionOptionID	AutoNumber	Primary key
QuestionID	Long Integer	Foreign key tblQuestion
QuestionOptionText	Text	Text describing the option
QuestionOptionValue	Text	Text describing the value

The Questions Table

There is one aspect of the question that you will need to specify in order to allow multiple responses. Only when a question is set to allow multiple responses will it permit the selection of more than one. This is the difference between a question that allows you to select one answer from multiple choices and a question that allows more than one of the offered responses to be chosen.

To specify whether we allow multiple responses to a given question, we have added a Boolean (Yes/No) field to tblQuestion and named it Question-AllowMulti, as shown in the relationship diagram in Figure 6-13, which is from the Questionnaire.mdb example file.

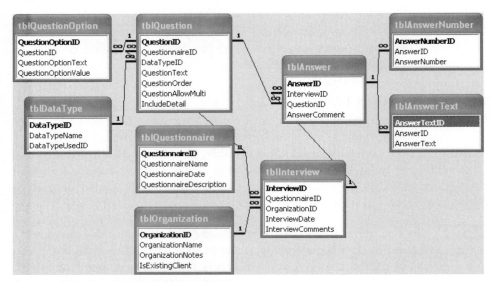

Figure 6-13: The Question relationships

Unlike the DataTypeID, the field QuestionAllowMulti does not affect the data in the Answer tables.

The Final Questionnaire

At this point, you have a flexible model that should accommodate a wide range of uses. To include a final set of considerations, we will take the functional questionnaire model and improve the appearance and user experience by looking at three potential enhancements.

- Questionnaire sections (grouping of questions)
- Organization contact interviews
- Question dependency

These are actually very simple to implement, and definitely worth the effort.

Questionnaire Sections

In the final example file for this chapter on the book's CD, Questionnaire_ Complex.mdb, we include a new table called tblQuestionnaireSection, with the fields as listed in Table 6-33. This serves as a mechanism to group questions into sections within a questionnaire. To incorporate sections, the relationship of the Question table will change from the Questionnaire table to the Questionnaire Section table. In turn, the Questionnaire Section table will relate to the parent record in the Questionnaire table.

Table 6-33: tblQuestionnaireSection

FIELD	DATA TYPE	DESCRIPTION
QuestionnaireSectionID	AutoNumber	Primary key
QuestionnaireID	Long Integer	Foreign key to tblQuestionnaire
SectionOrderNumber	Long Integer	Numeric ordering of section
SectionName	Text	Text describing the section

That's all there is to it. Now, you can group the questions under any heading that you want. And, using the section order number, you can also change the display sequence or use code to hide sections based on responses to other questions. The specifics for how to accomplish that are obviously beyond the scope of our discussion, but it is beneficial for you to realize that such things are not only possible, but relatively easy to achieve.

Organization Contact Interviews

This feature is equally simple to implement. From the earlier section of this chapter we established the relationship between organizations and contact individuals. So, to have interview results reflect both the individual and the organization that they represent, you only need to add tblOrganizationContact to the database and then replace the relationship between the interview and the organization with a similar relationship between the contact and the interview, as shown in Figure 6-14.

Unlike the previous example, with this design, the contact is required in the Organization Contact table before the person can be interviewed. Depending on the design of the user interface, that can seem like a simultaneous process to the user.

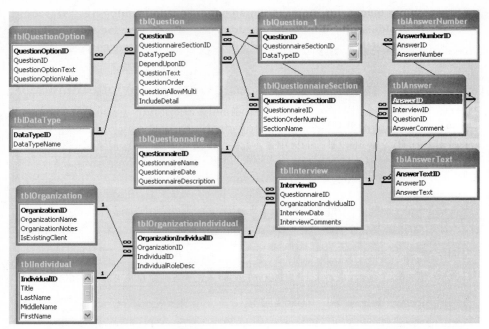

Figure 6-14: Relationships of the Questionnaire Section and Organization Contact tables

Question Dependency

While this technique also provides an example of a more comprehensive data model, the bigger benefits are derived from the way it can be used in the user interface. Being able to show or hide questions based on existing answers is a tremendous benefit to users. Consider how effectively this type of technique has guided you through surveys, to specific sales offers, into forums of interest and more. Obviously, this has the potential of becoming an invaluable tool among your database resources.

NOTE Although we have limited the consideration of user interface issues during our design of a solid schema, this example provides you with an additional learning opportunity and will add value to the user.

Often, a response to a given question will make several of the subsequent questions irrelevant. For example, if one of your first questions determines the sex of the respondent, subsequent questions that are gender-specific will not be relevant for the opposite sex. Only those questions that are now relevant to the gender chosen should be presented to the respondent. This type of question dependency is very common.

Ultimately, the easiest way to implement question dependency is to stipulate that a question can only be dependent on one other question. There will be exceptions to this, but you will need to decide if it's worth complicating the database design to allow for exceptions. The alternative would require a dedicated table to list the related questions that must be satisfied. In our scenario we stipulate that a question is dependent on only one other question. For simplicity's sake, we also stipulate that the master question will be either a Yes/No-type question or a numeric-type question with a value greater than zero. You might recall from early discussions that those two data types will employ very similar comparison techniques.

Adding the DependUponID field to the Questions table introduces a self-referencing join as the value of that field relates to the primary key QuestionID from that same tblQuestion. This type of join was discussed earlier in the discussion of tblDataType. You can also learn more about them in Chapter 3.

Specifying the parent question record in this way introduces a simple way to denote record dependency. You can then leverage this when designing your user interface.

The example data entered in the Questionnaire_Complex.mdb file on the book CD demonstrates both grouping of questions with questionnaire sections and the dependent nature of subsequent questions on the first introductory question.

NOTE An optional table that could be included might actually not play a part in your data design at all. It is sometimes helpful to provide a means of selecting certain records from a table. This is done simply by storing the primary key values from that table as a foreign key.

Such selection of question records in a "KeyQuestion"-type table might useful for querying specific questions that you intend to highlight for special reporting purposes. If such selection were to be a flexible reporting option, then this might be a situation where you leave that table local to your Access application. This allows each user to independently select their key question records and report accordingly without affecting other users. This is a good alternative to including a simple Yes/No field such as "KeyQuestions" in the Questions table to identify such records.

In the accompanying file, tblKeyQuestions has been included for that purpose, but it does not feature in the relationship diagram as it would not be included in the database file.

As you can see from these three examples, it can be relatively straightforward to customize your questionnaire to suit the specific situation.

Alternative Design: A Question Pool

An alternative design option is to maintain a central "pool" of questions. These questions are then available to be chosen from and assigned to a given questionnaire. This model would allow for the same question to feature in multiple questionnaires, without being duplicated.

Though we have not implemented this design in any of the examples for this chapter, it is simplicity itself to establish, and will provide immediate benefits if you encounter repetitive use of questions among different questionnaires. You would only need to add a junction table, tblQuestionnaireQuestion, with the fields shown in Table 6-34. This will establish the many-to-many relationship between tblQuestion and tblQuestionnaire and allow the assignment of questions.

Table 6-34: tblQuestionnaireQuestion

FIELD	DATA TYPE	DESCRIPTION
QuestionnaireQuestionID	AutoNumber	Primary key
QuestionnaireID	Long Integer	Foreign key to tblQuestionnaire
QuestionID	Long Integer	Numeric ordering of section
QuestionOrder	Long Integer	Order in this questionnaire
DependUponID	Long Integer	QuestionID this record depends on

As you can see, the link table includes fields for QuestionOrder and DependUponID, as these would now be details related to the use of a question in a particular questionnaire, rather than the question itself.

As we mentioned earlier, we have not incorporated this level of question reusability in the files for this chapter. We've mentioned it here so that you would have it in mind should it serve your purposes in the future. And with the number of examples that you've already completed, this will indeed be a breeze for you.

Marketing Combined

To integrate the database files discussed in this chapter, you need to step back to examine the core focus for your business and how you might want to use the features. It may be that you would implement a questionnaire at the very early stages of a marketing campaign. In that case, integration is as simple as including a foreign key to the CampaignID in your Interview table.

You may also conduct several questionnaires over a period of time to identify other potential requirements of existing client organizations, with the intention of cross-selling or exchanging referrals. In that case, your only link from the questionnaire to the earlier marketing section of this chapter would be through the shared Organization tables.

These options illustrate both ends of a spectrum of needs. With that in mind, find the approach for integration that works best for whatever your needs might be—and be confident that you have the resources and flexibility to support your marketing endeavors and their inevitable changing needs.

Summary

We began this chapter by discussing general marketing requirements and identifying the subjects required to describe individual campaigns. We then created a basic database model, which we further refined to provide additional features and the flexibility to respond to future needs.

Once the campaign design was in place we suggested various querying options, both to extract useful marketing information via searching across the separate tables and to act upon the data, giving you a head start when large-scale data entry may be required.

We then explored use of the questionnaire, beginning with a very simplistic database and then using an increasingly complicated model. Finally, by adding subjects to the design, you learned how to provide further questionnaire functionality such as allowing for multiple option answers, distinct sections, and dependent questions.

It's important to remember that the role of these combined database designs is to accurately predefine and record the information of your marketing efforts for both current reference and historical purposes. An application built to use this database may even have features to assist your marketing efforts. For example, it might produce mail merge documents or send out mass e-mails but, for the most part, your database needs only to record that these events occurred.

One of the benefits provided with Office 2007, is the capability to use Outlook to complete and return data questions via e-mail. So, if you create a questionnaire, you can now use Outlook to send it out and retrieve the results. You can choose to have the responses automatically incorporated in the database, view them individually, specify how many responses are entered automatically, and have the rest held.

You can leverage your newly gained skills for modeling a marketing campaign to help you record the data related to sales, which is the next and final chapter in this part of the book.

Sales is probably the most fundamental and comprehensive activity you need to consider when modeling a business, because almost everyone is selling some sort of product, whether it is manufactured in-house or purchased from another company. This chapter concentrates on companies that perform direct sales, whether they manufacture the products themselves or acquire them from a supplier or parent organization.

Sales is also a broad and varied subject—too broad and varied to consider the nuances for all sales options in one chapter, so here we give you the foundation for building a database tailored to your needs by using generic examples that can be applicable in concept and structure to whatever type of organization you are modeling.

Because you are modeling, at least in part, a *process*, this chapter provides an example of a *transactional* application. That means you will capture data about *events* as well as objects. Events (or processes) can age, and this chapter's example provides a way to manage that.

Almost every sales process will involve three core subjects: the customer, the order, and the product. As we create the database, the data related to these will be organized into tables. In addition, you need to consider the vendors that you purchase products from, business rules associated with a franchise, and any other factors that control or impact sales. Also, the sales process might include the need to create quotes and issue invoices. You will also want to be able to query the data to determine if payment has been received.

You begin by considering a company's individual requirements.

> **NOTE** Although services can also be sold, this chapter explains how to model the data associated with sales of products; Chapter 10, "Services," is focused on the sales of services.

Building the Model

Whether the database application is for your own use, for an organization, or for an individual, one of the first steps is to establish the overall purpose of the database and the critical objectives that it must accomplish. In identifying the data associated with sales, you will need to record information about both the processes and the items involved. You must identify all of the information that a company needs to record about themselves, their customers, their products, and anything else that forms a part of the sales process. This is often called *requirements gathering*. We've included some suggestions for this process in Appendix BB, "Gathering Requirements."

Although the sales order itself can be thought of as a somewhat abstract concept or a processing *event*, it will be the pivotal focus of the database. It is not an action of the kind that might be defined by a relationship. The sale has a very particular set of details all its own. These details must be identified before you actually begin designing the database itself.

Gathering Specification Data

The tables in your database will represent real-world components of the company's sales process. Management and staff understand the process of a sale, and that information needs to be extracted and converted into tables and records that will accurately model and support all of the business processes—and function efficiently to meet the users' needs.

Obtaining Information

You must consider the following core requirements, which may or may not be easily discerned from interviews with the intended users.

For our example, we will develop a database to support the sales tracking needs of a hypothetical organization: ABC Group. ABC Group manufactures and sells a range of products called *Magic Binders*. In response to your initial queries, they inform you that they have wholesale prices and quantities for sales to companies, and retail prices for sales to individuals. The Magic Binders are available in a range of models, so any sales order may include one or more models. They also allow salespeople to give special discounts in order to close a deal, essentially making the extended price less than the sum of the line item totals. And, as a further complication, the price of any type of Magic Binder can vary frequently due to fluctuation in factors such as manufacturing costs. However, once an order is established the price is set, so a subsequent change in product costs will not affect the existing order.

Without additional prompting, that is as much information as you might ordinarily receive from an initial visit with a company. But, to properly design your database, you will also need to get answers to the following questions:

- What details do they keep about customers, whether they are organizations or individuals?

- What details do they maintain that describe the products?

- Do the customer organizations or individuals have more than one address—for example, a delivery address and an invoice address?

- Is such an address specified when the order is made or is it a matter of record and part of the customer file?

- What details do you require for phone numbers and e-mail addresses? Will customers have more than one each?

- Is there a separate price list for wholesale versus retail orders? Are the values calculated differently? For example, wholesale prices may be 80% of retail prices. Is there a discount based on quantity?

- Do the different models of Magic Binders differ in price? This may seem obvious but it needs to be stated.

- Can an order ever consist of both wholesale and retail components?

- Can the same customer place either wholesale or retail orders at different times?

- Does tax at the time of order need to be recorded?

- Does the tax rate vary according to the type of order?

- Are delivery charges included? Does quantity, size, weight, or total price affect delivery charges? Do you need to accommodate expediting delivery?

- What's the largest quantity of a product that can be ordered?

- When offering special terms, does the salesperson offer a discount amount to be subtracted from the invoice after the invoice total is recorded, such as listed in a price adjustment, or is the discount reflected in the total price to be charged?

- Can a wholesale order be sold to an individual or must wholesale orders be to a company? If you can sell wholesale to an individual who is representing a company, how will you determine the appropriate contact information and account to bill?

▪ Can a product be ordered twice in the same order? For example, if a customer's request for Magic Binders is listed as "100 Extra-Long , 200 Short, and 50 Extra-Long," should the Extra-Long variety be restated as single entry of 150? In this scenario, might the original order list indicate the need to accommodate different pricing for specific packaging or packages? Perhaps the last 50 were older models or the packaging had been damaged.

▪ Do you record the actual delivery date of the order? Do you indicate and store an expected delivery date?

▪ Are orders invoiced individually or collected into batches?

▪ Do invoices have a fixed period for payment? If so, from what date—when the invoice is issued or when the product is delivered? Or can it be based on terms in wholesale customer accounts?

Questions like these often elicit other requirements for information that will influence the model's design. It is up to you, the developer, to flesh out as many of these details as possible. Try to ensure that your questions are answered with the level of detail discussed in the following paragraphs for the hypothetical ABC Group.

At ABC Group, wholesale orders are currently charged at 75% of the price of retail orders. This means that only one price or the other needs to be stored. Each product will have its own price, though some products may have the same price. A 7% tax is only charged on retail orders; there is no tax on wholesale.

Although a given customer may purchase at either wholesale or retail, a specific order can only be one or the other. Since it is rare for customers to change sales types, a default should be established when the customer record is created. This might be based on the customer being an organization or an individual. Although additional areas of categorization may also be beneficial to facilitate customer support, marketing and product planning, we will stick with the basics for our example.

Retail customers rarely represent repeat business whereas wholesale customers are highly repetitive customers. You should try to discern this sort of information during the initial requirements gathering process when interviewing the people who will be using the database.

Another important factor is that there is currently no capability to fill an order for greater than 25,000 of any type of Magic Binder. Also, delivery is included at a fixed rate for the entire order, one rate for wholesale and a different rate for retail. Further, wholesale customers will often have a delivery address that differs from the invoice address. Although this could be entered at order time, the information will be obtained manually from other customer paper records. A similar approach will be used if the customer has multiple phone numbers and e-mail addresses.

When a customer places an order, a salesperson quotes a fixed price based on the stored price of the items being ordered. Since more products may be added before the order is completed, the discount is not calculated until after all items are listed. When all the items are listed, the total price of the products ordered is calculated to determine the recommended total for the order.

Keep in mind, though, that there might be additional factors to determine the final order price. The price may vary based on the customer, particularly if it is a wholesale customer. And you will need to determine if the quantity of a specific product warrants a discount. If the process allows the same item to be listed multiple times, you will need a method of determining if the total number for the product should be discounted. As you can see, allowing multiple entries for a product can introduce significant complications, so we need to clearly define the related business rules in order to implement them correctly.

NOTE When designing for your actual requirements, you need to be sure that the pricing policy is explicitly stated and that each factor is listed. This is critical to ensuring that they are correctly implemented in the database. Pricing policies may not be enforceable purely by the database design but instead require application user interface logic. For examples of user interfaces see Chapter 14, "Implementing the Models."

When orders are placed, ABC Groups provides and records the expected delivery date. The actual delivery date will also be recorded as the two dates provided useful data points for analyzing processes. Invoices are issued for each wholesale order, and 60 days after the invoice is issued they are flagged as overdue. For wholesale orders, invoice and due dates are based on the date of delivery. However, retail orders must be paid in full before delivery, even if a deposit was made. As you can see, there is a lot of information to be documented about invoicing and delivery policies. These details are important and are the basis for business rules that your database must comply with and enforce.

At this point, you have an initial set of details, but requirements gathering is an iterative process, and at times even repetitive. For example, perfectly reasonable questions could still be, "Can you confirm that you need to store only retail or wholesale prices? Are you confident that the other price can always be calculated from the price stored? Can you conceive of a scenario where this won't be the case?" If so, you may need a method to accommodate exceptions.

You could also verify other aspects of the process that haven't been explicitly stipulated. For example, although it is not stated, you could infer that delivery charges can also change over time but that they become fixed when the order is placed. Even if it seems redundant, you should explicitly confirm such details.

This confirmation is important before you finalize the database design. Even if you are designing the database for yourself, you still need to ask these questions and note as many precise business rules and information needs as possible. As the designer, you are at liberty to choose the table structure, or schema, that you feel is appropriate to satisfy these rules and requirements. For example, you might choose to create a design in which both retail and wholesale prices can be entered into the database rather than have one calculated from the other. As long as the requirements are satisfied, you can "future-proof" the design to whatever extent is appropriate and fits within your timetable and budget. This can be balanced against the difficulties of making future changes.

Identifying the Requirements

After gathering all the preliminary information, you must ultimately be able to create a list so that you can represent each of the requirements in the database. Some will be related to others, and may even be consequences of others. You will be able to identify some of the requirements directly from your interviews, while others may be inferred from the possibilities mentioned above. You will even identify many factors that may become recorded as potential future considerations. Even the decisions that seem obvious to you will still need to be documented.

Based on the scenario described, we came up with the following basic list of requirements for the imaginary ABC Group.

- Customers can be either organizations or individuals.
- The names of both organizations and individuals must be stored.
- Customers may have several addresses.
- Customers can be categorized.
- Orders must be dispatched to the customer's delivery address.
- Invoices must be sent to a customer's appropriate address.
- The contact for the customer order must be recorded if known.
- Orders will be processed as either wholesale or retail.
- No order can contain both wholesale and retail components. (However, you can create separate orders for each type at the same time.)
- An order is limited to 25,000 units of any one product.
- Organizations and individuals may buy wholesale.

- Wholesale order product prices are 75% of retail, but this may change.

- The tax rate is different for wholesale orders versus retail orders.

- Tax is currently 7% for retail, 0% for wholesale; and these rates may change. (See note below about tax rates.)

- The rate of tax is fixed at the time the order is placed.

- The total price of an order is not necessarily equal to the sum of the extended product prices; adjustments and discounts may be given.

- A range of distinct products are available at individual prices.

- Products are grouped into parent categories.

- Products will have a description and line number; the prices may vary over time.

- The price of a product is fixed at the time the order is placed.

- A single product will only be listed one time in the order details. That means that you cannot have two prices for the same product in the same order.

- Delivery is charged at a fixed rate based on the order type: wholesale or retail.

- Delivery charges can vary over time, but the delivery rate is a flat rate and it is fixed when the order is placed.

- The expected delivery date of the order must be recorded.

- The actual delivery date of the order must be recorded.

- An invoice must be created for each wholesale order.

- An invoice will only be created for a wholesale order.

- Retail orders require full payment prior to delivery.

- Order details must include the order date, order type, due date, actual date, invoiced date, total price for the products, and either the amount paid or an indicator that the order is complete and closed.

- Payment due date for wholesale orders is based on the date the invoice is created.

- Invoices require a "date created" to determine when payments are overdue.

The preceding list for our hypothetical company is an example of what you might generate during your interview process. Once completed, your actual list should be confirmed with your established contact and signed off on as accurately describing the key factors and actions of the database. Even if your document is not comprehensive on your first attempt, it still provides a useful foundation for expanding the information later.

Identifying the Key Subjects

As the requirements gathering continues, the key elements involved in the process become apparent and will form the basis for the tables in your database. No matter how you go about the requirements gathering process, it must end with grouping of conceptually similar data. You can group the items and details as you go, or you can wait until you have your universe of requirements before breaking it into details and creating groups.

> **NOTE** Before we go any further, it seems important to mention that this chapter takes a slightly different approach than the rest of the chapters. In order to discuss some rather complex examples, we assume that you've gained a general understanding of relational data terminology and principles. So instead of sticking with general business terms and descriptions, we are jumping right in to the database design. We'll be referring to the tables, fields, and data types, and using proper naming conventions in the figures.
>
> As a bonus, we've also included some more advanced material. To help you visualize and understand how to retrieve data from multiple tables, we have provided some queries in both their graphic (design) view and written (SQL) forms. We also explain how the results—the data retrieved by the query—are affected by the relationship between the tables.
>
> We hope that the style and examples here help build more confidence in your ability to design a database structure for more complex scenarios. You shouldn't expect to instantly grasp every concept or to be fluent in interpreting queries. The point is to have the exposure when you have the benefit of being guided through the process.
>
> If you aren't familiar with database terminology or with the rules for relational data design, we encourage you to take a moment to review Chapter 3, "Relational Data Model." You will also find some valuable guidance on field properties and relationships in Appendixes A, "Field Properties," and B, "Relationships, Joins, and Nulls."

The requirements list clearly identifies rules governing the three main subjects of our model: customers, orders, and products. These are merely the starting point for the final data model as other subjects may become apparent during the design process. For example, the business rules that describe orders suggest inclusion of several data items for order date, the associated customer, product data, and price.

We also know that an order must be described by a type (retail or wholesale); and it will require some sort of reference number and potentially allow many products. Although we could put all this information in a single table, that would require duplicate fields for each product, price, and quantity, as shown in Table 7-1. This table structure is a violation of the table design rules for a relational database. (To learn more about how to properly design the tables and structure a relational database, we recommend that you review Chapter 3, which explains the more formal rules for normalization and the official meanings of the "normal forms.") In this chapter, we work towards a comfortable medium—to provide the explanation of how to properly design the tables, and to describe some alternatives and potential issues, without getting bogged down in formal terminology.

Table 7-1: Repeating Groups (Violation of Normalization)

FIELD	DATA TYPE
OrderID	AutoNumber
CustomerID	Long Integer
OrderDate	DateTime
Product1ID	Long Integer
Product1Price	Currency
Product1Quantity	Long Integer
Product2ID	Long Integer
Product2Price	Currency
Product2Quantity	Long Integer
. . .	. . .

These repeating groups represent a new subject that describes the products selected for an order, often known as "order details." If you have looked at other sales-based databases, such as the Northwind example that ships with Access, then it will come as no surprise that the core subjects, which will become the tables in our sales database, can be boiled down to the following:

- Customers
- Products
- Orders
- Order Details

These are related as shown in the relationship diagram in Figure 7-1. Their relationships can be described as:

- Customers have a one-to-many relationship with orders (a customer can have many orders, but an order can belong to only one customer).

- Orders have a one-to-many relationship with order details (an order may have many products included, but each one belongs to that one order).

- Products have a one-to-many relationship with order details. (A product may be included in many order detail rows but each detail record contains only one product.)

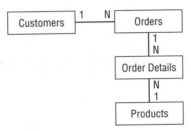

Figure 7-1: Simplified relationship diagram

NOTE Orders and Products share a *many-to-many relationship*. Simply put, that means that an order can contain many products and a product can appear in many orders.

Access does not directly support such a relationship between two tables. To resolve the relationship, we use an intermediate, or junction, table linked to each side of the many-to-many relationship. The order details serves as the junction table between orders and products.

The following sections explain the decisions made for each core subject. These subjects may require several tables to store the related information and they may also rely on data in other tables.

Designing the Tables

Using the simple, core subjects listed above, we now examine the required design with the goal of accurately modeling the data as it represents the business processes. We consider the consequences of the choices as we proceed. The first observation is that not all of the identified core subjects actually contain data about other subjects; so these can be represented by a single table.

NOTE Other chapters in this book describe a practice of including some standard fields, such as CreatedOn, CreatedBy, FieldChangedBy, FieldChangedOn. These fields can be just as applicable to a sales or any other database design and you're free to add them to your own implementation. However to keep the focus on the sales specific issues, we won't include them by default in the tables in this chapter.

Customers

As described earlier in this chapter, the customer requirements clearly suggest that at least two fields are needed: ReferenceNumber and DateRegistered. In addition you will likely need extra functional fields, such as a general-purpose Notes field and a flag which can be used to indicate that a customer is no longer active. Using a Yes/No field as a flag to mark a customer as inactive preserves the data for reporting purposes but can conveniently remove the customer from lookup lists. You should always consider future consequences before allowing any type of records to be deleted. One alternative is to use the Yes/No flag as a means of inserting an asterisk before the names of inactive customers and then sort those names at the end of the list.

Customer Options

As stated in the list of requirements earlier in this chapter, a customer can be either an individual or an organization. One obvious potential design is to have both types of customers as a single subject—however that introduces some significant challenges as it does not comply with the normalization principles as discussed in Chapter 3. Instead, you can create two tables that are specifically designed, one for individuals and one for organizations. How these relate to the Customer table is then an issue of great importance.

The concept of how a customer can be represented is important to several chapters and examples in this book. To provide you with greater design flexibility we have presented some options and examples in Appendix C, "Resolving Relationship Triangles." That way, you can determine the approach that works best for a specific scenario and incorporate the applicable tables and forms into your solution.

One Table for All Customers

To better focus on the sales-specific issues, we have deliberately chosen a basic Customer table design and given you the option to modify the tables based on an alternative design from Appendix C that might better suit the specific needs of your scenario. We will assume that any customer can be represented as an organization, but we will stipulate that an organization must be able to include related contact individuals. That will allow us to represent either type of customer in a basic, but sufficiently versatile, way. The result is the single Customer table shown in Table 7-2.

Table 7-2: Fields for tblCustomer

FIELD NAME	DATA TYPE	DESCRIPTION
CustomerID	AutoNumber	Primary key
CustomerName	Text	Customer company-type name
CustomerReference	Text	Assigned identifying reference
DateRegistered	Date/Time	Date became customer
CustomerInactive	Yes/No	Retired customer record

An advantage of maintaining customer data in a single Customer table is that the details are not separated based upon the type of customer—so you can find all of the base information in one table.

To record all the details about an individual, you will need a related table, tblCustomerIndividual. As you have seen in other examples in this book, this type of table structure uses a one-to-many relationship with the Customer table by placing the primary key from tblCustomer, CustomerID, as a foreign key in tblCustomerIndividual. The main fields are shown in Table 7-3.

Table 7-3: Fields for tblCustomerIndividual

FIELD NAME	DATA TYPE	DESCRIPTION
CustomerIndividualID	AutoNumber	Primary key
CustomerID	Long Integer	Foreign key to Customer table
Title	Text	Individual's title
LastName	Text	Surname
MiddleName	Text	Middle name/initials
FirstName	Text	First name(s)
BirthDate	Date/Time	Date of birth

If it is of value, you can further describe the individual within the context of the customer organization using a Role field or, to be more rigorous, a related

Role table referenced from the Customer Individual table. The relationship between the two main tables can be seen in Figure 7-2. The Role table is included in Figure 7-3.

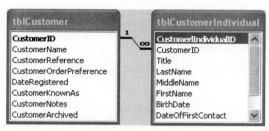

Figure 7-2: Simple customer model table relationship

This core customer pair of tables can be substituted with one of the more rigorous models offered in Appendix C. However, these alone don't describe everything we need to store about customers and their related data, so we next consider the other requirements and what customer-related subjects we have yet to implement.

In the requirements we identified the explicit need for storing multiple addresses per customer—for example, separate addresses for delivery and invoicing. This requirement extends to include the same consideration for other contact mechanisms such as e-mail addresses and phone numbers. These related customer contact subjects each form a table of their own: tblCustomerAddress, tblCustomerEMail, and tblCustomerPhone, which can be seen related to the Customer table in Figure 7-3.

We must also consider categorization of customers and, although a single field could allow for a descriptive category for the customer, a dedicated table listing all possible categories offers a more robust and user friendly selection. The resulting table tblCategory, shown in Table 7-4, uses a junction table, tblCustomerCategory, to relate to the customer.

Table 7-4: Fields for tblCategory

FIELD NAME	DATA TYPE	DESCRIPTION
CategoryID	AutoNumber	Primary key
CategoryName	Text	Identifying descriptive name
CategoryInactive	Yes/No	Field to mark category as inactive
CategoryNotes	Memo	Detailed notes on the purpose

The junction table tblCustomerCategory is shown in Table 7-5, and can be seen related to the customer in Figure 7-3.

Table 7-5: Fields for tblCustomerCategory

FIELD NAME	DATA TYPE	DESCRIPTION
CustomerCategoryID	AutoNumber	Primary key
CustomerID	Long Integer	Foreign key to Customer table
CategoryID	Long Integer	Foreign key to Category table
CustomerCategoryNotes	Memo	Optional notes on the association

Based on our interviews, requirements, and business rules, we now have a sound foundation for the customer information that needs to be managed. Even our simple model requires related tables for address, e-mail, and telephone contact details, but, should you choose to expand your customer tables, these related customer tables are still just as applicable. Figure 7-3 provides the relationship view of the customer tables that we have implemented. This design is avaliable in the file `Sales.mdb` for this chapter on the book's CD.

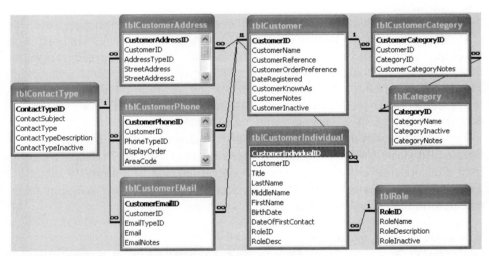

Figure 7-3: Customer detail tables and relationships

Products

We are now ready to review the requirements and details associated with products, continuing with the fictitious ABC Group and Magic Binders.

Required Product Fields

Based on our earlier analysis, we know that we will have both a product and a product category. We start by creating an initial list of fields based on the details that are directly related to each of those subjects.

The fields comprising the Product table, at least initially, include the current price as well as Name, line number, description, and a field indicating the current status of the product, ProductInactive. Based on the established requirements and the database designer's common sense for anticipated business needs, the Product table can be defined as shown in Table 7-6.

Table 7-6: Fields for the Product Table

FIELD NAME	DATA TYPE	DESCRIPTION
ProductID	AutoNumber	Primary key
ProductCategoryID	Long Integer	Foreign key to Category table
ProductName	Text	Product name
ProductLineNo	Text	Identifying number of product
ProductDescription	Text	Descriptive text
ProductRetailPrice	Currency	Current price of product listed
ProductNotes	Memo	Optional user-entered notes
ProductInactive	Boolean	Flag indicating "current" status

The CategoryID field is the foreign key to a related tblProductCategory table, as shown in Figure 7-4. If a category is mandatory for every product, then this field should be set as Required because, as stated earlier, referential integrity enforced by the relationship is not enough to dictate that a value must be present.

Figure 7-4: Relationship of the Product and Product Category tables

The ProductRetailPrice field holds the current price for the given product in a retail transaction. The requirements discussed earlier in this chapter specified that the wholesale price differs from this by a fixed percentage. Thus, storing the retail price alone is sufficient. But if the relative differences were not fixed across all products, then either another field for wholesale prices or a separate table to record the prices of the different types would be required.

Orders

The order is the central subject in our example design. It relates to the other subjects directly or indirectly and requires several data fields to provide all of the necessary details. Many of the requirements referring to orders are actually relevant only to the Order Detail table. Below are the items that become our Order fields that describe the order itself.

Required Order Fields

Based on the requirements that we listed earlier, you can determine that the Order table will require the fields shown in Table 7-7.

Table 7-7: Fields for the Order table

FIELD NAME	DATA TYPE	DESCRIPTION
OrderID	AutoNumber	Primary key
CustomerID	Long Integer	Foreign key to Customer table
CustomerContactID	Long Integer	Foreign key to contact in CustomerIndividual table
DeliveryAddressID	Text	Foreign key to Customer address table related to delivery
OrderType	Text	Wholesale or retail
OrderNo	Text	Identifiable reference number for the order
OrderDate	DateTime	Date order was created
OrderPrice	Currency	Total price agreed upon for goods
OrderTax	Double	Rate of tax at that time for the type Order Type
OrderDeliveryCharge	Currency	Defined delivery charge
OrderAmountPaid	Currency	Amount paid by the customer

FIELD NAME	DATA TYPE	DESCRIPTION
OrderDeliveryExpected	DateTime	Expected delivery date
OrderDeliveryDate	DateTime	Actual delivery date
OrderComplete	Boolean	Flag to indicate closed status
OrderNotes	Memo	Optional user-entered notes

In reviewing the fields for this table, we can also consider some concepts that you can apply to similar situations, such as storing the delivery address in a central table for addresses to accommodate a customer having multiple delivery addresses, not just more than one type of business addresses. We will also provide some examples of when you may need to use an alternative approach or table structure to that provided in our example.

NOTE Instead of providing multiple delivery address fields, included is the DeliveryAddressID field relating to a selected address record, which in turn is related to a given customer. This precludes duplicated data from addresses entered directly into orders. It requires use of an address record that already exists or that can be entered for a first-time customer. This would theoretically make our CustomerID redundant, and technically a fully normalized table would not include both. Only the DeliveryAddressID would be required. However, application requirements can override normalization rules at times. For example, when order records are first created, the delivery address might not be available while clearly the customer must be known. The CustomerContactID is not a required field and hence would not be a similar candidate.

The OrderTaxRate field is created to hold both the value of tax at the time of the order and the appropriate type of order. The requirements established different rates for wholesale and retail orders. The current tax rates will be stored in an administrative, or configuration, table containing such important values. This is sometimes a table with several, seemingly unrelated fields and only one record. It can be used to store data such as company logo, tax rate, bank routing, and other data that should have only one value and restrictions on who can change it. We discuss that in more detail later in this chapter.

This structure allows users to look up the appropriate value and preserve it with the order record. Although this may appear to be a clear case of redundant data, it is indeed storing a unique value for this particular record. Keep in mind that a table holding the current tax rates is dynamic, whereas the OrderTaxRate value is a deliberate snapshot of the rate at the time the order was placed. Therefore, subsequent reviews of the order will not use a different tax rate, and the integrity of the data regarding the amount the customer actually paid is maintained.

> **NOTE**   This type of scenario is quite common in sales, production, and other business models. For example, if you allow the sales price to be adjusted, you might store the sale price per item instead of the adjusted total price. So although we admonish against storing duplicate data, you will encounter several situations that require careful consideration to determine if the data is indeed unique to the record rather than repeating a value that can easily be obtained elsewhere.

Invoice data consists largely of order data, but in reviewing the requirements it is clear that not every order will require an invoice. Retail orders require payment in advance and do not have an invoice. Although the few additional data fields for an invoice could be included in the Orders table without breaking normalization rules, you can also introduce an Invoice table related to the order on the OrderID, as shown in Figure 7-5.

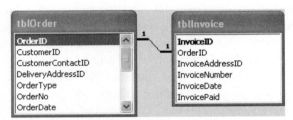

Figure 7-5: Relationship of the Order and Invoice tables

As we learned from indentifying the business rules and the requirements, the OrderPrice field is not redundant data as it might initially seem. Although it is based on the total of the ordered products, the salesperson is free to negotiate and arrive at an independent price, so you cannot rely on calculating the value. In addition to this, the OrderPrice field alone doesn't constitute the entire amount that the customer has to pay; there may be adjustments, taxes, service fees, and other considerations.

Consequences and Alternative Fields

Before you can determine how much the customer is required to pay, the total price to the customer for the order must be calculated. This will include the extended price for the products and the adjustments given by the sales person, plus the tax and any delivery fees. Keep in mind that your business model may be different. For example you may need to accommodate variable tax rates or you may have some product items that are taxable while others are not. You may also need to allow for adjustments and fees in addition to delivery charges.

Since our sales model incorporates all price adjustments into the value stored as OrderPrice, the tax, if any, will be levied against the OrderPrice, as indicated in the second factor in our calculation, shown below. Essentially, the price the customer must pay is the sum of three values, the OrderPrice, the OrderTax, and the OrderDelivery, as shown in the following calculation:

```
OrderPrice + (OrderTax * OrderPrice) + OrderDelivery
```

This returns the price for the given requirements of our example only. Other scenarios may see a non-flexible OrderPrice, using a discount field instead to allow alterations or relying totally on the flexible entries in the order details to total up to a desired amount.

> **NOTE** You might require a different basis for your tax calculation—check with your state and local jurisdictions, or any other agency that controls the taxes that you must collect and report. Your model might also need to cater for tax applied at the product level rather than the order as a whole, in which case the tax field would be an item in the Order Detail table, where it would be applied or not as required.
>
> Additionally, if the total of the products ordered will invariably be the price charged for the order, then you do not need a flexible OrderPrice field. In that case, storing this data would then indeed be duplication and a poor design. Alternatively, if it better aligns with your business model you could include a Discount field on the complete order to offer the customer a reduced rate upon the total of the product prices.

As a general rule, you will want to round the calculation of tax value to two decimal places to align with the other currency values to which it will be added and compared. By specifying in code that the numbers are rounded, you can avoid minor discrepancies in the total of very large orders. The differences, which can create havoc with customers and accounting processes, are a direct result of rounding. You can learn more about how data types and field properties effect calculations and rounding from Appendix A.

Since we are not storing the value for the order total, you will also need to use this calculation for rounding in any query used to determine the total price of an order. For example, if you want to know if an order has been paid in full, you will need to calculate the total price of the order, and then compare that to the payment recorded.

> **NOTE** Becoming comfortable with the SQL of queries isn't a requirement to building effective databases, but it can become a great asset and we show you more in due course.

ORDER PRICE QUERIES

Order price is a user-entered value for the charge for the products ordered. The amount the customer actually owes must be calculated by adding that to any due tax and delivery charges. This calculation is essentially:

```
OrderPrice + (OrderTax * OrderPrice) + OrderDeliveryCharge
```

The OrderTax field is stored as a fractional percentage which we need to multiply by the OrderPrice to determine the amount of tax to charge. Since we want currency values, it's worth rounding this value to two decimal places. This is then summed with the other prices. However, in databases if any field value is null (i.e. of an unknown value, equivalent to not having entered a value) then any operation performed upon it will result in null. (For more about database topics see Chapter 3 and Appendix B). To protect against this we use a function called Nz which allows us to perform a replacement on any null values.

To query for those orders that have not yet been fully paid, we can request records where the total amount due (as calculated above) is less than the amount paid by the customer. This query would look like the following figure.

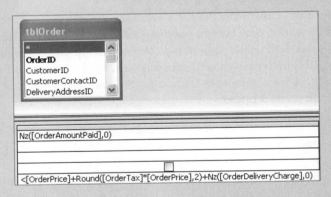

This appears in SQL view as the equivalent statement:

```
SELECT * FROM tblOrder
WHERE Nz(OrderAmountPaid, 0) <
    OrderPrice + Round(OrderTax * OrderPrice, 2)
    + Nz(OrderDeliveryCharge, 0)
```

There are times when a customer may have made payment in full before the complete order has been delivered or when you need to treat the order as closed or complete even though there is a balance remaining. But if you rely solely on the comparison of payment total to equal the order total as the indicator of the final order status, you will not have a means to identify the incomplete orders that are paid in full or the closed orders that have uncollectable balances.

One approach to overcome this is to add a Yes/No (check box) type field (OrderComplete) to indicate if an order should be treated as complete. You could then have users check the box if the order has received full payment or if they expect no further payment. This might be the case for a customer that has gone out of business, so the payment will never be received. The Yes/No field also makes it easy for you to query the data and list orders that are either complete or incomplete. You could also use this field in combination with the calculation for balance remaining to identify orders to which you might want to make adjustments to write-off the balance.

COMPLETED ORDERS

To create a query that returns those orders that are complete, you start with a new query and add the Orders table. Choose the fields you want to return and then apply the criteria on the OrderComplete field as in the figure.

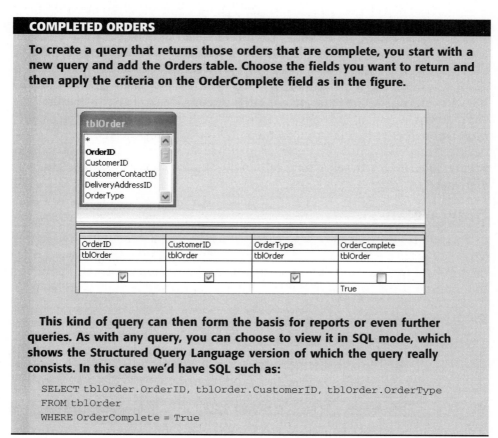

This kind of query can then form the basis for reports or even further queries. As with any query, you can choose to view it in SQL mode, which shows the Structured Query Language version of which the query really consists. In this case we'd have SQL such as:

```
SELECT tblOrder.OrderID, tblOrder.CustomerID, tblOrder.OrderType
FROM tblOrder
WHERE OrderComplete = True
```

Employing this simple Yes/No field to indicate that an order is complete or closed will often appeal to users. However, although ease of use is a major consideration for the user interface, it should not be your primary motivation for including a field or type of field in the table structure. Instead, you need to consider the bigger picture—because there might be other options that are better suited to your overall business needs and will offer greater benefits for the users.

Although we're currently only concerned with a completed status, another option would be to create the OrderComplete field as a different type of status field. For example, you might want to identify different stages of progress. In that case, you would create a table to store the list of status options and use it as a lookup table. Then, this field would become a foreign key to the new related Status table. This would enable you to indicate the order status such as prospective, confirmed, completed, cancelled, or returned.

The mention of "returned" prompts another consideration. Although you may have a specific policy for handling the return of an entire order, you may also need a way to accommodate the return of an individual item and relate it to the original order.

In addition, you might consider including a field in your table to display an order number to your users. You may want to include some specific formatting that combines several values to indicate the year, the store location, and the order sequence for that location. To this, you may want to add a suffix to indicate the purpose of the order, such as allowance, return, disputed, or supplement. These are just a few of the things that you may want to consider in order to modify the design to better suit your business needs.

Unfortunately, there aren't enough pages in this book to cover every likely action associated with sales, but you can modify the chapter examples to meet your needs.

Order Detail

OrderDetail is the only core subject for which we can list all of the details in a single table. The table tblOrderDetail provides the quantity and current price of each item ordered and includes the links to the related information, such as the product name. Although it does a lot, the table itself is quite simple.

Required Order Detail Fields

The fields that you need to include in the table OrderDetail are listed in Table 7-8.

Table 7-8: Fields for the OrderDetail Table

FIELD NAME	DATA TYPE	DESCRIPTION
OrderDetailID	AutoNumber	Primary key
OrderID	Long Integer	Foreign key to Order table
ProductID	Long Integer	Foreign key to Product table
Order DetailQuantity	Long Integer	Quantity of product type ordered
Order DetailtemPrice	Currency	Product item price at the time order was placed
OrderDetailNotes	Memo	Optional user-entered notes

In looking at the list of fields, it may seem that they are all self-explanatory and require little thought. However, that isn't necessarily the case. In fact, this table provides us with a good opportunity to explore some of the options for number fields and their implications.

We'll start with the data type for the DetailQuantity field. We chose a Long Integer based on the requirement that "an order may consist of up to 25,000 products." An integer data type has a maximum value of 32,767. This is enough to satisfy immediate requirements, but you also have an option to use the 2-byte Integer field size or the 4-byte Long Integer, which will accommodate needs that exceed 32,727.

With that in mind, you would want to consider what your business model allows for the upper end for the possible number of orders in a year and the potential for business expansion. Then add to that the likelihood that your application may be used for years to come. Clearly, if you anticipate any potential for even approaching the maximum values for an Integer, you should certainly take steps to avoid problems by choosing a different data type. This is just one of the choices that you will need to consider throughout your design process.

Another requirement on order details is that "a single product type may not be entered twice on the same order." Within the table structure, that means there can be no duplication of the ProductID within the same order. At the database level we can enforce the prevention of duplicate values by using a unique index. In this case, a unique index upon the ProductID field alone would prevent the same product from ever being ordered twice—regardless of the order. Obviously, that is not what we want to happen.

What we need to do is limit the restriction to a single order. We accomplish this by creating a unique index across two fields: the OrderID and the ProductID. This can be achieved by using the table designer or with a data definition query. We explain the table designer more in Appendix C, so for now we'll just show you the interface. Figure 7-6 illustrates how a unique index, idxOrderProduct, is based on both the OrderID and the ProductID.

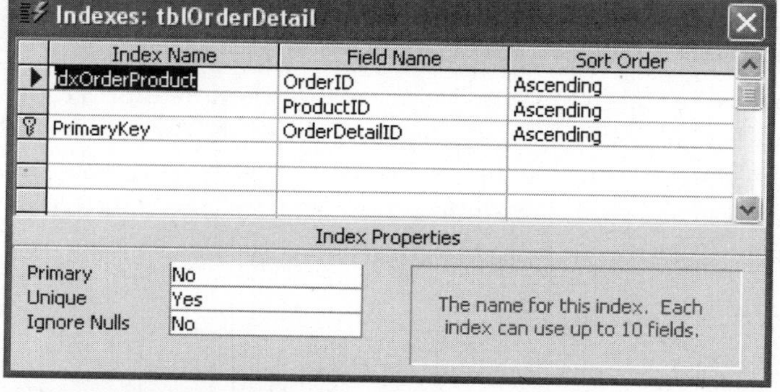

Figure 7-6: Multi-field unique index

By stipulating that the Index Property is Unique, the combination of the two fields will be unique, but the value of each field can be repeated numerous times in the table. Again there is a SQL alternative method to create data objects such as this index. In this case you would use the following syntax; either method provides the same result.

```
CREATE UNIQUE INDEX idxOrderProduct ON tblProductDetail
  (OrderID, ProductID)
```

Snapshot Data and the Lookup Alternative

The DetailItemPrice field is another instance of a field stored in a table whose value is based upon a field stored in another table. However, this is not truly duplicate data because the business rules mandate that the price of a product at the time of ordering must be stored. Therefore, although the order item price (DetailItemPrice) starts out the same as the product price (ProductRetailPrice) listed in the Product table, those two numbers are not likely to remain equal. Since the price as listed in a specific line item will not change over time, the values will diverge as prices get updated in the ProductRetailPrice field.

NOTE In a database such as Access, copying the value of a field is done through the user interface. In other words, it will also be your responsibility to provide the functionality in your forms to allow the user to look up the current price value and insert it into the Order Detail record. This is typically accomplished using a combo box. In this example, the Product table stores a value assuming the retail price. However, you will recall that wholesale orders are charged at 75% of retail. For those orders, a subsequent calculation must be performed before the value can be saved as part of the Order Detail.

Some database developers prefer to implement an alternative design to storing the current price in the Order Detail record. One option is that instead of preserving a snapshot of the product price, you can provide a schema whereby the price of a product would have to be calculated each time that it is used. This requires that every time the price of an item changes, you must preserve the price and the time of the change. As you can tell, this means that there could be an unlimited number of prices over time, which is accomplished by creating another table to store the price and the time that it took effect. Such a table would include the fields listed in Table 7-9. The table, tblPricePeriod, contains a field for the start date for a price. Since the price would be effective until a new date and price was entered for an item, the data range would be a calculation.

Table 7-9: Fields for the PricePeriod Table

FIELD NAME	DATA TYPE	DESCRIPTION
PricePeriodID	AutoNumber	Primary key
ProductID	Long Integer	Foreign key to Product table
PeriodBegin	DateTime	From date
ProductPrice	Currency	Product price for this time period

The Order Detail table would then store only the ProductID and the quantity. The calculations for product prices would use the date from the order. If you have lots of products and frequent price changes, you can imagine how quickly the PricePeriod table will grow. And you have another factor to consider—you will need to calculate the extended price and order total for every sales analysis report.

Although this design avoids the appearance of storing the same data in more than one location, it comes at the price of placing a greater burden on administration of the products in your application. Furthermore, it would prevent you from being able to make price adjustments. The operative phrase here is "the appearance of" since we have clearly illustrated that storing the sale price of an item does not duplicate the data stored as the product price.

Putting the Model Together

The `Sales.mdb` sample file for this chapter on this book's CD contains all of the tables that we have created so far. And there is only one table left to discuss: the Settings table, which we will use to store fixed value fields. At this point, this is only two fields, for the tax and the delivery charges that are used for lookup and insertion into detail rows on orders and quotes. This table is not necessarily related to any other table in the database, and there are several ways that it can be designed.

One option is to use a table that will have only one record, and it would have a field for each setting. The other option maintains a tall and thin table with fields to store the setting name and the associated value. See Chapter 16, "SQL Server and Other External Data Sources," for more detail on this table design topic.

Looking at the design of the first option provides an opportunity to explore field properties a little more. Our goal is to ensure that the table can only contain one record. This seems contrary to everything that we've seen, because all the tables thus far have been designed to contain essentially an unlimited number of records. But actually, with a little insider knowledge, you can easily force a table to be limited to a single-row. Simply create an Integer field and make it the primary key, which requires the value to be unique. Then, set the default value equal to 1 (=1) and include a validation rule that the field is always (=1), as shown for the field SettingID in Figure 7-7.

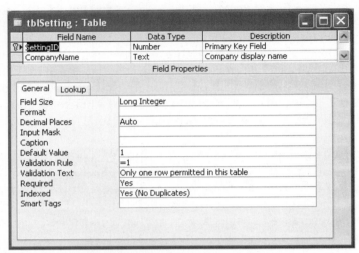

Figure 7-7: Field property settings that limit a table to one record

This combination of rules that the values must be unique (primary key) and yet must always be the same value, (in this case, 1), means that subsequent rows cannot be created. At least, you cannot create another row without changing one of these properties first. This can be applied to any similar table for which only a single row is required.

TIP   Many developers like to use "Administrative" or "Application" tables to store specific pieces of independent information that are limited to one value, rarely change, and are needed throughout the program. This might include your business number, bank routing number, business logo, and even the application name. Since each of these items can have only one value, they can all be stored in a single record. And, since they can have only one value at any given moment, you need to ensure that a second value cannot be stored. Therefore you need to ensure that the table can only have one record.

You can limit a table to contain one and only one record by using a specific combination of field property settings for the table's primary key. As shown in Figure 7-8, we are using a Long Integer, but you could use a different data type. The critical part is to set the default value for the field equal to what you set as the

validation rule; that forces it to be the only value allowed for that field. And, since the primary key must be a unique value, you can have one and only one record.

Again, in our example these are both 1. We also provide a nice message in the Validation Text in case a user finds a way to try to change the data stored as the primary key.

Once you have the necessary data in a table, you can use the values in countless ways. Typically, the data will be programmatically added to tables, forms and reports. This means that you will use code or set the default value of a field or control to the value of the field in your Settings table. This is just one of the many techniques that you will discover as you begin designing your own user interfaces. For now, we'll turn our focus back to the table structure and look at some other more advanced requirements and tables.

A More Complex Model

The example offered up to this point, though functional and adaptable to many types of sales-based databases, is not appropriate for all eventualities. You might have requirements that are more complex than the ones we've covered so far, so we will complicate the model further and demonstrate how you can modify the current example to better enable you to respond to additional needs.

First, let's get some additional requirements from ABC Group. You'll often face similar situations where you need to modify a database design. Perhaps it's that business needs have changed, or maybe you have not extracted sufficient information from all of the people who will be using the database or relying on the data. Be assured that when you are designing a database, more often than not you will discover a need for additional items as you and others begin using the application. Sometimes you just will not be able to ferret out every relevant piece of the puzzle regardless of how many questions you ask. This additional investment in the process as new requirements are added is known as *scope creep*. This will happen from time to time. Whether you are doing the development under contract, for an employer, or for yourself, remember that new scope also means that there will be an addition to previous estimates of time and budget. Project cost estimates must now change as a result.

Additional Requirements

ABC Group now offers their Magic Binders product in a variety of different grades. In fact, there are currently 10 grades: 15, 20, 25, 30, 35, 40, 50, 60, 75,

100; and new grades may be introduced in the future. But not every type of Magic Binder is necessarily available in every grade.

When an order is placed, the grade must be chosen for each product. And although it is possible for an order to include different grades of the same product, the same grade of a product can only be entered one time on an order.

After a price change occurs, a new printout of the current product list is created. It includes the types, grades, and categories of products. It also includes an image of each product. The stock image files are maintained on the server. The product list can also be printed in a brochure format.

During the order process, it is common for users to leave sticky notes on files for other users. Because a progression of notes can make unclear the order in which they occurred, it's important to maintain an accurate history of the notes. Some of these notes are critical and need to be brought to the attention of the people working with product orders; either when they are looking at a particular order or as an overview of all important notes.

It would be useful to know the type of note, such as a phone call, an important edit, and so on. As various comments are added together they can also provide a historic overview of the customer. In that case, the information is most useful when the notes are in chronological order. In order to serve both purposes, you will need to be able to group and sort the notes both by customer and by order.

It is also important to maintain a record of the employee who initiated the note as well as the employee who is responsible for an order. This is true for subsequent notes as well, so we will obviously need a full list of all employees, current, as well as past.

Occasionally, an employee will be required to give a customer or prospective customer an estimate or quote for a potential order. The products required for this prospective order must be listed with the prices, and a total order price must be provided. It should be possible to convert these quotes into orders when the customer accepts it.

With those business needs in mind, you will need to identify the key requirements. You might come up with a list similar to the following:

- There is a defined list of possible grades for the products, but not every product is available in every grade.

- The product grades may change as new grades are added.

- The different grades of each product are, or could potentially be, priced differently.

- The grade of product needs to be selected when ordering.

- An order may contain multiple grades of the same product; but cannot contain the same grade multiple times.

- Each product type has an image file stored on the server to be used for display purposes.

- A list of all company employees is required, both current and prior.

- Each order record must store the name of the employee who created it.

- Multiple notes may be attached to orders, to customers, and possibly to other subjects.

- The name of the employee making a note must be stored along with the note date, type, and a priority level.

One significant difference between this and the simpler model is the introduction of product grades. This fundamentally influences the design and assignment of products and their prices. A second significant difference is the emphasis on the use of notes.

Multiple Product Prices

Since we are now managing multiple grades for a product and allowing each grade to have a different price, you will need a mechanism for accommodating multiple prices for each product. The first step is to create a table to record all possible grades, which we will call tblProductGrade as shown in Table 7-10.

Table 7-10: Fields for the ProductGrade Table

FIELD NAME	DATA TYPE	DESCRIPTION
ProductGradeID	AutoNumber	Primary key
GradeName	Text	Simple name
GradeDescription	Text	Longer description
GradeInactive	Yes/No	Inactive= Yes; Active = No.

As you can see, we have only included the minimal number of fields. But, these provide the essential details about the grade: the name, which might be only the grade number, a description, and a flag to indicate if the grade is active. These are the only fields required for our example and they might be all that you need as well.

Since the price now depends on both the product and grade, you need to remove the price field, ProductRetailPrice, from the Product table. Consequently, you also need to create a table to store the price. In our example, it is called tblProductPrice and includes the fields that are shown in Table 7-11.

Table 7-11: Fields for the ProductPrice Table

FIELD NAME	DATA TYPE	DESCRIPTION
ProductPriceID	AutoNumber	Primary key
ProductID	Long Integer	Foreign key to Product table
ProductGradeID	Long Integer	Foreign key to Product Grade table
ProductPrice	Currency	Price for this product/grade

This provides the means by which to store a price for each required combination of product and grade. It also allows you to determine which combinations of product and grade are available, simply by the existence of records containing those combinations.

Previously, the Order Detail table required only a foreign key to the Product table, the new model reflects the choice of product and grade by a related entry from the product price table. Consequently the order detail stores the ProductPriceID and the overall structure appears as in Figure 7-8.

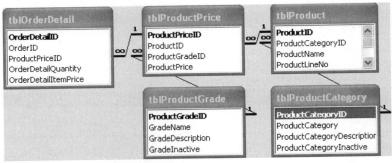

Figure 7-8: Product prices, including grade

MULTI-FIELD PRIMARY KEYS

In this book we have advocated implementing a single, AutoNumber surrogate primary key in all tables. There are advantages and disadvantages to almost any choice in databases, but this option makes for an excellent starting point. However it is entirely possible to include more than one field in an index, and in the primary key itself. In the additional CD file "c07Sales_ ComplexAlt.mdb" the product price table uses both the ProductID and ProductGradeID fields to form the primary key. This means that the foreign key in order details must also comprise of both of these fields. The relationships for this are shown in the following figure.

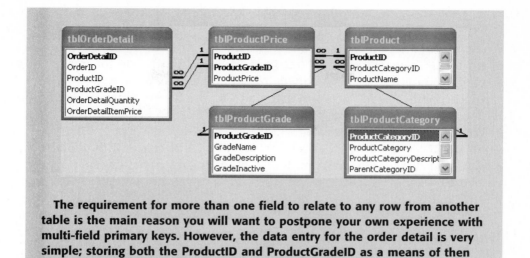

The requirement for more than one field to relate to any row from another table is the main reason you will want to postpone your own experience with multi-field primary keys. However, the data entry for the order detail is very simple; storing both the ProductID and ProductGradeID as a means of then looking up a related price will perhaps feel more natural than using a single field, ProductPriceID, as described in this section.

The previous multi-field index on tblOrderDetail across the OrderID and ProductID fields (shown in Figure 7-6) is now directly applicable by including the ProductPriceID field in the index instead to preserve the business rule that a specific product may be listed only one time per order.

NOTE The concept of product "grades" is used here to demonstrate how to manage more complex pricing requirements. In a real-world scenario, this could be almost any new product variable or property such as color or size. Any element of data regarding such an option for the product can be modeled in your design with a lookup table and a foreign key included as a new field in the ProductPrice table. In short, the core issue here isn't grades, but the existence of extra subjects affecting the price.

Product Images

Continuing with the product schema alterations, the requirement for an image can be handled very simply. In older versions of Access, many databases would implement an OLE Object field data type and use built-in Access functionality to insert images into this field type. This functionality is still available in Access today, but at the cost of very substantial file size bloat. In modern versions the Attachment data type is more appropriate because it compresses the physical file before storing it in the database.

Making use of an external image file can actually be as simple as storing the UNC path (complete listing of the computer, drive, directories, and file name) to that image file. Microsoft Access is now capable of binding an Image control to a ControlSource field that contains the file path, and the image will be displayed for users. This is equally true for images in forms or reports. You can incorporate this in our example by adding the ProductImageFile field to the Product table, as the image is another detail describing the product type, rather than being related to category, grade, or price.

Storing the text path can also save a great deal of space in the database, which still is fixed at the maximum of 2GB for an Access database. However, databases are getting better at compressing files, so you should choose the approach that works best for your situation.

Employees

An extremely common requirement in a database application is the list of employees, and this appears in the list of additional requirements earlier in this chapter. Although you might think that the information will be obtainable based on the user information for the computer operating system or Access application there are several reasons that you should not rely on that. The list of network, computer, and application will not usually include all of the current and past employees that may have worked with your customers.

In our simple model we have a table for customer individuals, and if we were to add the employee names to our database there will certainly be some similarity. There is no database design imperative that we must consolidate similar tables. However, consolidating similar data can make for convenient, searchable repositories of information, particularly in the instance of individuals data. To that end we can separate the person related fields of our existing Customer Individual table out into a new Individuals table. The resulting simplified searching can be used to determine if a person is already entered in the database, regardless of their role. As you can imagine, this greatly reduces the potential for recording someone's information in more than one place. Table 7-12 shows the new Individuals table.

And this leaves us with a Customer Individuals table which relates to the Individuals table and appears as in Table 7-13.

In addition to the standard individual type data, to represent employee information, we still need some employee specific data. We therefore create the Employee table to store additional details specific to employees, including their role and period of employment. We can link this table to the Individual table to store the name and contact information. The fields for the Employee table are listed in Table 7-14.

Table 7-12: Fields for tblIndividual

FIELD NAME	DATA TYPE	DESCRIPTION
IndividualID	AutoNumber	Primary key
Title	Text	Foreign key to Individual table
LastName	Text	Surname
MiddleName	Text	Middle name / initials
FirstName	Text	First name(s)
BirthDate	Date/Time	Date of birth
DateOfFirstContact	Date/Time	Optional first contact date

Table 7-13: Fields for tblCustomerIndividual

FIELD NAME	DATA TYPE	DESCRIPTION
CustomerIndividualID	AutoNumber	Primary key
CustomerID	Long Integer	Foreign key to Customer table
IndividualID	Long Integer	Foreign key to Individual table
RoleID	Long Integer	Foreign key to Role table
IndividualRoleDesc	Text	Description of specific duties

Table 7-14: Fields for the Employee Table

FIELD NAME	DATA TYPE	DESCRIPTION
EmployeeID	AutoNumber	Primary key
IndividualID	Long Integer	Foreign key to Individual table
RoleID	Long Integer	Foreign key to Role table
DateHired	DateTime	Date employee hired
DateLeft	DateTime	Date employee departed

Notice the way we indicate that a record is not active and therefore will not appear in the current select lists: the field DateLeft. For products, we used an Active/Inactive flag using a Yes/No data type field for a similar purpose. You need the information about current and past employees so that you can see the history of orders and notes. Also, you can use the inactive indicator to limit lists to current employees.

In this case, if an employee returns, you would need to remove the value from the DateLeft field so that their name could again appear in selection lists. And, since this is not intended to be any type of official tracking system for employee status, that should be all that you need. For that reason, you can safely consider the option of using a flag or yes/no field to indicate whether an employee is active.

> **NOTE**   If you want to maintain the history of an individual's hiring and leaving more than once, you need to move this information to a transaction sub-table linked to the employee table.

Tying the employee information to the order is done by storing the EmployeeID as a foreign key in the Order table. This allows you to record the information about the employee responsible for an order when it was created.

By including the employee role, you can use the information for filtering lists, understanding the perspective of the person writing a note, determining responsibilities and performing a variety of analyses.

Multiple Notes

In many of the tables implemented in the original design for this chapter, we created a general-purpose "Notes" field of data type Memo. This is a common practice, whether it is specified in the requirements or not, to allow users to enter general information about a record. Of course, notes themselves can warrant additional detail fields, if their relevance and importance is great enough.

> **NOTE**   Although a dedicated field of the appropriate data type is always the correct solution to any new data requirements, a general-purpose Notes field can handle unanticipated situations until a proper implementation can be incorporated.

In this case, there is a new requirement that you must now be able to hold multiple notes for an order so that you can review the chronology of information related to the order. This is similar to using "sticky notes," which have minimal structure but a great deal of flexibility. To learn more about how to structure a dedicated process progression model, see Chapter 10, "Services."

Multiple notes require a separate, related Notes table. To accommodate the chronology of notes, the table requires a NoteDate field that can store both the date and time that a note was created. For convenience and consistency, you could give the field a default value equal to Now(), to automatically record the exact date and time the record was created. You can learn more about this and other field property settings in Appendix A.

The final detail field is a description field, to summarize or provide the subject. If you limit this to a subject, you can use a list for users to select from. That would facilitate grouping and analyzing notes. However, you may also benefit by allowing users to enter a brief but descriptive narrative that conveys specifics about the note without having to read the full note text itself.

Based on the scenario that we've described, you would create the Note table with the fields as listed in Table 7-15.

Table 7-15: Fields for the Order Notes Table

FIELD NAME	DATA TYPE	DESCRIPTION
OrderNoteID	AutoNumber	Primary key
OrderID	Long Integer	Foreign key to Order table
NoteTypeID	Long Integer	Foreign key to NoteType table
NotePriorityID	Long Integer	Foreign key to NotePriority table
EmployeeID	Long Integer	Foreign key to Employee table
NoteDate	DateTime	Date and time note was created
NoteDescription	Text	Summary of note purpose
NoteText	Memo	Detailed text

Notice that most fields included are foreign key fields that describe the note—even the EmployeeID field, which relates back to the Employee table described in the previous section. NoteTypeID and NotePriorityID relate to Note lookup tables that are now required. The NoteType table will contain the list to select the type of note, such as phone, sales adjustment, and so on. The NotePriority table lists the terms for note priority, such as urgent, informational, follow-up, or close-out. Again, you will want to select the terms that will best serve your sales environments.

You can see examples of these in the sample database, c07Sales_Complex .mdb, for this chapter on the book's CD. The fields for tblNoteType and tblNotePriority are listed in Table 7-16 and Table 7-17, respectively.

Table 7-16: Fields for the Note Type Table

FIELD NAME	DATA TYPE	DESCRIPTION
NoteTypeID	AutoNumber	Primary key
NoteType	Text	Identify type of origin of note

Table 7-17: Fields for the Note Priority Table

FIELD NAME	DATA TYPE	DESCRIPTION
NotePriorityID	AutoNumber	Primary key
NotePriority	Text	Single word identifier for priority level
ImportanceRating	Integer	Numeric sequence priority

With these tables, you can manage the notes related to an order. The presence of such a table obviates the need for including one or more note fields in each main table or to have multiple note tables.

Order Quotes

Our final amendment to the database design could be either very minor or quite substantial. Given that a quote follows the same structure and intent as an order, it can even be considered as a type of order. This data could therefore be modeled as an Order record of a very specific status. By introducing a new Status field, orders could be labeled as being prospective, in other words—a quote. At its most simple, you could use a Yes/No data type field to indicate whether the record is Yes (a quote) or No (an order). Taking this further, you could use a field that describes the status of an order as it moves through various stages. This would allow you to identify a quote, and add more value to the order itself by making it easy to determine the status of an order. For our example, we will use the following statuses: Quote, Order, Delivered, Invoiced, Paid, and Closed.

> **NOTE** Such a Status field requires specific entry by a user. This offers a great deal of control, but also the potential for "out of date" status entries. Alternatively, the status could be determined based on the conditions and values from several fields.
>
> For example, a status of "Invoiced" could reflect the creation of an Invoice record.
>
> The status of "Paid" could be based on comparing the OrderAmountPaid value with the expected order's total price. If the values match, then the invoice could be deemed as "Paid." Similarly if the delivery date has passed, then the status would be "Delivered."
>
> You would need to identify all the appropriate comparisons that are needed to determine when each condition has been met. Then, you could design a query to check for each specific condition. However, the queries will soon become complex. The criteria that we've just discussed might use an expression such as the following:

```
Switch(Nz([OrderAmountPaid],0)=[OrderPrice]+Round([OrderTax]*
  [OrderPrice],2) +Nz([OrderDeliveryCharge],0),"Paid",
  [OrderDeliveryDate]<=Date(),"Delivered", [OrderAmountPaid]=0,"UnPaid")
```

The criteria as stated is ultimately inflexible and limited. You will need to weigh the benefits of a user-entered Status field against the challenges of relying on the user to properly and consistently update the data. If they do not, then why maintain it at all?

It is very possible that you will want to maintain the status history as it can be helpful to know what the original quote contained and which order it eventually became. You might want to compare quotes to orders to determine if they have the same products and prices. In fact, you might benefit from performing trending and business analysis on several stages of the order process—but for now we will focus on converting the quote into an order. In addition to calculating the ratio failed vs. converted quotes, you may also discover a trend in discounts offered or products added or dropped. Merely changing the status of an order does not maintain any of that chronology.

Adding a Quote table similar in design to the Orders table would be the clearest way to maintain both the historic chronology information and comparison data. When a quote becomes an order, you can use an *append query*—a special type of query used to add records to a table—to copy the existing quote data into the Order table, and another query to copy the quote details to the OrderDetail table. The order could still maintain the Status field if it were required, minus the "Quote" status, of course.

Using a separate table for quotes also allows you to include additional details that are specific to quotes and eliminate order-specific details. For example, order-oriented items such as OrderAmountPaid, OrderComplete, and the delivery date would not be needed for a quote.

Although you could include a field to indicate if the quote was converted, such as a "BecameOrder" flag, that field is not needed because you can discern the outcome of the quote based on whether or not there is a related record in the Order table. To do that, you need a way to relate the two records, either by saving the OrderID in the record for the quote, or storing the QuoteID in the record for the order. Since we are copying the quote into the order table, it seems logical—and is easiest—to include the QuoteID as part of that process.

To create the Quote table, you can start with a copy of the Order table; then rename it and remove the unnecessary fields. You will want to change some field names to refer to "Quote" rather than "Order" and add a few that are specific to your needs for tracking quotes.

As is the case for orders, you also need a table to list the products of the quote. Again, you do this the easy way: just make a copy of the OrderDetail table, rename the table to QuoteDetail, and rename and add fields as appropriate.

The relationships of the Quote and QuoteDetail tables to the product tables are shown in Figure 7-9. This is essentially identical to the relationship between the OrderDetail table and the product tables shown in Figure 7-8.

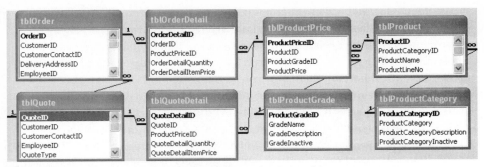

Figure 7-9: Quote and Quote Details tables and relationships

As you can see in Figure 7-9, the relationship between the Quote table and the Order table is based solely on the QuoteID being recorded in the Order table. This one field also provides the link for copying the quote details into the Order detail table.

COPYING QUOTE DATA

With customer and product data entered into a quote, it would be unreasonable to expect users of your database to manually re-enter that same data into a new order record. It makes sense to copy that data from the quote record into a new order record using an append query like that shown in the following figure. The process can be twofold: first create a new order record based on the quote record and then copy the selected product records from the quote detail table to the order detail.

Creating the main order record consists of the query appending to tblOrder by selecting values from tblQuote and including a parameter to specify the QuoteID to convert.

Notice that the OrderDate is not based on the QuoteDate value but defaults to the current date supplied by the `Date()` function. The SQL of this query follows:

```
INSERT INTO tblOrder (QuoteID, CustomerID, CustomerContactID,
   EmployeeID, OrderType, OrderDate, OrderPrice, OrderTax,
```

```
OrderDeliveryCharge, OrderDeliveryExpected)
SELECT QuoteID, CustomerID, CustomerContactID, EmployeeID, QuoteType,
Date() AS Expr1, QuotePrice, QuoteTax, QuoteDeliveryCharge,
QuoteDeliveryExpected
FROM tblQuote
WHERE tblQuote.QuoteID=[EnterQuoteID];
```

This query is named **qryAppendQuoteToOrder** in the accompanying file **Sales_Complex.mdb** on the book's CD. Notice that the QuoteID primary key is inserted into the QuoteID foreign key field value in tblOrder. This links the quote to its converted order.

Then you execute an append query to copy the quote detail records into order details. **qryAppendQuoteToOrderDetail** shows how you would do this. Notice that the query selects from both tblQuoteDetail and tblOrder, the latter is joined to acquire the OrderID of the newly created order record based on the QuoteID as inserted previously.

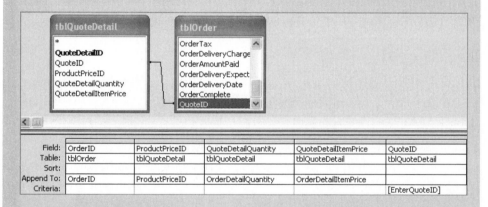

Field:	OrderID	ProductPriceID	QuoteDetailQuantity	QuoteDetailItemPrice	QuoteID
Table:	tblOrder	tblQuoteDetail	tblQuoteDetail	tblQuoteDetail	tblQuoteDetail
Sort:					
Append To:	OrderID	ProductPriceID	OrderDetailQuantity	OrderDetailItemPrice	
Criteria:					[EnterQuoteID]

The following is the code for this joined append query in SQL view:

```
INSERT INTO tblOrderDetail ( OrderID, ProductPriceID,
OrderDetailQuantity, OrderDetailItemPrice )
SELECT tblOrder.OrderID, tblQuoteDetail.ProductPriceID,
tblQuoteDetail.QuoteDetailQuantity,
tblQuoteDetail.QuoteDetailItemPrice
FROM tblQuoteDetail INNER JOIN tblOrder ON tblQuoteDetail.QuoteID
= tblOrder.QuoteID
WHERE (((tblQuoteDetail.QuoteID)=[EnterQuoteID]));
```

By sequentially executing these queries and providing the QuoteID, you can easily create a new Order record based on the selected quote without duplicating data entry effort. In your application, you would very likely change the parameter [EnterQuoteID] to refer to a form control value instead of the format Forms!FormName!QuoteIDControlName.

Now that you've created a simple sales database and explored some of the ways to accommodate more complex needs, it's time to discuss how to use the data after you get it into the tables.

Using the Database

Your ultimate design will be tailored in accordance with the requirements that you identify. With that in mind, you can design a table structure that meets user needs and expectations for features and performance.

In the following discussion, we consider some scenarios and how you might address them.

Querying the Database

The following sections examine two common areas that require queries for retrieving important information: invoicing and order pricing.

Invoicing

Our model implemented a separate Invoice table, which exists in relation to an order only in wholesale instances. By including a separate Invoice table, we have to include a table join in any query that concerns invoicing and monitoring of invoicing. The data from the order and invoice together then constitute what would be the invoice to the customer.

Earlier in this chapter, in the "Order Price Queries" sidebar, you saw a query that returns incomplete order records by calculating the total amount due for an order and comparing that to the amount paid. To extend this for invoices, you may want to query for results such as "all unpaid invoices that were dated more than sixty days ago." Whereas previously we performed a query to calculate the unpaid status of an order, the following query, shown in Figure 7-10, expands on that concept and joins the Order table to the Invoice table to also filter on the date it was issued.

> **NOTE**   The Nz() function converts null field values to 0, or to a different value that is stipulated in the formula. This function prevents what is known as *Propagation of Nulls*. Thinking back to basic multiplication, if any part of an equation is 0, the answer will always be zero; you'll have a similar effect with null values. Propagation of nulls has the effect that if any field in a formula is null the result of the formula will always be null. You can read more about this in Appendix A.

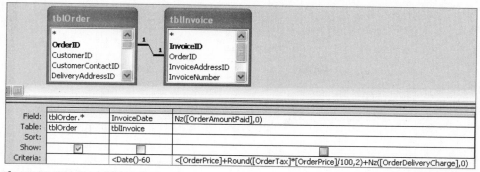

Figure 7-10: Unpaid invoices

In addition to the expression which compares the price to the amount already paid, shown in the "Order Price Queries" sidebar, we add the comparison to a date, comparing to the current date minus sixty days.

Looking at the SQL view of that same query, you can see how this translates from the design grid, with the criteria presented in the WHERE clause including both the date comparison and then our familiar price expression.

```
SELECT *
FROM tblOrder INNER JOIN tblInvoice
  On tblOrder.OrderID = tblInvoice.OrderID
WHERE InvoiceDate < Date() - 60
  AND Nz(OrderAmountPaid, 0) < OrderPrice +
    Round(OrderTax * OrderPrice/100, 2) + Nz(OrderDeliveryCharge, 0)
```

Any join between tables adds a certain amount of complexity to a query and joining too many tables in a single query may begin to negatively impact query execution time. But, for the most part, you should not need to worry about including joined tables in your queries. As long as they are included for good reason, it is more important to focus on creating a properly designed database that will execute efficiently and serve you well in the future.

Order Product Totals

Similarly to calculating order totals, during the creation of an order or quote, the salesperson needs to assign a "price" to the order. In our example this is a user specified value but it must be influenced by the calculated value of the products being ordered. Hence, this value should always be calculated and presented to the order taker. For this we need a totals query, which is a summary or aggregate query. The query would look like that shown in Figure 7-11, where you can see that the sigma ($\sum$) button on the toolbar is depressed to show the totals row.

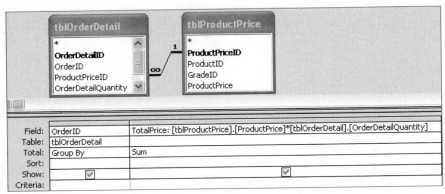

Figure 7-11: Order-Product totals qryOrderProductPrices

An aggregate query combines all records that meet the criteria of the query. In this query there are two calculations being performed simultaneously.

In the first calculation, the price of the product is multiplied by the quantity ordered; this is often referred to as the extended price.

The aggregate portion of the query then sums all of these extended prices grouped by the OrderID. This returns a single row for each OrderID with a total for that order, as illustrated in Figure 7-12.

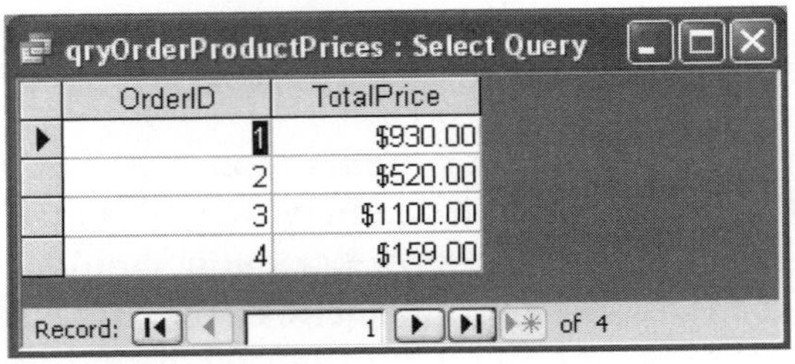

Figure 7-12: Order-Product totals results

This appears in SQL view as the aggregate query. Access will write this for you. By looking at the SQL view, you can learn a lot more about the logic involved with selecting and grouping the data and calculating the totals.

```
SELECT tblOrderDetail.OrderID, SUM( tblProductPrice.ProductPrice *
    tblOrderDetail.OrderDetailQuantity) AS TotalPrice
FROM tblOrderDetail INNER JOIN tblProductPrice
    ON tblOrderDetail.ProductPriceID = tblProductPrice.ProductPriceID
GROUP BY tblOrderDetail.OrderID;
```

The term inner join that you see in the SQL view refers to the join between the tables, as shown in the design view above. The results of this are shown in Figure 7-12.

This query is included on the book's CD in the file for this chapter named Sales_Complex.mdb.

Alternative Designs

The examples used in this chapter are deliberately broad to make it easier for you to modify them for use in your own database. Earlier, we discussed using "grades" to complicate the product model, or at least defining each product with a higher level of granularity. This additional granularity, or level of detail, could be anything that affects the price.

Product Grouping

Another possibility for added granularity in the context of products is the product category. In our example, they represent broad, generic groupings of the products offered. In databases that often contain a great many product types; it might make sense to have more groups or categories. Although new categories can be introduced, you may also need to create a hierarchy of categories. For example, "Product Model" or "Product Group" could be used if such arbitrary naming of a grouping level is appropriate for the organization being served by the database. This is often achieved by all of the levels of categories in the same table and providing means for one category to be a subset of another category. You'll see this type of "self-referencing" table in other examples in the book—in Chapter 16 when dealing with lookup tables and in Chapter 8, "Production and Manufacturing." Using our example here, you would need to include another field in the ProductCategory table, as shown in Table 7-18.

Table 7-18: Alternative tblProductCategory

FIELD NAME	DATA TYPE	DESCRIPTION
ProductCategoryID	AutoNumber	Primary key
ProductCategory	Text	Text name
ProductCategoryDescription	Text	More elaborate description
ParentCategoryID	Long Integer	Foreign key to a record in this table

The ParentCategoryID allows records of categories to "belong" to other categories. This Bill of Materials (BOM) type architecture is explained in more detail in Chapter 8, but as suggested here, it has many applications in databases.

Such hierarchical structures usually involve more application effort to implement and display to the user. For example, querying or reporting a BOM in an ACE database may involve some use of code, but it may allow for greater flexibility.

Notes Assignment

In the complex model for this chapter, the Note records are specific to a data table such as the Order table. This doesn't entirely satisfy the requirements presented for this database where notes may also be required for customers and other subjects. An alternative to this is a single notes table which can be related to each specific data subject table by implementing a junction table. For example, to allow orders to support multiple notes, you could use the structure shown in Table 7-19.

Table 7-19: Fields for the Order Note junction Table

FIELD NAME	DATA TYPE	DESCRIPTION
OrderNoteID	AutoNumber	Primary key
OrderID	Long Integer	Foreign key to Order table
NoteID	Long Integer	Foreign key to Note table

Figure 7-13 illustrates the use of many-to-many junction tables for allowing multiple notes per order and per customer. Notice the two junction tables, tblOrderNote and tblCustomerNote used for joining their respective data tables to the single Notes table.

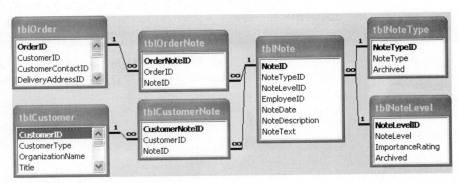

Figure 7-13: Notes related to orders

Additional Order Overview Option

It is always good to have alternatives—either completely different models to implement from the start or smaller concepts that you can offer to enhance the database beyond the initial set of requirements.

Consider, for example, the discussion on quotes. If it benefits the database's organization, the Order Status field could still be included in the Order table, despite the fact that there is a distinct Quotes table in the database. The order status would not include "Quote" as a status option, but it would still offer a potentially valuable identifying field to the Order table. You then have a new OrderStatus table, with the fields as listed in Table 7-20.

Table 7-20: Fields for the OrderStatus Table

FIELD NAME	DATA TYPE	DESCRIPTION
OrderStatusID	AutoNumber	Primary key
OrderStatusText	Text	Description of the display status
OrderStatusNumericLevel	Long Integer	Numeric level of the "stage"

Including the OrderStatusNumericLevel field enables you to query across all orders, whereas a text-based description will not. For example, you would not be able to ask to see a report on orders that pre-date the "Invoiced" stage, as that is an alphanumeric description. Instead, consider Table 7-21 showing the entries in the OrderStatus table.

Table 7-21: Sample Data from the Order Status Table

ORDERSTATUSID	ORDERSTATUSTEXT	ORDERSTATUSNUMERICLEVEL
1	Order Placed	1
2	Delivered	2
3	Invoiced	3
4	Paid	4
5	Closed	4

In this example, we have chosen to give equal status to both "Paid" and "Closed." This is entirely up to you or the eventual database owner. This field enables you to develop a query to return all orders that are not marked as Paid or Closed as shown in Figure 7-14.

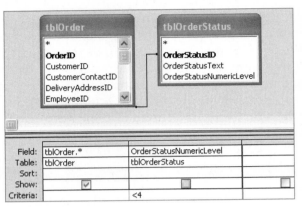

Figure 7-14: Order status querying

You could use a combination of values in the criteria. The criteria shown above will include all status levels less than 4. You are not limited to just one value, so you could, for example, request orders with status of 2 or 3. You can learn more about query criteria by exploring the Help file in Access.

The same query as the SQL code view described by the following code shows the join between the tables and the criteria in the WHERE condition that the level must be below four.

```
SELECT tblOrder.*
FROM tblOrder INNER JOIN tblOrderStatus
  ON tblOrder.OrderStatusID = tblOrderStatus.OrderStatusID
WHERE OrderStatusNumericLevel < 4
```

It is simple functionality to implement and is immediately powerful from a business point of view. The principle is applicable in similar situations across many of your tables and other databases.

NOTE   Looking at the order status example data it might seem tempting to use the OrderStatusID AutoNumber value as a numeric state. However, such an assumption about AutoNumber values is always a bad idea. You may want to later add lower-level values that would therefore make the increasing sequence inappropriate. In addition, assuming values of AutoNumbers at all is a discouraged practice because they are not guaranteed to be unique, sequential, or even ascending as the default behavior. Use your own assigned numeric level field to determine the state of a record.

Summary

Although very few sales-oriented databases will exactly fit the model of this chapter's example, with some minor modifications it will work for a wide variety of businesses. With some reworking or even a completely fresh design of your own, the principles to apply in acquiring the requirements and meeting them from a database schema perspective are the same. The same core subjects and tables are likely to appear: in one guise or another there will be customers, products, orders, and order details. It is the related tables and the breakdown of these into smaller subsidiary tables that uniquely builds the database and stamps your own design.

You have seen that, except in very rare circumstances, you always should enforce normalization guidelines. Even data that may appear denormalized upon first glance should be defensible from a schema perspective such as the product price stored at the time of the order.

You have seen the complexity of the model increased to include a commonly usable Notes mechanism that allows you to store multiple notes per order or customer. And the means to complicate the pricing structure of your products, in our example using product grades, but the same principle applies to any consideration which is a factor in your products finish and price.

Finally, you have walked through some example query techniques to begin to pull back out useful information from your relational data design.

Producing and Tracking the Goods & Services

In This Part

Production and Manufacturing

Manufacturing and production are complex operations, so you may find it challenging to properly represent them in a database. To be a useful tool for both management and production, the database must be able to capture and report a high-level overview of information that is important to the decision makers, and the very detailed, process-specific information important to the people managing production operations on the shop floor, as well as several other levels in between.

Moving past the various levels of detail required by management, you will find there are even greater variations in data requirements based on the actual production operations. For example, you might compare a company making paper plates to a company producing orthopedic implants. The paper plate manufacturer produces thousands of similar, but not necessarily identical, paper plates each day. The orthopedics manufacturer may produce only a few dozen implants in a week or a month, but each implant has to conform to very precise specifications. The processes and controls required by the paper plate manufacturer, obviously, can be quite different from those required by the implant manufacturer.

Fortunately for those tasked with creating the databases, there is a common thread that runs through the operations of both the paper plate manufacturer and the orthopedics manufacturer. That is, the processes used to make their products must consistently and reliably perform the task(s) they are designed to do.

Knowing the differences and commonalities among manufacturing operations is the first step of database creation: identifying what is important to the consumers of the data. With that knowledge, you can launch investigations aimed at discovering the details of the business model. Knowing what is important guides the design of a well-structured database to create a system that efficiently stores and retrieves data for its users.

In this chapter, we'll develop a sample database model that focuses on requirements shared by most manufacturers. We'll also take steps to ensure the design is scalable so that it can accommodate the requirements of different businesses. As you go through the examples in the chapter, you will learn how to customize the base model to meet your specific needs.

While creating the database model, we will follow the relational data modeling principles that were discussed in Chapter 3, "Relational Data Model." We will also refer to the content from Chapter 2, "Elements of a Microsoft Access Database." You will also find great benefit in the material from Appendixes A, "Field Properties," B, "Relationships, Joins, and Nulls," and BD, "Gathering Requirements" (on the book's CD).

> **NOTE** If you have not yet read Chapters 2 and 3, we encourage you to review the content in both chapters now. Pay special attention to any subject matter with which you are not familiar. Your understanding of the terms and concepts discussed in those chapters will help you create the database for this chapter.

Industry Terms

Before going further, it is important that we have a common understanding of how we are using a couple of the industry terms that will be used throughout the discussion: *production* and *manufacturing*. Although these terms are frequently used synonymously, there is a slight distinction between them. In this chapter, we use the following definitions:

- **Manufacturing:** The use of machines, tools, and labor (collectively referred to as processes) to make a product.

- **Production:** Broadens the scope of manufacturing by defining a plan as to how manufacturing processes will used in order to attain a goal or end result.

In other words, when we speak of manufacturing, we are referring to the processes that produce products, and when we speak of production, we are including the plan used to govern the management or use of those processes.

In some contexts, the words can be used interchangeably. We may even do so in this chapter. The potential that the distinction may be reversed in some environments only adds to the confusion. Ultimately, it is always important to know how the meanings of the two terms differ for each environment that you encounter, and whether that difference is important to your database model.

Enterprise-Level Systems

A manufacturing business will often look for specialized software designed for their production and manufacturing environment. You'll find that a lot of the software advertised as having the capability that you are seeking is *enterprise level*. Enterprise-level databases will have literally hundreds of tables in order to accommodate a multitude of scenarios. The options and flexibility are reflected in the design, maintenance, and overall cost. That is why many off-the-shelf applications offer much more than your business might need and at a price that is higher than your budget will accommodate. In addition, many businesses do not have the hardware required to support enterprise-level applications.

When you are creating a custom solution, you will often include many features that are provided by a commercial application. By following our example, you will see how to gain the benefits of tailoring those features to your needs rather than trying to organize your data into a generic model. Our database focuses on the information and functionality that are at the center of enterprise-level products. By keeping the scope compact, usable, and scalable, you can create a solution specific to your needs. The areas of functionality that we'll address include:

- Machines, tools, and labor are used to make products; these are collectively referred to as *processes*.

- Processes will be controlled or managed in order to produce a product at a given rate over a period of time.

- Processes will fail to function properly. In other words, processes will fail to meet production expectations.

- Processes that do not meet expectations will need countermeasures to put them into a condition that can meet the stated goals.

- General information regarding processes and what has, or will, affect them must be communicated.

NOTE Identifying your needs may extend beyond the items that we have listed. If that is the case, you should make a list of your additional needs. Then, as we develop the database, you can include them in the analysis process and incorporate them into the tables and fields as we go through examples.

Each item in our list contains one common element: processes. As mentioned, processes are the common threads that bind all manufactures together. Managing your manufacturing processes is the required foundation for consistently producing a high-quality product at optimum efficiency, with consideration for costs, production, and maintenance.

Purpose of the Database

Our example database is for a typical assembly operation. Think of a single production line in which many parts are stocked on each side of the line. Each station, or cell, of the line either adds more parts to the product or reinforces the assembly of previously set parts. A completed product comes out of the other end of the line.

Although this assembly line operation is the environment for which we developed the current model, our goal is to provide a base model that can be used by virtually any organization with processes to manage in a manufacturing environment. Therefore, as you read the following discussion, think of the ways our model applies to the processes in your environment and how you would adapt the model to fit them.

As mentioned, a manufacturing business needs to manage and monitor manufacturing processes; our goal in creating the database is to support that effort. We'll start with the concepts listed earlier and break them down into tasks that need to be done to reflect a process management philosophy. Whether you do this with software or not, you might come up with the following objectives:

- *Organize* processes the business uses to produce products.
- Track the *efficiency* of producing products.
- *Notify* appropriate personnel when a process is not meeting expectations.
- *Track maintenance, or countermeasure, activity* on a process that returns it to production-ready condition. In other words, track what was done to fix a process that is not meeting expectations.
- *Communicate miscellaneous items* with respect to processes that may be pertinent for others to know. Basically, "FYI"-type information.

By combining the model of managing processes with the areas of functionality that you need (listed earlier), you can define the purpose of your database. That purpose will guide the implementation of the concepts and functional tasks.

The purpose of our database is to store and manage data to support an application that can do the following:

- *Organize* all manufacturing *processes* used in the production of a product. The organizational functionality will involve creating a hierarchy of processes in order to reveal which processes belong to another process.
- *Provide manufacturing process efficiency* statistics for processes that are defined as monitoring points in the shop. A monitored process is often considered the "final" step before shipment to a "customer." A customer

may actually be the next process within the shop, or it could be a company at the dock awaiting delivery. Monitored processes are often called the *build processes* because they provide the statistics for the production *build* of a given day.

- *Notify people* when a process is not functioning as expected (this is called an *event*). Examples of events that would require notification include: a piece of equipment breaks down; a safety or ergonomic concern is affecting the operators; the quality of the resultant product is noncompliant with the standards of the business.

- *Record the countermeasures* used or applied to return the process to its standard operating condition, and the steps taken to correct situations indicated by notifications.

- *Provide a common repository of general information* regarding processes in order to facilitate communication, such as that required between shifts, or simply for reference by any interested party.

NOTE The purpose we've defined here is for a fictitious company. But you can use the same approach to review your business practices and the management of your manufacturing processes to determine how a database and application will integrate with them. That will help you develop a purpose honed to your specific needs. Once you have a draft of the purpose, you should review it with the people who will be using the database to ensure that it will meet their needs. This should include application developers as well as those who will use the application.

Defining the purpose of a database provides a framework for the subsequent steps. As you pursue other development activities, you can look back at the stated purpose to ensure that the activity addresses the overall goal to be achieved.

Identifying the Requirements

After deciding on the purpose of the database, you can begin identifying the list of requirements that it needs to fulfill. A great starting point in gathering requirements is to examine existing work flows, reports, and any other information available to you. These will help you understand the business processes—not to be confused with manufacturing processes—being addressed by the database application.

For example, by looking at our purpose, we can extrapolate that the application will need to address shift-to-shift communications regarding manufacturing processes and production builds. So, you will need to analyze the communication methods currently in place in your facility. In addition to the methods of communication, you will need to review the kind of information that is exchanged. And, of course, you always need to be vigilant about identifying needs that are not being met; undocumented needs are often the hardest to identify and respond to, but doing so can greatly increase the benefits that your application can provide.

Being limited to one chapter in a book, it's not possible to discuss a complete analysis of a company's documents and business practices. Instead, we'll help you to identify the requirements, and then we'll create a database based on the details that you can expect to discern during your own investigations. Because we are designing a database for an application that will store and retrieve information about manufacturing processes, we can determine that the database will need to accomplish the following tasks. It is important to clarify that this is what the database will do for the application, not what the application will do for the user. The database will:

- Store information about the manufacturing processes in a hierarchical manner.
- Store manufacturing build process parameters in order to calculate production metrics.
- Store information that defines or describes the conditions that prevent the process from performing as expected.
- Store information that defines or describes what was done to a process in order to make it function as expected, after a condition needing attention has been recorded.
- Store general information regarding processes and the production day.

Identifying User Expectations

Users will interact with your database, or data file, through a separate file, commonly known as the *front end, user interface, UI,* or simply as the *application.* The application will be designed specifically for their benefit. So one of our goals is ensure that we design the tables in such a way that the data will not be affected by the choice of the development tools used to create and provide the application—whether that is Microsoft Access, one of the .NET languages, or one of many web development languages.

In order to create a database model that will support multiple front end environments, and give application developers as much freedom as possible to decide how to work with the data, you should centralize as much business logic as you can for the database engine to handle. For example, using referential integrity with cascading updates or deletes will free the application from managing that task. We explain referential integrity, indexes and other database fundamentals in Chapter 2 and in Appendixes A and B.

As you design the tables, you may also want to include features that fit nicely with a particular application development environment. For example, if the application will be developed with Microsoft Access 2007 and forward, you may want to use a feature known as *attachment data* fields. This data type can compress and store files directly in the database, thereby reducing the complexity of your tables. We talk more about data types in Chapter 2 and Appendix A. If you aren't familiar with those, you may want to review the options for attachments and other new features.

Regardless of how the program is created, the people who use the application and the people who rely on the data will have their own expectations about what the application should be able to do. You will need to consider their needs and determine which ones must be accommodated in your database design. It is often best to involve people who will use the database to help determine the expectations. For an application focused on manufacturing processes, you might ask some, or all, of the following questions. The answers you receive may affect the final design.

- Are simple audit trails required? Is it important to know who entered records and when they did it?

- Who is the manufacturer or vendor of a process?

- Is the process a piece of equipment, a fixture, or a human process?

- What causes a process to require attention? One element of the database purpose stated earlier is that the application should notify people when a process is not working as expected. However, to improve processes, the cause of the problem or condition should also be identified.

- What methods are used to discover when a process is in a nonproductive state?

- Given that all efficiency losses are the result of a process, whether it is a machine, a tool, or labor, that did not function as expected, users will need to associate efficiency losses with the faulty or suspect process. In addition, users expect to have the ability to see and record the repair work done to a process.

As we develop our database, we'll identify additional items of information based on the application's purpose. When items are identified as details that need to be tracked, we will determine how they will fit into the tables of the database.

NOTE After you have identified all of the relevant details, you will go through a systematic process to determine if each detail directly describes the main subject or a different core subject. You might also discover that a detail actually represents a different subject that helps to support the main subject; or, it might describe a different subject altogether. Each of these subjects will be the basis for one or more tables in your database.

There are several approaches that you can use to analyze and group the details in order to identify and create the appropriate tables. In Chapters 8, "Production and Manufacturing," and 9, "Inventory Management," we are following a systematic approach that includes reviewing each detail against a list of four qualifying questions. The pattern of responses to those questions will help you determine how to handle the detail. This is one approach for implanting the normalization process you learned about in Chapter 3.

Undoubtedly, you will have a distinct set of user expectations based on the unique set of circumstances of your manufacturing environment and from any deficiencies that may be present in the current methods of gathering associated information. Be sure to list these items so that you can customize the sample database to meet your needs.

Manufacturing Overview: Identifying the Core Subjects

The general method for identifying the core subjects, and ultimately the tables that are needed to store your data, is to collect and review the information that you want to track, and then to group that information into distinct categories, or subjects. Your next step is to define how those subjects are related to each other.

Based on the database purpose and requirements, you will need to identify the initial set of categories for recording information about the manufacturing operation, the environment, and the specific needs of the people who will use the database and the data. The categories, or unique subjects, are often described by database developers as *entities;* they will become your *core subjects.* In our discussion, core subjects will typically become one of two distinct types of tables: core tables and support tables.

NOTE Database developers often use the term "entity" to represent a table, or group of tables, prior to its implementation into an actual database file. The process of analyzing data and creating the tables is the *modeling* phase. Consider, for example, "The Processes entity will be implemented as the table named tblProcess in the database." This statement illustrates that *entity* is the conceptual view of a table, while *table* is the physical implementation.

A *core table* represents a clearly defined and discrete subject that directly supports the database purpose. *Support tables* are related tables that provide additional information about the core subject. A support table may be, and often will be, associated with more than one core table.

Most databases have one topic as their focal point. We'll call the table that represents that focal point the *main table*. With the different terms and concepts we've introduced, this may seem confusing now, but it will become clear as you work through the example.

NOTE A *core table* is used to record the main information about the subject. It is either a *transactional* or an *operational table*, and will typically have frequent updates to the data. Conversely, a *supporting table*, also known as a *functional table*, is often used to provide reference information—for example, a list of U.S. states, or other items that might be provided in lists to allow users to select a value. For more information about the different types of tables in a database, please see Chapter 2, Table 2-1: "Common Table Types Used in Applications."

The Main Subject: Manufacturing Processes

Our goal is to create a database that stores information about a production and manufacturing operation. By examining the documentation, interviews, and lists of needs and expectations that have been gathered to this point, you can determine that the main subject, or focal point, to be represented by the main table in your database will be the *manufacturing processes*. We will often refer to the main topic simply as *process*.

A process can be anything that contributes to the manufacture of a product. A process could be a machine, a step performed by a human, or even a rack that holds parts, or a conveyance route that delivers parts. If you expand on this, you could think of a process as anything that may cause a loss of production or efficiency, if it is not functioning or performing as it was designed to. We will come back to this when we discuss the manufacturing processes a little later.

Additional Core Subjects

Looking again at the database purpose, requirements, and user expectations, we can identify additional subjects that provide the necessary details about the processes. We've listed the core subjects for our manufacturing process in Table 8-1. At this point, we will use these subjects, or categories, to group and manage the details that we need to record.

Table 8-1: Production and Manufacturing Core Subjects

SUBJECT	DESCRIPTION
Processes	The processes that contribute to the manufacture of a product. This was chosen as the main table because all components of the database purpose are centered around manufacturing processes.
Builds	The production statistics relevant to a production run, or build, of a process. This was chosen as a core subject because the purpose of the database indicated that efficiency statistics for selected processes were to be kept.
Notifications	Recording when a process is in a condition that requires attention or corrective action. For example, a process breaks down, is creating ergonomic issues, presents a safety concern, or simply needs preventive maintenance performed. This was chosen as a core subject because the database purpose indicated that people are to be notified when processes do not meet expectations.
Countermeasures	The actions applied to a process in response to a notification. This was chosen as a core subject because the database purpose specifies that the actions taken in response to a noncompliant process must be recorded.
General Notes	Basic notes regarding processes that may contain information such as reminders of upcoming changes to a process or group of processes. This was chosen as a core subject because the database purpose indicated that a communication mechanism for general information must be a part of the application.

Relationships between Core Subjects

Each of these core subjects relates to the others in some way. For example, processes have notifications, which need countermeasures. An interruption to a process identified in the notification may create lost time in the build. A general note briefly describes the notification if the lost time was significant. Figure 8-1 illustrates the relationships between the core subjects that we have identified.

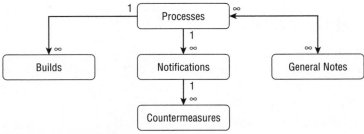

Figure 8-1: How the core subjects are related

The 1 and the infinity (many) symbol (∞) in the diagram indicate whether a specific item from one subject can be associated with one or many items in the other subject. The lines are drawn with the arrow pointing to the supporting details. With that in mind, you might "read" the diagram to say that one process can have many builds. It also indicates that each process can have several notifications, and each of those notifications can have several countermeasures. This might be the case if you have prolonged repairs or multiple attempts to correct the noncompliant condition indicated in the Notification.

You'll also notice that the line between Processes and General Notes has an arrow and an infinity symbol at both ends. This indicates that there will be a *many-to-many relationship* between the two subjects. That means that each process can have several notes, and each note can relate to several processes. We will explain how that is managed when we describe tables and fields. You can also learn a lot from the discussions in Chapter 2 and in Appendix B.

The relationships illustrated here are required to support the business requirements and user expectations driving your database design. In addition, Figure 8-1 illustrates the framework of a high-level work flow for your application that could be described as follows:

- A production day starts; a build is added for a process.

- If a process needs attention, a notification is entered into the database and the build stop time associated with the notification is recorded.

- Build stop time occurrences can be entered at any time and subsequently linked to the appropriate notifications as they are input.

- When a notification is addressed, information about the countermeasures applied is added in order to document the work performed.

- If general information about a process needs to be shared with a larger audience, a general note is added to the database.

The Approach for Reviewing the Core Subjects

At this point, we have identified the core subjects, but we still need to list and group all of the details so that we can determine the actual tables and fields that you will need to manage and integrate all of the relevant data. We have several core subjects, so we will tackle them one at a time.

But before we get immersed in the manufacturing details, we want to explain the approach that we will take to create the database. So, we'll take a moment to briefly describe the steps that we will use to analyze each subject. We'll also use this approach in Chapter 9. We want you to become familiar with the technique so that you are comfortable applying to your own projects.

Reviewing the Requirements

In each area in your own environment, you will need to investigate deeper to ensure that you have identified all of the requirements, user needs, expected reports, and other factors that might affect the data collection or reporting needs.

Identifying the Subjects

Just as you did for the overall purpose of the database, you will now group the details related to each core function into individual subjects. Each definitive subject will be the basis for a core table and associated supporting tables; a table may only store one item or detail, or it can have numerous details.

As we come across scenarios that involve special ways of handling the data, we will take the opportunity to explore both the business and manufacturing processes and how they get translated into details in your database. In the first example, you will look at the process hierarchy. In that discussion, you will learn a little about how hierarchal data can be represented in a TreeView design; you might envision the outline of a document, a decision tree, or the file explorer of Windows.

Identifying the Details

The next step is to carefully review each subject to ensure that you have identified all of the relevant details necessary to fully describe it, and you need to ensure that each detail is listed separately. These details will be represented as the *fields* in each table

A good example might be the details about a person; you might have name and eye color. Name is a general detail, so in order to list each item separately, you need the first name, the last name, and, depending on your business rules, you may also need the suffix, the middle name, and the title or courtesy address. Eye color cannot be further divided.

NOTE Database developers often use the term *attribute* to represent a field prior to its implementation in an actual table or database file, which is another step in the modeling phase. Consider, for example: "The Process Name attribute will be implemented in the table named tblProcess as the field named Process." This illustrates how "attribute" is the conceptual view of a field, while "field" is the actual implementation.

As we figure out how to record the details as fields, we come across several types of relationships between the tables. And, we will again take the opportunity to explore both the underlying business or manufacturing factors and the way that they are resolved in the database. This will help you to learn about various types of tables and relationships.

In creating the tables for the manufacturing business process, you will learn about child tables, lookup tables, and self-referencing tables. We will explore the concepts for each type of table so that you can apply them to similar scenarios in your own projects.

Grouping the Details into Subjects

After you have identified all of the relevant details, you will employ a systematic process to determine if each detail directly describes the main subject or a different core subject. You might also discover that a detail actually represents a different subject that helps to support the main subject, or it might describe a different subject altogether. Each of these subjects will be the basis for one or more tables in your database.

NOTE You can use several approaches to analyze and group the details in order to identify and create the appropriate tables. In Chapters 8 and 9, we are following a systematic approach that includes reviewing each detail against a list of four qualifying questions. The pattern of the responses to those questions helps determine how to handle the detail. This is one approach for implementing the normalization process that you learned about in Chapter 3.

While studying the examples in other chapters, you may have followed several different approaches. We believe you can benefit from experiencing different techniques that will help you become aware of some of the viable options. You can use the method or combination that works best for you in a given situation. Indeed, you may find a combination of techniques that suits you best, particularly if you use a less formal approach. When you are faced with a very complex scenario, or you are having difficulty determining the correct design, it may be helpful to follow a more structured analysis process.

Evaluating and Grouping the Details - The Four Questions

One of the first things that you will need to do is to decide if each detail, or field, represents the subject of the current table, or if it describes a different subject or table. Sometimes a field in your list may appear to do both. Our approach is to create a list of questions, then walk each detail through the list. Based on the set of answers, you can either create a field in the current table or identify the need for a new or different table; occasionally you may choose a different option, such as removing the detail altogether.

We will use the following questions to evaluate whether each detail needs to be in the current table or in another table. You can also use these questions with the details and fields in your existing database projects to see if they need to be modified, or normalized, to function more efficiently.

1. Is the field a property that directly describes the subject of the table?

2. Will the value of this field be limited to a set of known or standard values?

3. Can a single record have more than one value for this field?

4. Is the field redundant; does it describe or repeat another field in the table?

You may be asking yourself where these questions came from, or what is the intent of these questions. We use these questions as a way to organize, or "normalize," the data into tables that follow the guidelines for the relational data model, as explained in Chapter 3.

The first question directly relates to the ideal premise of the relational data model, which is that each field of a table represents a property that directly describes the discrete subject of the table. For example, in a table that is focused on people, you would not have a field for the name of a person's child because the name of the child does not directly contribute to the description of a person.

A No response to the first question often indicates the need for a separate table to represent that property or feature. The separate table may be a *lookup table*, *child table*, or even another *operational table* (or core table).

The second question helps you determine if the values expected for a field will be constrained to a fixed set. It they are, there are techniques that you can use to keep the data consistent regardless of who is entering the data. For example, if your table has a field for the color of an object, you may want to provide a limited set of choices to those using the application, such as a fixed set of colors like red, blue, green, black. This prevents entries like "turquoise," "baby blue," or "gren" (an obvious typo), and makes it easy to search and group the entries. As your needs change, you can modify the list of available values. Often, a Yes response to question 2 indicates the need for a *lookup table*, sometimes called a *domain or reference table*.

The third question helps you consider the *first normal form*, which prevents a record from having more than one field representing the same detail. For example, many people have more than one phone number, so it may be tempting to have a phone number table with enough fields to accommodate them, such as Phone1, Phone2, and Phone3. However, that would use several fields for the same detail. And, although it may seem easy to just add more fields, doing so makes it a lot more difficult to search and maintain your data. A Yes response to this question indicates the need for a child table.

The forth question relates to the *second normal form,* which is to prevent data redundancy. This means that a single detail can only be provided one time and can be in only one field; so, you should not include the same data in two or more fields in a table. For example, suppose you have table of product colors that has three fields: ProductID, ColorID, and ColorName. Both

ColorID (a foreign key from the Color table) and ColorName provide the same information.

The color name can be derived from the ColorID, so the field provides redundant data and should be removed. Using a single field to represent a single property promotes data concurrency. A response of Yes to question 4 indicates the need to simply drop a field from a table.

Asking these qualifying questions is a more formal technique for implementing the rules and guidelines for normalization than some developers usually follow. Asking a documented set of questions can help ensure consistency. For more detail on the relational data model or the normal forms, please refer to Chapter 3.

Creating the Tables and Fields

After determining how each detail will be treated, your next step is to create the core table and the related support tables. You'll find this step to be fairly easy because you will essentially be creating the tables and fields based on the way the details are grouped.

Your main tasks will be to a) assign a valid table name, b) create each field in the tables, establishing the necessary *field properties*, and c) ensure that you include the necessary fields to create the appropriate relationships between the tables. This process is called *defining the tables*.

You will need to pay attention to the field properties that you assign to each field. The field properties control the type of data that the field can store and the default display of the data. They can also help control data entry by limiting what users can enter, or by requiring them to select from a list. For example, you can use the field properties to limit a field to a 2-digit number if you know that the value must always be less than 100. See Chapter 2, Tables 2-3 and 2-4, and Appendix A for more information regarding field properties.

Reviewing the Relationships

After we have created all of the tables for a core subject, we will formally define the relationships between the tables. We'll look at the relationship view to see how they fit together.

We'll go through the same process for each of the core subjects. Then, we will see how all of the tables fit together by incorporating them into one relationship view. The big picture is the overall database schema.

Now that you have an idea of where we are headed and how we are going to get there, we can turn our attention back to the manufacturing processes.

Manufacturing Processes

We will start with the main focus for the database: the manufacturing processes. Details about the process will become the source for the fields in the tables. Before we jump into listing all of the details, we'll first discuss the manufacturing processes themselves and consider some of the user expectations and system requirements that we need to address.

Manufacturing Process Hierarchies

Processes in manufacturing environments typically nest within each other. For example: The entire production shop can be considered one process since a shop contributes to the manufacture of a product. And, when you look within the shop, you may find automated lines which are also individual processes, since they contribute to the manufacture of a product. As you look further into an automated line, you may find that there are three stations, which are, in turn, processes. In addition, each of these stations might have four robots, which are also considered to be processes. And even each robot can be broken down into several processes: the base, arms, and wrists. In designing your database, you will need to consider each of these unique, definable processes as potentially requiring separate tracking.

There is at least one more aspect to consider. Perhaps station 1 on the automated line requires parts that have to be added by a person. Therefore, you would need to identify a *parts set* process for that person; the process hierarchy would also need to include the fixture into which the person sets the parts.

If you have parts, you may also need to identify where they are. Suppose that you have a rack that holds the parts specific to that position at station 1. In that case, the storage rack is also a process because it "contributes to the manufacture of a product" as it holds the raw stock prior to it becoming part of the assembly.

As you can see, designing the database requires an in-depth analysis to identify and document the unique processes that are involved in manufacturing a product. To help you visualize this, we have listed all of the processes that we've just described in Figure 8-2 in their *process hierarchy*, commonly called a *process tree*.

Appropriate Depth of Your Process Tree

A process can be as high level as the entire plant or shop floor, which is often the *granularity*, or level of detail, used by corporate managers when discussing production goals and metrics. A process can also get down to the level of detail

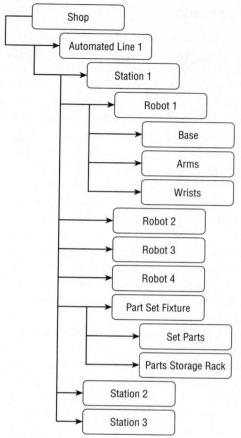

Figure 8-2: The process hierarchy

that defines a clamp holding a specific part; this might be the level of tracking required for maintenance personnel. You will need to determine the level of detail appropriate to support the current and anticipated needs of the people who will use and rely on the data from your database.

As a guideline, the depth of your process tree should not go beyond information that can be analyzed for the benefit of those using the data. For example, the process tree in Figure 8-2 could be taken to a depth that includes the bolts holding fixtures together. However, if the purpose of your database is to identify processes that cause production downtime, then identifying individual bolts and clamps would not provide useful information. Instead, if you collect the data to the process levels associated with a fixture, you could effectively group the data to report how and when the fixture affected production. That level of detail would support related business decisions.

Identifying the Details

Now that you are ready to create the tables needed to manage the data associated with the processes, you begin by listing details associated with the processes in your environment. These details will become the fields that will make up the core table and any supporting tables you identify. Creating a list of the details can help you to organize your thoughts. We recommend using a sheet of paper or an electronic format so that you can easily organize the fields into the appropriate groups that will become your tables.

Although you can do this in the Microsoft Access table designer, that would be jumping ahead because you haven't assigned the proper field names or properties. However, you may appreciate using an electronic format that allows you to view and work with the details of several subjects at one time. As you'll soon discover, it is very common to need to move or copy fields from one table to another.

We will start with the list of details that describe, and are important to, the manufacturing process, as shown in Table 8-2. Your list should contain the details that are necessary for your processes, so it will likely be somewhat different. Keep in mind that our model is intended to be relatively generic and easily modified.

The list of details in Table 8-2 may seem to be minimal, but for our purposes, it is sufficient to satisfy the database purpose and the user requirements. In addition, our goal is to provide you with a model database that is thorough, yet simple and easy to understand. The critical point to remember is that the list of details must include all of the details that you need to know—or will likely need to know—about your processes. Your list will probably grow in response to changes in your business needs. This could be a result of business expansion or new reporting requirements. But it is just as likely to come from further examination of your existing business practices that are related to the database purpose or user expectations.

Creating the Tables

The next task is to create the tables. As mentioned earlier, we will use a systematic approach to evaluate each detail against a list of qualifying questions to determine how the data should be recorded. This is one way to apply the principles for creating a properly normalized table design as we discussed in Chapter 3.

When creating the tables for a subject, you typically start with a core table. So, we will start with the Process table; following good naming conventions and using singular versions of the subject, we will name it tblProcess.

The purpose of this table is to store and manage the details specific to the manufacturing processes. In designing the table, we will also take steps to help ensure that the data is accurate and consistent. This is particularly important

Table 8-2: Manufacturing Process Details

DETAIL	DESCRIPTION
Process Name	Name of the process as it is known in the shop.
Process Type	The type of process, as defined by the people who will use the database. Often the information intended for this field is called class, or classification. You may use such terms as Autoline, Fixture, Parts Rack.
Description	A description of the process.
Location	The location of the process within the shop or plant. This might be the location of a piece of equipment or the exact location for storing replacement parts.
Process Parent	Identify the process directly above the current process. The parent process will appear as the next level up in the process hierarchy; the current process would be the child.
Vendor	The company from which you bought the process, if the process is a purchasable thing. Often a vendor sells processes or equipment from different manufacturers.
Manufacturer	The company that makes the process, if the process is made by a manufacturer. Sometimes a manufacturer sells what they make, but often a manufacturer is represented by a vendor—thus the need for two distinct fields.
Backed Up By Process	Identifies the process(es) that can back up the current process if the current process is in a nonproduction condition. You can use this information to help create a plan if you need to continue production while a process is out of commission.
Notes	Miscellaneous notes about the process.

because some field values will be repeated as new processes are added to the table. By following the guidelines to properly normalize the database, you can help ensure consistent data.

Explaining the Approach and Types of Tables

Once you have the list of details, you will need to determine how they will be recorded in the database. The approach that we're using in Chapters 8 and 9 uses the following questions to evaluate whether each detail item needs to be in the current table or in another table. You can also use these questions with the details, or fields, in your existing database projects to see if they could be modified to function more effectively.

1. Is the field a property that directly describes the subject of the table?
2. Will the value of this field be limited to a set of known or standard values?

3. Can a single record have more than one value for the field?

4. Is the field redundant? Does it describe or repeat another field in the table?

We will start with Process Name, the first detail in our list for the subject Process. We're looking for a response sequence of Yes, No, No, and No to identify items that can be added to the core table, tblProcess. And indeed, when you ask our questions of Product Name, your answer to the first question is Yes, and your answer to the remaining three is No. Therefore, you can conclude that Process Name directly supports the subject Process and should also become a field in tblProcess.

We will actually create the fields a little later; for now, our focus is on determining what to do with each detail in the list. We are determining whether to add it to tblProcess or to create a supporting table that potentially uses the field as the subject. So, you should continue asking the questions for the remaining items listed in Table 8-2.

As you do, you will find that there are two other details that give you the above response sequence. When you ask the questions for Description and Notes, the answers are also Yes, No, No, and No. Therefore, these will also become fields in tblProcess. Next, we will look at how to handle a different set of responses.

Potential Child Tables: Additional Details

As you ask the qualifying questions for certain details, you may notice that the responses will vary according to the specific scenario. So, although the Notes detail does not require an additional table in the current model, you may prefer to create a separate table for it in other situations. For example, you may want a separate table for notes if you are using the notes as an audit trail or in a database serving as a historical reference or archive.

Notes yields a Yes response to question number three, "Can a single record have more than one value for this field?" Since our primary goal is to provide a basic sample schema that is easy to learn from and customize, we will continue with a less complex model and keep the Note field in tblProcess. There are other examples throughout the book that show you how to put the Note field into a separate table when it is appropriate to do so.

Lookup Tables

The next detail is Process Type. When you ask our four qualifying questions, your answers are Yes, Yes, No, and No. The answer to question one is Yes, which reveals that the field should remain in tblProcess; however, there is a twist. You also answered Yes to question two, which asks if the values of the field are limited to a set of known or standard values.

This pattern identifies the potential need to create a support table that will provide the list of values. This is often called a lookup table, but it is also known as a *reference table* or a *domain table* (see the *Domains and Constraints* section of Chapter 3). We will create the table named tblProcessType to store a set of distinct values that can be used to identify the process type.

NOTE Allowing the user to select from a predetermined list of values not only saves time and minimizes the potential for entry error, but it also provides definitive values that can be used to select and group items to perform various types of analysis.

When the user selects the Process Type, a value is stored in the field of tblProcess. However, in this case, the value stored will be the value of the primary key for the specific process type selected rather than the name of the process itself. The ProcessType field in tblProcess is the foreign key, and it links to the primary key field in tblProcessType. The link between the two keys forms a relationship between tblProcess and tblProcessType. You can get a refresher on relationships and using primary key and foreign keys in the *Relationships* section of Chapter 2, and in Appendix B.

By using a lookup table, you can modify or add to the list of process types in one place, and the change will be reflected throughout the database. Modifications to Process Type in tblProcessType will be reflected everywhere the key values are used to represent the process type in other tables.

However, you may not always want to have existing records automatically updated. In that case, you can still use a lookup table in much the same way, but instead of storing the value of the primary key you would store the name of the process type. Just by changing which piece of data is actually stored in tblProcess, you can specify whether or not updates to data in the lookup table will be reflected in tblProcess.

NOTE Automatic updates can be accomplished by enforcing referential integrity and selecting the Cascade Update option. We will discuss that later in this chapter. You can also read more in Chapter 2 and Appendix B.

Now you're familiar with how lookup tables can be used, we'll proceed with the other three details that have the same response pattern as Process Type. You will get the same answers for Location, Process Parent, and Manufacturer. You will create those fields in tblProcess as foreign keys to supporting tables.

You will treat Location the same way you did Process Type. You will end up creating a lookup table and storing the value of the primary key in tblProcess. However, the other two items require a bit more discussion.

Self-Referencing Table

At first appearance, the Process Parent field suggests that you need to create a separate lookup table. But, if you look at the bigger picture, you can see that the processes are listed in the table tblProcess. So, now you need to figure out how to select the Process Parent from a list in the same table.

This illustrates an interesting concept known as a *self-referencing table*. This means that the field will "look up" the valid values from a field that is also in the same table. Simply stated, the parent process is just another process, so both the process and the parent process are represented by records in the same table, tblProcess. Because not all processes will have a parent process, not every record will have a value in that field. We will talk about some of the nuances associated with that when we create the actual field a little later in this chapter.

Choosing between Alternate Designs

The final detail that we flagged for a lookup table is the manufacturer. It gives us another opportunity to discuss some alternative designs. Once again, you start by asking our four qualifying questions. This time, we can answer either Yes or No to question 1, while the answers for the other questions are Yes, No, and No. Answering Yes to question 1 means that Manufacturer directly describes the subject of the table. The other answers indicate that values for Manufacturer come from a limited set of known values, and each process is provided by only one manufacturer (No to question three). However, you also should quickly recognize that there may not be a manufacturer for every process. For example, a human process of setting parts doesn't involve a manufacturer.

When a field is not applicable to a process, your answer to question 1 should be No, indicating that the field does not directly describe the subject of tblProcess, and, thus, it should not be a field in tblProcess. In a situation where there are two potentially valid approaches, you, the database developer, will need to decide what will work best. In this case, you can either create a junction table or accept nulls in the Process table.

- **Create a junction table:** One approach is to create a table to store all of the information about manufacturers, and then create a third table to make the connection between each process and the manufacturer that provides that process. The table that makes the connection between the two source tables is called a junction table. With this approach, you will not store any information about the manufacturer in the process table.

- **Accept nulls:** The other approach is to keep the Manufacturer field in tblProcess and accept that there will be *nulls*, or fields without a value for processes that do not have a manufacturer. Allowing nulls in tables goes against the concepts of the relational data model, but you could still avoid nulls by allowing users to select a response such as Not Applicable.

Although you could handle this situation with either approach, we will choose the first option, and use a lookup table and a junction table. This allows us to show you how to create and use a junction table. So, we will create a junction table, tblProcessManufacturer, in order to link tblProcess to tblManufacturer. Each record in the junction table will store the key value for a process and the key value for the associated manufacturer. If that sounds complex, don't be discouraged; it will make more sense when you view the figures illustrating our table designs later in this chapter.

Many-to-Many Relationship and a Child Table

The next field we will discuss is Vendor. In this case, your answers to the four qualifying questions will be No, Yes, Yes, and No. The Yes response to question 3 indicates that more than one value for Vendor can be associated with an item in tblProcess; that immediately suggests a particular type of supporting table, one that is often called a *child table*. A child table is a transactional table, just like a core table. However, each record in a child table must relate to a record in a parent table. In this case, tblProcess is the parent. It is also important to note that a parent table can have more than one child table, just like a person can have more than one child.

Since the child table will store all the vendors for a process, we will name it tblProcessVendor. As you are creating the table, you will also want to consider the implications of your responses to the other questions. Your answer to question two was Yes, so you know that the vendors need to be selected from a specific list. In this case, you will also need to create a lookup table for the vendors. We'll name that table tblVendor. This allows you to limit the selections to existing vendors.

The compound name tblProcessVendor indicates this table will store the key values from both the Process and the Vendor tables. And, because we determined that a given process can have more than one vendor, we know that a process can be listed multiple times; once for each of its vendors. Similarly, a vendor may provide more than one process. That is why this is called a many-to-many relationship. Again, this may seem a bit confusing at first. However, it is a rather common scenario, so it is important for you to know how to implement it in your database. You will see similar situations with employees and supervisors and throughout other organizations.

Self-Referencing Lookup Table

You have reached the last detail in the list. When you ask the qualifying questions about Backed Up By Process, you'll get a Yes for two questions: "Do the field values come from a known set of values?" and "Can a single record have more than one value for this field?" Based on these two Yes responses, you can determine that you need a lookup table.

You'll also notice that much like the Process Parent, the Backed Up By Process detail is limited to values that come from tblProcess itself. So, once again, you do not need to create a new table. However, because any given process may have more than one acceptable backup process, you do need to add a child table, which we have named tblProcessBackup. Using the child table, each process can have an unlimited number of backup processes.

Supporting Tables for Processes

At this point, you have reviewed all of the details that were identified for the main subject, processes. You evaluated each detail to determine if it would become a field in the Process table, or if it would be recorded in a different table. You also learned about several ways that tables can be related, so you can use information from more than one table. As we went through the details, you learned how some items could be handled in more than one way, and we explained the rationale for the methods used in our database. Ultimately, we identified the tables that we will use for our example, as listed in Table 8-3.

Table 8-3: Tables Representing Manufacturing Processes

TABLE	ORIGINATION
tblProcess	Natural choice for the core subject, Process. The table also provides lookup values for the Processes Parent and Backed Up fields.
tblProcessType	The list of process types used as a lookup table.
tblLocation	The list of locations used as a lookup table.
tblProcessManufacturer	A junction table to relate processes and manufacturers.
tblManufacturer	The list of manufacturers used as a lookup table for the tblProcessManfacturer table.
tblProcessVendor	A junction table to relate the processes and vendors.
tblVendor	The list of vendors used as a lookup table.
tblBackupProcess	The list of processes that back up other processes, a child table to the tblProcess table.

In order to understand the way tables and their data work together to fully describe the manufacturing processes, you also need to understand the relationships between tables. Figure 8-3 illustrates the relationships shared between each table. If you follow the lines, you can see how the data will flow. You'll likely recall from the earlier discussion about the symbols that the infinity sign indicates that there can be many instances of a record. For example, a given process type may be listed many times in the tblProcess table.

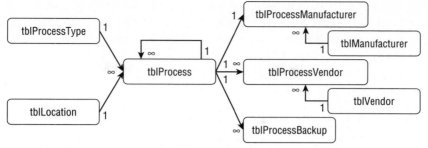

Figure 8-3: Table relationships for manufacturing processes

Using our process to normalize the data, we have determined that it will require eight tables to store the details about the manufacturing process, as shown in Figure 8-3. The core table tblProcess is supported by seven tables. It has one child table, tblProcessBackup, and four lookup tables:

- tblProcessType
- tblLocation
- tblManufacturer
- tblVendor

In addition, there are two junction tables; tblProcessManufacturer and tblProcessVendor. Additional details specific to the unique relationship created by the junction tables will be stored in the junction tables.

The self-reference within tblProcess, which identifies the parent process of a process, is represented by the one-to-infinity arrow pointing back to tblProcess.

Understanding Lookup Tables

It is important to note that lookup tables represent their own distinct subject. So, you will need to go through the process of defining the applicable fields for each lookup table, in much the same way that we just analyzed the core table tblProcess. Typically, though, analyzing a lookup table is relatively straightforward and quick; often it can be done in your mind without the aid of the qualifying questions. In general, lookup tables have fewer fields because they are primarily lists of data that can be used in another table.

Explaining the Fields

You now have the list of tables, and you understand how the data from each table will work together, so it is time to actually create the tables and fields. Your analysis determined both the tables that each field will go into and the relationship between the tables. Your next step is almost as simple as creating a valid field name for each field that belongs in a given table. The additional task is to select the correct data type for each field and set any field properties that are appropriate for your particular scenario. We'll discuss these items as we get to them, but you can also get a solid understanding from Appendix A.

Standard Fields

Before we deal with the fields that we've identified for the manufacturing process, we'll discuss some other, standard, fields that you may use in most, if not all, of your tables, and explain them now rather than every time that they appear in a table. We'll refer to these as *Standard Fields*.

Primary Keys

Look at the tables in the figures below; you will notice that all but one of the tables has a single field primary key which uses an AutoNumber as the data type. The only exception is the junction table, tblProcessManufacturer, and we will explain that shortly.

We did not discuss the primary key, or unique identifier, as part of our field analysis because the value in this field will not be derived from anything in the manufacturing process. We want the primary key to be a unique value that will be meaningless to the user, so we will use an AutoNumber. AutoNumbers are system-generated, unique values. The database system can use them to identify the individual item, or record, that is stored in a table. Moreover, although the AutoNumber is typically not seen by users, the value is used to find related records. This type of primary key is called a *surrogate key*. See Chapter 2 and Appendix A for more information.

Other Standard Fields

You will also find other fields in our table definitions that were not a part of the earlier discussion. Those fields provide functionality that is typically required or expected from an application. You can often use the field properties for these fields to set default values so that the system does most of the work. Since the fields are common to most tables and have standard settings and uses, we will refer to them as standard or common fields.

Table 8-4 lists the fields that you will find in most of the tables of our database. Not every field in this table will be present in every table, and you will quickly realize why they are not always needed. As you work with our model and incorporate the tables and fields appropriate for your scenarios, you may add other fields or manage these fields differently. An example of an alternative field definition would be to use a Yes/No data type for Inactive instead of a Date/Time data type. Another field that you may find helpful is a general note field, created as a text field, for administrative purposes—meaning for the database administrator. This type of note field may be especially helpful if you often need to import or mark data for future manipulation.

Table 8-4: Standard Fields

FIELD	DESCRIPTION
*<Identifier>*ID	The root of the table name is used for the identifier with the suffix of ID to indicate that it is the primary key of the table. For example, "VendorID." We use an AutoNumber data type to create a surrogate key. The database engine generates field values and, because we have selected the field as the primary key, each field will have a unique value.
Inactive	This uses a Date/Time data type to indicate when a row becomes invalid for use in the application. This is often used in lookup tables in order to prevent the display of values that are no longer used. By not deleting the record, the values will still be displayed in existing records.
CreatedDate	This field uses the Date/Time data type to store the date that a record was created. A common technique is to set the default value to Now(). Knowing when a record was created can be useful in several scenarios, such as identifying records that are incomplete or in a "half-baked" state and, thus, may require deletion. In addition, the information can be invaluable for traceability and a multitude of other purposes.
CreatedBy	This is a text field used to store the computer user's ID. The information is usually obtained by using code, and the user is not allowed to change the value. The data can be used for traceability and accountability.

NOTE We recommend that you have a primary key for every table. In addition, we recommend you use an AutoNumber data typed field as the single field primary key. If your table has other fields that need to have unique values, you can create a unique index to prevent duplicate values. The primary key and other field properties are discussed in Chapter 2 and in Appendix B.

Now that you know the basis for what we are calling the standard fields, you are ready to create the tables for the manufacturing process. We will start with the main core table, tblProcess.

Creating the Tables and Fields

Since we are building an application to represent a process management philosophy, the first table that we will create is tblProcess. You can look ahead to see the completed table in Figure 8-4. To build the table, we start by adding the fields from our list of standard fields. The first field is the primary key, ProcessID. You also need to add CreatedDate and CreatedBy. You will notice that those fields will have the same name and function in all of our operational tables.

However, before we add any more fields, we need to address some additional concepts. Understanding these will help you to leverage the capabilities of the database to provide more efficient solutions.

As you read about the tables and fields, we encourage you to review the actual tables in the chapter database that is provided on the companion CD. Looking at the tables themselves, you can read through the field definitions and investigate more of the field properties. With that in mind, we have purposely kept the discussions short in the book so that we focus on the concepts that influence the decisions about the designs.

Application Performance vs. Using Calculated Fields

As you study the fields shown in tblProcess, below, you will notice that we've included two other application-generated fields, ProcessIDPath and ProcessPath. These fields are generated and maintained by the application for the benefit of users.

Adding these fields to tblProcess deviates from the guidelines against including calculated fields in tables. Specifically, these fields violate the second normal form because they are the result of calculations. (For details on the second normal form see Chapter 3.)

The calculations that provide values for ProcessPath and ProcessIDPath evaluate the data in the table tblProcess to record the process names and ProcessIDs (respectively) for the complete hierarchy of a particular process. For every process that has a "parent," or value, in the BelongsTo field, the ProcessPath path field contains the concatenation, or text list, of all of the processes that you step down through to get to that level of detail. Similarly, the ProcessIDPath field contains the concatenated list of ProccessID values. As you can imagine, these are intense calculations, so rather than require the application to calculate values every time they are needed, we have decided to sacrifice a purist approach to database design in order to gain the performance benefits of storing the computed values for both fields.

> **NOTE** With self-referencing tables a TreeView control is an excellent tool for displaying and managing the hierarchy of records in the application interface. The database for this chapter on the book's CD includes a TreeView control. Microsoft did not provide a native TreeView control as a standard form control in Access 2010 and earlier. However, Microsoft does provide an ActiveX TreeView control that you can reference for this purpose.
>
> The ActiveX TreeView control provided by Microsoft is installed with the Office package. Later versions of Access may add a standard TreeView control to the application, so if you are using a version higher than Access 2010, you should verify that a native TreeView control does not exist in your install before using an ActiveX control.

The Process Table

The field names for table tblProcess in Figure 8-4 are fairly self-explanatory. It is also helpful (but not mandatory) to use the Description column to include additional notes about the fields, such as cautions or restrictions for the data, what the source is, how the data is generated, or other notes that you think might be helpful to you or your successor a year or 5 years down the road.

Field Name	Data Type	Description
ProcessID	AutoNumber	Unique row identifier
Process	Text	The process name
ProcessTypeID	Number	The type of process; Foreign Key to tblProcessType.ProcessTypeID
Description	Text	The process description
LocationID	Number	The physical location of the process; Foreign Key to tblLocation.LocationID
Notes	Memo	Notes about this process
BelongsTo	Number	The process in which this process belongs; Foreign Key to tblProcess.ProcessID
ProcessPath	Text	Application calculated. The hierarchy of the process using the Process field
ProcessIDPath	Text	Application calculated. The hierarchy of the process using the ProcessID field
CreatedDate	Date/Time	Date/Time the record was created
CreatedBy	Text	User ID of the person that created this record

Figure 8-4: tblProcess

As you create the tables, you have a lot of latitude for the field name and description. The first two columns shown in Figure 8-4 allow you to provide the absolute minimal information or controls required. However, each field also has several properties that give you the ability to speed data entry, format the display of your data, or validate the data as it is being entered. Chapter 2 and Appendix A provide detailed discussions concerning data types and field properties.

To create this table, you will also need to set the field properties as follows:

- ProcessID is identified as the primary key of the table.

- All fields with the Number data type have a FieldSize property of Long Integer.

- Process and ProcessTypeID are required.

The Process Manufacturer Table

The table tblProcessManufacturer, shown in Figure 8-5, is unique in that it does not have an AutoNumber primary key. That is because it uses the foreign key from tblProcess, ProcessID, as its primary key. Because primary keys are, by definition, unique values, using it as the primary key in the junction table forces a *one-to-one relationship* between the two tables: tblProcess and tblProcessManufacturer.

Serving as both a child table and a junction table, tblProcessManufacturer also has the field ManufacturerID, which is the foreign key from the Manufacturer table. Because the same ProcessID cannot be in two records, you are assured that there will only be one record for each combination of process and manufacture. In the comments field, you can record comments that are specific to the unique combination of the process and manufacturer.

| tblProcessManufacturer | | |
Field Name	Data Type	Description
⚹▸ ProcessID	Number	The process. FK to tblProcess.ProcessID
ManufacturerID	Number	The manufacturer of the process. FK to tblManufacturer.ManufacturerID
Comments	Text	Miscellaneous comments regarding the manufacturer of the process

Figure 8-5: tblProcessManufacturer

The Manufacturer Table

The table tblManufacturer, as shown in Figure 8-6, is a basic lookup table. As with many lookup tables, it includes fields for the primary key, the name of the manufacturer, and a description.

| tblManufacturer | | |
Field Name	Data Type	Description
⚹▸ ManufacturerID	AutoNumber	Unique row identifier
Manufacturer	Text	The name of the manufacturer
Description	Text	The description of the manufacturer
Inactive	Date/Time	Indication of when row became inactive

Figure 8-6: tblManufacturer

The Process Vendor Table

The table tblProcessVendor, as shown in Figure 8-7, is a basic junction table that consists of a primary key field and two foreign key fields. You should also include any other fields you have identified that directly describe the unique combination of a process and vendor subject of the junction table.

| tblProcessVendor | | |
Field Name	Data Type	Description
⚹▸ ProcessVendorID	AutoNumber	Unique row identifier
ProcessID	Number	The process. FK to tblProcess.ProcessID
VendorID	Number	The vendor. FK to tblVendor.VendorID
Comments	Memo	Miscellaneous comments regarding this vendor for this process
Inactive	Date/Time	Indication of when row became inactive

Figure 8-7: tblProcessVendor

The Vendor Table

The table tblVendor, as shown in Figure 8-8, is a basic lookup table. Additional information about the vendor, such as contact information, will be stored in other tables and connected through VendorID.

| tblVendor | | |
Field Name	Data Type	Description
⚹▸ VendorID	AutoNumber	Unique row identifier
Vendor	Text	Vendor name
Description	Text	Vendor description
Inactive	Date/Time	Indication of when row became inactive

Figure 8-8: tblVendor

The Process Type Table

The table tblProcessType, as shown in Figure 8-9, is a basic lookup table.

Field Name	Data Type	Description
ProcessTypeID	AutoNumber	Unique row identifier
ProcessType	Text	The process type
Description	Text	The description of the process type
Inactive	Date/Time	Indication of when row became inactive

Figure 8-9: tblProcessType

The Process Backup Table

The table tblProcessBackup, as shown in Figure 8-10, is a child table of tblProcess.

Field Name	Data Type	Description
ProcessBackupID	AutoNumber	Unique row identifier
ProcessID	Number	The process that is backed up. Foreign Key to tblProcess.ProcessID
BackedUpByID	Number	The process that provides the back up. Foreign Key to tblProcess.ProcessID
Comment	Text	Miscellaneous text describing the relationship

Figure 8-10: Table tblProcessBackup

As you may recall from our discussion of the Process Backup detail, tblProcessBackup includes a field, BackedUpByID, that identifies a backup process for each process. Each process can be backed up by any number of other processes, so this table can hold multiple records for each process, each associated with a backup process through the BackedUpByID.

The Location Table

Finally, tblLocation, shown in Figure 8-11, is the lookup table for selecting the location of a process.

Field Name	Data Type	Description
LocationID	AutoNumber	Unique identifier
Location	Text	The location description
Description	Text	Description/Comment about the location
Inactive	Date/Time	Indication of when row became inactive

Figure 8-11: tblLocation

Relationships

The next step in our design process is to fully describe and illustrate how the tables relate to each other. The work you've done, analyzing the data you need to document and monitor the activities associated with the manufacturing processes, has prepared you to formalize the relationships between the tables. Figure 8-12 is the relationship diagram that shows how the tables are related to each other.

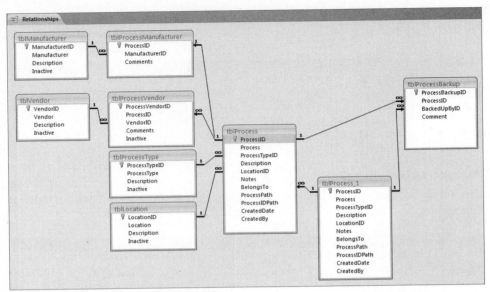

Figure 8-12: Relationship diagram for processes

NOTE In Figure 8-12, notice the table named tblProcess_1. We added the process table to the diagram twice in order to represent the self-join in the tblProcess table. The name tblProcess_1 is an *alias*. The aliased table view is pointing directly to the table tblProcess, so any relationship join lines, like the one shown between tblProcess_1 and tblProcessBackup, define a relationship between the table being aliased (tblProcess) and the other table.

Join Lines, Relationship Symbols, and Referential Integrity

Each relationship is identified with *join lines*. The 1 and the ∞ symbols at the end points of the join lines in Figure 8-12 represent the "one" side, or primary table, and the "many" side, or foreign table (a.k.a., child table), of a relationship.

In discussing table relationships, we follow a convention of calling out each relationship definition by the name of the table on the "one" side, followed by the name of the table on the "many" side. The primary key, abbreviated PK, and the foreign key, abbreviated FK, refer to the fields from the perspective of the primary table. In other words, the foreign key field is the same as a field in the primary table, typically the primary key. Values in the PK and FK fields must match in order to relate records from one table to another.

In addition to defining the relationship between two tables, you can also use the relationship to help manage the way data in the related tables is updated and deleted. Defined relationships have a property called *Referential*

Integrity. Referential integrity, abbreviated RI, ensures consistency between the records of related tables. Enforcing referential integrity prevents records from being added to a child table unless there is related record in the parent table. It also prevents a parent record from being deleted, leaving abandoned child records (called *orphaned records*). If you use the cascade delete option of referential integrity, when you delete a record on the 1 side of the relationship the database automatically deletes all related records on the ∞ side. If you use the cascade update option, changes to the value in the primary table are reflected in the fields in related tables.

You can learn more about relationships and the terms used to define them in Chapters 2 and 3, and Appendix B. As you can see from the list in Table 8-5, the relationships for the tables in the manufacturing processes rely on referential integrity being enforced, and they often use cascade delete.

Table 8-5: Relationships of Manufacturing Processes

RELATIONSHIP	TYPE	PRIMARY KEY FOREIGN KEY	REFERENTIAL INTEGRITY
tblLocation to tblProcess	1:M	tblLocation.LocationID tblProcess.LocationID	Yes
tblManufacturer to tblProcessManufacturer	1:M	tblManufacturer.ManufacturerID tblProcessManufacturer.ManufacturerID	Yes: Cascade Delete
tblProcess to tblProcessManufacturer	1:1	tblProcess.ProcessID tblProcessManufacturer.ProcessID	Yes: Cascade Delete
tblProcess to tblProcess_1	1:M	tblProcess.ProcessID tblProcess.BelongsTo	Yes: Cascade Delete
tblProcess to tblProcessBackup	1:M	tblProcess.ProcessID tblProcessBackup.ProcessID	Yes: Cascade Delete
tblProcess_1 to tblProcessBackup	1:M	tblProcess.ProcessID tblProcessBackup.BackedUpByID	Yes: Cascade Delete
tblProcess to tblProcessVendor	1:M	tblProcess.ProcessID tblProcessVendor.ProcessID	Yes: Cascade Delete
tblProcessType to tblProcess	1:M	tblProcessType.ProcessTypeID tblProcess.ProcessTypeID	Yes
tblVendor to tblProcessVendor	1:M	tblVendor.VendorID tblProcessVendor.VendorID	Yes: Cascade Delete
tblVendor to tblProcess	M:M	See relationships for junction table tblProcessVendor	—

Manufacturing Builds

Next, we'll analyze the information associated with the core subject Build. We'll follow the same steps with the manufacturing processes.

- Identify the details needed to describe the build.
- Evaluate the details to identify the core subjects and tables.
- Create the tables and fields.
- Put it all together by defining the relationships that link the tables together.

Identifying the Details

The first step is to identify all of the details that we need to include in the database. You'll need to create a comprehensive list that reflects the purpose of the database, which is to store production statistics relevant to a process production run, or build. As with other areas of the database, your field list may grow in response to business needs, or from further examination of your existing business practices related to the purpose of the database or user expectations.

Based on what we know of the manufacturing processes and production runs, we have created a list of details as shown in Table 8-6. As you look at the details, you will probably notice that some of them can be ascertained from other items in the list (e.g., Duration). This should prompt you to ask if all of the fields are necessary, or if some might be providing redundant data. You'll recall from our discussions in Chapter 3 that you should avoid storing redundant data in the database. We'll explain this further momentarily.

Table 8-6: Build Details

DETAIL	DESCRIPTION
Process	The manufacturing process for which the metrics are being tracked
Build Started	The date/time the build started
Build Stopped	The date/time the build stopped
Build Duration	The duration time that the build was able to produce products
Non Build Duration	The total time between the stop and subsequent start when the build process is stopped for a planned reason, such as lunch or breaks
Takt Rate	The pace at which one unit of product is produced
Stop Time	The total amount of time accumulated due to process stop throughout a build
Why stopped	The reasons why the build stopped when it was intended to be in production

Grouping the Details into Subjects

We will use a slightly different approach to the analysis to give you experience with a variety of techniques. We'll start with the core table that represents the subject of Builds, named tblBuild. The table will be similar in concept to the Process table. Next, we ask the four qualifying questions to determine what tables are needed to store the details.

1. Is the field a property that directly describes the subject of the table?
2. Will the value of this field be limited to a set of known or standard values?
3. Can a single record have more than one value for this field?
4. Is the field redundant? Does it describe or repeat another field in the table?

This time, we'll evaluate each detail with a process similar to a decision matrix. Putting the answers to the four questions into a matrix helps you see the results in a more graphic view, as shown in Table 8-7.

Table 8-7 contains the information and disposition for each of the details that we listed to describe Builds. You should pay particular attention to the discussion of redundant fields—a Yes answer to the fourth question.

Table 8-7: Analysis of the Details

DETAIL	RESPONSE PATTERN				DISPOSITION
Process	Y	Y	N	N	Remains in table tblBuild as the key that links to tblProcess.
Build Started	Y	N	N	N	Remains in table tblBuild.
Build Stopped	Y	N	N	N	Remains in table tblBuild.
Build Duration	Y	N	N	Y	Build Duration is elapsed time between Build Started and Build Stopped. If the field of Build Stopped is in the table, this field is redundant and should be dropped. If, however, you remove Build Stopped, the field can remain and Build Stopped can be calculated. Calculating the duration of the build yields a friendlier user interface, but you may find that you will take a hit in performance (albeit in the slightest of ways), since Build Duration is used in subsequent calculations. For the database of this chapter, Build Duration will be removed.

Continued

Table 8-7: *(continued)*

DETAIL	RESPONSE PATTERN				DISPOSITION
Non-Build Duration	Y	N	N	N	Remains in table tblBuild.
Takt Rate	Y	N	N	N	Remains in table tblBuild.
Stop Time	Y	N	N	N	Initially, this may seem to be a valid field for this table because of the response pattern. However, you'll recall from the database purpose and user expectations that each occurrence of build stoppage must be recorded. You can calculate this value based on the time stored in another table, tblBuildStoptime. The tables are related through a foreign key. The field is dropped.
Why Stopped	N	Y	Y	Y	This field does not directly describe the subject of the table, therefore it should not be in the table. This field is trying to capture the same data maintained in the Notification subject (discussed later) and is intended to support the Stop Time field. Because the Stop Time field will be in a different table, and the Why Stopped field supports the Stop Time field, you will need a junction table (tblBuildStoptimeNotification) that relates the two tables.

NOTE In more complex schemas, the build table may have a child table that contains build periods. That Build Period table would define each contiguous block of build time and contain the task time for that build period. You can then use the table to calculate the Build Started/Stopped and total Build Duration, thus eliminating the need for those fields in tblBuild. At that point, the Non-Build Duration would no longer be useful, so it would be dropped.

Based on the preceding analysis, summarized in Table 8-6, you can determine the need for three tables that will become the link between the process and a notification, as illustrated in Figure 8-13. We included the core tables tblNotification and tblProcess, which are shaded for distinction, in order to show you how tblBuild is related to the other core tables.

Creating the Tables and Fields

Your next step is to convert the details into actual fields in the tables. You will find that when you use this approach, the conversion of the details into fields is often relatively simple. Creating the fields of the supporting tables for tblBuild is no exception. Figures 8-14, 8-15, and 8-16 represent the tables and fields based on the analysis of the details listed above. The additional fields were explained in the discussion of the standard fields that are summarized in Table 8-4.

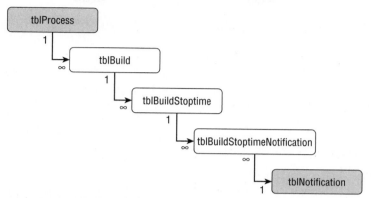

Figure 8-13: Table relationships for builds

The Build Table

The tblBuild operational table, shown in Figure 8-14, will store your production parameters for a tracked process.

Field Name	Data Type	Description
BuildID	AutoNumber	Unique row identifier
ProcessID	Number	The process that is being tracked. FK to tblProcess.ProcessID
BuildStart	Date/Time	Date/time the production day started
BuildStop	Date/Time	Date/Time the production day ended
NonBuildDuration	Number	Number of minutes between BuildStart and BuildStop that are non production
TaktRate	Number	Number of seconds to build one unit on the indicated process
QuantityBuilt	Number	Number of units produced at the conclusion of the build
CreatedDate	Date/Time	Date/Time the record was created
CreatedBy	Text	User ID of the person that created this record

Figure 8-14: tblBuild

The Build Stoptime Table

This child table is used to record each time the build process is stopped. If there are frequent build stops or if you need a finite measurement of stop time, the data in this table can automatically be populated using SCADA (Supervisory Control and Data Acquisition) or HMI (Human Machine Interface) software. Figure 8-15 shows the fields in the table tblBuildStoptime.

Field Name	Data Type	Description
BuildStoptimeID	AutoNumber	Unique row identifier
BuildID	Number	The build that was stopped due to this indicated Notification. FK to tblBuild.BuildID
StopTimestamp	Date/Time	The date/time the process stopped producing product
Duration	Number	Number of minutes the line/process was stopped (not producing products)
Comments	Text	Comments about this stop time occurrence
CreatedDate	Date/Time	Date/Time the record was created
CreatedBy	Text	User ID of the person that created this record

Figure 8-15: tblBuildStoptime

The Build Stoptime Notification Table

This junction table ties tblBuildStoptime to the table tblNotification in a many-to-many relationship by storing the fields BuildStoptimeID and NotificationID. Figure 8-16 illustrates tblBuildStoptimeNotification.

Field Name	Data Type	Description
BuildStoptimeNotificationID	AutoNumber	Unique row identifier
BuildStoptimeID	Number	FK to tblBuildStoptime.BuildStoptimeID
NotificationID	Number	FK to tblNotification.NotificationID
CreatedDate	Date/Time	Date/Time the record was created
CreatedBy	Text	User ID of the person that created this record

Figure 8-16: tblBuildStoptimeNotification

Reviewing the Relationships

Just as we did with the Process table, our next step is to fully describe how the Build table relates to the tables that contain the other details about the build. Figure 8-17 shows the relationships between the tables. The table tblNotification, (which will be discussed later), and the table tblProcess, are shaded because, although they represent other core subjects, they are related to the build process. You can see how the relationship between those tables closes the information loop.

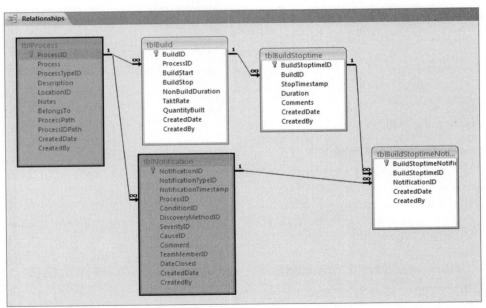

Figure 8-17: Relationship diagram for builds

You'll recall that the 1 and ∞ symbols shown in Figure 8-17 represent the primary table and the foreign table, or child table, of the relationship, respectively. If you would like more information on relationships and the terms used to define them, refer to Chapters 2 and 3, and Appendix B. To help you establish the necessary setting for referential integrity, we have summarized the relationships shown above in Table 8-8, and included the appropriate settings for referential integrity.

Table 8-8: Relationships of tblBuild

RELATIONSHIP	TYPE	PRIMARY KEY FOREIGN KEY	REFERENTIAL INTEGRITY
tblBuild to tblBuildStoptime	1:M	tblBuild.BuildID tblBuildStoptime.BuildID	Yes: Cascade Delete
tblBuildStoptime to tblBuildStoptime-Notification	1:M	tblBuildStoptime.BuildStoptimeID tblBuildStoptimeNotification.BuildStoptimeID	Yes: Cascade Delete
tblNotification to tblBuildStoptime-Notification	1:M	tblNotification.NotificationID tblBuildStoptimeNotification.NotificationID	Yes: Cascade Delete
tblProcess to tblBuild	1:M	tblProcess.ProcessID tblBuild.ProcessID	Yes: Cascade Delete
tblProcess to tblNotification	1:M	tblProcess.ProcessID tblNotification.ProcessID	Yes: Cascade Delete
tblNotification to tblBuildStopTime	M:M	See relationships for junction table tblBuildStopTimeNotification	—

Notifications

Next, we will analyze the core subject of notifications. Using the same procedure that you have been following, we will:

- Identify all details needed to describe notifications.
- Evaluate the details to identify the core subjects and tables.
- Create the tables and fields.
- Put it all together by defining the relationships between the tables.

Identifying the Details

The purpose of the notification is to provide users with a mechanism to store the details about a situation that affects a process and requires attention. A notification acts as a call or alarm to the appropriate personnel by identifing a process that needs to be fixed or adjusted. We have listed the associated details in Table 8-9.

Table 8-9: Notification Details

DETAIL	DESCRIPTION
Notification Type	This identifies the reason for or type of notification, such as an equipment breakdown, poor quality, a perceived ergonomic risk, or preventive maintenance.
Date and Time	The date and time that the issue was identified. This should not be confused with the time the notification was recorded.
Process	The process needing attention.
Condition	The condition that needs to be addressed.
How Condition Was Discovered	Indication of how the condition was discovered.
Severity	The severity level of the condition. This often affects how quickly attention is given to the process.
Cause of Condition	The reason that the process required a notification.
Comments	Additional notes to describe the situation.
Team Member	The employee who raised the notification.
What Was Done	Describes the response or actions taken.

Grouping the Details into Subjects

You'll quickly see that the analysis of the details follows the same procedure we used to review the details related to Builds. Since we have gone through this procedure before, you can repeat the steps without a lot of explanation. When you ask the same four qualifying questions, you should arrive at the results shown in Table 8-10, below.

1. Is the field a property that directly describes the subject of the table?
2. Will the value of this field be limited to a set of known or standard values?
3. Can a single record have more than one value for this field?
4. Is the field redundant; does it describe or repeat another field in the table?

Table 8-10: Analysis of the Details

DETAIL	RESPONSE PATTERN				DISPOSITION
Notification Type	Y	Y	N	N	Remains in table tblNotification as a key to the lookup table: tblNotificationType.
Date and Time	Y	N	N	N	Remains in table tblNotification.
Process	Y	Y	N	N	Remains in table tblNotification as a key that links to tblProcess.

DETAIL	RESPONSE PATTERN				DISPOSITION
Condition	Y	Y	N	N	Remains in table tblNotification as a key to the lookup table: tblCondition.
How Condition Was Discovered	Y	Y	N	N	Remains in table tblNotification as a key to the lookup table: tblDiscoveryMethod.
Severity	Y	Y	N	N	Remains in table tblNotification as a key to the lookup table: tblSeverity.
Cause of Condition	Y	Y	N	N	Remains in table tblNotification as a key to the lookup table: tblCause.
Comments	Y	N	N	N	Remains in the table tblNotification.
Team Member	Y	Y	N	N	Remains in table tblNotification as a key to the lookup table: tblTeamMember.
What Was Done	N	N	Y	N	Indicates a need for a child table, tblCountermeasure, which will be the core table for countermeasures.
What Builds Were Stopped	N	Y	Y	N	Indicates a need for a junction table that allows a BuildStoptime and tblNotification to share a many-to-many relationship. This will be similar to the table tblBuildStoptimeNotification.

As a result of this analysis, you can identify the need for the tables and relationships that are illustrated in Figure 8-18. We have shaded the tables that are defined in the discussion of other core subjects.

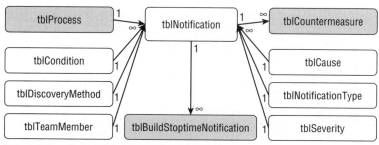

Figure 8-18: Table relationships for notifications

NOTE In addition to allowing each process to have numerous notifications, some scenarios may also need to allow one notification to be associated with more than one process. This would create a many-to-many relationship between processes and notifications. As in the earlier example, this would require a junction table between the Process table and the Notification table. In that case, the Countermeasure table would link to the new junction table instead of the Notification table.

Creating the Tables and Fields

The next step is to convert the details into fields. Figures 8-19 through 8-25 illustrate the tables used to provide the information related to notifications. The standard fields shown in these tables were discussed earlier and summarized in Table 8-4.

The Notifications Table

This table records the details concerning a process that is not meeting expectations or that might need attention. As the number of notifications accumulates, this table will help identify areas that receive the largest investment in time, and possibly money. Figure 8-19 shows fields that we included in the table tblNotification. The explanations of the new fields are provided in Table 8-10 above.

Field Name	Data Type	Description
tblNotification		
NotificationID	AutoNumber	Unique row identifier
NotificationTypeID	Number	The notification type. FK to tblNotificaitonType.NotificationID (Process, Quality, Ergo, Safety)
NotificationTimestamp	Date/Time	The date/time of the notification
ProcessID	Number	The process that a condition was identified on. FK to tblProcess.ProcessID
ConditionID	Number	The condition that was identified. FK to tblCondition.ConditionID
DiscoveryMethodID	Number	The method used to find the condition. FK to tblDiscoveryMethod.DiscoveryMethodID
SeverityID	Number	The severity of the notification. FK to tblSeverity.SeverityID
CauseID	Number	The core cause of the condition. FK to tblCause.CauseID
Comment	Text	Brief description of the notification or a comment to further define the notification
TeamMemberID	Number	The team member doing the notifying. FK to tblTeamMember.TeamMemberID
DateClosed	Date/Time	The date/time the notification was addressed
CreatedDate	Date/Time	Date/Time the record was created
CreatedBy	Text	User ID of the person that created this record

Figure 8-19: tblNotification

The Conditions Table

The table tblCondition, shown in Figure 8-20, is a standard lookup table that lists conditions and a description that might assist a user to select the most applicable condition.

Field Name	Data Type	Description
tblCondition		
ConditionID	AutoNumber	Unique row identifier
Condition	Text	The condition
Description	Text	The description of the condition
Inactive	Date/Time	Indication of when row became inactive

Figure 8-20: tblCondition

The Discovery Method Table

The table tblDiscoveryMethod, shown in Figure 8-21, is another standard lookup table. It has the list of ways an issue can be discovered. A finite list can help with data analysis for quality improvement and cost containment.

tblDiscoveryMethod		
Field Name	Data Type	Description
DiscoveryMethodID	AutoNumber	Unique row identifier
DiscoveryMethod	Text	The discovery method
Description	Text	The description of the discory method
Inactive	Date/Time	Indication of when row became inactive

Figure 8-21: tblDiscoveryMethod

The Team Member Table

The Team Member table is a standard lookup table. However, if you need additional information about a team member, you may need to add more fields. The tblTeamMember table, as shown in Figure 8-22, provides information for three core subjects: Notifications, and two more areas that we will discuss later. Although we'll list this table with each area, you will only create it one time, as the database will only contain one copy of the table.

tblTeamMember		
Field Name	Data Type	Description
TeamMemberID	AutoNumber	Unique row identifer
TeamMemberFirstName	Text	The team members first name
TeamMemberLastName	Text	The team members last name
Inactive	Date/Time	Indication of when row became inactive

Figure 8-22: tblTeamMember

The Severity Table

The table tblSeverity, as shown in Figure 8-23, is another standard lookup table with fields for a short name and a description to aid in selecting the most appropriate level. Having the severity level concisely defined and consistently applied is a significant aid in prioritizing repairs, and for management analysis.

tblSeverity		
Field Name	Data Type	Description
SeverityID	AutoNumber	Unique row identifer
Severity	Text	The severity
Description	Text	The description of the severity
Inactive	Date/Time	Indication of when row became inactive

Figure 8-23: tblSeverity

The Notification Type Table

The table tblNotificationType, shown in Figure 8-24, is a standard lookup table to provide a list of the types of notifications used.

tblNotificationType		
Field Name	Data Type	Description
NotificationTypeID	AutoNumber	Unique row identifier
NotificationType	Text	Notification type
Description	Text	A description of the notification type
Inactive	Date/Time	Indication of when row became inactive

Figure 8-24: tblNotificationType

The Cause Table

The table tblCause lists potential causes for stoppages. It is the final lookup table for notifications, and it contains similar fields and benefits offered by other lookup tables, as shown in Figure 8-25.

Field Name	Data Type	Description
CauseID	AutoNumber	Unique row identifier
Cause	Text	The cause
Description	Text	The description of the cause
Inactive	Date/Time	Indication of when row became inactive

Figure 8-25: tblCause

Reviewing the Relationships

Relationships for the tables that store the data directly related to notifications are represented in Figure 8-26. As with the previous relationship diagrams, we have shaded the tables that are explained in other core areas.

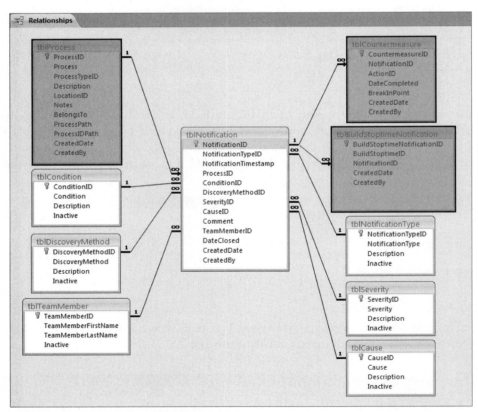

Figure 8-26: Relationship diagram for notifications

In addition to establishing the relationship between the tables, you will want to enforce referential integrity and use cascade deletes for some of the relationships. Table 8-11 summarizes the relationships shown in Figure 8-25 and includes the appropriate RI settings.

Table 8-11: Relationships of tblNotification

RELATIONSHIP	TYPE	PRIMARY KEY FOREIGN KEY	REFERENTIAL INTEGRITY
tblBuildStoptime to tblBuildStoptime-Notification	1:M	tblBuildStoptime.BuildStoptimeID tblBuildStoptimeNotification. BuildStoptimeID	Yes: Cascade Delete
tblCause to tblNotification	1:M	tblCause.CauseID tblNotification.CauseID	Yes
tblCondition to tblNotification	1:M	tblCondition.ConditionID tblNotification.ConditionID	Yes
tblDiscoveryMethod to tblNotification	1:M	tblDiscoveryMethod.DiscoveryMethodID tblNotification.DiscoveryMethodID	Yes
tblNotification to tblBuildStoptime-Notification	1:M	tblNotification.NotificationID tblBuildStoptimeNotification. NotificationID	Yes: Cascade Delete
tblNotification to tblCountermeasure	1:M	tblNotification.NotificationID tblCountermeasure.NotificationID	Yes: Cascade Delete
tblNotificationType to tblNotification	1:M	tblNotificationType.NotificationTypeID tblNotification.NotificationTypeID	Yes
tblProcess to tblNotification	1:M	tblProcess.ProcessID tblNotification.ProcessID	Yes: Cascade Delete
tblSeverity to tblNotification	1:M	tblSeverity.SeverityID tblNotification.SeverityiID	Yes

Countermeasures

The next subject we need to work with is Countermeasures. You will follow the same process to analyze the details. The steps are:

- Identify the details needed to describe the countermeasure.
- Evaluate the details to identify the core subjects and tables.
- Create the tables and fields.
- Put it all together by defining the relationships between the tables.

Identifying the Details

The tables related to countermeasures will provide users with a place to record details of what was done to a process in response to a notification. The ability to store relevant data about all of the activity related to a process can be quite beneficial for forecasting and for analyzing issue that are affecting productivity the most. Because a notification can have more than one countermeasure, you need to establish a one-to-many relationship between the tables. We'll review that in more detail shortly.

Based on our earlier discussions and work, we have determined that details listed in Table 8-12 are relevant to notifications.

Table 8-12: Notification Details

DETAILS	DESCRIPTION
Notification	The notification which prompted the countermeasure.
Action Done	The action applied to bring a process back to production condition, such as Repair, Replace, Adjust, and Fill.
Date Completed	The date/time when the countermeasure was completed or implemented.
BreakInPoint	A product indicator that identifies which product was the first product to run through the process after the countermeasure. This might be a Lot Number or Serial Number.
Steps To Implement	The steps needed to implement the action. This is basically a breakdown of the Action details.

Grouping the Details into Subjects

As in the past, we will evaluate each detail and determine how to place it into a table. As you repeat the steps using the same four qualifying questions, you should arrive at the results as shown in Table 8-13.

1. Is the field a property that directly describes the subject of the table?
2. Will the value of this field be limited to a set of known or standard values?
3. Can a single record have more than one value for this field?
4. Is the field redundant, or does the field describe another field in the table?

As a result of this analysis, you can identify the need for the tables and relationships that are illustrated in Figure 8-27. The table tblNotification is shaded to indicate that the table was defined in an early discussion.

Table 8-13: Analysis of the Details

DETAIL	RESPONSE PATTERN				DISPOSITION
Notification	Y	Y	N	N	Remains in tblCountermeasure as a foreign key to tblNotification.
Action Done	Y	Y	N	N	Remains in table tblCountermeasure as the foreign key to a lookup table, tblAction.
Date Completed	Y	N	N	N	Remains in tblCountermeasure.
BreakInPoint	Y	N	N	N	Remains in tblCountermeasure.
Steps To Implement	N	N	Y	N	Create a child table named tblCountermeasureStep that relates back to tblCountermeasure via a key value. This table will have fields that record the step number, the description of what was done during the step, and the duration (time) the step took to complete.
Who Is Doing the Work	N	Y	Y	N	Create a junction table named tblCountermeasureTeamMember that relates to tblCountermeasure using a foreign key. The table will also relate to the table named tblTeamMember using a foreign key.
Duration of the Work Done	Y	N	N	Y	This detail is the result of a calculation and therefore will not remain in tblCountermeasure. The calculation is a summation of the Duration field in tblCountermeasureStep.

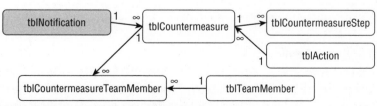

Figure 8-27: Table relationships for countermeasures

Creating the Tables and Fields

The next step, which you should find quite familiar now, is to convert the details into fields. Figures 8-28 through 8-32 illustrate the tables used to provide the information related to countermeasures. The standard fields shown in these tables were discussed earlier and summarized in Table 8-4.

The Countermeasure Table

This is the main table used to record what was done to a process in order to resolve a notification and to relieve the condition that required attention. As shown in Figure 8-28, the table includes the two foreign key fields and a field to record the date and time that the actions were completed. We have also included BreakInPoint to identify the first lot or product processed after the countermeasure is completed. You may find this and similar data to be quite helpful in audits and quality improvement processes.

Field Name	Data Type	Description
CountermeasureID	AutoNumber	Unique row identifier
NotificationID	Number	The notification that required actions. FK to tblNotification.NotificationID
ActionID	Number	The core action that is to be done. FK to tblAction.ActionID
DateCompleted	Date/Time	The date/time in which the countermeasure
BreakInPoint	Text	A production indicator that identifies when the countermeasure was in place (aka: Clean Point)
CreatedDate	Date/Time	Date/Time the record was created
CreatedBy	Text	User ID of the person that created this record

Figure 8-28: tblCountermeasure

The Countermeasure Team Member Table

This child, or detail, table is used to record the team members that participated in the countermeasure activity. The fields, as shown in Figure 8-29, are fairly self-explanatory.

Field Name	Data Type	Description
CountermeasureTeamMembe	AutoNumber	Unique row identifier
CountermeasureID	Number	FK to tblCounermeasure.CountermeasureID
TeamMemberID	Number	FK to tblTeamMember.TeamMemberID
Notes	Text	Brief note about the involvement of this Team Member for this Countermeasure
CreatedDate	Date/Time	Date/Time the record was created
CreatedBy	Text	User ID of the person that created this record

Figure 8-29: tblCountermeasureTeamMember

The Team Member Table

The table tblTeamMember, as shown in Figure 8-30, is a standard lookup table. When we put all of the tables together to look at the complete relationship diagram, you will see that tblTeamMember provides data to three tables: tblCounterMeasureTeamMember, tblGeneralNote, and tblNotification. For clarity and convenience, we are listing the table in each area, but the database will only contain one copy of the table.

tblTeamMember		
Field Name	Data Type	Description
TeamMemberID	AutoNumber	Unique row identifer
TeamMemberFirstName	Text	The team members first name
TeamMemberLastName	Text	The team members last name
Inactive	Date/Time	Indication of when row became inactive

Figure 8-30: tblTeamMember

The Action Table

The table tblAction provides the list of actions that can be taken as part of a countermeasure. The table, as shown in Figure 8-31, is a standard lookup table.

tblAction		
Field Name	Data Type	Description
ActionID	AutoNumber	Unique row identifier
Action	Text	The action
Description	Text	The description of the action
Inactive	Date/Time	Indication of when row became inactive

Figure 8-31: tblAction

The Countermeasure Step Table

You will find that it can be quite helpful to use this type of child table. In this case, it provides a detailed list of the tasks required for a countermeasure. In addition to documenting the steps taken, the data may be useful to determine or justify the number of people on hand to respond to notifications. Upon receiving a request for that type of analysis, you can use the data in this table to determine how much time each person spent implementing countermeasures.

Figure 8-32 displays the fields that we have included in the table tblCountermeasureStep. You will notice that the Duration field has a data type of Number rather than Date/Time. Our process will store the number of minutes invested rather than a start and stop time. You may find that a Date/Time field works better for your purposes.

tblCountermeasureStep		
Field Name	Data Type	Description
CountermeasureStepID	AutoNumber	Unique row identifier
CountermeasureID	Number	FK to tblCountermeasure.CountermeasureID
Step	Number	The step of this activity. Defaulted to a sequential number by the application.
Description	Memo	Description of the step of the implementation process of a countermeasure
Duration	Number	The length of time this step took, in minutes
CreatedDate	Date/Time	Date/Time the record was created
CreatedBy	Text	User ID of the person that created this record

Figure 8-32: tblCountermeasureStep

Reviewing the Relationships

Relationships for the tables that store the data directly related to countermeasures are represented in Figure 8-33. As with the previous relationship diagrams, we have shaded the tables that are explained in other core areas.

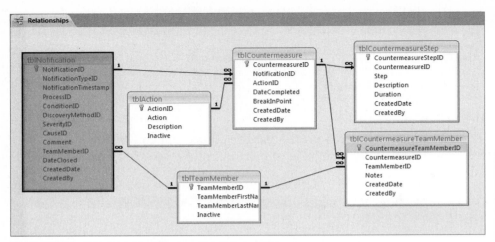

Figure 8-33: Relationship diagram for countermeasures

Table 8-14 summarizes the relationships that are illustrated in Figure 8-33.

Table 8-14: Relationships of tblCountermeasure

RELATIONSHIP	TYPE	PRIMARY KEY FOREIGN KEY	REFERENTIAL INTEGRITY
tblAction to tblCountermeasure	1:M	tblAction.ActionID tblCountermeasure.ActionID	Yes
tblCountermeasure to tblCountermeasureStep	1:M	tblCountermeasure.CountermeasureID tblCountermeasureStep.CountermeasureID	Yes: Cascade Delete
tblCountermeasure to tblCountermeasure-TeamMember	1:M	tblCountermeasure.CountermeasureID tblCountermeasureTeamMember.CountermeasureID	Yes: Cascade Delete
tblNotification to tblCountermeasure	1:M	tblNotification.NotificationID tblCountermeasure.NotificationID	Yes: Cascade Delete
tblTeamMember to tblCountermeasure-TeamMember	1:M	tblTeamMember.TeamMemberID tblCountermeasureTeamMember.TeamMemberID	Yes
tblTeamMember to tblNotification	1:M	tblTeamMember.TeamMemberID tblNotification.TeamMemberID	Yes
tblCountermeasure to tblTeamMember	M:M	See relationships for junction table tblCountermeasureTeamMember	–

General Notes

The last subject to analyze is general notes. We will use the same steps as we have in the past:

- Identify the details needed to describe general notes.

- Evaluate the details to identify the core subjects and tables.
- Create the tables and fields.
- Put it all together by defining the relationships between the tables.

Identifying the Details

The general notes table provides users with a place to record information regarding processes, such as general reminders or notifications of upcoming changes to a process or group of processes. This table can facilitate communication between the team members involved in the production process. Based on your knowledge of the processes and systems, and your experience with this example, you could likely create a list of details similar to the one that we have created in Table 8-15.

Table 8-15: General Notes Details

DETAILS	DESCRIPTION
Timestamp	The date/time the note was created.
Team Member	The team member creating the note.
Note Text	The note itself.
Process	The process to which the note pertains.

Grouping the Details into Subjects

As we did with the previous lists of details, we will evaluate each item and determine how to place it into a table. We will start with a main table, which we have named tblGeneralNote, and use the same four qualifying questions. The results of the analysis are listed in the decision matrix shown in Table 8-16.

Table 8-16: Analysis of the Details

DETAIL	RESPONSE PATTERN				DISPOSITION
Timestamp	Y	N	N	N	Remains in the tblGeneralNote.
Team Member	Y	Y	N	N	Remains in tblGeneralNote as a foreign key value to tblTeamMember.
Note Text	Y	N	N	N	Remains in tblGeneralNote.
Process	N	Y	Y	N	Create a child/junction table that relates to tblGeneralNote via a key value. In addition, the child table will have a key value to relate to tblProcess.

1. Is the field a property that directly describes the subject of the table?
2. Will the value of this field be limited to a set of known or standard values?
3. Can a single record have more than one value for this field?
4. Is the field redundant, or does the field describe another field in the table?

Based on these responses, you can determine the need for the tables and relationships that are illustrated in Figure 8-34. This includes two new tables, tblGeneralNote and tblGeneralNoteProcess, as well as two previously created tables: tblProcess and tblTeamMember. We have again shaded tblProcess, as it was previously described. And, although we already discussed the details for creating tblTeamMember, we will repeat the table and figure to provide a complete list of tables required for general notes. The benefit to readers who may be selecting specific modules outweighs our resistance to repeating the information.

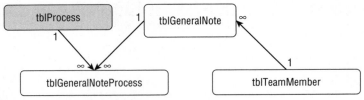

Figure 8-34: Table relationships for general notes

Creating the Tables and Fields

The next step is to repeat the familiar task of converting all the details into fields. Figures 8-35 and 8-36 illustrate the table designs used to store the data related to general notes. As with previous areas, the standard fields shown in these tables were discussed earlier and summarized in Table 8-4.

The General Note Table

The table tblGeneralNote, shown in Figure 8-35, is used to store information that needs to be shared with other people. When analyzing data in this table, you may find a variety of ways to leverage the combination of a note being active or not, and the time it was created.

Field Name	Data Type	Description
GeneralNoteID	AutoNumber	Unique row identifier
NoteTimestamp	Date/Time	The timestamp the note was (or will be) in effect
TeamMemberID	Number	The team member who created the note. FK to tblTeamMember.TeamMemberID
NoteText	Memo	The note text
CreatedDate	Date/Time	Date/Time the record was created
CreatedBy	Text	User ID of the person that created this record
Inactive	Date/Time	Indication of when row became inactive

Figure 8-35: tblGeneralNote

You may have noticed that there are two Date/Time fields in tblGeneralNote. The NoteTimestamp field allows the user to enter the date and time. It indicates when the note applies or when the note took effect; this is not necessarily the time that the note was entered. For example, if an issue arose at 1:00 P.M., the team member might not have time to create the note until much later. This could result in a note with a CreatedDate of 3:00 P.M. and a NoteTimestamp of 1:00 P.M.

The CreatedDate records the actual time at which the user entered the note. The data can be used to determine the amount of time between when the note was issued or needed, and when it was entered. You may also find it helpful for identifying notes that have been left incomplete for an extended period.

The General Note Process Table

The table tblGeneralNoteProcess, shown in Figure 8-36, is a standard junction table that is used to resolve the many-to-many relationship between tblProcess and tblGeneralNote. The junction table allows an unlimited number of notes to be associated with any given process, and also allows any note to be associated with multiple processes. For example, if the safety certification for all robots in a production line is going to expire at the end of the month, an operator could write a general note for the whole group by writing one note linked to all of the robots.

Field Name	Data Type	Description
GeneralNoteProcessID	AutoNumber	Unique row identifier
GeneralNoteID	Number	The parent general note
ProcessID	Number	The process the note pertains to

Figure 8-36: tblGeneralNoteProcess

The Team Member Table

The table tblTeamMember is the same lookup table that we created for Notifications and Countermeasures. It contains the two details fields, as shown in Figure 8-37.

Field Name	Data Type	Description
TeamMemberID	AutoNumber	Unique row identifer
TeamMemberFirstName	Text	The team members first name
TeamMemberLastName	Text	The team members last name
Inactive	Date/Time	Indication of when row became inactive

Figure 8-37: tblTeamMember

Reviewing the Relationships

The tables and relationships associated with the table tblGeneralNote are shown in Figure 8-38. Once again, we have shaded tblProcess because it represents a different core area.

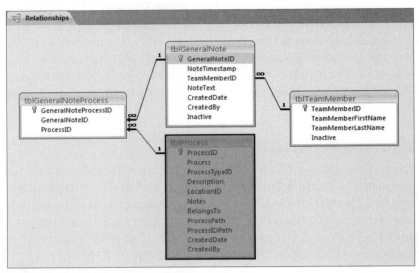

Figure 8-38: Relationships diagram for general notes

The diagram clearly illustrates how the junction table resolves the many-to-many relationship between tblGeneralNote and tblProcess. To assist you with creating the appropriate settings for referential integrity, we have listed the relationships and settings in Table 8-17.

Table 8-17: Relationships of tblGeneralNote

RELATIONSHIP	TYPE	PRIMARY KEY FOREIGN KEY	REFERENTIAL INTEGRITY
tblGeneralNote to tblGeneralNoteProcess	1:M	tblGeneralNote.GeneralNoteID tblGeneralNoteProcess.GeneralNoteID	Yes: Cascade Delete
tblProcess to tblGeneralNoteProcess	1:M	tblProcess.ProcessID tblGeneralNoteProcess.ProcessID	Yes: Cascade Delete
tblTeamMember to tblGeneralNote	1:M	tblTeamMember.TeamMemberID tblGeneralNote.TeamMemberID	Yes
tblGeneralNote to tblProcess	M:M	See relationships for junction table tblGeneralNoteProcess	—

Putting It All Together

We have now completed the task of fully describing each of the core subjects and analyzing the details to create the tables for a production and manufacturing database. We created five main areas and tables representing:

- The process
- The build
- The notifications
- The countermeasures
- The general notes

Up to this point, we have discussed each area as in independent module and indicated how they relate to other areas. Now that we have all of the tables, we can put them all together in relationship diagram, as shown in Figure 8-39.

This diagram, or schema, is the result of our analysis of the details that were derived from the database purpose and the evaluation of user expectations. The core tables are shaded for quick identification. As you look at the figure, you can see how the core tables are related, and you'll realize that they are just as we illustrated in Figure 8-1 at the beginning of this chapter.

Final Walk-Through

When putting any schema together, the final confirmation before deployment should include a walk-through of a standard work flow. This will help verify that the final design will indeed function as intended. We'll do that now with the final Production and Manufacturing schema. You might want to use the database itself, or an enlarged view of the relationship diagram, to follow the data through the tables.

Your production day starts. A *build* record goes into tblBuild for each process that is *tracked* from a production metric point of view (generally the upper hierarchy of processes).

If a process breaks down, shows a safety issue, creates ergonomic issues, or produces poor quality, your appropriate team member fills out a *notification*. The work flow assumes that your notifications are *monitored* by the production workers tasked with reacting to them (i.e., maintenance staff). After you have entered a notification into the system, the proper personnel will correct the situation and record *countermeasures* taken. So far, so good.

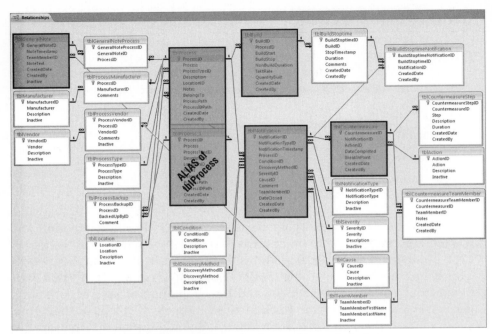

Figure 8-39: Relationship diagram for production and manufacturing

If your *build* loses production time, the lost time is recorded in tblBuildStop-time, which is a child table of tblBuild. Therefore, your stop time is grouped by the build process. You will account for stop time by linking lost time occurrences to your notifications. Note that lost time could also be entered on the same form a user completes to enter notifications (forms are part of the user interface, or UI, that will need to be designed). In any event, your goal is to account for all lost production time with a notification. It is also important that all notifications are addressed with at least one countermeasure.

In addition to process monitoring and management, you'll use the application to enable shift-to-shift communication, and to communicate simple observations that need to be shared among appropriate parties. The designated personnel of your organization can add *general notes*, containing information on a process or a group of processes. For example, a supervisor might record: "Process123 will be getting a new revision level of parts at midnight; be sure to record when the new parts hit the line." When the parts "hit the line," a *notification* can be written that records the condition of a new part, as well as a *countermeasure* that was performed (action and steps) in response to that—something like "verified quality and part interference, all checked out OK."

As you help your managers and analysts conduct research to report efficiencies in your processes, you'll use the data stored in tblBuild and tblBuildStoptime in order to provide metrics such as production time, lost time, and operational efficiency. You can do further analysis on tblNotification to identify which processes require the most frequent attention, and why that attention is required. Armed with that information, managers will be able to focus their staff on the problematic processes in order to rapidly improve the efficiency of your production builds.

Our database model passes this brief review, so you should be confident that it will support the data from your processes. Your next step will be to test with real data, and to create the basic forms and reports. As you do, you may discover additional information that would be helpful to incorporate into your database. Expanding and enhancing a database is a common and iterative process.

More Information

If you need more information on tools to provide business intelligence in the production and manufacturing environment, you are encouraged to search the Internet for key terms like Manufacturing Process Management, Manufacturing Executing Systems, SCADA (Supervisory Control and Data Acquisition), HMI (Human Machine Interface), and CMMS (Computerized Maintenance Management System). Those key terms should yield a wealth of information.

Summary

This chapter covered the process of creating the database model for production and manufacturing. We started by defining the overall database purpose: to monitor manufacturing processes.

Using that stated purpose, we identified the details that need to be recorded based on the manufacturing processes and user expectations. Then, we created and utilized a standard process to ensure that the design would follow the general guidelines and principles associated with the relational data model and normalization.

In reviewing the database purpose, user requirements, and user expectations, we identified five core subjects of the database:

- Processes
- Notifications
- Countermeasures
- Builds
- General Notes

Our next step focused on identifying and evaluating the details and grouping them into the areas represented by the five core subjects. Based on the principles and guidelines for creating a relational data model, we developed a list of four qualifying questions to ask about each detail. We created a decision matrix to determine if a detail would become a field and which table it would go into.

We systematically worked through the five cores subjects to evaluate each detail, so that we could identify and create the appropriate tables. Once we had the tables for a subject, we reviewed the relationships and determined the appropriate types of referential integrity. We summarized each area with a brief review of the relationship diagram.

After we had created all of the tables, we incorporated the tables and data from all five areas into one comprehensive model and looked at how the areas related to each other. The final step was a brief walk-through to confirm that we accomplished our goal and that the design will indeed support the information flow that we described.

Now that you've completed the database structure for a manufacturing environment, a natural next step might be to look at the tables required for data related to inventory. That is covered next, in Chapter 9.

Inventory Management

Nearly every business has an inventory of some sort. For some businesses, carrying inventory means keeping track of the products on hand for sale to customers. Usually, inventory also includes the supplies businesses need to run smoothly. Other businesses, such as manufacturers, must also keep track of the materials and supplies they need to build their products.

Sales consume inventory, so the functions for inventory and sales are often closely related. Therefore, in our commentary describing the inventory management model, we reference the sales model of Chapter 7, "Sales," and suggest a possibility for how you might link the inventory management model with the sales model presented in Chapter 7.

A database is the perfect tool for managing the information needed to keep track of the items you must have on hand to sell to customers, run the business, and make products. This chapter provides sample models designed for tracking the inventory of products a company or business sells to its customers.

While creating this database model we'll follow the data modeling principles and normalization guidelines from Chapter 3, "Relational Data Model." This chapter also relies on the content in Chapter 2, "Elements of a Microsoft Access Database," to guide you through the process of creating a database. In addition, Appendix BB, "Gathering Requirements," on the book's CD will help you develop the necessary information that defines what you need the database to do, in order to keep track of the inventory consumed, procured, and delivered.

NOTE Although inventory management is closely associated with sales and order fulfillment from vendors, this chapter does not expand to cover those areas.

However, we are not leaving you to merge the processes on your own. The CD for this book contains the sample database for this chapter, which emulates, in basic form, the integration of these functions.

NOTE If you have not yet read Chapters 2 and 3, we encourage you to do so before delving too deeply into the processes here. You will also benefit by reading Appendixes A, "Field Properties," and B, "Relationships, Joins, and Nulls." These provide reference material regarding field properties, table relationships, and working with queries. Your understanding of the terms and concepts discussed in those chapters and appendixes will help you follow the example and create the database for this chapter.

The Approach for This Chapter

We start with a discussion of the business function—inventory management—to identify the information and details that need to be recorded in the database. By reviewing general inventory processes, typical business needs, and user expectations, we identify the purpose and requirements of the database and draft a list of details to track.

We then identify the core subject areas and see how they are related. That leads to a discussion of the types of tables you will create, including a list of fields that will be standard in most of the tables. We next describe the process for evaluating your list of details and creating the appropriate tables and fields within the database.

At that point, we work through each subject area, starting with products, exploring some key database concepts—such as types of relationships and the factors to consider when you choose between alternative table designs and data types.

As we complete the tables for each subject area, we review how they are related. We'll do a similar review, with all the subject areas combined into one project, after all subject areas have been discussed.

NOTE The examples in other chapters have followed several approaches to identifying subjects and creating tables. We wanted you to benefit from experiencing different techniques so that you would be aware of some viable options, and be able to select the method or combination that works best for you. Indeed, you may find that a combination of techniques suits you best, particularly if you find yourself using a less formal approach, when you are faced with a very complex scenario, or when you are having difficulty creating or modifying your database.

This chapter and Chapter 8, "Production and Manufacturing," follow a systematic approach that includes reviewing each detail against a list of four qualifying questions. The pattern of responses to those questions will help you determine how to handle the detail. This is one approach for implementing the normalization process you learned about in Chapter 3.

We discuss this technique further later in this chapter, in particular in the "Evaluating the Details: The Four Questions" section.

The Inventory Management Database

To keep the development of the database compact yet usable, we focus on the primary functionality of inventory management. We've broken that down into three basic stages:

- Products are stored.
- Products are consumed.
- Products are replenished.

NOTE Identifying your needs as a retailer may extend beyond the concepts listed here. If that is the case, you should make a list of your additional needs. Then, as you develop the database in this chapter, you can analyze your specific needs and modify the database structure (the schema) to add additional fields and tables as needed. The *database schema* comprises the configurations, definitions, and rules that control how data is entered, stored, and retrieved. In other words, the database schema refers to your tables, queries, and relationships, and how they interact. Refer to Chapter 2 for more information about database schemas.

You can use these basic stages in many business models that require inventory tracking, although the level of complexity will vary by the business and the type of products or materials being tracked. For example, manufacturers may require several levels, or areas, of inventory tracking, including finished products, sub-assemblies, supplies, and so on. Retailers, conversely, will likely be able meet their primary inventory management needs with a single tracking level, focused solely on the products being sold.

Regardless of the level of complexity associated with the inventory management needs of a business, those inventory management systems share a common focus on the products. Managing your products through the three primary stages of inventory helps you to understand how your products move through your business. A better understanding of the product flow, combined with the specific details that you can extract from a database, can enable you to have better inventory controls—which can lead to greater profitability.

Purpose of the Database

The data you collect for an inventory management system should help you answer three primary questions, reflecting the three principles listed earlier:

- What do we have?
- Where is it?
- What do we need?

Our inventory model represents the part of a business process that tracks receiving (replenishing), storing, and selling (consuming) products. Imagine a store such as a home improvement center, where you walk in and are basically standing in the warehouse. You browse the store, select the products you want, and then check out.

From a business process perspective, the products you put in your shopping cart were stored (on shelves), consumed (by you, the customer), and now need to be replenished (by the store from a vendor). This shopping trip illustrates the business process of buying products from a vendor, storing those products on a shelf, and then retrieving those products from the shelf in order to sell to a customer. The scenario for this business process fits just about every retailer and wholesaler, as well as other business processes that involve storing, consuming, and replenishing inventory.

As previously mentioned, businesses need to manage and monitor the products they sell; our goal in creating the database is to support that effort. We'll start with the concepts listed earlier and break them down into tasks that need to be done to manage product stock. Whether you do this with software or on a piece of paper, you might come up with the following objectives:

- Identify the products you sell.
- Manage the vendors who can replenish those products.
- Keep track of the location of each product in the store.

As you can see from the objectives identified above, your product is the focal point of inventory management. Managing the product through the different stages of inventory status enables you to consistently identify your product needs and trends of consumption, and to make sound financial decisions about replenishing those products.

Identifying Your Requirements

Now that we have identified the purpose of the database, we can begin developing the requirements needed to fulfill that purpose. Of course, working with a fictitious company, we don't have actual workflow, documents, and so on to analyze. Therefore, our analysis for this example must depend primarily on the fictitious requirements we derive from thinking about our purpose.

When you seek out requirements for your own database, it is crucial that you analyze your existing workflows and the methods currently used to manage inventory. In addition, of course, you need to be careful to identify needs your existing system does not currently meet. Previously undocumented needs are often the hardest to identify and respond to, but including them can greatly increase the benefits that your application can provide.

Since the primary purpose of our database is to store and provide information for the inventory management business process, we can start by listing the key objectives. The database will need to accomplish the following tasks:

- Store information about products being offered to customers.
- Store information about the location of each product on-site.
- Store inventory transactions for each product the store offers.
- Store information about vendors who provide products.

These tasks identify what the database will do for the application, not what the application will do for the person using it. It is critical that you continually revisit this list to ensure that your database continues to meet your requirements. Again, we refer you to Appendix BB on the book's CD to review the techniques and tips it offers, to help you discern what users will need. They may not always know what the options are, and they likely won't be able to predict what they may be able to do with a new database solution. As you identify new requirements, you must either expand your scope to include them or identify them as being outside the current scope of your project.

User Expectations

As previously stated, we are designing the database model—the tables and fields—that will store the data supporting an application, often termed the *front end*, with which users will interface. The front end will contain the forms, reports, and queries, and it will connect to one or more data files, or *back ends*. Part of our goal is to centralize as much *business logic* as possible at the database level in our design by using the tables, fields, and relationships to implement requirements. Centralizing business logic at the database level leaves more options for application developers to choose from when they are designing the user interface. In other words, the data should not be affected by whether the application is developed using Visual Basic Classic, .NET languages, Microsoft Access, or one of the many web development languages. Our preference, of course, is to use Microsoft Access for the application layer with our models.

With that said, no matter which application development platform you choose, users of the application will have their own expectations about how the application should work. The database schema may need to accommodate those expectations. Several application-level expectations for an inventory management application items may affect the design of the model:

- A simple audit trail should be available; users may want to know who entered records, and when.
- A history of the vendor's product prices should be available in order to make sound purchasing decisions.
- The quantity on hand of a product should be available.
- Contact information for a vendor should be available.
- Overstock situations need to be accounted for; the application could also track alternative storage locations for overstocked items.
- The frequency of product movement should be known—for example, how many products were sold in a given time frame.
- Information about types of products should be available without having to physically see the products.

This list of user expectations is clearly not exhaustive, but it gives you a feel for the process. As you embark on developing your database, it is critical that you interview the future users of the application to determine what is important to them, and then adjust your schema accordingly. In addition, you may want to list some of these items now so that you can customize the sample database to meet your needs as well.

Inventory Overview: Identifying the Subjects

The general method for the first step in identifying tables that you will need to store your data is to gather the requirements and then determine the information you want to track. You can then group that information into distinct categories, or subjects. After establishing the categories, your next step is to define how those categories, or subjects, relate to each other. That will become the basis for the table design that will become your database schema.

Based on the information that you gathered about the inventory management process, environment, and specific needs of the people who will use the database and the data in it, you can identify the types of information that you need to store in the database. Defining the database's purpose and completing the requirements analysis will help you create a useful set of initial categories for grouping the data. The categories will typically become your core tables, which are sometimes referred to as *entities*. Our discussion in this chapter will often refer to two distinct concepts: *core tables* and *support tables*.

NOTE Database developers often use the term *entity* to represent the subject of a table (or a group of tables) during the modeling or preliminary design phase of the database development cycle. For example, the entity "Products" will be implemented as the table named "tblProduct" in the database.

In this chapter we use the terms *subject* and *table* in the modeling phase as we gather information about the data that needs to be tracked, as well as in the implementation phase when we are creating the tables, fields, and relationships.

Core and Supporting Subjects

A *core table (subject)* is a clearly defined and discrete subject that supports the database purpose. *Support tables* store related subject matter that provides additional information about the subject of the core table. A support table may be associated with more than one core table. Most database schemas have one topic that is the focal point of the database. We call this the *main core table*. The differing terms and concepts may seem confusing now, but they will become clearer as you work through the example.

NOTE What we define as a *core table* is known in database development terminology as a *transactional* or *operational* table—one that contains the data central to your business or activity. A *supporting* (or *functional*) table typically provide lists of information from which users can select. For more information about the different types of tables in a database, refer to Chapter 2, Table 2-1: "Common Table Types Used in an Application."

Core Subjects

Since our goal is to create an inventory management database, the next step is to identify the categories, or subjects, into which our information can be grouped. One question that arises is whether locations of the product should be the primary focus. Location often seems to be a viable option because as inventory is tracked, we typically look at a storage location, and when it is getting close to being empty, we acquire more products to fill it. Despite this important consideration, it is more logical to focus on the products themselves, so they will become the main core table. Products move through those storage locations, are purchased from vendors, and are sold to customers.

This database will, of course, need to manage other tables, but for the moment we will focus on the core concepts that the database will manage. Table 9-1 lists core tables that we derived by examining the information from the database's purpose, database requirements, and user expectations.

Table 9-1: Inventory Management Core Subjects

SUBJECT	DESCRIPTION
Products	Products that will be stored, consumed, and replenished. This is the main focal point of the database and is, thus, the main core table. Products are defined in this table as the business knows them.
Locations	Locations in which products are stored. You may know this as the "bin location," or by some other identifier that represents the location of the product being stored in your business environment.
Vendors	Businesses from which products are acquired.
Transactions	The transactions that occur for a particular product. For example, products can be sold, moved, replenished, etc. This table will be critical in providing the statistics users require, such as quantity on hand or consumption rate.

Relationships between the Core Subjects

All four core tables relate to one another. Products are purchased from a vendor and subsequently stored in a location. Products are removed from a location and sold to a customer. Figure 9-1 illustrates the relationships of the core tables in our sample database.

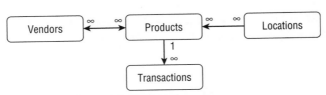

Figure 9-1: Relationships of the core subjects for Inventory

This core table diagram illustrates that one vendor can provide many products. In addition, one product can be supplied by many vendors. It also indicates that a single location can hold many products and that a product can be stored in more than one location, something you may need to do in order to address the overstock scenario.

In addition, Figure 9-1 illustrates the framework of a high-level workflow for your application:

- A product arrives in the store. An employee enters into the database the number of pieces received.

- The product is then stocked in the assigned sales location for that product. If an overstock exists, the excess product is stored in the overstock location.

- Once stocked, products are available to customers. As purchases occur, the company's Sales application automatically enters a transaction for each product purchased.

- As the in-stock quantity is reduced by sales, summary data indicates which products the business's purchasing software or department needs to reorder.

Although some functions listed above are not dependent on other functions, there may be reasons to consider them together in a work flow. For example, the data indicating which of your products needs to be reordered can be gathered at any time. However, you may find that inventory reporting is best done after the stock that has been received has been entered into the database.

Approach for Reviewing the Core Subjects

At this stage of development, the core tables simply represent distinct topics, or subjects, and are void of any fields. In order to fill that void, we will go through a process for fully defining, or describing, each core table. By consistently applying the process, you will do the following:

- Identify the details.
- Identify the tables that group the fields and see how the tables relate.
- Create the tables and define the relationships.

These steps should be very familiar to you if you went through the examples in Chapter 8.

Identifying the Details

The next step of building the relational model is to populate the tables with *fields* to store the data. Each field identifies a piece of information that specifically describes the subject matter of the table. Fields of a table are sometimes called details or *attributes*.

NOTE During the modeling phase of development, database developers sometimes use the terms *detail* or *attribute* to refer to a field prior to including it in an actual table or database file. For example, the attribute "Process Name" will be included in the table named tblProcess as the field named "Process".
"Attribute" is the term often given to a conceptual or generic view of a field, while the term "field" is the physical implementation that will contain the specific detail about an item. Refer to Chapter 3 for additional information.

The Standard Fields

As we create the fields for the core tables, we won't go into detail about the fields that are primarily for the benefit of the application or database engine, or the fields that store system administration information. Most of these field values are managed by the application, but they can also provide invaluable data for the database managers and users. We refer to them as *standard fields* in this chapter. Many of the standard fields may be used in most, if not all, of your tables.

Standard fields help provide functionality that is typically required or expected from an application. Table 9-2 lists the standard fields you will find in the sample database. Note that not every standard field will be present in every table, and you will quickly see why they are not needed in every situation. As you work with our model and incorporate the tables and fields that are appropriate for your scenarios, you may also need to create additional standard fields.

Table 9-2: Standard Fields

FIELD	DESCRIPTION
<Identifier>ID	The primary key of the table. It consists of the root of the table name, with the suffix of "ID". Example: *ProductID*. We use an AutoNumber data typed field and specify that it is the primary key so that the database engine will create a unique value for each record. This type of key is called a surrogate key. See Chapter 2 for more information.
Inactive	This field uses a Date/Time data type to indicate when a row becomes unavailable for use in the application. This field is often used in lookup tables (see Chapters 2 and 3) in order to prevent the display of values that are no longer used. Not deleting the obsolete value helps to maintain referential integrity and enables the old values to be included for historic purposes.
CreatedDate	This field uses the Date/Time data type to record when a record was created. A common technique is to set the default value to `Now()`, which stores the date and time to the precise second. Knowing when a record was created can be useful in identifying incomplete records, which may require deletion. In addition, the field provides valuable information for traceability.
CreatedBy	This is a text field used to store the computer user's ID. The information is usually obtained by using code, and the user is not allowed to change the value. The data can be used for traceability and accountability.

NOTE We recommend that you have a primary key for every table. In addition, we recommend that you use an AutoNumber data type field as the single-field primary key. You can also create a unique index on candidate key fields to help maintain data integrity. Key types and their uses are covered in Chapter 2 and Appendix A.

The Types of Tables

After you have identified the fields for your database, you will want to ensure that the design reflects relational data model principles in order to store the data efficiently and consistently. To do that, we will use a set of database development guidelines known as the *normal forms* and an activity referred to as normalization, or *normalizing the data*. The relational data model and normalization are discussed in detail in Chapter 3.

In the normalization process, which refines our tables to store data efficiently and consistently, we determine whether to keep a field in the core table, or create one or more additional support tables for each subject represented by our core tables. In the sample database, each core table requires more than one table. As we create the supporting tables, you should quickly be able to identify how the support table should be related to the core table.

Before going any further, we want to reassure you that the increasing number of tables is a typical outcome of this process. Although you might think that it would be easier to keep all the data in one table, that is rarely the case. Properly grouping data into tables and fields, makes it easier to maintain and ensure the integrity of the data.

As we go through the normalization process, we use several terms to identify different types of supporting tables. Table 9-3 lists those terms that identify the common types of supporting tables you will encounter both in our example and in many databases that you will create or examine.

As you absorb the information regarding core tables and supporting tables that follows, please keep in mind that a single table may be categorized as two different table types depending on how it is being used. For example, self-referencing tables are both a core table and a lookup table. In addition, a core table may be a lookup table to other core or supporting tables.

Creating the Tables and Fields

After you have completed the normalization process by defining and grouping your data into core and supporting tables, your next step is to define their respective fields and physically create the tables. You'll find this step to be fairly easy, especially since you will follow a well-defined model that can be consistently applied throughout the process.

Table 9-3: Supporting Tables

TABLE TYPE	DESCRIPTION
Child table (sometimes called a foreign table by database developers)	Each record in a supporting table describes a single record in the core table to which it refers. A child table can have more than one value, or record, supporting each item in the core table. For example, imagine that you have a core table of Parent. A single record in Parent can have more than one child. In order to properly associate the record in Parent with its children, you create a child table to represent Children of Parent. The two tables are related using a relational key. (Refer to the discussion of keys in Chapter 2 and Appendix B.)
Domain table or lookup table	A lookup table stores a set of possible values for a field in another table. For example, a core table may have a field named Color. You could create a color lookup table to store a list of available colors. In the core table, the color value stored will typically be the key value from the lookup table. In most situations, this will be an AutoNumber key value. However, in some situations, the key value may be the value of the field itself, such as "Blue."
	For lookup tables, it is quite common, and the practice of this chapter, to include a unique index on the main field of the lookup table in order to prevent duplicates. Using our table of colors, we would have the primary key of an AutoNumber field (ColorID) as well as a Unique index on a the main field of the lookup (Color). This will prevent duplicate entries in the Color field.
	A lookup table is not always directly associated with a core table's subject matter.
Self-referencing table	A self-referencing table has a special kind of parent-child table relationship because it involves only one table instead of two. The field representing the Parent stores a value from another record from the same table.
	A common example is employees and supervisors. The employee table contains one record for each person; it also has a field named "ReportsTo" to identify each person's supervisor. The ReportsTo field stores the primary key value from the supervisor's record in the records for each of the supervisor's direct reports.
	For each record, both the primary key and the foreign key are from the same table.

You need to assign valid names to the tables and fields, and then formally define, or create, them in the database file as a *table object*, often called a *table definition*. While defining each table and creating your fields, pay attention to the field properties that you assign to each field. Field properties determine the type of data you can store and the rules that govern, or validate, your data before it is stored. In addition, you can use the field properties to specify the default format in which the data will be displayed to the user. Refer to Chapter 2, Tables 2-3 and 2-4, and Appendix A for more information about field properties.

To help you implement, or build, the database, we will discuss each topic, or core table, individually. That way, you can focus on one aspect of the schema at a time. Breaking it down into these modules also makes it easier for you to incorporate sections of this example into your solutions.

Establishing the Relationships

After you have defined the core table and its supporting tables, you want to combine them into a single representation of the subject being modeled by formally establishing the relationships between the core table and its supporting tables. You do this in the Relationships window. The process is done by adding the tables to the Relationship view, then dragging and dropping the primary key onto the foreign key. A dialog box pops up, and you can confirm or change the properties as necessary.

Putting It All Together

Once you have analyzed the smaller pieces of your database represented by the core and support tables we have modeled and created, you will combine all of the distinct subjects (core tables) into a single schema by defining the relationships between the core tables of each distinct subject within the Relationship window. The schema will then represent a database for an inventory management business process.

Products

We begin with the core table of Products because it is the main topic of the database. First, we will identify any details we need to know about the product. Next, we will categorize the details into tables, and then represent the details with fields. Finally, we will put it all together with the relationship diagram that contains the data required for the core table, Products.

Identifying the Details

The details will change during the process, so as you're gathering and sorting the relevant information to be managed, you will find it helpful to use a note pad, cards, or an electronic format. Table 9-4 shows some details associated with the products to track in the database.

Table 9-4: Product Details

DETAIL	DESCRIPTION
Product Name	Name by which the product sells (as we know it).
Product Type	A generic type or category that enables you to group all products of the same type—for example, hardware, lumber, or tools.
UPC	The Universal Product Code for the product being sold.
Brand Name	Brand name under which the vendor sells the product.
Vendor Name	Businesses from which products are acquired.
Vendor Unique Identifier	Unique identifier the vendor uses for a product.
Vendor Product Name	Product name used in buying from the vendor.
Vendor Description	Description of the part, according to the vendor.
Unit of Measure	Unit of measure of a sellable unit.
Cost	Cost the business pays for a unit. Cost depends on the vendor.
Location	Where the product is stored at your business's premises.
Quantity on Hand	Quantity of a product you have on site.
Min on Hand	When the quantity (sellable units) drops to this level, you order more.
Max on Hand	The upper limit for the quantity (sellable units) on hand. Use this value to determine how much you want to buy to replenish your shelves.

As your inventory system becomes more complex to meet the expanding needs of your business, the list of details for your database will likely grow. Ideally, your initial list should include all of the things that you want to know—or will likely need to know—about your product. It's easier to include extra fields now with the expectation that they will be needed than it is to add fields later.

Identifying the Supporting Tables

The next task is to create the tables. As we do this, we'll apply relational modeling and normalization principles to the list of details.

We begin with the main core table that represents the topic being analyzed—in this case, Products. We will name this tblProduct, which is based on the subject, and has the prefix "tbl" in accordance with accepted naming conventions. The purpose of this table is to identify and describe the products that the business makes available to be consumed.

One of the first things you need to do is evaluate each detail and decide if it directly describes the subject of the current table, or if it actually represents the subject of another table. Sometimes a detail in your list may appear to do both. One way to help you decide is to create a list of qualifying questions, and then walk each detail through that list of questions. Based on the answers, you can either create a field in the current table or identify a different table in which to store the detail. In some cases, you may choose to remove the detail altogether because it does not belong in the database.

Evaluating the Details: The Four Questions

We will use the following questions to evaluate whether a prospective field needs to be in the current table, in another table, or removed completely. You can also use these questions with the fields in your existing database projects to help you determine if the tables should be modified. It is not uncommon to discover that, if you organize the data and fields to follow the guidelines for the relational data model, your database will operate more efficiently.

For each detail (or field of exiting tables), you should ask these four qualifying questions:

1. Is the detail (or field) a property that directly describes the subject of the table?

2. Will the value of this field be limited to a set of known or standard values?

3. Can a single record have more than one value for this field?

4. Is the field redundant, or does the field describe another field in the table?

You may be asking yourself where these questions have come from or what the intent of these questions is. We use these questions as a way to organize, or "normalize," the data into tables that follow the guidelines for a relational data model, as explained in Chapter 3.

The first question directly relates to the ideal premise of the relational data model, which indicates that each field of a table represents a property that directly describes the discrete subject of the table. For example, in a table that is focused on a people, you would not have a field for the name of the individual's child because the name of a child does not directly contribute to the description of a person. A No response to the first question often indicates the need for a separate table to represent that property or feature. The separate table may be a *lookup table*, *child table*, or even another *operational table* (or core table).

The second question helps you determine if the values expected for a field will be limited to a fixed set of values, thus allowing you to keep the data consistent regardless of who is entering the data. For example, if your table has a field for the color of an object, you may want to limit the choices presented to a person using the application to a fixed set of color names such as red, blue, green, and black. By doing this, you prevent entries like turquoise, baby blue, or magenta, plus you create a set of data that is easily searched due to the use of a constrained set of values. As your needs change, you can modify the list of available values. Often a Yes response to the second question indicates the need for a *lookup table*, sometimes called a *domain table* by database developers.

The third question helps you consider the *first normal form*, which prevents you from having more than one field in a record to represent multiple values of a single property (field). For example, many people today have more than one phone number, so it is tempting to add fields that are named Phone1, Phone2, and Phone3 in a phone number table. However, that would use several fields for the same property (phone number), which violates the first normal form. The impact is that it makes it a lot more difficult for you to search and maintain your data. A Yes response to this question indicates the need for a child table.

The fourth question is intended to help you adhere to the *second normal form*. The second normal form tells you to prevent data redundancy. That means that a single property, or descriptor, should only be provided one time and only in one field. You should not represent the same data in two or more fields in a table. For example, suppose you have a table of product colors that has three fields: ProductID, ColorID and ColorName. Both ColorID and ColorName provide the same information. So, you would need to remove the ColorName field.

It is likely that your colors are in a lookup table; thus, the value of ColorName can be retrieved from that lookup table by using the value of ColorID. Using a single field to represent a single property promotes data concurrency. A response of Yes to question four indicates the need to simply remove a field from a table since the information is redundant.

Asking these qualifying questions is a more formal technique for implementing the rules and guidelines for normalization than some developers usually follow. Asking a documented set of questions can help ensure consistency. For more detail on the relational data model or the normal forms please refer to Chapter 3.

For our first example in this chapter, we will go through the questions and steps in more detail, and refer back to the process in subsequent instances. For this set of four qualifying questions, a response sequence of Yes, No, No, and No identifies fields that can be added to the core table. Other sequences indicate that you should look for other alternatives for that detail.

We'll start with Product Name, the first item in the list of details for the subject of Products. Your response to the first question should be Yes, and to the remaining three it should be No. That fits the required sequence of answers for fields that belong in the table. There are no extraneous factors to consider, so you can conclude that Product Name directly supports the topic represented by the core table and should become a field in tblProduct.

Remember that we will physically create the fields later, during the implementation phase; for now, we are still identifying the fields and our focus is on determining what to do with each item in our list of details. We are only asking whether the detail should be added to tblProduct or put into a supporting table. If the other table does not yet exist, we would need to determine if the detail should be the subject of a new table. Now we can continue to ask our qualifying questions of the remaining details listed in Table 9-4.

As you work through the detail list, you will find other items generate the response sequence of Yes, No, No, and No. Those items are UPC, Min on Hand, and Max on Hand. Based on this response sequence, these items will become fields in tblProduct.

Note that Quantity on Hand yields a response sequence favorable to adding it as a field in tblProduct. However, this detail does not qualify as a field in tblProduct, and we'll explain why later. For now, you just need to recognize that it does not belong in tblProduct.

Using Transient Fields

Previously, we assigned fields in tblProduct for Min on Hand and Max on Hand. In many scenarios, these details could be categorized as *transient*. A *transient field* is one in which the value can change without affecting the item it describes. Transient fields do not describe the product. Thus, from the purist point of view, these details should be placed in a supporting child table.

In our model, we justified keeping the field in the products table because all products will always have a single set of values for these fields. Moreover, if the fields were moved to a separate table, the relationship to these values would be defined as a one-to-one relationship. For those two reasons, we use a less complicated design that will not jeopardize the integrity of the data.

Using Lookup Tables

Continuing to work through the list of details, we'll look at Product Type next. When we ask the four qualifying questions, the answers are Yes, Yes, No, and No. Because the answer to question one is Yes, you know that the detail should remain in tblProduct. However, we also answered Yes to question two, which asks if the possible values of the detail are limited to a set of known or standard values. This indicates that you need to create a support table, called a *domain table* or *lookup table* (see the "Domains and Constraints" section in Chapter 3). The lookup table will be named tblProductType, and it will store the set of distinct values for selecting a product type in order to give the people using the application a fixed list to choose from, thus preventing slight variations in the data being input.

To create the relationship between the tables, we will store the value of the lookup table's primary key field as a foreign key field in tblProduct. All of the lookup tables will be implemented this way. Another common characteristic that will be shared among all lookup tables is that the main field of the lookup table will have a unique index applied to it. For example, let's look at a lookup table that has two fields: an AutoNumber field and a text field that holds the item identifier. The AutoNumber field is also the primary key. In addition, we will create a unique index on the text field that is used to identify the item. This indexing strategy will prevent duplicate values in the lookup tables.

> **NOTE** Allowing users to select from a predetermined list of values not only saves time and minimizes the potential for entry error, but also provides definitive values that can later be used to select and group items to perform various types of analysis.

While we are thinking about lookup tables, let's examine the rest of the items in the list of details and identify other fields that have the same response pattern of Yes, Yes, No, and No. Two more qualify: Brand Name and Unit Of Measure. We'll create two lookup tables and call them tblBrand and tblUnitOfMeasure, respectively.

Many-to-Many Relationships and Child Tables

The next item from the list of details that we want to look at is Vendor Name. When you pose our four qualifying questions about the field, the response pattern is: No, Yes, Yes, and No. Answering Yes to the second question means that the Vendor Name field is limited to a known set of values, and that a single product can be associated with more than one Vendor Name. Since the answer to the first question was No, you know immediately that the Vendor

Name field belongs in its own table. This is a child table of tblProduct, named tblProductVendor. In addition, answering Yes to the third question means you will have a fixed set of values that identify a vendor for a given product. This may lead you to deduce that another lookup table and relationship is needed for vendors.

As you should recall, though, we already have the Vendor table; therefore, we can use that table for both functions. With respect to the Product table, tblVendor is a lookup table. It will also be the main table with respect to vendors. When we review the Vendor table, we will keep that dual functionality in mind.

While we're talking about tblProduct, however, also recall that the specification indicated that a vendor can provide more than one product. This leaves us with a many-to-many relationship between tblProduct and tblVendor because a product can have multiple vendors, and a vendor can offer multiple products.

As you look through the rest of the details, you will notice that one other detail, Location, fits the same response pattern as Vendor Name. You will treat that detail the same way, creating a lookup table named tblLocation, and you will also need to create a child table named tblLocationProduct. The combined terms in the name indicates that this is a junction table to resolve the many-to-many relationship between tblProduct and tblLocation. In addition, you should also note that Location is both a core table and a lookup table.

Now we can move on to the remaining details. Next, we'll look at Vendor Unique Identifier. The purpose of this field is to store the name of a product as the vendor knows it. The response pattern to our four qualifying questions is No, No, Yes, and No. This is a new pattern. The only Yes response indicates that a product can be represented by more than one value for Vendor Unique Identifier.

Also, you should recognize that the answers to question one (i.e., Does it directly describe the topic of the table?) and question three (i.e., Can a single record have more than one value?) are the same as those for the field Vendor Name. It is hoped that this triggers the thought that since we created the table tblProductName to accommodate the detail Vendor, and since the detail Vendor Unique Identifier field provides information directly regarding the topic of tblProductVendor, the detail could, and should, be stored in tblProductVendor.

The answers to our qualifying questions for details of Vendor Product Name and Vendor Description follow the same pattern and logic. Therefore, you should create fields for them in the junction table tblProductVendor.

Cost is the next detail. The response pattern to our qualifying questions for that detail is No, No, Yes, and No, which is the same pattern expressed for Vendor Product Name and some other details related to the topic Product Vendor—the vendor information for a single product.

However, we also have a business rule that the cost of the product must be tracked over time, which adds a twist that we will deal with by asking our four questions for the Cost field and considering tblProductVendor as the possible location of the field. In that case, you get a response pattern of No, No, Yes, and No, which indicates a child table. Because of the requirement to preserve pricing information, we need a table to store each price (or price change). To do that, we will add a child table, tblProductVendorCost, which will be directly related to the table tblProductVendor.

Design Alternatives for Quantity on Hand

The Quantity on Hand field is the last detail on the list. Here, the response pattern to the four questions is No, No, No, and No. With a response pattern like that, you may think the field does not belong in the Product table. You are correct, but we still need a way to handle it. There are several options, so you need to determine what will work best for your situation.

Many developers would store the raw value in a table and rely on processes in the user application to increment or decrement the value as products are consumed and replenished. Others consider Quantity on Hand a calculation because each product is tracked coming in and out of inventory. In that scenario, Quantity on Hand is calculated as the difference between the amount of products going in and the amount of products going out. Another, less popular, train of thought is to consider the field a transient field; this option requires a person to manually update the value every day.

Using a Transaction Table

Good database design rules indicate that the most correct implementation of Quantity on Hand is to calculate the value as needed in the application rather than storing it. Storing the calculation is essentially storing redundant data. To calculate the value for Quantity on Hand, we need to create a transaction table related to tblProduct to handle transactions involving products. These tables are linked in a one-to-many relationship. Our transaction table is named tblInventoryTransaction. The user application will get the business information it needs from the tblInventoryTransaction table when looking for products that need to be ordered, or when it is necessary to report on the Quantity on Hand.

Over time, products can become lost, stolen, or broken, which is sometimes referred to as *shrinkage*. The value returned by an application's Quantity On Hand function will, therefore, eventually be incorrect. Our transactional approach enables us to add a balancing transaction to make the computed Quantity on Hand match a manually audited value.

As you can see in the initial diagram of the subjects in our example, shown in Figure 9-1, Transactions is a core subject. This will become tblInventory-Transaction, which will contain the inventory transactions.

Table Relationships for Products

We've covered all the details for the core table named tblProduct; take a look at Figure 9-2 to see how the subjects supporting that core table are integrated. In addition to the key subject of products, we have core tables that represent vendors, locations, and inventory transactions.

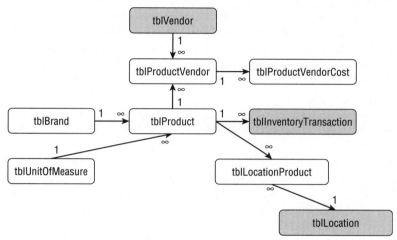

Figure 9-2: Relationships to tblProduct

Note that as we evaluated the details for the subject of Products, we also considered other core subjects. Although this happens frequently when you are defining the main core table of the database, it may not happen with every main core table.

It is also important to note that each new table that supports a core table should go through a similar evaluation. Because the process is the same, we will not go through the details of each table in this chapter. However, as you have just seen in the child table tblProductVendor, the field list can grow unexpectedly. With a larger number of fields in your supporting tables, it is more likely that you will benefit from ensuring that each table goes through an evaluation to ensure an efficient table design.

Creating the Tables and Fields

The next step is to create the actual tables and fields that we have described. The following discussion focuses on the tables directly related to the Products core table. Later in the chapter, you will look at the details for the tables that directly support the other core tables: tblLocation, tblVendor, and tblInventoryTransaction.

At this point, it will be fairly easy to convert the details into tables and fields. Our analysis has not only determined the tables each field will be part of; it also describes the relationships between tables. With that work done, the rest of the process is as simple as converting the name of the detail into a valid table or field name. Figures 9-3 through 9-9 illustrate the resultant table definitions for the core table of Products.

> **NOTE** As you create your tables, you have many options for how to name and define the fields. The figures illustrating the tables from our example show you the minimum amount of information needed to create a field. In addition, each field has several properties that enable you to speed data entry, display your data in specific formats, or validate the data as it is entered. See Chapter 2 and Appendix A for detailed information concerning data types and field properties.

The Product Table

tblProduct, shown in Figure 9-3, is the main core table of the database. We've already discussed each of the items from our list of details that are now the fields for this table. You can also see several standard fields.

Field Name	Data Type	Description
ProductID	AutoNumber	Unique record identifier, aslo the buiness identifier of this product
BrandID	Number	The brand name of the product being sold. FK to tblBrand.BrandID
UPC	Text	The Universal Product Code
ProductTypeID	Number	The product type. FK to tblProductType.ProductTypeID
Product	Text	The product name
Description	Text	A detailed description of the product
UnitOfMeasureID	Number	The unit of measure in which you purchase the product. FK to tblUnitOfMeasure.UnitOfMeasureID
ReorderLevel	Number	Reorder product when the quantity on hand reaches this level
OnSiteMaximum	Number	Number of products you do not wish to exceed to have on site
Inactive	Date/Time	Indication of when row became inactive
CreatedDate	Date/Time	Date/Time the record was created
CreatedBy	Text	User ID of the person that created this record

Figure 9-3: Design view of tblProduct

As you look through the field list, the fields with a data type of Number have a field size of Long, thus forcing whole numbers to be saved in the table. The text fields will have a varying field size and can be adjusted to suit your needs.

The Brand Table

tblBrand is a lookup table used to store values for the different brands available for the products. This table is great example for illustrating the indexing strategy of lookup tables explained in Table 9-3, and in the discussion. In order to prevent a brand from being listed more than one time, the field Brand will be indexed with no duplicates allowed. The design view of this table is shown in Figure 9-4.

tblBrand		
Field Name	Data Type	Description
BrandID	AutoNumber	Unique identifier for each row
Brand	Text	The brand's name
Inactive	Date/Time	Date the record became inactive

Figure 9-4: Design view of tblBrand

The Unit of Measure Table

tblUnitOfMeasure is a lookup table used to store the values of the different units of measure available for the products. The design view of the table is shown in Figure 9-5. The lookup indexing strategy is applied to the field UnitOfMeasure by creating a unique index on that field.

tblUnitOfMeasure		
Field Name	Data Type	Description
UnitOfMeasureID	AutoNumber	Unique identifier for each row
UnitOfMeasure	Text	The unit of measure descriptor
Description	Text	The description of the UOM
Inactive	Date/Time	Date the record became inactive for use

Figure 9-5: Design view of tblUnitOfMeasure

The Product Location Table

tblLocationProduct is a junction table between tblProduct and the core table Locations. The table will store the values of the different units of measurement available for the products. We included two fields, one from tblProduct and one from tblLocation (which we discuss later in this chapter). This allows us to record each location and product combination as a single record. We enforce a unique index on the fields to ensure that they are entered only once in the table. The design view of the table is shown in Figure 9-6.

tblLocationProduct		
Field Name	Data Type	Description
LocationProductID	AutoNumber	Unique system record identifier
ProductID	Number	The product. FK to tblProduct.ProductID
LocationID	Number	The location of the product. FK to tblLocation.Location

Figure 9-6: Design view of tblLocationProduct

The Product Vendor Table

tblProductVendor is a child table to tblProduct, as well as a junction table between tblProduct and the table of vendors. The tblProductVendor table will store information about a product offered by a vendor. Figure 9-7 shows the design view of tblProductVendor.

We have fully developed this table following the same process that we used with the core table of Products, so the figure shows all of the fields in design view. As you examine the fields, you may find that you have additional information that relates specifically to the association between a specific product and vendor. If so, you would need to add the appropriate fields to this table.

tblProductVendor		
Field Name	Data Type	Description
ProductVendorID	AutoNumber	Unique row identifier, system generated
ProductID	Number	The product that that is sold. FK to tblProductName.ProductNameID
VendorID	Number	FK to tblVendor.VendorID
ItemIdentifier	Text	The unique identifier this vendor knows this product as
VendorItem	Text	The name of the product according to this vendor chosen
Description	Text	Description of the product for this vendor
UnitOfMeasureID	Number	The unit of measure in which you purchase the product. FK to tblUnitOfMeasure.UnitOfMeasureID
SellableUnits	Number	For each purchase unit, number of sellable units per purchased unit
ProductNotes	Memo	Notes that may be pertinant about this product
Inactive	Date/Time	Indication of when row became inactive
CreatedDate	Date/Time	Date/Time the record was created
CreatedBy	Text	User ID of the person that created this record

Figure 9-7: Design view of tblProductVendor

Sometimes a short description is not enough to explain the purpose and design for a field. The following list provides additional information about the fields in this table that deserve some special explanation:

- **ItemIdentifier**: That field is used to allow you to store the identifier that the indicated vendor uses in regard to the product. Similar to the way that you refer to the product when communicating with your customers, your vendor will refer to the product by this identifier.

- **VendorItem**: Much like the ItemIdentifier field, except with the text of a product name. Some may argue that the information in this field is redundant because it is dependent upon ItemIdentifier, but since we do not have access to the vendors' data, we felt it appropriate to include the field, despite the redundancy.

- **SellableUnits**: When you purchase from a vendor, you may buy the product in units of a box that contains more than one sellable unit. This is where you would store how many sellable units you are buying when you purchase one UnitOfMeasure.

The Product Vendor Cost Table

tblProductVendorCost tracks the prices paid for a product at a given time and from a specific vendor. The fields, as shown in Figure 9-8, are fairly self explanatory.

tblProductVendorCost		
Field Name	Data Type	Description
ProductVendorCostID	AutoNumber	Unique record identifier
ProductVendorID	Number	FK to tbProductVendor.ProductionVendorID
Cost	Currency	The cost of the item from the indicated vendor
Inactive	Date/Time	Indication of when row became inactive
CreatedDate	Date/Time	Date/Time the record was created
CreatedBy	Text	User ID of the person that created this record

Figure 9-8: Design view of tblProductVendorCost

Establishing the Relationships

The next step in the design process is to fully describe and visualize how all of the tables used to store information about the products relate to each other. Based on our earlier analysis, we can now formalize the relationships between the tables in relationship view. Figure 9-9 illustrates the relationships of the tables associated with tblProduct. The other three core tables are shaded for clarity.

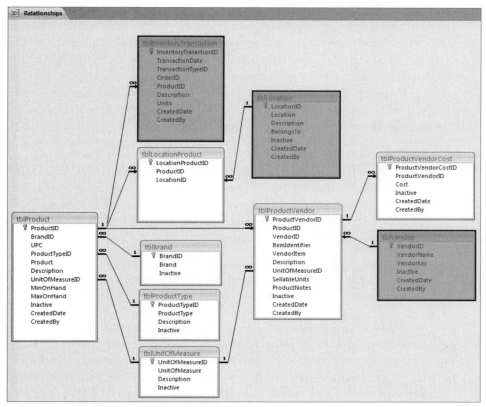

Figure 9-9: Relationship diagram for Products

> **NOTE** We will describe in detail each relationship in just a moment, but first note the "1" and "∞" symbols in Figure 9-9. They represent the "one" side, or primary table, and "many" side, or foreign table, of a relationship definition. Our standard method is to name each relationship definition by the name of the table on the "one" side, and then the name of the table on the "many" side—for example, tblProduct to tblProductVendor.

The relationship is formed using data in the primary key, abbreviated PK, which is stored in the primary table and in the foreign key, abbreviated FK, which represents the field in the foreign table. One way to think of this is that the foreign key represents data from another table, ergo, the term "foreign." In order to relate the individual records from one table to a record in another table, the values in the two fields must match. As a side note, the arrow you see represents the join that will be created if the two tables are used in a Query object and the AutoJoin feature is enabled. The presence of the arrow indicates that the relationship will automatically create an outer join (left or right). Chapter 2 explains joins in more detail.

In addition, relationship view is used to enable referential integrity (RI), as well as the referential integrity option of *cascading deletes*, which means that deleting a record on the "one" side of the relationship also deletes all related records on the "many" side. If referential integrity is not enabled, the "1" and the "∞" symbols will not appear. You can invoke the dialog box to edit the relationship by double-clicking on the join line that represents the relationship between the two tables. You will find more information on relationships and the terms used to define them in Chapters 2 and 3, and in Appendix B.

NOTE All of the relationships defined in this database have a primary key defined using an AutoNumber field. Because AutoNumber field values cannot be modified in the "one" side table, there is no need to enable the *cascade updates* option of referential integrity for these relationships. When you use cascade updates, the changes you make in the main record (field) will automatically be reflected in the related fields in other tables.

Also, with referential integrity enabled, records from the primary table cannot be deleted when there is a matching record in the foreign table unless the cascading delete option of referential integrity is also enabled.

Table 9-5 lists the relationships between each of the tables. Also indicated is whether referential integrity needs to be enforced, and if you specifically need to set the property to provide cascade deletes, which will automatically delete child records when the parent record is deleted. Note also that the last two relationships listed are called many-to-many, or type M:M. As pointed out earlier, this type of relationship is resolved by using a junction table, such as tblLocationProduct.

Table 9-5: Relationships between the Tables

RELATED TABLES	TYPE	PRIMARY KEY FOREIGN KEY	REFERENTIAL INTEGRITY
tblBrand to tblProduct	1:M	tblBrand.BrandID tblProduct.BrandID	Yes
tblProduct to tblInventoryTransaction	1:M	tblProduct.ProductID tblInventoryTransaction.ProductID	Yes
tblProduct to tblLocationProduct	1:M	tblProduct.ProductID tblLocationProduct.ProductID	Yes: Cascade Delete
tblProduct to tblProductVendor	1:M	tblProduct.ProductID tblProductVendor.ProductID	Yes
tblProductType to tblProduct	1:M	tblProductType.ProductTypeID tblProduct.ProductTypeID	Yes
tblProductVendor to tblProductVendorCost	1:M	tblProductVendor.ProductVendorID tblProductVendorCost.ProductVendorID	Yes: Cascade Delete
tblUnitOfMeasure to tblProduct	1:M	tblUnitOfMeasure.UnitOfMeasureID tblProduct.UnitOfMeasureID	Yes
tblUnitOfMeasure to tblProductVendor	1:M	tblUnitOfMeasure.UnitOfMeasureID tblProductVendor.UnitOfMeasureID	Yes
tblVendor to tblProductVendor	1:M	tblVendor.VendorID tblProductVendor.VendorID	Yes
tblProduct to tblLocation	M:M	See relationships for junction table tblLocationProduct	—
tblProduct to tblVendor	M:M	See relationships for junction table tblProductVendor	—

Vendors

The steps for analyzing the core table for vendors are the same as those used for our analysis of the core table Products.

- Identify and list all of the fields or details.
- Identify and relate supporting tables.
- Create the tables and define the relationships.

Identifying the Details

To create a list of the key items that you think are pertinent to the vendors, recall that a vendor replenishes your products, so your list of details should reflect that. Table 9-6 contains the list of fields we believe would be needed to address the purpose of the example database.

Table 9-6: Vendor Details

DETAIL	DESCRIPTION
Vendor Name	Name of the vendor
Address	Complete address of the vendor
Contact Name	Name of the contact person for a vendor
Job Title	Job title of the contact person
Phone	Phone number of the contact person
Email	E-mail address of the contact person
Products	Products that the vendor will supply

This list is relatively short. However, for the purpose of this database, it seems reasonable to have assembled a list of this size. Basically, we just need to know how to contact a vendor, how to order when we need to replenish stock, and where to send the check in order to pay the bill. Of course, your list may be much longer, but keep in mind that these are the key items and that some of them will be broken down into several fields.

Identifying the Supporting Tables

Since we have previously completed the steps to analyze fields, we are going to use a slightly different approach this time, which will give you a slightly different perspective and a greater learning opportunity. As you know, there is almost always more than one way of doing anything.

We start with the main core table that will represent the vendors, named tblVendor, similar in concept to the table for products. Next, we review the four qualifying questions you should ask when determining what tables to create from our list of details.

1. Is the field a property that directly describes the subject of the table?

2. Will the value of this field be limited to a set of known or standard values?

3. Can a single record have more than one value for this field?

4. Is the field redundant, or does the field describe another field in the table?

This time, we'll evaluate each detail with a process similar to a decision matrix, as shown in Table 9-7. The Response Pattern columns reflect the answers to the four qualifying questions for each field. This table contains the information and dispositions for the list of details generated earlier for the Vendors subject.

Table 9-7: Evaluating the Details

DETAIL	RESPONSE PATTERN				DISPOSITION
Vendor Name	Y	N	N	N	Remains in tblVendor
Address	Y	N	Y	N	Yes for question 3, having more than one value for a single vendor, indicates the need for a child table, tblVendorAddress. A single vendor can have more than one Address of different types, so we need to create a lookup table, named tblAddressType. The address will also need to be broken down into specific fields.
Contact Name	N	N	Y	N	Yes for question 3, having more than one value for a single vendor, and No for question 1, not directly describing the subject of the table, indicate the need for a child table, tblVendorContact. The contact name will also need to be broken down into specific fields.
Job Title	N	N	N	Y	Job Title will be moved to tblVendorContact because it supports the subject represented by tblVendorContact. Also, it would be redundant to have Job Title as a field of tblVendor.
Phone	N	N	Y	Y	As with Job Title, Phone is more closely related to the content of tblVendorContact. However, since a contact might have several phone numbers, we must make a child table to tblVendorContact. We'll call that tblContactCommunication.
Email	N	N	Y	N	Each contact can have more than one e-mail address, so this needs to go into a child table. But, since Email, like Phone, is a method of contacting a person, we can use the tblContactCommunication table by adding a field to identify the type of communication. The list of communication types can be stored in a lookup table that we will call tblCommunicationType.
Products Supplied	Y	N	Y	N	This pattern of responses indicates that we need a child table. However, as we discovered in analyzing the Products core subject, the table tblProductVendor fills this need.

Based on the responses in the decision matrix, we can determine that it will take seven tables to establish and maintain the data related to Vendors, as shown in Figure 9-10. You already have one of the tables, tblProductVendor, which is represented by a shaded object.

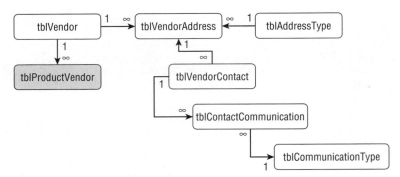

Figure 9-10: Relationships to tblVendor

Building on your experience from creating the tables and fields related to products, we will now create the tables and fields for vendors.

Creating the Tables and Fields

The next step is to examine the details that will go into each table so that we can create the appropriate fields. As you saw earlier, using a list of details as the basis for the fields can make this a relatively simple task, but it still requires you to examine each detail as you create the fields. In doing so, you will determine whether a detail needs to be separated into more than one field, as is the case with Contact Name.

You might also determine that it will be helpful to use some of the field properties to control what data can be entered into a field, such as preventing duplicate values by establishing an index with no duplicates (a unique index, described in Chapter 2 and in Appendix A).

The Vendor Table

tblVendor stores vendor names in the VendorName field. In addition, you will see a field named VendorKey. We added this field to permit flexibility in storing VendorNames prefixed with a short word, such as "The." The full name is stored in VendorName, but the VendorKey field can store a value by which you want to sort vendors. It is also indexed, and it does allow duplicates. Based on the suffix of Key, this field will be automatically indexed by Access unless the default AutoIndex options have been modified (see the AutoIndex Feature note).

For example, a VendorName of "The Bit Shop" would have a VendorKey of "BitShop." To assist a user with data entry for the VendorKey field, the application could set a default value for that field. Your users would have the capability to overwrite it.

AUTOINDEX FEATURE

As you may recall, fields that will be used heavily for sorting, or in relationships to other tables, should be indexed.

Access has an AutoIndex feature that will automatically index fields that end with ID, key, code, and num. This can be a benefit because you don't need to manually set the index properties, but it can also cause performance issues if you have fields indexed unnecessarily. These settings can be modified in the Access options; the Access Help file provides instructions on how to do that.

Figure 9-11 shows the design view of tblVendor. Also, note that two vendors may have the same name. To address that, you can force the vendor name to be unique by adding your own text to each vendor's name. For example: The Bit Shop (Ohio) and The Bit Shop (Washington). You can also add a description field to distinguish the two vendors. Alternatively, you can utilize the VendorKey field. The critical point is that you are aware of these types of scenarios, and that you develop a policy to deal with the situation. We have decided to create a unique index on the VendorName in order to force distinction.

Field Name	Data Type	Description
VendorID	AutoNumber	Unique identifier - system generated
VendorName	Text	The name of this vendor
VendorKey	Text	The sort key of this vendor
Inactive	Date/Time	Indication of when row became inactive
CreatedDate	Date/Time	Date/Time the record was created
CreatedBy	Text	User ID of the person that created this record

Figure 9-11: Design view of tblVendor

The Vendor Address Table

The table named tblVendorAddress is a child table of tblVendor. It stores the different addresses associated with a particular vendor. Figure 9-12 shows the design view for tblVendorAddress.

This table illustrates our earlier observation that some details may require more than one field when put into a table. You'll notice that the detail listed earlier as Address is now split into AddressBlock, City, State and ZipCode. In some situations, you may also need a country code, a second address block or street, or other address information.

tblVendorAddress		
Field Name	Data Type	Description
VendorAddressID	AutoNumber	Unique row identifier
VendorID	Number	FK to tblVendor.VendorID
AddressTypeID	Number	FK to tblAddressType.AddressTypeID
AddressBlock	Text	The address block (number and street name, suite, c/o etc)
City	Text	The city the vendor resides in
State	Text	The state of the vendor
ZipCode	Text	The zipcode or postal code of the vendor
Inactive	Date/Time	Indication of when row became inactive
CreatedDate	Date/Time	Date/Time the record was created
CreatedBy	Text	User ID of the person that created this record

Figure 9-12: Design view of tblVendorAddress

The Address Type Table

The table tblAddressType is a typical lookup table that stores lists of different address types: home, warehouse, or office would be viable terms. We included a Description field in the event that the short text of AddressType is not sufficient to describe the type of address.

This type of design is quite typical for lookup tables. Figure 9-13 shows the design view for tblAddressType.

tblAddressType		
Field Name	Data Type	Description
AddressTypeID	AutoNumber	Unique row identifier, engine generated
AddressType	Text	The address type
Description	Text	Decription of the address type
Inactive	Date/Time	Indication of when row became inactive

Figure 9-13: Design view of tblAddressType

The Vendor Contact Table

The table tblVendorContact is a child table to tblVendor. It stores information about the people your business could contact when you need to communicate with a vendor. Figure 9-14 shows the design view for tblVendorContact.

tblVendorContact		
Field Name	Data Type	Description
VendorContactID	AutoNumber	Unique record idenifier
VendorID	Number	FK to tblVendor.VendorID
NameFirst	Text	The first name of the contact
NameLast	Text	the last name of the contact
JobTitle	Text	The job title of this contact
Inactive	Date/Time	Indication of when the record became inactive
CreatedDate	Date/Time	Date/Time the record was created
CreatedBy	Text	User ID of the person that created this record

Figure 9-14: Design view of tblVendorContact

The Contact Communication Table

The table tblContactCommunication is a child table to tblVendorContact. This table stores the different phone numbers or e-mail addresses at which a VendorContact could be reached. Figure 9-15 shows the design view for tblContactCommunication.

tblContactCommunication

Field Name	Data Type	Description
ContactCommunicationID	AutoNumber	Unique row identifier, system assigned
VendorContactID	Number	FK to tblVendorContact.VendorContactID
CommunicationTypeID	Number	FK to tblCommunicationType.CommunicationTypeID
Identity	Text	The phone/email/etc that used to communicate with the indicated comm type.
DoNotContact	Yes/No	Communication through this information should not be used to make contact
Inactive	Date/Time	Indication of when row became inactive

Figure 9-15: Design view of tblContactCommunication

A special note about the field named Identity. This is not named according to convention, in the sense that it is common to see field names like PhoneNumber or Email. This table is used to store any type of communication method available for a contact. We will use the field name Identity because the phone number or the e-mail address is the "Identity" of the contact using the communication type indicated by CommunicationTypeID.

The Communication Type Table

The table tblCommunicationType is a lookup table that stores the different communication methods used in tblContactCommunication. Figure 9-16 shows the design view for tblCommunicationType.

tblCommunicationType

Field Name	Data Type	Description
CommunicationTypeID	AutoNumber	Unique row identifier, system generated
CommunicationType	Text	Communication type
Description	Text	Description of the CommunicationType
Inactive	Date/Time	Indication of when row became inactive

Figure 9-16: Design view of tblCommunicationType

Establishing the Relationships

Following the process that we used with the products core table, the next step is to fully describe and visualize how the tables that describe the vendor relate to each other. As a result of the work done in analyzing the core table, we can formalize the relationships between the core table and the supporting tables. Figure 9-17 illustrates the relational diagram of Vendors. As you can see, we have also included two tables that we created when building the tables for products, tblProductVendor and tblProductVendorCost, so that you can see how the vendor tables are related to the product tables.

As we previously explained, the "1" and the "∞" symbols in the figure represent the one side (or primary table) and the many side (also known as the foreign table or child table) of a relationship. In addition, the presence of the "1" and "∞" symbols indicates that referential integrity has been enabled.

Table 9-8 lists the relationships between each pair of the tables. It also indicates whether referential integrity needs to be enforced, and if you specifically need to set the property to provide cascade deletes; this will cause child records to be automatically deleted when the parent record is deleted.

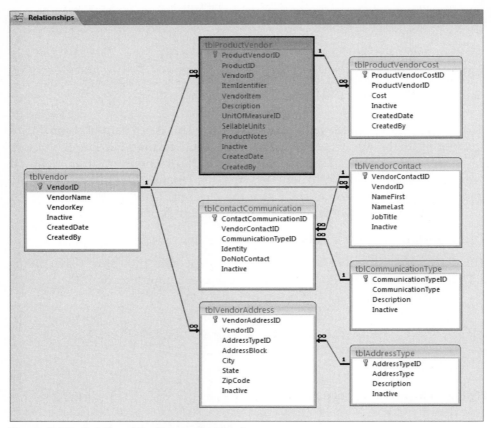

Figure 9-17: Relationship diagram for Vendors

Table 9-8: Relationships between the Tables

RELATED TABLES	TYPE	PRIMARY KEY FOREIGN KEY	REFERENTIAL INTEGRITY
tblAddressType to tblVendorAddress	1:M	tblAddressType.AddressTypeID tblVendorAddress.AddressTypeID	Yes
tblCommunicationType to tblContactCommunication	1:M	tblCommunicationType. CommunicationTypeID tblContactCommunication. CommunicationTypeID	Yes
tblVendor to tblProductVendor	1:M	tblVendor.VendorID tblProductVendor.VendorID	Yes
tblVendor to tblVendorAddress	1:M	tblVendor.VendorID tblVendorAddress.VendorID	Yes: Cascade Delete
tblVendor to tblVendorContact	1:M	tblVendor.VendorID tblVendorContact.VendorID	Yes: Cascade Delete
tblVendorContact to tblContactCommunication	1:M	tblVendorContact.VendorContactID tblContactCommunication. VendorContactID	Yes: Cascade Delete

Locations

We are now ready to examine the details related to locations. By this time you should be fairly well practiced at the process, but we'll list the steps once more to ensure that we're on the same page:

- Identify the fields.
- Identify and relate the tables.
- Create the tables and define the relationships.

Identifying the Details

The purpose of the Location table is to store information about storage locations for the products. Although this is pretty basic stuff, we will go through the same process to be consistent. Table 9-9 lists details that we need to record to identify where the various products are stored.

This is a very short list, but then we really did not expect that it would need too many details for locations. This example dramatically illustrates that the number of details required does not indicate the importance of what you are recording.

Table 9-9: Location Details

DETAIL	DESCRIPTION
Location	The location. Typically, this value is a code that can be interpreted to identify exactly where something is located.
Product	The product being stored in a location. This will relate to the Product table.
Description	A brief description of the location itself.
Parent Location	The parent location of the current location. This field enables you to build a hierarchy of locations. For example, at the top level you might have a store; under that, departments; under that, aisles; and under that, the bins in each aisle.

Indentifying the Supporting Tables

As before, we begin with the core table, tblLocation. Using the four qualifying questions, we determine whether we should add a field to the core table or create a new table. Table 9-10 summarizes the analysis of each item in the list of details.

To review, the questions are as follows:

- Is the field a property that directly describes the subject of the table?
- Will the value of this field be limited to a set of known or standard values?
- Can a single record have more than one value for this field?
- Is the field redundant, or does the field describe another field in the table?

The response patterns, as before, indicate how to handle each detail.

Table 9-10: Evaluating the Details

DETAIL	RESPONSE PATTERN				DISPOSITION
Location	Y	N	N	N	Remains in table tblLocation.
Product	N	Y	Y	N	Multiple values can be associated with a single record in tblLocation, which requires the creation of a child table. However, we already have the required table, defined while normalizing tblProduct and, tblLocationProduct. We also need a lookup table for the set of values for the product, but we also have the core table of tblProduct, which can easily double as a lookup table.
Description	Y	N	N	N	Remains in table tblLocation.
Parent Location	Y	Y	N	N	This pattern indicates that the field will remain in tblLocation. The value stored in this field will be a key pointing to a child table. However, the parent location is a foreign key to its own table. This is what creates a self-referencing table. More on that later.

In evaluating the details, we identified a new type of relationship: self-referencing. The hierarchy of departments in an organizational chart is a common example. All of the departments can be listed in one table, and as you move down the chart, each department reports to another department in the organization.

Explaining Self-Referencing Tables

The table tblLocation is a good illustration of the *self-referencing* table design mentioned in Table 9-3. To review, the value stored in the foreign key field is actually the primary key value of another record in the same table. In other words, the Parent Location listed in Table 9-10, gets its value from the list of records in tblLocation. The capability to do this is most often accomplished with the use of a Combo Box control on the form used to view and edit the data.

Figure 9-18 shows the relationship of the tables supporting the table tblLocation. Note that tblLocation is both the "one" side and the "many" side. As before, the shaded objects represent tables that were defined in another relationship with another core table.

Figure 9-18: Relationships to tblLocation

Creating the Tables and Fields

The next step is to create the tables and fields to fully describe the list of details.

The Location Table

The table tblLocation stores information about all of the locations at which you will store your products. This table is a self-referencing table and is capable of indicating a location as broad as the entire store or as finite as your smallest storage bin. The self-referencing table gives you an enormous amount of flexibility when defining and managing your locations.

As shown in Figure 9-19, we have used the field BelongsTo to store the LocationID of the parent location. The other fields are fairly self-explanatory.

Field Name	Data Type	Description
LocationID	AutoNumber	Unique identifier
Location	Text	The location description
Description	Text	Description/Comment about the location
BelongsTo	Number	The location this location is a part of. FK to tblLocation.LocationID
Inactive	Date/Time	Indication of when row became inactive
CreatedDate	Date/Time	Date/Time the record was created
CreatedBy	Text	User ID of the person that created this record

Figure 9-19: Design view of tblLocation

Because the tables for locations and products have a many-to-many relationship, you do not have a field in the table named tblLocation that relates to the tblProduct table. Instead, the primary keys from each of these tables become foreign keys in the junction table, tblLocationProduct. This was explained and illustrated earlier when we discussed the tables for products. You can see the design for tblProduct in Figure 9-3, and for tblLocationProduct in Figure 9-6.

Establishing the Relationships

Figure 9-20 presents the tables and relationships associated with information about the location of a product. The first thing you will notice is that the self-referencing relationship is represented in the Relationships window of Microsoft Access as an alias table, which is indicated with a suffix of an underscore and number, as shown here with tblLocation_1. There is not much more to note, except the inclusion of the table tblProduct, which was created out of the discussion surrounding the core subject of Products. It is shown shaded in Figure 9-20, in order to show the connection between the subject of Locations, implemented as tblLocation and the subject named Products, implemented as tblProduct. Figure 9-20 is complimented by Table 9-11, which follows shortly after the figure.

NOTE In Figure 9-20, you will notice the table named "tblLocation_1". We added tblLocation to the diagram twice in order to represent the self-join in the table tblLocation. The name "tblLocation_1" is known as an *alias*. The aliased table view is pointing directly to the table tblLocation.

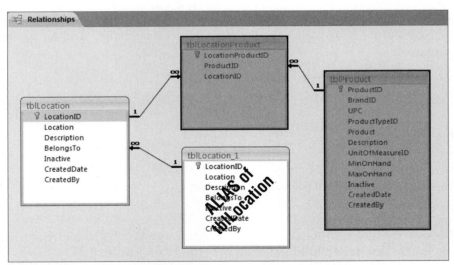

Figure 9-20: Relationship diagram for Locations

Table 9-11: Relationships between the Tables

RELATIONSHIP	TYPE	PRIMARY KEY FOREIGN KEY	REFERENTIAL INTEGRITY
tblLocation to tblLocation	1:M	tblLocation.LocationID tblLocation.BelongsTo	Yes
tblLocation to tblLocationProduct	1:M	tblLocation.LocationID tblLocationProduct.LocationID	Yes: Cascade Delete
tblLocation to tblProduct	M:M	See relationships of tblLocationProduct in Table 9-5	–

Transactions

The last core subject to analyze consists of the details associated with transactions. We will use the same process that we did with the last two core subjects, following the same steps.

Identifying the Details

When we were identifying the main tasks for the database, we noted the need to manage inventory. Since we want this database to record inventory levels, we decided to call this core area Transactions (short for Inventory Transactions). You will find that transactions for inventory are very much like those in a bank statement in the sense that you create a record to add or remove stock, or to adjust stock levels in your inventory, similar to the way you would handle deposits, withdrawals, and reconciliation. The general policy is never to delete records from this table. If your physical inventory numbers do not match with your calculated ones, you add a record to the Transactions table to adjust your calculated result.

Table 9-12 lists the main details that describe transactions.

Identifying the Supporting Tables

As before, we begin by identifying a core table, which we will name tblInventoryTransaction. Then, using the four qualifying questions, we will evaluate the details to determine whether they belong in tblInventoryTransaction or a different table:

1. Is the field a property that directly describes the subject of the table?

2. Will the value of this field be limited to a set of known or standard values?

3. Can a single record have more than one value for this field?

4. Is the field redundant, or does the field describe another field in the table?

Table 9-12: Transaction Details

DETAIL	DESCRIPTION
Transaction Date	Date the transaction took place.
Transaction Type	Type of transaction being recorded. Values include Received, Consumed, and Adjustment.
Purchase Order	Purchase order in which a transaction is to be processed against. For example: 10 units are received because of Purchase Order 123456, so the value 123456 would be written to this field.
Product Transacted	Product for which inventory is adjusted.
Description	Description of the transaction.
Units Transacted	Number of units involved in the transaction.

Table 9-13 summarizes the results of our evaluation.

Table 9-13: Evaluating the Details

DETAIL	RESPONSE PATTERN				DISPOSITION
Transaction Date	Y	N	N	N	This field remains in tblInventoryLocation.
Transaction Type	Y	Y	N	N	This field remains in the table as a foreign key field. The field will be related to the primary key field of a new lookup table named tblTransactionType.
Purchase Order	Y	Y	N	N	This field remains in the table. However, there is no lookup table from which to retrieve values. This field is available for future expansion as your functionality needs grow. This field will link to your purchasing application, which will generate purchase orders for your products. Chapter 7, "Sales," provides an OrderID column in the tblOrder, which is the type of value that this field is expecting.
Product Transacted	Y	Y	N	N	This field remains in tblInventoryTransaction and will use tblProduct as a lookup table to get its values.
Description	Y	N	N	N	This field remains in tblInventoryTransaction.
Units Transacted	Y	N	N	N	This field remains in tblInventoryTransaction.
Transaction Date	Y	N	N	N	This field remains in tblInventoryTransaction.

You will find that tblInventoryTransaction is a critical part of your database. It is the lifeblood of your Quantity on Hand reports; for example, you will use Units Transacted to calculate Quantity on Hand. You also use this table to determine the rate at which products are used or sold. This will help you determine how much product you need to order and when to order it.

The sample database for this chapter includes a few sample reports as well as Query objects and user-defined functions that illustrate how you can get common inventory-related values.

As shown in the diagram in Figure 9-21, relating this core table and its single supporting table is quite simple. However, as mentioned earlier, small and simple does not necessarily indicate insignificant.

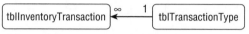

Figure 9-21: Relationship to tblInventoryTransaction

Creating the Tables and Fields

From the tables shown in Figure 9-21, you can anticipate the design of the lookup table that lists the types of transactions. The next step is to create the tables and fields.

The Inventory Transaction Table

As we just explained, tblInventoryTransaction will store details about the quantity of products on hand. Looking at the design view of the table, shown in Figure 9-22, you can see that most of the fields store data from other tables or are values created by the application.

The people using the application will typically be providing information in three fields: the description, the number of units, and the OrderID. You may be surprised that you might enter data into a field name with a suffix of ID. This field allows the user to indicate the purchase order that prompted the inventory transaction. The person inputting the data would likely get the purchase order information from the receiving paperwork of the product.

Remember that the Units are the number of sellable units received, and the description of the transaction will indicate the reason why the transaction is taking place; for example: "Shipment of two pallets totaling 20 boxes."

Field Name	Data Type	Description
InventoryTrasactionID	AutoNumber	Unique identifier
TransactionDate	Date/Time	Date of the transaction, default to Now()
TransactionTypeID	Number	Type of Transaction: FK to tblInventoryTransactionType.TransactionTypeID
OrderID	Number	The order id in which the product was shipped. Manually entered.
ProductID	Number	Product being transacted: FK to tblProduct.ProductID
Description	Text	A description of the transaction
Units	Number	The number of units in the transaction
CreatedDate	Date/Time	Date/Time the record was created
CreatedBy	Text	User ID of the person that created this record

Figure 9-22: Design view of tblInventoryTransaction

The Transaction Type Table

This table is a standard lookup table. The table provides the list of transaction types for inventory transactions. As you can see from the design view of tblTransactionType, shown in Figure 9-23, there are only two fields available to users.

For the most part, users will only be able to read values from this table in order to properly create an inventory transaction record. Any changes to the table's data will typically be done by a specifically authorized person.

tblTransactionType		
Field Name	Data Type	Description
TransactionTypeID	AutoNumber	Unique row identifer, system generated
TransactionType	Text	The transaction type
Description	Text	Description of the transaction type
Inactive	Date/Time	Indication of when row became inactive

Figure 9-23: Design view of tblTransactionType

After you have created the two tables, the final step is to establish their relationships.

Establishing the Relationships

The relationships for the core table of tblInventoryTransaction are shown in Figure 9-24. As before, we have shaded the objects that were defined in the analysis of other core tables.

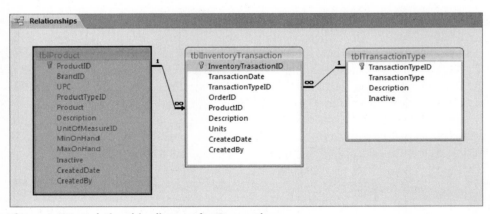

Figure 9-24: Relationship diagram for Transactions

Take note that the field OrderID in tblInventoryTransaction is to get its value from an application similar to one that would use the database example from Chapter 7—specifically, the table tblOrder.

LINKING TO EXTERNAL DATA

To link to external data, you can also include the linked tables in the relationship window. As we mentioned earlier when discussing getting data from the Sales database, you can use the Access Linked Table Manager or Get External Data Wizard to link to external databases and other data sources. Either approach will result in data being listed as a linked table along with your other Access tables. You can then add the table to the relationship window and establish the default join. You will not be able to enforce referential integrity, but you can define the AutoJoin type, which will be quite helpful when creating queries.

Table 9-14 lists the relationships for tblTransaction. Note that referential integrity is enforced in the relationships. You might also set additional field properties and use controls in the user interface to prevent a record from being inadvertently changed or deleted.

Table 9-14: Relationships of tblInventoryTransaction

RELATIONSHIP	TYPE	PRIMARY KEY FOREIGN KEY	REFERENTIAL INTEGRITY
tblTransactionType to tblInventoryTransaction	1:M	tblTransactionType.TransactionTypeID tblInventoryTransaction. TransactionTypeID	Yes
tblProduct to tblInventory Transaction	1:M	tblProduct.ProductID tblInventoryTransaction.ProductID	Yes

Congratulations! You have now created all of the tables and fields required for an inventory management database. Of course, you may need additional fields and tables for your solution, but now you know the process and logic for determining and creating a model appropriate for your needs.

Putting It All Together

Now that we have fully described each core table, we can put all the areas together to see the completed database schema. This schema is the result of identifying the database's purpose, the users' expectations, and other database requirements. Figure 9-25 illustrates the final schema as a relationship diagram. The core tables are shaded for simple identification. Looking at the figure, you can quickly see how the core tables are related. You'll notice that they are just as we anticipated when we reviewed the core subjects in Figure 9-1.

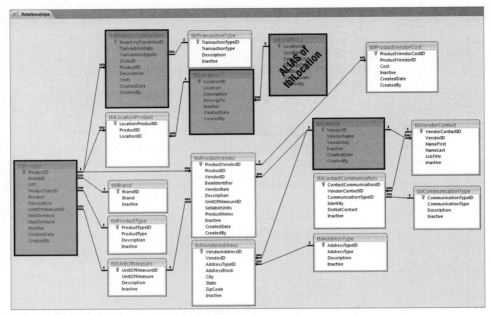

Figure 9-25: Relationship diagram for Inventory Management

Summary

This chapter showed you how to create the database schema for an inventory management database application. We started by clearly stating the purpose of the database: that is, to manage inventory.

We analyzed the database's purpose, requirements, and expectations to identify the core areas, which were then developed into the four core tables for the subjects of:

- Products
- Vendors
- Locations
- Transactions

We then systematically evaluated the details associated with each core area to identify all of the fields required for that area and determine the table to which they belong. Using a decision matrix, we asked the following four questions about each detail.

1. Is the field a property that directly describes the subject of the table?
2. Will the value of this field be limited to a set of known or standard values?

3. Can a single record have more than one value for this field?

4. Is the field redundant, or does the field describe another field in the table?

Based on the answers, we determined whether the detail should be added to the core table or a supporting table. We also considered whether the detail belonged in the database at all.

After creating the physical tables for each core subject (table), we established and explained how the tables related to each other and to the other core tables. Finally, we illustrated how the tables from all four core areas are represented in the relationship diagram.

In creating the database, we also explored some features and functionality that you will use in several other areas. One of the most important is the use of self-referencing tables. You will use this type of relationship in just about any scenario that resembles an organizational chart (supervisor of an employee) or family tree (parent of a child).

Chapters 8 and 9 used similar approaches for evaluating details and creating the database. The chapters work well together for manufacturing and inventory management. The next area that you will look at is tracking information related to services. In Chapter 10 you will create some databases to support a service business.

Services

In Chapter 7, "Sales," we covered only tangible products. That by no means describes every business. A large number of organizations provide a service, and this needs to be covered in a different way.

A service can be thought of as payment for time instead of a product. It is an agreement about the value of something performed in a period of time.

The cost of the service provided may be in direct correlation with the time it takes or it may depend upon how easily the provider can perform this task, especially if that provider can provide the service concurrently for many customers. Consequently, some companies simply aim to provide their service to as many customers as possible. In this way it is the process itself which has value, rather than the time spent performing it. This is usually because it's a special skill or requires a specific license. In such cases the service provider won't necessarily interact with the customer to perform the task.

For other organizations, there are only so many hours in the working day during which to sell their time. In such cases the organization has a fixed amount of resources with which to provide the service for a number of customers at any one time. This allocation of time to the customer needs to be scheduled and must include any other tasks such as preparing relevant equipment or compiling required information. Such appointment management is certainly nothing new in computer software. Anyone who uses Microsoft Outlook is familiar with the task of scheduling his or her calendar. Through shared calendars you can even check for conflicts with other users. But such software doesn't readily allow for the nuances of how your business works; it is time allocation without context.

When developing a database for services, the assignment of time to customers is only part of the service modeling process. Even when this is not a consideration, a database application can help in other ways. Most notably, the database can actually model the service provided, providing a step-by-step guide to both record and preview the service process and track progress. Such information in business is used for control and monitoring. You can know what stage of the process your customers are in and whether your staff is providing the service effectively.

This chapter describes managing appointments, and uses a simple example of a pet boarding company to demonstrate the booking concepts. By combining the new date and time concepts with established designs, we'll model process monitoring by looking at an events management database.

As part of the process, you will look at some situations that pose particular challenges for designing both the table structure and the user interface. We'll give you concrete guidance on some of the issues involved and the design alternatives. You will also see how to write queries to check for available appointment times, booking conflicts, and several other relatively complex tasks. The techniques that you learn in this chapter can be applied to many other scenarios and lines of business.

Database Terminology

As in other chapters, this chapter progresses by identifying the *subjects*, or entities, that make up the database. Each of these subjects represents a real-world concept such as order, customer, supplier, or invoice. Each subject translates into a table in your database or perhaps a group of related tables that describe it collectively. Each subject has various *items* of data that must be recorded and which describe the subject itself. These will be modeled as the fields of the tables.

The tables of the database all require a *primary key* to uniquely identify the records. These are all implemented as AutoNumber fields that provide a sequential number value automatically. These primary key fields are named for the table that contains them with the "ID" suffix. For example, a Customers table would be named "tblCustomer" and its primary key would be an AutoNumber named "CustomerID."

The tables you create must be joined together. The primary key of a table can be referenced from other tables to relate records from the two tables. The value of a primary key that represents a record in one table can be stored in a field in another table. The field in this related table referencing the primary key is called a *foreign key*. For example, a table tblJob may have a foreign key CustomerID which references the primary key from tblCustomers and identifies to which customer that job record belongs. That is a *one-to-many relationship*: one customer record may appear in many jobs but a job belongs to a single customer.

NOTE *Normalization,* described in Chapter 3, "Relational Data Model," is the process whereby you formally identify the individual tables that describe each subject. Roughly speaking, any tables which include items that actually describe more than one subject must be reviewed to determine what fields describe other subjects. These fields need to be extracted into new tables that will then be related to the original table.

When many items in one table can be related to multiple records in another table, it is referred to as a *many-to-many relationship*. This requires a third table, referred to as a *junction table*, to serve as a link between the two main tables, and is related to both by containing a foreign key to each. Occasionally this junction table will also contain additional data that is specifically and directly related to the link. You will often see that in sales, and we'll provided some examples in this chapter.

When you want to view the consolidated data in your application, you build a query that includes a *join* between the two tables, enabling their data to be returned as if stored in one table. In Access these queries are built graphically by using the query design view or built directly as Structured Query Language (SQL) behind the scenes.

Appointments Made Simple

In this chapter we're modeling appointments as a part of the services industry, but there's no denying that they are an important factor in many applications. Even for business databases that don't contain bookings or appointments, the concept of the apportionment of time is likely an important factor in some way. In the user interface of existing software, you may have seen onscreen implementations of appointment calendars that look more complicated than the simple model we'll show you. What you see in that existing software is the presentation layer of the application showing a convenient view of the data.

Any appointment may have various data items or *attributes*, depending upon its particular purpose and implementation. Ultimately, however, it's a measure of time between two fixed points. There you have your first choice. The definition of the appointment can be specified in more than one way. You can consider the appointment as one of the following:

- Between a start point in time and an end point in time

- A start point in time and then a specified length duration

- An end point in time after a preceding specified duration

In general you will only need the first option. It offers easy calculation of the duration of the appointment by considering the difference in time between the start and end while still allowing immediate comparisons for overlapping appointments. Everything else regarding the appointment is elaboration upon this core principle, but to see it in action we'll start our first example.

Pet Boarding Example

Although at first glance the choice of company for this example may not seem applicable to other businesses, the modeling of the services is generic and extendable. Ultimately, it's not the business itself that is of interest, but the common principles it introduces and the process of designing the database. Along with modeling appointments, one important concept we introduce is that this business provides two similar and related services. This could represent any organization that provides a service, even one that offers only one service but with various options regarding how it is conducted.

We'll begin by providing some simple business rules.

The Business Rules

This company, "Board & Groom," provides the following services:

- Kennel boarding for pets during the owner's vacations or emergencies
- Grooming, hygiene, and pampering for pets

The boarding, naturally, operates over a longer time schedule measured in days, whereas appointments are made for pet grooming during specific times within a single working day. Each activity requires different skills from the staff and specific information to be collected. For example, when booking a boarding, the dietary requirements of the pet must be known. Both services are geared toward dogs, although boarding is provided for other types of animals, too.

There are various types of each service reflecting different levels of luxury. Details of individual pet requirements must also be kept as both general pet data and information specific to each visit. While a single booking can include multiple pets, it can be for only one service type. Different services would require multiple bookings. One or more members of the staff are assigned the pets taken within a single booking, each staff member assuming a specific role.

In addition to standard contact details, a history of each customer's pets must be maintained to track and service repeat business. Based partly on these rules, the data requirements for a boarding booking are listed in Table 10-1.

Table 10-1: Boarding Data Items

DATA ITEM	DESCRIPTION
Customer Details	Standard customer information
Booking Date	Date booking made
Booking Status	State (e.g., confirmed, paid, etc.)
Start DateTime	Beginning date of stay
End Date Time	Ending date of stay
Booking Cost	Total cost of the booking
Booking Tax	Rate of tax charged
Booking Amount Paid	Amount already paid
Pet Name	For identity during stay
Staff Member	Members of staff assigned
Pet Type	Type of pet (e.g., dog, cat, etc.)
Pet Breed	Breed of pet (e.g., Labrador, Persian)
Pet Size	Size of pet
Pet Weight	Weight of pet
Pet Description	Brief text description of the pet
Pet Image	Optional image storage
Pet Special Requirements	Pet-specific information
Accommodation Type	Type of accommodation
Assigned Room No	Accommodation identification
Accommodation Experience	Quality level of booking
Dietary Requirements	Dietary requirements for stay
Special Requests	Owner requests per pet booking
Grooming Type	Type of grooming experience

It's important to note that slightly different elements are required for the different booking types. For example, in an accommodation there will be no requirement regarding the *type* of grooming to be performed. However, elements such as Assigned Room No and Dietary Requirements only relate to the pet's stay in the kennels.

Identifying the Subjects

Even before applying any analysis like normalization, you can reasonably identify core relational subjects and their details. If you need improvements they should become apparent later as you normalize your design. In this instance there is a clue due to the names, but purely from a business perspective we can identify initial table candidates as customers, pets, and bookings. We'll consider each of these in turn.

Customer Tables

Based on expected requirements and common sense, we will assume the existence of a standard customer table for individual identification, and related details tables for address and contact data. This level of customer detail wasn't presented in Table 10-1 for brevity. These tables are similar to those used in earlier chapters, and are shown in Figure 10-1.

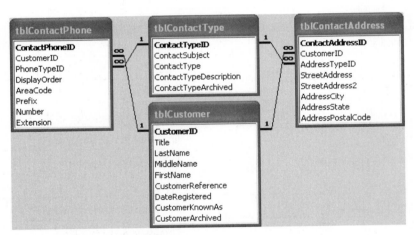

Figure 10-1: Simple customer tables

Pet Tables

When we consider the subject of Pets in conjunction with the items shown in Table 10-1, we can create a field list like the one shown in Table 10-2.

The field PetType indicates if it is a dog or cat, and the field PetBreed identifies the breed, such as Labrador, Springer Spaniel, Persian, Tabby, and so on, which are subclassifications of the PetType. The data entered in these fields will be repetitive, and could lead to inconsistent entries if not controlled. To solve this we create the related type and breed tables. Creating just a single breed table would lead to repetitive values for the type. For example, it would contain "dog" in a large number of rows. The tables and relationships for Pets are shown in Figure 10-2.

Table 10-2: Single Pet Table

FIELD	DATA TYPE	DESCRIPTION
PetID	AutoNumber	Primary key field
OwnerCustomerID	Long Integer	Foreign key to the "owner" customer
PetBreedID	Text	Foreign key to Pet Breed table
PetName	Text	For identity during stay
PetDOB	Date/Time	Date of birth of pet (to calculate age)
PetSize	Double	Size of pet
PetWeight	Double	Weight of pet
PetDescription	Text	Description of pet

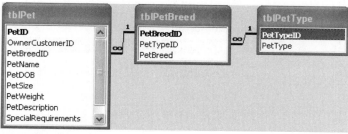

Figure 10-2: Pet tables

This table structure provides simplified listing functionality: instead of scrolling through hundreds of breed records from all animal types, a list filtered by a type offers a more direct selection. However, only the PetBreedID can be stored in a pet record or you risk having incorrect or conflicting information.

Booking Table

It's important to identify what items of a booking relate directly to a single, core booking table. We have established that certain data elements listed in Table 10-1 are specific to the type of booking being made. The fields that are considered to be dependent upon the activity type are listed in Table 10-3. (Bookings are discussed again later in the chapter in more detail, and in the context of appointments and availability.)

Table 10-3: Booking-Dependent Fields

FIELD	BOOKING TYPE
Accommodation Type	Accommodation
Assigned Room No	Accommodation
Accommodation Experience	Accommodation
Dietary Requirements	Accommodation
Special Requests	Both
Grooming Type	Grooming

Including these details in a booking record would create redundant fields because at least some of them will always be left unused. They are not entirely dependent on the booking and they describe the core booking. If we move these fields to a booking detail table, then we maintain better consistency and our table subject will be directly described by its fields. Table 10-4 describes the fields of a preliminary Booking table.

Table 10-4: Preliminary Fields for the Booking Table

FIELD	DATA TYPE	DESCRIPTION
BookingID	AutoNumber	Primary key field
CustomerID	Long Integer	Foreign key to Customer table
BookingDate	DateTime	Date booking made
BookingStatus	Text	Status (e.g., confirmed, paid)
StartDateTime	DateTime	Beginning date/time of activity
EndDateTime	DateTime	Ending date/time of activity
BookingCost	Currenncy	Total cost of the booking
BookingTax	Double	Rate of tax charged
BookingAmountPaid	Currenncy	Amount already paid

The established business rules state that a booking can be made for more than one pet, which is why there is no pet field in Table 10-4. There must be a one-to-many relationship between the Booking and Pet tables to model this requirement. You'll see that next.

Booking Detail Tables

The fields we have already identified as booking-type dependent need to be separated from the booking record and entered into appropriate detail tables. These are "detail" tables in that they describe the detail of a particular variation on the main booking. We require one detail table for each of the accommodation and grooming booking types. These booking-type details would normally exist in a one-to-one relationship with the booking record, but they describe the service that is to be performed for only one specific pet. For example, the accommodation table lists the actual kennel the pet will occupy. Therefore, these particular detail tables would exist in a one-to-many relationship with the Booking table. They are shown in Tables 10-5 and 10-6.

Table 10-5: Possible Accommodation Detail Table

FIELD	DESCRIPTION
BookingDetailAccomID	Primary key field
BookingID	Foreign key to Booking table
PetID	Foreign key to Pet table
AccommodationType	Type of accommodation
AssignedRoomNo	Accommodation identification
DietaryRequirements	Dietary requirements for stay
SpecialRequests	Special requests from owner

Table 10-6: Possible Grooming Detail Table

FIELD	DESCRIPTION
BookingDetailGroomingID	Primary key field
BookingID	Foreign key to Booking table
PetID	Foreign key to Pet table
GroomingActivity	Type of grooming performed
SpecialRequests	Special requests from owner

Notice that the detail table references the booking table using the BookingID and the pet table using the PetID foreign key fields. The accommodation and dietary fields are specific to accommodation only, but SpecialRequests relates to the pet in this instance. The same is true for the grooming detail shown in Table 10-6.

There is, however, a more logical design to implement, and following good database design practices can lead us to it. In both detail tables, the BookingID and PetID together represent a *candidate key* because they could uniquely describe any given record. The reason the combination of BookingID and PetID could be a candidate key is because you can't physically book the same pet more than once in the same booking. The SpecialRequests field is not dependent on the particular detail table directly. It is dependent on this combination of fields because it relates to the pet booking, not the accommodation or grooming.

These fields therefore separate out to form a new table which is described by the BookingID and PetID fields. We will maintain the practice of including a surrogate primary key AutoNumber field. This new table, tblBookingPet, is shown in Table 10-7.

Table 10-7: Booking Pet Table

FIELD	DATA TYPE	DESCRIPTION
BookingPetID	AutoNumber	Primary key field
PetID	Long Integer	Foreign key to Pet table
BookingID	Long Integer	Foreign key to Booking table
SpecialRequests	Text	Special requests from owner

This changes our detail table design and leaves us with the accommodation table described in Table 10-8.

Table 10-8: Revised Booking Detail Accommodation Table

FIELD	DATA TYPE	DESCRIPTION
BookingDetailAccomID	AutoNumber	Primary key field
BookingPetID	Long Integer	Foreign key to Booking Pet table
AccommodationType	Text	Description of type of stay
AssignedRoomNo	Text	Accommodation identifier
DietaryRequirements	Text	Dietary need for this stay

Similarly, a new grooming table is shown in Table 10-9.

Table 10-9: Revised Booking Detail Grooming Table

FIELD	DATA TYPE	DESCRIPTION
BookingDetailGroomingID	AutoNumber	Primary key field
BookingPetID	Long Integer	Foreign key to pet table
GroomingActivity	Text	Description of groom type

The AccommodationType and AssignedRoomNo fields in the accommodation table are descriptive and repetitive text fields. They are similar to the GroomingActivity field in the grooming detail table. Each of these can optionally be used to create dedicated tables to describe the AccommodationType, AssignedRoomNo, and GroomingActivity. It also provides the opportunity to expand these new tables into more fully descriptive subjects in their own right. For example, the new tblAccomodationType can exist as not only a text description, but also a description of the luxury level and the unit cost of such an experience.

These new tables relate to our previously identified core subjects and provide us with the general booking design shown in Figure 10-3.

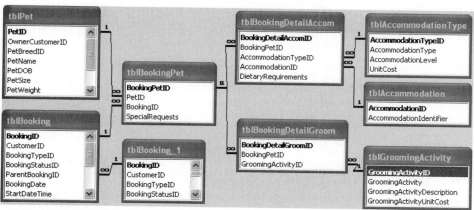

Figure 10-3: Final booking detail tables

We can now compile a list of core subjects for the database. As shown in Table 10-10, this is considerably different than our original list of only three items. However, we are far from done with our model. The booking table has been only partly modeled so far; now we will expand its design and examine how that can help with the day-to-day task of taking booking records.

Table 10-10: Identified Main Subjects

SUBJECT	DESCRIPTION
Customer	Customer details
Booking	Primary booking record
Pet	Pet details
Booking Pet	Pets assigned to a booking
Booking Accommodation Detail	Details of accommodation
Booking Grooming Detail	Details of grooming

The Booking Table Expanded

The booking table contains certain fields that we have yet to introduce but that play an important role in how you will view booking records and how you can query them.

Booking Types

To better describe the booking record we add a type field. The BookingTypeID is a foreign key related to tblBookingType and serves to distinguish between the two types of booking that we have—boarding or grooming. While this may seem redundant because we could infer the type of booking based upon which of the details tables have been entered, there are situations when this isn't enough. The reasons for including this field are as follows:

- **Time of subsequent data entry:** The detail records may not be completed when the initial booking record is created.

- **UI decision-making:** A field that determines which *type* of booking record can be used in an application to tell the UI the appropriate detail table to use.

- **Synonymous descriptions:** The same core types can be described in more than one way.

This final reason for the BookingTypeID is a concept that is worth expanding on. Although there are precisely two types of booking based upon the detail tables that exist, these same details might be used to serve bookings described in different ways. For example, there might be a charity booking type for the local animal sanctuary, which offers rudimentary housing for collected animals. This is a way of accommodating a new booking type while still using the same detail tables. It is the rows of tblBookingType that will describe these types. This presents a way for users to introduce new types into the system without changing the original design. Naturally, if a fundamental new service were introduced with its own data requirements, then a new detail table would be merited.

Booking Status

Also describing a booking record is the BookingStatus field. This would become a repetitive field that we could also separate out into its own table. This is similar in concept to the Status field in Chapter 7. Table tblBookingStatus is a convenient and flexible method of determining the progression of the service, from quote or provisional booking through to completion or cancellation.

> **NOTE** Regarding cancellations, a general notes field can be a useful field for any table. This was implemented in the Chapter 7. Maintaining a dedicated ReasonCancelled field in your service tables can also provide a valuable tool for improving your own business processes and increasing the ratio of enquiries to confirmed work.

As before, the status table contains a field BookingStatusNumericLevel, which provides a sequential indication of the stage at which a booking exists from a numeric perspective. In the c10Pets.mdb example provided on the book's CD for this chapter, you'll see the records illustrated in Figure 10-4.

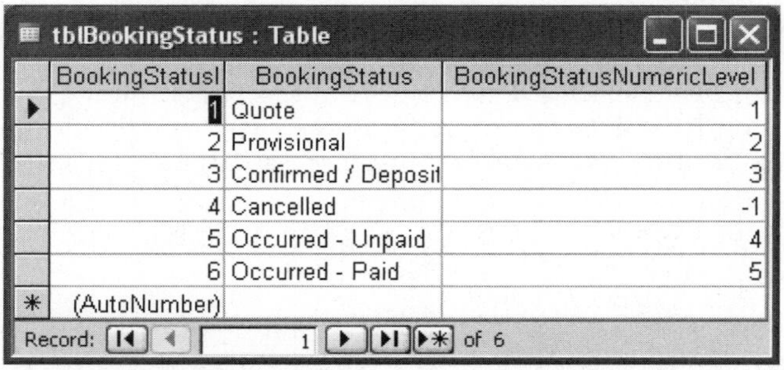

	BookingStatusI	BookingStatus	BookingStatusNumericLevel
▶	1	Quote	1
	2	Provisional	2
	3	Confirmed / Deposit	3
	4	Cancelled	-1
	5	Occurred - Unpaid	4
	6	Occurred - Paid	5
*	(AutoNumber)		

Record: 1 of 6

Figure 10-4: Booking status settings

This includes a row for cancelled bookings that includes a numeric indicator that is out of sequence (-1). Under normal circumstances you would query the numbers sequentially, for example, "Occurred - Paid" is logically a subsequent status to "Provisional." If you create your query criteria to exclude values less than zero, then you have an easy way to ignore the cancelled booking records.

For example, to find all bookings that have not yet started, while excluding those that have been cancelled, you use criteria to filter or limit the data that is returned (displayed to the user), as shown in Figure 10-5. This is the design view of the query using Access. We have used the criteria "Between 0 and 4." Because "Between" will actually include the two end values, the results will include records with level 1, 2, 3, or 4.

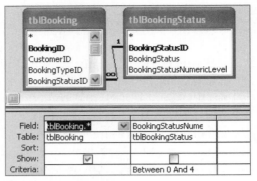

Figure 10-5: Querying active bookings

In Access, that same query can be shown in the SQL view as follows:

```
SELECT tblBooking.*
FROM tblBookingStatus INNER JOIN tblBooking ON
    tblBookingStatus.BookingStatusID = tblBooking.BookingStatusID
WHERE BookingStatusNumericLevel BETWEEN 0 AND 4
```

Booking Staff Members

The final booking table consideration based upon the initial data requirements is for staff members. We take a table similar to those implemented in models already shown for employees, such as in Chapter 7. The staff members are assigned to the booking record by employees, so an employee table will need to include the identification or name of the individual. You can include details that are necessary without responding to all of the fields. The Employee table, as implemented, is shown in Figure 10-6.

Field Name	Data Type	Description
EmployeeID	AutoNumber	
Title	Text	Individual's title "Dr, Mr, Mrs, Ms, Miss"
LastName	Text	Last Name
MiddleName	Text	Middle Name
FirstName	Text	First Name
DateHired	Date/Time	Date this employee was hired
DateLeft	Date/Time	Date this employee departed employment

Figure 10-6: Employee table

Because a booking record can be related to one or more employees, this requires a junction table between tblEmployee and tblBooking containing a foreign key to both tables. Such "junction tables" are common in database design because they support a many-to-many relationships that cannot be created directly between the two existing tables. We recommend that you try to identify the main subject or concept that each table represents, as this enables you to ensure that your schema is sound from a business perspective. In this case, the assignment can be thought of as just that, employees *assigned* to a booking to care for the pets in question. This makes sense for our business rules, as one requirement is to identify the role that each assigned staff member is fulfilling for that booking. The potential fields for a Booking Staff junction table are listed in Table 10-11.

Table 10-11: Proposed Booking Staff Junction Table

FIELD	DATA TYPE	DESCRIPTION
BookingStaffID	AutoNumber	Primary key field
BookingID	Long Integer	Foreign key to Booking table
EmployeeID	Long Integer	Foreign key to Employee table
RoleDescription	Text (255)	Description of role performed

As a free text field, RoleDescription provides the opportunity for inconsistent data and repeating values. This is another classic case for moving the field to a dedicated table, such as the Role table shown in Table 10-12.

Table 10-12: Role Table

FIELD	DATA TYPE	DESCRIPTION
RoleID	AutoNumber	Primary key field
RoleName	Text (50)	Name of role
RoleDescription	Text (255)	Description of role
RoleArchived	Yes/No	Role no longer performed

This table allows a more detailed description of a role (RoleDescription) while referring to it using a short name (RoleName) and storing a foreign key (RoleID) wherever required.

Given that we have a Role table to describe the role performed by staff members, we can provide the model to identify which employees are able to provide specific roles. This will also assist in the selection of staff members for a booking. We require another junction table between the Employee and the Role table, tblEmployeeRole, with the fields listed in Table 10-13.

Table 10-13: Employee Role Table

FIELD	DATA TYPE	DESCRIPTION
EmployeeRoleID	AutoNumber	Primary key field
EmployeeID	Long Integer	Foreign key to Employee table
RoleID	Long Integer	Foreign key to Role table

In Figure 10-7, you can see how tblEmployee, tblEmployeeRole, tblRole, and tblBookingStaff are related. It also shows how tblBookingType and tblBookingStatus relate to tblBooking.

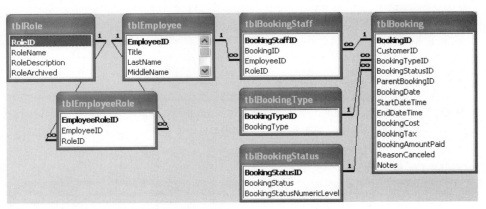

Figure 10-7: Booking-specific related tables

IMPLEMENTING CASCADE DELETE

Some relationships in this and other databases in this book enforce cascade delete, whereas other relationships don't.

Cascade deletes ensure that when a parent record is deleted, related child records are also deleted at the same time. This prevents the possibility of orphan records that have a foreign key value referring to a primary key value from a row that no longer exists.

There's a school of thought that cascade delete shouldn't be enforced in relationships, and policies in certain business sectors explicitly forbid it. However, it can be a useful tool for those who do want it. It is implicit and occurs without prompting on any deletion of a parent record, without exception.

You should enforce it only when it is appropriate for your model. Using our current example, if you delete a booking, then the related records indicating which staff members were assigned to that booking are also deleted, as cascade delete is enforced between those tables. However, it is not enforced between the Booking and Booking Status tables because we do not want the deletion of one status level record to delete all booking records that currently hold that state. The decision about when to implement cascade delete reflects personal preference, common sense, and business rules more than strict database procedure.

Cascade update similarly updates related foreign key values when a primary key is edited. However, it is not necessary in a database that uses AutoNumbers for the primary keys. These can never be edited once assigned. In other scenarios it will automatically update the "many" side table foreign key values with any updated primary key value in the "one" side of the join. As a good primary key is one that never, or at worst very rarely, changes, then this is implemented only as required.

Checking Appointments

As described at the beginning of this chapter, the "appointment" itself is merely the interval between two fixed time points. In this case the booking records start and end dates. How these are displayed in an application can be more complicated if you're trying to emulate Outlook-type functionality. First and foremost, we're modeling a database; and what we're interested in is the data stored in it, adding more and querying what's already there. Often, in an appointment-oriented service database, that means looking for *available* intervals.

NOTE There are numerous ways and means of making an application jump through hoops to achieve a certain goal, but Access's strength lies in its default functionality and very rapid building of data solutions. You can learn techniques to provide slick application functionality and include a grid-like user interface, but this is no reason to abandon the ideals of a normalized design.

What constitutes an available interval? An interval is available if it does not intersect with any existing appointments such that it would then cause the total of concurrent appointments to be greater than the maximum threshold permitted.

To place that in context of the current example, if there is a maximum of ten kennels, then no more than ten accommodation bookings can be taken that occur at the same time. These bookings need not share the same start and end points. Any overlap at all could still make the booking impossible to fully achieve. For example, a booking from July 1 until July 8 could be prevented by the presence of a booking whose dates range from June 25 until July 2 due to the overlap in dates on July 1. The fact that most of the requested time is available doesn't change the limitation that some of the booking can't be satisfied. There's also another alternative whereby conflicting bookings occur within the range of another. For example, in our July 1 through July 8 booking, there could be a short stay between July 2 and July 4. Indeed, there could be more than one in the same accommodation following that of, say, July 5 through July 7.

So how do you check for conflicts when you want to add a new booking record? Do you assume the maximum number of kennels available and calculate how many bookings already exist within the desired period for the prospective booking? Consider what is involved in that request. Checking for any bookings within that time period is relatively simple. You need to query for any booking that intersects with your proposed period. Figure 10-8 shows a diagram demonstrating the potential ways that our bookings could intersect.

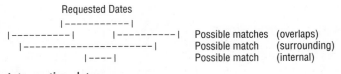

Figure 10-8: Intersecting dates

However, consider the diagram in Figure 10-9, which describes the records that we do *not* want to return, as they do not intersect with our proposed dates.

Figure 10-9: Non-intersecting dates

Clearly Figure 10-9 represents a simpler request of data than the several possibilities shown in Figure 10-8. To form a simple query that will find intersecting booking records, you want results that do not conform to the scenario shown in Figure 10-9—that is, you want bookings that do not occur entirely before the start or entirely after the end dates. We'll create a query with parameters, PropStartDate and PropEndDate, for which the user will provide the requested dates. The criteria for matching records is that the booking dates do not lie entirely before or entirely after the requested range. The query is shown in Figure 10-10.

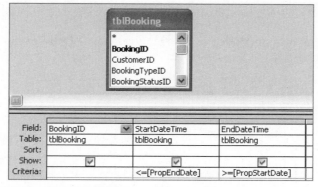

Figure 10-10: Intersecting query dates

USING A MATCHING QUERY

We arrive at the single, simple query shown in Figure 10-10 by considering the range of dates. We require both the start and end points of existing bookings to be outside the range of our requested parameters. If you use a table validation rule to ensure that bookings are entered with an end date subsequent to the start date, then we need only consider one end of the range. In other words, we have a match if the start of the requested range does not occur after a booking date, and the end of the requested range does not occur before it. The diagram for consideration is cut down to the following:

```
                    Requested Dates
                    |-----------|
            ---|                    |----
```

This gives a query in which we select records not outside the end of the ranges:

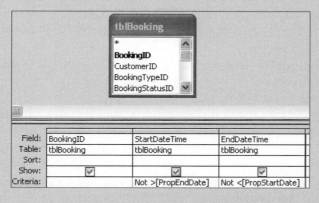

Continued

USING A MATCHING QUERY *(continued)*

From the query window, if you choose to view in SQL mode, you see that this is represented in SQL as follows:

```
PARAMETERS PropStartDate DateTime, PropEndDate DateTime;
SELECT tblBooking.BookingID, tblBooking.StartDateTime,
   tblBooking.EndDateTime
FROM tblBooking
WHERE Not StartDateTime>[PropEndDate] AND
   Not EndDateTime<[PropStartDate];
```

The Not operator in this query will cause the database engine to be unable to execute the query as efficiently as possible. This means slower performance as your database becomes larger. The equivalent query to this without using a Not operator would be as follows:

```
PARAMETERS PropStartDate DateTime, PropEndDate DateTime;
SELECT tblBooking.BookingID, tblBooking.StartDateTime,
   tblBooking.EndDateTime
FROM tblBooking
WHERE StartDateTime<=[PropEndDate] AND EndDateTime>=[PropStartDate];
```

This syntax is actually how Access would automatically reformat your query, giving us the query shown in Figure 10-10.

This query gives us a set of existing bookings that already fall within our requested date range. However, simply knowing that there are some other bookings does not indicate whether any kennels are free. The matching bookings aren't necessarily mutually exclusive. Some of them could run consecutively in the same kennel, rather than consume additional accommodation. Analyzing this further would involve more querying on the previous results to ensure that we don't include mutually exclusive entries. This becomes problematic very quickly and harder for you to maintain and for the database to execute.

So how can you easily determine availability? The answer is two-fold. Previously, we introduced the concept that each pet booking has an accommodation assigned to it, using the AccommodationID field in tblBookingDetailAccom. This value comes from the table tblAccommodation, which holds a record for each of the accommodation kennels that exist at the site. This full list of all possible kennels gives us a method to again turn querying on its head. So, we can query for any accommodation that is *not* occupied at *any* point during the proposed dates. If an existing booking ties up a given accommodation for any part of the proposed interval, then clearly it is unable to provide accommodation for the whole period. This query works because we have the table holding all possible accommodations to match against.

To simplify this process, we divide the request into two queries. The first, qryBookingAccommodation, joins the related booking tables together to provide a simplified source for subsequent querying. The tables tblBooking, tblBookingPet, and tblBooking DetailAccom are joined and the criteria is applied using the parameters previously demonstrated to find intersecting booking records, as shown in qryBookingAccomodation in Figure 10-11.

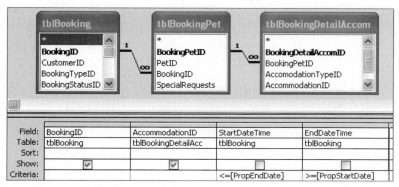

Figure 10-11: qryBookingAccommodation

This query provides us with bookings whose dates intersect in some way with our new required period. We then use these booking accommodation results in a final query, qryAvailableAccommodation, to find any accommodation that does *not* feature in that list. This requires an *outer join* between the full list of kennels, tblAccommodation, and the intersecting booking records' occupied accommodations, as shown in Figure 10-12.

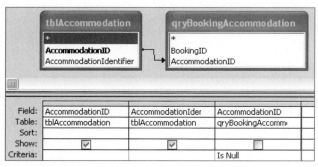

Figure 10-12: qryAvailableAccommodation

There are a couple of important concepts that you should notice here. The outer join is explained in the following sidebar and in Appendix B; the other point is that we are using a query as a record source for building another query.

As we indicated, you are using qryBookingAccomodation to limit or filter the records that can be included in the next query, qryAvailableAccomodations. This is a very important concept, as countless scenarios require more than one level of queries. A query used as a record source for another query is called a *subquery*.

USING A NON-MATCHING QUERY

Notice that this second query, shown in Figure 10-12, uses qryBookingAccommodation (Figure 10-11) as its source, joined to the tblAccommodation. The earlier query enables us to apply the parameters and return a set of matching bookings. It is this subsequent query's role to return all accommodation records not featured in that returned list. As mentioned, in our example this is achieved using an outer join. These are query joins between tables that "favor" one table over the other, returning all records from that table regardless of whether there is a match from the other side of the join. In the query design grid shown in Figure 10-12, this is achieved by right-clicking on the join in question and choosing the join type you require.

In SQL view that same query is as follows:

```
SELECT tblAccommodation.AccommodationID,
    tblAccommodation.AccommodationIdentifier
FROM tblAccommodation LEFT JOIN qryBookingAccommodation ON
    tblAccommodation.AccommodationID =
    qryBookingAccommodation.AccommodationID
WHERE qryBookingAccommodation.AccommodationID Is Null;
```

The left outer join favors the tblAccomodation records, so all entries from that table are returned along with any matching accommodation that has featured in the results from qryBookingAccommodation. We then apply some criteria to the AccommodationID field from that query's results, stipulating that it must be Null, i.e., have no value. The net result is that we keep only the entries from tblAccommodation for which no matching entry was found and returned in the conflicting bookings list.

This querying may look involved at first, but it breaks down into simpler constituent parts. The first query produces a single set of results that we can further manipulate, and it applies the parameters and criteria to identify the interfering bookings. The second query uses an outer join to return only those accommodations listed in the core tblAccommodation table that do *not* feature in the qryBookingAccommodation query. Therefore, these are the kennels that *are* available for the required period. If none are returned, then none are available.

You can learn more about queries and joins in Appendix C.

Extending the Database

You can add to the design of the database—for example, to support more types of bookings, by adding new detail tables. A general notes table such as the one shown in Chapter 7 can be a useful addition to any database.

There are also further considerations for which you might query your database. For example, instead of accommodation you could query for the number of groomer employees who do not have scheduled bookings within a prospective time frame. The Employee and Role tables provide the list of all suitable employees. Grooming activities have shorter intervals than accommodation bookings but that doesn't affect the theory behind the process. Appointment queries will work over minutes as easily as hours or days.

You've seen the basics of enabling a service within a given time period and the means of checking for availability using queries. The following sections describe an example that focuses on a concept other than appointments—that of describing the service itself.

Process Monitoring

Databases are often (and wrongly) thought of as relatively static repositories of data. This is not accurate in a very large number of cases. The transactional databases that you've examined in this book are adaptive and are constantly updated through direct user input, scheduled processes, and imports. For example, the sales records, financial entries, or production runs can change continuously. This up-to-date information is just as important as the historical entries, maybe more so.

Once a service record has been fully entered with details and dates, it too might be thought of as static until the service is completed and the record is changed by flagging it as complete.

The title of this section, "Process Monitoring," may sound like it refers to a manufacturing concept, but it's much broader than that. In fact, the concepts we look at aren't limited to service-related databases, but they are very commonly implemented in service databases.

Many services provided by companies either break down into a set of predictable sequences that comprise the entire service or they comprise a set of standard practices that are followed in preparing and providing the service.

A good example of such business types would be real estate title and sales services. Processes such as transfer of property require a fairly predefined set of steps performed at various stages, such as contact with clients, letters sent to inform parties of progress, completion and submission of documents, and inspections or searches performed on the property. They may not always necessarily be completed in the same order every time, but there is a process involved consisting of the same steps each time. It is this process that has value in modeling your database. The stages show users a great deal about what's been done, what is yet to be done, and anything that is taking longer than it should.

Almost any area for which there is a process to follow is an appropriate candidate for process monitoring. The method for describing a process is very simple, requiring only a few tables, but to give it context in our next example, we combine some concepts from the previous example before moving on to process monitoring.

Events Management

This example involves designing a database for a company that plans, prepares, and executes events for customers. These events can range from weddings to corporate activities, and they can involve some of the company's own staff as well as outside organizations.

We first discuss the principal requirements of the events management company, beginning by predicting some of the main subjects before examining the specific event items required for the business Then we consider the similarities between this database and the pet grooming example with which you're already familiar.

Previously in this chapter, you looked at the concept of a central booking table that had to handle two distinct types of business activities. Those two business types required two "detail" tables related to the core booking table to provide the appropriate fields for the given activities. The advantages of this concept become more obvious the more we increase the diversity of the business types.

Event Management Requirements

The events management company in this case plans and operates various types of events for their customers. The majority of customers come from providing the types of events shown in Table 10-14.

There is a wide degree of variation in the type of events provided. For example, there could be weddings with or without receptions, corporate shows inviting other organizations, or single companies doing team-building exercises. External companies are used to provide some of the required services that vary from one type of event to another. Corporate events, for example, typically have no need for a singer or a wedding cake, but there might still be catering and transport requirements.

Internal staff members also work the events, while other administrative staff monitor the status of pending and in-process events. Staff are responsible for preparing required equipment and personnel and, when required, arranging insurance policies. Events are referred to by customer name or other appropriate reference.

Table 10-14: Types of Events

EVENT TYPE	DESCRIPTION
Weddings	Including receptions and parties
Corporate Events	Corporate shows, group activities
Parties	Birthdays, anniversaries, etc.
Festivals	Music or art festivals
Misc	Other events not covered above

Queries from customers expressing interest in the company's services are answered in writing with brochures and documents offering written estimates. These answers are followed up by staff. Those that are accepted become provisional bookings and deposits are taken. The start and end date and times of the event must be recorded as well as the date the event was originally booked.

In this example we focus on only two event types: weddings and corporate events. The types of information stored in preparation for a wedding are shown in Table 10-15. Items for corporate events are listed in Table 10-16.

Table 10-15: Event Items for Weddings

ITEM	DESCRIPTION
Customer Details	Customer holding the event
Type of Wedding	Specific identification of event type
Venue	Location where event is held
Event Date	Date of event
Staff Assigned	Names of employees and roles assumed
Requires Disabled Access	Whether the venue requires disabled access
Start Time	Time event starts
End Time	Time event ends

Continued

Table 10-15: (*continued*)

ITEM	DESCRIPTION
Total Budget	Maximum cost for the event
Deposit Paid	Amount already paid
Caterers	Organization providing the catering
Menu Preference	Required menu type
Transport Providers	Organization providing the cars
Dress Makers	Organization providing the dress
Suit Hire	Organization providing the suits
Music	Organization providing the music/disco
Number in Party	Number requiring transport
Parties' Names	Names of all key players
Number in Reception	Total number of heads catered
Maximum Cost per Head	Highest budgeted venue and menu cost
Rehearsal Date	Date of rehearsal if manager is to attend
Photographer Required	Professional photographer to be used
Guest Book Required	Provide a book for guests to sign

Table 10-16: Event Items for Corporate Events

ITEM	DESCRIPTION
Customer Details	Customer holding the event
Type of Event	Specific event type (e.g., conference, release)
Speaker	Any individual performing or speaking
Number of Delegates	Total number of heads
Venue	Location where event is held
Event Date	Date of event
Staff Assigned	Names of employees and roles assumed
Requires Disabled Access	Whether the venue requires disabled access
Start Time	Time event starts

ITEM	DESCRIPTION
End Time	Time event ends
Total Budget	Maximum cost for the event
Deposit Paid	Amount already paid
Caterers	Organization providing the catering
Delegates Names	Names of selected or all delegates
Tag Line	Published name of the event
Publicity Required	Is notice in the press required?
Security Required	Is event sensitive and requires security?
Projector Required	Large screen projector to be supplied?

The subjects of this database could be wide and varied, consisting of both individuals and organizations that provide a range of different products or services. We'll progress through the core subjects first, identifying those already familiar to us from the pet boarding example. Then we'll confront the new issues.

Identifying the Subjects

Whereas our previous service example had a central booking subject, we are clearly now dealing with events, and we'll name our core subject accordingly. There are customers for whom the events are provided, and we create customer detail tables modeled on previous customer tables you've seen in this and other chapters in this book. If you need specific information not included in this design, you can add those fields as appropriate.

NOTE It's a good idea to reuse existing table designs if you can. If possible, you could use the actual tables that have been used in other databases. Sharing database tables and data across databases can provide a great resource for finding "individual records." Although the records may have been created in multiple files, they can still be retrieved from a single location.

Many of the items listed in Table 10-15 and 10-16 are common to both types of events, making them excellent candidates for a core events subject table. It is equally clear that there are items which do not appear in both. This is the common scenario for organizations that provide more than one service. Event-specific data that is not the same for all event types will form a set of event detail tables.

Customer Data

Given the existing customer model from the boarding and grooming service example presented earlier in this chapter, we can implement the same customer and related contact tables, in this case including e-mail as a valid means of communication. The contact detail tables for address, phone, and e-mail are again stored as tables related to the customer, as shown in the relationship diagram in Figure 10-13.

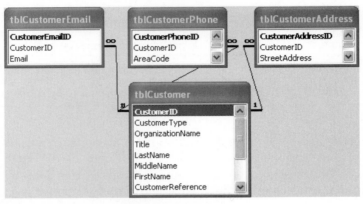

Figure 10-13: Customer and contact method tables

Employees, Individuals, and Roles

Tables for employees, individuals, and roles are implemented just as they were in several other examples in this book, by maintaining a single Individuals table and relating subjects such as employees with a foreign key to this table. A Role table is used to categorize the employees. This time it describes the functions that a member of the staff can perform in relation to events. As mentioned earlier, it serves as a useful querying aid to determine availability of employees to provide events.

Identifying the Event Subjects

The Event table must contain only fields that depend entirely on the primary key of this table. Items that depend on the type of event must be separated out. The core event table is described in the following section.

The Core Event

We've identified the event items in Table 10-17 based on the requirements described in the ''Event Management Requirements'' section and items stipulated in Tables 10-15 and 10-16 that are common to each event type. Table 10-17 shows the items and where the requirement came from.

Table 10-17: Items for the Core Event

ITEM	OBTAINED FROM
Customer	Items list (Tables 10-16 and 10-17)
Event Type	"Event Management Requirements" text
Event Status	"Event Management Requirements" text
Event Venue	Items list (Tables 10-16 and 10-17)
Event Description	"Event Management Requirements" text
Event Booking Date	"Event Management Requirements" text
Start Date Time	Items list (Tables 10-16 and 10-17) and "Event Management Requirements" text
End Date Time	Items list and "Event Management Requirements" text
Event Budget	Items list and "Event Management Requirements" text
Amount Paid	Items list and "Event Management Requirements" text
Staff Assigned	Items list and "Event Management Requirements" text
Caterers	Items list (Tables 10-16 and 10-17)
Insurance	"Event Management Requirements" text
Requires Disabled Access	Items list (Tables 10-16 and 10-17)

These items describe the core event. Before we create a table to model this subject, we need to consider both the rigorous process of normalization and the experience of the previous example.

Related Event Subjects

We have already identified the customer as a distinct subject and modeled this as separate tables. We have done the same for the subjects of event type, event status, and staff assigned. Event status is a concept we can implement directly as before. Shown in Figure 10-14, this table provides the numeric sequence to allow for effective and versatile querying.

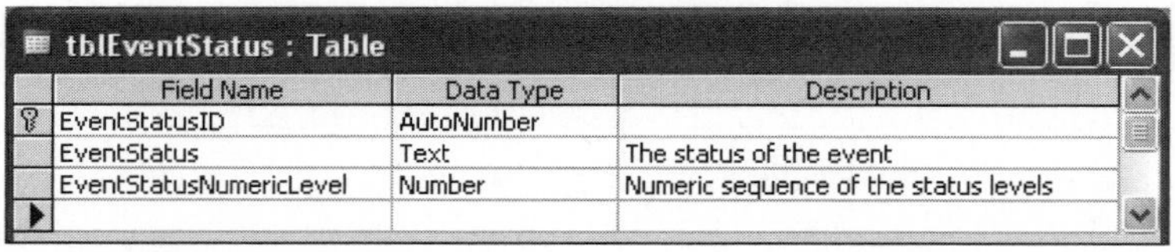
tblEventStatus : Table

Field Name	Data Type	Description
EventStatusID	AutoNumber	
EventStatus	Text	The status of the event
EventStatusNumericLevel	Number	Numeric sequence of the status levels

Figure 10-14: Event Status table

The staff is similarly represented as before. As shown in Figure 10-15, the staff are modeled using tables for employees, roles, and an employee's role in an event.

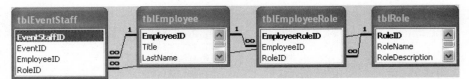

Figure 10-15: Event staff tables

The Booking Type table was described in the pet boarding example, but there were only two types there, and this example has six core types of events. However, only two of these types have specific requirements. This requires a type subject, to manage the items listed in Table 10-18.

Table 10-18: Items for Event Type

ITEM	DESCRIPTION
Event Type ID	Identifier
Event Type	Describes the event type (e.g., marriage (hotel), team building, etc.)
Data Category	One of the main groups (Wedding, Corporate, Party, Festival, Misc.)
Has Data Table	Requires specific data to be recorded

This would make a reasonable table. The example data for it is shown in Table 10-19.

Table 10-19: Data for Event Type

EVENTTYPEID	EVENTTYPE	DATACATEGORY	HASDATATABLE
1	Marriage (Hotel)	Wedding	Yes
2	Marriage (Church)	Wedding	Yes
3	Marriage (Office)	Wedding	Yes
4	Corporate Event	Corporate	Yes
5	Team Building	Corporate	Yes
6	Christening	Party	No

Note the telltale repeating rows and that the HasDataTable field is dependent upon the DataCategory. This actually requires a pair of tables, tblEventType and tblEventDataCategory, to be modeled correctly, as shown in Figure 10-16.

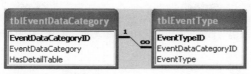

Figure 10-16: Event category and type tables

NOTE The use of separate data tables that essentially represent the same subject—in this case, the wedding details and corporate details tables—does not strictly adhere to accepted guidelines for relational data structure. This is an intentional choice.

While this book does not offer specific advice on developing a user interface, we want to minimize its complexity. Offering this structure should help with this goal. This is an example of an either-or type of relationship, meaning that only one of the detail tables would be used for a given event type. This structure can also be extended to allow more than two detail tables should that be necessary. Appendix B, "Relationships, Joins, and Nulls," has more examples demonstrating how to deal with either-or relationships.

The event subject is better defined now, but other subjects can be determined from our list in Table 10-17. Venues could be modeled as a single table, as shown in Table 10-20, with reasonable descriptive fields added to better describe the subject.

Table 10-20: Possible Further Items for Venues

ITEM	DESCRIPTION
VenueID	Primary key
VenueName	Name of venue
VenueType	Type of venue (e.g., church)
VenueDescription	Description of venue
VenueNotes	Further notes

Given the type of values, we have repeating values for VenueType. This suggests the need for a dedicated table. We also have the potential, just as with employees, to describe the different types of event a venue could fulfill. This is illustrated in Figure 10-17.

NOTE If there is a requirement to allow an event to take place at more than one venue, then Venues would become a junction table in a many-to-many relationship with the Events table. An example of that would be a wedding that required event organization at both a church and a reception hall. There are several examples of junction tables in the database. This scenario is demonstrated in the Events Complex example database for this chapter on the book's CD.

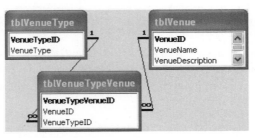

Figure 10-17: Event venue tables

New Event Subjects

In the events item list of Table 10-17, caterers are still an outstanding repeating group that would be represented better as a subject itself; but before we create a dedicated caterers table, we need to recognize that other organizations are required in the database as well. From the wedding detail item list alone we have the following:

- Transport providers
- Dress makers
- Suit hire
- Music

All of these are services obtained from an external provider or organization. Creating dedicated tables for each is an option, but you can quickly end up with a spider's web of nearly identical tables. Such distinct tables prohibit immediately searching across all types at once. It's better to implement caterers as just one instance of a more generic subject of organizations.

We need to identify the required data items for organizations such as caterers. (If you're building a database for someone else, asking them for this sort of information is a standard part of the requirements gathering process and simply an extension to the questionnaire you started with.) We'll consider the simple example table for organizations shown in Table 10-21.

A similarly simple table describing the services that organizations perform for events is required. This is shown in Table 10-22.

Table 10-21: Organization Table

FIELD	DATA TYPE	DESCRIPTION
OrganizationID	AutoNumber	Primary key field
OrgName	Text	Name of organization
OrgAddress	Text	First line of address
OrgAddress2	Text	Second line of address
OrgAddressCity	Text	City line of address
OrgAddressState	Text	State line of address
OrgAddressPostalCode	Text	Postal/zip code of address
OrgNotes	Memo	General notes field

Table 10-22: Service Type Table

FIELD	DATA TYPE	DESCRIPTION
ServiceTypeID	AutoNumber	Primary key field
ServiceType	Text	Name of service performed

Given that design, you may wonder where the service field type exists in tblOrganization. It's conceivable that an organization may be capable of performing more than one type of service. Consequently, the same organization details would need to be entered repeatedly for multiple services if we included a foreign key. Therefore, we have a many-to-many relationship between Organization and Service Type, and create a junction table called tblOrganizationService.

The relationship between these tables is shown in Figure 10-18.

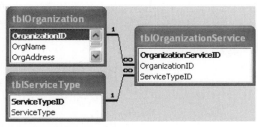

Figure 10-18: Organization service tables

You could then relate organization records to the event tables by including the foreign key fields such as CatererID, which stores the primary key value from the tblOrganization. However, we have an opportunity to make the design more flexible. Many organizations can be involved in an event; and each organization may be included on many events over time. Using a many-to-many relationship allows us to add organizations to events as they are required, producing a more flexible model to improve those event types that don't require a dedicated detail table.

This design requires a table that relates events to organizations and describes the service they perform in that event, as shown in Table 10-23.

Table 10-23: Event Service Provider Table

FIELD	DATA TYPE	DESCRIPTION
EventServiceProviderID	AutoNumber	Primary key field
EventID	Long Integer	Foreign key to Event table
OrganizationID	Long Integer	Foreign key to Organization table
ServiceTypeID	Long Integer	Foreign key to Service Type table
ServiceExtraDescription	Text	Describes any nuances

Thus we arrive at the organization relationships shown in Figure 10-19.

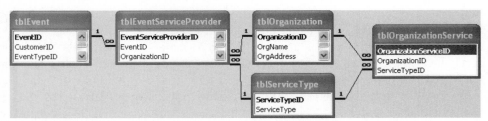

Figure 10-19: Relationships for organization and event service providers

Note that this design doesn't prevent the selection of an organization along with a role that it doesn't provide. This reflects a business scenario where you can segue organizations into roles that they're not otherwise listed as performing. You could then query the database to find occasions where organizations have filled roles outside their specified services. If you wanted to force the selection to be limited to the previously specified services, you would need to incorporate the restrictions in the application rather than through the the design.

The Final Event Table

Table 10-24 shows the final Event table, which includes the foreign keys to the customer, type, status, and venue tables, but not keys for organizations.

The foreign keys enforce the relationships among these tables, as shown in Figure 10-20.

Table 10-24: Event Table

FIELD	DATA TYPE	DESCRIPTION
EventID	AutoNumber	Primary key field
CustomerID	Long Integer	Foreign key to Customer table
EventTypeID	Long Integer	Foreign key to Event Type table
EventStatusID	Long Integer	Foreign key to Event Status table
VenueID	Long Integer	Foreign key to Venue table
EventDescription	Text	Description for ease of reference
EventBookingDate	Date/Time	Date booking received
StartDateTime	Date/Time	Date and time event starts
EndDateTime	Date/Time	Date and time event ends
EventTotalBudget	Currency	Maximum cost for the event
AmountPaid	Currency	Amount already paid (deposit or full)
InsuranceReference	Text	Reference to any insurance taken
RequireDisabledAccess	Yes/No	Will the venue require disabled access?

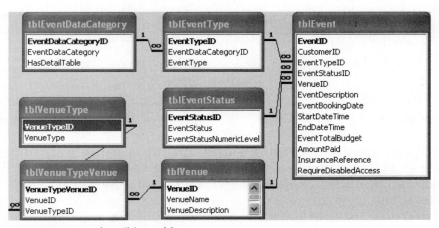

Figure 10-20: Event-describing tables

Event Detail Tables

You should not expect to automatically create distinct detail tables in a services database like this. The required fields will dictate whether that is necessary. In some cases, such as the scenario we've created here, you might not need a detail table for some of the types, or you may need more detail tables than we created in this case.

For this example, the requirements dictate two specific event types that have dedicated items identified. Are we ready to specify those as containing the remaining fields not modeled in the events table? Before that, in the wedding data items, we have an entry of Parties' Names, which is a summary of the names of all key individuals. These would also be foreign keys, which all relate to specific entries in the individuals table. Within each detail table we could provide a carefully planned set of fields to accurately describe the major players in the event type described.

For example, in our wedding example there could be a bride, groom, best man, groomsmen, bride's father, and so on. If you're not already convinced that this represents a problem, then ask yourself a few questions: How many groomsmen? How would they be identified ? Groomsmen1 and groomsmen2? Whatever their designation, it is hoped that the nature of the repeating groups becomes clear. Therein lies the flaw with identifying individuals in this manner. While it's often vital to have detail tables that accurately describe the nature of the event detail, you must carefully consider what it is you're describing and whether there are other ways it could be modeled.

You can consider this modeling of individuals to be very similar to the service organizations previously discussed. Figure 10-21 shows the Event Individual tables from the database diagram.

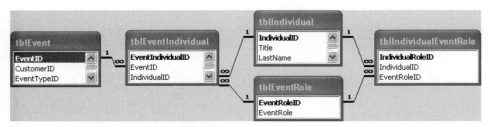

Figure 10-21: Event individual tables

At an extreme, this reasoning could extend to almost any individual or organization. For example, if the customer were instead modeled purely as an individual, it might be tempting to remove the CustomerID foreign key from tblEvent and implement that as an entry in the related individuals table. Personal preference and common sense will both play a part in your design. The customer is a fundamental subject in any model and the relationship diagram will ultimately be a form of self-documentation for your database.

Relating a customer to an event purely through record entry would obfuscate this relationship, and ultimately the database stops making sense.

As a result of this flexibility of related individuals and organizations, our detail tables become less pivotal to the description of the event type. However, there remains a legitimate case for detail tables when you have fields that are not relevant to every scenario and can't be represented by a flexible, related table such as individual or organization. In the events example, the detail tables for weddings and corporate events remain. The fields they consist of are shown in Figure 10-22.

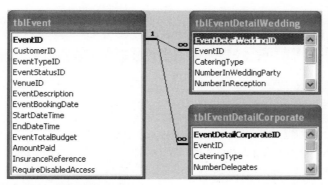

Figure 10-22: Event detail tables

Querying Events

Concurrent events may be less likely than concurrent pet bookings, but whatever the maximum number is, some conflict checking will need to be performed. Rather than a maximum number of accommodations, the decisive factor may be availability of staff to run an event. You can query this in a similar way to the pet boarding example (see qryEventAvailableStaff in the Events example database for this chapter on the book's CD) to return the list of all "Event Manager" type employees who are not already occupied within a specified time interval. However, you may need to account for employees being unavailable for reasons other than other events, such as holidays and vacation. If required, you can include a table to maintain the planned holidays for each employee in your schema and use queries to check for availability.

The Process Model

In considering this subject we are not attempting to model the process itself in our database design. Such an attempt would be inflexible and almost certainly reflect poor normalization. Instead, we provide users with the tools to model their own process inside a versatile "process template" table structure. You know your own business, its requirements, and the stages involved in completing the service or services it provides. As the developer of the database, you must be familiar with the business and its rules to create the database. Other users may also be empowered to maintain and add to the described process over time. The process that describes the service when first modeled may not accurately reflect that process a few years later. Bear in mind that this is much more than a checklist; this should be a one-stop information snapshot of where each of your service records stands.

Table 10-25 shows some example stages in planning and providing a corporate event. The example data is deliberately abbreviated to easily illustrate the concept. Your own processes may have as many steps as needed.

Table 10-25: Corporate Date Event Plan Steps

STEP	TIME
Send quote to customer	Pre Event
Confirm venue dates	Pre Event
Confirm menu with customer	Pre Event
Confirm catering booking and provide final menu	Pre Event
Confirm transport of equipment/stands	Pre Event
Confirm sound system availability	Pre Event
Event - Introductions	Event
Event - Speaker	Event
Event - Refreshments	Event
Event - Close	Event
Invoice raised	Post Event
Invoice paid	Post Event
Parties' invoice paid	Post Event
Follow-up contact with customer	Post Event

Modeling this process as fields in a table would be irresponsible. If you were to include each step as a field in a table, what data type would it be? Should it be a Boolean (Yes/No) field to indicate that it occurred, or perhaps a text or numeric key to describe the stage of the step? Each step would likely require a Date/Time field to describe when it occurred and a Text field to list any problems, and such repeating groups of fields are unacceptable and the field structure would be entirely inflexible to an end user.

You need a model for the process step structure that does all of the following:

▪ Describes the process for an event of each particular event type

▪ Holds description, status, date, sequence, and free text data

▪ Is easily adaptable, rather than schema-bound

This is achieved by breaking the concept down into the following three table components:

▪ A steps template, which is dependent upon event type

▪ A status lookup table, which describes the status options of any given step

▪ The process steps, which are the actual step records created one at a time for a specific event referring to the appropriate template

The template is the set of steps for a given event type. Records in this template, each describing an individual step, will collectively constitute a single process. It must include a foreign key of the Event Type table and the fields to describe the step in the process. At a minimum, that consists of a sequential identifier of the step (as within each set of steps we require order) and a text description of the step. If you look at tblProcessStep in the example file c10Events.mdb on the book's CD, you'll see the steps entered for a corporate day as described in Table 10-25. The design of the table is shown in Table 10-26.

Table 10-26: Process Step Table (Template Steps)

FIELD	DATA TYPE	DESCRIPTION
ProcessStepID	AutoNumber	Primary key field
EventTypeID	Long Integer	Foreign key to Event Type table
EventStepNo	Long Integer	Step sequence number
EventStepDescription	Text	Description of this step

The lookup table for the possible stages that a step can move through is provided in the file c10Events_Complex.mdb and includes the stages "Begun, Pending, Complete, Overdue, and Canceled." Table 10-27 shows the design for this.

Table 10-27: Process Stage Table (Status Options)

FIELD	DATA TYPE	DESCRIPTION
ProcessStageID	AutoNumber	Primary key field
ProcessStepStageOrderNo	Long Integer	Stage Order sequence
ProcessStepStage	Text	Text description of stage

Finally, we need to implement the process described by a template for specific event records. There is no requirement to identify which template we're using. That can be inferred from the event record EventTypeID. We need only to include the EventID to relate to the parent event we're working from. To identify any step with an event, we reference the primary key of the process step record, ProcessID. To describe a step status, we need a foreign key to the stage, ProcessStepStageID. To round out the description of a step's status we include date and optional note text, which are included as ProcessStepDateTime and ProcessStepNote. The full Event Process Step table is shown in Table 10-28.

Table 10-28: Event Process Step Table (Event Steps)

FIELD	DATA TYPE	DESCRIPTION
EventProcessStepID	AutoNumber	Primary key field
EventID	Long Integer	Foreign key to Event table
ProcessStepID	Long Integer	Foreign key to Process Step table
ProcessStageID	Long Integer	Foreign key to Process Stage table
ProcessStepDateTime	Date/Time	Date and time step was executed
ProcessStepNote	Text	Note regarding the step

The relationships between all the process-monitoring tables is shown in Figure 10-23.

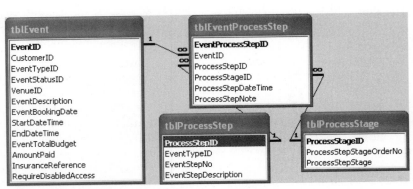

Figure 10-23: Process step tables

Without discussing user interface considerations, we will explain how this is implemented. The execution of individual steps is carried out directly on tblEventProcessStep. This records the live step but it needs to be joined to tblProcessStep to provide the step context, as this table stores all step description.

In our example, given that any event has an event type attributed to it, the template to be used is clearly identifiable at any time by query. It requires the display of all rows from tblProcessStep where the EventTypeID is that of the currently displayed Event record. From any EventID it's always possible to show the steps that should be involved in that process—as shown in Figure 10-24, which shows qryProcessStepsEvent from the file c10Events.mdb (available on this book's CD).

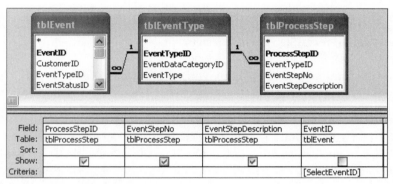

Figure 10-24: qryProcessStepsEvent

This query can display the appropriate steps to the user. If you inner join this to the tblEventProcessStep table on the ProcessStepID fields you'll see only those steps that have had an action performed against them in the event. It's more powerful to see an overview of all the steps. To see which steps you've implemented and to see all the steps yet to be taken, you need an *outer join*. Join queries are described in Chapter 3 and Appendix B.

The query displayed in Figure 10-25 is qryProcessStepsEventAll.

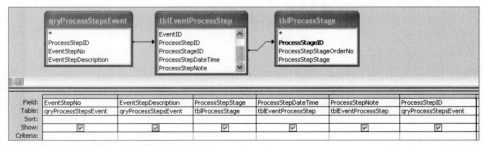

Figure 10-25: qryProcessStepsEventAll

The results of this query for the example data with EventID value 3 are shown in Figure 10-26.

qryProcessStepsEventAll : Select Query

EventStepNo	EventStepDescription	ProcessStepStage	ProcessStepDateTime	ProcessStepNote
1	Send quote to customer	Complete	29/08/2009	Agreed after negotiation
2	Confirm venue dates	Complete	31/08/2009	
3	Confirm Menu with customer	Pending	31/08/2009	Waiting for confirmation
4	Confirm catering booking - provide final menu			
5	Confirm transport of equipment / stands			
6	Confirm sound system availability			
7	Event - Introductions			
8	Event - Speaker			
9	Event - Refreshments			
10	Event - Close			
11	Invoice Raised			
12	Invoice Paid			
13	Parties invoice paid			
14	Followup contact with customer			

Record: 1 of 14

Figure 10-26: qryProcessStepsEventAll results

With information like this displayed, the progression through a process of any kind becomes immediately apparent. This kind of information offers control.

NOTE **In a user interface using an Access form you can use conditional formatting to implement color-coding based on the value of the Stage field to further enhance the "at a glance" functionality of your process steps.**

It's also worth mentioning that because a template is stored separately from the individual events step records, any changes to the core step process are reflected in all events of the same type. This is the result of employing a relational model in which updates do not need to be manually propagated. If you wanted to operate differently and maintain a permanent imprint of the steps as they were at the moment of creation, then you would need to maintain a near duplicate of the tblProcessStep table, and append the matching rows from tblProcessStep into this table at the moment of event record creation. This kind of duplication is best avoided if you don't need it, and there's much to be said for the versatility of an immediately flexible template.

You might want to include your own specific fields in the steps tables to accommodate whatever data is appropriate for your needs. This can extend to providing functionality from your application, such as e-mails or mail merge. The settings which drive this functionality must come from the template in tblProcessStep.

Event Notes

As a final element to the design of this example we have included event notes. Again, this is informed by options discussed in previous chapters that are relevant here.

You can describe the step status with additional text. For anything not related to the steps, you need the versatility of the related notes table. Given the dynamic nature of the services model, well-identified notes with your event record are crucial. Figure 10-27 shows the tables that comprise that functionality.

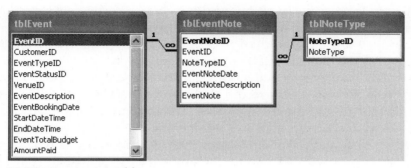

Figure 10-27: Event notes tables

Providing note types such as Key Information, General Note, Feedback Comment, and Reason for Cancellation can give the Notes entries real meaning and offer easy searching capabilities.

Variations of the Theme

Earlier in this chapter we listed other business implementations of this type of model. To consider some briefly, events management need not be an external affair. Organizations that provide activities entirely in house have much to gain by modeling not only their own process, but also their own supply of equipment. Whereas we have modeled external organizations and individuals, such a company could include equipment and individuals to complete a given activity type and model the process in a very similar way.

In these events examples and in legal or real estate businesses, your application user interface may use the lists provided in this chapter to initiate the creation of documents or e-mails that submit forms for completion and monitor results.

Summary

In this chapter you've seen that appointment-like scheduling in the service industry needn't be complicated. If you keep your user interface consideration out of the picture initially, the database design which models and drives that functionality is surprisingly simple. In the pet boarding example, you saw some examples of how to implement such a booking-type database and how a core type of data can have related detail tables to maintain consistency and avoid redundant fields.

The principal of both appointments and detail tables was reexamined in the subsequent events management example. You learned how the details table can become less necessary by optionally including related subject data, and that junction tables often do have a real-world meaning in themselves.

Finally, you saw the concept of process control modeling whereby a process can be modeled without specifying it at the data design level. A particular set of tables enables you to enter and modify data that describes the service process, row by row. Related tables record the status of each stage of this process, describing the overall progression. This process control is especially relevant to the service industry, where, by definition, you are performing some set of actions to satisfy the customer. However, applications of this type of model extend beyond services alone and into any database for which you want to track a process, such as a sales process, marketing, or customer relationships.

To create your own services database, you will likely need to disregard some of the design options offered in this chapter. Your organization will undoubtedly require different subjects or different fields in the tables. That's natural, and this model isn't offered as a definitive implementation but as a model from which to begin. Universal concepts such as checking for conflicting bookings and process control can be implemented in many scenarios, and benefit future work. The model presented here empowers you to make the best database consistent with your own needs.

Next, we'll move on to exhibit control of a different kind, that of financial control with the tracking and analyzing of financial data.

Tracking and Analyzing Financial Data

In This Part

Accounting Systems: Requirements and Design

Did you ever have a lemonade stand when you were a kid? Many kids have plunged headlong into free enterprise by selling cool glasses of refreshment in front of their house. Accounting for lemonade stands was simple. All you needed to do was to record sales. Mom furnished the materials and equipment necessary to make and sell the product and supplied a rent-free location to set up shop. She may have provided some cash to have available for making change.

As soon as one glass of lemonade was sold, you had a profit. No complicated accounting formulas to get in the way of the good times to come later at the five and dime store or, in more recent years, the mall.

Now fast forward 30 years. You have finished your MBA and you and a friend are successful in your field and are starting a business. Since Mom probably will not provide the entire inventory, equipment, and cash needed to begin production, you will need to record a lot more than just sales. You will need to record inventory purchases, capital expenditures, liabilities, general expenses, and sales. You also need to comply with a host of tax regulations related to the multiple jurisdictions that apply to your business.

To record the financial data, you can buy off-the-shelf accounting packages. Two of the more common packages are Peachtree Complete Accounting and QuickBooks Pro from Intuit. High-end customizable packages like Microsoft Dynamics GP and Microsoft Dynamics SL are also available from value-added retailers. Another option is professional custom-designed software, whose cost can range from a few thousand dollars to many thousands of dollars. You also have the option of creating your own accounting system.

Accounting systems can be old-fashioned manual systems or automated computer systems, from shoe box to mainframe. Since you are reading the chapters of this book devoted to accounting and finance, you are probably interested in moving from a manual system or an off-the-shelf package that will not easily adapt to your needs to one you hope to design and create yourself.

This chapter provides the foundation for building an accounting system. Chapter 12, "Accounting: Budgeting, Analysis, and Reporting," will enable you to revise and extend the framework to perform budgeting and reporting functions.

Double-Entry Accounting

We recommend using a *normalized structure* when designing any database, and this accounting model is no exception. (Normalized structure design is covered in detail in Chapter 3, "Relational Data Model.") Our accounting database models will all be based upon *double-entry accounting*, described in the following paragraphs. While it may be easier for the non-accountant to use a simple *single-entry accounting* system, single-entry systems will probably create future problems resulting from growth in the business or new accounting requirements. Single-entry accounting systems resemble a simple checkbook register. The entries are usually two columns; in one column the increases are recorded, and in the other the decreases are recorded. Although single-entry accounting is easier to learn, it is much more difficult to produce financial reports needed by businesses.

While this chapter is not intended to be a refresher course in accounting, we will discuss the basics of double-entry accounting. Double-entry accounting is describing what is necessary for every transaction entered into the system. Assets are increased with a debit entry; liabilities and owner's equity are increased with a credit entry. Expenses and costs are *debits,* and income and gains are *credits.*

At least two entries must be made for each transaction, and the debits and credits must be equal. Prior to automated accounting systems, debits and credits were always positive numbers. With the advent of normalized relational accounting systems, debits are represented with positive numbers and credits with negative numbers (at least for open systems where the user is designing the table structure). (See Chapter 2, "Elements of a Microsoft Access Database," for a detailed discussion of *normalization.*) This is necessary because in a normalized *relational database system (RDBS)* there is only one field in the journal table for the transaction amounts. If the debits and credits equal each other, the total of the credits subtracted from the debits will equal zero. In a normalized RDBS system, you use aggregate queries to summarize the data. After closing at the end of the accounting period, the general ledger (GL) entries should summarize to zero.

To illustrate the basic concept, let's look at a simple purchase of office supplies for a business. The owner purchases paper goods for $12,000 from a local store. The transaction is made using $12,000 cash. A second transaction is made to buy an office chair for $600 with cash.

The entries would be made as follows in a traditional paper-based accounting system:

Paper Goods Expense	12,000	
Cash		12,000
To record purchase of paper goods		
Office Chair	600	
Cash		600
To record purchase of office chair		
Depreciation Expense	200	
Accumulated Depreciation (Office Chair)		200
To record depreciation for the office chair		

Because paper goods represents an asset, the $12,000 debit increases the balance of that account. The net profit or loss of the business is affected directly by the acquisition of these assets because the business expects to use all of the paper within the period. The *matching principle* in accounting requires recognition of expenses in the period when the benefit was received. Since the life of the paper goods is short, the expenses are immediately recognized.

The life of the chair is expected to be three years, with no salvage value, and the expenses related to the chair will be recognized over a three-year period through a method called *depreciation*. At the end of three years, the value of the asset will have been reduced to zero or the estimated salvage value.

The GL now shows a $12,200 loss for the period due to the expenses to purchase the paper and the depreciation for the chair. Cash was reduced by the $12,600 paid at the purchase.

To illustrate the same transaction in a single table in a RDBS, we can record the same entries using debits as positive numbers and credits as negative numbers.

Paper Goods Expense	12,000
Cash	−12,000
Office Chair	600
Cash	−600
Depreciation Expense	200
Accumulated Depreciation (Office Chair)	−200

It may seem counterintuitive to record expenses as a debit, but both income and expenses are closed into the *retained earnings account*, which is an equity account and has a credit balance. A debit for an expense is actually reducing the equity account.

The description of the transaction has been removed from the General Ledger table and moved to a header or batch record that describes a series of transactions. This helps eliminate the storage of duplicate data.

Chart of Accounts

A *chart of accounts (COA)* is a detailed listing of the general ledger accounts and the *account numbers* assigned to the accounts. The chart of accounts is the heart and soul of any accounting system. All of the entries in the general ledger must use an account number from the COA. Traditionally, GL accounts use a numbering scheme in which the first digit indicates the type of the account: Asset = 1, Liability = 2, Equity = 3, Income = 4, and Expense = 5. A scheme with four-digit or eight-digit account numbers is usually sufficient for most small businesses. With an eight-digit system, the first four digits represent the major account groups, and the last four digits are reserved for variations of the main account.

The following list provides an example of a COA showing how the numbering scheme works:

10010000 Petty Cash

10010001 Petty Cash – HR Dept

10010003 Petty Cash – Marketing Department

10100000 Cash – First National Bank Checking

10100001 Cash – Third First National Bank Checking

10200000 Furniture and Equipment

10200010 Accumulated Depreciation (Furn and Equip)

10300000 Leasehold Improvements

10300010 Accumulated Depreciation (Leasehold Improvement)

10500000 Accounts Receivable

20000000 Accounts Payable

20100000 Notes Payable

30000000 Common Stock

30100000 Additional Paid-in Capital

30500000 Retained Earnings

40000000 Sales

50100000 Office Supplies

50100001 Printer Paper

50300000 Sales Tax Expense

51000000 Rent Expense

51500000 Depreciation Expense

This allows grouping and sorting the various account types. It is also possible, for reporting purposes, to group on the first four digits and to aggregate the similar accounts into one account group.

The table that stores the COA consists of a primary key, the account number, a short description, and a long description. An optional field may be a date field to indicate that the account is no longer used.

When choosing primary keys, we prefer to use surrogate keys over natural keys. (See Chapter 2 for a detailed discussion.) In the case of the COA, the natural key would be the account number itself. The major drawback to using the account number as the primary key is the extra work required to change the account numbers if later the decision is made to renumber the COA; with a natural key, you not only need to change the account number in the COA table, it is necessary to change all of the foreign keys in other tables that relate back to the COA table. With a surrogate key, only the entry in the COA table is changed, because the primary key remains the same.

General Ledger

The general ledger (GL) is the main feature of an accounting system. It is in this ledger that all transactions are recorded, either in detail or summarized from subsidiary ledgers (subledgers). In a manual system, the subledgers are external to the GL. Every debit and credit entry is recorded in the GL. The account balances are the total of all entries, both debits and credits, for each account.

A *trial balance* is used to verify that debits equal credits and that the individual accounts are correct before producing the financial statements at period end.

Assets, liabilities, and equity are always summarized for all periods in the accounting system, while income and expenses are usually summarized for the current period only. The *balance sheet accounts* (assets, liabilities, and equity) are never closed; the *income statement accounts* (income and expenses) are closed at the end of the fiscal period.

A period-end close of an income statement account requires an entry for each account that returns the balance to zero. The total of the closing entries is made to the equity account *retained earnings*. Because only the income and expense accounts are closed, the total of these entries equal net income or loss for the period. For example, if in the first year of business the total of a company's income statement accounts equals $1,000,000 profits, the retained earnings account would be credited (increased) with a $1,000,000 entry. The next year, the company's income statement accounts show a $500,000 loss. The retained earnings account would be debited (decreased) $500,000. The balance of the retained earnings account would now be $500,000, which shows the profitability of the business since its inception.

If the sales account has a $2,000,000 balance and the expense accounts have a $1,000,000 balance at the end of the period, these would be the entries to close the period:

Sales	2,000,000	
Expenses		1,000,000
Retained Earnings		1,000,000

To close the year

The next year, the sales account has a $2,000,000 balance and the expense accounts have a $2,500,000 balance at year end:

Sales	2,000,000	
Retained Earnings		500,000
Expenses		2,500,000

To close the year

After the period has been closed, summarizing both balance sheet and income statement accounts will result in the correct balance for the year. For shorter periods, such as monthly or quarterly, the income statement accounts must be restricted to the transactions made in the period, whereas the balance sheet accounts must include all transactions in those accounts regardless of when they were made.

Subsidiary Ledgers

The use of subledgers enables the detail transactions to be recorded in related groups, such as cash subledgers, sales subledgers, accounts payable (AP) subledgers, and accounts receivable (AR) subledgers. In a subledger, only the entry that relates to that account is recorded. For example, in an AR subledger, you would record the charge to the customer's account, but not the sales entry. When the customer makes a payment to the account, the credit to the account is made in the subledger, but the cash is not.

The reason for only recording one side of the double-entry transaction is to allow for more detail than is available in the GL. Each cash transaction should have a bank account number related to it to facilitate reconciliation of the account to the bank statement. Each sales transaction should have information about the salesperson and buyer to track how well a salesperson is performing and how much a customer is purchasing. The AP subledger keeps track of who and how much the business owes each vendor, while the AR subledger details the transactions of customers who are allowed to purchase on credit.

Depending on how large a subject is and how many transactions are recorded, it may require multiple tables to store the data and to archive the data of previous periods. In smaller enterprises, it is possible to record all of the transactions in the GL and use queries to create virtual subledgers. A field that is a foreign key to the *AR/AP Vendor/Customer table* for example, allows a query to return only the records that are related to specific types of entries, such as AR or AP entries. An AR subledger would include only AR-related entries, and the entries returned would show both the charges and the payments for each customer. The query can be designed so that the results can be grouped by each customer or client to summarize the data and return the balance for each account.

Cash Subledgers

A *cash subledger* would be used much like a checkbook. Depending upon the need, each check and deposit would be recorded and the balance of the account would be reconciled to the bank statement received from the financial institution. In instances where check registers are produced in another system, such as the claims-paying system of an insurance company, summarized entries with the total of the checks issued on a given day would be recorded in the cash log. Deposits are recorded in the same manner, and the level of detail usually depends on the source of the deposits. All AR receipts, cash sales, and cash from other receivables would be aggregated and a single entry made.

The cash entries relating to other subledgers should reconcile to the entries indicating cash payments or cash receipts in the AP or AR subledgers.

Investment Subledgers

An optional *investment subledger* is used to keep detailed records of securities owned by the business as an investment. After a security is purchased, many types of transactions need to be recorded. Stocks have dividends and splits to record, bonds have interest payments, accrual of premium, and accretion of discount, and mutual funds have dividends, interest, and capital gain distributions.

Each publicly traded security has a Committee on Uniform Security Identification Procedures (CUSIP) number. The CUSIP number uniquely identifies a security. This number would be recorded in a table for securities, along with purchase date, price, coupon rate, and other specific information about the security. The transactions related to the security would include a foreign key to the Security table and the GL account recording the entry.

Queries can again be used to create virtual subledgers that group and aggregate the transactions down to the security level. This enables the reconciliation of the securities with the security statements furnished by the brokerage firm.

Accounts Receivable Subledgers

The more activity in specific receivable accounts, the more likely the account is a candidate for an *accounts receivable subledger*. When a company places a security deposit for the lease of office space, this amount is recorded in a specific GL account. Because there are no transactions other than recording the deposit and the return of the deposit, it would be a waste of resources to use a subledger.

However, trade accounts with customers are a different matter. A hardware store may sell items daily to contractors who are purchasing supplies and materials to build houses. The hardware store is a good candidate to use a subledger to record the credit sales made to its customers because the credit sales are continuous and routine. Conversely, a burger joint that only sells on credit on the sixth Friday of the month would not be a candidate for a subledger to record credit sales, as there will be no entries.

By adding a field in the GL table that is a foreign key to the AR/AP Vendor/Customer table, it is then a simple task to create a query or view that allows single accounts, with the outstanding balances to be viewed on a form or report. With this view, the details of the individual accounts can be used for an itemized statement or for reconciling the accounts to source documents.

Accounts Payable Subledgers

Most businesses purchase supplies and inventory on credit from their suppliers. These are obvious candidates for an *accounts payable subledger*. Less obvious candidates may be the many taxing authorities—local, state, and federal. As wages are earned by employees, there are associated taxes due from the company to the federal, state, and local taxing authorities, and these taxes must be accrued as liabilities and then paid to the tax authorities when they are due.

However many accounts are needed, it is imperative that the information is readily available to the company's management to ensure that these accounts are kept up to date.

Recording the vendor or creditor in the AR/AP Vendor/Customer table creates a key to use as a foreign key in the GL subledger field. With this simple method it is easy to return the balances and transactions to a single vendor or summarize the current balance of all AP accounts.

Database Design Considerations

An accounting system should have built-in controls to ensure that only authorized users enter and view the data, and the system must use methods that force users to enter and modify data only through the forms or other user interface provided by the developer. If users can enter or delete records without restrictions or rules, the integrity of the database cannot be guaranteed.

All entries should be made in batches, and the total of the positive debits and negative credits in the batch must equal zero. To correct an entry that is in error, a correcting entry should be made so that a valid audit trail is present. Users should never have direct access to the data through tables or queries. The data should be exposed only through the use of forms or reports.

Data validation is also a consideration to the developer; for example, users should not be able to create general ledger accounts on the fly. A manager, or other designated user, should be the only user to have permission to make additions or changes to the chart of accounts. Users should be given options using drop-down lists and/or radio buttons to enter most required data, rather than free-form text boxes.

Some RDMSs, such as SQL Server, have *triggers* at the table level to perform actions other than those requested by the user, such as an INSTEAD OF DELETE trigger. When a delete action is requested, the action is intercepted and another action is processed. For example, instead of deleting the record, a field in the record could be updated to show that the record is deleted, leaving the record intact. Another example of a trigger would be updating the value in the field that records when a record is modified. Access does not have triggers, so these actions must be implemented using *Visual Basic for Applications (VBA)*, or some other means, to duplicate the functionality of triggers.

A database designed in Microsoft Access should always be split into two parts, or tiers. The front end or user interface has the forms, queries, and VBA code, and the back end, or a database, contains the tables and relationships. A third, or middle tier, is sometimes used to house the VBA code that contains implementations of business rules. The advantage of having a multi-tiered system is that it is easier to maintain the objects in the front end and the code in the middle tier. A developer can update the code without disturbing the data. Data corruption is also minimized in a multiuser system if the database is split.

NOTE Many books and online help forums can provide additional information about developing user interfaces. See Appendix E, "References and Resources," for a list of resources.

Accounting Database

The minimum requirements for an accounting system designed in a RDBS will have at least the following tables:

- **Accounts table:** Chart of accounts
- **General Ledger table:** Main entry table
- **Ledger Type table:** Lookup table for ledger type
- **AR/AP Vendor/Customer table:** Lists all customers and vendors; the account type is specified by a link to Ledger Type table
- **Cash Ledger table:** Cash subledger for detail cash account information
- **Batch table:** Master batch records
- **User table:** Authorized users
- **Reporting Type table:** Indicates to which statement the account is reported
- **Transaction Type table:** Lookup table for type of transactions
- **Type table:** Entry type (i.e., financial, budget, statistical, etc.)
- **Report Header table:** Used to select the previously designed report
- **Report Detail table:** Junction table used to define which GL accounts are assigned to each line item in a report
- **Investment Master table:** Individual security master information (optional)
- **Investment Detail table:** Subledger for detail information on securities (optional)

The Accounts table is a junction table to identify the various general ledger accounts listed in a chart of accounts. The descriptive name of the account is associated with a GL account number and a unique value, or primary key. In this book, we prefer to use surrogate keys instead of natural keys. There are strong arguments, pro and con, for both methods, but for an inexperienced developer, the surrogate key, such as Access' AutoNumber data type, is much easier to implement and use.

The General Ledger table is the heart of the accounting system. In this table, all of the accounting entries are recorded, including budget entries. Each record identifies the account, a description of the entry, the batch, the user, whether the entry was a budget entry or an actual entry, the transaction date, and the date and time the entry was recorded. The account, the batch, the user, and possibly the type of entry would all be foreign key entries to the primary keys in the Accounts table, the Batch table, the User table, and an Entry table.

The Ledger Type table is a lookup table for storing the type of ledger being used. An entry for "None" is provided for entries not using subledgers, and the rest of the entries indicate whether the subledger is Accounts Payable, Cash, and so on. A foreign key entry in the General Ledger table identifies the ledger and is used to return entries only for that ledger.

The AR/AP Vendor/Customer Number table stores information about customers and vendors. The primary key is used to identify entries in the GL that relate to the AR and AP subledgers—typically, the vendor/customer name, address, phone number, and so on. See Chapter 13, "Managing Memberships," and Chapter 4, "People, Organizations, Addresses," for more details.

The Batch table identifies and describes an individual, unique batch or group of related entries, and tracks when the batch was created and posted. Batch entries can be used to group related entries and facilitate displaying information regarding the entries in the batch. For each day, all entries relating to cash received could be placed in a single batch. Reconciling an account is usually easier if smaller segments of the entries in the account can be individually analyzed, and placing related entries in a batch enables the entries to be grouped by a batch ID.

The User table identifies users authorized to use the system, and associates users with batches and entries that they create.

The Reporting Type table identifies to which financial report an individual general ledger account will be assigned. Assets, liabilities, and equity are reported on the balance sheet, and income and expenses are reported on the income statement. Using a value in the Accounts table to indicate this simplifies the selection of an account in a query.

The Transaction Type table is a lookup table to store the types of transactions being recorded, i.e., deposit, check, transfer, and so on. It can be used with multiple ledgers, but primarily the cash subledger.

The Type table is used to identify an entry as a financial entry or a budget entry. It's also possible to create multiple budgets, with each budget using a specific entry in the Type table.

The Report Header table is used to identify reports and to store the name of the report and the dates that the report is an active report. A report ID will be used by the Report Detail table.

The Report Detail table is a junction table, which may also be referred to as a crosswalk table, join table, or bridge table, as it is used to create many-to-many relationships. Specific GL accounts are assigned to specific lines in a report using this table.

The optional Investment Master table is used in conjunction with the related table for investment detail. Information for each security that does not change with individual transactions is recorded in the master table—CUSIP number, date issued, par, maturity dates, type of security, and so on.

The optional Investment Detail table is used to store details about specific securities and track the transactions related to the investments owned by the company. The master information for each security is stored in the master table.

Table Structure

Each table should have a field defined as the primary key. A *primary key* is a unique value to identify a single record in the table. The Access AutoNumber data type is an ideal candidate for a primary key. Access creates a unique value automatically for each record when the record is created. All the remaining fields are used to describe the entry. The description, amount, and date entries are values from the accounting transaction itself. Other fields are foreign key entries to related tables and are directly related to the RDBS itself. Using related tables enables the storing of information in only one place in the database. If a value (e.g., the account name) changes, only a single record needs to be modified and the change is reflected globally, instead of having to identify and change all affected records in the table.

Designing a table requires reviewing what information is expected to be stored in the table. But before we get into the specific details for each required table, let's review some fields that will be standard to most tables in our examples.

Standard Fields

Each table has a single field primary key, with a data type of AutoNumber, and was discussed in the breakdown of the core Accounts earlier in this chapter. The primary key is not discussed in the remaining tables because the field is a system-generated unique record identifier and does not describe the subject being represented by the table.

We also have three other fields that are not discussed in the description of each table. These fields will almost always have application-generated values that can be used for various system administrative functions. The standard fields are listed in Table 11-1.

The Account Table

The Account table includes the details shown in Table 11-2.

First, the table needs a name, and using an accepted naming convention, the table will be named tblAccount. The accounting staff uses the chart of accounts as a road map of the accounts. In an accounting system, the table also functions as a lookup table to display the account information as needed. The primary key field of the table, tblAccount, is used to relate records in the Accout table to records in the General Ledger table, instead of using the actual account numbers.

Table 11-1: Standard Fields

FIELD	DESCRIPTION
Inactive	A Date/Time data type that provides an indication of when a row becomes inactive or invalid for use in the application. Often used in lookup tables in order to prevent or group the display of values that are no longer used. By not deleting the obsolete value, referential integrity can be maintained, while presenting the user with valid values.
CreatedDate	Also a Date/Time data type, it holds the date a record was created. This type of information is helpful if records are in a "half-baked" state and thus may require deletion.
CreatedBy	The computer user's ID. Used for traceability.

Table 11-2: Details in the Account Table

DETAILS	DESCRIPTION
Account number	Number assigned to GL account
Account name	Name of GL account
Description	Short narrative describing the purpose of the account
Reporting ID	Indicates to which report the account is assigned

As discussed earlier, each table needs a primary key. In most cases in Access tables, an AutoNumber is the appropriate data type to use for the primary key. It is considered best practice to provide meaningful names for all fields, but with a standardized naming convention. Names for primary keys usually include the table name or abbreviation and ID; so we'll use the name AcctID.

Beginning with account number, it is proper to abbreviate the table name and begin each word in uppercase with no spaces, a practice called *camel case*. AcctNumber will be used as the name of the account number field. The value stored in this field can be either numeric or text, and can include special characters. It is common practice in GL number schemes to use segmented account numbers, and dashes to separate the segments, e.g., 101-2100 or 1020-001200-0100. The data type for this field would normally be text.

The next detail is the name of the GL account. This is also a text field and it is used to quickly identify an individual account with a name that is more meaningful than an account number. AcctName will be used as the name of this field.

In this table, as in other tables, it is usually good practice to use data validation on certain fields. Every account should have a name and a number. Although the primary key is used by the related tables to identify a record, blank account names and numbers would not be meaningful on the financial reports. Access enables the developer to force a field to be a required field. This property is set in the property sheet of the table.

Description, the next detail, is also a text field and is used to describe the purpose of the account and other information as needed. The name of the field will be AcctDescription.

The field, ReportingTypeID, is a foreign key to the Reporting Type table and is used to identify to which report a GL account is mapped for reporting. The fields for the Account table are shown in Figure 11-1.

Field Name	Data Type	Description
AcctID	AutoNumber	Primary Key
ReportingTypeID	Number	Indicator to show which financial statement this acct is used.
AcctNum	Text	Actual account number that is shown on the chart of accounts
AcctName	Text	Name to be displayed as the account name
AcctDescription	Text	Short narrative describing the purpose of the account
CreatedDate	Date/Time	The date a record was created.
CreatedBy	Date/Time	The computer user's ID. Used for traceability
Inactive	Date/Time	Indication of when a row becomes invalid for use. Often used in lookup tables in order to prevent the display of values that are no longer used

Figure 11-1: tblAccount in design view

General Ledger Table

The General Ledger table has the two details as listed in Table 11-3

Table 11-3: Details in the General Ledger Table

DETAIL	DESCRIPTION
Description	Short narrative describing the purpose of the entry
Amount of entry	Debit or credit representing the amount of the transaction

The name used for the General Ledger table is tblGL. This is the table used to store all financial and statistical transactions. All financial reports and virtual subledgers are based upon this table.

The first general detail in the General Ledger table is the Description field. This self-explanatory text field contains a short description of the entry to facilitate the reconciliation of the accounts.

The other detail that will be included in the table is the amount of the entry. The entry is either a debit (+) or a credit (−) and is denominated in the currency used by the company. The data type should be currency, not because financial transactions are being recorded, but because the currency data type is a fixed decimal data type, rather than a floating-point decimal. Floating-point data types are approximations of the value of a number, whereas fixed decimals are accurate to four decimal places. As each entry is completed, the sum of all financial entries should total zero. Double-entry accounting requires that the total of debits equals the total of credits; and because debits are positive and credits are negative, the result of summing all entries will result in zero.

The remaining five fields are foreign keys to other tables. They all use the long data type, as they need to link to AutoNumber fields in the tables to which they are related. Figure 11-2 shows the General Ledger table in design view in Access.

Field Name	Data Type	Description
tblGL		
GLID	AutoNumber	Primary Key
AcctID	Number	Foreign Key to tblAcct
BatchID	Number	Foreign Key to tblBatch
ArApVendorCustID	Number	Foreign Key to tblArApVendorCust
UserID	Number	Foreign Key to tblUsers
TypeID	Number	Foreign Key to tblType
Description	Text	Free form description of entry.
AmtEntry	Currency	The dollar amount of the debit or credit.
DateEntry	Date/Time	Accounting transaction date.
CreatedDate	Date/Time	The date a record was created.
CreatedBy	Date/Time	The computer user's ID. Used for traceability
Inactive	Date/Time	Indication of when a row becomes invalid for use. Often used in lookup tables in order to prevent the display of val

Figure 11-2: tblGeneralLedger in design view

Lookup Tables

Lookup tables are often used to provide lists of data for users to select from and provide an excellent means to efficiently enter standardized data. They can minimize the chances for data entry errors and for storing multiple versions of the same data. An additional benefit of having standardized entries is that you can more easily group and analyze data. It is important to know you can either store the value that the user sees or store a hidden value that you specify (typically the primary key of the selected record). In our examples, you will store the value of the primary key of the selected record from the lookup table as the foreign key in the main table.

Ledger Type Table

The Ledger Type table is a lookup table used to identify the type of ledger or whether the entry represents a vendor or a customer. The table is named tblLedgerType. You will only need to add one field to this table, the Text field AccountType, which will provide the description of the account type. The description will appear in selection lists on forms, as headers in reports, and it will be used for grouping entries.

The design view of the Ledger Type table is shown in Figure 11-3.

	tblLedgerType		
	Field Name	Data Type	Description
LedgerTypeID	AutoNumber	Primary Key
AccountType	Text	Free-form description of type of ledger or sub-ledger
CreatedDate	Date/Time	The date a record was created.
CreatedBy	Date/Time	The computer user's ID. Used for traceability
Inactive	Date/Time	Indication of when a row becomes invalid for use. Often used in lookup tables in order to prevent the display of values that are no longer used.

Figure 11-3: tblLedgerType in design view

Transaction Type Table

The Transaction Type table is another lookup table and is named tblTransactionType. This table has the field TransactionType. This field will provide the list of the "types of transactions" that will be in subledgers. Examples of entry types are cash, deposit, check, ACH in, ACH out, and so on.

The field data type is Text and the descriptions should be as concise yet descriptive as possible. The design view of the Transaction Type table is shown in Figure 11-4.

	tblTransactionType		
	Field Name	Data Type	Description
TransactionID	AutoNumber	Primary key
TransactionType	Text	Description of transaction type
CreatedDate	Date/Time	The date a record was created.
CreatedBy	Date/Time	The computer user's ID. Used for traceability
Inactive	Date/Time	Indication of when a row becomes invalid for use. Often used in lookup tables in order to prevent the display of values that are no longer used.

Figure 11-4: tblTransactionType in design view

Vendor/Customer Table

The next table is a lookup table used to store vendor and customer information used in the GL, cash, accounts receivable, and accounts payable subledgers. Using the standard abbreviations for accounts receivable and accounts payable, the name of the table is tblArApVendorCust. The table includes fields to record the details that you need in table.

The first detail field, named ExternalAccountNo, is a text field used to store an account number that is assigned externally, not as part of your accounting system. This would be the account number for a vendor account, and it could also store the accounts receivable account number. This field needs to be a text field, as users have no control over the numbering schemes used by external sources.

The next field, named EntityName, is also a text field. It is used to record the name of the entity, either a business or a person, that the record is describing. This field can record the customer's name or the name of the vendor. Because there is usually other information such as addresses or phone numbers that need to be associated with these entities, you will need additional tables to store the relevant data. The additional tables will be related to this table by storing the primary key of this table.

LedgerTypeID is a foreign key to the Ledger Type table and is used to indicate whether the entry is for a vendor or a customer. Since this is a foreign key, you will need to use a long integer data type.

The design view of the table, tblARAPVendorCust, is shown in Figure 11-5.

Field Name	Data Type	Description
ArApVendorCustID	AutoNumber	Primary Key
LedgerTypeID	Number	Foreign Key to the tblLedgerType i.e. Vendor, Customer, ect.
ExternalAcctNo	Text	Vendor or Bank assigned account number, also internal account number to use if formatted account numbers are required
EntityName	Text	Vebdor name, customer name, etc.
CreatedDate	Date/Time	The date a record was created.
CreatedBy	Date/Time	The computer user's ID. Used for traceability
Inactive	Date/Time	Indication of when a row becomes invalid for use. Often used in lookup tables in order to prevent the display of values that are no longer used.

Figure 11-5: tblARAPVendorCust in design view

Cash Ledger Table

The next table is the Cash Ledger table, named tblCashLedger. The cash ledger is a subledger used to record the details of entries to the cash accounts. The details that you need to record in the Cash Ledger table are listed in Table 11-4.

Table 11-4: Details in the Cash Ledger Table

DETAIL	DESCRIPTION
Check number	The number of the check, or a range of check numbers, used in the complete transaction.
Paid to	The name printed on the check, or, if a range of check numbers, the source of the payment—e.g., medical claims payable, etc.
Transaction amount	The total amount of the transaction, or range of transactions, being recorded.
Transaction date	Date on the check or checks included in the entry.

Those details become the fields in the Cash Ledger table as shown in Figure 11-6.

Field Name	Data Type	Description
CashLedgerID	AutoNumber	Primary Key
ArApVendorCustID	Number	Foreign Key to tblArApVendorCust table and the stored bank account number
AcctID	Number	Foreign Key to tblAcct and the COA GL number
TransactionTypeID	Number	Foreign Key to tblTransactionType Check, Deposit, ACH in, ACH out, etc.
CheckNo	Text	Actual check numbers or range of check numbers
PaidTo	Text	Payee name. It can also be a foreign key to a Payee table if desired.
AmtTransaction	Currency	Dollar amount of transaction
DateTransaction	Date/Time	Date of actual transaction
CreatedDate	Date/Time	The date a record was created.
CreatedBy	Date/Time	The computer user's ID. Used for traceability
Inactive	Date/Time	Indication of when a row becomes invalid for use. Often used in lookup tables in order to prevent the display of values that are no longer used.

Figure 11-6: tblCashLedger in design view

Batch Table

The next table is the Batch table, named tblBatch. This table identifies groups of related entries and specifies whether a batch has been posted. Posted batches should not be modified. Instead, any corrections to a posted batch are made using additional entries that adjust or reverse the previous entry using approved accounting procedures. Table 11-5 lists the details that are recorded in the Batch table. The design view of the table is shown in Figure 11-7.

Table 11-5: Details in the Batch Table

DETAIL	DESCRIPTION
Batch header name	Free form description of the batch and its purpose
Batch posted date	Indicates if and when a batch has been posted

	tblBatch		
	Field Name	Data Type	Description
⌘	BatchID	AutoNumber	Primary key
	UserID	Number	Foreign key to Users table
	BatchHeaderName	Text	Description of the batch.
	BatchPosted	Date/Time	Date the batch was posted. A posted batch should not be modified, any modifications after posting should be correcting entries instead.
	CreatedDate	Date/Time	The date a record was created.
	CreatedBy	Date/Time	The computer user's ID. Used for traceability
	Inactive	Date/Time	Indication of when a row becomes invalid for use. Often used in lookup tables in order to prevent the display of values that are no longer used.

Figure 11-7: tblBatch in design view

User Table

Next is the User table, named tblUser. The User table is a lookup table that holds information about each authorized user and the date range during which the user is authorized to use the system. It is considered best practice to store names as title, first, middle, last, and suffix, rather than storing the full name in a single field. In this example, only the first name and last name fields are used. Table 11-6 lists the details that will be recorded in the User table. The design view of the table is shown in Figure 11-8.

Table 11-6: Details in the User table

DETAIL	DESCRIPTION
Last name	The last name of the user
First name	The first name of the user
User effective date	The first date the user is authorized to use the system
User end date	The ending date that the user is authorized to use the system

	tblUser		
	Field Name	Data Type	Description
⌘	UserID	AutoNumber	Primary Key
	LastName	Text	User's sir name
	FirstName	Text	User's given name
	UserEffective	Date/Time	Beginning date a user is authorized to use the system.
	UserEnd	Date/Time	Ending date a user is authorized to use the system.
	CreatedDate	Date/Time	The date a record was created.
	CreatedBy	Date/Time	The computer user's ID. Used for traceability
	Inactive	Date/Time	Indication of when a row becomes invalid for use. Often used in lookup tables in order to prevent the display of values that are no longer used.

Figure 11-8: tblUser table in design view

Report Header Table

The next two tables are used to create reports. The first report table is a Report Header table that is named tblReportHeader, and the second is the report detail table, tblReportDetail. These two tables are used in conjunction to identify and define the details of the reports.

The Report Header table creates an ID used by the Report Detail table to select the correct records that are used in any given report. The Report Header table also stores the name of the report and the dates when it is active. There is only one detail that you will need in the Report Header table, which is the ReportName. It is a Text field, as shown in the field list in Figure 11-9.

tblReportHeader		
Field Name	**Data Type**	**Description**
ReportHeaderID	AutoNumber	Primary Key
ReportName	Text	Name of Report
CreatedDate	Date/Time	The date a record was created.
CreatedBy	Date/Time	The computer user's ID. Used for traceability
Inactive	Date/Time	Indication of when a row becomes invalid for use. Often used in lookup tables in order to prevent the display of values that are no longer used.

Figure 11-9: tblReportHeader in design view

Report Detail Table

The second report table is the Report Detail table, named tblReportDetail. It is a junction table and is used to create many-to-many relationships. It is here that the GL accounts are mapped to specific rows in specific reports. Table 11-7 lists the details that you will record in the Report Detail table.

Table 11-7: Details in the Report Detail Table

DETAIL	DESCRIPTION
Account number	The GL account number that is mapped to this specific line in the report
Line name	The text that will be displayed on the report
Line grouping level	Assigns an order to a group of line items in a report
Line sort order	Assigns a sort order to the individual lines of a report

To assign GL accounts to specific report lines, an entry would have the account number or foreign key of an account number, and the line number. An aggregate query, or GROUP BY query, is then used as the record source of the report. This aggregating enables multiple accounts to be assigned to the same report line. ReportHeaderID and AcctID are foreign keys to tblReportHeader and tblAccount, and so they need to use a long integer data type. Figure 11-10 shows the design view of the Report Detail table.

Field Name	Data Type	Description
ReportDetailID	AutoNumber	Primary key
ReportHeaderID	Number	Foreign key to tblReportHeader
AcctID	Number	Foreign key to tblAccount
LineName	Text	Text to appear on a line in report
Level	Number	Number indicating section of report for grouping and aggregating
SortOrder	Number	Number indicating placement of line in the report
CreatedDate	Date/Time	The date a record was created.
CreatedBy	Date/Time	The computer user's ID. Used for traceability
Inactive	Date/Time	Indication of when a row becomes invalid for use. Often used in lookup tables in order to prevent the display of values tha

Figure 11-10: tblReportDetail table in design view

Optional Tables

Four tables used in the "Budget" section of Chapter 12 are used to demonstrate how to work with data from this or other systems to create a budget. The structure of these optional tables varies according to the source and type of data that will be imported. Therefore, instead of starting with a list of details for each table, we will move directly to list the fields that we will include in our example database.

NOTE Appendix D includes VBA code used in Chapter 12 to populate the Work Day table. The code and instructions on how to use it are provided in the database for that appendix on the book's CD, ADD_BonusResource.mdb.

Holiday Table

The first table, tblHoliday isused with VBA code that counts the work days in a month. Any date in this table will not be counted as a workday. If the table is empty, every work day will be counted. Since we are using VBA code to calculate the number of work days in a month, the table is required even if you do not have a holiday in a given month.

Figure 11-11 shows the design view of the Holiday table.

Field Name	Data Type	Description
HolidayID	AutoNumber	Primary key
HolidayDate	Date/Time	Actual date of a holiday
CreatedDate	Date/Time	The date a record was created.
CreatedBy	Date/Time	The computer user's ID. Used for traceability
Inactive	Date/Time	Indication of when a row becomes invalid for use. Often used in lookup tables in order to prevent the display of values that are no longer used.

Figure 11-11: tblHolidays in design view

Rate Table

The next table, named tblRate, holds the salary and hourly rate for each employee. A query is used to calculate and spread the daily labor costs over the 12-month budget period. Figure 11-12 shows the design view of the Rate table.

Field Name	Data Type	
RateID	AutoNumber	Primary key
Department	Text	Budgeting departmet name
Employee	Text	Employee name
SalaryRate	Currency	Current pay rate as bi-weekly salary or hourly rate
EmployeeNumber	Text	Employee number from payroll system

Figure 11-12: tblRate in design view

Department Table

The Department table used in the example in Chapter 12 is a lookup table for the various departments or segments of the business. The name of this table is tblDepartment, as shown in the design view in Figure 11-13.

Field Name	Data Type	Description
DepartmentID	AutoNumber	Primary key
HomeDepartmentDescription	Text	Department where employee works and payroll expenses attach
DeptCode	Text	Department code from payroll system
GLUnit	Text	General ledger unit or account number attached to the department
GLProject	Text	General ledger project or account number that may further define the employee's department

Figure 11-13: tblDepartment in design view

Work Day Table

The next table used in Chapter 12 is a table that holds the date of the first day of each month of the budget period (field WorkMonth) and the corresponding number of work days for the month (field WorkDays). The value stored in WorkDays is calculated using a VBA routine. Although there are other ways of performing this calculation, this provides a clear demonstration of how to allocate a budget over a 12 month period. The table is named tblWorkDay as shown in design view in Figure 11-14.

Field Name	Data Type	Description
WorkDayID	AutoNumber	Primary Key
WorkMonth	Date/Time	First day of month for each month of the budget period.
WorkDays	Number	Number of work days in each month.
CreatedDate	Date/Time	The date a record was created.
CreatedBy	Date/Time	The computer user's ID. Used for traceability
Inactive	Date/Time	Indication of when a row becomes invalid for use. Often used in lookup tables in order to prevent the display of values that are no longer used

Figure 11-14: tblWorkDay in design view

Investment Master Table

The Investment Master table, named tblInvestmentMaster, contains the names of the investments currently or previously held. It includes the fields listed in Table 11-8. The design view of the table is shown in Figure 11-15.

> **NOTE** Additional fields may be added as required, but bear in mind that the fields should describe only the actual security, not transactions involving the security.

Table 11-8: Fields in the Investment Master Table

FIELD NAME	DATA TYPE	DESCRIPTION
InvMasterID	AutoNumber	Primary key
CUSIP	Text	CUSIP number of security
Description	Text	Describes the security
DateIssued	Date	Date security was issued
DateMaturity	Date	Maturity date of security
DateVoid	Date	Date record was voided

tblInvestmentMaster		
Field Name	Data Type	Description
InvMasterID	AutoNumber	Primary Key
CUSIP	Text	CUSIP number of Security
Description	Text	Detailed information describing the security
DateIssued	Date/Time	Date security was originally issued or offered for sale
DateMaturity	Date/Time	Date security matures
CreatedDate	Date/Time	The date a record was created.
CreatedBy	Date/Time	The computer user's ID. Used for traceability
Inactive	Date/Time	Indication of when a row becomes invalid for use. Often used in lookup tables in order to prevent the display of values that are no longer used.

Figure 11-15: tblInvestmentMaster in design view

Investment Detail Table

The Investment Detail table, named tblInvestmentDetail, includes the details about each investment. Since there may be several transactions for each investment holding, there will be a one-to-many relationship between the Investment Master and the Investment Detail tables. The table will include the fields listed in Table 11-9, as shown in design view in Figure 11-16.

tblInvestmentDetail		
Field Name	Data Type	Description
InvDetailID	AutoNumber	Primary Key
InvMasterID	Number	Foreign Key to tblInvestmentMaster
AcctID	Number	Foreign Key to tblAccount
TransactionTypeID	Number	Foreign Key to TransactionType i.e. bought, sold, dividend, gain, etc.
TransDescription	Text	Description of investment
Units	Currency	Number of shares or units etc
Price	Currency	Total dollar amount of security aquired
DateTrans	Date/Time	Date of financial transaction
CreatedDate	Date/Time	The date a record was created.
CreatedBy	Date/Time	The computer user's ID. Used for traceability
Inactive	Date/Time	Indication of when a row becomes invalid for use. Often used in lookup tables in order to prevent the display of values

Figure 11-16: tblInvestmentDetail in design view

Queries

Now that we've discussed how to separate the data so that it can be stored in exactly the right tables; you must be wondering how you are going to pull it back together. That's one of the jobs of a query. When creating your ledgers and reports, you will need to use queries to pull data from multiple tables.

Table 11-9: Fields in the Investment Detail Table

FIELD NAME	DATA TYPE	DESCRIPTION
InvDetailID	AutoNumber	Primary key
InvMasterID	Number	Foreign key to Investment Master
AcctID	Number	Foreign key to COA
TransactionTypeID	Number	Foreign key to TransactionType—e.g., bought, sold, dividend, gain, etc.
TransDecription	Text	Description of investment
Units	Currency	Number of shares or units, etc.
Price	Currency	Total dollar amount of security acquired
DateTrans	Date/Time	Date of financial transaction
CreatedDate	Date/Time	The date a record was created. This type of information is helpful if records are in a "half-baked" state and thus may require deletion.
CreatedBy	Date/Time	The computer user's ID. Used for traceability.
Inactive	Date/Time	Indication of when a row becomes inactive or invalid for use in the application. Often used in lookup tables in order to prevent the display of values that are no longer used

Queries are the workhorses of a database. Queries enable multiple tables to be joined and the information displayed as one recordset. A *recordset* is essentially what the name says, a set of records. It can be all the records in one table, or it can be selected fields from several tables. And you can further limit the data to only the records that meet stated criteria.

Joins are relationships applied by the query to single or multiple fields in multiple tables. There are four basic types of joins in an Access database, and at one point or another, you will use them all.

- **Cross join** (or, in Access, no defined join): Produces a *Cartesian product*; where every record in table 1 will be multiplied with every record in table 2, and every record in table 3, etc. For example, if one table has 50 records, the second table has 10, and a third table has 2 records, the results of the query would have 1,000 records. There are uses for this type of join; but you can easily see that accidental use can cause problems and return large recordsets with duplicated data.

- **Inner join:** The default join in the Query Designer in Microsoft Access. This will only return the records for which the joined field matches in both tables.

- **Left join** and **right join:** Returns all the records in one table and only the records in the second table where the joined fields match.

- **Full outer join:** Access does not inherently support a full outer join; however it can be simulated by creating multiple queries and then combining the queries in a Union query.

    In other RDMS that do provide this functionality, a full outer join will return all records in both tables even if the joined fields are not equal. Unlike the cross join, a full outer join does not produce a Cartesian product. Instead, the fields selected from the table on the side of the join that do not have matching entries in the second table will be returned as null.

Using Queries to Create a Virtual Ledger

In a manual system, creating a subledger requires making the detail entries in the subledger and then creating summary entries in the GL to record the total of the detail entries. Queries use a similar process to create a virtual ledger which can be restricted to provide the information about a single account type and account number. You can create a subledger, either on screen or printed, that contains only the entries that pertain to a single GL account, a single AR account, a single vendor account, or any other stated criteria. With the structure that we've provided, the only difference between an AR subledger and an AP subledger is the criteria applied.

The information is presented using forms and subforms which will display the type of subledger and the accounts or transactions to be returned. The following example, shown as SQL below and in the query design view in Figure 11-17, returns the records in the GL for AP transactions for Ink Drop Printing, formatted for readability.

In this example, a series of queries can be created using the same basic structure and then modifying the criteria to change the function of the query. The primary table in the query is the general ledger table tblGL. The accounts table tblAccount, and the accounts receivable-accounts payable-vendor-customer table, tblArApVendorCust are lookup tables and provide related values for foreign keys in the GL table.

Add the three tables, tblGL, tblAccount, and tblArApVendorCust in a new query in query design view. Create relationships between the three tables by adding joins to the tables. To create a join, click on the AcctID field in the tblAccount table and drag it to the AcctID field in tblGL. Access will automatically create an Inner Join using this method and it is correct for this join. Create a second join using the field ArApVendorCustID in the tables tblGL and tblArApVendorCust field ArApVendorCustID. This join needs to return all records in tblGL and only those records in tblArApVendorCust that are equal. To do this, right-click on the join line between the tables, select Join Properties, and select option 2.

Include the fields shown in Figure 11-17 in the query grid; for the criteria row for the ArApVendorCustID field, enter 3, and for the AcctID field, enter 10. Save the query as qryAcctsPayableByAccountBalance. The SQL from this query is shown below.

```
SELECT tblGL.GLID
    , tblGL.AcctID
    , tblGL.BatchID
    , tblAccount.AcctNum
    , tblAccount.AcctName
    , tblArApVendorCust.EntityName
    , tblGL.ArApVendorCustID
    , tblGL.UserID
    , tblGL.TypeID
    , tblGL.DateEntry
    , tblGL.Description
    , tblGL.AmtEntry
From tblAccount
    INNER JOIN (tblGL
        LEFT JOIN tblArApVendorCust
        On tblGL.ArApVendorCustID = tblArApVendorCust.ArApVendorCustID)
        On tblAccount.AcctID = tblGL.AcctID
WHERE tblGL.ArApVendorCustID = 3
And tblGL.AcctID = 10;
```

This query, or SQL statement, can be adapted to create multiple types of ledger views by modifying the WHERE clause, such as changing the 3 in the ArApVendorCustID field to another vendor. To create an AP ledger, change the criteria for the ArApVendorCustID field to 1 and the criteria for the AcctID field to 21. This will return all of the transactions for Mike's Steaks N

Margaritas, a receivable account. A date range can be entered to return only current period activity if desired.

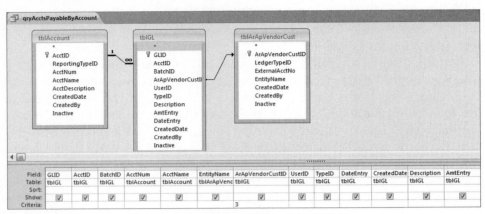

Figure 11-17: Design view of qryAcctsPayableByAccount

Aggregate Queries - Account Balances

The account balance for the individual accounts, either AP, AR, Vendor, or Customer, are calculated using an *aggregate*, or *totals*, query. To create an aggregate query from the previous query, click on the $\sum$ Totals icon (found on the Ribbon or Toolbar) and Access will add a Totals row to the query grid.

Before viewing the query results (running the query), you need to remove all but the fields AcctNum, AcctName, EntityName, AmtEntry, AcctID and ArApVendorCustId, as shown in Figure 11-18. In the Total row, use the dropdown list to select Group By for the first three fields and Sum for AmtEntry. Select WHERE for AcctID and ArApVendorCustID; and enter the selection criteria of 10 and 3, respectively. The result is the current balance for the accounts used in the previous query. The SQL statement for this query is provided below, followed by the Access design view.

```
SELECT tblAccount.AcctNum
    , tblAccount.AcctName
    , tblArApVendorCust.EntityName
    , Sum(tblGL.AmtEntry) as AmtEntry
FROM tblAccount
    INNER JOIN (tblGL
      LEFT JOIN tblArApVendorCust
        On tblGL.ArApVendorCustID = tblArApVendorCust.ArApVendorCustID)
      On tblAccount.AcctID = tblGL.AcctID
WHERE tblGL.AcctID = 10
    AND tblGL.ArApVendorCustID = 3
GROUP BY tblAccount.AcctNum
    , tblAccount.AcctName
    , tblArApVendorCust.EntityName
```

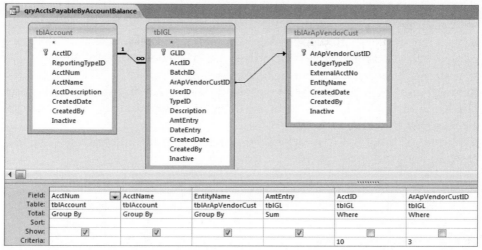

Figure 11-18: Design view of qryAacctsPayableByAccountBalance

You can limit the results to a specific time frame by including the field DateEntry from tblGL and adding criteria to it. Using criteria to return data less than or equal to a specific date will provide a balance at that date. For example, in the WHERE clause example shown below, DataEntry <= #6/30/2009#, would return the account balance as of June 30, 2009.

```
WHERE tblGL.AcctID = 10
      AND tblGL.ArApVendorCustID = 3
      AND tblGL.DateEntry <= #6/30/2009#
```

Relationships

In Access, relationships are defined in the Relationships window, as shown in Figure 11-19. Defining relationships enables the database itself to enforce *referential integrity*. In brief, referential integrity can be explained as requiring that a record is established in the primary (parent) table before an entry can be created in the child table; typically the "many" side of a one-to-many relationship between tables. The value in the foreign key field of the child table must equal a value in the primary key field in the parent table; otherwise the database will not allow the record to be created in the child table.

When referential integrity is selected, there are two additional relationship options, *Cascade Update Related Fields* and *Cascade Delete Related Records*. Cascade update will update the related fields if the value in the parent field is changed, while cascade delete will delete the related record if the parent record is deleted.

The decision to use either cascade update or cascade delete should be made with care. Both have a useful purpose, but they may also create unintended consequences. For example, if cascade delete is selected and a user deletes a parent record, all related child records will also be deleted.

You can learn more about relationships in Chapter 3, "Relational Data Model," and in Appendix B, "Relationships, Joins, and Nulls." For the purposes of our discussion, it is crucial that you understand the importance of establishing the relationships.

In this example, all relationships enforce referential integrity and neither cascade update nor cascade delete are selected.

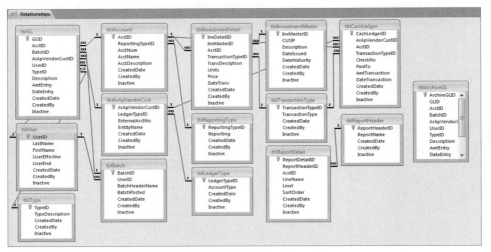

Figure 11-19: Relationship diagram for the accounting tables.

Creating and Using Archive Tables

In a large accounting system, after the accounting year has been closed, it is common to move data from active tables to *archive tables*. This might improve performance by reducing the number of records a query must process to return the correct results. If you are considering the need to archive your accounting data, you will also need to understand how accounting systems work and what the balance or balance forward is based on.

Balance sheet accounts, i.e., assets, liabilities, and equity accounts, all have the current balance calculated from the opening entry of the account to the last entry in the table. Income statement accounts, i.e., income and expenses, calculate only the current balance from the beginning of the current accounting period.

Unless the performance of the queries and forms is degraded due to a large number of records, we recommend not using archive tables. That's because once the data is archived, especially in balance sheet accounts, it makes it more difficult to get the historical information of each account. Income statement accounts are easier to work with, as the beginning balance in each account at the beginning of the fiscal year is zero because of the closing entries made to each account and to the retained earnings account.

Creating an Archive Table

If an archive process needs to be created, the best option is to only archive the income statement accounts. To create the archive file, you would make a copy of the General Ledger table and add a new AutoNumber field to use as a new primary key. The current field that is used as a primary key in the original table would be changed to a number, long integer, data type. Changing the AutoNumber to a long integer will allow the existing primary key to be preserved. You should also add a Date field to store the date on which the archive was added. Table 11-10 lists the fields in ArchiveGL table. Figure 11-20 shows the General Ledger Archive table in design view.

Table 11-10: Fields in the General Ledger Archive Table

FIELD NAME	DATA TYPE	DESCRIPTION
ArchiveID	AutoNumber	Primary key
GLID	Number	Original primary key
AcctID	Number	Foreign key to tblAcct
BatchID	Number	Foreign key to tblBatch
ArApVendorCustID	Number	Foreign key to tblArApVendorCust
UserID	Number	Foreign key to tblUsers
TypeID	Number	Foreign key to tblType
Description	Text	Free form description of entry
AmtEntry	Currency	Dollar amount of the debit or credit
DateEntry	Date/Time	Accounting transaction date
DateArchived	Date/Time	Date the records were archived
CreatedDate	Date/Time	The date a record was created. This type of information is helpful if records are in a "half-baked" state and thus may require deletion.
CreatedBy	Date/Time	The computer user's ID. Used for traceability.
Inactive	Date/Time	Indication of when a row becomes inactive or invalid for use in the application. Often used in lookup tables in order to prevent the display of values that are no longer used.

tblArchiveGL		
Field Name	**Data Type**	**Description**
ArchiveGLID	AutoNumber	Primary Key
GLID	Number	Original Primary Key
AcctID	Number	Foreign Key to tblAcct
BatchID	Number	Foreign Key to tblBatch
ArApVendorCustID	Number	Foreign Key to tblArApVendorCust
UserID	Number	Foreign Key to tblUsers
TypeID	Number	Foreign Key to tblType
Description	Text	Free form description of entry.
AmtEntry	Currency	The dollar amount of the debit or credit.
DateEntry	Date/Time	Accounting transaction date.
DateArchived	Date/Time	The date the records were archived.
CreatedDate	Date/Time	The date a record was created.
CreatedBy	Date/Time	The computer user's ID. Used for traceability
Inactive	Date/Time	Indication of when a row becomes invalid for use. Often used in lookup tables in order to prevent the display of values that are no longer used.

Figure 11-20: tblArchiveGL in design view

A routine that is only accessible to users who are authorized to close accounting periods should be created. You can use that routine to automate a process to append the current year income statement account data from the GL table to the GL Archive table, validate that totals agree in both tables, and then delete the original data from the GL table. Automating the routine not only saves staff time, but it also ensures that the process occurs in exactly the correct order and minimizes the potential for errors.

Verifying Income Statement Accounts

Because income and expense accounts are based on an accounting year, you should verify that the account balances are zero at the beginning of each accounting year. So, when you are making the year-end entries and posting all the batches for the year that is to be archived, you should confirm that all income statement accounts have a zero balance. You can do this quite easily with a query that returns all entries for income statement accounts for the specified accounting period.

You can modify this query to create a new GROUP BY query, sum all of the entries to get a check figure, and then add a field to count the records. Since the accounts have been closed into retained earnings, the check figure should be zero. Figure 11-21 shows the design view of qryArchiveAcctBalanceAndCount, a query that uses a GROUP BY function to calculate the ending balance and the number of records that were selected by the criteria.

As you can see, the query includes just the two tables, the General Ledger and the Account list. You should save this query so that you can use it in the future.

Appending Data to an Archive Table

Next, change the query type from a select query to an append query. This will retain the criteria from the original query and continue working with the same set of records. When you change the query to an append query, you will be prompted for the name of the table to receive the records. For this example, it is tblArchiveGL. Figure 11-22 shows an append query, qryGLArchiveAppend that can be used to add records to the ArchiveGL table. You should save this query for future use.

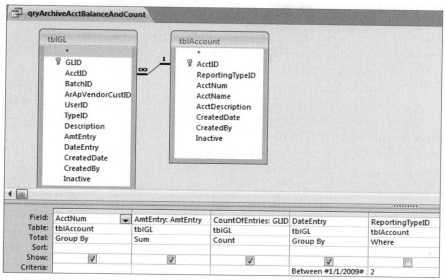

Figure 11-21: Design view qryArchiveAcctBalanceAndCount

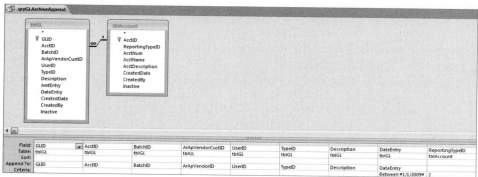

Figure 11-22: Design view of qryGLArchiveAppend

You can now confirm that the amounts and the record counts in the original table and query match what was appended to the Archive table. If the records match, you can convert the append query to a delete query by again changing the query type. When you run the delete query, it will delete the archived records from the General Ledger table. You should save this query for future use. By saving each query as it is modified, you can repeat the archive process as needed by following these steps and using the appropriate selection criteria.

Posting Ending Balances to the General Ledger

To archive the balance sheet accounts, the ending balance needs to be posted to the General Ledger table to replace the entries being archived. Create an append query from a query that returns the year-end balance of each account. You can do this by opening the query, qryAcctsPayableByAccountBalance, and saving it with a new name. When you change the query to an append query, you will be prompted for the name of the table to receive the records. Select tblGL. You also need to append January 1 (or the first day of your fiscal year) of the new accounting year to the field DateEntry; and use "Beginning Balance" or other appropriate terms as the description. Since the income statement accounts were closed to the retained earnings account, the total of all accounts should equal zero.

After appending the beginning balances, create another query to append all of the previous year entries to the Archive table. The total of this query should also be zero. If the total is correct, then you can create and run a query to delete the records from the General Ledger table. You can follow the same process as we used earlier for selecting, changing, and saving queries.

Access, and many other database systems, can process the series of queries in transactions and will only commit the records to the tables if there are no errors. Access uses VBA to process records in transactions, while SQL Server can process transactions using the T-SQL language.

It is also a good practice to require both a complete backup of the data before archiving and a compact and repair after completing the routine. When records are deleted in Access, they are not actually removed from the database; instead, they are marked as deleted and are not available for viewing. The deleted records are removed and the space is reclaimed after running the built-in compact and repair function.

You can use select queries and union queries to report the information from multiple years.

Summary

In order to successfully document and analyze the performance of a business, financial records must be accurately recorded according to standardized accounting practices. To successfully report on the data, it will typically be stored in an automated accounting system. However, not every business, especially very small businesses, will go that route.

As stated earlier, off-the-shelf packages such as Peachtree Complete Accounting or QuickBooks Pro from Intuit, and high-end customizable packages such as Microsoft Dynamics GP or Microsoft Dynamics SL, are all good accounting package choices to monitor your business. But, accounting packages, like business needs, will change over time. And you may not have found the right system for your needs; or you may want to supplement an existing system to accommodate special needs for a particular department or activity.

We intentionally did not provide a model database for a payroll system. The basic accounting for payroll is relatively simple, but the process of accounting for and calculating payroll taxes, unemployment taxes, employee benefits, and so on, is a daunting task. For most businesses, it would probably be best to use a commercial payroll system or outsource those processes. Designing the electronic reporting required by the various taxing entities and the multiple tax schedules for various governmental agencies would be difficult to create and maintain for the average accountant or payroll department staff.

If the decision is made to build your own custom accounting system, then care should be taken to maintain the integrity of the data. When the user interface is created, users should not be allowed to edit or view the data directly in tables or queries. It is imperative that users only have access to the data through a form or a report that provides the controls appropriate to prevent inadvertent modifications to the data. Otherwise, there is a much greater risk of compromising the data.

There are several business rules that you will need to enforce through the user interface. Since accounting processes rely on batches, the batches must balance before they are posted. This rule needs to be enforced at the form level. Instead of deleting a record, records should be updated to indicate that they are void, and then the record can be excluded from future reports. For example, if a check is voided, you cannot simply delete the record. Instead, you need to mark it as void and record that check number as being issued and zeroed out.

Auditors and other external examiners who audit the firm's books and records will more readily accept the numbers from a system that has sufficient controls to enforce data integrity. If users or developers can change data directly in the tables, all of the firm's books and records may be considered suspect. To pass even a base litmus test for accountability, it is imperative that the system use correcting or reversing entries to provide some form of audit trail.

Microsoft Access provides many tools to help you ensure the integrity and accuracy of your data. It has a multitude of features to make it as simple as possible to create a user interface for recording, viewing, and reporting your financial data. You have a lot to look forward to as you learn how to create forms and reports that are tailored to your needs.

While your mom may have trusted you when you told her that you and your friend made a total of $15.50 at the lemonade stand and you each received $7.75, you can be sure that stockholders, partners, lenders, and especially the IRS will not be as trusting. Make sure that your application uses sound methods to ensure that the data is correct and stays correct.

Based on what we have discussed in this chapter, you now have a solid set of tables that you can modify to fit your specific needs. So, the next step is to see how to use these tables with your data to create budgets, financial analysis and other reports. You'll learn about that next, in Chapter 12.

Accounting: Budgeting, Analysis, and Reporting

Accounting methods and systems were designed in response to requirements to provide information to both internal and external users.

In the simplest form, a business needs to determine whether its income is exceeding its expenses. In small enterprises, like a lemonade stand, this is done simply by recording the sales and purchases, and then using simple math to calculate whether the venture produces a profit or a loss.

As a business grows, more detailed accounting and reporting is required to satisfy the demands of the users of information. What began as a simple *cash basis accounting* now needs to be *full accrual accounting*. The Internal Revenue Service requires full accrual accounting in most businesses where product inventory is used.

Full accrual accounting, in its essence, matches income and expenses to the period when the income is earned. A cash basis system cannot do this, and the financial results are skewed as a result. Unless all income and expenses fall in the same accounting period, the net results may show a large net income in one period and a large net loss the next.

Employing full accrual accounting produces results as close to the actual results as possible. Consider *depreciation*, for example, which affects the assets a company purchases, such as machinery. In a cash basis system, the total cost of $3,600 would be charged against income when you buy it. In an accrual basis system, the life of the machinery would be used to expense only the portion used in each period. If the useful life is determined to be three years, only 1/36th of the total cost is expensed in a given month. *Amortization* of income is another example. If a three-year service contract is sold to a customer, each month 1/36th of the total contract price is recorded as income.

The recording of financial transactions, the creating and using of budget data, using the financial and budget data for analysis, and using the data to produce reports is discussed in this chapter.

Once the transactions have been recorded to the correct accounts, the information can be used to produce financial reports, and the data can be used to analyze the profitability of the entity, and to generate forecasts and budgets.

Although we will briefly cover some fundamental accounting concepts, this chapter is not intended to be an accounting primer. It relies on your having some familiarity with the business involved; it uses the tables that we described and created in Chapter 11, "Accounting Systems: Requirements and Design." The focus in this chapter is on extracting information from the data in those tables. To do that, we use queries to combine data from several tables.

So, unlike other chapters in this book, this chapter is more about creating queries than tables. In several examples, we'll show the queries in Access design view and explain the tables, fields and criteria that you will need to use to retrieve data for your reports and analysis. You can also find additional information on tables, relationships, and queries in Chapters 2, "Elements of a Microsoft Access Database," and 3, "Relational Data Model," and Appendix B, "Relationships, Joins, and Nulls."

Budgets

Budgets are specialized managerial reports used both to express formal financial goals and to measure the financial results. There are three major types of budgets: *cash budgets*, *operating budgets*, and *capital budgets*.

A budget showing projected cash inflows and outflows is a cash budget. Small businesses need to be able to track and predict the cash flows of the business in order to meet payment requirements on time.

A budget that is used to control and predict the income and expenses of a business is an operating budget. Operating budgets are usually prepared for the fiscal year of the business and reflect the natural business cycle of the company. Operating budgets also need to use the same general ledger classifications as the actual accounting in order to later compare the actual results with the projections made in the budget. By creating a budget and then comparing the actual financial results throughout the year with the budget, management can identify exceptions and make adjustments to operating practices in a timely fashion to improve the operating efficiency of the business.

A budget that is used to control the acquisition and disposal of assets such as property, plant, and equipment is a capital budget. Another function of a capital budget is to predict, prepare for, and keep under control the liabilities necessary for capital improvements. In this discussion, we will focus on the operating budget. It is the most commonly used budget.

Creating an accounting system with budgeting capabilities is actually only an extension of a basic accounting system. Budget entries are made using the same double-entry accounting principles that are used to record the actual expenses and income. The difference is that amounts are identified as budget entries. Thus, there's one set of aggregated numbers that are the actual results, and another set that are the budgeted numbers.

Budget Basics

The budget of an entity should be viewed as one of the most important parts of the overall strategy and planning necessary for successful results. The finished budget is a great tool, but the detailed examination of processes and procedures at the departmental level that are required to develop a budget can lead to improved efficiencies and savings that would normally go unnoticed.

Some of the problems of implementing a budget include managers who do not fully understand their own business model. Some managers lose sight of the overall business and become compartmentalized in their thinking. For example, a manager may reduce the costs in his or her own department by eliminating a quality inspection. However, the costs to another department are increased due to a higher failure rate of the product because the defect was not detected before it was sold. Managers may also be guilty of not recognizing the benefits and importance of an accurate and complete budget process. These managers will record only what is necessary to get the budget approved. Opportunities to identify expenses that can be reduced or eliminated are missed because the manager only expended the minimum effort.

Managers must be vigilant in their efforts to identify anything that impacts the bottom line of the company, not just the department for which they are responsible. If managers are isolated in their own little fiefdoms, proper planning cannot be easily done. Managers must communicate with each other and anticipate areas within the company that may become problems if action is not taken. The budget process, if done properly, can assist in interdepartmental cooperation.

Budgets should be prepared to match the meaningful reporting periods for the organization. If a budget is prepared only at the annual level, management cannot use it to measure the company's performance until the end of the year. Conversely, if it is prepared and recorded on a monthly basis, it can be utilized as a tool each month. When management is able to identify and determine the causes of the variances, proactive measures can be taken to exploit variances that are beneficial and mitigate variances that are having a negative impact on the bottom line.

Startup businesses must use estimates of expenses and income that are based on pure estimates, whereas existing businesses can rely more on the experience of the previous operations. Either way, the key to a successful budget is realistic estimates that have income and expenses properly matched to the correct accounting periods. For example, if a Christmas store has $300,000 annual revenue and $270,000 annual expenses, the matching principle would not dictate that $25,000 monthly revenue and $22,500 monthly expenses are recorded as budget entries when 90% of sales and variable expenses were generated in November and December. The monthly entries would be adjusted to best reflect the activity that should actually occur for each month.

The more accurate budget estimates are, the more meaningful actual vs. budget variance analysis can be.

Creating a Budget

Undoubtedly, the most difficult step in the budgeting process is producing the estimates of revenues and expenses. Instead of being seen as a tool that enables management to reduce costs and increase revenues, a budget is often seen as an annual exercise in futility. Preparing a budget takes hours that many managers do not feel they have to spare. Some don't give the process their best efforts. To make the budget preparations as easy as possible, tools should be provided and detailed instructions given to those who will prepare the budgets.

Budget Tools

There are commercial software packages, like Budget Maestro, Tagetix, Microsoft FRx Forecasting, and PROPHIX, that can assist in budget preparation and then integrate the results with commercial accounting packages. Most small to medium, and even some large, businesses use spreadsheets, such as Microsoft Excel, to allocate the budget numbers meaningfully throughout the year.

Using Excel for the budget has many benefits. Most managers use Excel on a regular basis for routine business activities, so they are comfortable working with spreadsheets. Using built-in or customized formulas, managers can spread annualized costs over each month with little trouble. Excel data in one department's spreadsheet can be linked with all departments to create a master spreadsheet for the entire company.

Base Budget Data

To prepare a budget, an estimate of revenues and expenses must be developed. Unless the budget is for a startup company, there should be a history of accounting and payroll data to use as a starting point.

Most accounting and payroll systems can export the financial and payroll data to a format that Excel can import. This simplifies the preparation by eliminating manual data entry.

Base financial data can be annual account totals, monthly totals, or an amount that will use statistical data as a multiplier to result in accurate period data. Payroll data is probably most accurate if it has the latest employee pay rate information with any planned pay increases and employee headcount changes.

Getting the Data into Excel

If the accounting model described in Chapter 11 is going to be used as the accounting system, or if the accounting data will be imported to an Access table, preparing a spreadsheet can be easily automated.

There are two basic methods to automate the process to move the data from Access to Excel. Access can export the data, or Excel can import it. Both methods need to use a query to select the correct data to be used.

Export and Import Methods

The easiest way to export data from a table or query to Excel is to copy the data in Access and paste it into Excel. Another easy process is to use an Access or Excel wizard help you. Linking to text files, Excel spreadsheets, or other databases is also an option available from Access.

Both Access and Excel include several import and export options. The data import and export wizards allow the user to control how fields and columns are mapped to a destination table or worksheet. If the file is a text file, either fixed width or delimited text, a file specification can be created, saved, and reused the next time the import or export is performed.

The External Data option in Access has icons allowing the user to import or link to multiple types of data. Clicking on an icon will invoke a wizard to either import or link the data. When external data is linked, it is not stored in the local database, but remains in the original file or database. After the data has been linked, the data can be queried as if it were in an Access table.

EXPORTING DATA TO EXCEL USING VBA OR A MACRO

If you frequently need to use the same export routine, you might want to automate as much of the process as possible. An automated routine can be created that will allow a user with little technical knowledge to select a file and import or export it by clicking on a command button from a form in Access.

You can do that several ways, but a couple of the more popular are to use either VBA or a macro. That is beyond the scope of this book, but we'll touch

Continued

EXPORTING DATA TO EXCEL USING VBA OR A MACRO *(continued)*

on it briefly here so that you are aware of the options. We encourage you to explore more when you are creating the user interface.

To export the data to Excel, you can use code or the VBA method `DoCmd` `.Transfer Spreadsheet`. The arguments for the `TransferSpreadsheet` method are `TransferType`, `SpreadsheetType`, `TableName`, `FileName`, `HasFieldNames`, and `Range`.

Alternatively, if you want to use a macro, the `OutPutTo` Macro action's arguments are `Object Type`, `Object Name`, `Output Format`, `Output File`, `Auto Start`, `Template File`, `Encoding`, and `Output Quality`.

All of the options we've mentioned—using a wizard, using the VBA methods, and the Macro actions—can use an Access query as the source of the export. Excel can use queries located in Access as the source of pivot tables or worksheets.

The query used to export can be a simple data dump that enables Excel to do all the forecasting work, or the query can pre-calculate specific information. Adding a table that holds the periods comprising the budget period enables the data to be spread over each month. Adding the number of work days in the month table also enables labor hours to be accurately spread over the budget period.

For example, by importing dates that indicate in which months employees are due a rate increase along with the payroll data, the new pay rates can be spread to each following month in the budgeting period. This can be accomplished with the built-in functions in Access and a query.

Usually the employee data will be imported from a payroll system and, of course, the model for a table with payroll-related data is dependent on the format being imported. Most exports from commercial systems will be a flat, denormalized text file. Since the file will not be used as a part of a transactional system, it is OK to use the flat file as is. Ideally, the file will include the employee ID number, name, pay rate, department, and anniversary dates—or dates of expected merit or cost of living rate changes.

Spreading the Data Over the Budget Period

If the imported file lists the correct departments for the budget period, then the single flat file should work to create the budget. If employees will be moved from department to department, it would be a benefit to create a department table and a junction table to store the employee ID and department ID fields. In the following example, a department table is imported. A query to return only unique combinations of Department Code, GL Unit, and GL Project from the temporary department table is used.

An essential table for this process is one that lists all of the months and working days included in the budget period. See tblWorkDay in Chapter 11.

To get the desired results in a query that will return a projected gross monthly salary for both salaried and hourly employees, the Working Days table is used in a special way. A *Cartesian join*, or *cross join*, is used. A Cartesian join is a join that is not defined to join specific fields between two or more tables. It will produce a Cartesian product, i.e., if one table has 10 records and the second table has 35 records, then the result will have 350 records. Each of the 10 records from the first table will return 35 records from the second table.

Figure 12-1 shows the design view of a query to spread the payroll data over the 12-month budget period using a Cartesian join. Notice that there are no join lines to tblWorkDays.

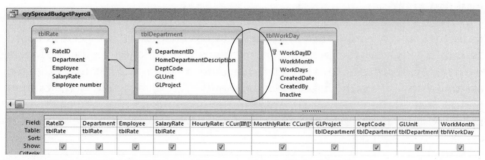

Figure 12-1: Design view of a payroll query using a Cartesian join

Using the Cartesian join in this example, where the goal is to spread the monthly salary totals through each month of the year using the actual working days, simplifies this process. All employees have one record in the Rates table that includes either their bi-weekly salary amount or their hourly rate. The Work Days table has 12 records consisting of a date indicating the payroll month and a field that indicates how many working days are in the month. When the query is executed, each employee will have twelve records that now include Employee ID, Employee Name, Pay rate, Pay Month, and hours in the month. With the results of a Cartesian product, it is simple to add field expressions to calculate the gross pay for all months in the period.

A simple formula to calculate the hourly pay rate for salaried employees can be used with the single field that contains both hourly and salaried rates. The following expression shows the logic when using the

`IIf()` function to calculate the hourly rate and apply a planned rate increase in March:

```
HourlyRate:CCur(IIf([SalaryRate]>1000,([SalaryRate]*26)/2080,
    [SalaryRate])*IIf(Month([workmonth])>=3,1.035,1))
```

The logic in the `HourlyRate` calculation above assumes that no hourly employees earn in excess of $1,000 per hour. If the employee's rate is greater than $1,000, then the rate is bi-weekly; otherwise, an hourly rate is used. The bi-weekly salary is then annualized and converted to an hourly rate. The company uses bi-weekly pay periods, so there are twenty-six pay periods in a year, and 2,080 working hours in a year. (2080 ÷ 26 = 80 hours per pay period)

The second `IIf()` function is used to spread a company-wide pay increase of 3.5% beginning in March to each employee. This calculation could be adapted to determine planned increases on the employee's review date if that value is included in the payroll import.

A second field expression is used to calculate employee gross pay according to the actual working hours in a month. Most businesses use accrual-based accounting, whereby expenses and revenues are matched to the period in which they occur, not to when they are paid or received. For this example, assume a payday on the first day of the month. The cash is paid in the current month, but all the expenses occurred in the previous month. The calculation below spreads the budgeted expenses to the correct months.

```
MonthlyRate: CCur([HourlyRate]*8*[workdays])
```

The Cartesian join returned the working days from the Work Days table that corresponds with a month in the budget period. The hourly rate is multiplied by eight hours, and then multiplied by the number of days in that month. The result is the labor dollars that apply to that month. Figure 12-2 shows the results of the qrySpreadBudgetPayroll.

Getting Data to Excel for Additional Analysis

Excel has built-in methods that allow it to connect directly with the Access database to execute a query from within Excel. In Excel 2007, use the Data menu item on the Ribbon, choose the From Access icon, and select your Access database. Figure 12-3 shows the Ribbon in Excel and the menu to import external data.

When the Import Data dialog opens, select Pivot Table Report to start the Pivot Table Wizard, as shown in Figure 12-4.

Rate	Department	Employee	SalaryRate	HourlyRate	MonthlyRate	DeptCode	GLUnit	GLProject	WorkMonth
21	012301	Hennig, Ms T	$2,786.43	$36.05	$6,633.09	012301	FRA1	CORP	3/1/2010
21	012301	Hennig, Ms T	$2,786.43	$36.05	$6,344.69	012301	FRA1	CORP	7/1/2010
21	012301	Hennig, Ms T	$2,786.43	$36.05	$6,056.30	012301	FRA1	CORP	5/1/2010
21	012301	Hennig, Ms T	$2,786.43	$36.05	$6,344.69	012301	FRA1	CORP	8/1/2010
21	012301	Hennig, Ms T	$2,786.43	$36.05	$6,344.69	012301	FRA1	CORP	4/1/2010
21	012301	Hennig, Ms T	$2,786.43	$36.05	$6,633.09	012301	FRA1	CORP	12/1/2010
21	012301	Hennig, Ms T	$2,786.43	$36.05	$6,344.69	012301	FRA1	CORP	9/1/2010
21	012301	Hennig, Ms T	$2,786.43	$36.05	$6,344.69	012301	FRA1	CORP	6/1/2010
21	012301	Hennig, Ms T	$2,786.43	$36.05	$6,056.30	012301	FRA1	CORP	10/1/2010
21	012301	Hennig, Ms T	$2,786.43	$34.83	$5,572.86	012301	FRA1	CORP	2/1/2010
21	012301	Hennig, Ms T	$2,786.43	$36.05	$6,344.69	012301	FRA1	CORP	11/1/2010
21	012301	Hennig, Ms T	$2,786.43	$34.83	$5,851.51	012301	FRA1	CORP	1/1/2010
13	013201	Bradly, Truitt L	$3,585.26	$46.38	$8,534.71	013201	SAL1	CORP	3/1/2010
13	013201	Bradly, Truitt L	$3,585.26	$44.82	$7,170.51	013201	SAL1	CORP	2/1/2010
13	013201	Bradly, Truitt L	$3,585.26	$46.38	$7,792.56	013201	SAL1	CORP	5/1/2010
13	013201	Bradly, Truitt L	$3,585.26	$44.82	$7,529.04	013201	SAL1	CORP	1/1/2010
13	013201	Bradly, Truitt L	$3,585.26	$46.38	$8,163.64	013201	SAL1	CORP	6/1/2010
13	013201	Bradly, Truitt L	$3,585.26	$46.38	$8,163.64	013201	SAL1	CORP	4/1/2010
13	013201	Bradly, Truitt L	$3,585.26	$46.38	$7,792.56	013201	SAL1	CORP	10/1/2010
13	013201	Bradly, Truitt L	$3,585.26	$46.38	$8,534.71	013201	SAL1	CORP	12/1/2010
13	013201	Bradly, Truitt L	$3,585.26	$46.38	$8,163.64	013201	SAL1	CORP	8/1/2010
13	013201	Bradly, Truitt L	$3,585.26	$46.38	$8,163.64	013201	SAL1	CORP	11/1/2010
13	013201	Bradly, Truitt L	$3,585.26	$46.38	$8,163.64	013201	SAL1	CORP	9/1/2010
13	013201	Bradly, Truitt L	$3,585.26	$46.38	$8,163.64	013201	SAL1	CORP	7/1/2010
1	010901	Flirt, Traci D	$33.28	$34.44	$6,337.84	010901	FIN1	CORP	12/1/2010
1	010901	Flirt, Traci D	$33.28	$33.28	$5,324.80	010901	FIN1	CORP	2/1/2010
1	010901	Flirt, Traci D	$33.28	$34.44	$6,062.28	010901	FIN1	CORP	11/1/2010
1	010901	Flirt, Traci D	$33.28	$34.44	$6,337.84	010901	FIN1	CORP	3/1/2010
1	010901	Flirt, Traci D	$33.28	$34.44	$6,062.28	010901	FIN1	CORP	7/1/2010
1	010901	Flirt, Traci D	$33.28	$34.44	$6,062.28	010901	FIN1	CORP	4/1/2010

Figure 12-2: Results of qrySpreadBudgetPayroll

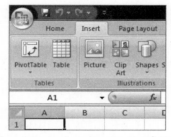

Figure 12-3: Using Excel to execute an Access query and create a pivot table

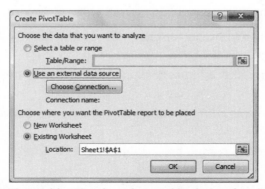

Figure 12-4: Excel's Pivot Table Wizard can be used to design the pivot table.

Use the wizard to lay out the pivot table with the month as the column head and the other desired fields as row labels. The result is the projected payroll expenses for the budget period.

Budget Entries: Manual Entry or Import

Getting the entries from the spreadsheets to the accounting system can be relatively simple or excruciatingly tedious. Manual entries may be the most efficient system in smaller entities.

A properly designed budget entry spreadsheet can be used to enter and prepare the budget and to upload the data to the accounting system. To import a prepared batch entry, the user would add an entry to the batch table. For example, assuming there are 50 income and expense accounts in the general ledger, then there will be 600 budget entries, one entry per month per account. If there are multiple departments or units, and each department or unit uses the same 50 accounts, there will be 600 entries for each department. At a minimum, all that is required to upload the budget entries from the budget spreadsheet is properly formatted spreadsheet data. This can be accomplished using formulas on a worksheet in Excel that format the required fields needed by the accounting system.

You can also use VBA code from either Access or Excel to pull the values from specific locations in the budget spreadsheets, format the entries to fill the fields in the GL table, and then upload the entries as a batch.

Process Flow Control

Usually, one central employee supervises the budgeting process. This employee varies from company to company, but it is usually a finance department employee. Be it the CFO, the controller, or the head bookkeeper, someone needs to ensure that correct information is supplied by those preparing the budget.

The budget manager is responsible for all of the following:

- Ensuring that the budget templates are in the hands of the department heads in plenty of time for accurate and timely input

- Answering any and all questions and supplying additional information if needed

- Receiving and compiling completed templates and approving or rejecting the submissions, and

- Ensuring that the completed budget data is loaded into the budgeting system.

Although a discussion of flow control is out of the scope of this book, most commercial budgeting software packages provide some form of flow control in their software package. Products like Budget Maestro, Microsoft's FRx Forecaster, Tagetix, and PROFIX, mentioned earlier in this chapter, are examples. These all include features that enable the budget manager to send the templates, view the progress of the preparers, document the steps, view any notes added to the budget, and track the approvals and rejections. Some include processes to automate variance reporting.

Applying the Budget

Once the budget has been created, either on paper or in a spreadsheet like Microsoft Excel, it is necessary to ensure that the budget accounts correspond with the financial chart of accounts. Once the budget is in the correct form, the entries can be manually entered into the GL as budget entries. The Access developer can create an optional automated process to upload entries from Excel. When the entries are posted as budget entries, the entries do not affect, in any way, the financial entries that are recording the actual accounting transactions from day to day.

Ideally, for each account there should be summary budget entries that, if all the estimates are perfect, match the total of all the entries for each of the financial accounts. In reality, there will be variances in most of the accounts.

Reporting Variances in the Budget

An Actual vs. Budget report, also called a *variance report*, is an extension of a basic income statement or profit and loss statement. The source for the variance report is the query used in the income statement. It is a simple aggregate, or Group By, query that sums the balances in each income statement account and an added column that also sums the budget entries for each income statement account. The original column is designated as Actual, and the new column is designated as Budget. The variance from the expected budget can also be calculated as a percent variance. The variance calculations can be preformed either in the query or in the report.

In the following example, we created a query that returns the actual and budget account balances for the first quarter of 2009 for all income statement accounts. The dollar variance is calculated in the query. If a percentage variance is desired, the additional calculation can be performed in either the query or the statement. Figure 12-5 is the design view of a query used to create a simple variance report. Note that "Between" is an inclusive operator, so the query criteria "Between #1/1/2009# And #3/31/2009#" will include results for January 1 and March 31.

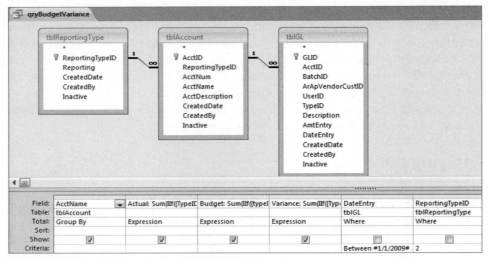

Figure 12-5: Query used to create a variance report

Once a variance is identified, detailed reports for the specified GL accounts can be requested and displayed in a form or a report. Figure 12-6 shows the design view of a query used to show the detail records that make up the transactions included in a variance.

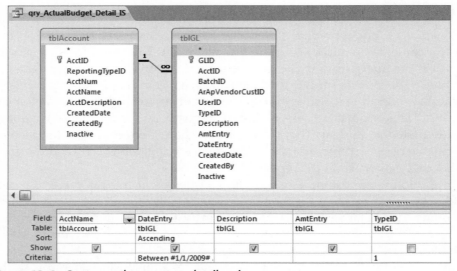

Figure 12-6: Query used to create a detail variance report

This enables the user to more easily identify the entries that are more than or less than the originally estimated amount. If the variance is going to be temporary, then only an explanation is necessary. If it is going to be an ongoing variance, such as the result of adding a new employee subsequent to generating the budget document, then it may be appropriate to modify the budget. The additional budget entries would increase the affected budget account balances thereby eliminating the recurring variances in reports for future periods.

Analyzing Profitability

After an accounting system is created, and the information for the first accounting period is entered, it is time to verify that the accounts are in balance, i.e., debits equal credits. Then, we can produce the reports and other information needed by management, investors, customers, and regulators.

The balance sheet and the income statement (also known as the profit and loss statement) are the two primary reports used by management, financial analysts, and other interested parties. The balance sheet is used to present a summary of the assets the company owns, a summary of the liabilities owed to others, and the basic ownership structure of the company. The income statement summarizes the revenues, cost of goods sold, and expenses for the period.

Ratio analysis is used to further evaluate the financial data in an effort to explain the performance of the company. These ratios are divided into types of ratios and include activity ratios, profitability ratios, net operating ratios, and others. Ratio analysis, like most analysis, is not an exact science. The results are only indicators. To be a valuable tool, they should be used with other analytical processes.

Reports

Although many types of reports are possible in an accounting system, we are going to focus on three main reports: the Trial Balance, the Balance Sheet, and the Income Statement.

Trial Balance

In order to create a report for presentation, the data must be available in the proper form. Using the chart of accounts, a simple query can create a trial balance that shows the ending balances of each General Ledger account. Figure 12-7 shows a design view of a query to create a trial balance.

This query, qryTrialBalancePrevPeriodClosed, will work for the balance sheet accounts, as it sums all of the entries in those accounts from inception. The income statement accounts may not be correct if the prior period's closing entries were not made. Figure 12-8 shows the results of the trial balance query in Figure 12-7.

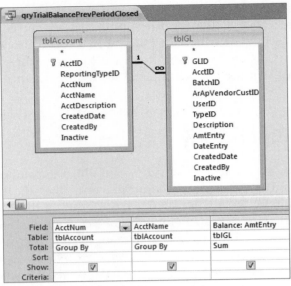

Figure 12-7: Query design for a trial balance

Account_N	Account_Name	Balance
10100000	Cash - First National Bank Checking	$73,250.00
10200000	Furniture & Equipment	$1,250.00
10200010	Accumulated Depreciation - Furniture & Equipment	($25.00)
10300000	Leasehold Improvments	$25,000.00
10500000	Accounts Receivable	$2,000.00
20000000	Accounts Payable	$0.00
30000000	Common Stock	($1,000.00)
30100000	Additional Paid-in capital	($99,000.00)
40000000	Sales	($2,000.00)
50100000	Office Supplies	$500.00
51500000	Depreciation Expense	$25.00

Figure 12-8: Example of records returned for a trial balance

Income statement accounts are closed at year end into the retained earnings account. A credit balance has a debit made to the account to zero it out, and the credit is made to retained earnings. The total of these entries is equal to net income or loss for the period.

To ensure that only current period entries are returned, the ReportingID field is used to sum the correct accounts needed. The ReportingID field is used to indicate financial entries, budget entries, or statistical entries. In addition to the ReportingID criteria, the income statement accounts are limited to transactions occurring in the current period. To limit the period to a specific range of dates, criteria is entered in the DateEntry field. The criteria arguments are passed to the query at runtime using form references. They are not hard-coded as they are in this example.

Several methods are available to create a query that enables the summation of differing time periods. A *union query* is used in this example. For ease of design and design changes, instead of having to write the query all in SQL, two queries are designed to return the information, and they are used in a union query to return the desired results.

The two queries, qryTrialBalanceBalShSec (see Figure 12-9) and qryTrial-BalanceISSec (see Figure 12-10), are designed using Access' graphical Query Designer.

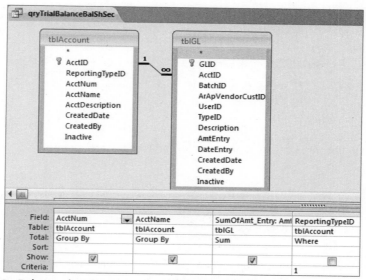

Figure 12-9: Balance sheet accounts for the trial balance query

The query design tool cannot be used to create a union query; SQL must be used to develop it. There are two types of union queries, UNION and UNION ALL. The two types work the same except that the UNION operator will, by design, aggregate all duplicate records. The UNION ALL returns all records; and, as a result of not aggregating records, it runs faster. We have used the UNION ALL in these examples.

Figure 12-11 demonstrates how to combine the two queries into a very simple SQL statement. As long as both queries have identical fields in the recordset that is returned, the individual fields do not need to be listed. Figure 12-12 shows the results of the union query.

To produce a trial balance for a previous period, criteria would also need to be applied to the balance sheet accounts to only sum the entries through the ending date requested.

If a single report is needed to show the beginning balances, period activity, and ending balances, it can be done using a single union query.

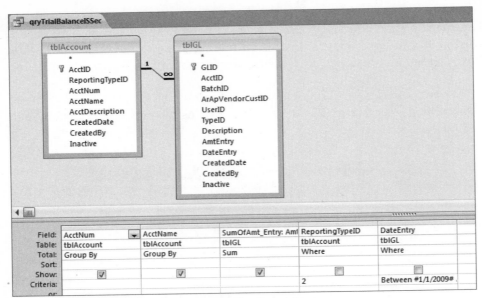

Figure 12-10: Income statement accounts for the trial balance query

qryTrialBalanceUnion

```
Select * From qryTrialBalanceBalShSec
UNION ALL Select * From qryTrialBalanceISSec;
```

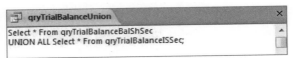

Figure 12-11: Union query combining the balance sheet accounts and income statements

qryTrialBalanceUnion

Account_Num	Account_Name	SumOfAmt_Entry
10100000	Cash - First National Bank Checking	$73,250.00
10200000	Furniture & Equipment	$1,250.00
10200010	Accumulated Depreciation - Furniture & Equipment	($25.00)
10300000	Leasehold Improvments	$25,000.00
10500000	Accounts Receivable	$2,000.00
20000000	Accounts Payable	$0.00
30000000	Common Stock	($1,000.00)
30100000	Additional Paid-in capital	($99,000.00)
40000000	Sales	($2,000.00)
50100000	Office Supplies	$500.00
51500000	Depreciation Expense	$25.00

Record: 1 of 11 No Filter Search

Figure 12-12: The records returned by the union query

Four queries are needed to create a single union query to return the beginning balances, period activity, and ending balances. It is necessary to add placeholder fields to each query, as all segments of the union query need to have the same number of fields. The queries are as follows:

qryTrialBalancePreviousPeriodBS, shown in Figure 12-13

qryTrialBalancePreviousPeriodIS, shown in Figure 12-14

qryTrialBalancePreviousPeriodCurActivity, shown in Figure 12-15

qryTrialBalancePreviousPeriodEndingBalance, shown in Figure 12-16

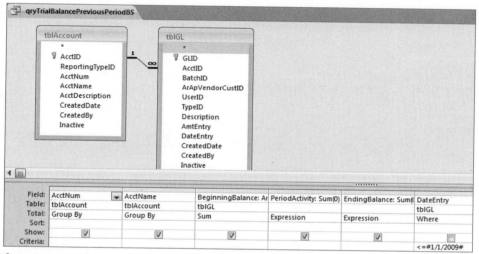

Figure 12-13: Query to return beginning balance sheet account balances

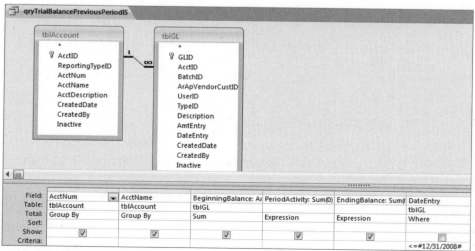

Figure 12-14: Query to return beginning income statement account balances

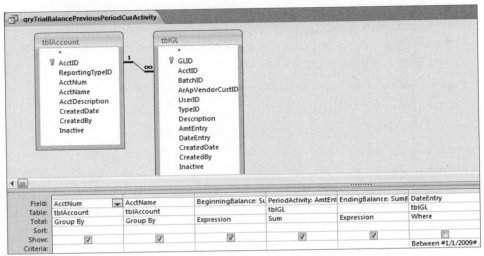

Figure 12-15: Query to return current period activity

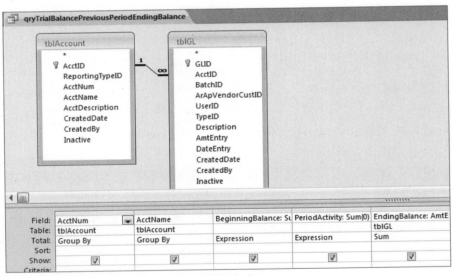

Figure 12-16: Query to return period ending balances

Figure 12-17 illustrates a union query used to combine the results of the four queries into a single recordset.

Figure 12-18 shows how to aggregate the results of the union query into a recordset that will include a single record for each account and fields to show the account's beginning balance, the period activity, and the ending balance.

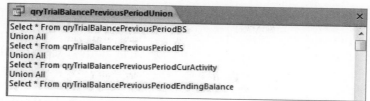

Figure 12-17: The four queries are combined into a single union query.

| | qryTrialBalancePreviousPeriodFinal | | | | |

qryTrialBalancePreviousPeriodUnion

*

AcctNum
AcctName
BeginningBalance
PeriodActivity
EndingBalance

Field:	AcctNum	AcctName	BeginningBalance: Be	PeriodActivity: Period	EndingBalance: Endir
Table:	qryTrialBalancePrevio	qryTrialBalancePrevio	qryTrialBalancePrevio	qryTrialBalancePrevio	qryTrialBalancePrevio
Total:	Group By	Group By	Sum	Sum	Sum
Sort:					
Show:	✓	✓	✓	✓	✓

Figure 12-18: Design view of a query that creates the detail trial balance

Figure 12-19 shows the results of an aggregate query used to sum the beginning balance, current activity, and ending balance fields to create the trial balance.

	qryTrialBalancePreviousPeriodFinal			
Account_Num	Account_Name	BeginningBalance	PeriodActivity	EndingBalance
10100000	Cash - First National Bank Checking	100000	-26750	73250
10200000	Furniture & Equipment	0	1250	1250
10200010	Accumulated Depreciation - Furniture & Equipment	0	-25	-25
10300000	Leasehold Improvments	0	25000	25000
10500000	Accounts Receivable	0	2000	2000
20000000	Accounts Payable	0	0	0
30000000	Common Stock	-1000	0	-1000
30100000	Additional Paid-in capital	-99000	0	-99000
40000000	Sales	0	-2000	-2000
50100000	Office Supplies	0	500	500
51500000	Depreciation Expense	0	25	25

Record: ◄ 1 of 11 ► ►I ⚹ No Filter   Search

Figure 12-19: The final records for the trial balance, showing beginning balance, current activity, and ending balance

Alternatively, a report can be used to aggregate the balances, allowing all amounts for each account to display on a single row. Simple check figures can be added to the report to indicate whether the report is out of balance.

Balance Sheet

For the next two reports, we must introduce a method to map the correct values to the correct lines on the reports. A *junction table*, named tblReportDetail, is used to map individual accounts to specific lines in a report. The chart of accounts includes all accounts, usually in numerical order. The accounts do not usually appear on the balance sheet in the order or detail of the chart of accounts. Many accounts may be aggregated into a single line item of the report.

To accomplish the correct ordering and aggregation, we will use the Report Detail table. In a working accounting database application, an entry form would be created. Table tblReportHeader would be used to select the report and line detail would be entered through the form or subform. In addition, there should be a form to add, modify, and remove accounts from the chart of accounts. Part of this process should include a screen to add the account to the proper reports. At creation time, the user should know on which reports the account should be placed and the proper location on the reports. Forcing the designation at creation time prevents out-of-balance errors caused by accounts not being included in the financial reports.

To create the detail of the report, entries are made that assign each GL account to a line on the report. The sort order of the report line is also entered here. The Level field is used to indicate if the line should be included in the Assets, Liabilities, or Equity section of the report.

Then the queries are designed, using a query based upon the union query similar to the one used for the trial balance. But this time, it will only return the balance sheet accounts, and it will use a join to the junction table to retrieve the balance sheet line name and amount. Each line in the balance sheet will aggregate the GL accounts assigned to that line in the Report Detail table.

In addition to including the balance sheet accounts, the balances of all income statements must be summarized and aggregated into the Retained Earnings line on the balance sheet. Figure 12-20 shows the query to create a balance sheet.

Income Statement

The same method that was used to create the balance sheet is used to create the income statement. This is done with a query similar to the one used to create the balances for the income statement accounts in the trial balance; it uses the same joins to the tblReportDetail and tblReportHeader tables.

As in the balance sheet, the line-by-line entries are generated by the GL entries and the report detail entries are from the query, qryIncomeStatement, as illustrated in Figure 12-21.

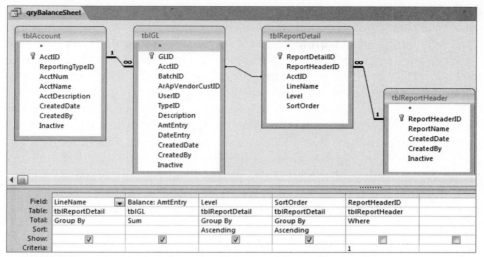

Figure 12-20: Design view of the query used to create a balance sheet

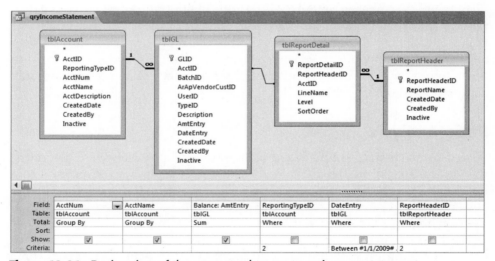

Figure 12-21: Design view of the query used to create an income statement

Common-Size Statements

Common-size statements are statements that use a percentage of a line item, such as a percent of sales, for each line item in an income statement. They may also use a base period and then state the values for each subsequent period as a percentage of the base period. Common-size analysis is a valuable tool because all of the values are expressed as a percentage of a common number. Vertical analysis, whereby each line is expressed as a percentage of a base amount, shows what proportion each item is compared to the base amount. Horizontal analysis, which includes multiple years of common-size statements, gives the analyst a way to find trends not easily discerned from fixed amounts, although the chapter file does not include queries to conduct this type of analysis, you can create some basic queries using the following steps.

To create a vertical analysis, you can start with the same query used to create either of the balance sheets or income statements. Add a hidden control to calculate the amount that all fields will use as the base amount. You can use a domain aggregate function to populate the control. Then add a control to the detail section of the report to display the percent of sales or other base amount. The vertical common size is easily included on currency-based reports, and the common-size column is usually an additional column added to the right side of the currency column, expressed as a percentage.

Horizontal analysis requires a little more work, as a query needs to be modified to return multiple years of data. This can be accomplished using another SELECT statement in the UNION query. This method allows all report line amounts to be summarized into a single line on the report. Instead of displaying the currency amount, add a formula in the controls to calculate a percentage of the base amount. The ideal layout of the report would be one that is identical to the currency-based report. A report with the current year and one or two previous years could be designed as the standard report, with a version to include currency amounts, and another version to include only common sized data.

Ratio Analysis

Successful businesses are managed using some form of analysis to determine the enterprise's strengths and weaknesses. Whether it is a comparison to a benchmark of similar businesses, a comparison of previous period results to current results, or a comparison to direct competitors, the comparisons usually use numbers that are not always on the financial reports.

There are many types of ratios and many different ratios within the various types, including profitability ratios, liquidity ratios, coverage ratios, income ratios, and many more. They are all used to reduce the data to simple numbers that are easily compared to other periods or companies.

The data for the various ratios usually come from an easily identifiable line in either the balance sheet or the income statement. After the correct GL accounts that compose the line item in the statement are identified, the use of a simple DSum() function used on the qryBalanceSheet query or on the qryIn-comeStatement query will return the correct values. You can also use a query designed to return scalar values relating to the statement line item. A simple formula that utilizes the values is all that is needed to calculate the ratio.

Profitability Ratios

Return of Capital Employed (ROCE) is used to assess how much the invested capital has earned during the period. Return on capital is a measure of the opportunity costs for a potential investor. The current ROCE should be compared with previous years' ROCE, with market interest rates available to the potential investor, and with the ROCE of other companies in the same industry. ROCE is calculated as follows:

$$\text{Earnings before interest and taxes} \div (\text{Current Assets} - \text{Current Liabilities}) = \text{ROCE}$$

Figures 12-22 and 12-23 show examples of queries that can either be the record source for a recordset or used with a domain aggregate function such as `DLookup()`.

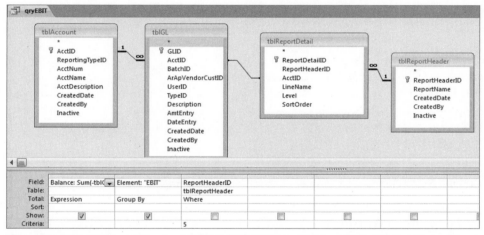

Figure 12-22: Design view of qryEBIT, which returns earnings before interest and taxes for the ROCE ratio

Figure 12-23: SQL view of the Union query, which returns the elements needed to calculate ROCE

In Figure 12-23, the two single queries are combined into a single Union query to return all elements needed to calculate ROCE.

This query, qryROCE, returns three values: earnings before taxes, total assets, and current liabilities. These values are all that is required to calculate

ROCE. Use the values in the Report Detail table with criteria to limit it to a specific line or lines.

The second method is the preferred method. It allows changes to be made without having to update the SQL. This enables the end user to make changes due to a changing chart of accounts.

Return on Equity (ROE) is used to measure the return on investment. It measures the return to shareholders. ROE is calculated as follows:

$$\text{Net Income} \div \text{Shareholder's Equity} = \text{ROE}$$

Figure 12-24 shows a design view image of the query to return net income.

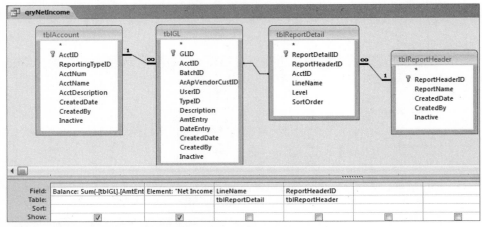

Figure 12-24: Design view of query to calculate net income.

The query to calculate the equity of the shareholders, qryShareholders Equity, is shown in Figure 12-25.

Next, both queries are combined to return both elements of ROE, as shown in Figure 12-26.

Figure 12-27 shows the results of qryROE.

Profit Margin on Sales Ratio indicates what rate of profit the company is earning for each sales dollar earned:

$$\text{Net Income} \div \text{Net Sales} = \text{Profit Margin on Sales}$$

Earnings Per Share (EPS) is used to quantify the earnings of an individual share of company stock:

$$\text{Net Income} \div \text{Weighted Shares Outstanding} = \text{EPS}$$

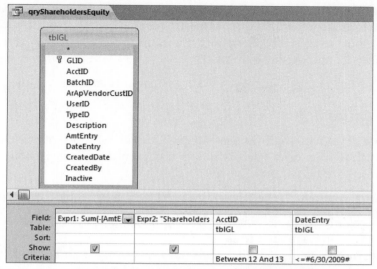

Figure 12-25: Design view of query to calculate shareholder's equity.

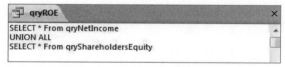

Figure 12-26: SQL view of Union query for ROE query

Figure 12-27: Recordset returned from the ROE query

Liquidity Ratios

Current Ratio is used to compare short-term assets with short-term liabilities and can be used as an indication of whether sufficient assets are available to service the short-term debts. Generally, 2:1 is the recommended ratio. Liquidity problems may be indicated when the ratio is under 2:1. Over 2:1 may indicate that the company is not utilizing its current assets to their fullest potential.

$$\text{Current Assets} \div \text{Current Liabilities} = \text{Current Ratio}$$

Quick ratio, or acid-test ratio, indicates the ability of a company to use its liquid (cash) and somewhat liquid assets (investments and accounts receivable) to pay its short-term debts. Generally, the ratio should be 1:1 but it may vary significantly from industry to industry.

$$(Cash + Marketable\ Securities + AR) \div Current\ Liabilities = Quick\ Ratio$$

Activity Ratios

Receivable Turnover Ratio is used to provide an estimate of the quality of the receivables and how successful the company has been in collecting its receivables:

$$Net\ Sales \div Average\ Trade\ Receivables\ (ATR) = Receivable\ Turnover\ Ratio$$

ATR is calculated by averaging the beginning and ending balance of the receivables accounts related to sales.

Asset turnover ratio is used to see how efficiently a company utilizes its assets:

$$Net\ Sales \div Average\ Total\ Assets\ (ATA) = Asset\ Turnover\ Ratio$$

ATA is calculated by averaging the beginning and ending total asset balances.

Summary

Budgets can be powerful management tools if they are properly used. A carefully considered and designed budget planning process enables management to compare the goals set forth in the annual budget with the actual results. Budget planning that is not well thought out, or not realistic, will render any variance analysis useless. Overall, the process is difficult and can be frustrating, even under the best circumstances. However, managers who put forth the extra effort to develop a budget that realistically reflects attainable goals and the prevailing business climate will have a great tool to evaluate the company's performance.

A database developer should always design and implement systems using methods and designs that follow the guidelines of normalization to the extent possible, and that provide a level of data integrity suitable for the intended function of the application.

An accounting database is not a solution that assures a successful business, but it is an important tool to make a business successful. The key to a successful budget system in an accounting database is not how the database stores and reports the information; it is the business strategy translated into financial numbers that makes the system work.

The data stored in an accounting system can hold the key to a successful business, but only if it is used correctly. If the owners or management only use the data to meet the minimum required reports, important trends will be missed. It is hard to take advantage of strengths that the analysis is revealing if the analysis is not done at all. Also, a weakness may be overlooked and earnings may suffer.

Financial statement analysis or ratio analysis will not always uncover problems that exist in a company. Analysts or business owners must not rely on a single ratio or comparison to base their decisions. The financial statements of small businesses may not be audited by external auditors, and may not be accurate.

Comparing the financial results of your company to similar companies may not be an apples to apples comparison. Accounting practices may differ significantly from company to company. Similar companies on different fiscal years may have very similar annual results, but analysis of inventories at fiscal year-end may result in very different conclusions that are actually due to the seasonal cycle.

Industry averages are not exact. Only if all businesses included in the average have the same product lines, will it be a perfect fit. Your product line may only include pots and pans, while the other companies in the average also make stoves. As long as the analyst is aware of the differences, ratio analysis can provide useful results. Knowing the limitations is as important as performing the analysis.

Don't rely on a single ratio. Ratio analysis works best when many ratios from different ratio categories are used. The analyst should look at all of the results, and look for trends and patterns that may indicate adverse conditions.

Examining relationships between different statements and finding trends in those relationships is the definition of analyzing profitability. Making the examination easy to accomplish is key to timely analysis. Set up correctly, the financial statements and analysis can be printed at the touch of a button. The easier it is to produce the statements and to produce the ratio analysis, the more likely that management will take the time to try and find problems before they become serious.

The data is available. You, the developer will need to make it easy for management to find and to digest it. Access has a set of graphical tools to display the information as charts and graphs. Access also works very well with Microsoft Excel and other applications that have more robust graphical tools.

Part

V

Independent Areas

In This Part

Managing Memberships

Almost all of us can claim membership in one or more organizations. If you belong to a church, a club, a lodge, a civic group, a study group, a computer user group, a baseball team, a committee, a parent teacher association, a lending library, or a buying group, then you are a member of an organization. Whether commercial or noncommercial, all but the smallest and most informal organizations need to manage memberships and related functions. Although your small circle of high school friends who still get together on a regular basis might be an exception, a larger group such as your high school class can benefit from a database application to keep track of classmates and notify them of reunions, homecoming events, and other activities. The purposes and requirements of the organization determine which features and functions of a database application will serve it best, but all organizations share some basic needs.

HOW THIS CHAPTER IS ORGANIZED

Many of the tables in this chapter are identical to or minor modifications of tables from earlier chapters, in particular Chapter 4, "People, Organizations, Addresses" and, to a somewhat lesser degree, Chapter 5, "Customer Relationship Management."

In those chapters we followed a common process to create the database. They started with a discussion of the business function to identify the information and details needed to support it. Then, the details were grouped into subjects, which we illustrated in diagrams. We followed with a detailed discussion of how those subjects were converted into the tables and fields of

Continued

HOW THIS CHAPTER IS ORGANIZED *(continued)*

the example database. As we completed the discussion of each main area, we looked at a relationship diagram to see how data and tables fit together.

Rather than repeat the same process to create essentially the same tables in this chapter, we focus on the business functions of managing memberships and create the example database to support those business functions.

NOTE Both people and organizations can be members of an organization. In the case of organizations, references to people may be in connection with the individual's position in the member organization. We covered the basic table structures and suggested data content for both people and organizations in Chapter 4. Since the topic of this chapter is closely related to that, you may find it beneficial to briefly review Chapter 4.

STANDARD FIELDS USED IN MOST TABLES

An in-depth discussion of surrogate, primary, and natural keys, indexing fields singly and in combination, audit trail information, note fields, and using memo fields in a table in combination with other fields or in a separate table can be found in the "Standard Fields Used in Most Tables" sidebar and the subsequent "Memo Field" sidebar in Chapter 4. Please review that discussion before proceeding and refer to it if you wish to clarify as you progress through this chapter.

Membership Management Functions

Whether the members are people, organizations, or both, a typical membership organization has to add new members, renew memberships, and modify membership information. Provision for modifying membership information should be available as a separate operation of the database application in addition to being part of the renewal process. This is because a member's information can change without being associated with renewal.

A relationship diagram illustrating the schema of the tables that participate in managing membership data is shown in Figure 13-1. Some tables in this diagram also participate in other schemas, for which relationship lines are not included here.

Member information may already exist in tables, word processor, spreadsheet, or another application's data format. This data can be copied into your database with Access's Get External Data feature. You can then either add fields to existing tables or create new linked tables with the additional fields you need.

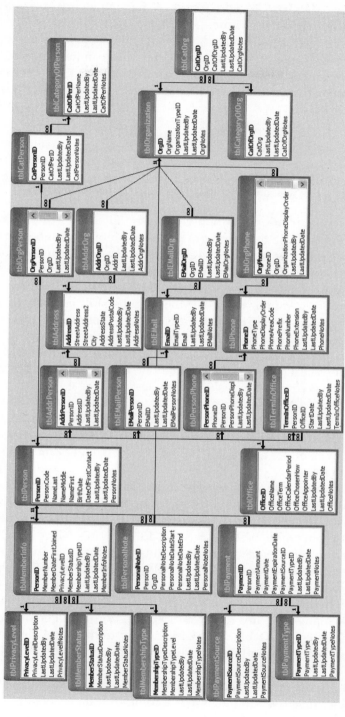

Figure 13-1: Relationships of the Membership Management tables

In the example database for this chapter, the tables are tblPerson and tblMemberInfo. As shown in Figure 13-2, the tables are linked one-to-one so that tblPerson can be maintained separately if used in other database applications in your organization. If you prefer, you can add the fields now included in tblMemberInfo to tblPerson and eliminate tblMemberInfo to simplify the structure of your membership database application.

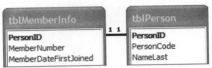

Figure 13-2: One-to-one relationship of the Person and Member Info tables

In the one-to-one relationship shown, PersonID is an AutoNumber in tblPerson, and PersonID in tblMemberInfo is a long integer number. In each of the two tables, field PersonID serves as both the primary key for the table itself and as a foreign key to the other table. Because the relationship between the tables is built with two primary keys, it forces the relationship to be one-to-one.

To create a more common example, the membership consists of people, rather than organizations. In the latter case, the Member Information table would have been joined one-to-one with the Organization table.

However, if both people and organizations can be members, the tables would be joined in a "not-strictly-normalized" manner, which we have described in Appendix C, "Resolving Relationship Triangles" as the "either-or" relationship. The examples in Appendix C provide an approach to manage the data so that a record in a parent table may be related to a record in one or the other of two child tables, but not to both. This means that the Member (a record in the parent table) can be either a person (tblPerson child table) or an organization (tblOrg, a child table).

In such a scenario, with both people and organizations as members, you would also require a different structure to support the relationship between the Person table and the Address table and the many-to-many relationship between the Organization table and the Address table. Since the Address information for both people and organizations is maintained in the Address table, the table in this chapter will differ from the Address table (a table by the same name) discussed in Chapter 4.

For our membership example in this chapter, the Address table will participate in two many-to-many relationships: one with the Person table and one with the Organization table. Each of the many-to-many relationships will actually be resolved into one-to-many relationships, as demonstrated later in this chapter.

Several tables used in the example for this chapter are identical or nearly identical to tables discussed in detail in the complex data model in Chapter 4,

"People, Organizations, Addresses." Those tables are listed in Table 13-1, and you will find the detailed discussion of the tables and fields, along with the image of the design view, in Chapter 4. You will also notice that we have abbreviated some of the table and field names.

Table 13-1: Tables Referenced from Chapter 4

CHAPTER 13 TABLE NAME	CHAPTER 4 TABLE NAME	FIELDS OMITTED FROM THE CHAPTER 13 TABLE
tblPerson	tblPerson	PersonCategoryID, TitleID, TitleSuffixID
tblOrganization	tblOrganization	OrganizationDateOfFirstContact
tblAddress	tblAddress	AddressTypeID, CountryID
tblOrgPerson	tblOrganizationPerson	TitleSuffixID, RoleID
tblAddrOrg	tblAddressOrganization	
tblAddrPerson	tblAddressPerson	
tblEMailOrg	tblEMailOrganization	
tblEmailPerson	tblEMailPerson	
tblOrgPhone	tblOrganizationPhone	
tblPersonPhone	tblPersonPhone	

This model only requires one table in addition to those copied from Chapter 4. The Member Information table is unique to the membership business functions, so it was not included with the general people and organization functions.

The Member Information Table

This table, named tblMemberInfo (shown in Figure 13-3), contains member information. It can be associated with a person in a one-to-one relationship, as already discussed. The fields for tblMemberInfo are as follows:

MemberNumber is a Text field holding the membership number.

MemberDateFirstJoined is a Date/Time field that contains the initial date of membership.

MemberPrivacyLevelID is a Long Integer field that is used as a foreign key to tblMemberPrivacyLevel.

MemberStatusID is a Long Integer field that is used as a foreign key to tblMemberStatus. Alternatively, if you are confident that the list of status options will not change, you could store the value of the status and eliminate the relationship but still use tblMemberStatus as a lookup table.

MembershipTypeID is a Long Integer field that is used as a foreign key to tblMembershipType. Similar to MemberStatus, if you are confident in the stability of the list of member types, you could store the text instead of the value of the foreign key. This would eliminate the relationship between the two tables but still provide the benefits of using a lookup table.

Field Name	Data Type	Description
PersonID	Number	Primary key, uniquely identifies this record, foreign key to Person table for one-to-one relationship
MemberNumber	Text	Membership Number
MemberDateFirstJoined	Date/Time	Date of initial membership
PrivacyLevelID	Number	Foreign key to tblPrivacyLevel
MemberStatusID	Number	Foreign key to tblMemberStatus
MembershipTypeID	Number	Foreign key to tblMembershipType
LastUpdatedBy	Text	User who last updated this Record
LastUpdatedDate	Date/Time	Date/time when this record was last updated
MemberInfoNotes	Text	Optional, unstructured comments or notes about this record

Figure 13-3: The Member Info table

Organization information is maintained in tblOrganization. Telephone numbers are stored in tblPhone, which has relationships between a phone number and a record in either tblPerson or tblOrganization through separate junction tables. Both are discussed in Chapter 4.

Adding and Renewing Memberships

The membership database would be designed around a member table, which stores information about the current members. There can be good reason for maintaining information on former members, and possibly prospective members as well. The member table would contain information on the members, including the officers. If you want to include other personal information, you could incorporate fields or tables from Chapter 4. A user interface (in Access, a form or screen) must allow initial entry of member data, editing of member data, and entry of a renewal record.

Keeping Track of Members

Because members are the focus of "membership organizations," it is common to maintain more personal information than is the case in business scenarios where information about the person is secondary to other information. An event table containing records of civic or technical activities or honors, educational achievements, career advancements, and personal events may be useful. An example using this type of information would be a membership organization that occasionally issues a press release mentioning a member. Having that information in your database makes it easy for you to retrieve it, obviating the need to search library or Internet publications.

This same event table could record the offices or positions held by each member, using one entry for each term in office. For clarity and simplicity, however, the example database for this chapter contains a separate table for members' terms in office. The trade-off of an additional table to simplify understanding and working with the database seemed worthwhile. In fact, if your membership organization does not need to maintain this kind of personal information, this table can be omitted without interfering with having a record of the organization's officeholders.

Following the principles of good database design, each event record will contain information about only one activity, honor, achievement, career advancement, personal event, or office held in the membership organization. Each record will allow the option to record start and end dates. Because of the wide range of personal information that may be appropriate, this is not conducive to using a lookup table to the options. If the description field is limited in length to 255 or fewer characters, a text field can be used and a query returning the distinct entries from this field can be used as the row source of a combo box. This also allows a new description to be added if none of the existing ones are satisfactory.

If the types of items needed for a given organization are limited, a foreign key and a lookup table for note type can be easily added to the database. You could model this after the earlier discussions of the Membership Type table to which the Member Information table refers as a simple structure, or the Person Category junction table, which allows a person to be included in more than a single category.

In the examples for this chapter, we will collect information about an individual in the table named tblPersonalNote, described in the following section.

The Personal Note Table

This table, named tblPersonalNote (shown in Figure 13-4), contains personal information about a person, accomplishments, civic or technical activities, and personal events.

The fields for tblPersonalNote are as follows:

PersonID is a Long Integer field that is used as a foreign key to tblPerson, identifying the person to which this note applies.

OrganizationRelated is a Long Integer field that is used as a foreign key to tblOrganization, if pertinent.

PersonalNoteDescription is a Text field that describes a civic or technical activity or honor, educational achievements, career advancements, or personal events. An Access Text field can contain a maximum of 255 characters; if that is not enough, replace it with a Memo field.

PersonalNoteDateStart is a Date/Time field that records the date if there is a single date or the start date if there is a date span.

PersonalNoteDateEnd is a Date/Time field that records the expiration or end date, if pertinent.

Field Name	Data Type	Description
PersonalNoteID	AutoNumber	Primary key, uniquely identifies this record
PersonID	Number	Foreign key to tblPerson, the person to which this applies
OrgID	Number	Foreign key to tblOrganization, use if related to an organization
PersonalNoteDescription	Text	Describes civic or technical activity or honor, educational
PersonalNoteDateStart	Date/Time	Date or start date
PersonalNoteDateEnd	Date/Time	Expiration or end date, if pertinent
LastUpdatedBy	Text	User who last updated this Record
LastUpdatedDate	Date/Time	Date/time when this record was last updated
PersonalNoteNotes	Text	Optional, unstructured comments or notes about this record

Figure 13-4: The Personal Note table

Offices and Elections

If the organization has officers or a governing board, that information is usually kept in a table related to the Member Information table described earlier. In cases where organizations are members, it would be related to the Person table, which in turn is related to the table of member organizations. If members' positions or offices held are covered in the Personal Notes table, it may not be necessary to keep other election information in the database, in which case you would not need the additional table.

Tables as Implemented in the Example Database

For simplicity of understanding and maintenance, the example database for this chapter contains an Office lookup or reference table, the Office table. It provides a list of the offices of the membership organization and related information. It also has a Term in Office table to record each chronological term of office and the member who filled the office.

The Office Table

This table, named tblOffice (shown in Figure 13-5), describes the offices that members may hold in the membership organization that is the subject of your database application. The fields for tblOffice are as follows:

OfficeName is a Text field that contains the name of the office (e.g., president, secretary, treasurer).

OfficeTerm is a Long Integer field that shows the number of months or years for the term of office (null or zero = unspecified or no limit).

OfficeCalendarPeriod is a Text field that indicates the time period unit of measure for the Long Integer in the previous field (m = months, y = years, null = unspecified or no limit).

OfficeChosenHow is a Long Integer field that is used to record the election/appointment method (1 = elected by members; 2 = elected by board; 3 = appointed).

OfficeAppointer is a Text field that holds the name of the office of the appointer, or "board," if indicated by the previous field.

Field Name	Data Type	Description
OfficeID	AutoNumber	Primary key, uniquely identifies this record
OfficeName	Text	Name of office (e.g., President, Secretary, Treasurer)
OfficeTerm	Number	Number of months or years, null or zero = unspecified or no limit
OfficeCalendarPeriod	Text	Abbbreviation: "m" = months, "y" = years, null = unspecified or no limit
OfficeChosenHow	Number	1=elected by members, 2 = elected by board, 3 = appointed
OfficeAppointer	Text	If appointed, the name of the office of the appointer, or "board"
LastUpdatedBy	Text	User who last updated this Record
LastUpdatedDate	Date/Time	Date/time when this record was last updated
OfficeNotes	Text	Optional, unstructured comments or notes about this record

Figure 13-5: The Office table

The Term in Office Table

This table, named tblTermInOffice (shown in Figure 13-6), indicates the person holding an office in the membership organization that is the subject of the database application, and the dates during which the member held that office. The fields for tblTermInOffice are as follows:

PersonID is a Long Integer field that is used as a foreign key to tblPerson.

OfficeID is a Long Integer field that is used as a foreign key to tblOffices.

StartDate is a Date/Time field that records the start date of the term in office. The end date will be calculated based on the start date and the established term for the office.

Field Name	Data Type	Description
TermInOfficeID	AutoNumber	Primary key, uniquely identifies this record
PersonID	Number	Foreign key to tblPerson
OfficeID	Number	Foreign key to tblOffices
StartDate	Date/Time	Start date of term of office
LastUpdatedBy	Text	User who last updated this Record
LastUpdatedDate	Date/Time	Date/time when this record was last updated
TermInOfficeNotes	Text	Optional, unstructured comments or notes about this record

Figure 13-6: The Term in Office table

Lookup Tables

Lookup tables enable a method of providing lists from which users can select. When there are very limited options that are not expected to change, they can be stored directly in the field using a value list. This is sometimes referred to as being *hard-coded*. Alternatively, for longer lists and lists that may change, you can use a lookup table. Information from lookup tables can be stored in a field by either saving the value itself, such as the name of an office, or by storing the foreign key value.

If there is only one place where the information is entered, and the value is a short one, the value list approach works well. If there is a possibility that the value may need to be selected from multiple places in the application's user interface, then having the information in a value list can lead to maintenance complications because there are limited options for updating the list.

For most situations, you will find it easier to use lookup tables. That still leaves you with the option of storing the value of the field, such as the name of an office, or the primary key value. The main determining factor is whether you want the data stored in the record to be automatically updated should the data in the lookup table change or whether you want the record to retain the original value regardless of future changes to the lookup table.

If you want the data in the record to be preserved, then you need to store the actual value in the lookup field. Alternatively, if you want changes in the lookup table to be reflected in the existing records, you need to store the primary key value of the lookup table in the Foreign Key field of the data record, so the tables will be joined and the value always retrieved from the lookup table.

Along with privacy (discussed in the section "Reporting Member Information" later in this chapter), lookup tables are defined for the type of membership (such as student, regular, family, emeritus, or honorary), which is recorded in the Membership Type table, shown below in Figure 14-10, and for the status of the member (deceased, prospect, active, or former), which is recorded in the Member Status table, shown below in Figure 14-11. Note that the lookup tables for Person Categories and Organization Categories are discussed in Chapter 4.

The Membership Type Table (a Lookup Table)

This table, named tblMembershipType (shown in Figure 13-7), will provide the list of options for selecting the membership type. The fields for tblMembership-Type are as follows: MembershipTypeDescription is a Text field describing the type of membership. Because you do not want to have two identical descriptions, this field is indexed with no duplicates. Because each value will be unique, this field is a natural key.

MembershipTypeLevel is a Long Integer field that is used as a level of membership or rank, if applicable.

tblMembershipType : Table

Field Name	Data Type	Description
MembershipTypeID	AutoNumber	Primary key, uniquely identifies this record
MembershipTypeDescription	Text	Initial Date of Membership
MembershipTypeLevel	Number	Level of membership or rank, if applicable
LastUpdatedBy	Text	User who last updated this Record
LastUpdatedDate	Date/Time	Date/time when this record was last updated
MembershipTypeNotes	Text	Optional, unstructured comments or notes about this record

Figure 13-7: The Membership Type table

The Member Status Table (a Lookup Table)

This table, named tblMemberStatus (shown in Figure 13-8), will provide the list of membership status options that a user may select. The fields for tblMemberStatus are as follows: StatusDescription is a Text field that describes the member's status. Because the field is indexed and allows no duplicates, it can also be used as natural key.

	Field Name	Data Type	Description
▢	MemberStatusID	AutoNumber	Primary key, uniquely identifies this record
	MemberStatusDescription	Text	Description of status, indexed no duplicates
	LastUpdatedBy	Text	User who last updated this Record
	LastUpdatedDate	Date/Time	Date/time when this record was last updated
	MemberStatusNotes	Text	Optional, unstructured comments or notes about this record

Figure 13-8: The Member Status table

Junction Tables

All of the junction tables used in the examples for membership management are the same as those described in the complex data model in Chapter 4 as listed in Table 13-1.

Documenting Memberships

Common documents for members include certificates of membership or membership cards. In an Access application, these can be produced as reports, with information obtained from the tables described in Chapter 4 in conjunction with tblMemberInfo, described in this chapter. If membership carries privileges such as qualification for a credit union or discounts from vendors, the membership database should make it easy to validate that the member is active and in good standing and meets any other criteria stipulated to qualify for the benefit. Information for these reports should be extracted with queries so you do not need to create additional tables for this purpose.

However, for faster processing and to preserve data as it was reported while also allowing updates to the underlying data in the database, some membership databases store a "snapshot" of the data until the next reporting period. You can create permanent tables in your database application for the purpose of storing those snapshots.

Reporting Member Information

Periodic reports about other members are almost always needed, whether they are printed on paper or previewed on screen. Member information is needed by the organization's board of directors, committees, and officers. Additionally, the organization may share some information about members to other members. Phone lists, address lists, interest areas, and volunteer lists may fall into this latter category. As with information for documenting memberships, the information for these reports should be extracted with queries. See the earlier discussion on storing a "snapshot" of data results.

For any release or publication of member information, you must be acutely aware of the need to respect members' privacy and to have an organizational privacy policy. Although there are statutes that apply to other subject areas, none are as widely known as those governing the privacy of medical information: the *Health Insurance Portability and Accountability Act of 1996 (HIPAA) Privacy Rule*. This is mandated by federal law, overseen by the U.S. Department of Health and Human Services, and enforced by the Office for Civil Rights.

According to the HHS website:

The Privacy Rule provides federal protections for personal health information held by covered entities and gives patients an array of rights with respect to that information. At the same time, the Privacy Rule is balanced so that it permits the disclosure of personal health information needed for patient care and other important purposes.

Don't rely just on your own interpretation. Get competent legal advice because penalties can be significant.

The Privacy Level Table

In addition to legal requirements governing privacy, it is considerate and polite for membership organizations to allow members to specify a level of privacy desired. The example database for this chapter includes a table for this purpose: the Privacy Level table. It has a one-to-many relationship with tblPerson. To facilitate implementation, the organization should decide on a default privacy level to be used, and it may even want a different default for prospective, former, and inactive members.

This table, named tblPrivacyLevel (shown in Figure 13-9) contains the privacy information. There is only one unique field for tblPrivacyLevel.

PrivacyLevelDescription is a Text field that describes the level of privacy desired by the member. This field is indexed with no duplicates. Therefore, it can also be considered to be a natural key.

Field Name	Data Type	Description
PrivacyLevelID	AutoNumber	Primary key, uniquely identifies this record
PrivacyLevelDescription	Text	Description, indexed no dupes
LastUpdatedBy	Text	User who last updated this Record
LastUpdatedDate	Date/Time	Date/time when this record was last updated
PrivacyLevelNotes	Text	Optional, unstructured comments or notes about this record

Figure 13-9: The Privacy Level table

Recording Expiration and Payments

Most modest-sized membership organizations that need to record membership payments will choose from one of two approaches. They will either maintain the financial data in a commercial accounting program or record the financial data within the membership database. But, even if you use a separate accounting program for the financial aspects, you will still want to have the member's expiration date in a table in the membership database. You may also choose to include additional financial information that will assist with analysis and planning.

If you plan to store all of the payment and membership date information in the membership database, you will typically need the following three tables: an Expiration Date table for determining which memberships need to be renewed and sending a reminder and two lookup tables, one for the Payment Source and the other for the Payment Type.

The Payment Table

This table, named tblPayment (shown in Figure 13-10), contains the record of payments and expiration dates of memberships. Although it may seem that expiration date could be calculated from date of renewal, some renewals may be done early or late, may be for a longer period, or the organization may offer extensions as a reward. The fields for tblExpirationDate are as follows:

PersonID is a Long Integer field that is used as a foreign key to tblPerson or tblMemberInfo.

PaymentAmount is a Currency field containing the amount of the dues payment.

PaymentDate is a Date/Time field that records the date this payment was made.

A multi-field index with no duplicates allowed is defined for the table, including PersonID and DateOfPayment to prevent the same relationship being inadvertently stored multiple times.

PaymentExpirationDate is a Date/Time field that contains the date this paid membership expires.

SourceID is a Long Integer field that is used as a lookup key to tblSource.

PaymentTypeID is a Long Integer field that is used as a lookup key to tblPaymentType.

Field Name	Data Type	Description
PaymentID	AutoNumber	Primary key, uniquely identifies this record
PersonID	Number	Foreign key to tblPerson or tblMemberInfo (related one-to-one, thus have the same key)
PaymentAmount	Currency	Amount of the dues payment
PaymentDate	Date/Time	Date this payment was made
PaymentExpirationDate	Date/Time	Date this paid membership expires
PaymentSourceID	Number	Foreign key to tblSource
PaymentTypeID	Number	Foreign key to tblPaymentType
LastUpdatedBy	Text	User who last updated this Record
LastUpdatedDate	Date/Time	Date/time when this record was last updated
PaymentNotes	Text	Optional, unstructured comments or notes about this record

Figure 13-10: The Payment table

The Payment Source Table

This table, named tblPaymentSource (shown in Figure 13-11), records the source of the payment. The field for tblPaymentSource is:

PaymentSourceDescription is a Text field that contains the name of a single source, e.g., website, meeting, postal mail.

Field Name	Data Type	Description
PaymentSourceID	AutoNumber	Primary key, uniquely identifies this record
PaymentSourceDescription	Text	Name of a single source, e.g, website, meeting, postal mail
LastUpdatedBy	Text	User who last updated this Record
LastUpdatedDate	Date/Time	Date/time when this record was last updated
PaymentSourceNotes	Text	Optional, unstructured comments or notes about this record

Figure 13-11: The Payment Source table

The Payment Type Table

This table, named tblPaymentType (shown in Figure 13-12), records the type of payment. The field for tblPaymentType is:

PaymentType is a Text field that describes the type of payment; for example, cash, check, PayPal.

Field Name	Data Type	Description
PaymentTypeID	AutoNumber	Primary key, uniquely identifies this record
PaymentType	Text	Description of the type of payment, e.g., cash, check, PayPal
LastUpdatedBy	Text	User who last updated this Record
LastUpdatedDate	Date/Time	Date/time when this record was last updated
PaymentTypeNotes	Text	Optional, unstructured comments or notes about this record

Figure 13-12: The Payment Type table

Information from these tables can be combined with the other membership data to create reports needed by officers, sponsors, the members themselves and outside entities. Content commonly found in detail reports includes the member's identification number/code, contact information, and expiration and renewal dates. Depending on the purpose, the reports may also include the office or position within the membership organization and other pertinent information.

Summary reports to the organization's directors and officers might provide statistics on things such as the number of current members or the number of memberships expiring this period. You could also review trends or evaluate the effectiveness of a membership drive by looking at the number of renewals and number of new members over a given period of time. As mentioned, the specific financial information may be kept separately in a commercial accounting software package, but it could be included in a custom database application.

You can also generate data as required for reports to governmental entities to maintain the nonprofit status of an organization. The requirements vary according to jurisdiction but might include membership summary, attendance at meetings, and information to show that the organization is fulfilling the purpose for which it was chartered.

Communication

A membership organization will, on occasion, need to communicate with its current members, former members, and potential members about such matters as meetings, renewals, elections, and so on. These communications may be sent electronically by e-mail or by mailing a hard copy. Often the same information will be posted on an organization's website, but that is usually just an additional source for the information, rather than a substitute for sending individual notices. Our discussion and model address tracking data related to individual communications rather than published notices.

Keep in mind that electronic methods of dissemination rely upon the member visiting the website or accessing e-mail (the member must come to the information), whereas the postal service does not rely on any actions or special attention on the part of the member—other than to pick up and read the message. Of course, mailings can be significantly more expensive in terms of both time and money.

- **E-mail communication:** You can handle e-mail communication in multiple ways. A common approach is to use COM-compliant mail software to create and send the e-mail under control of your Access database application. This can create impressive e-mail messages, individually addressed and individually "tailored" to contain the addressee's own information. It is likely to take more time and effort than other approaches. At the other end of the spectrum, you can simply export or use VBA code to write a text file of addresses, and then manually copy that file into the BCC line of an e-mail. Depending on your e-mail client, the message itself may be impressive or rather plain. If your Internet Service Provider limits the number of e-mails that you can send, you may also need to use batches.

- **Letter or memo communication:** These can be created and sent by using Access to control Microsoft Word or other COM-compliant word processing software to print individualized letters, along with either envelopes or mailing labels. However, it is usually just as effective, and easier to implement, if you create a "mail-merge" list in a file, and use it with Microsoft Word or other word processing software to create the individual letter or memo communications. Another way, much simpler and easier to develop if you do not need extensive formatting, is to print the letters as pages of an Access report. Alternatively, you can print each copy as a separate report, print as an Adobe Acrobat portable document format (.pdf) file, and e-mail that. Printing the letters as pages of one large report won't work with .pdf because you cannot mail .pdf pages separately.

  Envelopes can usually be printed directly from Access Reports, or these too can be created with a mail-merge list in Word. To save the extra work of printing the addresses on envelopes, you can carefully place the address information in either an Access Report or a Word document so that it can be folded to show in a window envelope. The latter approach also avoids the possibility of mismatching the letter and envelope if they are printed separately.

- **Communicating activities:** The range of activities for membership organizations is broad, depending on the organization's interest. Many such organizations have regular or occasional meetings and "projects" or activities for which invitations, reminders, records, reports, and notices may be required. You might handle this by posting information to a website, sending an e-mail to all or a pertinent subset of members, sending postal mailings to some or all members, or a combination of the above. If preparatory work is needed for an activity, similar communication may be required to and from the members or officers involved which may be treated as a separate activity.

  To prepare the communication, you will use a table about activities and the associated information. This table defines the activities but is not directly related to a person in the membership tables. Because at least some of the activities may have relationships to many members, and many members to the activities, you may need to have an *Activity-Member* junction table to support the many-to-many nature of the relationship.

Other activities may be for "all hands" which are the easiest to deal with. An activity is, in fact, a form of simple event and in our scenario it requires less documentation. In the example database for this chapter, activities will be kept in the Event tables, described and pictured below. If you have activities that require additional, separate planning, tracking, and other functions, you can use the model provided in the next section, "Events."

■ **Communication record:** In general, membership databases are not used to track individual correspondence. Tables are included in some other functions described in this chapter for a similar purpose. The Event Documents table for keeping a record and a link or file address to allow viewing external documents in various file formats: text processing, portable print formats, etc. The Sponsor Contact table is for tracking contacts with prospective and active sponsors with links to or information about a particular contact.

Communication and events use the same schema, shown in Figure 13-13.

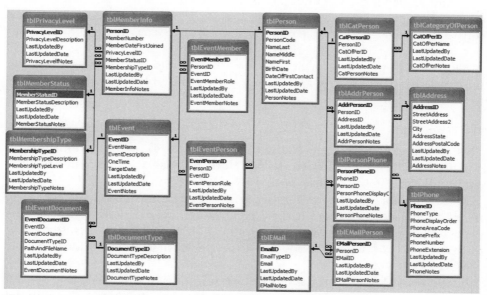

Figure 13-13: Relationships of the Communication and Event tables

Some of the tables shown in this schema have other relationships that are not shown here because they are included in schemas for other functions discussed in this chapter.

Events

"Events" discussed in this section are "happenings" outside the normal meetings or normal, regularly scheduled activities of the membership organization.

This database application does not attempt to cover all facets of a membership organization, and the normal schedule of "things" is not included. Such events typically are handled as special projects, requiring planning, staffing, contracts for facilities and services, registration, and after-the-event analysis and follow-up. This differs somewhat from regular meetings and activities because those tend to be the same each time (whatever the time interval). They are held most often with the same designated staff and, therefore, require less tracking of what is planned and done.

As with several other topics, basic tables for holding data on individuals and organizations involved are as described in Chapter 4 with additional tables.

Planning Events

When an event is suggested, accepted, and you have reached the planning stage, it is time to enter the event into the database and start documenting information on the planning activities. Details may be recorded in the table, but you will typically also use hyperlinks or file references to external documents created with word processing, project management, spreadsheet, or other software. Access provides a more-or-less simple way to display external documents using a hyperlink field.

Because a single event or activity may have multiple documents, the file references are kept in a separate Event Document table related one-to-many to the Event table.

The Event Table

This table, named tblEvent (shown in Figure 13-14), contains information about events. This table does double duty because we use it in both the communication and the event business functions.

In conjunction with communication, the events are associated with the member and we used them to send congratulations or greetings for various events. As you'll recall, communications had both recurring events, such as birthdays and anniversaries, and one-time events, such as educational or civic achievements.

In the event business function, we are referring to the event as a special happening or occasion. In this perspective, a one-time event might be a special gathering of members, a prominent speaker, or recruiting at a public event.

Our model is not specifically designed to manage recurring events in the literal sense because that would require additional tables in a one-to-many relationship. However, there are a couple of approaches where you might consider using the provided tables to record quasi-recurring events:

- You could incorporate a unique identifier such as the year into the name of the event, allowing you to retain all related data for each event occurrence.

- If you don't need to retain all the related data, you could merely change the event date each time the event occurred.

Whatever your needs, you can take advantage of the OneTime event field and the event date in conjunction with the event name to help with grouping, reporting, and comparing events. The fields for tblEvent are as follows:

EventName is a Text field that holds the name of the event.

EventDescription is a Memo field that may contain a long description.

OneTime is a Yes/No (Boolean) field that indicates whether this is a one-time event. The meaning of the values are as follows:

- Yes indicates a one-time event such as receiving a civic honor if used in the communication business function, or a one-time event such as holding a training session if used in the event business function.

- No indicates a repeating or recurring event such as an anniversary or birthday or the annual company Independence Day picnic.

TargetDate is a Date/Time field that records the designated date for the event. As mentioned earlier, if this is a recurring event, you will need to change the date when preparing for the event.

Field Name	Data Type	Description
EventID	AutoNumber	Primary key, uniquely identifies this record
EventName	Text	Name of Event, indexed no dupes, a natural key
EventDescription	Memo	Long or detailed description of event
OneTime	Yes/No	Yes = one-time event; No = scheduled event
TargetDate	Date/Time	For one-time event (optionally, next date for recurring)
LastUpdatedBy	Text	User who last updated this Record
LastUpdatedDate	Date/Time	Date/time when this record was last updated
EventNotes	Text	Optional, unstructured comments or notes about this record

Figure 13-14: The Event table

The Event Document Table

This table, named tblEventDocument (shown in Figure 13-15), records references to electronic documents about an event. The fields for tblEventDocument are as follows:

EventID is a Long Integer field that is used as a foreign key to the Event table to identify the event with which the document is associated.

EventDocName is a Text field that contains the name or brief description of a document.

DocumentTypeID is a Long Integer field that is used as a lookup key to the Document Type table.

PathAndFileName is a Text field that is includes the complete path and filename of a document; for example, `C:\OrgName\Events\Summit\Invite2010`.

	Field Name	Data Type	Description
🔑	EventDocumentID	AutoNumber	Primary key, uniquely identifies this record
	EventID	Number	Foreign key to tblEvent
	EventDocName	Text	Name or brief description of document
	DocumentTypeID	Number	Foreign key to tblDocumentType
	PathAndFileName	Text	Fully-qualified path and filename of document stored online
	LastUpdatedBy	Text	User who last updated this Record
	LastUpdatedDate	Date/Time	Date/time when this record was last updated
	EventDocumentNotes	Text	Optional, unstructured comments or notes about this record

tblEventDocument : Table

Figure 13-15: The Event Document table

Schedule and Tasks

Early in the planning for a project, a schedule will be determined. This may be tentative to allow for options or firmer if the event must coordinate with some other event, such as a holiday, spring break, school terms, and so on. If external scheduling software is used to record and modify the schedule, this can be handled with hyperlinks or file references. For the purpose of this discussion, we will assume that schedule information will be kept in our membership database application in a Task for Event table.

The Task for Event Table

This table, named tblTaskforEvent (shown in Figure 13-16), records the tasks necessary to execute an event. The fields for tblTaskForEvent are as follows:

EventID is a Long Integer field that is used as a foreign key to tblActivity.

TaskName is a Text field that contains the name or brief description of an activity.

PlannedDate is a Date/Time field that records the date when the activity is to be performed.

ActualDate is a Date/Time field that records the date the activity was actually completed.

Information is a Memo field that contains additional detail information about the task.

	Field Name	Data Type	Description
	TaskID	AutoNumber	Primary key, uniquely identifies this record
	EventID	Number	Foreign key to tblEvent
	TaskName	Text	Name or brief description of task
	PlannedDate	Date/Time	Date the task is or was due
	ActualDate	Date/Time	Date the task was actually completed
	Information	Memo	Additional detail information about the task
	LastUpdatedBy	Text	User who last updated this Record
	LastUpdatedDate	Date/Time	Date/time when this record was last updated
	TaskNotes	Text	Optional, unstructured comments or notes about this record

tblTaskForEvent : Table

Figure 13-16: The Task for Event table

Event Staff

Information about the individuals who will serve on event staff can be kept in the People table, such as the one used in Chapter 4. In that case you would need to add a separate table containing event-specific information. Since you will often have the same people working on different events, the two tables will be joined in a many-to-many relationship using a junction, or intersection, table named tblEventMemberJunction.

In addition to identifying the event and the member, this table includes the role or position of the member in the event. In that case, you may have multiple entries for one member. For example, one person could serve as a planner of the event, a registration clerk, and a speaker. The same person could be involved with more than one event.

The Event-Member Table (a Junction Table)

This table, named tblEventMember (shown in Figure 13-17), links members and the events with which they are associated. The fields for tblEventMember are as follows:

EventID is a Long Integer field that is used as a foreign key to tblEvent.

MemberID is a Long Integer field that is used as a foreign key to tblMember.

EventMemberRole is a Text field that describes the role or position of the member in regard to this event or activity. If you have identical roles that you are using time after time, this is a candidate you should consider for linking to a lookup table.

Create on the table a multi-field index using EventID, MemberID, and EventMemberRole, with no duplicates, to prevent the same relationship from being recorded more than once in this table.

tblEventMember : Table

Field Name	Data Type	Description
EventMemberID	AutoNumber	Primary key, uniquely identifies this record
PersonID	Number	Foreign key to tblMemberInfo
EventID	Number	Foreign key to tblEvent
EventMemberRole	Text	Role or position of member in re: this event or activity
LastUpdatedBy	Text	User who last updated this Record
LastUpdatedDate	Date/Time	Date/time when this record was last updated
EventMemberNotes	Text	Optional, unstructured comments or notes about this record

Figure 13-17: The Event-Member table

Contracts and Contacts

If contracts for facilities or services are required, they can be summarized in a separate table or they can be linked from the event table to external files. Unless the organization's events are very repetitive in nature, it would make little sense to create a table for detailed information on such contracts. In our example database, the links to contracts will be entries in tblEventDocument, shown earlier.

Conversely, you need to keep track of numerous contacts for each event. Since you already have tables for the event and for people associated with your organization, you only need to create a relationship between the two tables. As in previous examples, this requires a junction table.

The junction table between the Events table and the Person table, will contain a foreign key from each table. It might also contain information about the role a nonmember has in the event, dates and times of involvement, and other pertinent information. This differs from the Event Member junction table, in that the nonmember person's information will be found in the Person table, not in the Member Info table. In the example database for this chapter this table is the Event-Person table.

The Event-Person Table (a Junction Table)

This table, named tblEventPerson (shown in Figure 13-18), associates a person with an event. A person can be associated with multiple events, and an event can be associated with multiple people. This table can record the association of nonmembers as well as members. The fields for tblEventPerson are as follows:

PersonID is a Long Integer field that is used as a foreign key to tblPerson.

EventID is a Long Integer field that is used as a foreign key to tblEvent.

EventPersonRole is a Text field that records the role or position of the member in regard to this event or activity. If you have identical roles that you are using time after time, this is a candidate you should consider for linking to a lookup table.

Define a multi-field index with no duplicates allowed on the table, including PersonID, EventID, and EventPersonRole to prevent the same relationship being inadvertently stored multiple times.

Field Name	Data Type	Description
EventPersonID	AutoNumber	Primary key, uniquely identifies this record
PersonID	Number	Foreign key to tblPeople
EventID	Number	Foreign key to tblEvent
EventPersonRole	Text	Role or position of member in re: this event or activity
LastUpdatedBy	Text	User who last updated this Record
LastUpdatedDate	Date/Time	Date/time when this record was last updated
EventPersonNotes	Text	Optional, unstructured comments or notes about this record

tblEventPerson : Table

Figure 13-18: The Event-Person table

Event Execution and Follow-up

You may have several other business functions associated with the execution of and follow-up to your events. Your current list of tables and fields may contain all of the data you need to track and follow up on these additional tasks. If not, you can incorporate new fields and tables to meet your needs.

The following list discusses some of the areas that you may want to consider for events. For the most part, you will already have the necessary data. Additional tables and fields are noted where they may be needed.

- **Documenting event preparations:** It is useful to track actual execution of the planning activities, meetings, and other features of the event, including the people who are serving as event staff. By using the appropriate junction tables to join existing tables, you will likely be able to track all of the necessary data, but that will depend on the specific details associated with the various kinds of events that you hold, as well as their tracking requirements. For example, meetings, lunches, committee meetings, and other gatherings often record attendance. Table tblEventTask shown earlier is an appropriate place to record planned activities and their completion. If this event is large or has a multitude of tasks, you should investigate whether one of the project management software packages would be a better choice. Two such commercial software packages are Microsoft Project and Oracle's Primavera.

- **Preregistration:** Events often require that attendees be registered and identified. They may also invoice, receipt, and record payments. In order to make certain that planned attendance will be sufficient to warrant holding the event, you may require preregistration. Some organizations offer a discount for early preregistration.

  Attendee registration will be recorded in a table whose details, again, depend on the nature of the event. This table, or the junction tables to which it is joined, will have foreign keys to other tables in the membership database.

  Before the event, you may wish to prepare personalized identification for attendees. Alternatively, with today's improved (faster, more flexible) printer hardware, you may decide to create a badge when the attendee checks in. Because of the differing requirements and types of events, our example does not include a separate table for preregistration data. Instead, we are providing a more streamlined scenario that uses the role of "preregistered" in tblEventMember or tblEventPerson.

- **Registration:** As attendees arrive, you will want to check them in to record their appearance. This uses the same tables described for preregistration. Even if the event was fully booked, there may be no-shows, so you may need a way to add registrants on-site. The new people can be registered and their appearance recorded at the same time. For our purposes, this would be accomplished by having a role of "registered" in tblEventMemberJunction or tblEventContactJunction. For some purposes, such as required continuing education, attendees must stay for the entire event, so attendance would have to be checked again, on exiting. One way to encourage this, often used at software product launches or presentations where an evaluation sheet is required, is to have some kind of prize or giveaway which isn't made available until the attendees are exiting.

- **Post-event analysis and follow-up:** Organizations that successfully host events use the records generated before and during the event to report, chart, and analyze the outcome. They can then use this information to improve the process for future events. The criteria for success must be defined by those responsible, but they can utilize the information captured in the previously described topics on events.

When the data has been collected and organized, it can be presented in charts and reports. From this "initial" data analysis, you may determine that additional detailed analysis is required, for which data can be exported into one of many formats (interoperability is one of Access' traditional strong points) for analysis by other programs such as Microsoft Excel. Even if you do not normally use a server database as the "back end" to store your data, you might want to export event data to Microsoft SQL Server tables in order to take advantage of SQL Server's extensive analytical capabilities.

You will use queries to extract attendance, registration, schedule, and other information from your existing tables. The data can then be exported to the analytical software of your choice. If "events" are the primary purpose of your database, it is likely that some analysis features are included. If so, the results can easily be converted to Access Reports. Alternatively, you can create custom reports in Access. No separate tables are necessarily required for post-event analysis and follow-up.

Recruiting

Most membership organizations must also recruit new members. An old adage states that any organization is either growing or dying. These functions can be combined with the membership database, which, as we've discussed, will already have "infrastructure" that is useful—communication, recordkeeping, and reporting. The benefit of combining membership and recruiting functions is that maintenance and enhancements to the infrastructure components will only need to be done once.

Even so, some organizations prefer to keep the operations and data separately, transferring information when a prospective new member actually joins. Assuming, as we do here, that the recruiting operation is large enough to benefit from automation, the infrastructure is often copied from the membership database to reduce time and effort. Figure 13-19 shows the relationship diagram illustrating the schema of recruiting functions.

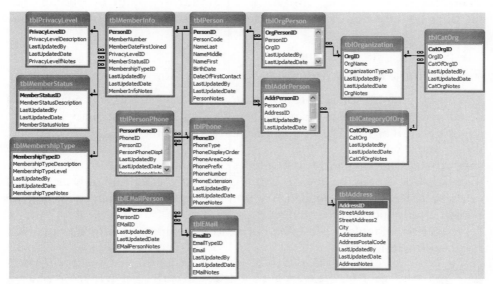

Figure 13-19: Relationships of the Recruiting Functions tables

Getting New Members

There are many ways to obtain "leads" for prospective members, such as referrals, website inquiries, newspaper and radio advertising, and others. The options and details are beyond our scope here, but once the leads are obtained, there are two major factors you need to consider: where to keep the list of prospective members and how to follow up and contact the prospects.

NOTE For our discussion, we will assume the list of prospects is going to be kept in the Person table of the Membership database. We'll accomplish this by adding "Prospect" as a member type.

There are several options for tracking follow-up contact with the prospects. For even the simplest of these, you need a list or report of the prospects that includes their contact information. Since we are using Prospect as a member type, it will be an easy matter to use this as a criteria in a query to extract a list of prospects. In fact, you might even be able to make a copy of some previous query that had different criteria and modify it for your current needs.

Once you've saved the new query, you can also use it as the data source for a mailing list to use with a mail merge operation.

Another good idea is to send meeting notices and other promotional material to prospective members. If you are sending the material as an enticement, you should also consider which material to send and over what period of time. It is the role of the organization's leadership to determine whether extending "free" mailings provides an incentive to join or perhaps has the opposite effect of encouraging people to prolong their "free of charge" benefits.

Re-recruiting Former Members

The opportunity to contact previous members is one strong argument for not deleting records for members who become inactive. By using our approach to flag the record as inactive, you still have their most recently reported contact information which may or may not still be current. Therefore, it is relatively easy to send an invitation and attempt to persuade them to renew their memberships. Again the infrastructure will already exist, and only additional selection criteria will be needed. You can also maintain the historical links to related information in other tables.

No additional tables need to be introduced to support the former member re-recruiting functions.

NOTE It is a good idea to mark but not delete members, not even those who are deceased. The time may well come when your historian, your members, or you would like to have a history of your group.

Sponsorships

Many organizations would find it difficult to continue to exist and operate at the level they have attained without sponsors who donate funds, material, or services. And, of course, the weight of a sponsor's name can influence other potential sponsors and prospective members. Keeping information about prospective and former sponsors as well as active sponsors in the database is far better than keeping the traditional file of physical business cards or the formerly ubiquitous Rolodex. Just as you can try to re-recruit former members, you can try to re-interest former sponsors into becoming active again. It may also be of historical interest who were sponsors in the past.

Given the benefits of working with sponsors, we will incorporate the sponsorship functions into our existing database. Figure 13-20 shows the two new tables as tblSponsorContacts and tblSponsorInfo.

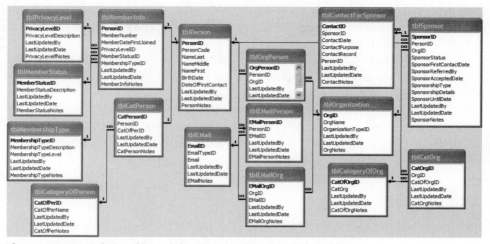

Figure 13-20: Relationships of the Sponsorship Functions tables

You may want to consider the benefit of having different types of information based on whether you are contacting a prospective sponsor or an active sponsor. The following discussion may prompt you to think of other factors that are important to the interactions with your sponsors. Two types of sponsor that you will surely need are:

- **Prospective sponsors:** Although your purpose in contacting prospective sponsors is different from your reasons for contacting prospective members, they use the same methods and approach with respect to the database. Therefore, you already have the infrastructure as part of the membership database. Can you see a pattern developing here? You need to capture additional data to indicate the type of sponsorship being sought, status of discussions, and the results. The type of information needed will vary based on your organization, the sponsor, and the type of sponsorship provided.

- **Active sponsors:** Keeping in touch with your sponsors is typically of key importance. Although the method of contact and the content that you send to sponsors may differ, you can use the information in the database to create personalized mailings.

  You also need to track the results of contacting sponsors. For example, are they going to donate an item, sponsor an event, provide facilities, or make other in-kind donations? The results data for sponsors who have agreed to assist can be kept in the same tables as the similar data used in the process of obtaining sponsorship.

Simply by including an Inactive field in the Sponsor records, you can accommodate former sponsor information. You may have an opportunity to work with them in the future.

A limitation here is that our structure will support only one person or organization for a sponsor record. That is by far the most common case in the real world. Should two sources of sponsorship be identified in one organization, they are likely somewhat different types or subjects of sponsorship, and would need to be entered as separate sponsors. Since our model will work well for the majority of cases, we will stay with a basic design and avoid unnecessary complications to the design of tables and the user interface.

The Sponsor Table

This table, named tblSponsor (shown in Figure 13-21), holds information about prospective, active or former sponsors. The fields for tblSponsor are:

- PersonID is a Long Integer field, used as a foreign key to the Person table, if a person is the sponsor.
- OrgID is a Long Integer field, used as a foreign key to the Organization table, if an organization is the sponsor.

Only one of the PersonID and OrgID fields may contain a non-zero value. We recognize that this is not a preferred table configuration and that it requires special handling when the application or user interface is designed. However, database development, like many other areas of business, requires tradeoffs and practical resolutions. This type of "either or" table configuration is not uncommon. In fact, you will see it in several examples in this book. We have provided two approaches to resolving relationship triangles in Appendix C.

SponsorStatus is a Text field that denotes that the prospect is active or has some other status, as needed. Alternatively, if you have many status values that are used repetitively, this would be a candidate to be implemented as a lookup table.

SponsorFirstContactDate is a Date/Time field that records the date of first contact with the sponsor or potential sponsor.

SponsorReferredBy is an optional Text field that identifies who referred this sponsor or candidate.

SponsorAcceptedDate is a Date/Time field that records the date this sponsor accepted the sponsorship and agreed to any terms and conditions associated with being a sponsor.

SponsorshipType is a Text field that provides a brief text description of the type of sponsor. Alternatively, if you have many sponsorship type values that are used repetitively, this would be a candidate to be implemented as a lookup table.

SponsorshipDetails is a Memo field that records details about the sponsorship, if needed to further describe the sponsorship agreement. In this area especially, it pays to be flexible.

SponsorUntilDate is a Date/Time field that indicates the term of sponsorship to which the sponsor agreed.

Field Name	Data Type	Description
SponsorID	AutoNumber	Primary key, uniquely identifies this record
PersonID	Number	Foreign key to tblPerson, if a person is the sponsor
OrgID	Number	Foreign key to tblOrganization, if an organization is the sponsor
SponsorStatus	Text	Prospect, active, or other as needed
SponsorFirstContactDate	Date/Time	Date of first contact
SponsorReferredBy	Text	Who referred this sponsor or candidate, optional
SponsorAcceptedDate	Date/Time	Date this sponsor accepted
SponsorshipType	Text	Brief text, type of sponsor
SponsorshipDetails	Memo	Details, if needed to be flexible
SponsorUntilDate	Date/Time	Term of sponsorship
LastUpdatedBy	Text	User who last updated this Record
LastUpdatedDate	Date/Time	Date/time when this record was last updated
SponsorNotes	Text	Optional, unstructured comments or notes about this record

Figure 13-21: The Sponsor table

The Contact for Sponsor Table

This table, named tblContactForSponsor (shown in Figure 13-22), enables you to keep a record of your contacts with both prospective and active sponsors, the subject, and the outcome of the contact. It is not a list of individuals who can be contacted for this sponsor. The fields for tblContactForSponsor are as follows:

SponsorID is a Long Integer field that is used as a foreign key to tblSponsor to identify the sponsor whose contact information is in this record.

ContactDate is a Date/Time field contains the date (and perhaps the time) the sponsor was contacted.

ContactPurpose is a Text field that briefly describes the purpose of this contact.

ContactRecord is a Memo field that records what was discussed and agreed upon.

PersonID is a Long Integer field that is used as a foreign key to tblPerson to identify the person who was contacted.

Field Name	Data Type	Description
ContactID	AutoNumber	Primary key, uniquely identifies this record
SponsorID	Number	Foreign key to tblSponsor
ContactDate	Date/Time	Date when contacted
ContactPurpose	Text	Brief description of why this contact
ContactRecord	Memo	What was discussed or agreed
PersonID	Number	Foreign key to tblPerson -- person who was contacted
LastUpdatedBy	Text	User who last updated this Record
LastUpdatedDate	Date/Time	Date/time when this record was last updated
ContactNotes	Text	Optional, unstructured comments or notes about this record

Figure 13-22: The Contacts for Sponsor table

Small Membership Organizations

It is difficult to draw a sharp distinction between membership organizations that might be considered "small," which we have not emphasized in this chapter, and "modest," which we took as the lower limit. You can make your own decision about what database application functionality will work best for you. Your organization may benefit from some of the approaches laid out earlier even though you think it has few members. And some larger organizations may find that their needs are well served by our model because it is simpler, more specific to their needs, and easier to customize than many commercial options.

If you call your organization a "team," a "committee," or a "club," it may fall into a category in which there are more specific needs that can be addressed by a simpler model with fewer options and complications. In that case, you might want to incorporate some of the tables and options from our model.

If you have a limited number of members and they are all people, rather than organizations, and you don't have a great need for employer information, or for background and history information on the members, then you might be able to use a simplified data structure.

In that case, you could refer to Chapter 4 and start with the Person table. Rename it as tblMemberInfo and add a single field for Employer (if that serves your purposes). You would also include fields for limited, single-option contact information, such as a physical address. Add any other pertinent fields that we haven't addressed elsewhere in this chapter but that you find useful. Keep in mind that it is desirable to follow relational database design principles when you add tables or fields.

It seems prudent to allow for multiple options for payments, member types, and phone numbers, so you will probably want to have a Phones table and a Phone Type table. If you collect dues, you may well want to have a one-to-many related Payment table showing the date paid and the time period covered (including or implying an expiration date). If you simplify matters by having annual memberships all due on the same date, you can have a very simple Table of Payments. If you have only one "class" of member, you may not need any Membership Type information to determine how much to charge for dues.

Most such clubs have officers, so it is often helpful to have an Office table and a Term in Office table.

In a team or committee environment you might have more frequent individual communication with members and require a communication record showing the date and type of contact, subject, conclusions, and/or links to external documents.

Depending on the scenario, you may benefit from having a schedule of meetings particularly if you don't have a regular, permanent meeting place, giving the date and time, address, host/hostess, speaker, and subject. As an adjunct, you may keep a record of attendance in a table with foreign keys to the Member table.

If you have door prizes, you may wish to have a Prize table with a record of prizes related to meetings with a description and a field to record the winner. Add a Meeting Agenda table, with some additional fields, and you may be able to replace your secretary's text or word processor files of meeting "minutes." In this environment, other organization-specific information can also be included by adding a field to record whatever is useful to you in your organization in your circumstances.

WARNING Bear in mind that not all members may have access to the database, so don't design your database to store data that would require you to give all members access unless that is desirable.

Summary

This chapter discussed aspects of managing memberships and membership organizations. Common functions include adding and renewing memberships, keeping track of past, current, and prospective members, and recording information about offices, office holders, and officers and elections. We also discussed various reports you can create using the information you gather.

You will likely want to communicate with members and others through e-mail and postal letters or memos about activities. We explained how to create the tables to support communications with members, prospects, and sponsors. You learned how to create the tables to support recruitment drives for the purpose of signing up new members or re-recruiting former members. And you saw how the same table structure can be used to support membership, recruiting, and sponsors. After all, you may need to obtain new sponsorships and maintain relations with current sponsors.

And, of course, you will likely be planning events which may entail scheduling event activities, event staff, event contracts, event contacts, executing events, pre-registration, registration, and post-event analysis and follow-up.

Therefore, you looked at the tables that you would use to incorporate event planning into your database.

The basic information for a membership organization's database will be about people and organizations, a subject covered in detail in Chapter 4. Reviewing that chapter will give you some additional insights and perspectives for creating your membership database.

As described in the definition of membership organizations, you can also have commercial membership organizations such as discounting, members-only sales, and lending libraries. Chapter 7, "Sales," provides additional functions and information that will be useful in a database for that type of organization. For additional ideas on recruiting members and sponsors, see Chapter 6, "Marketing." Finally, it is worth mentioning that members are the customers of a membership organization, so a review of Chapter 5 will also be worthwhile.

Membership application, renewal, update, and maintenance can also be accomplished using a web-based application for access to data, both by the members and by the organization's administration. The administrators may access the application via the Internet or via an Access database on a local area network (LAN). Although some of the tables that we've designed here may be suitable for some forms of web-based distribution, they are not specifically designed with that in mind. If you are working towards a web-based scenario, you might consider a server database solution that can be accessed from an appropriate website or web application. Microsoft products that you might consider are Microsoft's SQL Server, Expression Studio, SharePoint, and Visual Studio.

CHAPTER 14

Implementing the Models

This chapter combines models from three other chapters to illustrate how easy it is to design and implement a powerful database. Earlier chapters walked you through several approaches to creating the necessary tables and fields; this chapter builds on that experience. We briefly describe the business model to be addressed and provide the required tables. Then we move directly into discussing the user interface by showing you how to create some basic forms and reports, and the queries that they rely on.

We'll show you, step by step, how to create a functional application, including multiple ways to accomplish the same results. As with most areas of database development, there is more than one way to achieve the desired outcome. We will show you the easy way to create database objects using built-in wizards, and we'll also demonstrate how to build objects from scratch.

Our sample application is based on a fictitious not-for-profit organization (NFP), the National Spreadsheet Developers Support Group (NSDSG). It has dues-paying members and donors, and sells specialty merchandise to produce revenue. This organization is staffed by volunteers, and most supplies and operating expenses are donated or purchased using the money from dues.

The organization intends to track the membership and the donors by maintaining mailing addresses, e-mail addresses, and phone numbers for every customer, member, and donor. They must also bill members for annual dues and record the payments. Donations must be tracked by type of fundraiser; and the donors must be identified with each fundraiser in order to maximize future fundraising efforts.

Not-for-Profit Organizations

There are many NFP organizations around the world. Some are large, well-funded, multinational organizations, but most are small, local, and operating with limited budgets. Usually NFP's have some form of tax exempt status.

In the United States most NFP organizations are 501(c)(3) organizations. 501(c)(3) organizations are exempt from paying most taxes and can receive donations that are deductible as itemized deductions on the donor's income tax return.

In smaller volunteer organizations it is possible to pass the donated funds directly to the intended beneficiaries of the organization without deducting administrative costs. However, the major NFPs usually operate at anywhere from 60% to 85% margins. Labor costs, office expenses, and advertising expenses are the bulk of the administrative costs. Our focus is on the smaller organizations.

Tracking Membership

The NSDSG has asked for assistance in creating a database to make it easier to run the organization. The members are the backbone of this organization. The members support NSDSG by providing the labor necessary to run the fundraisers and collect the donations. They also pay dues or membership fees in order to maintain their membership. The organization uses dues exclusively for general operating expenses such as rent, utilities, office supplies, and mileage and travel reimbursement for the members.

Membership Types

There are three types of members, Active, Inactive, and Life. Active members pay the full annual dues amount and are expected to assist with the fundraising efforts of the NSDSG. Inactive members pay reduced dues and are not required to help at the events of the organization. Life members are exempt from paying dues and may participate at events if they desire.

Dues Collection

Dues for existing members are payable on an annual basis. They are set by a majority vote of the organization and can be changed for the next calendar year any time prior to October 1st of each year.

Currently, the dues for active members are $120 per year; dues for inactive members are reduced by 50 percent, to $60. Dues for new members are prorated on a monthly basis from the date of membership to the annual renewal date. No refunds of dues are given when a member withdraws from the organization.

Billing

Dues notices are sent on, or near, October 1st of each year. Each member is billed according to his or her membership status at the time notices are prepared. The notice is sent via US mail with a return envelope.

The process for billing the dues will create an entry for each member and record the date posted, the member's ID, and the amount due from the member.

Receipt of Payment

Members mail payments to the secretary/treasurer of NSDSG. Upon receipt, the secretary/treasurer records payments and deposits the checks and cash in the organization's checking account. Credit card transactions are processed through the bank.

When posting the payments, the secretary/treasurer creates a record for each payment, showing the date the payment was received, the member's ID number, the amount received, and optional information about the payment such as check number, cash, credit card, and so on.

Member Information

The contact information for each member and donor needs to be recorded in the database. Physical and mailing addresses, e-mail addresses, and phone numbers are the heart of the NSDSG's operations. Without this information the organization cannot operate. In addition, other demographic information is needed for both the members and donors.

Contact Information

Current, accurate, and complete information is a must for smooth and efficient operations of the NSDSG. Inaccurate mailing addresses incur additional postage costs and forwarding fees. Late delivery of fundraiser information could reduce donations.

Electronic addresses are becoming more important to NFPs. The cost of sending an email is almost nothing; but regular postal rates are rising fast. However, keeping email addresses up to date is a never-ending task because users change email addresses more frequently than they change mailing addresses.

Phone numbers are also very important for both fundraising and keeping in touch with individual members. Phone calls can be used to contact individual members and donors for activities and campaigns, by a formal phone committee or informally, when necessary, by an officer of the organization.

Demographic Information

Information about each member and donor, such as occupation, date of birth, date of the first contact with the NSDSG, skills, special needs, and donor preferences, needs to be easily accessible so that it can be used to target members and donors for special fundraising and member activities.

Dates recording the end of membership, either by death or termination, are also recorded. Recording the end of a donor's relationship with the organization is very important. If a former donor continues to receive communications after requesting not to be contacted, this can, at the least, create ill feelings toward the organization and, at worst, violate federal Do Not Call laws.

Tracking Donations

Fundraising campaigns are usually targeted to specific segments of the community. For example, golf tournaments are targeted to golfers and golf-related businesses. Fundraisers for theater groups or symphonies are targeted to donors who are supporters of the fine arts. Some fundraising activities are tax-deductible and some are not. Distinguishing the two is imperative, and mixing the two can possibly create an illegal use of the funds.

Each donation will need to be identified to indicate the donor and the intended use of the funds. If the donation was tax-deductible, the record must be identified as such for reporting purposes.

Tracking Sales

The organization sells merchandise with the organization's logo to customers, members, and donors. Although logo items promote the organization, most of the selling price is used to cover the cost of the item.

Sales are tracked by item and by customer. Customers can be members, donors, or casual purchasers. In some fundraising campaigns the same merchandise is given to donors, so zero-dollar sales are recorded, and the cost of the merchandise is charged to the fundraiser's direct expenses.

Designing the Database

To build the membership application, you will use portions of the database models from Chapter 7, "Sales," and concepts from Chapter 11, "Accounting Systems: Requirements and Design."

All models used in this example use *surrogate keys* as the primary keys in the tables, which simplifies the combination process. We will use an AutoNumber data type as the primary key. If *natural keys* had been used, it would have been necessary to modify the key structure for the additional tables added to the schema.

Tables

The schema from Chapter 7 will be the primary model used, since the majority of the functions of this organization are related to an individual, in this case, a member. We will add seven tables to the Sales model:

- tblDuesReceivable
- tblPaymentDetail
- tblDuesType
- tblDuesRate
- tblIndividualDuesType
- tblIndividualDetail
- tblDetailType
- tblAccount (Optional)

Dues Receivable

The Dues Receivable table records both dues billed to each member, and payments made by the member. The concepts used in this table were discussed in Chapter 11. Debits and credits are used to indicate if the record is a bill, which is a positive number, or a payment, which is a negative number.

The table tblDuesReceivable contains four fields, shown in Figure14-1, but the AcctID field is optional. If the account is going to be used with a Chart of Accounts in an accounting module, it is considered a best practice to use a table for the Chart of Accounts and create a relationship with the tblAccount table. This allows for more flexibility in assigning accounts to be used for each billing.

tblDuesReceivable		
Field Name	Data Type	
DuesReceivableID	AutoNumber	Primary Key
IndividualID	Number	Foreign Key to tblIndividual
AcctID	Number	Foreign Key to tblAccount (Optional)
TransDate	Date/Time	Date of Transactions
DuesAmt	Currency	Monetary value of the transaction

Figure 14-1: Design view of tblDuesReceivable

Payment Detail

The purpose of the Payment Detail table is to record the check number and date of the check, plus any comments for a record. CheckNo is an easy to recognize field name, but you may prefer to replace the word *Check* with Payment or another term. The field CheckNo is used to record the identifier for all types of payments, including credit card confirmations, electronic fund transfers, and cash receipt numbers. Figure 14-2 shows the design view of tblPaymentDetail.

Field Name	Data Type	
PaymentDetailID	AutoNumber	Primary Key
DuesReceivableID	Number	Foreign Key to tblDuesReceivable
CheckNo	Text	Check Number, Cash, Credit Card confirmation, etc
DateOfCheck	Date/Time	Date check issued or date of credit card transaction
Comment	Text	Freeform comments

Figure 14-2: Design view of tblPaymentDetail

Dues Type

The Dues Type table, shown in Figure 14-3, is used to store the different types of membership dues and is a lookup table for these values.

Field Name	Data Type	
DuesTypeID	AutoNumber	Primary Key
DuesType	Text	Description of type of dues
DuesTypeActive	Yes/No	Active dues type

Figure 14-3: Design view of tblDuesType

Dues Rate

Dues rates change frequently, and this requires a flexible means to assign dues rates to each member, depending on the membership type and date of billing. We have included fields for both the beginning date and end date to help track the period that a particular rate was in effect and to allow for retroactive billing. The DuesRateVoid field indicates that a particular rate is not in effect and is not available for use. Figure 14-4 shows the design view of tblDuesRate.

Field Name	Data Type	Description
DuesRateID	AutoNumber	Primary Key
DuesTypeID	Number	Foreign key to tblDuesType
Amount	Currency	Dues amount
BegDate	Date/Time	Rate effective date
EndDate	Date/Time	Rate end date
DuesRateVoid	Yes/No	A rate is void if it is no longer applicable; It is not available for historic billing.

Figure 14-4: Design view of tblDuesRate

Individual-Dues Type

The Individual Dues Type table, shown in Figure 14-5, is a *junction table* for the tables Individual and Dues Type. The purpose of a junction table is to create a many-to-many relationship with two tables. This provides a mechanism for defining which dues type a member is assigned and, subsequently, the effective dues rate associated with that dues type.

	tblIndividualDuesType		
	Field Name	Data Type	
🔑	IndividualDuesTypeID	AutoNumber	Primary Key
	IndividualID	Number	Foreign key to tblIndividual
	DuesTypeID	Number	Foreign key to tblDuesType
	BegDate	Date/Time	Type effective date
	EndDate	Date/Time	Type end date
	IndividualDuesTypeActive	Yes/No	Yes No Indicates active type

Figure 14-5: Design view of tblIndividualDuesType

You can also use an index with no duplicates allowed to prevent an individual from being assigned more than one dues type at a time. We'll take this opportunity to go through the steps to create a multiple field index. This is a valuable lesson that you will find many opportunities to apply. Using the following steps, you will create a multiple field index on the IndividualID field, the DuesTypeID field, and the BegDate field.

1. With tblIndividualDuesType table open in design view, click on the Design tab on the Ribbon, and then click on Indexes.

2. To create a multi-field index, enter the name of the index, DuesType, in the Index Name column.

3. Add the IndividualID in the Field Name column, and select Yes for the Index Properties Unique field.

4. Repeat steps 1–3 for the other two fields named above, but do not fill in the Index Name on these fields.

Figure 14-6 shows the Indexes dialog box for tblIndividualDuesType.

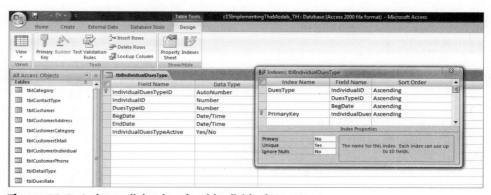

Figure 14-6: Indexes dialog box for tblIndividualDuesType

Individual Detail

The Individual Detail table, shown in Figure 14-7, will store additional, optional facts about the related individual in tblIndividual.

tblIndividualDetail		
Field Name	Data Type	
IndividualDetailID	AutoNumber	Primary Key
IndividualID	Number	Foreign Key to tblIndividual
DetailTypeID	Number	Foreign Key to tblDetailType
DetailDate	Date/Time	Effective Date of Detail Type

Figure 14-7: Design view of tblIndividualDetail

Detail Type

The Detail Type table, shown in Figure 14-8, is a lookup table that stores the detail type categories used in the related tblIndividualDetail table.

tblDetailType		
Field Name	Data Type	
DetailTypeID	AutoNumber	Primary Key
DetailType	Text	Description of Detail Type
DetailActive	Yes/No	Yes No indicates active type

Figure 14-8: Design view of tblDetailType

Defining Relationships

Now, relationships need to be created to include these new tables in the original Sales database. Three of the new tables have relationships defined with tblIndividual: tblDuesReceivable, tblIndividualDetail, and the junction table tblIndividualDuesType. Figure 14-9 is a relationship diagram of the tables in the combined database.

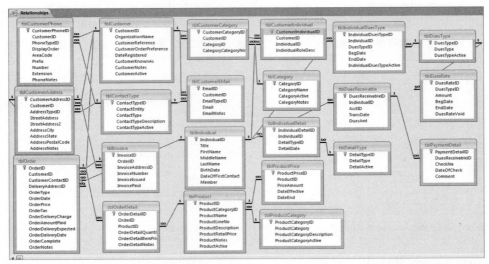

Figure 14-9: Relationship diagram showing how the additional tables are related to the original tables in the Sales database

Components of the User Interface

After you've created the schema, which is the foundation of the database, it is time to create the queries, forms, and reports that compose the user interface, which allows users to access the data.

Queries

Queries are used to return data from the tables. A query can be as simple as returning the data in a table or as complex as combining specific data from multiple tables and including complex expressions that perform calculations.

Queries can be the record source for forms, reports, list boxes, combo boxes, and VBA recordsets. Access has built-in *Domain Aggregate Functions* like `DSum()` and `DLookUp()` that can use queries to return a value.

Parameter Queries

The records returned by a query can be restricted by providing parameters or arguments in the criteria or a WHERE clause of the query. Parameters can be hardcoded in the query, and Access also has multiple methods available to pass the parameters to the query at runtime.

The design view of an Access query allows the developer to enter text in the *Criteria row*, surrounding the text with square brackets—for example, [**Enter Customer Name**]. The query will return only those records that match the criteria.

However, rather than having users respond to the parameter query each time it runs, you can allow them to enter the value on a form and then refer the query to the form. This is considered a better practice, as it allows users to enter data or to select from dropdown lists one time.

By using dropdown lists, check boxes, or other controls, you can apply logic to validate and control the data entered by a user. In addition, using a control on a form to enter criteria allows the criteria to be entered a single time and then used for multiple queries or reports. To do this, you can use *form references* in the query. The syntax to pass the values using a form reference requires the name of the form and the name of the control. For example, the following string, using the correct object names for your query, would be entered or pasted into the criteria row of the query:

```
Forms!frmYourFormName!YourControlName
```

When the query is opened, the criteria is passed from the form to the WHERE clause of the query, and only records that match the arguments will be returned. Note that the form referenced by the criteria must be open for the query criteria to find and use it.

Another method of supplying arguments at runtime is to dynamically create the WHERE clause, or the entire SQL string, using VBA. The dynamic construction of a query is beyond the scope of this book, but Access 2007 VBA Programmer's Reference (Wrox) would be a good source for additional information about using VBA in an Access application.

Types of Queries

Two types of queries in Access are used from the query design tool: *select queries* and *action queries*.

Select Queries

Select queries return only records. They do not delete, append, or update any data. They return data. *Field expressions* can be used to calculate values by using formulas and functions. Multiple tables can be *joined* creating a single recordset composed of portions of each table.

Union queries are a special subset of select queries. Union queries combine two or more identically structured recordsets into a single recordset. When working with denormalized data, union queries can be used to create a normalized data set. Union queries can also be used to combine data from two tables with similar data, when a relationship exists to join the two tables. Each SELECT statement in a union needs to have the same fields in the same order. By design, union queries omit duplicate records in the resulting recordset. However, if you need to return all records, including duplicates, you can use the *ALL keyword*, that is, *Union All*.

Action Queries

There are three types of action queries. Because these queries add, change, or delete data in your tables, Access displays a warning to the user before completing the action. You can suppress warnings, which are turned on by default.

Append queries return records from a table and add those records to another table. The records are not displayed as a recordset, and an append query cannot be used as a source for a form or report, or used in another query. The Where clause can specify that only certain records be processed or be omitted so that all records are included.

Update queries modify data in specific fields in a table. Like append queries, criteria can be used to restrict the update to only certain records. Expressions and functions can be used to manipulate the data being updated.

Delete queries delete records from the underlying tables. The resulting deletion of data is permanent, although warnings are displayed to the user first. Because the deletion is permanent, you should be careful to select only the records that need to be deleted.

Forms

Forms are typically what the users will see on their monitors; forms are the workhorses of the user interface. All data should be entered and maintained through forms. End users should not have access to the raw tables or queries in a *transactional* database.

Forms also allow for *validation of data* before it is entered in the tables. By using list boxes and combo boxes, you can offer valid preselected choices to the user instead of allowing freeform entries. Invalid data, such as numbers that are out of the range of acceptable values, invalid ID codes, invalid date values, and improperly formatted string values can be intercepted and handled using VBA, macros, or other validation rules before the data is committed to a record.

The data that the user enters may need processing before it is stored. Partial dates may need to be converted to valid dates before saving them to a table. For example, users could enter a month and year because that is all they ever have. Instead of forcing the user to enter the correct day also, a built-in function can be used to add the day value to the month and year as the record is being saved.

Forms can also serve as menus and as places to enter criteria for forms, subforms, reports and queries.

Reports

Reports are used to display, analyze, and distribute the information in the database. Reports can include complex calculations and aggregations that can be viewed on the screen, printed to paper, or exported to PDF or other file formats. Access is capable of producing management reports, user reconciliation reports, charts, and many other types of reports.

Modules

Modules are containers for VBA code. There are private modules for forms and reports, and there are public modules for code that is to be available throughout the entire project. VBA is beyond the scope of this book, but *Access 2007 VBA Programmer's Reference* (Wrox) is an excellent source of VBA information.

Backup during Development

To prevent the loss of new database objects during the design process, we recommend that you save a copy of the database multiple times during the day. Multiple backups allow you to return to an earlier, working copy if a change causes the database to become corrupt. Frustratingly, you may not immediately know about the corruption, but having multiple backups allows you to search for and preserve as much work as possible.

An alternative to saving a copy of the actual database is to use a method that works with VBA to save the objects to a text file. Some developers use the undocumented `SaveToText` method throughout the day, in case of corruption. By using the `LoadFromText` method, corrupt database objects can be replaced by reloading a previously saved text file. We've provided the instructions and code module in the upcoming "How to Save an Object to Text" sidebar. The module is in this chapter's database and in the Bonus Resources database, both on the book's CD.

These are undocumented features in Access, and the methods can be removed from the program at any time, so you should not rely on them as a part of the user interface to export or import objects. However, using these methods as a backup during development should not present any risks unless you upgrade your version of Access during development.

As you'll notice in the list of objects backed up and in the code that follows, we do not include tables or queries. Although there is code for working with tables and queries, we have had inconsistent results with it, so we did not include the code in our examples. As an alternative, we recommend that you use the database Documenter to provide the information about these two objects. Although this does not allow you to automatically recreate the tables or queries, it does preserve the specification so that you can confidently set the correct properties. The Documenter can be found under Tools ➤ Analyze.

HOW TO SAVE AN OBJECT TO TEXT

All you need to run the backup code is a simple form with a single command button that calls the `sub` procedure. You can create a new form and use the Control Wizard to create a command button that runs the `DumpAllObjects` procedure. The sample form in the database for this chapter is called frmSaveToText. There is also a version of the same form in the database for Appendix E, "References and Resources," on the book's CD—frmSaveToText is in ADD_BonusResource.mdb. You can import or copy that form into any database, along with the `DumpAllObjects` code. You can then use the form to run the code.

The code will save each form, report, macro, and module in the database to a separate text file. Each file will have the name of the object along with the date and time that it was saved to text. This allows you to create multiple versions of your database throughout the day without overwriting the previous backups. If you need to recover an object, you load the selected objects from text. The process to load objects is done one at a time and requires that you provide the name for the new object and the name of the text file. Here is the SaveToText code:

```
Sub DumpAllObjects(Optional strFilePath As String = "")
  Dim obj As AccessObject
  Dim strName As String
  Dim strDate As String


  On Error GoTo HandleError
  If strFilePath = "" Then
    strFilePath = "C:\CodeBackup" 'Access.CurrentProject.Path
'Note: if you want to save to a different location, replace c:\
'codebackup with the path and folder that you want to use, or pass
'the location as an argument in the Sub.
  End If
  strDate = Format(Now(), "yyyymmddhhnnss")
  For Each obj In Access.Application.CurrentProject.AllForms
    Access.Application.SaveAsText acForm, obj.Name, strFilePath &
    "\" & strDate & obj.Name & ".txt"
  Next
  For Each obj In Access.Application.CurrentProject.AllReports
    Access.Application.SaveAsText acReport, obj.Name, strFilePath &
    "\" & strDate & obj.Name & ".txt"
  Next
  For Each obj In Access.Application.CurrentProject.AllMacros
    Access.Application.SaveAsText acMacro, obj.Name, strFilePath &
    "\" & strDate & obj.Name & ".txt"
  Next
  For Each obj In Access.Application.CurrentProject.AllModules
    Access.Application.SaveAsText acModule, obj.Name, strFilePath &
    "\" & strDate & obj.Name & ".txt"
  Next
ExitHere:
  Exit Sub
HandleError:
  Select Case VBA.Err.Number
    Case Else
      MsgBox Err.Number & " " & Err.Description
  End Select
  Resume Next
End Sub
```

How to Load an Object from Text

In the event that you need to replace a database object, or all of the objects in the database, you can recover an older version of the object from a saved text

Continued

HOW TO SAVE AN OBJECT TO TEXT *(continued)*

file. You will need to run the `LoadFromText` code that follows in the immediate window. This will require that you provide the `FormName` and the path of the saved text file.

```
LoadFromText acForm, "FormName", "C:\CodeBackup\FormName.txt"
```

This may sound tedious, but most developers rely on this process as the surest bet. We refer you to another tool that we've provided in the Bonus Resource database on the book's CD that saves the names of all objects to a text file. Having a list of the object names allows you to save time and minimize errors by using copy and paste rather than typing the name of each object. It can also provide a helpful checklist to ensure that you recreate all of the objects if you are starting with a new container.

To reduce the possibility of continued corruption issues, we strongly recommend that you start with a blank database, then import the tables and queries from the "best copy" that you have of the suspect database, before loading the objects from text.

User Interface Design

The foundation for our database is complete now that the tables have been designed; it is time to begin building the visible structure of the database.

The NSDSG needs a database to track and control three main activities: keeping track of members, customers, and sales.

Activities Focused on Individuals

The database tracks members and customers for three reasons: contacting members for member-related activities, contacting individuals for sales-related reasons, and managing the office staff of the organization.

The first step in creating the application is to create a way to enter the information about the individuals. After data is entered, we will need to be able to find individuals and specific groups of individuals.

Entry Form

The following steps will help you create a data entry form. The steps and figures are specific to Access 2007 and show the standard Windows Ribbon. Prior versions of Access use a menu, toolbar, and database window. Access wizards can help you create a new form in prior versions.

NOTE One common approach with prior versions of Access is to open the database window. Then, from the Objects list, click on Forms. Next, click "Create form by using wizard." Follow the steps in the wizard using the table, tblIndividual, and add all of the fields. We typically recommend using a query rather than a table for the record source; however, the table works quite well for our demonstration.

You can arrange the fields and add additional formatting to suit your preferences. After that, skip to step 12 below to see how to change to form view, and then move on to the next section, "Add Functionality."

The following steps apply to Access 2007.

1. Use the Create menu item on the Ribbon to begin creating a form.

2. Select the Blank Form option, as shown in Figure 14-10.

Figure 14-10: Select Blank Form.

3. Use the View dropdown menu to select the Design View option, shown in Figure 14-11.

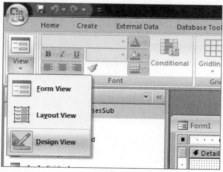

Figure 14-11: Select Design View

Form1 is now open in design view, ready for you to add controls and formatting. Form1 is the default name, but it is not an appropriately descriptive name for the form. So, the next step is to rename the form.

4. Save the form as frmIndividual.

The prefix "frm" indicates that the named object is a form, and "Individual" indicates that the form has something to do with an individual.

One of the worst things you can do is to use cryptic or default names for database objects; instead you should use concise, informative names that will help you recognize the purpose of the object. It does not matter which naming convention you use, but it does matter if you do not use one. Using prefixes and meaningful names helps to self-document the database.

The purpose of this form is to enter information about individuals, so our next task is to use the Property Sheet to select the record source for the form. The record source determines which data the form will use.

5. Right-click the black square just below the form's name, or click on the Property Sheet icon in the Tools section on the right side of the Ribbon. Figure 14-12 illustrates both of these ways to open the property sheet.

Figure 14-12: Right-click the black square or the property sheet icon on the Ribbon

6. If you selected the property sheet from the Ribbon, it will be open; if you chose to right-click on the black square, you will then need to select Properties, as shown in Figure 14-13.

Figure 14-13: Click on Properties

Access allows the data to be bound, or directly connected, to a form or report by specifying the record source. A similar option is also available for several controls.

7. Click on the Data tab of the Property Sheet, shown in Figure 14-14. This tab lists the data-related properties you can set in design view.

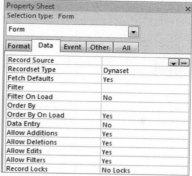

Figure 14-14: Select the Record Source property

8. Click the dropdown arrow on the right side of the Record Source property, and select the entry for tblIndividual, as illustrated in Figure 14-15.

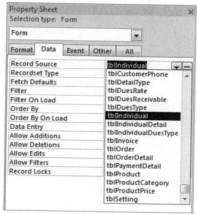

Figure 14-15: Select tblIndividual from the dropdown

With the record source specified, the next task is to add the fields to the form.

9. Click on the Add Existing Fields icon in the Tools section of the Ribbon, and the Field List of tables in the database will be displayed, shown in Figure 14-16.

Figure 14-16: Click on the Add Existing Fields icon to display the field list

10. You can double-click on a single field or select multiple fields. Figure 14-17 shows all fields selected.

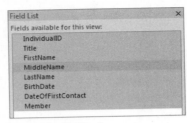

Figure 14-17: Select all fields in tblIndividual

11. Drag and drop all of the fields from tblIndividual onto the detail section of the frmIndividual. Figure 14-18 shows all fields after they are placed in the detail section of the form.

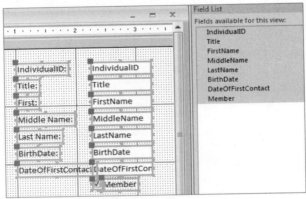

Figure 14-18: Drag all the fields onto frmIndividual

The controls can be arranged in any manner that is acceptable to end users. Forms can be as simple or elaborate as the developer or end user desires. For this example, we will create simple forms intended to demonstrate basic functionality.

12. Select the View icon in the Views section on the left side of the Ribbon, and the form will open with the data that is stored in the table. Figure 14-19 indicates the position of the View icon on the Ribbon.

Figure 14-19: The View icon

Limited functionality in the form, as it now stands, allows data entry and management of records for individuals. However, the form provides no data validation, and it does not have a method to search for individuals or to enter information about an individual that is stored in other tables.

Add Functionality

First, we need to add a method to find the individuals that need to be accessed through the form. The following steps provide instructions for adding controls with VBA functions behind them. Although the Ribbon and menus may differ depending on the version of Access you are using, the basic process remains the same. And, the code will work with Access 2000 and above. As an alternative to VBA, you can use macros. The processes and structure for creating and managing macros has changed significantly over the versions. So, we will refer you to the Access help and online resources for detailed instructions on macros.

Adding the list box Control

To add a list box control to the form, follow these steps.

1. Add a page header to the form by right-clicking on the Detail section bar of the form and selecting Page Header/Footer. Figure 14-20 shows the pop-up menu used to add a Page Header.

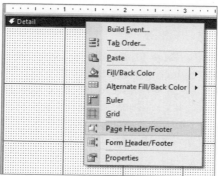

Figure 14-20: Add a page header

2. Next, you need to expand the section so that it is about 1.5 inches high to allow room to insert some controls. Figure 14-21 shows the expanded Page Header section.

Figure 14-21: Expand the Page Header section

3. Click on the Use Control Wizards icon, shown in Figure 14-22.

Figure 14-22: Use the Control Wizards icon

4. Select a list box control, shown in Figure 14-23.

Figure 14-23: Add a list box to the page header

For older versions on Access, you will typically find the list box control on the Form Design toolbar.

5. Draw a control in the Page Header with dimensions of about 1 inch high and 4 inches wide. Select "I want the list box to look up values in a table or query." Figure 14-24 shows the list box that was added to the form, with the label "Find Individual." The list box will provide the selection list for the form. The following steps walk you through the process of completing the list box in the wizard.

6. Select tblIndividual.

7. Add the fields IndividualID, LastName, FirstName, MiddleName, and Member.

8. Sort by LastName, FirstName, and MiddleName, all in ascending order.

9. Make sure that Hide key column is selected.

10. Use Find Individual as the label.

11. In the property sheet, rename the control as lboFindIndividual. The prefix, "lbo", stands for list box.

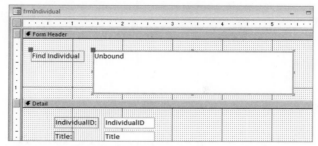

Figure 14-24: Add a list box to the page header

Adding VBA to the List Box Control

To make the list box work, you must add VBA code to the After Update event of the list box. The following steps help you add that code.

1. In design view, select the lboFindIndividual list box, and in the property sheet on the Event tab, click on the ellipsis control in the leftmost column of the After Update Event to invoke the Choose Builder dialog. Figure 14-25 shows the location of the ellipsis on the property sheet.

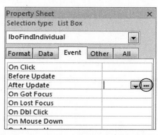

Figure 14-25: Click on the ellipsis located on the After Update event

2. Select Code Builder and click OK. Figure 14-26 shows the Code Builder selected.

Figure 14-26: Invoke the Code Builder on the After Update event

The following code is used to select member records for viewing or processing. Add this code to lboFindIndividual_AfterUpdate().

```
Private Sub lboFindIndividual_AfterUpdate()
    'find the record that matches the individual in the list box.
    Dim rs As Object
    Set rs = Me.Recordset.Clone
    rs.FindFirst "[IndividualID] = "& Str(Nz(Me.lboFindIndividual, 0))
    If Not rs.EOF Then Me.Bookmark = rs.Bookmark

End Sub
```

3. Save the form and open it using the View icon. Select an individual—the record for that member is now displayed in the main body of the form.

Adding a Subform for Dues History

We need functionality to view the individual's dues history and to post payments and adjustments. To accomplish this, we add a subform to the main form. First, a modification to the main form's layout needs to be made. Arrange the controls horizontally at the top of the Detail section to allow room for a subform below the existing controls.

1. Open the Form Wizard to create a new form based on the table tblDues-Receivable, and name it frmIndividualDuesReceivableSub.

2. In the property sheet for this form, set the default view to Datasheet and save the form.

3. Open frmIndividual in design view.

4. Increase the height of the Detail section to about 4 inches.

5. Drag and drop form frmIndividualDuesReceivableSub onto the Detail section of frmIndividual. Figure 14-27 shows the subform after placement on the form.

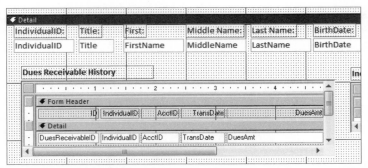

Figure 14-27: Add frmIndividualDuesReceivableSub to the detail section of the form

6. Open the Property Sheet and set the master/child relationship using Link Child Fields and Link Master Fields in the Data tab, as shown in Figure 14-28.

Adding a subform and creating a relationship between the record sources of the two forms allows users to select a record and see the related records from the other table or record source. In this case, the dues history of the individual is displayed, and additions, adjustments, or deletions to dues history are possible.

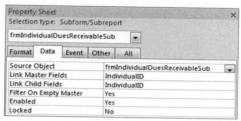

Figure 14-28: Set the Link Master Fields and Link Child Fields in the property sheet of frmIndividualDuesReceivableSub

Related Forms

The following forms are used to enter supporting data, and for navigation and menu creation purposes.

Dues Supporting Forms

Additional tables are related to dues. The tblDuesRate table is directly related to the dues collection process, but it does not have a direct relationship with individuals. The table stores data that the application needs to do other tasks.

Dues Rate Entry   A form is needed to facilitate entering and archiving the dues rates. The completed form, frmDuesRate, is shown in Figure 14-29. Follow these steps to create the form:

1. Create a new form based on tblDuesRate, and select all fields to be included in the form. Again, the exact layout and formatting of the form are up to you. The layout can be columnar, tabular, or datasheet.

2. Name the form frmDuesRate.

3. Open the form. Figure 14-29 shows the Dues Rate form.

Dues Rate Entry						
DuesRateID	DuesTypeID	Amount	BegDate	EndDate	DuesRateVoid	
1	1	$120.00	1/1/2009		☐	
2	2	$60.00	1/1/2009		☐	
3	3	$0.00	1/1/2009		☐	
4	1	$100.00	1/1/2007	12/31/2008	☐	
5	2	$50.00	1/1/2007	12/31/2008	☐	
6	3	$0.00	1/1/2007	12/31/2008	☐	
8	1	$17,000.00	1/1/2009	1/1/2009	☑	
* (New)	0				■	

Figure 14-29: frmDuesRate open in continuous form view

Adding a Control to Open the Form   To make the Dues Rate form easily accessible, add a command button to the main Individual form. Use the following steps to create a command button and add the necessary code.

1. Open frmIndividual in design view.

2. With the Control Wizard on, draw a small command button to the right of the search list box. The wizard will guide you through the process of creating the code behind the button to open the form.

3. Select Form Operations, then Open Form, and frmDuesRates.

4. Add the text Dues Rate Entry to display on the button, and name the command button cmdDuesRateEntry.

5. View frmIndividual, then click on the new command button to open the form.

The code behind the command button that the wizard created is listed here:

```
Private Sub cmdDuesRateEntry_Click()
On Error GoTo Err_cmdDuesRateEntry_Click

    Dim stDocName As String
    Dim stLinkCriteria As String

    stDocName = "frmDuesRates"
    DoCmd.OpenForm stDocName, , , stLinkCriteria

Exit_cmdDuesRateEntry_Click:
    Exit Sub

Err_cmdDuesRateEntry_Click:
    MsgBox Err.Description
    Resume Exit_cmdDuesRateEntry_Click

End Sub
```

Recording Billings and Payments To create billing entries and record dues payments, we use a form with command buttons to perform the following tasks:

- Preview members prior to posting the dues so that pre-posting adjustments can be made.
- Post the dues billing.
- Print one or more dues notices.
- Record payments and adjust individual dues amounts.

Prior to billing the members, the secretary/treasurer will need to preview the members being billed and confirm that the billing amounts are correct. Follow these steps to create a query to verify billing.

1. Create a new query in design view from tblIndividual.
2. Drop in the fields IndividualID, LastName, FirstName, and Member; then, from tblDuesRate, drop in Amount, BegDate, and EndDate. In this query, the AcctNo and TransDate fields are field expressions, which are not in a table, and return the values coded in the expression.
3. Add the AcctNo field expression to the query: `AcctNo: 4001`
4. Add the TransDate field to the query: `TransDate: Date()`
5. Add the criteria for the Members field to the criteria row: `<> 0`. Access recognizes Yes/No fields as 0 for No and -1 for Yes.

   It is helpful to know that, in this scenario, any number that is not 0 will be interpreted as a Yes.

6. The criteria for the BegDate field is an expression that calculates the first day of the next year and finds a rate that is less than or equal to the first day of the next billing year: `<=DateSerial(Year(Date()),12,32)`

   The DateSerial function has three arguments, Year, Month, and Day. All arguments in the DateSerial function are integers.

   The year argument uses the `Year()` function to return the current day's year. The month argument is 12, or December. The day argument is 32. Access knows that December, or any other month, does not have 32 day; it adds one day to the end of the month and returns the first day of the next month—in this case January 1, 2010, assuming 2009 as today's year.

   As with most areas of development, this is just one of many techniques that will work.

7. The criteria for the EndDate field uses an expression in the criteria to return a date greater than or equal to today's date.

The field expression is `EndDate: Nz([tblDuesRate].[EndDate],#12/31/9999#)`

The `Nz()` function returns a replacement value for a field if the field is Null. In this expression, a Null value will return December 31, 9999.

Allowing for Null values is required in this instance because if the rate is active, it most likely will be Null, and the criteria that will be applied will not work with Null.

8. Add this criteria expression to EndDate. It is almost the same as in the BegDate field, with the difference that we use greater than or equal to first day of the next year instead of less than: `>=DateSerial(Year(Date()),12,32)`

9. Add the field DuesRateVoid to the query, and add 0 as the criteria. DuesRateVoid is True if the rate is void, and should not be used in any calculation. Access stores true as -1 and false as 0, so a record that is not 0 would be excluded from the records returned.

10. Save the query as qryDuesPrePost.

11. Create a blank unbound form, and name it frmDuesSwitchboard. It does not need to be bound to any table since it is not being directly used to view or modify data.

12. Use the Control Wizard to add a command button to open the query. Name that command button Open Dues Pre-post Query.

Figure 14-30 shows the pre-post query in design view.

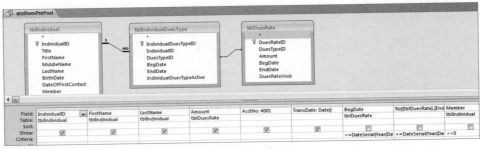

Figure 14-30: qryDuesPrePost shown in design view

After the pre-billing has been verified, we need to create a billing record for the same members' accounts. The query, which returns the pre-billing records, can be modified to append the records to the dues receivable table.

To create the query to post the dues, follow these steps:

1. Save qryDuesPrePost as qryDuesPost.

2. Change the field expression for the TransDate field from `TransDate:`
   `Date()` to `TransDate: DateSerial(Year(Date()),10,1)` to post the
   billing as of October 1 of the current year.

3. Change the type of the query from a select query to an append query,
   and select tblDuesReceivable as the table to append to.

4. Remove the LastName and FirstName fields from the query.

5. Set the IndividualID field to append to the IndividualID field.

6. Set the Amount field to append to the DuesAmt field.

7. Set AcctNo field to append to the AcctID field.

8. Set TransDate field to append to the TransDate.

9. Save the query.

10. Add a command button to frmDuesSwitchboard to run qryDuesPost.

Creating a Dues Notice   A dues notice can be either a simple mail merge with
Microsoft Word, or an Access report. In this example we will use an Access
report to serve as a bill to the member.

1. Create a new report, basing it on qryDuesPrePost.

2. From the Property Sheet of the new report, open the query from the
   Record Source by clicking on the ellipsis on the right-hand side of the
   record.

3. Add tblCustomerAddress.

4. Create a join between CustomerID in tblCustomerAddress and IndividualID in tblIndividual.

5. Drop the necessary address fields into the query.

6. Change the query to SQL view, and copy and paste the text for the SQL
   into the Record Source of the report. Saving the SQL statement in the
   report property is an alternative method of binding a record source to an
   object.

The SQL is now fully contained and saved in the report. One drawback to
using this method is the potential for having to make the same changes in
multiple reports, instead of in one saved query that is used by all the reports.
However, a benefit is that the record source is always kept with the report.

Next, we design a report using text boxes with concatenated string literals
and data from the query by completing the following steps:

1. Start by adding a text box to the Detail Section of the report, and delete
   the Label control that Access added.

2. Concatenate the First and Last names in the text box:

```
=([FirstName]+" ") & [LastName]
```

CONCATENATION OPERATORS "+" AND "&"

Notice the use of both the + concatenation operator and the & concatenation operator. The + operator propagates nulls, while the & operator does not.

Using the + operator with the field FirstName and the space prevents an extra space before LastName if FirstName is Null. FirstName and the space will be Null and not a space. Then the Null and LastName are combined using the & operator, and the result will equal the value in LastName, since Nulls are not propagated using the & operator.

3. Add two more text boxes for the address fields.

4. Concatenate the City, State, and Postal Code fields in another text box to finish the address block.

5. Add an additional text box and create a date for the bill:

```
=Format([TransDate],"mmmm d"", ""yyyy")
```

6. Add another text box for the dues notice and expand it to a size that will hold the main body of the text.

7. Next, add the text below to the dues notice, concatenating string literals and field values to complete the text. Note that Chr(13) and Chr(10) are the codes for carriage returns and linefeeds to add the proper line spacing.

```
="Dear " & [Title] & " " & [LastName] & Chr(13) & Chr(10) & Chr(13)
& Chr(10) & "The dues for the National Spreadsheet Developers Support
Group are due and payable. Please take a moment to place a check in the
mail for " & Format([amount], "Standard") & "." & Chr(13) & Chr(10) &
Chr(13) & Chr(10) & "The dues of the membership fund the operating
expenses of the organization and by doing so increase the percentage of
donations that we can give to the deserving recipients." & Chr(13) &
Chr(10) & Chr(13) & Chr(10) & "Thank you for your support."
```

8. Create a command button on the switchboard form (frmDuesSwitch-board) to run the billing query.

Figures 14-31 and 14-32 show the design view and print preview of the dues notice, respectively.

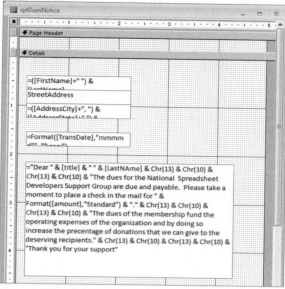

Figure 14-31: Design view image of the dues notice

Figure 14-32: Print Preview image of the dues notice

Recording Payments To post the payments, we'll add another command button to the Dues Switchboard form and open frmIndividual. We will use the dues history subform (frmIndividualDuesReceivableSub) to record all payments and adjustments directly on the form.

Customers and Donors

Customers of the organization can be members, donors, or both. Customers can purchase merchandise from the store or make donations to the organization.

Keeping track of donations and fundraising events is essentially an extension of sales; fundraising campaigns and events can be considered products, and donations can be considered sales. In that sense, the donors are customers. So, an order is created using the campaign as the product, and the price is entered either as predefined units with a fixed price or as a single unit at a variable price.

Customers

Customers can be individuals or businesses. The Sales database has a table for customers, tblCustomer, and a table for individuals, tblIndividual.

Data Entry Forms

To enter data in the Customer tables, we will use a form much like frmIndividual. However, to illustrate other options available in Access, we'll create the Customer form with a *Tab control* to hold multiple subforms instead of placing subforms directly in the detail section of the main form.

Tab Controls We will again start by creating the main form based on one table. We can then add data from related tables to the Tab control in the subform.

1. Use the Form Wizard to create a form based upon tblCustomer.

2. Add all fields from tblCustomer to the form.

3. Select Columnar as the layout of the form, and choose an appropriate style. Next, select the option to open the form in design view.

4. Save the form as frmCustomers.

5. Increase the width and height of the detail section of the form to about 6 inches high and 6 inches wide.

6. Draw a Tab control in the area below the existing controls; make the Tab control about 3 inches high and 4 inches wide.

7. Save and close the form.

8. Using the wizard, create a new form based on tblCustomerAddress.

9. Select all fields and use the datasheet view for the layout.

10. The title will be frmCustomersAddressesSub.

11. Select Modify to modify the design of the form.

12. In the property sheet, change the caption to Customer Addresses.

13. Save and close the form.

14. Open frmCustomers in design view, and drag frmCustomerAddresses onto the first tab of the Tab Control.

15. Set the Link Child Fields and Link Master Fields properties to CustomerID. The field names will likely be there by default, but it is good to check.

16. Change the caption for the first page of the Tab control to Addresses.

17. Save and open the form.

    You will need additional tabs, or pages, to add more subforms.

    To add pages to the Tab control, select the Tab control while in design view, right-click, and select Insert Page.

18. Repeat the steps above and create a form using the tblCustomerEMails. Name it frmCustomerEMailsSub, then drag it onto the second tab of the Tab control.

19. Rename the tab to Email Addresses.

20. Save and open the form.

To Look Up Individuals

Add the same search feature you added to frmIndividual to frmCustomers. Modify the VBA code to use the correct primary key field, which should be CustomerID. Save the control as lboFindCustomer, and modify the new search control's name in the VBA code so that it is lboFindCustomer.

You can add other customer-related tables to new or existing pages on the Tab control or directly on the detail section of the main form. As the developer, you can add as little or as much functionality as appropriate for the situation.

Products

The product table stores all products that the organization sells or uses for fundraisers. Each product, or fundraiser, should be a record in the tblProduct. Users will need to add, archive, and modify the product information, so you must create forms to allow users to easily perform these functions.

Product Maintenance

There are two tables that directly relate to the sales of products and donations to the organization. The tblProduct table stores the information that describes the products, including the price. The tblProductCategory table defines and describes the categories of the different products. Since we need to maintain a price history, we will add a third product table to record prices, as shown in Figure 14-33, and create a relationship with the Product table, as shown in Figure 14-34.

tblProductPrice		
Field Name	**Data Type**	
ProductPriceID	AutoNumber	Primary Key
ProductID	Number	Foreign Key to Product Table
PriceAmount	Currency	Price of Item
DateEffective	Date/Time	Beginning Date of Price Span
DateEnd	Date/Time	Ending Date of Price Span

Figure 14-33: Design View of tblProductPrice

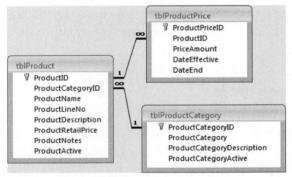

Figure 14-34: Relationship diagram for the Product-related tables

Fundraising Product Design

The organization should create business rules that dictate how the product records will be structured based on whether the product is fundraising or receipt of a donation. A donation that is not associated with any formal fundraising activities should use a permanent product and category. The price related to that record should be 1 unit of the local currency. With the price per unit set up in this manner, a donation of $1000 would be the equivalent of purchasing 1000 T-shirts. No modifications in how the donations are processed are necessary.

Formal fundraising campaigns can be added as a product, allowing both the source and the amount of donations to be traced back to the donor. In addition, if the donation entitles the donor to receive something of value in return for the donation, say a tote bag with the organization's logo on it, the value of the tote bag could be subtracted from the tax-deductible value to report the correct amount of donations made by the individual at year end.

Data Entry Forms

To show you some additional features of Access 2007, we'll used the Split Form Wizard, following the steps below, to create the Product data entry form.

1. Click on tblProduct to select it from the Navigation Pane, but do not open the table.

2. After selecting the table, click on the Split Form icon in the Forms section of the Create Ribbon, as shown in Figure 14-35.

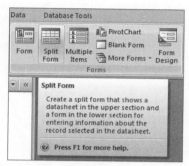

Figure 14-35: The Split Form icon on the Ribbon

The Split Form Wizard creates a form that simultaneously displays data in both datasheet view and form view. Data entry can be performed in either section of the form. Records selected in datasheet view are displayed in the form above.

Adding a Product Price Subform In the form view section, we will add a subform that can be used to view and enter the price of the product items. To add the subform we will start by creating a new form based on the tblProductPrice.

Use the following steps to create a new form and insert it as a subform into the Product form.

1. Click on the tblProductPrice table in the Navigation Pane.

2. Click on the Form Design icon on the Ribbon. Access will create a form named tblProductPrice.

3. Open the form in design view, and save the form as frmProductPriceSub.

4. Open the property sheet, set the default view as datasheet view, and set Allow Datasheet View to yes.

5. Change the Caption to Price Entry.

6. Save the form and close it.

7. Open frmProduct in design view and make the Detail section about 4 inches high.

8. Next, drop frmProductPriceSub onto frmProduct.

9. Set the Link Child/Link Master properties to the correct key values if the wizard did not resolve the links.

   The Link Master Field should be ProductCategoryID from tblProduct, and the Link Child Field should be ProductCategoryID from tblProduct-Category.

10. Adjust the size of the subform and the form sections to get the correct view of the data. Figure 14-36 shows the completed Products form.

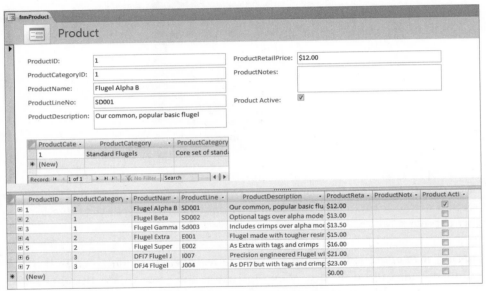

Figure 14-36: The Product form with the Product Price subform

Product List Reports

You will typically need various reports to list the merchandise that is for sale. A simple report can easily be created to list all of the information in the Product table.

1. Click on tblProduct and click on the Report Wizard in the Reports section of the Ribbon.

2. A dialog box will pop up asking which fields are needed on the report. Select all and move to the next dialog form.

3. Select Product Category to group the report data, then move to the next dialog and set the sort to Product Name. The next dialog form defines formatting information.

4. Select the default settings and proceed to the next dialog.

5. Choose the default style and click next.

6. Click Finish and the report will open.

7. Switch to design view and change the report title to Products.

8. From the Property sheet change the caption to Products.

9. Save and close the report.

Figure 14-37 is the completed Product report.

ProductCategoryID	ProductName	roductID	ProductLineNo	ProductDescription	ductRetailPrice	ProductNotes	Pr
1							
	Flugel Alpha E	1	SD001	Our common, popular basic	$12.00	☑	
	Flugel Beta	2	SD002	Optional tags over alpha mc	$13.00	☐	
	Flugel Gamma	3	Sd003	Includes crimps over alpha	$13.50	☐	
2							
	Flugel Extra	4	E001	Flugel made with tougher re	$15.00	☐	
	Flugel Super	5	E002	As Extra with tags and crimp	$16.00	☐	
3							
	DFI7 Flugel J	6	I007	Precision engineered Flugel	$21.00	☐	
	DFJ4 Flugel	7	J004	As DFI7 but with tags and cri	$23.00	☐	

Friday, November 27, 2009   Page 1 of 1

Figure 14-37: The completed Product report

Product Price Report

To create a list of products with prices, you will need to use a query for the record source and join the Product table with the Product Price table. We will create the report by starting with an existing report and modifying the record source and the report layout.

Using the following steps, we'll create a new report called Product Prices.

1. Open the Product report and save it as rptProductPrices.

2. Open the Property sheet to the Data tab.

3. Click on the ellipsis on the right side of the Record Source column. This will invoke the Query Designer on tblProduct.

4. Drop the tblProductPrice table into the Query Designer. The designer should automatically create a join between the two ProductID fields.

5. Change the Retail Price field to use the Price Amount field from the Product Price table.

6. Run the query to see if it returns the expected results. To return every product, there must be a related price for each product in the Product

table. Any product without a matching price will not be listed by the query as it is currently designed.

To include all records in the Product table, regardless of whether or not they have a price in the Product Price table, the join needs to be changed from an inner join to a left join. (Joins are discussed in Appendix B, "Relationships, Joins, and Nulls.")

7. Right-click on the join line between the two tables in query design view. This will open the Join Properties dialog box.

8. Select option 2, "Include all records from 'tblProduct' and only those records from 'tblProductPrice' where the joined fields are equal." Figure 14-38 is a view of the Join Properties dialog box.

9. Close the query and click "Yes" when prompted to save changes and update the record source property of the report.

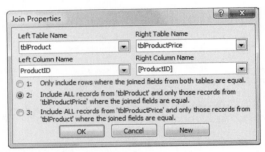

Figure 14-38: Change the inner join to a left join

The original ProductRetailPrice control will now need to point to PriceAmount. This can be changed in the property sheet or in the control directly. Make the change and preview the report.

Orders and Sales

Chapter 7 has a detailed discussion on using the order tables. Reviewing that chapter before attempting to implement an order system will help you understand the concepts described here.

The Orders table is the hub of the Order system. It is the master record for all sales. The table has three foreign keys; they relate to the Invoices table, the Order Details table, and the Individuals table. OrderID, the primary key for the table, is the unique identifier for each order. The Order Details table holds the detail entries for each order and uses the OrderID value to group all of the detail for orders with the same IDs to aggregate quantity, products, and price.

Order Entry Form

To create an order, a record in the Order table must be created first, and then the individual detail records can be added in the Order Detail table. Because of this relationship, the correct method to use is a form/subform. Follow these steps to create the form and subform:

1. Create a new form and use the Order table as the record source, using any of the methods previously demonstrated in this chapter.

2. Add all fields in the Order table to the form.

3. Save the new form as frmOrders.

4. Change the caption for the form's title to Orders.

   If you used a wizard, the controls that were added will probably need to be resized to be more appropriate for the data that they will display. You can, however, change the size of several controls at a time.

5. Use multi-select to select the column of text box controls on the left side and reduce the width to about 1 inch wide.

6. Move the labels and text boxes on the right column to the left until the labels are about .25 inches from the right side of the left text box controls.

7. Adjust the width of the text boxes in the right column using a similar technique.

8. Increase the height of the detail section to about 5 inches, and save the form.

Create the Order Detail Subform

Next, we will create the record source for the order detail subform:

1. Create a new query and name it qryQrderDetail.

2. Drop tblOrderDetail into the Query Designer.

3. Select all fields and add them to the query.

Create a Calculated Field in the Query

You also need a calculated field in this query:

1. To calculate the total cost of each line item, create a field expression and add it to the query. The expression calculation is Units * Price and is expressed this way:

   ```
   TotalCost: [OrderDetailItemCost]*[OrderDetailQuantity]
   ```

2. Save the query.

Create the Order Detail Subform

With the query saved, we can create the subform:

1. Create another new form for the Order Detail subform by dropping the query qryOrderDetail on the detail section of the Orders form. Let the wizard create the subform.

2. Save the form as frmOrderDetailsSub.

Add a customer lookup

The Orders form is now partially functional and can create orders, but it cannot add customer or purchaser information unless the user knows the specific record ID; that is not going to be the case. So, using the following steps, we will add a Lookup control to search for and select customers.

1. Create another new form for the Order Detail subform by dropping qryOrderDetail on the detail section of the Orders form. Let the wizard create the subform.

2. Save the form as frmOrderDetailsSub. The Orders form is now partially functional and can create orders, but it cannot add customer or purchaser information unless those IDs are known by the user.

3. With the Use Control Wizards icon selected, draw a list box control to the right of the controls on the main form.

4. Use the default option and choose the option to use a query or a table for the values for the list box.

5. Select the Customers table and add the CustomerID and theCustomer-KnownAs fields to the form.

6. Sort in ascending order by the CustomerKnownAs field.

7. Adjust the width of the field to display the names of the customers.

8. Select "Store the value in this field;" then select the CustomerID field.

9. Name the field lboCustomers.

Adding the Customer Address Subform

To add an address record for an order, we will add a subform to the Order form by dropping the Customer Addresses table on the Detail section. You may also want to use a Tab control and place the subforms on separate pages of the control. The functionality is essentially the same with both methods, but you may find that one is easier for your intended users.

At this point, you can look up customers and view their orders. The form displays the order details and address associated with each order. The sample form shown in Figure 14-39 was created by following the preceding steps. It is named frmOrders and can be found in the database provided for this chapter.

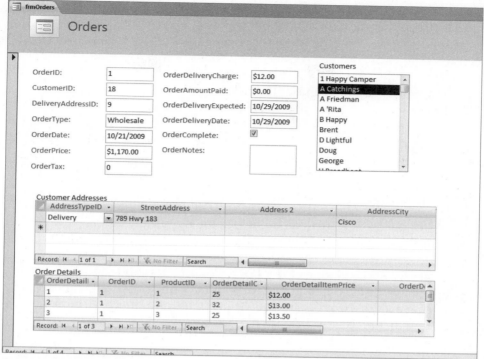

Figure 14-39: The Orders form

Tab Stops and Tab Order

When the user opens the form to prepare an order, the tab order should place the cursor where the logical first entry will be. By default, the wizard sets the OrderID control as the first tab stop. OrderID is an AutoNumber type and cannot be edited, so it does not make sense to place the cursor in that field. Similarly, the next two values, Customer ID and Customer Contact ID, are provided by the Customers and Customer Contact list boxes. So again, these fields should not be tab stops.

Logically the Customers list box should be the first tab stop. You can set the tab stop order by following these steps.

1. From the design view (or layout view) of frmOrders, open the property sheet. The tab stop properties are located on the Other tab.

2. Set the value for Tab Stop for the OrderID, CustomerID, and Customer-ContactID controls to No. Then, set the Tab Index on each of the remaining controls to the order that makes sense for your form. Keep in mind that the first stop is numbered 0 and not 1.

Order Totals

Chapter 7 provides a detailed discussion about storing denormalized data in the Order table. Although storing calculated values or storing redundant data is usually not recommended, Chapter 7 sets forth reasons that order totals and tax rates should be stored with the order details in cases such as this.

The last phase of creating an order form is to add the various totals to the record in the Orders table. We need two totals: Order Price and Order Tax. Order Price is the sum of the Item prices in the Order Detail table. Order Tax is a computation based on a taxable amount and a tax rate.

In this example, the tax rate calculation will not be done as an internal process. Tax methods vary greatly from jurisdiction to jurisdiction, and it would be impossible to cover all methods in this exercise. The delivery charges are also external calculations and not included in this example; the charges could be a mixture of fixed amounts or from a schedule based on distance, weight, or both. Amount Paid is used for cash purchases and to recognize partial prepayment of the order. Delivery Date is the expected delivery date. The default can be a calculated amount, but it is typically better if the control is pre-populated with a default date that can be changed by the user. Notes and Complete are manual entries.

One method of calculating Order Price is to use the `DSum()` function. `DSum()` is a domain aggregate function that is included with Access. The function will sum all of the values from a single field in a table or a query. Arguments can be provided to limit the records aggregated to a specific value.

The syntax of `DSum()` is

```
DSum(expr, domain [, criteria] )
```

`expr` is the numeric field that is to be totaled, `domain` is the name of the table or query, and `criteria` is an optional argument used to restrict the records to a specific value or range of values. If the argument is not supplied, all records in the domain will be used to calculate the total.

Another possibility is the `DLookUp()` function. The syntax is the same as that of the `DSum()` function. `DLookUp()` returns a scalar value. It will return a single value from a table or query. To have this method return the total order price, an aggregate query that sums the orders would be created, and the `DLookUp()` function would be executed against that query, with the value returned as the total.

A third option uses VBA to retrieve the value from the saved aggregate query to populate the Order Price field.

Using the `DSum()` function is done to update the order after the dirty event of the Orders form in the manner shown in the following code.

```
Private Sub Form_Dirty(Cancel As Integer)
    Dim f As Form
    Set f = Forms!frmOrders

    f.OrderDate = DSum("TotalCost", "qryOrderDetail", "OrderID =" & _
f.OrderID)

End Sub
```

Invoices

After the order has been entered, the invoice is ready to be created and printed. But to print the invoice, a record must exist in the Invoice table. The Invoice table and the Order table are related in a one-to-one relationship. The records in the two tables appear as one record after the Invoice table is populated with the Order ID. Once the Order ID field in the Invoice table is populated with a corresponding Order ID from the Order table, an invoice can be created.

To create an invoice, you need a way to add a record with a specified OrderID to the Invoice table. We will do that by using a form to create an invoice.

Invoice Form

The starting point for the invoice is a simple form bound to the Invoice table. You can use the Form Wizard to create a form based on tblInvoice. When you create the form, shown in Figure 14-40, you will need to leave room at the bottom for a command button to preview the invoice.

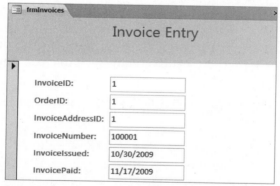

Figure 14-40: Invoice Entry form

Invoice Report

The next step is to prepare a report that will be the printed invoice. The first step is to create the record source for the report.

Creating a Query for the Record Source

We'll use the following steps to create the query for the invoice report.

1. Create a new query.
2. Add the Invoice table and the Order table to the designer.

3. Join the Invoice table and the Order table with an inner join on the field OrderID.

4. Add the Customer Address table and join it to the Invoice table on the fields AddressID and InvoiceAddressID.

5. Add the query qryOrderDetail and join it to the Order table on the field OrderID.

6. Add all fields to the query grid.

7. Save the query as qryInvoicesOrders, as shown in Figure 14-41.

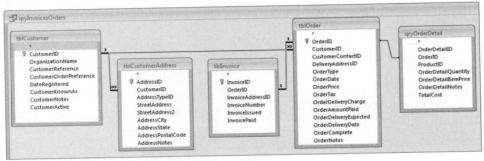

Figure 14-41: Design View of qryInvoicesOrders

Creating the Invoice

With the record source ready, you can continue with the process to create the invoice itself. We'll briefly list the main steps to create the sample report shown in Figure 14-42.

1. Use (select) the query qryInvoicesOrders as the record source for the invoice.

2. Create a blank report and add the fields needed to create the invoice.

3. Place the customer and address information in an address block in the Page Header section on the left side of the report.

4. Organize and format the invoice number, order date, and delivery date in the upper right of the report.

5. Arrange the order price, tax, delivery charge, and amount paid, as shown below.

Next, create a calculated control to display the amount due.

1. Add a text box control to the form, and in the text box control's source (on the Data tab of the property sheet), add the following formula:

```
=[OrderCost]+[OrderTax]+[OrderDeliveryCharge]-[OrderAmountPaid]
```

2. Place the detail information in the detail section of the report. Include the fields OrderDetailQuantity, OrderDetailItemPrice, and TotalCost.

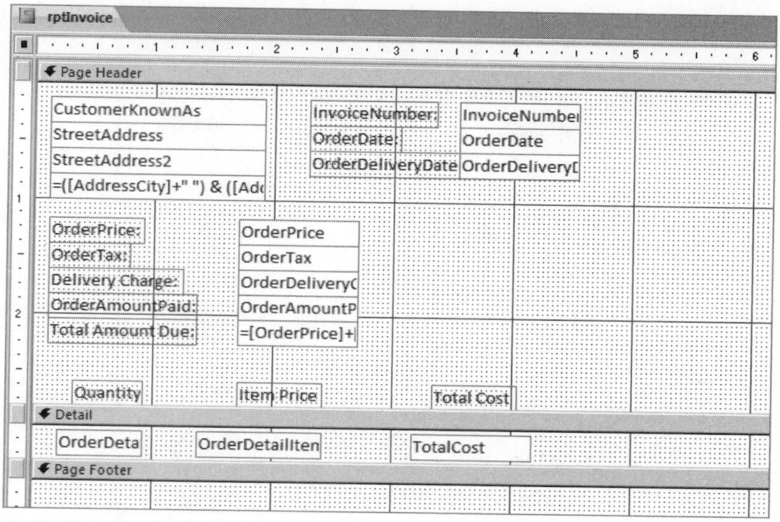

Figure 14-42: Invoice in design view

This provides you with a basic invoice. You may want additional fields, such as date printed, a company logo and letterhead, and other details appropriate for your scenario. You can also can arrange the fields and add additional formatting as you deem appropriate.

Summary

We have demonstrated that it can be relatively simple to combine tables from different databases if they follow consistent naming conventions and were designed according to the rules of normalization. However, when acceptable design standards have not been followed, it can be challenging to combine tables from multiple sources.

Because the databases in this book were designed using an AutoNumber as the primary keys, it was much easier to incorporate additional tables into the database and relate the records. And, we did not need to make modifications to the key structure to add the additional tables.

Access is well suited for rapid database development. The database designs presented in this book are a great starting point for a customized solution to fit your business needs. There are many online resources to help you through the design and implementation process (see Appendix E, "References and Resources," for a list of excellent resources). The Microsoft newsgroups are a great source for assistance. UtterAccess.com is another community of willing and capable database experts. Do not hesitate to ask for assistance at one of the many help sites; chances are good that someone has already experienced your problem and has a solution.

SQL Server and Other External Data Sources

Although this book is intended to help you design databases in Access, the principles of good database design are not dependent on the software you use to build your database. The same rules, processes, and relationships apply across the board and if you design first on paper, as many professionals do, then the database software does not even need to be a consideration during your design phase.

However, when you build the database, the software platform you choose can subtly affect the design. That is because considerations beyond the normalization and design process have to be taken into account. For example, how is your database going to be used? Will the company that uses it be adding a hundred new records a month or a hundred thousand? Will it be accessed by five users at once or fifty? How secure will it need to be? Such considerations are a fundamental part of choosing what software you will use to implement your database, for there is a choice to be made. That choice can influence the design and, more importantly, how you work with your data.

Server databases, and in particular Microsoft SQL Server, are very common tools for the Access developer. So, although this book is about Microsoft Access, you still have database choices available to you and in this chapter you will see what they are, how you make them, and what benefits they can provide to your organization.

Before we get into the technical details, we want to share a few assumptions. Since you're reading about SQL Server, we're assuming that you are somewhat familiar with the concepts of relational data design and are comfortable with the terminology. Because the different platforms may treat certain types of data differently, we will also be discussing various data types. You don't need to be an expert to follow the process. It is important for you to be aware of the differences and to investigate further when you are preparing to work with different platform. And, if you feel the need for a refresher on relational data modeling or terminology you can turn to Chapters 2 "Elements of a Microsoft Access Database," and 3 "Relational Data Model," and Appendix B, "Relationships, Joins, and Nulls."

Client-Server Databases

In this section, we introduce the concept of client-server development, why you may need it, and what should determine your final decision to use it. We also briefly cover the processes involved to better prepare you for the optimization suggestions later in the chapter. Very simply stated, a client-server solution involves two files. One file provides the user interface, the client. This is often installed on the user's computer and provides the forms and reports required to enter, edit, and retrieve data. The other stores the data and is referred to as the server; you might think of it as serving the data back to the client. The files can be on the same computer, on a local network, or connected only through the Internet. The physical location of the two files can be relatively independent, as long as they can make some sort of network connection. Of course, there is a lot more to it. We'll begin by discussing the file server.

File-Server Limitations

The default Access database engine, known as ACE (which stands for Access Connectivity Engine), is the successor to Jet, which was the engine used prior to Office 2007. It is understandable if you are wondering about the term "database engine" because that seems to be used synonymously with both Access and database. Access is the application that provides the user and developer environment. ACE, or the database engine, is actually the software that the database uses to create and manipulate the data that is stored. When you install Microsoft Access 2007 or later, it automatically installs ACE. Prior versions of Access installed Jet.

ACE is a File-Server database. This means that the database engine runs on the client, or local PC of each user. The server or PC hosting the database with the data acts primarily as a central file storage location. This offers the performance convenience of distributing the data processing load among the user PCs that are making those requests. It also has the considerable benefit that it offers very convenient distribution and setup. To install a data-oriented software solution you literally drop the data file in place and there's your database; the engine—or program—will be provided in conjunction with the front end.

NOTE A *database engine* is the software that, for all intents and purposes, really *is* the database. The data itself is stored in a structured file, which is generally thought of as the database, but that file structure is very specific to each type of database and of little use by itself. The engine is the software that reads from that format, performing the queries, optimizations, and all updates and maintenance to that file data. It's an example of some very accurate naming as it truly is the engine that drives your database.

However, there is a fundamental disadvantage associated with the sharing requirements placed on a single file. The actions of multiple users simultaneously accessing or changing data on a single file is a complex process for the various operating systems and database engines to deal with. Consequently, a file-based database engine has limitations. These limitations can affect any or all of the following: concurrency, speed, robustness, size, security, integrity, and recovery. That is not to say that ACE is lacking in all of these areas. ACE is a powerful, robust, and responsive database engine that will provide excellent results and efficiency when used with properly designed databases. Its fundamental limits merely mean that it should not be used beyond the scope of its intended purpose. If you use a horse to pull a trailer intended for a truck, you cannot very well blame the horse when it does not get very far. But there are still plenty of areas where a horse is appropriate and a truck would not fit.

The classic example of the effect of these limitations is that in multiple user environments both performance and reliability can degrade if the number of simultaneous users grows too high. In addition, a file-server database can contain only a finite number of records—currently ACCDB files are limited to 2GB in size. Additionally, they do not support certain useful functions such as transaction logs for database recovery after a disaster or other loss of data.

However, not all performance impacts can be attributed to the database engine; more often than not they are a consequence of poor database design and implementation. And that is why we are writing this book; we want to help you enjoy the benefits of a well-structured database and to avoid undue challenges.

Server Databases

On the other hand, a database server operates as a process that runs continuously on the server receiving requests for data operations from client PCs. The database server performs the required actions on the data or returns the requested data (records) to the client application. Known as *client-server*, this process is less likely to suffer from the limitations described in the previous section. A client-server offers greater data integrity and scalability because its single service performs the entire database operations.

Consequently, in order to provide the necessary level of performance for all users, a client-server must meet substantial hardware specifications. Although a client-server application is often considered to be the inevitable solution to speed problems, this is a misconception. Because it is so important to take advantage of the server side processing of data requests, you need to make every effort to ensure that your design allows that to happen. A poor file-server database generally translates into a poor client-server one; in fact, the conversion can even make things worse. We will offer some suggestions later in the chapter what will help you to ensure efficient data operations.

There are other reasons to make the move to a server database, but the potential performance of a server database relies upon the assistance of efficient data requests and a solid schema within which to form them. You will find no official documentation about where the line is for determining when to move to a server database. Generally, it is when at least one of the following applies:

- Your number of concurrent users grows beyond a "reasonable" level.
- You need to more tightly secure your data.
- Your volume of data is surpassing reasonable use or the physical file size limit for ACCDB/MDB.
- You require a robust data recovery plan or need tracking such as an audit trail of data operations.
- You need some other server-based extended functionality.

NOTE The issue of how many users necessitate moving to a server database platform is a contentious one. Opinion varies widely as to a reasonable cut-off point. For a well-designed file-server database, around 20 users is reasonable but it could easily be more for applications that have light use or are used mainly to look up and retrieve data. It could also be substantially fewer; depending on the efficiency of the database design and the type of data manipulation involved. Perhaps a better answer is, "When the number of users is harming performance and reliability."

Of course, the potential shift in platform to a database server does not mean that you will not continue working in Access. It's not always understood that Access is a database application development environment, not ACE, the data engine itself, as we mentioned earlier. But the two work closely together and since ACE ships with Access, it easily gives the impression that it is a single product. It is often convenient to refer to ACE tables as being "native" to Access, but Access is very capable of working with the software of other database providers including server-based database engines.

The key to Access's ability to use other data sources is in ACE's support of *Open Database Connectivity (ODBC)*. ODBC is a set of standards that enables individual software vendors to provide an interface to their database systems without having to supply language specific requests. The appropriate use of any Access application is with linked tables, even when linking to another ACCDB (or MDB) data file as the "backend." Access is capable of using ODBC drivers provided by other products to link to those tables instead. Such ODBC linked tables still pass through a layer of ACE wrapping, as the links themselves are data objects in their own right, as illustrated in Figure 15-1. The end result is that this effectively enables you to work with linked data from external sources very much as you would with "native" tables.

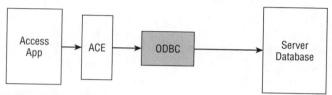

Figure 15-1: Figure 15-1: ODBC data requests

As long as you have the appropriate drivers installed on the client, the linked tables can reference a wide range of database products such as Oracle, MySQL, AS400, Excel, text files and, of course, Microsoft SQL Server.

Microsoft SQL Server

SQL Server (pronounced "sequel server") is Microsoft's enterprise-level database application. It consists of a powerful server database engine and the accompanying language (Transact-SQL, or T-SQL), and includes administration, reporting, and analysis tools.

Second to ACE, SQL Server is likely to be the database engine you most often encounter; and it is the most common server platform used with Access. As it does with other databases, Access links to SQL Server using an ODBC provider. With both ACE and SQL Server being Microsoft products, they are frequently used together and there are several tools specifically designed for using Access with SQL Server.

Many projects that start out as "native" ACE databases are later upsized to SQL Server databases to take advantage of its more wide-ranging abilities and performance options. There are tools to help with the conversion, including the Upsizing Wizard that is shipped with Access, the SQL Server Migration Assistant that is downloadable from Microsoft, and SQL Server's own Integration Services. You will also find a host of dedicated third-party utilities. These are capable of converting an existing MDB or ACCDB solution to a SQL Server-based database. In your Access front-end application the local or "native" linked tables are replaced with ODBC linked tables, offering a user and development experience very much like that before the upsize moved the tables.

Data Type Comparisons

Does this linked table convenience mean you are able to continue exactly as before? To a certain extent, yes, in some cases. There are some differences in both the data types offered and the implementation of functionality, but the wrapping that is provided by ACE through linked tables actually means much of these differences are not applicable to your Access application—or at least may not have an apparent impact.

For example SQL Server `varChar` data types will appear in your linked tables as the ACE `Text` data type and `Integers` on the server will appear and behave as their ACE `Long Integer` counterpart and so forth. AutoNumber fields are equivalent to SQL Server Identity columns (fields in Access are often referred to as columns in SQL Server, but the terms are interchangeable). As with an Access AutoNumber, the Identity column can provide an auto-generated incrementing value, so they are commonly used as the primary key index for a table. And here again, the Identity column is not a required column, and SQL Server will not automatically insert it or make it the primary key.

For more information on surrogate and primary keys, see Chapter 3 and Appendix B. One important difference to note is that SQL Server generates the Identity value only when a new record is committed, or saved, whereas ACE issues it upon record creation—even if the record is deleted before it has been saved.

NOTE Although the practice of inserting an Identity column's value as the record is committed makes sequence gaps less likely; it's important to stress that this gap doesn't matter simply because the value of the surrogate key is merely a unique record identifier. Some applications choose to expose this row identifying field in the user interface, but the value is most often only used internally by the application. If you need a consecutive numeric sequence, then you should use a separate field rather than relying on an AutoNumber/Identity column to provide it.

Table 15-1 provides a list of the common data types that are used in an ACE-based database and their SQL Server counterparts.

NOTE A lot of the discussion will focus on SQL Server data types, their characteristics, and their similarities and differences from those in Access. In this chapter, data types are presented in monofont to help draw attention to the names of the data types as they are discussed in the narrative.

Table 15-1: SQL Server Data Type Equivalents

ACE (AND JET)	SQL SERVER	SQL SERVER DIFFERENCES
Text	varChar, nvarChar	Not limited to 255 chars
Date	DateTime, SmallDateTime	(see comments in the following section)
Integer	SmallInt	
Long Integer	Int	
Decimal	Decimal	
Double	Float	
Single	Real	
Byte	TinyInt	
Currency	Money, SmallMoney	
Boolean (Yes/No)	Bit	Allows Nulls
Binary	nvarBinary	
Memo	nvarChar(Max), Text	
OLE	nvarBinary(Max),Image	

Date Data Types

Dates are especially important when considering a source other than ACE. There are several additional data types in SQL Server that can store date data including `DateTime2`, `Date`, `Time`, and `DateTimeOffset`. The `DateTime` and `SmallDateTime` are the data types you are most likely to encounter, and they are the closest to the Date type found in ACE. When viewing your linked tables design in Access, both ACE and the ODBC provider will hide many of the differences between the data types, so you will see your linked tables presented with the familiar ACE data types.

In both ACE and SQL Server, dates are stored internally as numeric values, with a unit of measure equal to days. The numeric value is based on the number of days from a base date. The whole number portion of the numeric value represents the days offset from the base date. The decimal portion is the fraction of a day that represents the time. SQL Server uses Jan 1, 1900 as the base and ACE uses Dec 30, 1899 as the base, so the difference must be accommodated. For example, 12pm on Dec 12th, 1943, would be stored in SQL Server as 16050.5, but in ACE as 16052.5, a difference of two days. The ODBC provider is aware of this and properly handles the offset during communication between ACE and SQL Server so the dates are correctly represented in both locations. It is important to note that ODBC cannot allow for differences in time detail or for the difference in the permitted range of allowed dates. ACE and SQL Server date types have noticeably different valid ranges as shown in Table 15-2.

Table 15-2: Acceptable Date Data Type Ranges

DATA TYPE	DATES FROM	DATES UNTIL	ACCURACY
Date (ACE)	Jan 1, 0100	Dec 31, 9999	1 second
DateTime (SQL)	Jan 1, 1753	Dec 31, 9999	33.3 milliseconds
SmallDateTime (SQL)	Jan 1, 1900	Jun 6, 2079	1 minute
DateTime2 (SQL 2008)	Jan 1, 0001	Dec 31, 9999	100 nanoseconds

If these differences in range might be a factor in your database, you will need to know which data type is being used on the server. Even though when viewed through a linked table in design view from the Access user interface they will all appear simply as Date/Time, you might need to adjust the formulations and equations in your application to ensure that the dates are managed correctly.

Text Data Types

The Text data type in ACE is analogous to the varChar (or nvarChar as it supports Unicode) in SQL Server. The key difference is in the field length or size. There is no upper limit to the maximum size of a varChar column if defined as varChar(Max). And the upper limit for a pre-defined size is varChar(8000), which is still much larger than the 255 characters that an ACE Text field can support. Therefore, any varChar or nvarChar column defined above a length of 255 will appear as a Memo in your linked tables.

Boolean (Yes/No) Data Types

Bit fields in SQL Server are a two-state data type (storing 0 or 1) that can also permit null values. The ACE equivalent Boolean (or Yes/No) data type has a value of 0 or -1 but cannot accept null values. This discrepancy can be a source of problems in the conversion of Bit to Boolean by ODBC and especially for updates through linked tables in Access. To reduce the potential for these issues, you should create Bit fields in SQL Server with nulls disallowed and with a default value, which is often set to 0 (or False).

Numeric Data Types

Though both ACE and SQL Server support Floating Point number types, the nature of these types of numbers is, by definition, inexact. With a fixed allocation of memory to store the numeric value, only so many characters can be stored precisely. Beyond that it's an approximation. After all, computers count in binary, not decimal as we do. In ACE these floating precision data types are Double and Single and in SQL Server they are Float and Real.

A non-trivial consequence of the limits to precision is that non-integer numbers stored in these data types do not necessarily return a match when compared against what could be considered to be the same value. This can cause ACE to mistakenly believe the server table row has been updated by another process while it was also being edited in the current application. The result is an error message to indicate the row is locked. If you encounter this situation, then you have some options to consider. You can usually substitute a different numeric data type that supports exact precision, such as Money or Decimal. Alternatively you can fix the locking issue by including a TimeStamp field in the server table.

Contrary to what the name suggests, the TimeStamp field is not a reference to a Date or Time value, rather it is an incremental row version check updated by SQL Server. ACE uses this field to determine the record status, thus avoiding the record-locking issue that results from the misinterpretation that a record had been changed. In theory this can also have a performance enhancing effect as ACE needs only check this one field to determine if there has been an update as opposed to checking each field in the record. Bear in mind that TimeStamp data types can have their own issues updating data through an Access application user interface, so it is only worth implementing a TimeStamp field in a table for a particular reason rather than as a general practice.

SQL Server also supports a larger type of integer data type called BigInt. This permits a huge range of values. The maximum permitted is 9,223,372,036,854,775,807. Because ACE has no equivalent data type to this, when viewed from a linked table in Access any BigInt fields will be listed as Text type. This may seem like quite a disparate pairing of types and it certainly isn't ideal, however ACE does not have a numeric field that can accommodate that many digits, using a text field at least allows users to retrieve and work with the values.

Binary (File) Data Types

SQL Server has several options for storing what, in Access, would be referred to as an OLE Object. To store these in Access, you will typically use an OLE Object field, which is merely a Long Binary data type. OLE objects are typically external files such as images or documents, so the files can be quite large. Despite the sizeable capacity of a SQL Server database, storing the object directly in the database is not necessarily the best choice. It is more common to store the text version of the UNC path to the files, which would typically be stored on your server's hard disk. When object storage is required, the SQL Server Image data type has largely been superseded by varBinary(Max). You can also use either of those file types for OLE object functionality in Access. In a full SQL Server database there's usually more storage space to accept that kind of functionality if it's required whereas an ACCDB will bloat very quickly.

ACE's Attachment data type and the Multi-value field data type are not supported in SQL Server. If you have any multi-value data types in your Access tables, you would need to replace them by creating additional tables to store the data directly at the table level rather than within the field. Many developers would tell you that this is a better approach anyway. The ACE `Attachment` data type uses the same complex data type strategy used in Multi-Value fields. To transfer the files for storage in SQL Server, you would need to use a different data type, such as `varBinary(Max)` or `Image`. But it is worth mentioning that it is more common to merely store the UNC path in the database and store the file elsewhere on the server. However, this is a less portable solution than having the file or attachments directly in the database.

Other Data Types

There are several other data types that SQL Server offers, such as the `XML` data type and the newer `Spatial` and `Hierarchy` data types that have no equivalent in ACE. If you only have previous experience with "native" Access databases then you're unlikely to be concerned with these.

Server Functionality

In addition to the data type differences, you will find that SQL Server offers numerous capabilities beyond what Access can provide. These are derived from the tools that ship with the product and from the functionality that is inherent in the engine itself.

Server Robustness

We have only mentioned in passing the more functionally rich backups offered by a server database. These are made possible due to the extensive logs that SQL Server maintains on data operations. The logs permit a range of backup functionality, which can be complete or incremental. This provides server administrators a comprehensive recovery strategy to minimize data loss after a disaster.

Naturally, backups can be performed on a file-server database such as ACE by simply copying the ACCDB or MDB file to an archive location. However, this is an "all or nothing" solution. It also places locks on the file during data writing operations, which can cause conflicts and errors when the database is in use. Server databases such as SQL Server do not suffer from such limitations and offer greater robustness.

The security model employed by SQL Server is much more comprehensive; this alone can be a valid reason for choosing SQL Server for data storage. There's only a certain amount of protection that can ever be provided for an ACCDB data file as exposure of the physical file to each user is inherent to a file-server database. SQL Server offers more comprehensive security to both the physical protection of the database files and the flexibility of the security applied to the database and its objects. SQL Server supports both its own security login model as well as Windows authentication. This can be a very attractive option for many applications.

Server Objects and Transact SQL

Perhaps the single greatest difference between SQL Server functionality and ACE is that of the query language itself. ACE SQL supports a wide range of the ANSI standard syntaxes for working with data and manipulating data objects. Ultimately, ACE centers on making single-statement requests for data or updates. There is no programming control of execution flow, no real decision-making or handling of errors. SQL Server's own dialect, Transact SQL (or T-SQL), offers all of these and more.

Views are the closest analogy to an Access select query. A view is a single T-SQL statement that selects data from one or more tables, effectively creating a virtual table which itself can be selected from or updated. If there are columns of data you wish to obscure from certain users, then a view that selects all but those columns provides a logical object to which users can be granted access. Being granted access to a view does not grant access to the table itself.

It is also common to create views that compile data from several tables into a single set of records. Similar to the queries we've created in Access, views can be a useful core object to use in subsequent queries and they can be used as a linked table in Access applications. In many respects they can be treated as "virtual tables."

Server objects such as *stored procedures* (SP's), *user defined functions* (UDF's) and *triggers* are all programmatic objects defined in T-SQL. A stored procedure is a single object that is comprised of a set of T-SQL statements. Therefore, they can include logical comparisons, loops, and conditional execution as well as execute SQL statements to select or perform actions upon data. Stored procedures can accept parameters somewhat similar to ACE queries, but they offer much more functionality.

User defined functions fill a similar role but can be used to return values or entire datasets for selection in other database querying and do so in a well optimized, re-usable object for maximum efficiency.

Triggers are special stored procedures that run on a specified data action for a given table, similar in concept to Access form events. For example, you can specify that an AFTER UPDATE trigger should be executed after any update is performed upon a particular table. The trigger enables you to work on the entered data or perform other database actions at that time. Trigger types include UPDATE, INSERT and DELETE and can be assigned for AFTER or INSTEAD OF actions.

Creating linked tables in your Access application to your SQL Server tables or views will not offer any mechanism for working directly with the stored procedures or user defined functions themselves. But Access does support other functionality that enables you to fully utilize SQL Server's capabilities. We discuss those briefly in the "Optimization Suggestions" section. You can also use triggers to work with data that is in SQL Server. Triggers are run independently by the server on any data operations, regardless of how they are initiated. This means that any actions you perform on the server data through linked tables, or any other means, will invoke the associated trigger. Without adding code to your application, you can use triggers to provide functionality such as to clean (sanitize) entered data or maintain an audit trail of data operations.

SQL Server Editions

Various flavors of SQL Server are available, beginning at the top with the Enterprise edition, which offers the full power of the engine and a complete array of packaged tools. These tools range from the standard console of Management Studio (MS) to the powerful Integration Services (IS), formerly known as Data Transformation Service or DTS, to full Business Intelligence (BI) options. The Standard edition offers a lot of the same core database functionality, and differs mostly on the specific tools included in each area, such as with the BI options. The workgroup edition is more limited again on both database and bundled tools, but it still offers the same core SQL Server engine with enough tools to satisfy many smaller organizations. The editions progress all the way down to SQL Server CE, an extremely lean version designed especially to operate efficiently on small devices, such as PDAs.

For many initial Access-centric conversions, there is the downloadable SQL Server Express edition. SQL Server Express offers the core server engine and Management Studio enabling you to really get a look into the server's objects. It offers an opportunity to experience a server database environment. Indeed, many of the large database vendors offer a no-frills free version of their flagship product, so you have several ways to begin working with server data and making your database applications more "bullet proof" with increased functionality.

Server Database Design

As in previous chapters which considered specific business applications, our goal here is to form an appropriate analysis of requirements for a server database. Based on the earlier list for considering when to employ database software, we need to answer the following questions:

- How many concurrent users need to be supported?
- How many records do you add per week/month/year?
- How secure does your data need to be from employees and others?

- Is the data business critical? Can you afford any loss of data or downtime?

- Does the organization have the funds for a potential server database outlay or does it already have server database licenses?

The answers to these questions will help you determine if a server database is appropriate. As you gain experience, you may be aware of functionality you require in your database that can only be achieved in a server database; as the developer, this is another question that you can often ask and answer yourself. Once the decision to use a server database has been made, you need to avoid certain pitfalls when designing the tables and associated relationships and permissions. In the next section we look at the implications a server database has on your table schema.

Design Considerations

Do the differences between file-server and client-server development affect database design? To a considerable extent, it can be argued that the difference in database platforms does not affect design and that a well-designed database is similar in almost any environment. Using a server database does not equate to implementing a data warehouse, so a normalized, relational schema still rules supreme in creating a great many transactional database applications.

Narrow and Long Tables

When you're considering the actual physical design of the application, there are important principles to bear in mind. Selecting fewer fields—only those specifically required to satisfy a particular purpose—in an ACE database table makes little difference in terms of performance and efficiency. However, with a SQL Server database the data from all selected fields will be sent across the network, so the more specific the request, the better the performance will be. In other words, SQL Server will reward you for selecting fewer fields in your queries in a way that ACE does not. In table design this is known as maintaining a "narrow and long" mindset. Making sure your tables are well normalized is the best possible start to achieving this. Tables of only a few fields with many rows are the preferred schema; selections are made among those rows to satisfy a request.

To illustrate the concept of how to minimize the data requested, we'll use a table named tblDateSettings, shown in Table 15-3, that stores report selection criteria. The same table implemented with a single row of data is shown in Table 15-4.

If this settings table were required for multiple users, then an additional field could be included to identify each row for a specific user name.

Normalization mandates that you do not allow repeating groups, so your attention is quickly drawn to the data fields, as they appear to have repeating settings. Bearing in mind that this table supports the application rather than storing data about a subject, it does not necessarily qualify for normalization. From a practical standpoint, consider that if we extend that table, adding more and more columns for additional selection criteria, the width would soon become noticeable. In a server database, querying the table for only a required column is one option to improve the efficiency. One example of such a query might be to select only the password expiration data. For this example, that query would be:

```
SELECT Password_Expiry_Date FROM tblDateSettings
```

Table 15-3: Example of a Settings Table

FIELD NAME	DATA TYPE	DESCRIPTION
ID	Identity	Primary key
Report_From_Date	DateTime	Current reports from filter
Report_Until_Date	DateTime	Current reports until filter
Search_From_Date	DateTime	Current search from filter
Search_Until_Date	DateTime	Current search until filter
Last_Used_Date	DateTime	Last date app was used
Password_Expiry_Date	DateTime	Date password expires

Table 15-4: Example Settings Table Data

ID	REPORT_ FROM_DATE	REPORT_ UNTIL_DATE	SEARCH_ FROM_DATE	ETC...
1	01/01/2009	01/01/2010	12/01/2009	

However, consider the alternative schema in Table 15-5 where each setting has become an individual row, with several rows used to describe all the required settings. The data stored would then appear as shown in Table 15-6.

This vertical rather than horizontal layout means that you retrieve settings by using a query that has to use two fields to retrieve the password expiration date: the SettingName and the SettingValue. The query would be written as:

```
SELECT SettingValue AS Password_Expiry_Date
FROM tblDateSettings
WHERE SettingName = "Password_Expiry_Date"
```

Table 15-5: Alternative Settings Table

COLUMN NAME	DATA TYPE	DESCRIPTION
ID	Identity	Primary key
SettingName	varChar	Name of property
SettingValue	DateTime	Stored value
SettingDescription	varChar	Description of property

Table 15-6: Alternative Settings Table Data

ID	SETTINGNAME	SETTINGVALUE	DESCRIPTION
1	Report_From_Date	01/01/2009	Current reports from filter
2	Report_Until_Date	01/01/2010	Current reports until filter
3	Search_From_Date	12/01/2009	Current search from filter
4	Search_Until_Date	12/31/2009	Current search until filter
5	Last_Used_Date	12/12/2009	Last date app was used
6	Password_Expiry_Date	02/01/2010	Date password expires

Though this is only an illustration of the concept, the example can be extended to include settings for multiple users and settings of data types other than just the DateTime type. Some would suggest that you should include a column for every possible data type. However, this inevitably results in unused columns. Alternatively, a single varChar type column (as the most versatile data type) can have almost any data stored as text, and the data can be converted to the required data type after it has been selected. Table 15-7 shows what this would look like.

Table 15-7: General User Settings Table

COLUMN NAME	DATA TYPE	DESCRIPTION
ID	Identity	Primary key
UserID	Integer	Foreign key to identify a User
SettingName	varChar	Name of property
SettingValue	varChar	Stored value
SettingType	varChar	Description of data type
SettingDescription	varChar	Description of property

If you chose this particular design then this can be further normalized to provide greater flexibility. Both the SettingType and SettingDescription fields are dependent on each individual SettingName (which is a candidate key in this instance). Therefore, you would separate the fields into two tables: tblUserSettings is shown in Table 15-8 and the related table, tblSettings, is shown in Table 15-9.

Table 15-8: General User Settings Tables

COLUMN NAME	DATA TYPE	DESCRIPTION
UserSettingID	Identity	Primary key
UserID	Integer	Foreign key to identify a user
SettingID	Integer	Foreign key to identify a setting
SettingValue	varChar	Stored value

Table 15-9: General User Settings Tables

COLUMN NAME	DATA TYPE	DESCRIPTION
SettingID	Identity	Primary key
SettingName	varChar	Name of property
SettingType	varChar	Description of data type
SettingDescription	varChar	Description of property

The effort of implementing this generic table design is rewarded with several benefits. As you might expect, this design can help prevent the selection of unnecessary fields in queries. It also provides another real advantage, which allows for the dynamic creation of new settings simply by adding appropriately named records to the tables rather than by attempting to create new fields in the table design. Although the need to add new fields should be a rare occurrence in tables modeling your business data, business requirements can change, and that can result in the applications evolving. The need for new settings is closely linked to this evolution.

AMBIGUOUS DATA FORMATS

In a situation such as storing various data types in a Text type field, you must protect against any ambiguity. Date data offers the greatest likelihood of such ambiguity as its format varies from region to region.

If you are sure that the application viewing or displaying the data has the same regional setting as the application inserting the data, then the conversion back to date display will go smoothly. However, any potential change could result in completely misinterpreted data. For example, December 1, 2009 in U.S. date format mm/dd/yyyy appears as 12/1/2009; but many other regions use dd/mm/yyyy, so it would be presented as 1/12/2009. This would typically be interpreted as the 12th of January, 2009, in the U.S. calendar.

The best solution when storing dates in `Text` data types is an international format. The ISO 8601 standard, yyyy-mm-dd, is the most internationally recognized format. Using it for the preceding example, the date would appear as 2009-12-01 in either region. Values stored and retrieved in that format aren't open to interpretation and will retain their meaning in any region. This format is also available for use when constructing your queries, whether they are local to Access, which uses ACE SQL, or on your SQL Server, which uses T-SQL.

Keep in mind that you can format the way data is displayed independent of the way that data is stored; so users need not be concerned with or affected by the formatting at the table level. Your priority is to ensure that the data is correctly stored and interpreted.

Lookup Tables

The term *lookup table* can attract some controversy. In practice these tables are used to refer to tables that serve no purpose other than feeding values into the foreign key of the tables that model the main entities of the database. They often consist of nothing more than a primary key identity for use as a foreign key in the related tables and a text field for the display value. Lookup table results are almost always presented in applications in list form for convenience in the user interface or, using referential integrity, to force a permitted set of values only. In other words, having a related table of lookup values forced selection of only one of those values as opposed to a free choice.

Since some developers prefer using lookup tables as a means of controlling their application lists, you might find several such tables in a single application. Although we've recommended using a surrogate primary key identity field in every table, another school of thought is that this is redundant in simple lists. Since only the value itself is required in the lookup table and the value can be inserted directly into the field in the main table, the lookup table can consist of only a single field containing descriptive data. This does not violate normalization, as no other fields are dependent on this single value. The classic "defense" for a surrogate primary key in lookup table is that if you need to change or update a value, you will only need to change it in one place—the lookup table. You will not need to worry about cascade updates to make sure the revised value is consistent in all related tables.

It is suggested that each lookup table you create should represent an identifiable entity and not be considered purely a user interface mechanism shoehorned into the database for convenience. If you can name the single entity that each table represents in your database then you are less likely to have introduced any convoluted choices. It's for this reason that the term "lookup table" isn't universally liked. Despite this ideal, some of your database tables may ultimately only exist for functional, rather than data modeling, purposes.

> **NOTE** Lookup tables are certainly not confined to server database development. They are used in almost every relational database design regardless of the platform. However, in a server database it's even more likely that you will encounter the trend towards accumulating the various lookup subjects (tables and fields) into a single conglomeration. For this reason, the relative merits and drawbacks of this practice are discussed in this chapter to show why you might want to store all of the lookup lists in one table, and, more importantly, to explain why this might not necessarily be a good choice.

To illustrate lookup table evolution, take the example demonstrated earlier in this book for looking up values of U.S. states and abbreviations. It consists only of an identifying key field and a simple descriptive field. Suppose you want to include countries and their abbreviations in that convenient table. In order for these values to be used in lists to assist users in making simple and correct data entries in related tables, we need to know what type of data is being described. Therefore, the table might change as shown in Table 15-10. And a selection of possible data from such a table of U.S. states is shown in Table 15-11.

Table 15-10: List Lookup Table

COLUMN NAME	DATA TYPE	DESCRIPTION
Abbrev	varChar	Primary key (abbreviation of state or country)
ListType	varChar	Identifying group type (such as state or country)
ListValue	varChar	Value displayed (name of state or country)

Table 15-11: List Lookup Example Data

ABBREV	LISTTYPE	LISTVALUE
WY	State	Wyoming
YT	State	Yukon Territory
AF	Country	Afghanistan
AL	Country	Albania

As you can see, much like the thin tables previously, this makes it easy to add more details (states and countries) and to create new categories (perhaps regions or continents) merely by adding new rows with the appropriate ListType to distinguish them. But this versatility is offset by the need to specify two fields, both the type and value, in order to work with an abbreviation.

Ever more generic examples exist of similar concept lookup tables culminating in what's known as the One True Lookup Table (OTLT). This is a single unified source of simple data used in many information lists in an application. The reason for the existence of OTLTs is understandable as many lookup values are simple text. To form a related record we need merely a surrogate primary key, usually an `Identity` field, and the single display value. As in the earlier application settings table example, you could maintain a separate table that describes the different lists and another which actually contains the values for the lists. Consider the following tblListTypes and tblListEntries tables. The former is shown in Table 15-12. The values of which would be used in tblListEntries, which is shown below in Table 15-13.

Table 15-12: Generic List Type Table (tblListTypes)

COLUMN NAME	DATA TYPE	DESCRIPTION
ListTypeID	`Identity`	Primary key
ListType	`varChar`	Type for filtering or display

Table 15-13: Generic List Lookup Table (tblListEntries)

COLUMN NAME	DATA TYPE	DESCRIPTION
ListID	`Identity`	Primary key
ListTypeID	`integer`	Foreign key to tblListTypes
ListValue	`varChar`	Value displayed

Together these tables can describe a wide range of lookup lists without requiring a dedicated table for each list. Table tblListTypes stores the types of lists available that would otherwise be modeled using separate lookup tables. The field values in tblListEntries reference the ListValueID from tblListTypes to determine which list the values comprise. Table 15-14 shows sample data for list types, and Table 15-15 shows some example data for the list values.

Table 15-14: Generic List Lookup Types

LISTTYPEID	LISTTYPE
1	States
2	Countries

Table 15-15: Generic List Lookup Data

LISTID	LISTTYPEID	LISTVALUE
1	1	Wyoming
2	1	Yukon Territory
3	2	Afghanistan
4	2	Albania

You can remove the requirement for two tables to model your lists. But this comes at a price as it complicates the queries used to retrieve the list values. The single flexible lookup table includes the ListTypes as other "parent" rows in a new tblListEntries design. Furthermore there's nothing preventing these parent groupings from being more than a single level deep. For example, consider a subdivision of Sales categorization where a master set of "Categories" is subdivided into "Retail" or "Wholesale," each of which is divided into further categories such as public, trade, and suppliers. This hierarchical structure is shown in Table 15-16. Sample data that could be used to create a hierarchy of categories is shown in Table 15-17.

Table 15-16: Single Lookup Table (tblListTypes)

COLUMN NAME	DATA TYPE	DESCRIPTION
ListID	Identity	Primary key
ListTypeID	integer	Foreign key to ListID of this table
ListValue	varChar	Visible description value

Table 15-17: Single Lookup Table Sample Data (tblListTypes)

LISTID	LISTTYPEID	LISTVALUE
1		Categories
2	1	Retail
3	1	Wholesale
4	2	Retail to public
5	2	Retail to trade
6	3	Wholesale to trade
7	3	Wholesale to suppliers

The major benefit of this versatile structure is how easy it becomes to add new entities to the list and to create multiple levels of those lists. However, it can be much more complicated to query; as explained in the following sidebar.

RETRIEVING DATA FROM A HIERARCHICAL TABLE STRUCTURE

To retrieve a list of main categories, instead of using a trivial query like:

```
SELECT tblCategories.Category FROM tblCategories
```

you have to refer the lookup table to itself and then request the list of categories, as shown here:

```
SELECT T2.ListValue As Category
FROM tblListEntries As T1 INNER JOIN tblListEntries As T2
ON T1.ListID = T2. ListTypeID
WHERE T1.ListValue = "Categories"
```

And, if you also need a list of all the subcategories, you will need to go one level deeper and your query could be constructed similarly to the following:

```
SELECT T2.ListValue As Category, T3.ListValue As SubCategory
FROM tblListEntries As T1 INNER JOIN
(tblListEntries As T2 INNER JOIN tblListEntries As T3
ON T2.ListID = T3. ListTypeID)
    ON T1.ListID = T2. ListTypeID
WHERE T1.ListValue = "Categories"
```

Although such a hierarchical set of lists may well be adding complexity that you would rather avoid, this type of flexible lookup table is relatively common in database design where application design and even user interface considerations come into the equation. The concept can extend further into describing other areas requiring lists, essentially any hierarchical structure that includes the "level above," such as tables, fields, rows, and even values. But your single table then describes a wide range of complex entities and begins to look more like a data dictionary.

A *data dictionary* consists of a table (or small set of tables) that lists and describes all the tables and fields in the database. There's nothing wrong with data dictionaries. SQL Server maintains its own set of system tables and views which provide this kind of definition functionality automatically. But you do not want to turn your lookups into such an extensive concept and incorporate every possible entity modeled in the database.

NOTE In theory, any table could be reduced to such a structure based on single elements that reference some parent element, which in turn has a parent. That is, individual fields all have a parent table and so could be modeled as records joined together by a common parent record. Such a labor-intensive construction is nonsensical for anything but the application responsible for putting the rows back together into meaningfully grouped data.

Though adding new fields to your "database" is then a versatile process, the performance hit would be prohibitive; and naturally you will not want to implement database solutions like this. Microsoft SharePoint actually implements lists in a similar way in order to support the requirement for flexibility, but it also has a performance threshold as a result.

The One True Lookup Table is not favored by many database professionals. The concept is not consistent with an entity-driven relational database design. However, the single biggest reason to not employ the OTLT concept over a set of distinct lookup tables is enough to avoid them: the performance hit can be great. Regardless of how powerful your server is, selecting a small set of rows from one much larger table is always going to be less efficient than selecting from a small, dedicated table. The comparison is even worse for the OTLT when a hierarchical query is required to choose that data.

The design axiom of "narrow and long" is a good rule of thumb, but when you start making tables unnecessarily "long," then you are going to affect the performance of doing lookups within those lists. From an Access perspective, another influence on this is where linked table data is loaded into the application user interface. Access can initially request the full primary key index of that table and then filter and request by other fields as required. A larger table means a larger index, and there's no need to make it larger than it needs to be.

So where do you draw the line? At what point is a table list part of a database design or a tool for convenient application data entry? As soon as a table takes on more than one meaning, or stores more than one entity, then it could be thought of as a dictionary fueling your application. Always consider the purpose of your database. If you can see the single entity in each table in your database then you will not go far wrong.

Design Optimization

Rather than a radically different methodology, databases designed for servers generally just incorporate subtle nuances. These nuances are generally made to enhance performance, but they can also make use of the server's abilities.

Denormalizing

The process of deliberately removing normalization principles from a given table design is always a contentious issue. If the decision is taken to even slightly denormalize a table structure, then it should be done only after great deliberation. You should understand the consequences, an understanding which should be based on experience from implementing fully normalized solutions. In most cases you can implement an alternative instead.

Many databases are denormalized in order to improve performance. However, a normalized database will generally perform very well. Even when it does not, performance is not the ultimate goal of normalization and there are other optimization techniques to try first, such as those listed in the "Optimization Suggestions" section later in this chapter. In some structures the burden of normalization hinders simple development of your user interface. You must not let that be a factor when making the decision. You can learn to leverage the inherent features in Access and VBA techniques to be able to develop a functional user interface based on a fully normalized table structure. Maintaining a versatile, normalized schema will enable you to more safely handle future data requirements.

So when and why might you want to design a schema that does not conform (or may appear to not conform) to the standards we have been consistently encouraging you to adopt? An example of data which is not necessarily normalized was shown in Chapter 7, "Sales," in the example database's Order Details table. You might think that storing both a foreign key ID to the item in question and the unit cost of that item, which is then a value dependent upon another key value in that table, could be considered to violate the third normal form.

As shown in that chapter, it is a common option that allows for the changing values of the item over time, thereby recording the price at the moment the order is created. It also allows for a possible business rule stating that this price may be negotiable which would then require including the order-specific price field. With either of these considerations, it can be argued that this value is a separate piece of information from the default item price. In a client-server database this decision makes even more sense to avoid convoluted queries upon a historic price range table. If you have a table that stores a range of possible prices per item, then you have even more historic data to store and more table joins to perform in your query.

Connecting multiple tables in a query isn't necessarily an expensive operation in a database, so it isn't an excuse to denormalize the tables. At the same time, you don't need to complicate queries any more than is absolutely necessary.

Assisting Optimization

Optimization is the process whereby a database engine prepares the execution method of a query to make best use of the resources available in order to provide the best possible processing and return time of the data. The best design practice you can follow to assist optimization is to properly normalize and appropriately index your tables.

One of the simplest axioms of normalization is the requirement that each field store precisely one value, also known as data atomicity. To illustrate the benefits, we'll consider a scenario where a poor table design stores all of the address information in one field. If this data will be filtered, searched or linked to, then the field is usually a good candidate to be indexed. But fields that contain multiple details will not reap the maximum benefits from being indexed. Consider storing all address data in a single field. In order to search for a state or zip code, we would have to isolate the specific component that we want. For example, if we know that the zip code is the last 5 digits, we could use a SQL statement such as the following to query for records with the zip code "90210":

```
SELECT * FROM tblEntity WHERE Right(AddressField, 5) = "90210"
```

This type of query will prevent the database engine from making proper use of any index upon the Address field, as it forces the engine to perform a function (`WHERE Right(AddressField, 5)`) on every record as in order to apply the criteria. In addition to obviating the use of an index, these types of function calls can have a very significant hit on performance. In contrast, with a properly designed model, the zip code and state fields could be indexed, and the query could use the zip code to efficiently filter for "90210" and then pull up only the records that match.

This principle extends to scenarios where the data being stored really is atomic. An example would be a single field for the entry of a manufacturer's reference code for a machine where a section of the data may be important by itself, such as the last four characters to identify the year of manufacture. An index would not substantially help the execution of the query. Instead, you might store this code separately in a distinct field that allows for direct querying. In a server table you could hide this functionality from the user and employ a trigger to maintain a separate field holding this searchable field. This would be denormalization of a different sort and could be avoided by concatenating the fields together when queried. Although this is not advised as a general practice, it is an example of how business requirements and rules can affect your design.

A similar situation that is also important for you to consider is related to stored date values. In a database which stores date and time values, it is standard to include both date and time in a single field. For example, EmployeeA clocks in on December 12, 2009, at 23:00; the data is stored as ClockIn 12/12/2009 23:00:00.

If one of your application's primary functions was monitoring shift times, such as when employees were late, then querying this in Access would look something like the following:

```
SELECT * FROM tblTimeLogs WHERE TimeValue(ClockIn) > #23:00#
```

Again, this would negate ideal index use on that field; and it requires that you use a function to call it. Based upon the business requirements of the application, you would need to decide whether to store the date and time values separately. The converse can be equally true where your business rules require the combination of date and time; such as to determine the time lapse in a multi-day experiment.

These are some of the more common factors to consider for optimizing performance. You will also need to pay particular attention when converting specific types of tables and fields.

Problem Tables and Conversions

Many databases that move to a server platform started in a file-server format. They often operate for years before moving to the server; so even if you think you are only building a temporary solution or a prototype, it's clearly better to get it right in the beginning.

But, as many developers have experienced, you may be faced with converting a database structure that deviates from best practices with results that are less than optimum in a client-server scenario. After your conversion, and especially if you are not able to improve on the structure, you must determine how you can maintain the database as efficiently as possible.

From a database design perspective it's important to keep one eye on the goal of having the server perform the bulk of the data operations. Sometimes this can only be achieved by using a slightly more advanced development techniques than linked tables alone. But even then, a good design is always the best possible starting point.

Since the tables provide the foundation for your entire application, if you are working with a poorly designed table structure, you should not discount the option of starting the design again from scratch. The time it may take is often saved by avoiding the problems you would encounter using the original design. And, moving to a new design does not mean that you need to sacrifice existing data. You can use the old database to fill the new one by using a series of carefully designed append queries. For example, denormalized data can often be normalized by using union or pivot queries. *Union* queries allow you to list the results of multiple queries by creating a record for each instance that meets the stated criteria. *Pivot* queries essentially switch the rows with the columns.

The following examples will help illustrate what we mean. We'll start with the data shown in Table 15-18.

Table 15-18: Denormalized Conversion Data (tblPay)

EMPLOYEEID	PAYRATE1	PAYRATE2	PAYRATEOT
1	$100	$120	$200
2	$150	$170	$300

This is not a properly normalized table because each employee has several pay rates. A better structure is to have each record list the employee, the pay rate type and the pay rate, essentially turning one record per employee into three records.

To do that, you start with a query or select statement to get the records for the first pay rate (PayRate1) and list all employee IDs with the pay rate. You would also need the lists for PayRate2 and PayRateOT. Each query provides a list of records for the specified pay rate. Then, using a union query, you can combine all three lists.

By putting the select statements or queries in a union query, you can create a list of all of the employees along with their rates for each pay rate type. For our example, you can use the following SQL statement for the union query.

```
SELECT EmployeeID, `PayRate1´ As RateType, PayRate1 As PayRate
    FROM tblPay
UNION ALL
SELECT EmployeeID, `PayRate2´ As RateType, PayRate2 As PayRate
    FROM tblPay
UNION ALL
SELECT EmployeeID, `PayRate3´ As RateType, PayRate3 As PayRate
    FROM tblPay
```

Because this is a union query, it will not display in query design view, either in Access or in SQL Server. However, once you become accustomed to the terminology, the statement itself is fairly self-explanatory. This query returns the data as shown in Table 15-19.

Table 15-19: Normalized Data Results from Union Query

EMPLOYEEID	RATETYPE	PAYRATE
1	PayRate1	$100
1	PayRate2	$120
1	PayRateOT	$200
2	PayRate1	$150
2	PayRate2	$170
2	PayRateOT	$300

Such a union query can be used in an append query to insert the results into a new table of the appropriate design. As you can see, we used the three SELECT statements to essentially un-pivot the data and turn the columns to rows, creating a row for each type of pay rate. We then used a union query to put the three sets of data together in one display.

Optimization Suggestions

In this section we offer a few hints and methodologies that can help make an application perform faster and more efficiently. In reaching for the best possible use of the database, some of the practices may ultimately need to be implemented through your own user interface; and many will likely rely on VBA code, or at least on macros. We want to offer as much efficiency as possible without employing code.

Appropriate Use of Indexing

One of the most important steps to making your database perform more efficiently is to create indexes in your tables. As the name implies, indexes contain a separately stored set of values that function as a pointer for determining the values stored in a record. The concept of indexes is discussed in Chapter 2, and in Appendix A. To summarize briefly, a database engine uses an index as you would use the index of a book to get to the single page you want to read. Indexes created for a given table can contain one or more fields from that table. The database engine will use indexes for a given query request if it determines that they are of benefit. Hence to leverage this functionality, you need to ensure you index the appropriate fields.

When you build tables in ACE using the Access table designer, you get some indexing assistance right out of the box. By default if you create a field name with the suffix "ID," "key," "code," or "num," Access will automatically add an index to that field. You can change that setting in the Options for Access. Access will also create an index when you establish a foreign key relationship; although the index will not be listed in the Indexes dialog, it is visible in code. If you want to remove these or add more indexes, it is a simple change in the field properties. To change indexes, you can open the Index dialog for that table and make the desired changes. Alternatively, you can add or change the index and other field properties for a specific field by opening the table in design view, selecting the field, and making the desired changes. Indexes can also be created by executing *Data Definition Language* (DDL) SQL statements in ACE.

In SQL Server you have to take a bit more responsibility for your own indexing and that's not such a bad thing. Just as too few indexes can limit the potential performance of querying a table, too many will impact the performance of inserting and updating data in your table. The individual indexes need to be updated at the same time as the table data itself is updated. This means that you are not only updating the data viewed by the user, but also the index value for field that is indexed.

How do you know what makes a field or group of fields a good candidate for indexing? Being familiar with the business requirements is an excellent starting point. Apart from the key fields likely to be used in query joins, you will recognize the fields that are likely to be frequently searched or sorted. In addition, fields that contain a high level of uniqueness make good index candidates. Conversely, you may not notice any difference at all if you place an index on a `Bit` field, for example. Because there are only two possible values, a table scan isn't going to be much more expensive than an index.

It's also true that an appropriate use of indexing is not just confined to the choice of fields on which to index. As we have already mentioned, an index on a field used in criteria may or may not be usable by the database engine due to other factors. The classic example is when there's a need to perform a function on the field (an action taken with that field for every record), which ensures that the table data itself will be read instead of just the index or a small portion of the records. Any calculation on the field in the query will do likewise, such as appending a prefix or suffix, adding a value, and similar operations. The following sidebar explains this in more detail.

FUNCTIONS IN QUERIES

Functions in Access are a method of returning a value in VBA code or an expression in your forms, reports, and queries. Commonly used functions like `Date()` and `Now()` return a value for you to use and are very valuable in queries. For example when you want all records whose date field matches today then you can use:

```
SELECT * FROM tblEmployee WHERE DateHired = Date()
```

which would appear in an Access query design view as shown in the following figure.

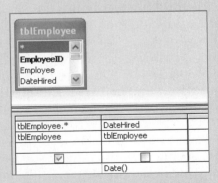

Many functions accept parameters passed to them and return a value based on that parameter. For example, in Access you can use the function DateValue to return only the date portion of a value that contains both date and time components. Therefore if the DateHired field in the previous example contained a time component, it would fail to match against `Date()` alone, as an exact match is performed on the values. So a simple answer is to use a function call.

```
SELECT * FROM tblEmployee WHERE DateValue(DateHired) = Date()
```

tblEmployee.*	Expr1: DateValue([DateHired])	
tblEmployee	.	
☑	☐	
	Date()	

If DateHired contained the value 12/12/2009 12:45:00 then the return value from DateValue would be just 12/12/2009 and it would match the criteria if today happened to be December 12. Such function calls prevent the database engine from making query optimizing use of any index placed upon the DateHired field. This will harm database performance.

A better alternative you can use in your own queries is to form a request around the date you want. Ask for records whose date field lies after the beginning of today but before tomorrow. This translates as:

```
SELECT * FROM tblEmployee WHERE DateHired >= Date() AND DateHired
  < Date() + 1
```

tblEmployee.*	☑	DateHired	
tblEmployee		tblEmployee	
☑		☐	
		>=Date() And <Date()+1	

If you want to format the result of a field for display purposes as returned from the query, this will not impact your query's optimization. You just incur the relatively smaller overhead of calling the function for each row of your query. You probably won't even notice the difference in the time it takes to execute.

```
SELECT tblEmployee.* , DateValue(DateHired) As JustDate
FROM tblEmployee WHERE DateHired >= Date() AND DateHired < Date() + 1
```

tblEmployee.*	JustDate: DateValue(DateHired)	DateHired	
tblEmployee		tblEmployee	
☑	☑	☐	
		>=Date() And <Date()+1	

These concepts apply to both ACE and SQL Server.

Query Operators: Selection Criteria

Performing a Like operator comparison in your query and using wildcards in the criterion can also affect efficiency. The Like operator itself is a perfectly valid comparison of field values to maintain efficiency. Used alone, it will only return values that are an exact match to the criteria, so it is often used in conjunction with a wildcard or other criteria. For example, `Like ``Mar*´´` would return Margaret, Marie, and Martin. It is important to realize that when you include wildcards in your request, you make it progressively more difficult for an index to be used.

For example, it is better to put the wildcard in the middle or at the end of the criteria, because then the query can use the index values for a field. But if you begin the criteria with a wildcard, the query cannot take advantage of an index and must search each section of every field individually. That would be analogous to searching a book index without knowing the word's initial characters. Consequently, you should use caution when creating queries that add wildcards by default to parameters passed. For example, consider the following query in Access. It asks for every surname that includes a certain set of characters, regardless of where it is in the name:

```
SELECT * FROM tblClients WHERE ClientSurname Like "*" & [SurnameParam]
   & "*"
```

The preceding query will perform noticeably slower than this one that will only return values that match the criteria:

```
SELECT * FROM tblClients WHERE ClientSurname Like [SurnameParam]
```

Keep in mind that because the query starts with SELECT *, they will both provide the complete record for each item that matches the criteria. To provide maximum flexibility for users, it is often best to give users the option to use wildcards or not. You can help them make educated decisions by including some suggestions in your user interface, such as to lead with a character and then wildcard, for example, `"Sp*"`.

Linked Table Implications

When you link to SQL Server data, certain practices related to "native" data (or data in Access tables) still remain the same. Indexing behavior does not change all that much; and we have already discussed some issues to consider when forming query requests from Access. But what if you need to request data in a format other than how it's stored and you have not denormalized any values? In that case, you must rely on a function call. The critical factor is to ensure that the query is executed on the server. By having the server do the heavy lifting and return the filtered results to the Access application, you are on track for a faster, more scalable database.

Consider the earlier example from the "Assisting Optimization" section earlier in this chapter:

```
SELECT * FROM tblTimeLogs WHERE TimeValue(ClockIn) = #23:00#
```

SQL Server has no function directly equivalent to `TimeValue` that is supported directly in ACE. Consequently, with no local evaluation of the function to be performed, the server yields to Access to filter the results. The whole table is sent from the server and ACE applies the criteria to provide the required records. This is a scenario that you want to avoid. The goal of client-server database work is to move as little as possible over the network. Remember that all of our communication in these requests is made possible by ODBC. This convenience can often disguise the fact that there isn't a seamless gap between the databases.

Not all query results are as efficient as others. However, with a slight modification, the query request just discussed will enable the server to substitute a function of its own. It can then execute the request locally (on the server), thereby improving performance. Instead of `TimeValue`, we use the `DatePart` function to get just the hour from the value stored in the ClockIn field, as shown in the following SQL statement.

```
SELECT * FROM tblTimeLogs WHERE DatePart("h", ClockIn) = 23
```

This demonstrates the value of knowing which functions are recognized by each system and how they are processed. Unfortunately, knowing which functions have an ODBC and T-SQL equivalent is usually gained only through experience, trial and error, and reliance on good reference material. You can increase your learning curve by checking the executed queries on the server using the SQL Server Profiler utility. Your goal is to see queries that closely emulate those you made in Access.

QUERY PERFORMANCE USING ACCESS EXPRESSIONS

Problems with creating efficient queries are sometimes presented to imply that using Access expressions such as Form values will result in client-side filtering. If you create parameter queries in Access you may have used examples such as:

```
SELECT * FROM tblTimeLogs WHERE ClockIn =
    Forms!frmOptions!txtChooseClockIn
```

Continued

QUERY PERFORMANCE USING ACCESS EXPRESSIONS (continued)

However, these and other Access form expressions are evaluated first, on the client-side. An interpretable query is then passed to the server. For example, if you had the value "23" in the `txtChooseClockIn` form textbox, then all the server receives is a query request for:

```
SELECT * FROM tblTimeLogs WHERE ClockIn = 23
```

SQL Server isn't aware of the Access form, and it doesn't need to be; it is the job of Access to interpret the statement first and make strong requests to the server wherever possible. Since that form value ("23" in the preceding example) is fixed and does not vary with each row in the query, the server can further optimize the request.

Applying criteria in queries is not the only way that Access allows you to limit results. ACE is, generally, well-optimized for performing joins. In an ACE database, you should use the join properties between two tables (or another query) to limit records returned where possible. For example, if you have a long list of record ID values you want to return, a query that joins to a table of those values is more efficient than including the limitation as criteria on a field.

However, this is not true when joining tables using a *heterogeneous join*—where the join is between tables from separate sources such as in a query involving a linked SQL Server table and an ACE table. By contrast, a homogeneous join, which involves tables from a single database, is a very efficient operation. A heterogeneous join in Access can result in multiple query requests on the server, one of which includes a full index or table read. Although heterogeneous joins are something you'd generally want to avoid, for relatively small local tables, Access will construct the most sensible query it can to make use of server resources. There are other querying options available to you to guarantee the best performance from your database.

As your local queries become more complex, it becomes more unlikely that ODBC translation will successfully parse those requests to use server-side processing. There is no definable line that is crossed where this will occur, you just have to make the best queries that you can and watch for the results.

Other Access Functionality

Linked tables are the workhorse of Access. They provide the default function-ality when working with an ACE database and offer an immediate avenue into server-based development. They behave similarly whether linked to server data or to an ACCDB or MDB database. Using linked tables allows your existing native queries to run, even though you may have to work to optimize those a bit. However, if your needs justify it, Access offers other functionalities for working with server data. When we include VBA code, many intricate data operations become possible; but even the default Access functionality includes some powerful tools. The following sections briefly cover some of functionality native to Access.

Pass-through Queries

When the requirements placed on a native Access query, fail to produce the desired results, or fail to produce them in a timely manner, then it may be because of the unwanted client-side processing of the data that was received from the server. But, even if you avoid unnecessary processing on the data, there is still some inherent overhead involved because the ACE must "wrap" or package requests, and linked table requests are generally executed on the server as a series of statements to provide the required results.

Pass-through queries are an alternative query, which Access will "pass through" to the server (bypass the local ACE database engine) so that the query will run directly on the server. Like the linked tables, these queries use an ODBC connection, but without much of the associated performance cost. This gain comes with some effort on your part. The definition of the pass-through must be written by hand—you cannot directly use the Query-By-Example (QBE) grid in Access to make your query, but you can start with the QBE to generate the SQL statements that can become the basis for your pass-through query. The query must be written in the dialect of the database to which you are connecting. For SQL Server, that is T-SQL. In addition, the results of a pass-through are read-only; but that isn't entirely unfavorable.

Although the pass-through query is read-only (so you cannot update the returned data), there may be immediate benefits anywhere that you display read-only data in an application. For example, both when printing reports and offering selection lists in forms, read-only data is used. That the results of a pass-through query are not updatable is a deliberate and effective means of making them more efficient. The overhead associated with updatability isn't required in many circumstances, so why incur it?

CONNECTION STRINGS

Both linked tables and pass-through queries have a property called `Connect`, which stores a connection string containing a set of values that allow the ODBC connection to be made. It typically looks something like:

```
ODBC;DSN=DSN_Name;DATABASE=DB_Name;UID=User_Name;PWD=Password
```

Continued

CONNECTION STRINGS *(continued)*

which reflects an ODBC DSN (Data Source Name) that exists on the client PC. For example, a connection string could resemble:

```
ODBC;Driver=SQL Server;Server=Server_Name;Database=DB_Name;
   Trusted_Connection=yes;
```

The completed string contains the necessary information for the local database to connect to the appropriate server and database file. When you begin to link a table in Access and choose an ODBC source, the wizard dialogs that appear will present a list of DSNs for your system as well as give you the opportunity to create a new one. The same dialog is available when you create a new query and select it to be a pass-through, and then click the ellipses next to its `Connect` property.

We might as well get the rest of the bad news out of the way at this stage. At present pass-through queries don't support use as subforms or subreports, at least not with the standard benefits expected based on the link between the Master and Child fields for automatic filtering. While that's not catastrophic in a subform scenario, it largely rules them out for subreport use until some future functionality is implemented.

In addition, due to their self-contained nature, pass-through queries do not accept parameters in the way that native Access queries do. This prevents them from being used to request different data based on an external value. Again this may change in the future, but for now you can work around this limitation by employing some very simple VBA code in your application to alter the definition of the pass-through statement. In effect, you can change everything about it.

A query originally designed to return all values from a lookup list can be made to select a single value from an entirely different table. Fundamentally you can also alter data on the server database through a pass-through by using the same functionality to create and execute an UPDATE, INSERT, or DELETE statement. For example, the following statement is valid T-SQL syntax, and would add a client named "John Jones" to the tblClients table:

```
INSERT INTO tblClients (ClientSurname, ClientForename) VALUES
   (`Jones`, `John`)
```

Because your code executes directly in the SQL Server environment, you can also execute stored procedures and refer to user defined functions. Indeed you can do almost anything that T-SQL supports.

If you intend to use pass-throughs, it's common to maintain a core set that you use for various functions such as specific list displays on core data for lookups. In addition, you might have two or more pass-throughs whose definition can be altered at runtime as your application requires: one to select data and another to update it. There is a "Returns Records" property of the query that expects by default either to select data or to update data.

Although you can use pass-throughs in a local Access query, you should avoid selecting a server table from a pass-through with the intention of applying criteria to the pass-through locally. Applying the criteria locally means that the entire set of data will be fetched onto the local machine (client) before it is filtered. So you might retrieve 800,000 records, before filtering them down to the 20 for customers named Margaret. This is a behavior you want to avoid in client-server development. It would be preferable to use a linked table for such criteria. If you want to apply criteria to a pass-through, then you should use code to alter its definition so that the criteria is incorporated into the pass-through as the filter is applied on the server.

Local Table Storage

A major benefit of using a client-server query is the opportunity to leverage the server's capacity for query execution. As a result, the network has less to do, because only the filtered results are passed. However, there will be times—for example when you're working with lists using lookup table values—when you want an unfiltered list, in which case the network traffic in not reduced.

In these cases, you can help reduce network traffic by creating locally cached (stored) sets of data that are commonly used and are not often filtered on the server. The more static a set of data is, the better a candidate it is for a local cache. Obvious examples are things like a list of U.S. states, countries, and any other non-varying list. Because Access has such close integration with ACE, it makes perfect sense for these data caches to be held in local ACE tables. They can be tables local to the ACCDB that houses the application or merely local to the client PC and used in the application as linked tables. The crucial point is that the data does not need to be transferred over the network.

Even with static or rarely changing value lookup lists, you may want to make sure you have the latest set by refreshing your local cache as your application launches. This can be accomplished simply by deleting the previous contents of the local table and inserting the records from a server table. This is a perfect scenario for using a pass-through query as discussed in the previous section. The results do not need to be updatable and you are importing a full table of records. Alternatively, you can choose to cache data that updates a little more often and decide how often you need to perform an update of that table. You might determine that it is sufficient to update the data only when the application is launched, or you may use a little code to schedule updates. Another option is to allow users to perform the updates on demand.

Using the local table for the lists on your forms can save numerous round-trips to the server. You may wonder what benefit there is to having the data stored on the server and locally. Why not just use the local tables? Fundamentally the server acts as a master list and any changes that do occur will be made there. Then they propagate down to the clients as desired. Also, remember what we said about heterogeneous joins: If you need to join together data from a lookup table and another entity table, then using server tables for both optimizes that process. The local table remains for the fast provision of lists without network traffic, giving users the best of both worlds.

Local tables can perform other functions, too. Some common uses are as an intermediate repository for data during complex calculations, storing imported data to be cleaned up before insertion into live tables, or storing pass-through query results used to generate reports.

The value of Access as an application development environment can be seen in circumstances like this, even when linking to SQL Server for all of the live data.

Access Data Projects

ADPs, or Access Data Projects, are an alternative format application in Access. They have a different file extension to distinguish them from MDB and ACCDB files. ADPs were introduced in Access 2000, so the .adp file extension is used in that and all later versions of Access.

In an ADP there is no local query engine. ACE is not implemented in an ADP, so all processing is done by connecting directly to a SQL Server database. This has various advantages and disadvantages. Chief among the advantages is that, by definition, all data processing is done on the server. The ADP has built-in functionality to make use of server features such as binding forms directly to stored procedures and user-defined functions. The ADP forms and reports support properties that are not present in an ACCDB. This enables you to pass parameters to the stored procedures where you would have used a form expression in a query. The connection to the server is made through the SQL Server OLEDB provider rather than ODBC, which among other things provides a slight performance advantage.

Some of the limitations with an ADP will be immediately clear. There can be no local tables because there is no engine to store or process them—not even when Access is installed on the client machine. There are no linked tables either. One connection, and only one connection, is made to a SQL Server database; and all tables that the user has permission to use are then available in the application. To bind directly to stored procedures that allow data to be changed or updated, users need permission on the underlying tables.

Several types of functionality that you can use quite easily in an ACCDB need to be implemented differently in an ADP. For example, cascading combo boxes are a common feature in Access applications. In an ACCDB they can be created using parameter queries and a very small amount of VBA code. With an ADP, you will have to create this functionality yourself. The SQL Server engine cannot interpret expressions based on Access objects.

All your querying must be done either through a query designer or directly in T-SQL. You might have experience with VBA code in an ACCDB using DAO, but you will now need to learn ADO. This isn't a particularly large transition; many of the objects and concepts are the same. But it will take some time to become completely familiar with ADO and ADPs.

In ADPs, although the data definition will always be available through the designer in Access, it will only be functional when the ADP is connected to a SQL Server version of the same age or older. For example, you cannot update the schema of a SQL Server 2008 table through Access 2007, whereas Access 2010 does support it. In such situations you still have Management Studio for design work and, of course, it offers a great deal of other SQL Server-specific functionality besides merely design views of objects.

ADPs can provide a great deal of power and efficiency, but to make the most use of them, you need some coding knowledge. That may be a significant contributor to ADPs not being as commonplace as they might be. Microsoft does not promote them as their recommended method for SQL Server connectivity, and instead demonstrates a preference for linked tables in an ACCDB.

The limited adoption of ADPs is likely due to many factors, but one strong possibility is that they are specifically designed for connection to SQL Server databases. A great strength of Access has always been its ability to rapidly build robust and functional applications against a range of different data sources. Next we take a brief look at just what some of those are.

Other Data Sources

Although ACE and SQL Server comprise, by far, the largest proportion of the source data for applications developed in Access, to consider those alone does not do justice to the variety of choices. It's now easier than ever to see several of the main external data sources supported by Access. The Ribbon has an External Data tab, shown in Figure 15-2, from which you can select your preferred source.

In previous versions of Access the same core set of sources are available from the Import menu option. In Figure 15-2 the source option for ODBC Database is shown expanded. It is the first stop for establishing links to SQL Server and any other ODBC data source available to you.

Figure 15-2: Figure 15-2: External Data tab

Other Server Databases

Despite its huge success as the common alternative database platform for Access, SQL Server isn't even the largest database provider. Any database vendor that provides an ODBC driver for Windows can be linked to using Access. This includes database providers such as Oracle, MySQL, DB2, PostgreSQL, Sybase, and others. Many organizations already have existing database solutions and servers in place either as part of their own IT infrastructure or installed as the source of proprietary software.

Applications created in Access that link to and supplement existing databases on one or more of the platforms just mentioned are an excellent way to bring together otherwise disparate information. You can then use Access to create reports, monitor activities, and even make updates to the original data file where permitted. You also can create your own table structures to hold data which you import from external software products. This gives you the opportunity to design a schema more appropriate and suited to your needs than the proprietary software itself may otherwise permit. Once you have your linked tables in Access you are empowered.

Bear in mind that much of what you have read in this chapter about linking to SQL Server databases is directly applicable to other databases too. There is not a lot preventing you from supplementing your existing Oracle or MySQL server databases by creating new tables and giving yourself the precise database application you need by incorporating any pre-existing data. The same rules of good database design, as discussed throughout this book, will still apply.

Data Formats

This section briefly covers some of the other common data formats available to you that do not necessarily conform to relational database formats, but nevertheless enable you to access and work with data from almost any source in your Access database.

Excel Spreadsheets

The most common request made of Access with regard to external sources is perhaps "I need to import or export this data with Excel."

Though Microsoft Excel is massively popular in its own right as the default spreadsheet application for the world, many database users view spreadsheets with derision. Their "flat file" nature is by definition non-normalized, and is the antithesis of what you should be aiming for in a database. But spreadsheets needn't attempt to model relational data. They are so fundamental in everyday business and personal life that they should be embraced. The snapshots of data that they can hold and then easily transfer are in a format that is recognized across the business world. Who has not received an Excel spreadsheet attached to an email at some stage?

Access has always enjoyed a strong integration with Excel. Though linked table data to Excel is currently non-updatable, the ability to view the up-to-date values in real time still has significant benefits. However, it is in importing and exporting of spreadsheet data where the bulk of the work is done. Creating a summary query in Access of an otherwise very large, relational set of data and exporting results to Excel is available from the user interface without requiring a single line of written VBA code. You can store the process as a Saved Export or Import to be executed again instantaneously in the future. This was formerly known as an Import Specification and Text File integration.

SharePoint

As a platform for collaboration and sharing of information and documents for both businesses and individuals, Microsoft SharePoint has truly gone from strength to strength.

Access can link to and import and export from your existing Share-Point server lists. You can now move your existing Access database to SharePoint, taking advantage of the functionality that the server offers while maintaining your existing forms and reports. This can be done through the simple wizards in the External Data tab. Once complete, you have access to the SharePoint list data for updating.

SharePoint offers the security and reliability of server data. It supports both online and offline data, so that users can work remotely and synchronize data during a subsequent connection. There are currently some trade-offs—for example, referential integrity is not supported, and there is a threshold on the number of rows before performance degrades. But the gains include wide availability of your data and features such as the SharePoint Recycle Bin, a safety measure Access was unable to implement previously without some manual VBA coding intervention.

A full discussion of how Access can make use of SharePoint is beyond the scope of this chapter, but some fascinating and exciting changes such as web apps in Access 2010 have deepened their relationship and integration will continue to get stronger in the future.

Text Files and CSVs

We are going "old school" here but the popularity and need to support text-file-based data demands attention. For many years now, if data needed to be transferred from one location to another, then a predictable formatted text file holding that data has been the choice. Ultimately all that's required when transferring data is predictability—to be able to interpret the data exported when it is imported at the other end. It's still very simple.

Comma-separated values files (*CSVs*) are text files used to store data in rows generally separated by carriage returns. The values on any given row are, by default, separated by commas, ergo the name. You have the option to have the first row contain the field names to assist with interpretation of the data at the other end. An example is:

```
ClientID,ClientSurname,ClientFormname
1,Hennig,Teresa
2,Bradly,Truitt
3,Spaulding,Brent
4,Linson,Larry
5,Purvis,Leigh
```

You also have the option to have the data *delimited*, which means that the value in each field will be enclosed in the specified characters, often the double quote. The fields will still also be separated by a comma. So the first record in the example above would be "Hennig," "Teresa."

Although the burden is on the export process to provide the values as expected that doesn't mean that the import process will always go as planned.

As with all data import processes, it's a common practice to maintain a local "work" table for temporary record storage rather than to import directly to your live data table. Importing into a work table gives you the opportunity to confirm that the data imported successfully and contains the data you expected before adding it to the application tables. A work table enables you to examine and clean the data if necessary before inserting it into your live data tables. It is also possible to create a linked table to a text file and even update the data within the text file. If you work with text files in that manner, it is important to note that they are not designed for sharing and become locked until released (the connection or query is closed).

XML

eXtensible Markup Language (*XML*) is now present in almost every facet of information technology because of its universal interpretation. XML is just a specification for structuring data. You can examine any XML file you receive or produce from an export in a multitude of applications, from a dedicated XML editor to Notepad.

The content of XML data appears within elements or tags and can contain attributes that are optional properties of an element. There is a simple example export file in the folder for this chapter on the book's CD. Here is a small example:

```
<tblPeople>
    <PersonID>2</PersonID>
    <NameLast>Bradly</NameLast>
    <NameMiddle>L</NameMiddle>
    <NameFirst>Truitt</NameFirst>
</tblPeople>
```

XML files can be used somewhat like a CSV file to conveniently transfer data. But XML provides the added advantage of including instructions for the data type and formatting the display. We've provided a brief explanation in the following sidebar.

XML REPRESENTATION OF HIERARCHICAL DATA

A vital benefit of XML over standards such as CSV, is how easy it is to represent hierarchical data. The elements of your data can have child nodes to represent the data elements of related data. For example, relating a table "People" with child records stored in "Phone" would appear as follows:

```
<People>
    <PersonID>2</PersonID>
    <NameLast>Bradly</NameLast>
    <NameMiddle>L</NameMiddle>
    <NameFirst>Truitt</NameFirst>
    <Phone>
        <PhoneNo>555 123456</PhoneNo>
        <PhoneType>Landline</PhoneType>
    </Phone>
    <Phone>
        <PhoneNo>555 111111</PhoneNo>
        <PhoneType>Cell</PhoneType>
    </Phone>
</People>
```

Similar to its markup language cousin, HTML, XML also supports attributes of each element, appearing as named properties of the element. This can allow for an entire description of an element without using the nested child elements shown in the previous example, which would now appear as:

```
<People PersonID="2" NameLast="Bradly" NameMiddle="L"
  NameFirst="Truitt">
```

Continued

XML REPRESENTATION OF HIERARCHICAL DATA *(continued)*

```
        <Phone PhoneNo="555 123456" PhoneType="Landline"/>
        <Phone PhoneNo="555 111111" PhoneType="Cell"/>
</People>
```

This structure does not necessarily make the XML any better or more efficient to use, but it is an alternative that is common.

For Access to be able to import this data using native functionality while maintaining the relational nature of the data, you can either transform the data itself or make sure you include the required join fields in the data. In the previous example that would involve PersonID appearing in the Phone records, as shown next.

```
<People PersonID="2" NameLast="Bradly" NameMiddle="L"
  NameFirst="Truitt">
    <Phone PersonID="2" PhoneNo="555 123456" PhoneType="Landline"/>
    <Phone PersonID="2" PhoneNo="555 111111" PhoneType="Cell"/>
</People>
```

However this is not generally required to represent related data in XML.

In addition to the data, a description of the data structure and the individual data types can be included in the XML file or as a separate document: the *XSD*. The *XML Schema Definition* can be interpreted by the application reading that schema document. So an XML file conveys both the data and the specific display instructions.

A database will very commonly export a table or query results into XML format. Access has been able to import and export XML for many years. Complex data in XML, such as data that includes both the parent and child records, can be imported into distinct tables. But there is an inevitable limitation to what the default import process can achieve in that respect. The significant hurdle is that the imported tables do not maintain relationships between the hierarchical data (parent-child table relationship).

To allow the newly imported Access tables to recover the links between related records you would have to include the primary key of the parent in the child elements, as described in the sidebar above. There's a simple example export file for this chapter on the accompanying CD.

Access doesn't currently support linking to XML data; so you cannot provide live updates to an XML source. This is understandable since XML can represent relational (or at least hierarchical) data, it is used primarily as a storage and transfer medium to facilitate cross-platform communication.

Summary

In this chapter, you have seen the basic concepts describing how a client-server database functions and how it differs from working with ACE file-based databases.

In particular you learned the implications of working with SQL Server and the options that Access offers. As you can see, the guiding principles of database design remain largely the same for server databases. You learned about some table design options that can assist in performance to make better use of the power of the server and the efficiency it can bring your application. To assist with performance we reviewed the benefits of linked tables using ODBC. We recommended how to get the most benefits by using ODBC to link to SQL Server, having properly constructed queries and supplementing them with local data and pass-through queries.

You saw briefly the various data formats that are commonly required to be read and used from Access and how they fit in to the data transfer process.

The bottom line is that, essentially, wherever your data is stored and whatever platform it might come from, Access and ACE are capable of working with it. As SharePoint features expand and as SQL Server moves ever more into the Cloud, Access will have greater opportunities for remote data source connections. So you might say that, for Access, the sky is literally the limit.

Part

VI

Appendixes

In This Part

Field Properties

This appendix expands on some of the concepts you've learned in this book as you were creating the tables and fields. In several examples in the book, you need to set specific field properties to control the type of data that could go into the field. There were also times that specific field properties were required in order to support relationships between the tables.

Rather than leave you to learn from experience, in this appendix we explore field properties in detail so you can learn to use them to your advantage.

Using Field Properties

You have seen summaries of field properties in some chapters. Now, we'll examine field properties in more detail. Properties available for a field depend, in part, on the data type assigned to values in that field. Therefore, we'll have to look at several different fields in order to cover all of the properties you can set. We'll start with one of the simpler ones to configure—the AutoNumber.

Access generates a new, unique value for an AutoNumber field each time a new record is started in a table. As soon as a record is started, Access records that AutoNumber value as "used" and cannot reuse it, even if the record is not saved. When a record is deleted, Access abandons the value of the AutoNumber in that record and cannot reuse it. This makes the AutoNumber an excellent choice for surrogate primary keys.

Take a look at the field properties for an AutoNumber field, shown in Figure A-1.

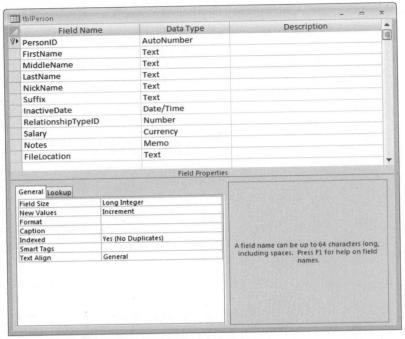

Figure A-1: Field properties for an AutoNumber field

The primary key in the Person table is PersonID. It is defined as an AutoNumber data type. The General and Lookup property tabs in the lower part of the design view list its properties.

Properties of AutoNumber Fields

AutoNumbers play a special role in Access, a role that is often misunderstood by people new to them and their uses. In discussing their properties, we also consider how they should be used.

First, AutoNumbers are really useful only as the data type for a primary key field. They are unique within a table, they can never be null, and they cannot be changed once inserted into a record—these specific properties are requirements for primary keys.

> **NOTE** In normal circumstance, this is a true statement. We are aware that in the case of table corruption, Access can end up *trying* to regenerate an existing value for an AutoNumber. It is important to realize that this is always an indication that the table is corrupt and must be repaired.

In Figure A-1 you can see that Access displays the small key symbol in the leftmost column of the PersonID field. Access uses that symbol to identify fields designated as primary keys.

In the lower portion of the table design view are two tabs—General and Lookup. The General tab contains the following seven properties defined for the AutoNumber data type:

- Field Size
- New Values
- Format
- Caption
- Indexed
- Smart Tags
- Text Align

Of those seven properties, there is only one that you cannot configure; it will be indexed and you cannot make adjustments to that setting. Let's take a look at each of these properties and the options available for them. We'll offer some comments on why you might, or might not, want to select certain options. Some choices do boil down to personal preference.

Field Size

AutoNumbers are defined, by default, as long integers, but they can be set up as Replication IDs, also known as Globally Unique Identifiers, or GUIDs.

Long integers, as you learned in Chapter 2, "Elements of a Microsoft Access Database," are stored in 4 bytes (32 bits). Long integer values range from −2,147,483,648 to 2,147,483,647, which means you can create up to 4,294,967,296 records in a table, which has a primary key defined as an AutoNumber with Long Integer data type. That ought to be sufficient for most Access databases. If you have more than 4.2 billion records in a table, you probably should be looking at alternatives, such as migrating to SQL Server.

Replication IDs, on the other hand, are 128 bit (16 Byte) values. A Replication ID randomly generated as an AutoNumber in an Access table might look like this:

{3C0D3E7E-694D-47A0-89B8-B2C674D5D2A5}

The total possible number of Replication IDs, or GUIDs, is 2^{128}. According to Wikipedia, that's 340,282,366,920,938,463,463,374,607,431,768,211,456 different values. Because the possibility of duplicate values being generated is so very small, they are almost guaranteed to be unique, regardless of where and when they are generated.

Given the values and properties of each, when and where would you decide to use Replication IDs instead of long integers for your AutoNumber primary keys? In the great majority of cases, there is no reason to select Replication IDs. There is, however, one situation where they may be useful, if not required—replication. Database replication is beyond the scope of this book, but suffice it to say that if you need to replicate your Access database, you may need to have the AutoNumbers defined as Replication IDs. Otherwise, it is not necessary. Moreover, as we've learned from personal experience in our own development, managing GUIDs as primary keys in Access is not a trivial task and should not be undertaken lightly.

New Values

There are two configurable properties for creating new AutoNumber values: *Increment* and *Random*. They apply only to AutoNumbers defined as long integers.

Increment means each new value generated is one greater than the previously-generated value. That does not mean they will remain sequential. As pointed out above, Access generates a new value each time a new record is started, whether that record is saved or not. Although Access does not duplicate existing values, it can reuse deleted or abandoned AutoNumber values.

Random means that Access selects new values at random. Although deleted numbers can be reused, that is an extremely rare occurrence with random numbers.

The default property is Increment and you should almost never have any reason to select Random. The one special case where you might select Random would be in a replicated database in which you did not define the primary key AutoNumber as a Replication ID.

If you have selected Replication ID as the Field Size, the New Values property is not available. All Replication IDs are, by definition, randomly generated.

Display Formats

Interestingly enough, you can set display formats for AutoNumbers, just as you can for other fields. Most experienced developers agree that end users should never see AutoNumbers, so display format is almost always a non-factor in a professionally developed database. Nonetheless, you have the option, if you want to use it. Figure A-2 shows your choices. The property sheet does not say this, but you should be aware that the Format property affects only the way values are displayed in a form or report, not the way they are stored.

Because long integer AutoNumbers are numeric, the format options are also numeric, ranging from currency through scientific. If you must show your users primary keys in forms or reports, you can format them as one of the formats shown in Figure A-2.

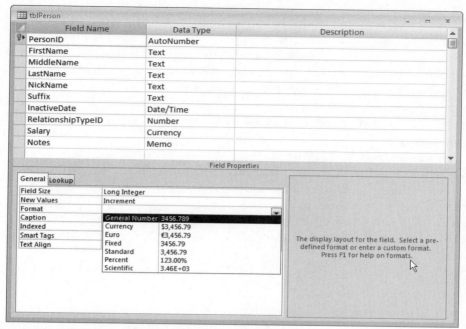

Figure A-2: Display formats for long integer AutoNumbers

If you have selected Replication ID as the Field Size, the Format property is not available.

Caption

If you follow a standard naming convention for objects in your database, you'll have field names like "PersonID" or "InactiveDate." By default, Access displays those names as label captions for those fields in queries, forms, and reports. Since you usually don't want users to see them, you have two options. One is to edit labels each time you add the fields to forms and reports. That is tedious. The other option is to define a default label here. If you do that, Access will use it everywhere. It is a good practice, therefore, to create captions for fields you plan to show to users.

For example, you would use a caption like "Person" for the PersonID field. Anywhere that field is displayed on a form or report, or in a query, the label Access creates for it will also be "Person."

> **NOTE** The Caption property is not relevant for an AutoNumber field, which you won't show to your users.

Indexed

The Indexed property is important. Chapter 2 explained how indexes are created and how they work, so if you need a quick review, refer to that chapter. Here, we'll talk about how to define indexes on fields, using the tools available to you.

Since we are discussing the properties for a primary key field, the index must be defined as Yes (No Duplicates). All primary key fields are indexed. A no-duplicates index will not permit duplicate values to be entered. There are other options, which we'll take a closer look at when we review other fields in this table. However, for a primary key, "Yes (No Duplicates)" is the only option permitted.

As you learned in Chapter 2, there can be performance trade-offs with indexes. Retrieving, filtering, and sorting data, for example, is much faster when it is done on indexed fields. Queries are faster when joins are created on indexed fields. However, too many indexes, or indexes on the wrong fields, can actually slow down data entry, because Access has to update indexes on multiple fields, and possibly multiple tables, each time an update or insert occurs.

As a guideline, then, you should limit non-primary key indexes to fields which:

- You often search on
- You often sort on
- Participate in relationships

While it is possible to walk down the field list in the table design view, setting indexes for each field, it is better to have a complete look at all of the indexes at once so you can manage them more effectively as a whole. The Index property sheet allows you to do that. In Access 2007, the icon to open it is shown in Figure A-3.

Figure A-3: Icon to launch the Index property sheet

When opened, the Index property sheet looks like Figure A-4.

Note that the primary key field, the one on PersonID, is identified by the same key symbol as in the table design view. Also, the properties at the bottom of the sheet are set to Yes for Primary and Unique, and No for Ignore Nulls. Those are defining characteristics for primary keys.

As you can also see in Figure A-4, there has been a second index defined for PeopleID. One of the reasons you want to open the Index property sheet for each table is to look for instances like this where, for one reason or another, multiple indexes have been defined on some fields. Duplicate indexes are not useful and can be a drag on performance, so just delete them. In this case, of course, the index named PersonID is the one you delete; you can't delete the primary key index without removing the primary key designation from the field.

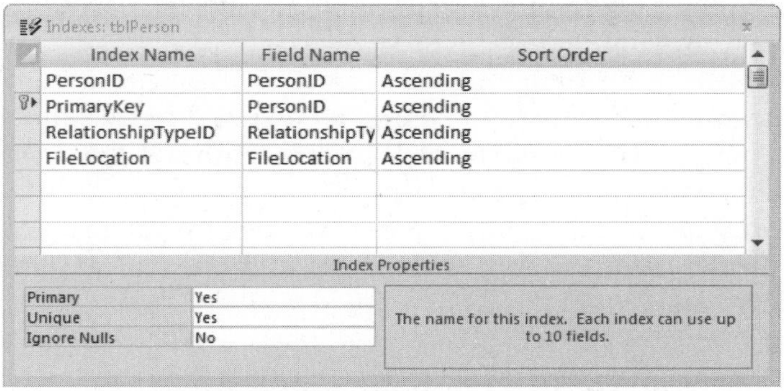

Figure A-4: Index property sheet

Other indexes have been defined on this table for RelationshipTypeID, which is a foreign key from the Relationship Type table, and for FileLocation. We'll look at FileLocation later in this appendix.

We'll take another look at indexes when we consider other, non-primary key fields.

Smart Tags

As a practical matter, Smart Tags should not apply to primary key fields, so we will consider them later, when we consider other, non-primary key fields. Basically, Access permits you to assign Smart Tags to fields in order to identify them as things like "Telephone Number," or "Person," which permits you to then take specific actions on those fields, such as "Place a Call," by clicking on the Smart Tag for that field in a query or form. A full discussion of Smart Tags is beyond the scope of this book.

Text Align

The last property available for AutoNumber fields is Text Align. You can choose to display values in this field as:

- General - Text aligns to the left; numbers and dates align to the right (the default property).

- Left - Text, numbers, and dates align to the left.

- Center - Text, numbers, and dates are centered.

- Right - Text, numbers, and dates align to the right.

- Distribute - Text, numbers, and dates are evenly distributed.

For most purposes, the default alignment, General, is appropriate. However, if you want to override the alignment for text—for example, so that every value in a field aligns to the right in forms and reports—you can set it here.

Whatever you set here is the default setting for the field. You can choose to override it in forms and reports.

Again, we are explaining the field properties that you can configure, although, as previously noted, you normally do not display AutoNumbers to user at all. These properties are available to most other data types, so we will not repeat the explanations for each type.

Before we move on to consider the next field in our example, and the properties for the data type in it, we need to add one important observation about AutoNumbers.

When Should You Not Use an AutoNumber?

The properties of AutoNumbers make them an excellent choice for primary keys, but not much else. A common mistake made by new users is to try to use AutoNumbers as a sequencing or sorting field. That works, as long as you do not count on having consecutive values in the field. Remember, starting a record generates a new, unique, value every time. If that record is abandoned, the value is lost and a gap appears in the sequence. If one or more records are deleted, again, gaps are left in the sequence. Large gaps are easily created if you start an append query and then cancel the action just before they are added to the table. It should be obvious, therefore, that AutoNumbers are really not suited to such uses.

Properties of Text Fields

The next field in tblPeople is FirstName, shown in Figure A-5. It is a text field, meaning that it will treat any values entered in it as strings of characters or text.

There are a total of 15 properties you can set for a text field, as compared to the 7 you just saw for AutoNumbers. All of the properties are configurable, so we review each one. Since we've already covered several of these, we'll augment but not repeat what we've previously discussed.

- Field Size
- Format
- Input Mask
- Caption
- Default Value
- Validation Rule
- Validation Text
- Required
- Allow Zero Length
- Indexed
- Unicode Compression
- IME Mode
- IME Sentence Mode
- Smart Tags
- Text Align

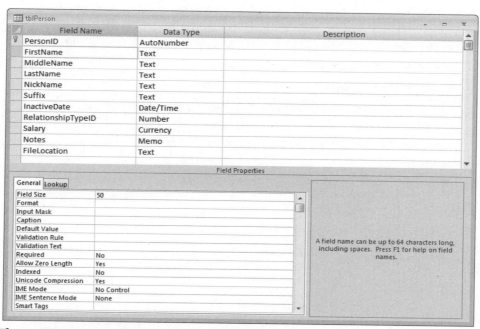

Figure A-5: Properties for FirstName, a Text field

Field Size

Text fields can hold up to 255 characters. The default number of characters is set at the database level. Depending on the type of values you intend to store, you might want to specify fewer. For example, you might want to limit the number of characters that can be entered in a field to keep the data within the display parameters for a form or report.

Another reason to specify a limited number of characters is to help ensure that valid entries are made in fields for phone numbers and zip codes. Used in conjunction with input masks, setting a phone number field to 10 characters, for example, or a zip code field to 9 characters, can help prevent users from entering extra digits. Granted, limiting the number of characters does not ensure the accuracy of what is entered, but it helps.

The "Database Defaults for Tables" sidebar looks at how you do that in Access 2007.

DATABASE DEFAULTS FOR TABLES

In Access 2007 the database options are available by clicking on the round "Office" icon in the upper left corner and selecting Access Options from the fly-out. Look for Object Designers on the menu and click it to see and set the properties.

As you can see in the figure below you can choose:

■ **The default data type for all new fields as you create them in a table**

■ **The default field size for new text fields**

■ **The default number field size**

■ **Whether to create indexes on certain field types automatically, and if so, which types to index**

■ **Whether to show the property update options button**

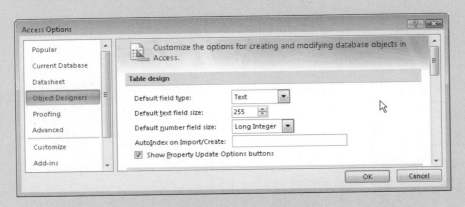

The default for Default field type is Text. Text is the most "generic" of all data types, so it does make sense to have it as the default.

Text defaults to the maximum, 255. Again, it makes sense to default to this value, and let the user select smaller values, when appropriate.

For numbers, the choice of Long Integer as the default seems a bit arbitrary. However, some other choices, such as Replication ID, would make no sense, and others like "byte" or "Decimal" would not be appropriate in as many situations as the Long Integer, which actually is the best of the choices.

The next property—which determines which fields, if any, Access should index automatically—can be considered an area where Access, in trying to be helpful, just bites off more than it can comfortably chew. For example, if you put the letters "ID" in this field, Access automatically creates indexes on any field which has "ID" in the first or last position of the field name. That might be helpful; but if it is not used carefully, it can lead to a proliferation of indexes, some of which you don't even know about and which might be a drag on performance. It is generally considered a good practice, therefore, to limit entries here to one or two for which you know you will *always* want to create indexes. Some developers even make it a practice to eliminate all automatic indexes, preferring to control all of them directly.

Return to the table now and take another look at the field size for the Text field illustrated in Figure A-5.

You should use the smallest reasonable Field Size property setting. In Figure A-5, therefore, the field size for FirstName was changed from the default for this database to 50. Most people's first names should fit comfortably into that length. You may also find that smaller field lengths help constrain data entry and encourage proper use of the space allowed. For example, a field length of 20 would limit the opportunity for including extraneous data or descriptions with the first name, such as "Traci (Teresa's cousin)."

Format

There are no default or predefined formats for Text fields. That makes sense, of course, as text can be virtually anything you want to enter in the field.

Input Mask

The input mask property can be applied to fields to specify a pattern for all data entered into a field. Input masks consist of the following three parts, separated by semi-colons:

- The input mask itself
- Whether literals should be stored or only displayed
- The character to display as a placeholder in the input mask

Two examples are telephone numbers and zip codes; let's save a more detailed discussion for the other table, tblPhone.

Caption

We looked at the Caption property briefly when talking about the AutoNumber primary key field. Creating a good caption is relevant for name fields, considering that you *do* want to show them in your forms and reports. Therefore, for fields in the so-called "CamelCase" format, for example, you can create a caption like "First Name" instead of "FirstName" on forms and reports and in queries.

Default Value

Depending on the nature of the field, you may want to define a default for each new record. For FirstName, that probably makes no sense—you obviously can't predict what the first name for each new person will be. In other cases, it might make sense. When we look at the properties of the Date/Time field later in this appendix, we'll see how a default does make sense.

Validation Rule and Validation Text

Validation rules help you implement business rules by controlling data entered into fields. We'll discuss this in more detail when we look at the properties of the Date/Time field later in this appendix, where a simple example can be defined.

Required

We'll discuss the importance and potential use of the Required property Appendix B, "Relationships, Joins, and Nulls," when we dive into a discussion about nulls. This is where you set it. The default is "No," meaning that this table would accept nulls for First Names. In Figure A-5, it is changed to "Yes" because the business rule is that First Name is always required.

Allow Zero Length

This property enforces a business rule which allows, or disallows, *zero-length strings* (*ZLS*). When set to "Yes," you can enter a ZLS for a person's first name. Again, Figure A-5 shows that the default, "Yes," has been changed to "No." We want first names for everyone and " " is not acceptable.

Note that a ZLS essentially indicates nonexistent data for a Text or Memo field. This is represented by two double quote marks without any space between them (" ").

We'll tell you more about zero-length strings later in this appendix. For now, you can think of a ZLS as a string of text with no characters in it. The important thing there is that defining a value as a ZLS means that we *do* know what is in it (nothing).

Indexed

We have covered indexing previously. In this table, we decided not to index FirstName because we don't anticipate searching, sorting, or filtering on it. If that is not a valid assumption, we can come back and change it later.

Unicode Compression

The default value for Unicode Compression is "Yes" and you should just leave it that way. Unicode is a method of encoding characters in Text, Memo, and Hyperlink fields. It requires more storage space because each character is stored as 2 bytes. Allowing Unicode compression permits Access to store those strings more efficiently.

IME Mode and IME Sentence Mode

IME Mode refers to the way kanji characters, used in Japanese, are displayed. You do not need to change the default, "No Control," unless your database will require Japanese characters.

Smart Tags

We briefly touched on Smart Tags earlier. With the FirstName field, you might find a use for them. If you click on the builder button at the right end of the property field, the dialog shown in Figure A-7 opens, showing you some options.

In Figure A-6, we've selected the "Person Name" option for the FirstName field. That means a Smart Tag will appear anywhere the FirstName field appears in a datasheet or form. Clicking the Smart Tag will open a dialog offering these actions: Send Mail, Schedule a Meeting, Open Contact, Add to Contacts. If any of these actions appeal to you, you can set them for the appropriate fields in your tables.

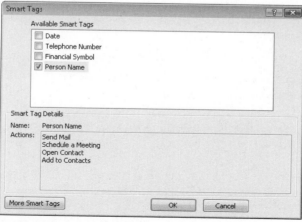

Figure A-6: Smart Tag options for FirstName

Text Align

We covered the issues regarding this property earlier. The default is "General," but if you want first names, for example, to appear right aligned instead of left aligned in every place in your database, you can set that property here. Text alignment can be overridden in a form or report.

Since we've had a fairly comprehensive review of the properties for text fields, we'll skip over the next few fields, which are also text fields. The next field with a new data type is the InactiveDate field. It is a Date/Time data type and has some additional properties for us to learn about.

Properties of Date/Time Fields

Figure A-7 displays the properties for a Date/Time field.

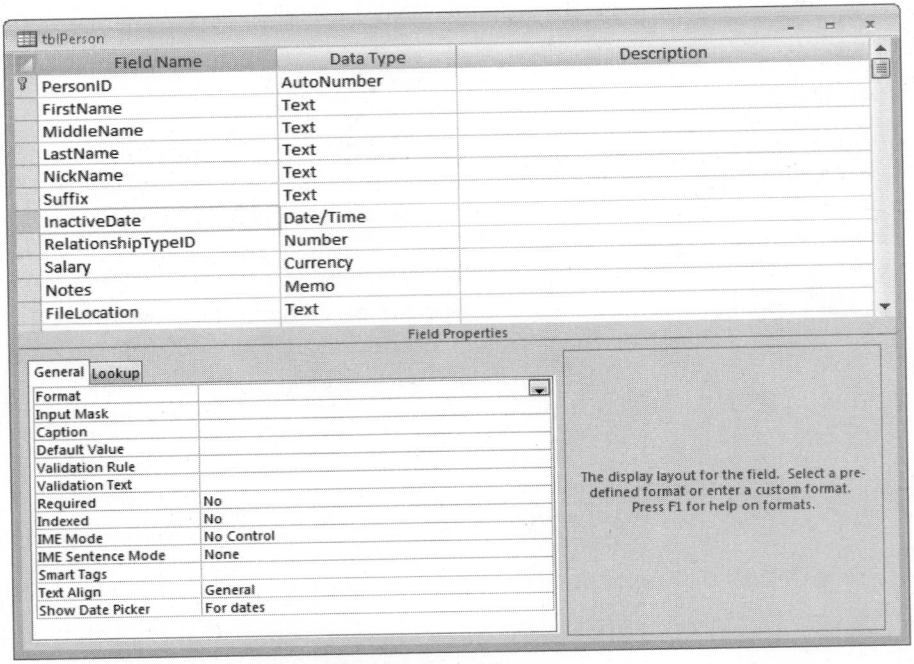

Figure A-7: Field Properties for Date/Time fields

There are 13 configurable properties for Date/Time fields.

- Format
- Input Mask
- Caption

- Default Value
- Validation Rule
- Validation Text
- Required
- Indexed
- IME Mode
- IME Sentence Mode
- Smart Tags
- Text Align
- Show Date Picker

We've already covered some of them, so once again, we'll only look at these selected ones: Format, Input Mask, Validation Rule, Validation Text, and Show Date Picker.

Format and Input Mask

The Format property allows you to define a default format for dates entered in this field. Most of the time, you'll probably want to control date formats in forms and reports, where context determines which is most appropriate. Therefore, at the table level, there are probably only three commonly used masks:

- General Date
- Short Date
- Medium Time

When you specify "General Date" for the format property, dates entered with a time component are displayed as: mm/dd/yyyy hh:mm:ss AMPM.

However, the result you get depends, in part, on how you enter the date. When you don't specify the time portion, Access displays only the date portion entered. Therefore, even if you've defined the Format property as a general date (which includes both date and time), the value may still be displayed as just the date portion when time is not entered along with the date. However, if the user (or system) enters both the date and time, General Date format displays both values in the field.

NOTE The statement that "Access displays only the date portion entered" can be somewhat misleading, but a full discussion is beyond our scope here. In fact, all dates do include a time portion, which is not displayed for values entered with a time specified.

Short Date means that the value in the date field always displays in mm/dd/yyyy format. Again, the underlying date field retains the value entered, including the time when it is included, but the display will not include the time when the Short Date format is applied.

Medium Time means that the value in the field is displayed as a time in hh:mmAMPM format. And as before, the actual date and time stored in the field is not changed. This property only affects the display. For values entered with a time component, that time component displays. For values entered as dates without a time component, the displayed value will be 12:00AM.

The important thing to remember about Date/Time formats is that they determine how the values in the field are displayed, not how they are stored.

The Input Mask property, on the other hand, controls how users can enter dates. A typical Input Mask looks like this: 99/99/0000;0;_.

The Input Mask has three parts separated by semi-colons: the format required, whether literals are stored with the values, and the default place-holder for fields. In an input mask, the digit "9" indicates it requires either a digit or a space, whereas "0" indicates a digit is always required. In the Input Mask just shown, the forward slash is stored as part of the value, as specified by the 0 in the second part of the Input Mask. The placeholder is the underscore. Users must enter all dates in the format specified by Input Mask. The help file in Microsoft Access provides several examples for using the Input Mask.

Default Value

Typical choices for Default Value for Date/Time fields are Now() and Date(). The Date() expression returns the current system date. The Now() expression returns the current system date and time. Depending on your business rules, you might require one or the other. If it is important to know both, for example, on which day and at which time a record was entered, Now() is the right choice. If it is only important to know on which day a record was entered, Date() is sufficient.

Validation Rule and Validation Text

You can enforce certain business rules at the table level by implementing a Validation Rule. For example, with regard to the InactiveDate field in this table, you may want to specify that only values equal or prior to today's date are valid on the assumption that we can't predict when a person will become inactive. To enforce that rule, you can add the following to the Validation Rule property: <=Date()

That will prevent inserting or changing a date with a value greater than today.

To present users with a friendly message, you can specify the Validation Text to show when an invalid value is supplied:

"Please enter dates less than or equal to today's date."

Validation rules, by the way, don't apply to existing values. If you've already added records to the table, and later apply the validation rule, Access will check for, and warn you about, such values. However, you can apply the rule anyway, retaining all of those nonconforming values. Trying to edit any of them, however, will invoke the validation rule.

Show Date Picker

The Date Picker, new in Access 2007, is a little icon which can appear next to all date fields on forms. Clicking it pops up a calendar from which you can select a date. It is handy, but you might not always want to see it on forms. By default it is turned on. You have the option of setting the property to "Never" if you don't want users to have access to it.

This property can also be configured on forms. Therefore, most of the time you'll probably want to leave it set to the default at the table level, and change it to "Never" just in those forms where it is not appropriate. You will have ample opportunity to learn more about the properties associated with forms as you create and modify the user interface for your databases.

Further Study on Dates and Time

That's a very brief overview of the properties for Date/Time fields. With regard to the Date/Time values themselves we've only scratched the surface in the preceding discussion—just enough really to help you deal with field properties in tables. You may wish to pursue further reading on the subject. In this book, you can refer to Chapter 2 for more details.

Properties of Number Fields

Next up for review is the Number field, shown in Figure A-8.

There are 12 properties for number fields, as shown in Figure A-9. One of the properties, Decimal Places, is only configurable for some types of numbers, and another property, the Input Mask, is not configurable.

- Field Size
- Format
- Decimal Places

- Input Mask
- Caption
- Default Value
- Validation Rule
- Validation Text
- Required
- Indexed
- Smart Tags
- Text Align

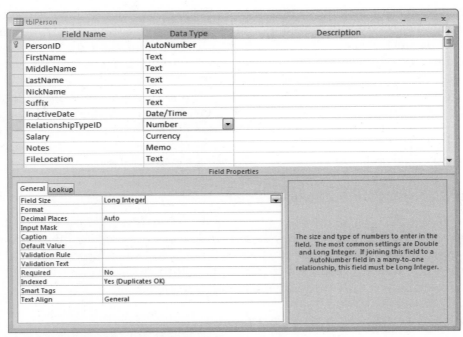

Figure A-8: Field properties for Number fields

Again, we'll only discuss those properties that we've not already covered with previous data types, with the exception of Field Size, Format, and Default Value. Although some properties offer different choices than for previous field types, such as options for Validation Rules, we assume you'll be able make those choices to reflect your business rules.

Field Size

As with dates, a full discussion of field sizes for numbers is well beyond our scope. We'll stick to the most important characteristics and considerations involved in choosing field size for your tables. Keeping in mind that the size of the values stored in numbers has some impact on performance and storage (however minimal it may be on modern computers), you usually prefer the smallest field size that will adequately store the values you require.

A second consideration is the precision with which those values are stored. It is beyond the scope of this appendix to discuss the complexities involved in that, but suffice it to say that numerical precision might simply be thought of in terms of how many places to the right of the decimal you need. We typically see two places with money, and there are not many business situations that need more than 3 or 4 places. For our purposes, just be aware that the trade-offs you might face are greater precision vs less precision and accompanying impacts on performance.

The default value for Field Size is Long Integer, which we discussed earlier. The other choices, for number fields include:

- Byte
- Integer
- Single
- Double
- Replication ID
- Decimal

You already know what Replication ID means. Let's quickly look at the other options and where you might use them.

Byte

This choice stores whole numbers from 0 to 255. If you need a simple counter field which has a range of possible values that can never exceed 255, the byte field might be a valid choice. Of course, that will depend on your scenario; if you are counting attendance and expecting 800, this would not work.

Integer

Integers are whole numbers. In Access, the Integer data type ranges from −32,768 to 32,767. If you need a number field which can never exceed 65,536 different values, Integer would be a valid choice.

Long Integer

Long Integers are whole numbers from −2,147,483,648 to 2,147,483,647. The total available, 4,294,967,296, makes them a good choice for the primary key value of Access tables, and it is the default for AutoNumbers. If you need a number field for which values will exceed the total available as Integers, or if values in the field will exceed 32,767 (the size of Integers), the Long Integer is the choice.

Single (aka Float), Double and Decimal

It's easier to discuss these three number types together because the differences between them have more to do with the precision, or number of decimal points, with which they can store fractional (such as 7/8 or 1/3), or decimal values, than with the range of numbers they can represent, although there are some differences. Singles (sometimes called Floats) represent fractional values up to 7 decimals of precision. Doubles can represent up to 15 decimals. Decimal numbers can store up to 28 decimals of precision.

Another difference is that floating point numbers (both single and double) can not accurately store all values in the range they cover, while decimals can. On the other hand, while more precise (up 28 decimal points vs. 15 for Doubles), decimals handle a smaller range of values than singles or doubles. Therefore, the choice here is largely determined by how you plan to use the numbers, as well as how large or how small they will be in your database.

If your field will contain only whole numbers, the choice is between Byte, Integer, and Long Integer. In that case, the range of available values is the primary consideration.

If your field needs to handle decimal values, and great precision is required, your first choice would be the Decimal type, or possibly the Currency type, which we'll see later.

If your database requires decimal values with a lesser degree of precision, you can select the Single or Double type and expect possibly better performance. However, unless the calculations are quite intense, this may not be a significant factor.

Decimal Places

The next configurable property for numbers is the number of decimal places to *display*. Of course, this does not apply to whole numbers, or integers which do not have a decimal portion. Also, it only determines how many digits are displayed, not how many are stored.

Your choices are Auto, which follows the precision specified in the Format property, or a value from 0 to 15. 0 means no digits are shown to the right of the decimal. Controls on forms and reports inherit this setting for bound fields.

Default Value

In versions of Access prior to 2007, the default value for numbers was always 0. You could change that, of course, but this was often a source of frustration. One of the most common uses for number fields was foreign keys. And foreign keys were usually related to primary keys defined as AutoNumbers. The problem, as you might have guessed, was that by default AutoNumbers start at 1 and increment. Having a default of 0 for a foreign key just did not work! Fortunately, that was changed in Access 2007. The default is now null for number fields, and that works just fine for most foreign keys.

When we discuss relationships later in this appendix, we'll revisit the use of null as the default for foreign key values. For most other uses, it's not a problem.

Sometimes you might choose another valid value to be the default. For example, let's say you have a domain, or lookup, table in which you have a list of resources. The first choice is always Engineering Aide because two-thirds of all assignments go to them. It is easy to select the primary key for Engineering Aide from the Resources table and make it the default. Users only have to select a new value in one-third of the records they enter, as opposed to all of them.

We've already discussed the remaining properties as they apply to other data types. You'll make different choices, of course, but the principles are the same.

Properties for the Currency Data Types

The next field we'll consider is a Currency data type, Salary, shown in Figure A-9. Although we use it here with a field that stores money, the built-in features of the Currency data type can make it an excellent choice for other purposes as well, as you'll soon find out.

The Currency data type has the following 11 properties:

- Format
- Decimal Places
- Input Mask
- Caption
- Default Value
- Validation Rule
- Validation Text
- Required
- Indexed

- Smart Tags
- Text Align

Figure A-9: Properties for the Currency data type

We only need to look at two properties for the Currency data type. The others are similar to those you've already read about.

Format

It might seem a bit surprising to see that currency can actually be formatted as something other than dollars or Euros, as shown in Figure A-10.

There is a very good reason for these options, though, and it has to do with the accuracy of the Currency data type. Currency data typed fields only store up to four decimals. However, while they are not as precise as Single or Doubles, they are quite accurate within their level of precision. Therefore, when accuracy is extremely important, you can select the Currency data type, *even if the values being stored are not monetary*, and count on that accuracy up to the four decimals presented. Further, by selecting a format like Standard, you can display the values in a format that makes sense for the context.

Of course, if the values in the field are monetary, the Currency data type is appropriate while ensuring the same accuracy.

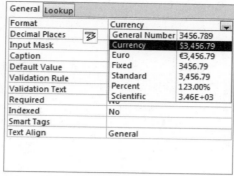

Figure A-10: Currency data type formats

Decimal Places

Interestingly, you can still elect to *display* more than four decimals for Currency, up to 15 as with other number fields. However, the Currency data type is limited to four decimal places, as noted in the previous paragraph, so Access displays 0s for all decimal places after the first four.

In summary, currency fields are accurate for 15 spaces to the left of the decimal and 4 spaces to the right.

Properties for the Memo Data Type

The Memo data type can hold up to 63,999 characters when they are entered directly, and it can store more if the data is entered programmatically—that is, through code. The format is not configurable. The Notes field shown in Figure A-11 is a Memo data type field.

Memo fields are useful for situations requiring extensive notes. You can use automation to insert large amounts of text in memo fields. The limit for text entered programmatically is the size of the entire Access database—2GB. In other words, a single memo field in a single record could, at least theoretically, fill all of the available space in an Access database.

There are some known problems with Memo fields, so you should use them with appropriate caution. Among other factors, Memo fields are known to be a cause of corruption in databases. For that reason, many developers prefer to create a separate table for notes, linked to the main table. That way, if a memo field in that table does become corrupted, it doesn't impact its parent table.

Unique Index Enforced for a Text Field

We only have one more field to look at in this table, shown in Figure A-12. It's also a Text field, with all the same properties of the Text field we discussed previously. However, in this example, we've added a unique index, which is set under the Indexed property. We'll discuss it briefly as an introduction to the next section, in which we'll move on to discuss relationships between tables.

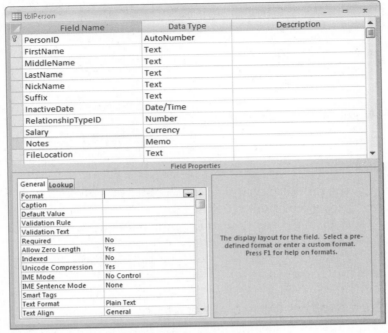

Figure A-11: Field properties for the Memo data type

Single Field Index

Figure A-13 shows a Text field, FileLocation, on which a unique index has been enforced. The Indexed property displays that choice as Yes (No Duplicates).

Although this field is not a primary key, we do not want to permit any value—in this case a file location—to be entered more than once.

FileLocation is a reference to a specific folder, or file, containing the paper copies of all personnel records for each person in the table. Each file, of course, is unique to one person, and therefore has a unique FileLocation identifier. To help ensure that data entry makes no errors in recording the same FileLocation for two different people, we have imposed a table-level constraint on this field.

Multiple Field Index

It is possible to combine two or more fields in a unique index. To see an example of this, let's quickly switch to a different table, tblPhone, where a unique index has been created for two fields, as shown in Figure A-13.

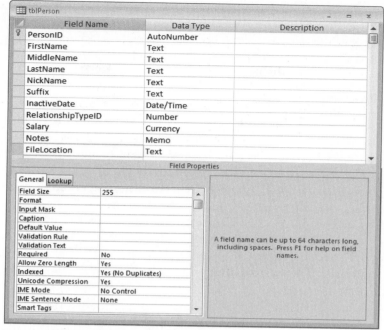

Figure A-12: Text field with a unique index enforced

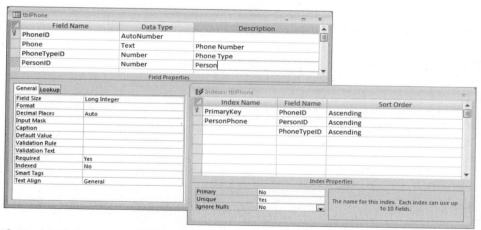

Figure A-13: Compound field unique index

In order to create an index on two fields, you need to open the Index property sheet. We showed you how to do that earlier (see Figure A-3).

Figure A-14 displays the index PersonPhone which defines a multi field index for PersonID and PhoneTypeID in the Phone table. We created the index by selecting the first field, PersonId and typing in a new name for it in the Index Name column (PersonPhone). Then we added the second field, PhoneTypeID, by selecting it in the next row. Note that the Index Name field is empty in that row. This tells Access to combine the fields in a single index.

Unique Property

Finally, we change the Unique property for this new index from "No" to "Yes." Now, Access will only permit each PersonID to be entered with a phone type once. In other words, each person will be allowed a single work phone, a single home phone and a single mobile phone.

What additional fields would benefit from indexes? Looking at the fields in the people table, LastName appears to be a candidate. Remember, indexes can speed searches, filtering and sorting. If your workflows include frequent searches for specific people by last name, an index on this field is a good idea. LastName will not be defined as a primary key, of course, and it should not be defined as Unique. That would limit you to one "Linson," one "Bradley," one "Hennig," and so on.

Ignore Nulls

Your business rules will dictate whether you want to set the Ignore Nulls property to "Yes" or "No". If you choose, the default, "No," the field will accept nulls, meaning you can enter a person's record even if you only know their first name. You will learn more about nulls in Appendix B.

Properties for the Yes/No Data Type

We need to look at one more data type, but to do that we'll switch to a different table. Take a look at the Customer table in Figure A-14, which includes a field called CustomerInactive. It's defined as a Yes/No data type. In addition to explaining the data type, we're going to demonstrate how to use the field values to group records. The table and queries that we'll use are provided in the BonusResource.mdb provided with Appendix E's files on the book's CD.

Most of the available properties for Yes/No fields are similar to those you've already learned about for other data types, so we'll focus on only two. On the General tab, we'll discuss the Format, and on the Lookup tab we'll discuss Display Control.

You'll notice that many of the examples in the book include an "inactive" field to flag records which are no longer active, but which we do not want to remove. For example, we might flag a customer as inactive because they went out of business and we do not expect to receive any further orders from them. However, we cannot remove that customer from our database because we need to retain their order information. Retaining information about customers who did not make purchases may provide data that is beneficial for various analyses. So, we need to keep the customer records for historical purposes, but we don't want them mistaken for current entries by users inputting new orders because that could lead to data entry errors. But we also need a mechanism to control how and when the records are displayed and used. Adding the CustomerInactive field gives us the control and flexibility we need.

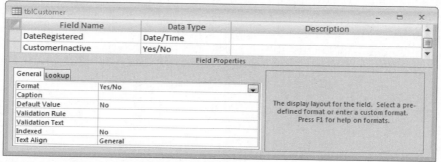

Figure A-14: tblCustomer with a Yes/No field

CustomerInactive accepts one of only two possible values for each record: "Yes" or "No." The technical term for fields of this data type is *Boolean*, although we usually refer it by the more common name "Yes/No."

A Yes/No field can be formatted as True/False, Yes/No, or On/Off, as illustrated in Figure A-15. Note that the Format property refers to the way values are *displayed* to users, not the underlying *value*. Access actually stores a -1 for "Yes" and 0 for "No." You can also define custom formats when as appropriate for your database.

NOTE Access stores Yes/No fields as either -1, for "True," "Yes," or "On," and 0 for "False," "No," or "Off." We can take advantage of the underlying numeric values when doing calculations in code or SQL statements (queries). We will show you one way to do that later in this appendix.

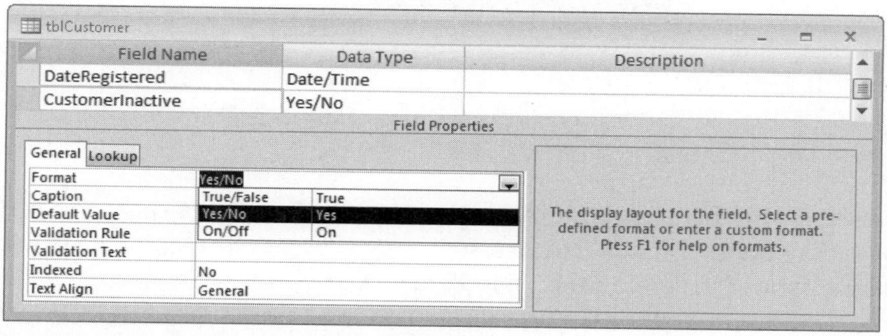

Figure A-15: Format option for Yes/No field

The numeric values raise another important consideration. Other database engines, such as SQL Server, use 1 for "True" instead of -1. So if you are working with other data platforms, you will need to know what that platform uses for Yes/No fields and how the conversion is managed. One technique is to use the absolute value of the field. For 1, that is ±1. A full discussion is beyond the scope of this book, so for now, just remember that you can refer to these values with either literals (e.g. "Yes") or numerics (e.g. -1).

In this case the default option, Yes/No, is appropriate for our CustomerInactive field. "Yes" means that they have gone into inactive status, "No" means their status has not changed to inactive. Figure A-16 shows that one customer has been flagged as Inactive in this Customer table.

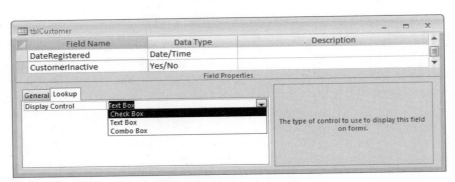

Figure A-16: A customer flagged as inactive in a Yes/No field

As Figure A-16 shows, the default display option for Yes/No fields is a check box, which is a good visual presentation for many uses. However, there are other options, as shown in Figure A-17.

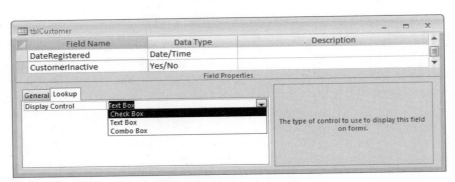

Figure A-17: Display options for Yes/No field

Selecting the Text Box option for Display presents text values Yes or No, True or False, On or Off. You can also create a custom format, using different combinations of values, as shown in Figure A-18, where we selected Text Box as the Display option, and also changed to the format property to Inactive [Red]; Active [Blue].

Note that "Inactive" corresponds to "Yes" or "True," and "Active" corresponds to "No" or "False." Although this type of formatting is available at the table level, we recommend that it be used in the controls on the forms or reports where you want to highlight this detail. "Active" is displayed on the new record line because that is the default value of the field.

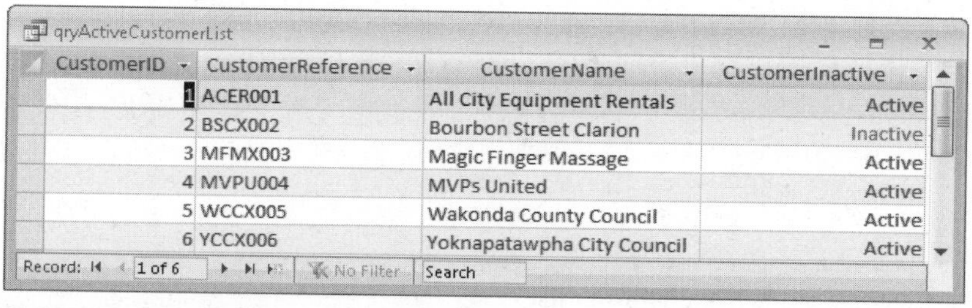

Figure A-18: Custom display of a Yes/No field

The third option, selecting the Combo Box display, presents the values to users in a dropdown box in the field.

Using Yes/No Fields in Queries

We selected this Customer table as an example of Yes/No field properties so that we can show you how you can take advantage of this field type when creating filtered queries and custom displays for users. Let's start with a filtered query, as shown in Figure A-19, which will only return records where CustomerInactive equals No.

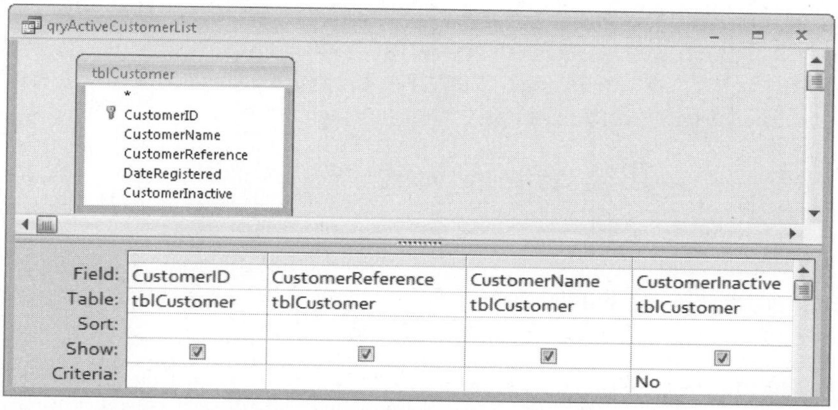

Figure A-19: Filtering a query on a Yes/No field

The query in Figure A-18 will return a list of all active customers, excluding those where the CustomerInactive field is set to No. Remember that this equation is essentially a double negative—we have asked for customers that are not marked Inactive.

Compare Figure A-20 to Figure A-16, and you will notice that the filtered list does not include the record for CustomerID 2, because the record has Inactive or "Yes" in the field CustomerInactive.

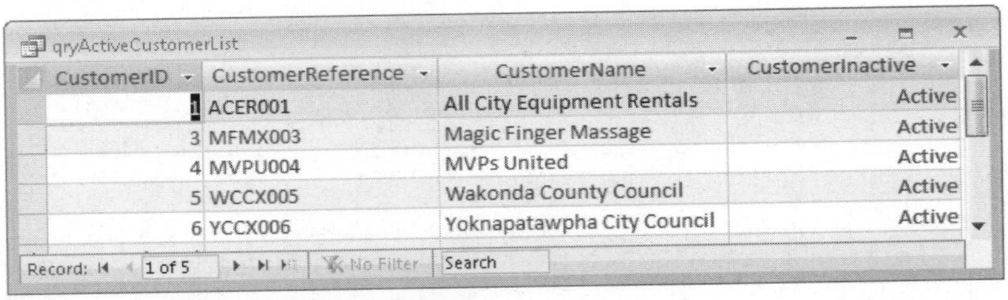

Figure A-20: Filtered active customer list

You might want to use this query to filter records for a report showing only currently active customers.

If you are familiar with your data, you may already be thinking that there are more than two possible values for this field. If the field does not require a value, some records may not have one. It is often helpful to require a value for check box fields. Otherwise, you will need to check for and accommodate null values. Fields without a value are either nulls or zero length strings (ZLS). Appendix B has a discussion and examples of how to work with those.

Custom Presentation Using Yes/No Fields in Queries

For our final example, we'll show you a way to display a customized list of customers, both active and inactive, with a visual marker for inactive customers. Take a look at the query as shown in Design View in Figure A-21, and in the SQL View in Figure A-22. We'll explore the contents of the SQL after we look at the query results.

Figure A-21: Query to select a customized list of active customers

The resulting recordset is shown in Figure A-23. The inactive customer, Bourbon Street Clarion, is flagged with an asterisk (*) and it is also sorted to the end of the list, moving it out of the sequence of active customers at the beginning of the list. Any existing orders from that customer will show correctly; you will see the customer with their existing (historic) orders. But we now have two visual cues to help prevent assigning new orders to an inactive customer.

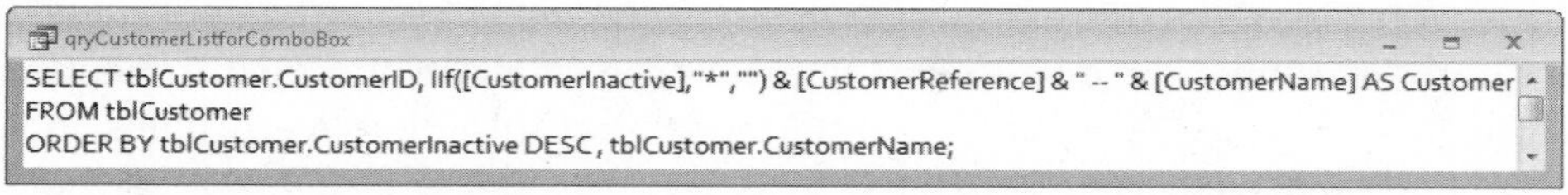

Figure A-22: SQL string for a query to select a customized list of active customers

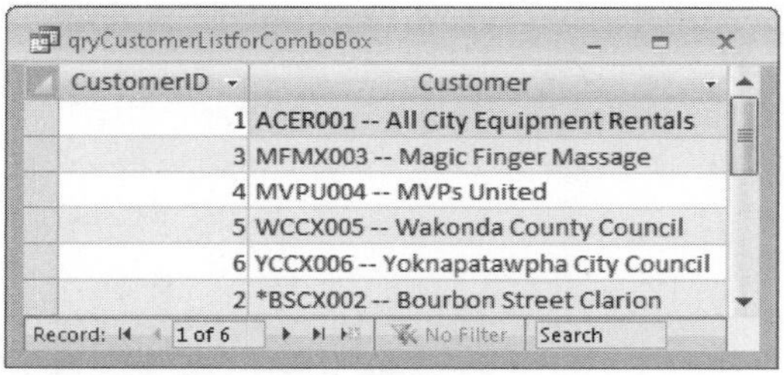

Figure A-23: Customized list of active customers

To show you how it works more clearly, here's the SQL statement for this query, reformatted to fit this page:

```
SELECT tblCustomer.CustomerID,
IIf([CustomerInactive],"*","") & [CustomerReference] & " -- " &
  [CustomerName] AS Customer
FROM tblCustomer
ORDER BY tblCustomer.CustomerInactive DESC, tblCustomer.CustomerName;
```

We used the Immediate If function (IIF) to append the asterisk to the front of names of inactive customers. Then we concatenated the customer reference number and customer name into that string. As shown in Figure A-23, the result is the string *BSCX002 – Bourbon Street Clarion, which is displayed to the user in a combo or list box.

IIF Statements

A quick refresher on IIF statements will help explain the process. IIF takes three arguments: the expression to be evaluated, the option to select if the expression is True, and the option to select if the expression is False. In this case, we evaluate the Yes/No field itself, which can only be True or False (Yes or No). If it is True, we select the "*", if not, we select a ZLS. You learn more about ZLSs in Appendix B.

To achieve the sorting we want, we took advantage of the fact that Access stores Yes/No fields as numbers, -1 and 0. Sorting an active field in descending order means that "Inactive" customers (flagged as -1) come after "Active" customers (flagged as 0), because 0 is greater than -1.

Then, we applied the more traditional alphabetic sort on CustomerName so that all active customers are displayed alphabetically first, then all inactive customers alphabetically.

That concludes our discussion of field properties. In the next appendix, Appendix B, you learn more about the relationships between tables in a relational database.

Relationships, Joins, and Nulls

This appendix expands on some of the concepts that you've learned in this book. Specifically you'll learn more about:

- Tools in Access to manage table relationships and query joins
- Nulls and their uses
- Concepts you need when creating and using lookup tables

We'll start by discussing relationships and joins.

Relationships and Joins

All of the database schemas you've studied in this book require you to identify and define relationships between tables. You've also seen examples of, and used, joins in queries. In this appendix, we take a closer look at the tools Access provides to manage those database components. We also demonstrate the effect that the type of relationship or join has on record sets using the data.

NOTE A *record set* is a group of records. This can be as basic as the records in a table or the results returned by a query involving one or more tables.

Note that we used two terms, not just one, to refer to the process of establishing relationships between tables: *identify* and *define*. Moreover—unlike in some chapters—we specifically avoided the term *create* in this context. We'll explain why we make those distinctions shortly, but first, let's briefly review relationships as they exist in databases.

As you recall from Chapter 2, "Elements of a Microsoft Access Database," there are three types of relationships in a database: one-to-one, one-to-many, and many-to-many. In each case, the fundamental principle at work is this: two tables, each representing one subject, relate to one another in some way.

All too often, English and other languages can be ambiguous, something the "language" of a database should never be. The language of a database serves one purpose: it must be precise and specific. Therefore, to be of any value to the database, relationships between tables must be precisely and explicitly defined. Our focus here is to show you how to identify and define the proper relationships between tables.

It's All Been Done Before

The first step, of course, is to identify the subjects of interest in our database and create a table for each subject—for example, a People table and an Address table. The next step is to identify how the subjects of those tables interact. It's import to recognize that you are not creating or establishing relationships. You are formalizing, in a database-specific way, a definition for the relationships that already exist among the subjects in the real world.

Consider the example of a personal contact database containing tables for contacts and phone numbers. We create that database to capture information about the contacts with whom we want to stay in touch and the methods we can use to do so. One table lists those people (contacts); the other lists phone numbers.

There are hundreds of thousands of phone numbers in use throughout the U.S., and probably millions in the world, but we only want to include them in our Phone Number table if they already have a relationship to people in our Contact table. If, for example, you make a random number in "phone format," such as 999-555-0000, you should not be able to just stuff it into the Phone Number table in your contacts database. That number has no relationship to anyone. Phone numbers belong to contacts—that's why they belong in the Phone Number table in this database.

Telling It Like It Is

Once we've satisfactorily identified (and possibly refined) all of the relationships between the tables in a database, it's time to share those insights with the database itself. You've seen examples of this in the relationship diagrams throughout this book. What we want to illustrate now is that, when you add the Contacts and Phone Numbers tables to the relationship diagram window, they are already related. The Relationships window is a just a tool through which you can tell Access everything it needs to know about that relationship. Once that is done, you can turn the responsibility for monitoring and enforcing the relationship over to Access.

> **NOTE** Although we are discussing the most common use of the relationship diagram, which is to show and control relationships between tables, the tables in a relationship diagram do not have to be related. You can, in fact, include tables that have no dependency on other tables. You may want to do this if you are reviewing all of the tables in the database.

As described in Chapters 2, "Elements of a Microsoft Access Database," and 3, "Relational Data Model," in particular, but in other chapters as well, you saw diagrams like Figure B-1.

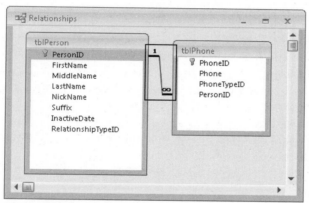

Figure B-1: Relationship line

In this image, concentrate on the area between the table lists—that's the relationship line. It defines—for Access—the relationship between the two tables in the Relationships window. It is there to formalize in the database the definition of the relationship between people and their phones.

Let's walk through the steps you need to take to make this happen. Although we're showing you the tools found in Access, other relational database management systems, such as SQL Server, have tools that perform the same functions.

The first step is to place your tables in the Relationships window. The following discussion is based on the design interface in Access 2007. If you are using an earlier version, the steps will be similar, even though the components you use (Database Container vs. Navigation Pane) are somewhat different.

1. If you are using Access 2007, select Database Tools from the Ribbon, then click Relationships. That will open an empty window, as shown in Figure B-2.

Figure B-2: Initial Relationships window

2. There are several ways to get your tables into the Relationships window, where you can define and customize relationships. One is to select them in the list of tables in the Navigation Pane (Database Container in previous versions) and drag and drop them into the Relationships window. Another method is to use the Ribbon, as shown in Figure B-3.

Figure B-3: Insert tables from the Ribbon

3. With your tables in the Relationships window, you are ready to tell Access about the relationships between them. I hope you noticed that, when you first add tables to the Relationships window, as shown in Figure B-4, there are no lines between any of the tables.

Remember that the relationship already exists in a logical sense; we know that because we identified it during the modeling phase. Here in the Relationships window we're defining it formally—that is, we're telling Access about it. It's obvious that Access doesn't know about the relationship, because it initially shows the two tables without any relationship lines connecting them.

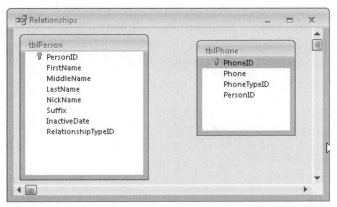

Figure B-4: Initial view of the Relationships window after adding tables

4. To define the relationship in Access, select one of the two key fields you inserted in your tables. You can start with either the primary key from the parent table or the foreign key from the child table. Although Access is not smart enough to know which fields you want to use ahead of time, once you have identified them for the application, it is smart enough to help you complete the definition of the relationship by identifying the data types of the fields and, more importantly, whether they have already been defined as primary keys.

   A field becomes a foreign key by virtue of having been recruited to participate in a relationship with a primary key in another table. Access can only identify the foreign key when it knows about the relationship that defines it.

5. Click on the field you selected, and drag the cursor over to the other table, making sure that the cursor is highlighted on the corresponding key field in that table. Let go of the mouse, and wait for the Edit Relationships dialog, shown in Figure B-5, to open for you.

6. In Figure B-5 you can see that an important assumption has been made by Access, based on the characteristics of the two fields involved in the relationship you are defining. Access recognizes that you've picked the primary key field in tblPerson, PersonID, and dragged it onto a field in tblPhone.

   Access knows all about the properties of those two fields and uses one of those properties to decide what kind of relationship this is. In tblPerson, PersonID is a primary key, which means in part that each value in it must be unique. In tblPhone, on the other hand, PersonId is defined to permit a value to be entered more than once. Those two facts tell Access this is a one-to-many relationship, and that PersonID must, therefore, be the corresponding foreign key. The fact that they have the same name is irrelevant to Access in this context. It's the relationship itself, and the properties of the fields, that matter. In a later section of this appendix, when we take a closer look at field properties, we'll return to this point.

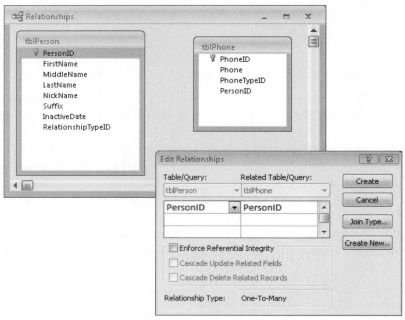

Figure B-5: Edit Relationships dialog

If you stopped here, Access would now know there is a one-to-many relationship between tblPerson and tblPhone but nothing more than that. Look at Figure B-6.

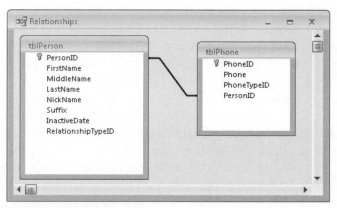

Figure B-6: Basic relationship defined

The unadorned relationship line in Figure B-6 tells Access that the relationship exists. However, if you stop here, Access will not enforce referential integrity on that relationship. As you should recall from Chapter 2, without referential integrity in place, Access will permit you to enter key values into the "many" side table even though they don't already exist in the "one" side table. Recalling our earlier example of a made-up phone number, Access would quite happily let you stuff "999-555-0000" into the phone number table and assign it to a nonexistent person; that is to say, you could use any value for PersonID even though that value does not exist as a primary key value in the Contacts table. You can prevent that by telling Access to enforce referential integrity.

NOTE The one exception to this rule is the case of a null in a foreign key. However, that discussion requires us to consider the nature of nulls. We do that later in this appendix.

7. The check box for Referential Integrity is right there on the Edit Relationships dialog, as shown in Figure B-7. Click to check it. That activates the other two choices, which you learned about in Chapter 2 as well.

You can click:

- Cascade Update Related Records
- Cascade Delete Related Records
- Both
- Neither

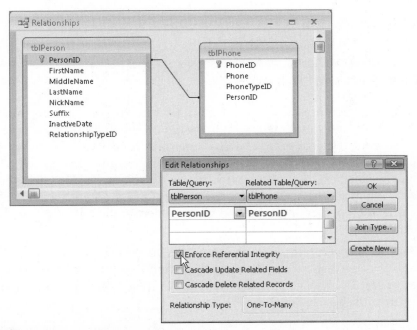

Figure B-7: Click to enforce referential integrity

With Cascade Update enabled, changes in the primary key field will cause an update in the foreign key for related record(s). With Cascade Delete enabled, deleting a record in the "one" side table also deletes any related records in the "many" side table.

Which of these options you choose, if any, depends to a certain extent on business rules that apply, but also on your personal preferences. Refer to Chapter 2 to refresh your understanding of the effect and consequences of selecting these options.

8. The relationship line is now adorned with two symbols—1 and ∞ (as shown in Figure B-8)—which, in part, indicate that the Person table is on the one side of the relationship and that the Phone table is on the many side of that relationship (one person can have many phone numbers). The convention in Access is that explicitly showing these symbols in the diagram also means that referential integrity is enforced on that relationship.

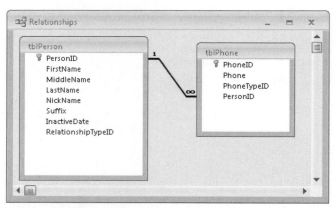

Figure B-8: Referential integrity enforced

So, with referential integrity in place on this one-to-many relationship, Access knows you do not want to assign phone numbers to people who don't exist (at least as far as this database is concerned). So, now, if you want to insert "999-555-0000" into the Phone Number table, the first step will have to be telling Access which person it belongs to. That helps ensure data integrity because you must first insert a record, with a primary key value, for a person in the person table, subject to the following important exception.

As you may recall from Appendix A, "Field Properties," we promised to tell you more about the "Required" property for fields. Here is a good example of when you would want to set it to "Yes" so that a non-null value must always be entered.

By default, Access will let you insert an "orphaned" phone number in the Phone table. If you don't try to assign a foreign key to it—that is, if you leave it null—Access accepts that record without a foreign key. You can prevent this behavior by setting the Required property for the PhoneNumber field to "Yes." Still, that would not be a restriction on the relationship itself, only on the field.

Change Happens—Redefining Relationships

Particularly in the early stages of design and development, changing your mind is not uncommon. Let's say, for example, that you started out with a table in which you used a natural key for the primary key. Later you realize that is not a good choice and decide you want to use a surrogate key for the primary key instead. However, you've already defined a relationship on that field and maybe even added some records to both tables. That makes it harder, but not impossible, to change things. Let's take a quick look at a simple example of a making that change, starting with Figure B-9.

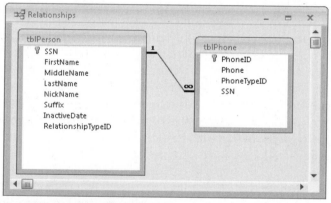

Figure B-9: Existing inappropriate relationship

As you can see in Figure B-9, this relationship illustrates a poor choice because the table uses the Social Security number (SSN) as the primary key. As you have read several times in this book, we strongly recommend using an AutoNumber for the primary key. Additionally, Access does not provide adequate safeguards appropriate for confidential data such as a Social Security number. Also, although SSN's are widely used for identification, there is no guarantee that they are unique nor that everyone will have one. Because one of the requirements for primary keys is that they must be unique, SSNs fail on that count as well.

Correcting this relationship will require several steps, starting with the addition of appropriate key fields, as shown in Figure B-10.

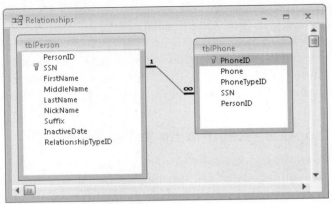

Figure B-10: Adding appropriate primary and foreign key fields

One of the reasons for starting out with new fields, rather than trying to repurpose one of the existing fields is that we have to select compatible data types for our primary and foreign keys. You can't see this in Figure B-10, but the new PersonID field in tblPerson is an Access AutoNumber, whereas the new PersonID field in tblPhone is a Long Integer. AutoNumbers are, as you learned in Chapter 2, Long Integers with additional properties required to ensure uniqueness in any given table.

SSN, on the other hand, is a Text field in both tables. Under some specific circumstances, we could rename SSN in the child table and convert it to a Long Integer in order to keep it as the foreign key; however, it really doesn't make sense to do so. And, once you've added records, it is not feasible to do so anyway. Instead, we use the existing fields to update the tables with their new primary and foreign key values, and then drop the redundant fields.

As an aside, it's worth noting that the new field, PersonID, in the Phone table is not yet a true foreign key. The relationship between tblPerson and tblPhone is still defined on SSN, meaning that it is still the foreign key.

Because the new field, PersonID, in tblPerson was defined as an AutoNumber, Access immediately generates new values for PersonID for every existing record in the table. That saves us the trouble of having to do so manually. In tblPhone, on the other hand, PersonID has no values yet. We created the new field for the table, and made it a Long Integer data type, but we haven't put anything in it yet. As you should recall from discussions in several chapters, this is a good example of a field with nulls instead of values. (Later in this appendix, we'll examine nulls in more detail.)

The next step is to update the values for our soon-to-be foreign key field in the child table. An update query will do that. Figure B-11 shows the query grid views of this update query. Figure B-12 shows the SQL view.

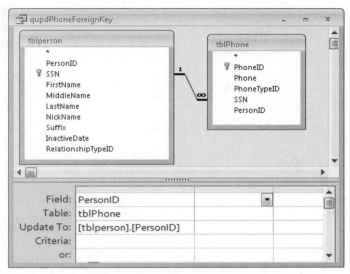

Figure B-11: Update new foreign key field: query grid view

Figure B-12: Update new foreign key field: SQL view

We'll explain this in more detail later, but we'd like to call your attention to the join line between tblPerson and tblPhone in the upper section of the query grid in Figure B-11. It looks exactly like the relationship line in the Relationships window because it fills a similar, but somewhat different, role.

Figure B-12 shows the SQL syntax Access generated to execute the update. Again, we will cover it in more detail in the next section, but note that the relationship between tblPerson and tblPhone is rendered as an INNER JOIN in the update query. For now, the important point is that this query updates each of the values for PersonID in tblPhone, to match the PersonID values from tblPerson. Remember, Access has generated those values for us in tlblPerson because PersonID is an AutoNumber data type in tblPerson. On the other hand, PersonID in tblPhones still has nulls in that field in its records.

When run, this query copies the PersonID values from each record in tblPerson to all records in tblPhone that have matching SSNs. As an aside, you might have recognized already that, after the query runs, the tables can be "matched" or "joined" on either SSN, PersonID, or both. You can see this in

Figure B-11 and in Figures B-13 and B-14, which illustrate different join lines for the fields in these tables.

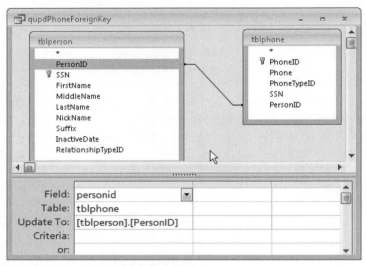

Figure B-13: Inner join defined on PersonID only

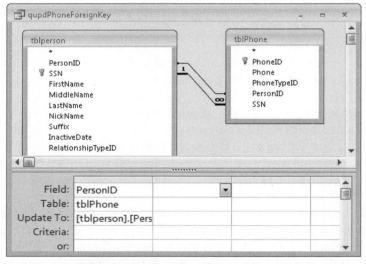

Figure B-14: Inner join defined on both SSN and PersonID

Figures B-11, B-13, and B-14 show that the query window gives you quite a bit of flexibility in defining joins. You can use the existing relationship(s) defined between fields in the tables, as in Figure B-11, or you can create your own joins as in B-13 and B-14. The resulting record sets may be, and usually will be, different, depending on how the joins are defined.

Before we take a closer look at the differences between the two join lines in Figure B-14, let's finish the task of correcting the primary and foreign key fields in tblPerson and tblPhone.

After the update query shown in Figure B-14 runs, all of the PersonID fields in tblPhone contain the value of the matching primary key from tblPerson. The SSN field, therefore, is now redundant in tblPhone.

> **NOTE** We won't debate here the pros and cons of keeping SSN in this sample table. We only added it to our sample tables to illustrate a point regarding changing relationships. Suffice it to say that confidentiality and good sense make it undesirable to store data of this type in an Access database, so we would normally remove it now.

In Figure B-15, we go back to the Relationships window and remove the relationship on the SSN field so that we can change the primary key to the proper field. Access won't let us make the change if there is a relationship on the existing primary key.

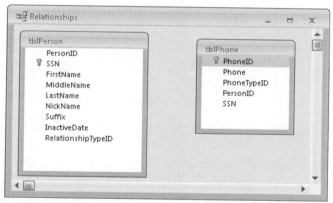

Figure B-15: Relationships removed to allow change in primary key

With the relationship definition removed in the Relationships window, you can open tblPerson in design view and designate the new AutoNumber field, PersonID, as the primary key for tblPerson. You can also open tblPhone and remove the redundant SSN field there. Then, you can come back to the Relationships window and complete the conversion, as shown in Figure B-16. Be sure to check the option to enforce referential integrity.

Before we move on to a closer look at the join lines in queries, and how they differ from the relationship lines we've examined so far, let's take a quick look at the Join Type option on the Edit Relationship dialog, as shown in Figure B-16. When you click it, the dialog shown in Figure B-17 opens.

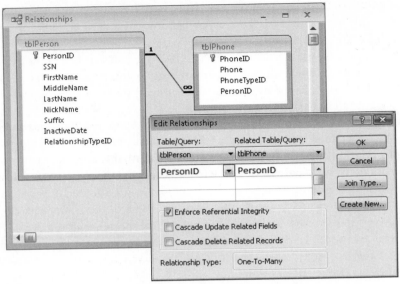

Figure B-16: New relationship defined on valid primary key field

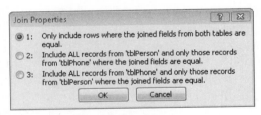

Figure B-17: Join properties for table relationships

There are three ways to define joins for table relationships, as shown in Figure B-17.

The default, and generally preferred, join type is called an inner join. That's option 1 in the dialog. As the dialog explains, any query based on the tables in that relationship returns only rows, or records, where the joined fields (that is, the primary and foreign key fields) are equal.

The second type of join, option 2 in Figure B-17, is called a left join. Again, the dialog explains how records are returned in queries based on tables related on this type of join: all records from the left-side table and only matching records from the right-side table.

The third type of join, a right join, is the opposite of the left join in the sense that it returns all records from the right table and only matching records from the left table.

In most working databases with which we are familiar, the default join type—the inner join—is the preferred type. That is true, in part, because we can easily change that join type in any query where we want to achieve a different result from that returned by an inner join.

And that observation leads us directly to our next topic, join types in queries.

Automatic and Custom Joins in Access Queries

Access has a very nice query editor. One of the best things about it is that it uses information from the relationships you define to automatically create joins on tables when you place them in the editor. It uses the default join type you defined in the Relationships window. You saw an example of that in Figure B-11.

However, the Access query editor has two other useful features.

First, you can set a property on your databases to create auto joins in queries. With that property set, Access makes some educated guesses about tables as you add them to the query editor, even if you haven't defined relationships between those tables before inserting them into the query editor. Access looks for fields with the same name in both tables. If it finds matching names, it looks for matching data types. Then, if identically named fields have the same data type, and if either one of those fields is a primary key, Access assumes that there is a one-to-many relationship on those fields. It also assumes that you intended to define it, even if you haven't gotten around to it yet. Therefore, Access helpfully steps up and creates the join for you automatically.

As noted in Chapter 2, however, auto join only works when the table has a single primary key field; it doesn't work with compound primary keys.

This behavior goes back to a point we made in the opening paragraphs of this appendix. Relationships between tables exist independently of whether we define them for Access. This default auto join behavior in queries is based on that fact.

Second, when the default joins are not appropriate for a particular task, the query editor assists you in changing them as needed. Consider the default inner join created in the query editor shown in Figure B-18.

If you want to see a list of contact persons and their phone numbers, this query will do it. But what do you do if you need to see all of the contacts in your list, even if they have no phone? The inner join shown in Figure B-18 won't give you that result. You've already seen the answer, though; it's the left join. To alter the default inner join autogenerated by Access, double-click directly on the join line in the query editor.

Clicking on the join line pops up a Join Properties dialog very much like the one you saw earlier in the Edit Relationships window when you were learning how to enforce referential integrity. The same choices are offered, and you simply select the one that promises you the result you need. That would be, of course, option 2. When you close the Join Properties dialog, the query editor now looks like Figure B-19. You can see the small arrow head, which Access added to the join line to indicate that this is now a left join. Drag the fields you want to see (LastName and Phone, in this example) into the field list.

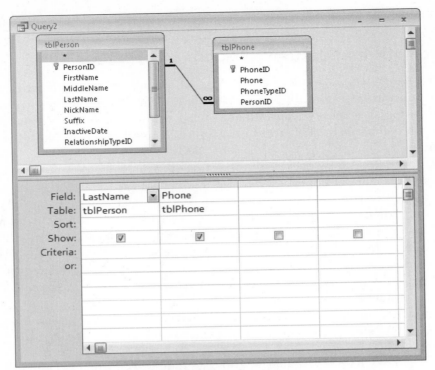

Figure B-18: Default join automatically created by Access

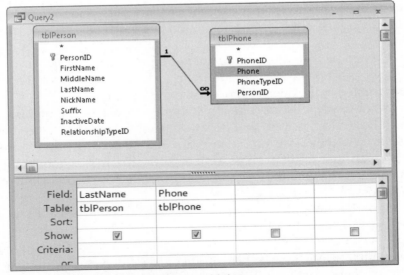

Figure B-19: Left join defined for TblPerson-tblPhone

When you run the query, you'll see results as illustrated in Figure B-20. The person shown in the first record has a valid phone number; the second person doesn't. The value of that field, in fact, is null, a special value you'll learn about later in this appendix.

Figure B-20: Query results returned by a left join

How does the SQL statement differ for left joins? Figure B-21 shows the LEFT JOIN syntax.

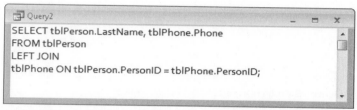

Figure B-21: Left join in an SQL statement

The right join returns a record set which includes all records from the table on the "right" side and only matching records from the left. The SQL is shown in Figure B-22.

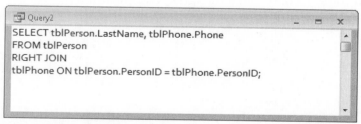

Figure B-22: Right join in an SQL statement

The resulting record set is shown in Figure B-23.

In Figure B-23, there is only one record returned rather than the two records from the left join shown in Figure B-21. This is because there are no records in the table on the many side (tblPhone) that do not have a matching record in the table on the one side. That couldn't happen anyway, because we've enforced referential integrity on the relationship between them.

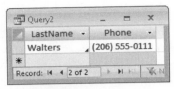

Figure B-23: Record set returned by a right join

Finding Missing Values

Another useful thing we can do with left joins is to limit the list of contacts to show only contacts for whom we do not have phone numbers. To do that, we use the left join and our other friend, null. The SQL looks like Figure B-24.

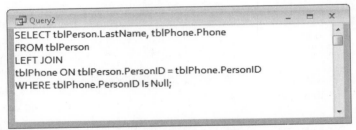

Figure B-24: Left join with null criteria to limit result list

The result set returned is shown in Figure B-25. Compare it to Figure B-23. The other record, the one with a foreign key value, is not returned.

Figure B-25: Results from a query to return unmatched records

Why does this work? The null criteria in the WHERE clause in Figure B-24, does it: WHERE tblPhone.PersonID Is null.

Understanding Null

To fully understand how null works, it will help to take a closer look at the it. A full discussion of nulls would cover ground well beyond the design of table schemas and queries. We'll keep our comments here to a minimum, though, and emphasize the areas where nulls are required in queries like this one. Nonetheless, we hope you pursue the topic of nulls further. Understanding how nulls work, not just at the table level but also in expressions in VBA, and in forms and reports, is an essential skill you need to design and build useful databases.

If It's Not Something, Is It Nothing?

As you've just seen in the query to return unmatched records in two tables, nulls can be a very handy tool, but until you get a good handle on what they are, they can also be a bit obscure. To use them effectively, you have to know what a null is, and just as importantly, what it is not.

Many folks think of null as "undefined" or "unknown." However, it's equally important to understand that null is not zero, and it is also not an empty string.

Zero, represented as 0 in mathematical calculations, is a known quantity. If you have five children, and three of them get married and move out, and then the other two go away to college, you now have zero children living at home.

However, if you wanted to know how many children the authors of this book happen to have living in their collective homes, the answer would have to be, "I don't know." It might be zero. It might not be zero. It might be one. It might be greater than 10. You just don't know. That's closer to the concept of null.

So why is it that null is not an empty string? An empty string is also known as a *zero-length string* and is often referred to with the acronym ZLS. It is represented as two quotation marks with no space between them: "". The distinction is that you don't know what a null might represent, whereas the concept of a ZLS is quite clear and precise. It is a text string with no characters in it.

Having eliminated the things a null is not, we reach the conclusion that a null is "undefined" or "unknown." The following discussion should make this easier to understand.

What a Null Is

Null is a special value for fields in tables and for variables used in VBA and other code. Although fields (or columns) of most data types can accept nulls, VBA variables with the data type of "Variant" are the only valid recipients of the value null. Although our focus is on the database structure, we wanted to reiterate the VBA aspect so that you are aware that nulls are an important concept for you to explore from that perspective as well.

The Difference between ZLS and Null

Often the best way to explain an abstract concept like "null" is to look at some common examples of what it is and what it isn't. We're all familiar with contact lists, so we'll use that.

When we record the people's names, we put each name in a separate field, so we'll use FirstName, MiddleName, and LastName. Although first and last names are required, middle names will be optional. Those become our business rules, and we can use some properties at the table level to help enforce those rules.

Because the FirstName and LastName are required, we can set the Allow Zero Length property to "No" for those fields. However, the MiddleName is not required, so the Allow Zero Length is set to "Yes," which will allow a ZLS in that field.

This allows the MiddleName to either have a value or be left blank. But just because a field is blank does not mean that it is or should be a ZLS. There are two possible reasons for those "blanks": they are null or they are a ZLS.

Nulls The MiddleName could be left null because when the record was created, we did not know the middle name of the person. This is essentially an "unknown," but that does not mean that there is no middle name—it more likely means that we failed to get that data. The middle name could be "Marie" or "Traci," or it might indeed be nonexistent.

At this point, we don't know whether the name exists or not, and if it does exist, we don't know what it is. That exemplifies null.

ZLSs The MiddleName field could be intentionally entered as a ZLS. As we said, the middle name is optional—it is not required even if known. So either we know that there is no middle name or we know that there is a name, but it is intentionally not provided.

In this case, the field is either blank because we know that there is no name or because we know that there is a name but we are not providing it. That exemplifies a ZLS.

Therefore, the MiddleName field will be a mix of:

- **Strings:** The middle names of contacts for whom we have the values.
- **Nulls:** The records where we failed to get any information on middle names.
- **Zero-length strings:** The records where we know the contact has no middle name.

In looking at the field, whether it is in a table or on a form, we can't see any difference between a ZLS and a null. But the important thing is that Access can not only tell the difference but also can treat them differently. So you should learn to use this to your advantage.

Thus, null is useful when creating queries like the one you saw in the previous section. In that query, we used the fact that no records contained certain primary keys from the contact table to identify contacts without phones. They match nothing in the phone table.

Zero would not work for that purpose, because zero is a value that could be matched by another zero. Likewise, ZLS would not work because that is also a value that would match other ZLSs.

Now that you understand nulls better, let's take another look at the SQL from the query in Figure B-24. It should be clear to you why the SQL was written this way, with "Is Null":

```
SELECT tblPerson.LastName, tblPhone.Phone
FROM tblPerson LEFT JOIN tblPhone ON tblPerson.PersonID =
    tblPhone.PersonID
WHERE tblPhone.PersonID Is Null;
```

And why it was not written this way, with "=Null":

```
SELECT tblPerson.LastName, tblPhone.Phone
FROM tblPerson LEFT JOIN tblPhone ON tblPerson.PersonID =
    tblPhone.PersonID
WHERE tblPhone.PersonID = Null
```

In a database it makes no sense to ask if any value is equal to null. There is no way to know whether they are equal or not, so the answer always has to be "I don't know," or "null." That, in turn, means that the second SQL statement would have to return an empty record set ("Access doesn't know if any records match or not") instead of the record set shown in Figure B-25.

Learn More about Nulls

In this appendix, we've only touched on a few aspects of nulls and null behavior. Really, just enough to explain this one query. There is a great deal more to know about them, and we strongly encourage you to make it a point to learn about them.

Domain (or Lookup) Tables

In several chapters in this book, we created domain, or lookup, tables when we needed to provide a pre-defined list of values for certain attributes in our tables. For example, we saw two domain tables, tblManufacturer and tblLocation. As you may recall, both consisted of four fields: a primary key, a field for the name of the subject of the field, a field for an extended description of the subject, and an invalidated field, to indicate when such fields are no longer valid for the purposes of the database. Let's take a more detailed look at lookup tables.

For the most part, we can classify domains, the subject of domain tables, as *open* or *closed*, and identify characteristics of the subject of those tables that help us decide how to construct and use them.

Closed and Open Domains

One consideration is whether the range of potential values for a domain is open or closed. As is often the case, examples are the best way to explain this.

Names of weekdays are a closed domain. There are seven. There will never be more; there will never be less. Names of the months in the Gregorian calendar are also a closed domain. There are 12. As long as we continue to use the Gregorian calendar, that number will remain the same. The names of the states of the United States also make up a closed domain, albeit with some ambiguity. There 50 states. But for some purposes, we want to include the District of Columbia. And for other purposes, we'd like to include U.S. territories, such as Puerto Rico and Guam. While it is definitely a closed domain, inclusion of all members is not 100% consistent across all circumstances. Moreover, although it's unlikely, new states could be formed someday.

And, finally, the names of the members of the U.S. Senate are not a closed domain. There 100 Senators. That means there are 100 members of that domain of names. It is likely, if not quite certain, that there will be one or more members replaced every two years. Therefore, the domain, while it is constant in size, is open.

Closed domains are those for which there is virtually no chance of additions or deletions. Open domains are those for which there are virtually guaranteed to be additions or deletions.

However, as the example of U.S. senators illustrates, there are open domains that act a little bit like closed domains. They are limited in size to a predetermined number of values, but the members of the domain change at regular intervals.

Domain Size

Another consideration for domain tables is their relative size. Domains like weekdays and months are relatively small, having 7 and 12 members, respectively. The U.S. Senate domain is somewhat larger, consisting of 100 members.

And as we've seen, the domain of states is not quite fixed, ranging from 50 or 51 to 60 or more.

Other domains may contain quite large numbers of members. A common example of this is a catalog of items used in a construction business. The organization maintains a catalog of all of the items needed to build its projects, things like pipes of various size, length, and materials—for example, 6-inch-diameter steel pipe, 8-inch-diameter aluminum pipe, and so on. At any given time, the catalog consists of several thousand items. Moreover, it can change quite often as new items are added and old items are dropped.

Defining Your Domain Table Structure

The characteristics outlined above are useful in helping us to decide which fields to include in domain (lookup) tables, and how to incorporate them into a schema.

Open Domain Lookup Tables

Let's start with one that is relatively easy to handle, from Chapter 8, "Production and Manufacturing." tblVendor lists the vendors from which an organization will secure the materials and products it needs. It contains four fields:

- Primary Key
- VendorName
- VendorDescription
- Invalidated

This is an open domain. New vendors are approved, existing vendors go out of business, and so on. This domain also varies in size. Without looking at a specific implementation for a specific organization, we can't know how many members it might have, of course, but the number is certain to be greater than one and it is certain to change from time to time.

With open domains like tblVendor, we have to insert the appropriate primary key as a foreign key in the related table. This conforms to our standard requirements for primary and foreign key fields.

Closed Domain Lookup Tables

However, there are times when it makes sense to consider whether we need a surrogate primary key for a domain table. Consider, for example, a closed domain, consisting of states. Several things about this domain make it different from the open vendor domain. First, it is relatively small and easy to remember. It is closed; no matter how long our database is in production, it is quite unlikely we'll need to modify the lookup table. And finally, its members are unambiguous, even when abbreviated as "WA" or "FL" or "TX." We should have no trouble recognizing valid members when they are presented as choices in a dropdown.

In such cases, some developers elect not to use a surrogate primary key for the domain table. Instead, they select the values of the domain itself as natural primary keys. And it is also clear that there is no need for the Invalidated field in this lookup table. Whether or not the table should consist of one field (StateAbbreviations) or two (StateAbbreviations and FullStateNames) is largely a matter of preference.

Note, of course, that if you do elect to use a natural key as the primary key, you will have to ensure that the data type for the primary key matches the data type of the foreign key field in the table for which it supplies values.

Summary

This concludes our expanded review of relationships and query joins, nulls, and domain tables. In this appendix we discussed the steps you will follow in defining relationships between tables, and implementing joins in queries. We explained nulls and their use in field properties and gave you an example of one use of nulls in queries. Finally, we explained how to set up and use domain, or lookup, tables.

In the course of our discussion, we identified a number of areas where you may benefit from further reading in subjects too complex to consider in detail here. That includes nulls and the Date/Time and Number data types in Access.

Resolving Relationship Triangles

In several chapters of this book, we've presented models for managing customer data in a manner that allows a customer to be either an individual or an organization, but not both. As is often the case, implementing a table design to support this business rule leads to hard choices between options because there is more than one viable way to do it, and any approach will involve both the design of the tables and the user interface. In this appendix we take a quick look at two basic approaches to resolving relationship triangles.

Non-Normalized Schema to Support a Less Complex Interface

In the first approach we will demonstrate a way to keep the tables and forms as basic as possible. In doing so, we deliberately opted not to enforce 3rd Normal Form (3NF); so we have included fields that do not directly describe the main subject of the tables in order to make the interface somewhat less complex. We've selected a generic set of table names in order to make the example more generally applicable:

- tblParent
- tblChildtheFirst
- tblChildtheSecond

"Parent" corresponds, in the context of table schema to support customers, for example, to "Customer," while "Child the First" and "Child the Second" correspond to "Individuals" and "Organizations."

Figure C-1 shows the tables and the relationships between them.

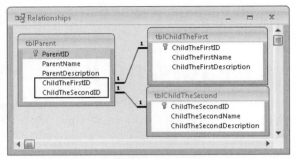

Figure C-1: Parent and multiple child tables with two foreign key fields in the parent table

Note that there are two foreign key fields in the Parent table, either of which can identify a child record. While this violates 3NF, we believe that it is acceptable to do so in this case, because it supports a less complex and, perhaps more intuitive, interface design for assigning child records.

Also note that the relationship diagram Figure C-1 indicates that the relationship between the Parent table and the Child tables is 1 to 1. That prevents a single child from being assigned to more than one customer record. To support this rule, the Indexed property for the ChildTheFirstID field is defined as Yes (No Duplicates), as shown in Figure C-2.

In addition, we have also implemented validation rules on the parent table to enforce the business rule which states that a customer (Parent record) can be either an individual (Child the First) or an organization (Child the Second), but not both. Look at the Table level validation rule in Figure C-2.

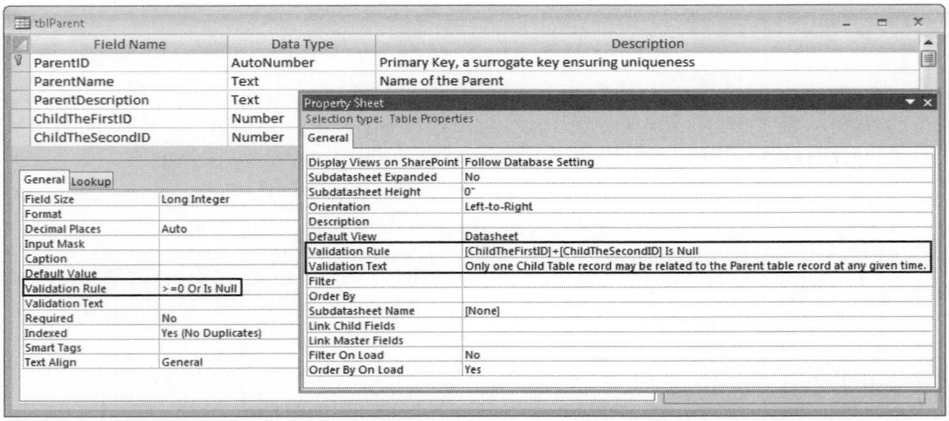

Figure C-2: Table level validation rules for ensuring a single child is assigned

Using the Law Of Propagating Nulls to Validate

As you can see in the table property sheet in Figure C-2, the table level validation rule is stated as [ChildTheFirstID]+[ChildTheSecondID] Is Null.

This validation rule relies on the Law of Propagating Nulls (LOPN). The LOPN states that adding any value to null returns null. We discussed some of the other properties of Nulls in Appendix B—refer to that discussion if you need to refresh your understanding. Basically, because null is not known, we can't logically add any value to it and know the result, so the result must be null. In this validation rule, therefore, if either of the two fields, ChildtheFirst or ChildtheSecond, is null, adding them together will return null.

However, if both of the fields have a non-null value, adding them together would *not* return null, so the validation would fail.

Figure C-2 also shows the field level validation rule applied to the foreign key fields, ChildtheFirst and ChildtheSecond. It states > = 0 or Is Null.

This validation limits child foreign keys to non-negative values and nulls.

With these rules in place, Access itself enforces the "either/or" choice for the child foreign key. Only one of the two fields can be populated for any given record, thereby enforcing the business rule established for this application.

Figure C-3 shows a simple form to demonstrate one way to provide a user interface using this table design.

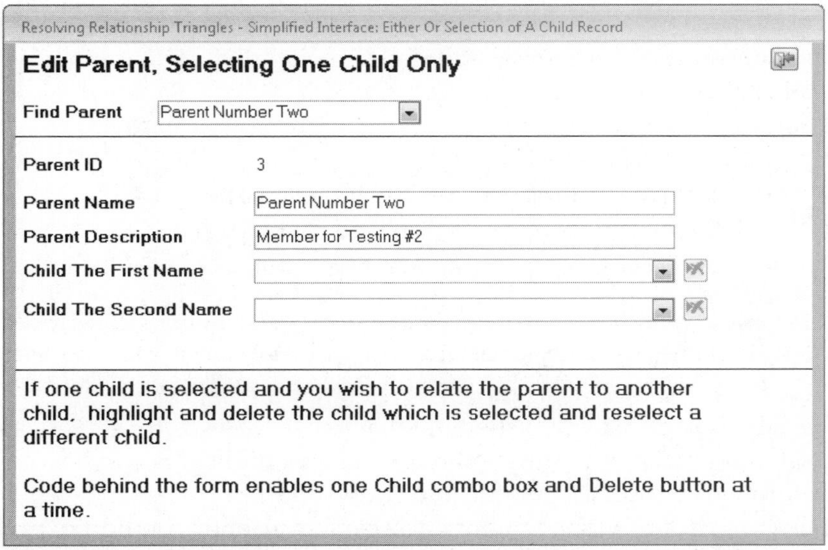

Figure C-3: Initial status of the user interface to implement either/or child assignment, with no child assignment

At this stage of data entry, users can select one child from either combo box.

In Figures C-4 and C-5 you'll see updates in the user interface reflecting selections in one of the two child combo boxes.

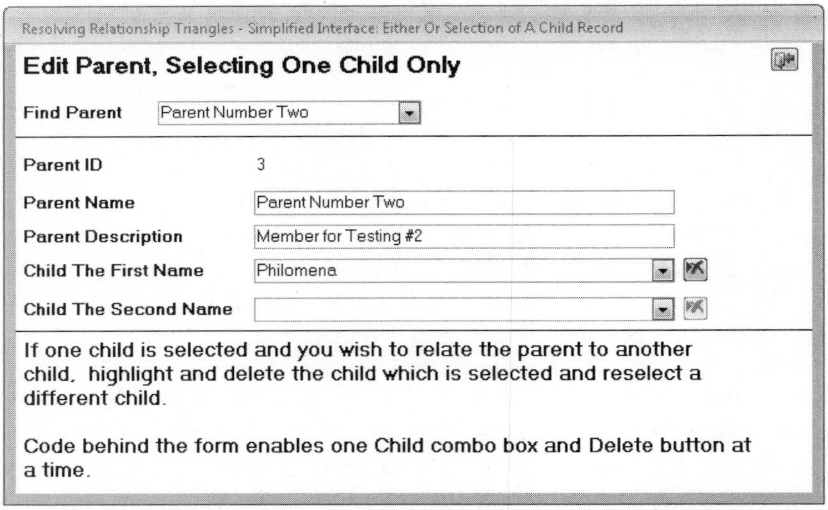

Figure C-4: User interface to implement either/or child assignment, child one selected

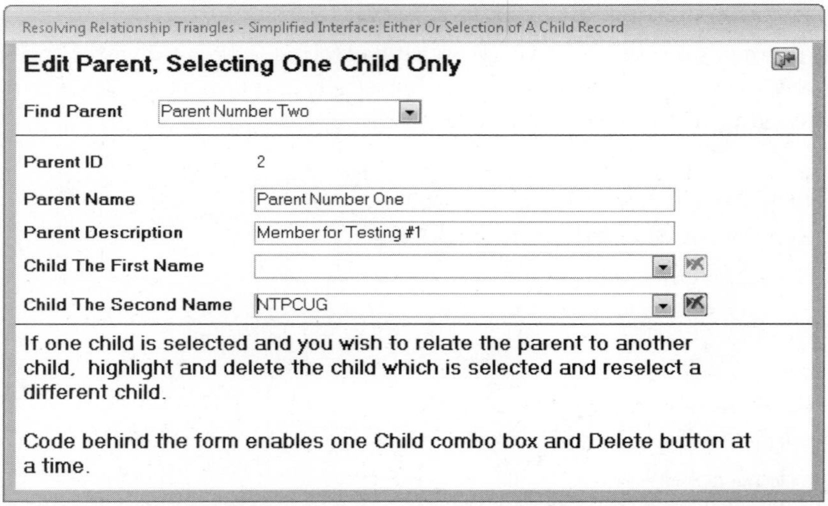

Figure C-5: User interface to implement either/or child assignment, child two selected

The combo box called Child the First Name gets records for its row source from tblChildTheFirst, and the combo box called Child the Second Name gets records for its row source from tblChildTheSecond.

Because we do not want to allow a selection in both combo boxes, code in the form disables the combo box and Delete buttons for the child foreign key not selected. Of course, with a validation rule in the table, as shown in

Figure C-2, Access would also prevent two assignments as well. We believe that managing the available choices in the interface is a more user-friendly approach.

The tables, forms, and code for this "Either/Or" relationship triangle are provided in appCResolvingRelationshipTriangles_Simplified.mdb, on this book's CD.

Normalized Tables Supported in a More Complex Interface

Next, let's look at a second table design which also supports the requirement that a customer can be either an individual or an organization, but not both. The tables in this model are normalized, although the relationships established are somewhat more complex, as you can see in Figure C-6.

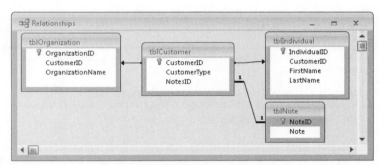

Figure C-6: Parent and multiple child tables with customer type in Parent

In this design, the attribute "CustomerType" is defined in the customer table. Each customer must be identified as an Organization or as an Individual. Child tables for Organizations and Individuals link to the customer table via the CustomerID foreign key. As with the first table design, the child tables store the details specific to the subject of that table.

The input form for this table schema is shown in Figure C-7. It uses a combo box to search for records, as shown in Figure C-7. Selecting a customer in this combo box makes that customer the focus of the form, as shown in Figure C-8.

In this implementation, code in the form runs when a customer type is selected for a new customer. One of the functions of that code is to make the selection of customer type permanent by disabling the customer type combo box. We've done that to ensure that the customer type cannot inadvertently be changed. You could create a new record for a customer who was created with the wrong type.

The form also includes two subforms, one for the names of organizations and one for the names of individuals. Only one of these subforms will display at a time, so when one of the subforms is displayed, the other is hidden. Code behind the combo box for selecting a customer will display the appropriate subform when a customer is selected, as illustrated in Figures C-8 and C-9.

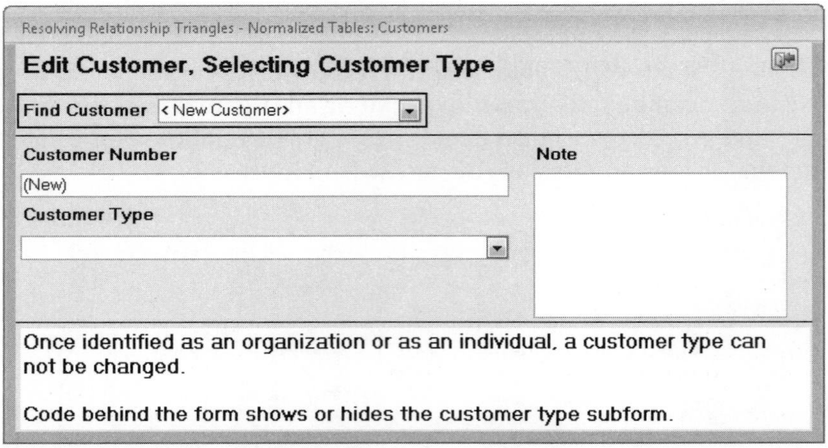

Figure C-7: Input form for new customers

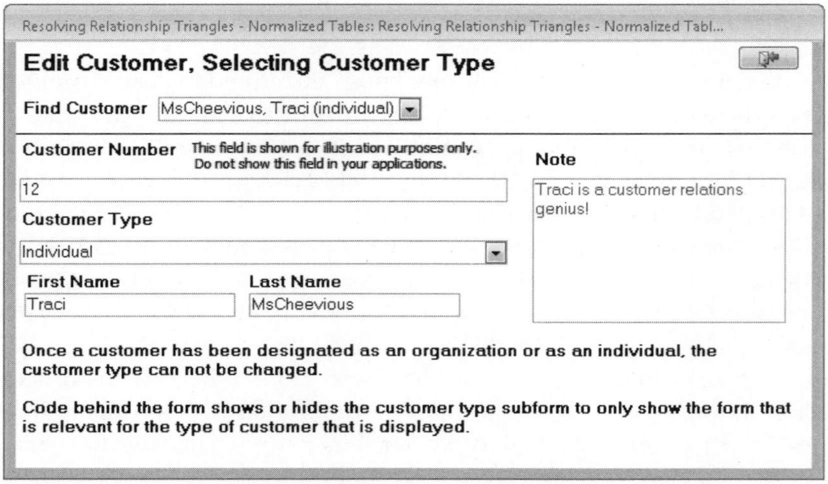

Figure C-8: Input and lookup form for an individual customer

Sub-table for Notes

The sample database created for this model also illustrates use of a sub-table for notes. The Note table is linked to the Customer table in a one-to-one relationship, as shown in Figure C-6. Because we used a memo field for notes, we have moved the field into a separate table to minimize the risk of data loss should a memo field become corrupted. You read about tables like this in several chapters. You can download the sample database, appCResolvingRelationshipTriangles_Normalized.mdb, to study how it is implemented here.

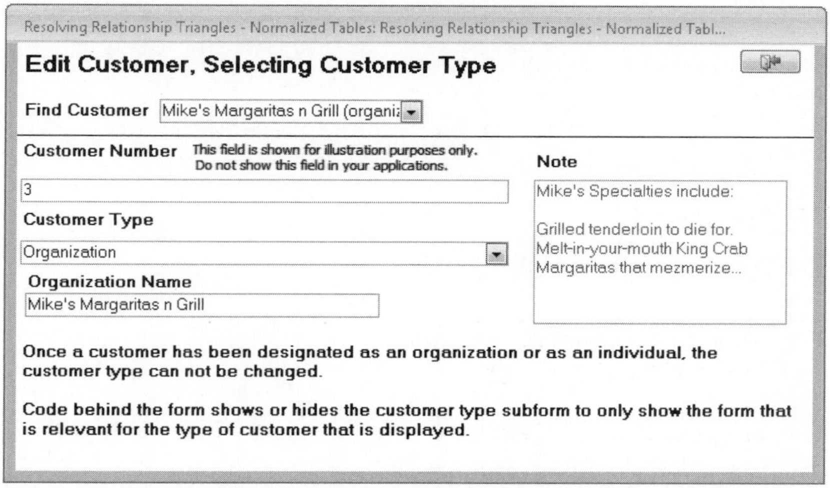

Figure C-9: Input and lookup form for an organization customer

Summary

In this brief overview, we've shown you two methods for implementing a customer table schema that allow a customer to be either an individual or an organization, but not both. This is a relatively common relationship triangle that you will see in several business scenarios, not just those related to customers. Although the table schema for the first approach is not normalized, the second example follows the guidelines for normalization. The choice of a table schema also influences interface design, specifically with regard to an input form. In both methods, we use code to make the form hide, display, or enable controls that pertain to one customer type or the other.

In your own databases, you may find yourself facing similar choices between two or more possible table schema. While we would always encourage a normalized design, we also recognize that there are times when a choice also involves selecting a method which is easier and more intuitive to implement in the user interface.

Measures: Financial and Performance

Measures are used to evaluate the performance of a business, or of segments of a business. Financial measures, like the financial ratios and ratio analysis discussed in Chapter 12, are based on financial results. On the other hand, performance measures often are applied to data that is not strictly financial in nature, such as customer satisfaction.

By using quality and time measures to uncover exceptions to standard procedures, tracking performance in carefully selected key areas can identify both inefficiencies and exceptional results. These select measures are *benchmarks* that will be used to compare or measure the actual results. The benchmarks act as the *scorecard* for management. The scorecard can be an actual report that uses the selected measures, or easy-to-find comparisons in standard period report packets such as quarterly reviews and annual reports.

Most of the data models discussed in this book contain data that can be used to measure the performance of a company or organization. But you may also need to use additional tables or external sources, like Excel spreadsheets, to hold the additional information needed to measure performance.

There are endless variations of measure types, so your goal should be to select the measures that match your industry and your specific needs. Some measures are required for specific reasons for specific purposes. A specific custom measurement that is unique to the individual company may be advantageous. Measures are an integral part of a cost accounting system and developing suitable measures for your business will assist with both the financial and the nonfinancial decision making processes.

This appendix describes and provides examples of various measures and how to use them. Because the focus is on how to select the appropriate data for conducting analysis and providing worthwhile results that you can use to improve your operations, we will not be walking you through the process of creating the tables. However, we have provided a database on the book's CD and will point out some of the tables and queries available there to help you get started with your own analysis.

NOTE Also read Appendix G, "Data Warehousing Concepts," which describes a data warehouse and how it may be used to make reporting an easier process.

Whether you are working with a standard database or a data warehouse, applying measures to both the financial and nonfinancial data requires designing the measures and creating a place to store the data that is used in the comparisons.

Financial and Nonfinancial Measures

A measure is a property of the data that can be used to calculate averages, counts, or other aggregates on summarized data. This concept works with many different types of measures. For example, the square footage of a department can be used as one measure to arrive at administration expenses by square feet. Most lines of business rely on some form of measures to manage production, evaluate success, and even comply with regulations. You will find measures or metrics used by vast ranges of businesses and processes, including:

- Retail stores—comparing monthly sales year-to-year
- Departments—comparing net profits between departments
- Locations—comparing transportation costs
- Employees—setting performance standards and conducting annual reviews
- Members or customers—evaluating customer satisfaction or percentage of repeat customers
- Orders—analyzing order size, quantity, profits, total orders in a sale, or visits
- Date and/or time of purchase—determining staffing requirements, calculating return patterns
- Medical procedures—calculating risks, costs, success rates
- Doctor office visits—determining utilization levels

- Hospital admissions—observing trends in inpatient services
- Emergency room visits—identifying chronic ER abusers
- Policies sold—determining agent productivity
- Billable hours—gauging the productivity and profitability of professionals
- Labor hours—identifying inefficiencies and deviations from standard costs
- Machine hours—determining variances from standard costs and schedule required maintenance
- Engine hours—calculating billing for rental equipment and determine maintenance schedules
- On-time deliveries—recognizing those involved in the delivery process
- Late deliveries—identifying problem areas in the delivery process
- Miles allowed—calculating the variance between miles allowed and miles driven
- Miles driven—determining when scheduled maintenance is due

Establishing the Baseline

The standard costs, or benchmarks, are the direct cost of materials for a unit and the direct labor costs. The benchmarks are established prior to the actual work being performed. Usually they are established in the planning or budgeting phase. The difference between the actual costs and the standard costs is the total variance. The *total variance* can be divided into 2 parts. The first part is the efficiency variance or quality variance, and the second part is the price variance or rate variance. From this variance analysis, it can be determined if the cost variance is due to substandard materials, inefficient labor processes, or the improper estimating of the cost of the materials needed to assemble the product.

Selecting the Correct Measures

Measures must fit the needs and goals of the management of the company and of the people doing and supervising the work. The time period being measured should have a good fit with the process being measured. An alternate method of measuring the process should also be designed. Using multiple methods to measure the same process allows the opportunity to provide multiple perspectives into the scorecard. For example, you wouldn't want to celebrate exceeding your production quota just to discover that it was at the expense of 50% rejection rate for poor quality.

Using the right measures is critical to the success of the scorecard. A measure using board feet of lumber used to construct a building would not be a useful measure to use for an all-steel building. Conversely, comparing the number of labor hours used over a twelve-month period would not be a good time horizon to calculate hours required to construct a unit, unless all units are started and finished in the same twelve-month period.

As you are matching the measure to the task, you should be considering the two basic classes of performance measures: qualitative and quantitative. These are discussed in the following sections.

Qualitative Measures

Qualitative measures include worker related functions such as a person taking on more responsibility and thereby being more productive or workers increasing productivity by increasing their job skills. It also includes process areas such as reviewing and modifying procedures to eliminate waste, improving identification and allocation of costs, identifying automation candidates and using it to perform routine repetitive jobs, or adding more features to the product while keeping the manufacturing process efficient and simple. These are just some of the examples of qualitative measures.

Quantitative Measures

Quantitative measures basically compare numbers, either over time or between entities. There are two types of quantitative productive measures: financial and nonfinancial.

Financial Measures

Financial measures use financial data in at least one of the components of the comparison. The financial component could be salary and wage expenses, sales revenue, administration expenses, or owner's equity. The other component or components of a measure can be either financial or nonfinancial data such as machine hours, square footage, or labor hours, just to name a few.

You would use financial measures to calculate labor savings from using temporary or part-time workers instead of full-time workers, to draw a comparison of labor expenses to industry averages, or to track advertising campaigns and the revenue created for each advertising dollar.

Other common examples of financial measures include return on investment, increase in cash flow, cost of reengineering the manufacturing process, change in the cost of production from previous periods, market share by product lines, change in revenue from previous periods, and reduction in waste from increased efficiencies in production methods.

Nonfinancial Measures

Nonfinancial measures are used with data that is statistical and not financial in nature, such as square footage, billable hours, on-time deliveries, average time on a call for a call center employee, number of items per minute checked by a grocery store cashier, wins and losses by a sports team, and so on. All components of a nonfinancial measure will be statistical and their purpose is to provide a common size for certain key business functions to identify trends and to compare results to other companies in the same industry.

Examples of common nonfinancial measures include the number of sales transactions, number of customer complaints, time between product conception market, on-time or late deliveries, production process time, and number of new prospects to new sales. If you are considering or have just implemented related changes, you may also make a comparison of direct to indirect labor before and after automation or track the proportion of waste materials generated before and after implementing process changes.

Variances as Measures

By variance analysis it is possible to analyze why a process or a product did not perform as expected. Using a purchase price variance may lead to the detection of a loss in quality or it may reveal the reason for an increase of returns. An increase in waste may indicate that a process is either designed poorly or there is a deviation in the prescribed procedures. If a process manager increases production to have a more favorable volume variance, the end result may be too much unusable inventory.

Examples of Measures

Once you understand some of the ways to collect data that can be used for comparisons, you will be able to identify what data will be required for your analyses. In many cases you will be able to use data that is already captured in existing systems. In other cases you may need to create ways to identify and capture more data points. By reviewing some common scenarios, you will have a better idea of what will work for you.

General Examples

Each industry has specific measures that allow for a better comparison of information between multiple companies.

In the health insurance industry, premiums and medical benefit expenses are measured using per member per month or PMPM. PMPM is simply the count of active members, or lives insured, for each month. Health insurers also use admissions and bed days to measure hospital costs. Physician encounters and non-physician encounters are tracked and used to measure professional medical expenses.

If a segment of the health insurer's business had 120,000 members over the course of a year and the plan had $20,000,000 in premium revenue and $15,000,000 in medical benefit expenses then the premium revenue PMPM is $166.67 and the medical benefit expense PMPM is $150.00. If the overall business of the insurer had 10 times the members, revenue, and expenses, the PMPM amounts would still be the same, and as a result are easily comparable with the smaller segment.

Manufacturers use a variety of measures to determine how well processes and the business in general are performing. Labor hours and labor dollars are used extensively in cost accounting to measure budget variances. Benchmarks are set for processes and the number of hours required to build a unit are established and the cost in dollars is determined by calculating the cost of materials.

Professional services use billable hours to measure performance. When an attorney is on the phone with a client, in a meeting with a client, doing research, or in court representing a client, you can be assured that the billable hours are adding up. There are many other labor hours for the attorney and the staff that are not directly billable to the client. The receptionist's time is not directly associated with a single client, the pro bono case is not billed to any client, and the office manager's time is also not directly billed to a client. Instead, these are absorbed by all clients through administrative overhead.

If there were 30 billable hours to a client, there were probably at least that many hours that need to be included in the total overhead of the law firm. The accounting records will reflect the total expenses for the firm for the period. The total billable expenses divided by the total billable hours for all attorneys in the firm will allow the costs to be allocated to each lawyer based on the billable hours recorded for each attorney. A single attorney may bill 30 hours at $300 per hour, having $9,000 in revenue. Using the allocation of the total overhead, the single hour standard overhead rate is multiplied by 30 and the overhead is assigned to the individual attorney. Conversely, overhead can be calculated at the total rate per period, usually a month or a year, and divided amongst the principles according to a pre-arranged formula whether or not any hours were billed.

Measures for Construction

In a construction business the stakeholders want to know how effectively the raw materials are being converted into the finished building because it directly relates to the return on their investment. Many types of measures are required to determine the results. One approach is to compare what was planned, the benchmark, with what actually happened, the actual costs. And you would need to state if the comparison was done with or without considering overhead charges.

For this example, consider that the plan specification for the foundation of a building called for 10 cubic yards of concrete and it usually takes no more than an eight hour shift with one supervisor and five workers to pour the foundation. The standard cost of the foundation would be 10 yards of concrete x the cubic yard cost of concrete + 1 supervisor x hourly rate x 8 + 5 workers x hourly rate x 8.

The concrete vendor billed for 11 yards of concrete and this indicates a standard quantity allowed variance or a variance in the quantity that had been predetermined to be needed to produce the foundation. Management would need to determine why the additional concrete was invoiced. Was there an error in the calculation of the specifications for the foundation? Did the crew waste more concrete than was necessary? Did the vendor bill for more than was actually delivered?

If the estimate used for the bid calls for the supervisors pay rate to be $40 per hour and the laborer's rate to be $25, then the total standard labor cost for the foundation should be $1,320. When the actual direct labor costs are recorded the total is $1,500. Management would need to investigate further to find the reason for the variance. Was the original estimate of the time needed to pour the foundation accurate? Were the pay rates of the workers correct? Were there delays in the pouring process and, if there were delays, were they attributable to external sources or to internal sources?

Measures Using Standard Costs

Most of us are subjected to standard costs when we take a vehicle to the auto repair shop. For years, auto mechanics have used a standard costing model for the labor charges that end up on the repair bill.

The auto repair industry historically relied on books with the standard time published for every possible repair anyone would ever need. Now the same information is provided electronically and is built into the billing system. The practice of using standard costing allows for accurate estimates of repair costs for the customer and it allows for a reliable method which the shop owner can use to measure how efficiently the mechanics are performing the work.

A car needs a new fuel pump installed. The car owner is given an itemized estimate of the costs for the repairs. The manual states that the labor for the repair should take 1.5 hours. The mechanic may take one hour or three hours to complete the repair, but the shop will pay the mechanic only 1.5 hours at the standard labor rate. The incentives of the standard labor rate encourage mechanics to complete the repairs in less time than listed, thus allowing for the potential to bill for additional projects during the same time period. They also encourage quality workmanship so that mechanics avoid doing rework without additional pay.

Measures for Sales

The volume of widgets at Wal-Mart would be much greater than the sales of the same widget at the local corner store. It is difficult to compare $100 gross sales to $100,000 gross sales of the same product. But if you compare the average price of widgets sold the number has much more meaning. Wal-Mart sold 9,850 widgets and the corner store sold 10 widgets. The average price of the widgets at Wal-Mart was $10.15 each, while the corner stores price was $10 per widget. With an apples-to-apples widget it is easy to make a meaningful comparison of the two sales figures. The question that this measure highlights is why is the corner store selling the widgets at an average price that is less than Wal-Mart's average price. It is the analyst's job to seek the answer to that question. And, we may just have the explanation in a follow-up example; we'll at least look at some factors to consider.

The corner store will usually have a higher per unit *profit margin*, the difference of the sales price of an item and the cost of the item, than Wal-Mart. Wal-Mart can demand lower costs for the merchandise purchased due to their very large purchasing volumes. If the corner store purchases the same widget that Wal-Mart does, the cost per item will be higher. For the corner store, the profit per item will need to be higher per item.

Big ticket items like new cars have a very large profit margin built in to the sticker price. The dealer can then afford to bargain with a buyer and seemingly appear to lose money on the sale by allowing the buyer to arrive at a fantastic price. In actuality, the dealer still has enough of a profit margin built in to the price to pay the sales commission, income taxes, and still make a profit. Most big ticket items have sufficient margins to allow for spirited negotiations and still make a profit.

Example Tables

In this example we create three tables and four queries to demonstrates how to track and quantify how well or how poorly either a single delivery person or all delivery personnel perform their duties.

The Invoice table and the Employee table in this example are used only to supply values for the Delivery table. The design of these tables will not be discussed in this appendix. Figure D-1 is the design view of the Invoice table.

Figure D-2 is a design view of a simple Employee table. The table has only a minimum number of fields for this example.

The Delivery table's only purpose is to schedule and record the scheduled delivery date and time and the actual delivery date and time. Using the recommended naming convention, the table will be named tblDelivery.

As recommended throughout this book, each table should have a primary key. In most instances the primary key should be an AutoNumber. In the

tblInvoice		
Field Name	Data Type	
InvoiceID	AutoNumber	Primary Key
OrderID	Number	Foreign Key to Orders table
InvoiceAddressID	Number	Foreign Key to Address table
InvoiceNumber	Text	Invoice number
InvoiceIssued	Date/Time	Date invoice issued to customer
InvoicePaid	Date/Time	Date invoice paid by customer

Figure D-1: Design view of the Invoice table

tblEmployee		
Field Name	Data Type	
EmployeeID	AutoNumber	Primary Key
EmployeeLastName	Text	Last Name of the employee
EmployeeFirstName	Text	First Name of the employee

Figure D-2: Design view of the Employee table

delivery table the primary key will be DeliveryID and it will be an AutoNumber. The next two fields are foreign keys to the Invoice and Employee tables and are named EmployeeID and InvoiceID.

The two fields that are needed to describe the delivery are Date/Time fields. In these fields both the date and time for the scheduled delivery and for the actual delivery are recorded. Names of the fields are DatePromised and DateDelivered.

An optional field was added to include notes concerning the delivery and is a Text field named DeliveryNote. In this example a single note was all that is needed. If multiple notes are expected, a notes table should be added to the database and a foreign key should be used to relate the delivery and the notes tables. Figure D-3 shows the design view of the Delivery table.

tblDelivery		
Field Name	Data Type	Description
DeliveryID	AutoNumber	Primary Key
EmployeeID	Number	Key to Employee table
InvoiceID	Number	Key to Invoice Table
DeliveryNote	Text	Description of delivery exceptions
DatePromised	Date/Time	Date and time the delivery was promised
DateDelivered	Date/Time	Date and time of actual delivery

Figure D-3: Design view of the Delivery table

To illustrate how the three tables are related to each other, Figure D-4 shows the relationships for the three tables.

Example Queries

Delivering your product as promised is essential in retaining customers who rely on the items being delivered on time. Whether a customer's reason for

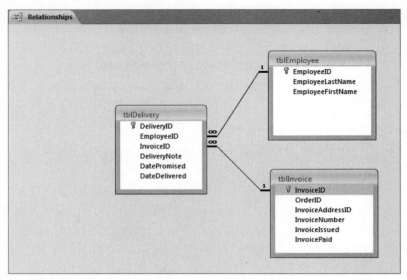

Figure D-4: Relationships of the delivery status tables

needing the product is a birthday present or is business operation-critical material, late delivery can result in lost future sales.

In order to determine if the deliveries are being made on time, the promised delivery time must be entered at the time the order is made. The delivery person must then report the actual delivery time. GPS systems can also be used to determine if the delivery vehicle was actually at the location at the recorded time.

Once the delivery time is recorded, the DateDiff() function can be used to evaluate if the delivery was on time or not. Figure D-5 shows the design view of a base query, qryTrackDelivery. This query is used by the rest of the queries to determine the delivery statistics for the company.

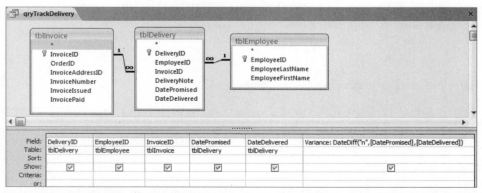

Figure D-5: Design view of the query used to calculate the number of minutes between the promised delivery time and the actual delivery time

The next query, shown in Figure D-6, is used to determine the overall delivery statistics for the company.

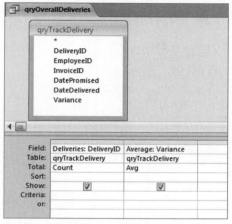

Figure D-6: Design view of qryTrackDelivery used to determine the overall average delivery time for the company

The remaining queries isolate the early, on time, and late deliveries. They can be further restricted to an individual employee by applying additional fields to group by the employee. Figure D-7 is the design view of the early deliveries. Note that the criteria allows up to ten minutes before it is considered late. Changing the criteria to >= 0 would change the query to return all late deliveries.

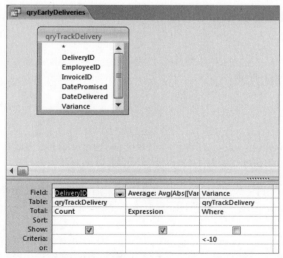

Figure D-7: Design view of qryEarlyDeliveries used to determine the early deliveries for the company

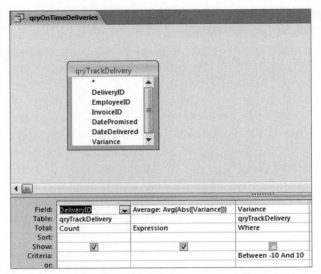

Figure D-8: Design view showing the criteria for qryOntimeDeliveries, used to determine the on-time deliveries for the company

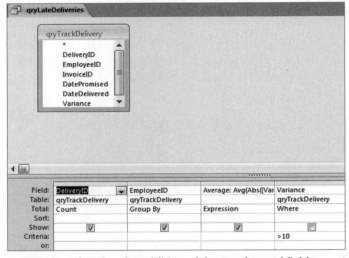

Figure D-9: Design view showing the addition of the EmployeeId field to qryLateDeliveries used to determine the on-time deliveries for individual employees

Figure D-8 shows how to apply the criteria to determine if the delivery was on time. Again note the + or − 10 minutes used to create a window for an on time delivery.

In the next query, we add the employee to the query. By doing this, the delivery statistics for each employee will be returned. Figure D-9 is showing how to add the EmployeeID field.

Summary

Using measures to perform analysis on the results of your business, as well as the public statistics of your competitors, analysts and managers can see trends and outliers that may indicate that an operational change is needed or provide assurances that a process is working correctly.

Both financial and nonfinancial measures are valuable tools the analyst can use to dig deep into the inner workings of a business. Properly designed measures that are used consistently can identify both deficiencies and efficiencies in the processes and procedures of the business. Early detection can be used to increase the profitability of the segment and of the business as a whole.

Measures allow for detailed examination of thousands of data points and let you look at them in ways where they can be directly compared with other similar information. Without some method of common sizing the analysis, the currency values would be meaningless; even worse, it could be misconstrued and cause a significant detriment. Comparing Wal-Mart's billions of dollars revenue to the corner stores thousands of dollars revenue would be impossible.

Digging deeper, Wal-Mart's analysts may look at the corner store's $10 widgets and find that the store bought ten widgets and all ten went out the door, but they actually sold for $11.11 each, rather than $10. Since the store manager gave one widget away free, in looking at sales totals, the price appeared to be only $10.

References and Resources

We initially set out to have this appendix contain a list of resources for you to draw on whenever the inevitable questions arise while you're developing your databases. But we soon realized that we could provide an invaluable bonus just by compiling several of our own database tools into one file. So, in addition to providing you with the database models and explaining the rationale for their design, we are giving you the Bonus Resource database that includes some tools to help you analyze, work with, and create your own database solutions.

Our Favorite Starting Points

When you first start searching for help online, chances are you will be inundated with a lot of hits. Then you are faced with not only finding a reference that really relates to your specific issue, but you also need to know that you are getting good advice. To help you get started, we, the writers and the editors, would like to share some of the sites that we use when we are looking for inspiration and help. These include newsgroups, blogs, personal or group sites, and forums. Since most of the resources listed here are online, we have provided the information in electronic format on the book's CD, as well as here in the book. After all, database developers are all about eliminating duplicate effort!

To keep this list short, we are only listing a few of our favorite starting places for finding a solution. With that in mind, we did not include the sites of third party vendors. However, we do want to mention that in addition to selling powerful, time saving tools, several companies offer newsletters and tips. That said, we've restricted this list to places that we use ourselves to find free tips and tools. As you visit each of these sites, you'll also find links and references to a multitude of other sites.

Access MVP (www.accessmvp.com)

This site offers collections of tips, modules, and sample files from Access MVPs.

Sergei Gavrilov's Access Utilities (www.accesstools.narod.ru)

This site offers several utilities for Microsoft Access.

Allen Browne's site (www.allenbrowne.com)

Allen's site is a virtual encyclopedia of Access tips and techniques, including good coverage of known Access bugs, plus a helpful section on preventing and recovering from database corruption.

SQL-Server FAQ (www.aspfaq.com/faq/)

On this site, you'll find answers and tips for select versions of SQL Server.

Microsoft Access Team Blog (http://blogs.msdn.com/access/)

The Access team blog provides you with information about Access directly from the Access Development team. Get insights into new features, tips from the community, and links to tutorials and other great resources.

Candace Tripp's site - Access Downloads
(www.candace-tripp.com)

Candace's website is a good resource for all Access developers, from beginners to experts. It is dedicated to providing links to Web resources, free example projects and databases.

Tony Toews' site (www.granite.ab.ca)

Tony is an Access MVP, and his site provides tips and tools to resolve corruption issues, merge with e-mail programs and upsize to SQL Server. He also offers a front-end application updater for split databases.

Stephen Lebans' site (www.lebans.com)

Stephen's site has hints, tips, and free source code that you can use in your own Access database projects, whether they are personal or commercial. Although Stephen retired from all things Access, the knowledge he shares in his site is invaluable. (Stephen retired from Access as of September 2009, but it's worth the visit if the site is there!)

The Access Web (www.mvps.org/access/)

This FAQ site is designed to help Microsoft Access developers find answers to some common questions. All code, utilities, and add-ins provided here are free and you are allowed to use them as part of your own applications.

MZ-Tools 3.0 (www.mztools.com)

If you start using VBA, get MZ-Tools. MZ-Tools is a free add-on tool that helps you to write code, find code, design your forms, and document and review your applications faster and more efficiently.

Rick Fisher's Find and Replace (www.rickworld.com)

This site offers Find and Replace, a helpful utility for working Access objects.

Database Design Forum on MSDN/TechNet

(http://social.msdn.microsoft.com/Forums/en-US/databasedesign)

Under the SQL Server group, this forum is focused on database design. The discussions include Access database design. Several of the authors and editors from this book are moderators and contributors to the forum.

Michael Kaplan's own site (www.trigeminal.com)

If Michka tells you a rooster can pull a train, you can go buy your ticket. This site offers presentations and samples for free download.

Utter Access Discussion Forums (www.utteraccess.com)

Utter Access (UA) is a moderated discussion board. While the main topic is Access, you will find help for other database engines and various software applications. The site includes forums for specific topics—from normalization and table design to user interface suggestions. There are also plenty of code samples to download and use.

Database Publishing WhizBase (www.whizbase.com/)

This site offers a free version of WhizBase to add database functionality to an existing website.

Greg Reddick's site (www.xoc.net)

Learn about naming conventions commonly used in Access applications. Whether you follow them or not, you should at least be familiar with them.

Websites of the Authors and Tech Edit Teams

As Access MVPs, the authors and editors are all very active in the Access community. In addition to their own site, many manage or are key contributors to websites of their user groups and other organizations. In addition to giving you another perspective about the authors, their sites also provide valuable links, tips, and information about current events and opportunities.

And now that we've mentioned user groups, we cannot over emphasize the benefits of being involved with a user group, especially if you have the luxury of being able to attend the meetings in person. User group meetings provide an invaluable opportunity to network with other people who are involved with projects similar to yours. The members welcome visitors and will happily help you to understand, learn, and master database development. We encourage you to look for a local user group; and if that doesn't pan out, you can always sign up for newsletters from other groups.

TEAM MEMBER	TYPE OF SITE	WEB ADDRESS
Teresa Hennig	Database development	www.DataDynamicsNW.com
George Hepworth	Samples tools and tips	www.GPCData.com
Larry Linson	Samples and articles	http://accdevel.tripod.com
Arvin Meyer	Tips, samples and links	www.DataStrat.com
Leigh Purvis	Database samples and tools	www.databasedevelopment.co.uk/examples.htm
Armen Stein	Tips and sample code	www.JStreetTech.com
NTPCUG Application Developer Issues SIG	User group site	http://appdevissues.tripod.com
	Presentations and free sample files	http://sp.ntpcug.org/accesssig/
Seattle Access Group	User group site	www.SeattleAccess.org

Newsgroups

Microsoft provides a user community in the form of Microsoft newsgroups. The newsgroups are heavily supported by MVPs, and are also visited from time to time by Microsoft staff as well, so this can be a great place to get answers right from the source, and from recognized experts. We've also added the MSDN forum for SQL Server as that includes some discussions of database design. The Office-specific newsgroups listed below can be accessed in a number of ways.

Microsoft's Community site: www.microsoft.com/office/community/en-us/default.mspx

Microsoft's MSDN Community site: http://social.msdn.microsoft.com/Forums/en-US/category/sqlserver

Google's Groups: `http://groups.google.com`

The most popular way to access Microsoft's busy newsgroups is to use an NNTP newsreader such as Outlook Express. Complete instructions for setting up Outlook Express to communicate with the newsgroups can be found at the following URL:

`www.microsoft.com/windows/ie/community/columns/newsgroups101.mspx`

Books

Understanding database models and the rules and guidelines for creating the tables and fields to support your requirements is only part of the process. You also need to design a user friendly interface that allows people to easily enter, retrieve, and modify data. After all, being able to store your data without being able to efficiently retrieve and use it is like having an amazing library, but being unable to find or use anything in it.

The team would like to recommend a few of their favorite books. Again, our personal preferences are shared for your benefit; along with the caveat that each person will have their own needs, interests, and styles. What feels like a perfect fit for one person might be uncomfortable for someone else. Our goal is to share our passion for Access and to help others to enjoy the benefits that it offers.

TITLE AND PUBLISHER	AUTHOR	WHY WE RECOMMEND IT
Grover Park George On Access: Unleash the Power of Access Holy Macro! Books, 2004	George Hepworth	Team pick for the 2010 version. All versions are great resource books.
Database Design for Mere Mortals: A Hands-On Guide to Relational Database Design Addison-Wesley Professional, 2003	Mike Hernandez	Basic concepts on database design in plain and simple English. The first book Teresa read about dababase design.
Access 2007 VBA Programmers Reference Wrox, 2007	Teresa Hennig, Armen Stein, and others	A book for intermediate to advanced level users that teaches how to use VBA and other tools to provide a better user interface.
Expert Access 2007 Programming Wrox, 2007	Rob Copper, Mike Tucker	While not meant for beginners, it's definetely a book worth having after you cut your teeth on database design.

Bonus Resource Database

While we were pulling together the sample databases for this book, we realized that we could provide an invaluable bonus just by compiling several of the database tools that we use into one convenient place, so we created the Bonus Resource database that includes some tools to help you analyze, work with, and create your own database solutions.

The database includes selected forms, tables, queries, and modules from the chapter files. We've also included several bonus modules from the authors that will help you efficiently create, manage, and analyze tables. We've also provided several pre-populated reference tables that you can copy into other applications.

This database makes an excellent starting point for you to build your own database development toolkit. Whenever you come across something that you could use in other databases, consider adding the objects to this database so you'll always have the right tools for the job.

The ADD_BonusResource.mdb includes the following:

Forms

- frmBackupYourObjects: A utility that creates text definitions of all of your database objects. In addition, a text file is created that includes a command to restore each individual object. All code used for this utility is behind the form (the code is not in a standard module).

- frmRemoveAllData: A utility that removes all data from every local table in your database. All code used for this utility is behind the form (the code is not in a standard module).

- frmUSysValueList: A demonstration of using a hidden table. The form displays the values of the hidden table to allow editing of the records. In addition, a demonstration of a user function that retrieves the values from this table is shown. frmUSysValueList_Values is used as a subform for this demonstration.

Queries

- qryContiguousCalendarDays: A query that uses three tables (tblYear, tblMonth, and tblDay) to create a contiguous list of days. When you need to add another year, simply add the year value (ie: 2010) to the table named tblYear.

- qryRelationship: Returns the defined relationships from a database. The query calls on code contained in mod_Miscellaneous; fRelationshipType() and fRIEnforced().

- qryUSysValueList_Exposed: Allows you to view the data contained in the hidden table USysValueList.

- qryActiveCustomerList: A query illustrating the use of a Yes/No field to filter active from inactive records.

- qryCustomerListforComboBox: A query illustrating the use of a Yes/No field in conjunction with concatenated field names to create a custom list for display in a combo box. Appendix A, "Field Properties," explains how to use these two Yes/No queries to group records of inactive customers and display them at the bottom of lookup lists.

Modules

MOD_MISCELLANEOUS

- IsTable(strTableName): Returns true if the table name provided is a table in the database.

- fUIDataType(lngDataType): Returns the Access data type as shown in the table designer that corresponds to the value provided.

- fRIEnforced(lngRelAttribute): Returns relationship characteristics of the value provided.

- fRelationshipType(lngRelAttribute): Returns the relationship type (1:1 or 1:M) as indicated by the value provided.

- UTV(strField): Retrieves the value associated with the field provided from the hidden table USysValueList.

MOD_WORKDAYS

- fNetWorkdays(dtStartDate, dtEndDate, [blIncludeStartdate]): Returns the number of work days between the two dates provided. Optionally includes the start date.

- fAddWorkdays(dtStartDate, lngWorkDays): Adds the specified number of work days until the date provided.

- fNetWorkDaysByMonth(lngYear): Inserts the number of work days per month into the table named tblWorkdays.

Tables

- tblChild: Used to support the query qryRelationship.

- tblCustomer: Used to support the queries qryActiveCustomerList and qryCustomerListforComboBox

- tblDay: Used to support the query qryContiguousCalendarDays.

- tblHolidays: Use to store the dates that are not work days, used by fNetWorkdays().

- tblMonth: Used to support the query qryContiguousCalendarDays.

- tblParent: Used to support the query qryRelationship.

- tblStateRef: A table used for lookups that provides the full name and official abbreviation of states.

- tblWorkdays: Created/used by fNetWorkDaysByMonth().

- tblYear: Used to support the query qryContiguousCalendarDays.

What's on the CD-ROM

This appendix provides information about the contents of the CD that accompanies this book. For the latest and greatest information, please refer to the ReadMe file located at the root of the CD. Here is what you will find:

- System Requirements
- Using the CD with Windows and Macintosh
- What's on the CD-ROM
- Troubleshooting

System Requirements

Make sure that your computer meets the minimum system requirements listed in this section. If your computer doesn't match up to most of these requirements, you may have a problem using the contents of the CD.

- **For Windows Systems:**
  - Windows Vista, Windows XP, or Windows 2000 or later. Microsoft Office 2007 only works with these operating systems.
  - Windows 98 will Support Office 2000, 2002 and 2003.

- A PC with a fast processor running at 500 MHz or faster (800 MHz for Windows Vista).

- At least 256MB of total RAM installed on your computer (512MB RAM for Windows Vista). For best performance, we recommend a minimum of 512MB for all versions of Windows.

- 2GB of free disk space (for installation of Microsoft Office 2007).

- You will need additional disk space for working with larger database solutions.

- **For Macintosh Systems:**
  - Mac OS running Virtual PC for the MAC or VMWare, Bootcamp, or similar programs that support virtualization of an appropriate Windows operating system. We recommend Windows XP or later and Microsoft Office Access 2003 or later.

NOTE   **The sample databases will not work with Office for the Mac as that does not include Microsoft Access.**

The CD files need to be placed into the Windows environment.

- **For All Systems:**
  - Although it is not required, it is helpful to have an Internet connection to get updates to Microsoft files and to use Microsoft Office Help online files and resources.

  - A CD-ROM drive.

  - Microsoft Access 2000 or newer to open and use the database files.

  - Microsoft Word 2000 or a reader to open the File Guide, CD Guide and other Word documents.

  - A PDF reader, such as Adobe Reader, to read the bonus content.

Using the CD

To access the content on the CD, follow these steps.

1. Insert the CD into your computer's CD-ROM drive. The license agreement appears.

2. Read the license agreement and click the Accept button if you want to use the CD.

3. The CD interface appears. The interface allows you to browse the content and to copy the files and folders to your computer.

NOTE TO WINDOWS USERS

The interface won't launch if you have autorun disabled. In that case, click Start ➤ Run (For Windows Vista, Start ➤ All Programs ➤ Accessories ➤ Run). In the dialog box that appears, type **D:\Start.exe.** (Replace D with the proper letter if your CD drive uses a different letter. If you don't know the letter, check how your CD drive is listed under My Computer.) Click OK.

NOTE TO MAC USERS

The CD icon will appear on your desktop, double-click the icon to open the CD and double-click the "Start" icon.

Office for the Mac does not include Access. You will need a version of Microsoft Office that includes Access or a stand-alone version of Access.

Mac users must load the files into the virtual platform for Windows and Microsoft Office.

What's on the CD-ROM

The authors are proud to provide you with the companion files and bonus content that complement and expand on the discussions in the book. The CD provides the single most comprehensive set of database models and guides available — a total of 76 files! It includes Bonus Material of a complete chapter and four appendixes as PDF files. We have invested thousands of hours creating, deliberating on, and reviewing the concepts, methods and techniques that will provide you the greatest benefit. Our goal is to provide you with a structured learning process and functional designs that correlate to real-world scenarios.

We have created both simple and more complex models and offered numerous design alternatives so that as you gain the experience of building and modifying the tables, you will also understand the rationale for choosing between options. The CD Content includes 31 database models that are ready to be incorporated into your solutions. Each time you use one of the models, it will pay for the book dozens of times over.

Access Database Designs Files

Example files for *Microsoft Access Small Business Solutions: State-of-the-Art Database Models for Sales, Marketing, Customer Management, and More Key Business Activities* are provided on the CD, on the tab named CD Content. The folders and files are in a directory named "AccessDatabaseDesigns," behind the button, "Open CD Contents." If you click the button, you will see the 18 folders that correlate to the chapters and appendixes indicated by the folder names. We recommend that you copy the entire directory to your personal documents folder on your computer.

Alternatively, you may also leave the files on the CD and only copy selected files to the folder of your choice. Please note that Access files typically do not run from a CD. Files copied from a CD may default to a read-only setting; if you experience that, please read the troubleshooting tips.

Below the AccessDatabaseDesigns directory there are 12 folders named *cxxchaptertitle* and four folders named app*appendixtitle*. There are also two folders with a prefix "B" that contain companion files for the bonus chapter and one of the appendixes that are on the CD. Each folder contains all the files necessary to follow the examples in the corresponding chapter or appendix. The file names indicate the chapter and subject, such as c07sales.mdb.

A few chapters and appendixes have no example files, so they do not have a corresponding folder on the CD. Most chapters contain one or more Access database files with an mdb file extension. We used the mdb file format so that the files can be used with the greatest range of Access versions—they can be opened and used with Access 2000 and greater. All of the table structures and most of the forms and code will work with Access 2010. However, the 64 bit version of Access 2010 does not support the TreeView control (see Chapter 8). It is also important to know that a database can occasionally have problems with references. Since this is often associated with using the file with a different version of Access or in a different system environment, we have provided some instructions for checking references. Please review the troubleshooting section below for several helpful tips.

Each folder also contains a Word document with an explanation of the files in that directory. This briefly describes the database examples, the operations or functions that they address and some of the key features that they provide. It also mentions some of the bonus material that offers a broader benefit, such as several of the example queries, some populated lookup tables, and a few modules to help you document your database.

Many of the folders also contain one or more text files that provide the code, modules, or SQL write-ups from the chapter. In the folder for Chapter 15, you will also find some XML files and an XSD file. The files can be opened and edited with Notepad or with other programs that allow editing of XML files. If you are looking at the folders using Windows Explorer, you will find the chapter folders in the folder named AccessDatabaseDesigns.

Using the Files

As you go through the files, you will find many alternative solutions and/or database schemas that compliment or expand on the topics covered in each chapter. You can use these as a learning tool to investigate the field properties and the relationships between the tables. We encourage you to add some sample data as it will help you to understand the database design and to determine what modifications are necessary to meet your needs.

By working with the companion files as you read a chapter, you will see first hand how a particular schema is being implemented. Not only that, but most of the ground work has been done for you to create a database following the examples in each chapter. This will save you countless hours when implementing any of these solutions for your business.

We are especially proud to provide you with the Bonus Resource database. It contains many of the tools, shortcuts, and resources we use in our own Access applications. Collectively, the contributors to this book and bonus CD have well over 100 years of combined experience with Microsoft Access. This can serve as the start of your personal database development toolkit. We added this file to Appendix E, which started out as a list of some of our favorite websites and resources.

We have invested several thousand hours (without exaggerating) in designing, reviewing, deliberating on, and developing the database models and chapters so that they would provide a strong and versatile foundation to support most business needs. We've included many optional features and explained how you can modify the models to represent and accommodate the dynamics of your business. We hope that you enjoy and benefit greatly from our efforts.

Folders, Files, and Features

The following is a brief guide to the purpose and features of the files that you'll find on the CD. There is a more complete list of files and benefits in the *File List* and *Access Database Designs CD Guide*. Additionally, each folder contains a File Guide that highlights bonus features, such as queries and populated lookup tables. These are Word documents, so you can easily print them.

We wanted the book to be as self-contained as possible so that it provides what you need, right at your fingertips. There was so much that we could not fit it between the covers of the book, but rather than forego valuable content, we have included one chapter and four appendixes on the CD. You can open the files from the Bonus Content button on the CD Content tab. Part of the bonus is that you can save the files to you computer, which allows quick searches, copy and paste, and click to open references. And, of course, you may also want to print and store the hardcopy with the book.

Chapter 4: People, Organizations, Addresses

People and organizations are topics you will find in many serious business database applications whatever the business function that application addresses. They are the primary topics of contact list or contact management, personal information manager, or address book applications. The tables and databases that are provided in this chapter can be used in conjunction with or incorporated into other applications.

- **c04PeopleSimple.mdb** is the example database for the simple model of people and organization data described in Chapter 4. This example is for business functions that are not people- and organization-centered, and are not large or demanding with regard to flexibility. Adapted to your needs, this can cover a wide range of business functions.

- **c04PeopleComplex.mdb** is the example database for the complex model of people and organization data described in Chapter 4. This is an example for business functions that are people- and organization-centered and are large, with complex relationships. It covers a different range and allows more flexibility than the simple model. It can also be adapted to your needs.

The databases in this chapter contain several pre-populated lookup tables that may be useful in several applications. We encourage you to change the values to those that suit our own needs and to leverage the tables to your advantage.

Chapter 5: Customer Relationship Management

Customer Relationship Management software is considered a must-have for any enterprise that deals directly with a great number of customers, or for medium-to-large organizations with lots of customers. It's a subject of "buzz" that has held up well for years in the bag of tricks carried by successful consultants. The downside for small-to-medium businesses has been that the price of the commercial packages is prohibitive.

In this book, however, we let you in on a secret that the producers of those commercial packages would just as soon you didn't know: you can create your own application. In this chapter, we coach you on creating the tables, and we also provide a model that you can use as a "starter" to adapt to your specific business needs. We leverage the tables described in Chapter 4 and adapt them to the requirements identified in this chapter. At the final count, there are 52 tables in this chapter.

The databases in this chapter contain several pre-populated lookup tables that may be useful in several applications. We encourage you to change the data to those that suit our own needs and to leverage the tables to your advantage.

- **c05CRM.mdb** is the example database for CRM for small-to-medium sized organizations. It addresses activities associated with knowing and corresponding with your customers. It also allows you to track how well your sales, service and support are really serving your customers, and to monitor marketing activities. You can also capture data related to employee training and awareness.

Many of the tables contain information used in multiple areas, so adapting to your business-specific requirements is likely to be easier than you expect. Much of the information about the business is kept as data in the tables rather than being encoded in the application itself, which will ease your task of making this application your own.

Chapter 6: Marketing

Chapter 6 content is divided into two sections. The first section, "Marketing Campaigns," is represented by a single database file that provides a basic and customizable model that allows you to keep track of customers, business types, contact information, and various stages of marketing campaigns.

For the second section, "Questionnaire," we provide three database files that correspond to the progression of features being incorporated and the database design used to support them. The chapter indicates when content is relevant to a particular file and whether it is the preferred implementation or an alternative example provided for your information and use in the future.

The concepts used to support a questionnaire are applicable to a multitude of purposes, from marketing campaigns to inspection reports, and from satisfaction surveys to providing book reviews. We create three distinct models plus some optional features, providing you with the foundation for supporting simple polling tasks and conducting interactive surveys that use current responses to select subsequent questions—much like many online surveys.

- **06Campaign.mdb** is the database design as fully described in the chapter's "Marketing Campaigns" section. The design represents the process of conducting a marketing campaign, storing organization contact details and progressively contacting those organizations as part of the campaign process. This complete database, including its queries, is described in the chapter. In particular, the queries qryOrganizationUnavailable and qryOrganizationAvailable are instructive in providing functionality that would form part of an organization's mailing efforts, and allow a user to determine who to contact, and who to no longer contact.

- **c06Questionnaire_Simple.mdb** is a very simplistic example from the "Questionnaire" section found in the latter half of the chapter. It complements the previous marketing campaign concept, as questionnaires often form a lot of marketing groundwork, while being easy to understand and implement but remaining versatile and flexible. This is a smaller file that serves as an introduction to the concepts being explained in the chapter content. Despite its simplicity, this model may be all that you need to support a simple yet effective marketing campaign or questionnaire.

■ **c06Questionnaire.mdb** builds on the structure that supports a simple database and incorporates additional capabilities. As explained in the chapter content, this file presents a more comprehensive and flexible questionnaire database. In particular, it allows for data type-specific answers and multiple choice responses.

■ **c06Questionnaire_Complex.mdb** is the final database file, which adds the final refinements of "Questionnaire" sections, including "Question Dependency," which uses a self-referencing join. Question dependency allows you to automatically present subsequent questions based on the response to a specific question.

Self-referencing tables can be used to provide a multitude of solutions. Learning how to use them will be a tremendous benefit. Similarly, the concepts for a questionnaire also apply to a multitude of areas, from researching employee satisfaction to having your group vote on where to hold the next party.

■ **qryInterviews** is a bonus query that relates to Questionnaires. (There is no example in the chapter of bringing interview data together.)

Chapter 7: Sales

Sales is one of the most fundamental and comprehensive of business activities. The concepts for database design can be applied to a vast range of businesses, whether the products sold are manufactured in-house or purchased from another company. This chapter concentrates on companies that perform direct sales and provides several variations to help you tailor a solution to your needs.

Chapter 7 contains three database files that chart the progression of the database design structure described in the chapter. The complex model includes several queries, and we encourage you to pay close attention to the discussion of how to create and use the crosstab query, qryProductsPrice-Crosstab. The chapter indicates when content is relevant to a particular file and whether it is the preferred implementation or simply an alternative example provided for your information. We encourage you to review the database along with the chapter.

The databases for this chapter also include tblSetting that demonstrates how to limit a table to one record. This technique can be used for many purposes, such as to contain your company logo, server location, and other items that will only have one value at time.

■ **c07Sales.mdb** is the database design as initially created and described in the chapter. This represents the most simplistic design and contains only tables and their relationships without any queries.

- **c07Sales_Complex.mdb** is the more advanced database created in the second section of the chapter. Apart from a greater number of tables and more complex interactions, this file contains all the required queries that were discussed throughout the chapter.

- **c07Sales_ComplexAlt.mdb** is a variation of the more advanced database created in the chapter. As explained in the chapter content, this file presents a subtly alternative table design and includes only the queries that are implemented differently due to those variations. Two of the special features include the use of a multi-key product price table and the use of a single table for notes that allows a note to be associated with multiple subjects.

Chapter 8: Production and Manufacturing

Tracking data related to production tracking can be remarkably complex. The example shows how to identify multiple stages in a production process, to log incidents and down time, and to record the associated notes. The example files include several bonus items that can easily be incorporated into other applications; such as a TreeView control and a demonstration of how and when to use calculated fields.

- **c08ProductionAndManufacturing.mdb** is the database created by following the instructions in the chapter. The database provides the structure for identifying the process, parts, staff, and suppliers associated with your manufacturing processes. It allows you to record process start and stop times, identify production issues, and track their resolution. We also provide and discuss examples that allow notes to be recorded about processes and subprocesses.

  In addition, the form, frmProcessManager, contains a sample of a TreeView control and the code used to manage the data of the self-referencing table, tblProcess. This form demonstrates how to manage and display hierarchical data using a TreeView control. You often see TreeView controls used for menus, file lists, process controls, and organization charts.

- **qryRelationships** is a bonus feature to create a list of table relationships from the database. It provides the table names, the related fields, the relationship type, and the associated index properties.

- **frmProcessManager** provides a user interaction demonstration and also illustrates a technique for storing the result of a calculation, often called a "calculated field." While this practice is discouraged in database design, you may encounter situations where you want to use a calculated field. One example is provided in the chapter under the heading "Application Performance vs. Using Calculated Fields."

Chapter 9: Inventory Management

The database examples for inventory management provide the tables for managing inventory, tracking quantity on hand, and determining replacement orders. We have included some queries to show you how to retrieve the data and perform the basic calculation. In addition, there is a quick data entry form to help you understand how to enter and search for inventory.

We've also included a basic point-of-sale database to demonstrate how to integrate inventory management with sales by linking to data in another application. This allows the inventory to automatically be depleted as items are sold. You must have both databases in the same folder in order to ensure proper functionality of the files.

- **c09InventoryManagement.mdb** is the database created by following the instructions in the chapter. In addition, the file contains a sampling of queries to return data for the quantity on hand, products that are overstocked, and products that need to be ordered.

- **c09PointOfSale.mdb** is a very small database to illustrate inter-application linking. This database is not described in the chapter; however, it effectively demonstrates the desired concept.

Chapter 10: Services

The examples for this chapter demonstrate how to create a database model to support a basic service business. We begin with a single database representing a pet grooming and accommodation service. With that foundation, we incorporate additional requirements to accommodate setting appointments and avoiding appointment conflicts.

The second section of the chapter demonstrates how to create the tables to support holding or managing events. We start by creating a basic model, which becomes the base for a second model that can accommodate more complex interactions and business requirements.

- **c10Pets.mdb** is the full database design for the pet grooming and accommodation service. It begins with a relatively simple customer model, and then introduces the concept of bookings and occupancy which have direct implementations well beyond the pet-based example.

  - The query **qryAvailableAccommodation** demonstrates a relatively simple yet powerful query that allows the database to determine what accommodation availability there is in any time period.

- **c10Events.mdb** supports the chapter's Event Management example. This also offers booking functionality, but the focus is on the ability to prepare and provide a given service, and most importantly, to monitor the progression of planning and execution. We do this using simple process monitoring templates.

- **c10Events_Complex.mdb** builds on the Events database developed in the chapter to gradually introduce more advanced concepts. As discussed in the chapter, this example includes a greater number of tables and more complex interactions. It includes centralized contact details to help ensure that an address or phone number is never entered twice. It also manages basic event fees and allows for multiple venues.

Chapter 11: Accounting Systems: Requirements and Design

This chapter explains the tables, data, and concepts involved with creating a database to support the accounting needs of a small- to medium-sized organization.

By creating the tables, you will learn some of the fundamentals of accrual accounting and how to design a chart of accounts. You'll also see how to create and use an electronic general ledger and sub-ledgers. After that, we'll walk you through a process to archive historic data; a task often associated with year-end accounting activities.

- **c11AccountingSystems.mdb** is the database created by following the instructions in the chapter. This database, combined with the discussion in the chapter, will prepare you to create a basic model for an accounting system. This chapter explains the tables, data, and concepts involved with creating a database to support the accounting needs of a small- to medium-sized organization.

Chapter 12: Accounting: Budgeting, Analysis, and Reporting

This chapter focuses on creating financial reports and creating the queries for financial analysis. The chapter and database help you learn and apply techniques to record financial, statistical, and budget data, and to report on the data with standard accounting reports. You learn to create the queries for several key tasks, such as those required for the trial balance, balance sheet, and income statement.

In looking at budgeting and analysis, we'll develop a base set of numbers that will be used to predict future results. Then we will demonstrate how to report variances by comparing the budgeted amounts with actual results. The files also include the queries for performing ratio and financial analysis.

In addition, you learn about creating and using two types of union queries: the Union query and the Union All query. These queries cannot be represented in the query design view, so they are presented in the chapters in SQL, along with an explanation.

- **c12AccountingBudgetReportingAnalysis.mdb** is the database for this chapter. The tables were created in Chapter 11. The queries are explained and created in Chapter 12.

Chapter 13: Managing Memberships

We are all members of one organization or another. Those membership organizations vary in type, subject, and character, but only the very smallest and most informal do not need to manage memberships. The database model provides the ability to add and renew memberships, record payment of dues, manage information about the organizations offices or positions, and will allow you to create the associated reports. It also support activities associated with holding events and recruiting new members.

- **c13Memberships.mdb** is the example database for data used to manage the memberships, communicate with members, manage events, conduct recruiting activities, and manage information about sponsors. The database is intended to be generic so that it can address business functions that are common to many membership organizations from small to large.

There are 37 tables in this database. Several of the tables were copied from the example databases for Chapter 4 and 5. Some of the tables are exact copies but others have been modified to accommodate the specific needs of the membership database. Sample data has been pre-populated in several tables. We encourage you to change the values to those that suit our own needs and to leverage the tables to your advantage.

Chapter 14: Implementing the Models

We based this example on a fictional not-for-profit organization (NFP) to help you learn how to integrate tables and functionality from several business functions into one database. The database is not meant to be a complex and comprehensive solution; rather, it is primarily a tool to demonstrate some techniques and recommendations for how to create and use forms, reports and queries.

The database is intended to help you learn how to add tables to new or existing databases and quickly create a functional application. When working with tables from other databases, you will often find that the table and field names do not exactly match the conventions that you have established for your own files. As you will see, that can easily be accomodated.

- **c14ImplementingTheModels.mdb** supports a not-for-profit (NFP) organization that has dues-paying members, donors, and sales of specialty merchandise items that produce revenue for the organization. This organization is staffed by volunteers and most supplies and operating expenses are donated or purchased from the dues revenue of the members. They maintain mailing addresses, e-mail addresses, and phone numbers for every customer, member, and donor. They bill members for their annual dues and record the payments. Donations are tracked by type of fund raiser, and donors are associated with each fund raiser in order to maximize future fund-raising efforts.

The database includes more than a dozen forms to help you learn how to create the user interface for entering and viewing data. It also has several sample reports, including a dues notice that is a friendly letter of reminder to send to your members.

Chapter 15: SQL Server and Other External Data Sources

The content of Chapter 15 covering SQL Server does not relate to any specific database design. The chapter uses hypothetical scenarios and examples to illustrate points. Consequently there is no accompanying database file or script that supports the discussion of SQL Server.

In support of the section on XML files there are five files that provide examples of data in XML format or data to be put into such a format. They expand on the example snippets in the chapter content. Notepad is a perfectly valid option for viewing and working with both XML and XSD files. One way to specify that they open in Notepad is to right click the file name and select Open With and then select Notepad.

- **c15XMLData.mdb** is an Access database holding just two tables: People and Phone. The latter is related to the People table by a foreign key. This data is what needs to be represented by the following XML files.

- **c15PeoplePhone.xml** is an XML file which holds the previous MDB data in its hierarchical structure using full Child Element format.

- **c15PeoplePhoneAttribute.xml** is an XML file which holds the exact same MDB data in its hierarchical structure, however this version uses Element data in Attribute format.

- **c15tblPeople.xml** is an example of exported XML data of just the data in the People table. This data alone has value, but not much more meaning than a CSV file. The XML data, by itself, is essentially a list; however it can be easily formatted. Combing the XML file with an XSD file provides the data definition required to format and configure the data.

- **c15tblPeople.xsd** is the accompanying XSD file for the previous XML People data. You can clearly see the definitions for each element in the XML, so that, given both, you could make informed decisions about what to import into appropriate data types and structures.

Appendixes A and B: Field Properties and Relationships, Joins, and Nulls

The tables described in Appendixes A and B illustrate field properties and relationships between tables in a simple customer contact database. We've included additional tables, forms, queries and a report to provide a basic, yet functional customer contact application. Please note that the file also includes four tables that should NOT be used in your applications. The tables are used to demonstrate poor designs that were discussed as not recommended, and are included to help you recognize and avoid some pitfalls that you might otherwise encounter.

▪ **appABFieldsAndRelationships.mdb** contains the tables used for the examples in both appendixes. It contains additional tables, forms, queries and a report to provide a simple customer contact database.

Appendix C: Resolving Relationship Triangles

The databases described in Appendix C illustrate two possible approaches to designing the tables that support a specific business rule: A customer can be categorized as either an organization or an individual, but not both. This type of either-or relationship triangle is quite common, and is by no means limited to dealing with customers or even people. As is often the case, implementing a table design to support this business rule leads to hard choices between options because there is more than one viable way to do it—and they all require controls in the user interface, or forms.

We included these databases to show you how different choices influence the interface design required to work with the data model chosen. However, as developers, our strong preference is always normalized over non-normalized tables.

▪ **appCResolvingRelationshipTriangles_Simplified.mdb** is the database illustrating a less normalized table schema and interface.

▪ **appCResolvingRelationshipTriangles_Normalized.mdb** is the database illustrating a more normalized table schema and interface.

Appendix D: Measures: Financial and Performance

Measures are used to evaluate the performance of a business, or segments of a business. Financial measures, like the financial ratios and ratio analysis discussed in Chapter 12, are specific to financial results. Performance measures are often applied to data that is not strictly financial in nature, such as customer satisfaction. This appendix and the companion files provide instructions and examples that will help you compile and analyze data to support making sound business decisions.

▪ **appDMeasures.mdb** is the database that contains the tables and queries discussed in the chapter. It demonstrates how to track and quantify how well, or how poorly, either a single delivery person or all delivery personnel perform their delivery duties. This includes using a function to report the time difference, a feature that is helpful in scheduling, tracking, calculating average time spent, and a multitude of other tasks.

Appendix E: References and Resources

While we were pulling together the sample databases for this book, we realized that we could provide an invaluable bonus by compiling several of the database tools that we use into one convenient place. So, in addition to providing the database models described in the book, we are have created the Bonus Resource database that includes several tools to help you analyze, work with, and create your own database solutions.

The database contains selected forms, tables, queries, and modules from the chapter files. We've also included several bonus modules from the authors that will be quite helpful when you design and work with other database files. They will help you to efficiently create, manage and analyze tables. It also has several pre-populated reference tables that you can copy into other applications.

This database makes an excellent starting point for you to build your own database development toolkit. Whenever you come across a something that you could use in other databases, consider adding the objects to this database so you'll always have the right tools for the job.

- **ADD_BonusResource.mdb** A database with selected forms, tables, queries, and modules from the chapter files that you will find to be helpful as you design and work with other database files. Several of the modules will help you create, manage and analyze tables.

Chapter B1: Knowledge: Intellectual Property, Structural Capital and Intellectual Capital

It is an old axiom: Knowledge is power. In today's environment, you can expand that to: knowledge is vital to survival and crucial to success. This chapter addresses three categories of knowledge that are important assets: intellectual property (with file b1IPTracking.mdb), structural capital (with file b1ProcessInfo.mdb), and intellectual capital (with files b1EmployeeRel.mdb and b1SupplierTrk.mdb). It includes a separate database for tracking those.

- **b1IPTracking.mdb** is the example database used for tracking various types of intellectual property that you own or that you use in your organization. Reminders of the need for actions, a record of activities performed, and regular reports are typical database application features you might implement with the tables defined.

- **b1ProcessInfo.mdb** is the example database that is the modern replacement for the employee manual of the past. It contains information about jobs (positions), business structure (departments), the work done in the departments, the business functions executed to perform that work, and details.

- **b1EmployeeRel.mdb** is the example database for collecting and keeping information about your employees so that you can let them know that you appreciate them. It provides tools to recognize their achievements and to record additional skills or expertise that they may have in areas not directly related to their job that might qualify them for a promotion or openings in different business areas.

- **b1SupplierTrk.mdb** is the example database for tracking activities and transactions with suppliers to your organization. You would create a database application based on the tables and fields defined in this database to collect data that you can analyze. Although we don't provide the queries and reports in this chapter, the table structure that we do provide will make it easy for you to learn how to create queries, forms, and reports to suite your needs.

Appendix BC: Data Warehouse Concepts

The concept of a data warehouse is introduced in this appendix. A data warehouse is a set of tables designed specifically to make reporting easier—as such they usually do not conform to the forms of normalization required in a relational database. Most tables will have data that has been summarized, and calculated fields, repeating groups, and in many cases, the same values will be stored in multiple tables. All of this is done to increase the efficiency of designing and generating reports. With an Access application, you might incorporate some of the concepts when creating selected work tables or temporary tables for specific purposes.

- **bcDataWarehouse.mdb** is the database created by following the instructions in the chapter. This contains fact tables that include summarized data with pre-calculated values that make reporting and analysis easier and more efficient for users. Dimension tables are used to describe the data in the fact tables. They are much like lookup tables. The query demonstrates how to gather, group, and perform calculations on data from multiple tables.

Troubleshooting

If you have difficulty installing or using any of the materials on the companion CD, try the following solutions:

- **If you open a database and it indicates that it is "Read Only,"** you will need to follow the "Help" instructions for your version of Access to change the properties. Older operating systems may treat files that are copied from a CD as read only files.

- **If you receive a "Security Warning" when opening an Access database,** you will need to select the response that correlates to have the file "Open."

- **Trusted Locations – Access 2007 and greater.** If you are running Access 2007 or greater, you may find it convenient to add the folder "Access-DatabaseDesigns" (or whatever name you have used for the main folder that stores CD content) as a trusted location. Follow the directions provided by the version of Access that you are using.

- **Converting Database Files to Other Access File Formats (versions).** The table structures that we have created are in the Access 2000 file format so that they will function as designed in most, if not all versions of Access. If you want to convert the file to a different version, you should follow the instructions provided by Access help.

- **Features Not Supported in All Versions.** In addition to tables, we have provided some other tools, such as forms and reports, to help you work with the data and create complete solutions. Although some features are not supported in every version of Access, they provide valuable examples. We've noted some known issues, such as with the TreeView control in Access 2007 and greater. Regretfully, we did not know of a reliable solution at the time of this printing. We recommend that you turn to the online resources for assistance if you encounter challenges incorporating features in newer versions of Access.

- **References.** Working with a database in a different version of Access will occasionally result in problems with references, but this rarely occurs with files that have only tables and queries. However, many of our files contain forms and code, so we wanted to give you some guidance on references. You may get an error message as soon as you try to open the database or you may get an error message when you click on an object or command on a form. Following the prompts typically opens the Visual Basic Editor (VBE) or code window. That is also where you check references. With a database open, clicking Ctrl-G will also open the VBE.

The files should work with the standard references for each version of Access from 2000 through 2010. The only exception is Chapter 8, which contains a form with a TreeView control that requires Microsoft Windows Common Controls 6.0 (SP6).

To check or fix the references, follow these steps:

1. Hold down the shift key as you open the database; that is when you click on the Open button.

2. Open the VBA Editor; you can do that by clicking Ctrl-G.

3. Click on Tools, then References. This will open a dialog box where you can browse through available references and add those that are

needed. The selected references are listed at the top with a check in the box.

4. After you have selected the appropriate references, you should compile the code by clicking on Debug, then Compile.

In addition to knowing how to check the references, we thought it would also be helpful for you to know the default references for the previous versions of Access.

Access 2000

Visual Basic For Applications

Microsoft Access 9.0 Object Library

OLE Automation

Microsoft ActiveX Data Objects 2.1 Library

(Note: Microsoft DAO 3.6 Object Library is installed by Access 2000, but not referenced by default)

Access 2002

Visual Basic For Applications

Microsoft Access 10.0 Object Library

OLE Automation

Microsoft ActiveX Data Objects 2.1 Library

(Note: Microsoft DAO 3.6 Object Library is installed by Access 2002, but not referenced by default)

Access 2003

Visual Basic For Applications

Microsoft Access 11.0 Object Library

OLE Automation

Microsoft DAO 3.6 Object Library

Microsoft ActiveX Data Objects 2.1 Library

Access 2007

Visual Basic For Applications

Microsoft Access 9.0 Object Library

OLE Automation

Microsoft Office 12.0 Access database engine Objects

▪ **Turn off any anti-virus software that you may have running.** Installers sometimes mimic virus activity and can make your computer incorrectly believe that it is being infected by a virus. (Be sure to turn the anti-virus software back on later.)

- **Close all running programs.** The more programs you're running, the less memory is available to other programs. Installers also typically update files and programs; if you keep other programs running, installation may not work properly.

- **Reference the ReadMe:** Please refer to the ReadMe file located at the root of the CD-ROM for the latest product information at the time of publication.

Customer Care

If you have trouble with the CD-ROM, please call the Wiley Product Technical Support phone number at (800) 762-2974. Outside the United States, call 1(317) 572-3994. You can also contact Wiley Product Technical Support at http://support.wiley.com. John Wiley & Sons will provide technical support only for installation and other general quality control items. For technical support on the applications themselves, consult the program's vendor or author.

To place additional orders or to request information about other Wiley products, please call (877) 762-2974.

Index